I0868694

Cases on International Business Logistics in the Middle East

Islam Abdelbary
Arab Academy for Science, Technology, and Maritime Transport, Egypt & University of Plymouth, UK

Sandra Haddad
Arab Academy for Science, Technology, and Maritime Transport, Egypt

Ghada Elkady
Arab Academy for Science, Technology, and Maritime Transport, Egypt

IGI Global
PUBLISHER of TIMELY KNOWLEDGE

A volume in the Advances in Logistics, Operations, and Management Science (ALOMS) Book Series

Published in the United States of America by
IGI Global
Business Science Reference (an imprint of IGI Global)
701 E. Chocolate Avenue
Hershey PA, USA 17033
Tel: 717-533-8845
Fax: 717-533-8661
E-mail: cust@igi-global.com
Web site: http://www.igi-global.com

Library of Congress Cataloging-in-Publication Data

Names: Abdelbary, Islam, DATE- editor. | Haddad, Sandra Samy, editor. | Elkhady, Ghada, DATE- editor.
Title: Cases on international business logistics in the Middle East / Islam Abdelbary, Sandra Samy Haddad, and Ghada Elkhady, editors.
Description: Hershey PA : Business Science Reference, [2022] | Includes bibliographical references and index. | Summary: "This book contributes to filling the wide knowledge gap in the field of logistics and supply chains, specifically in the Middle East region, based on applied evidence with case studies that deliver insights into contemporary findings of logistics and supply chain to officials and academics "-- Provided by publisher.
Identifiers: LCCN 2022012041 (print) | LCCN 2022012042 (ebook) | ISBN 9781668446867 (hardcover) | ISBN 9781668446874 (paperback) | ISBN 9781668446881 (ebook)
Subjects: LCSH: Business logistics--Middle East--Case studies. | COVID-19 Pandemic, 2020---Economic aspects--Middle East--Case studies.
Classification: LCC HD38.5 .C276 2022 (print) | LCC HD38.5 (ebook) | DDC 658.500956--dc23/eng/20220503
LC record available at https://lccn.loc.gov/2022012041
LC ebook record available at https://lccn.loc.gov/2022012042

This book is published in the IGI Global book series Advances in Logistics, Operations, and Management Science (ALOMS) (ISSN: 2327-350X; eISSN: 2327-3518)

British Cataloguing in Publication Data
A Cataloguing in Publication record for this book is available from the British Library.

For electronic access to this publication, please contact: eresources@igi-global.com.

Advances in Logistics, Operations, and Management Science (ALOMS) Book Series

John Wang
Montclair State University, USA

ISSN:2327-350X
EISSN:2327-3518

Mission

Operations research and management science continue to influence business processes, administration, and management information systems, particularly in covering the application methods for decision-making processes. New case studies and applications on management science, operations management, social sciences, and other behavioral sciences have been incorporated into business and organizations real-world objectives.

The **Advances in Logistics, Operations, and Management Science** (ALOMS) Book Series provides a collection of reference publications on the current trends, applications, theories, and practices in the management science field. Providing relevant and current research, this series and its individual publications would be useful for academics, researchers, scholars, and practitioners interested in improving decision making models and business functions.

Coverage

- Operations Management
- Political Science
- Finance
- Organizational Behavior
- Computing and information technologies
- Marketing engineering
- Decision analysis and decision support
- Production Management
- Services management
- Information Management

IGI Global is currently accepting manuscripts for publication within this series. To submit a proposal for a volume in this series, please contact our Acquisition Editors at Acquisitions@igi-global.com or visit: http://www.igi-global.com/publish/.

The Advances in Logistics, Operations, and Management Science (ALOMS) Book Series (ISSN 2327-350X) is published by IGI Global, 701 E. Chocolate Avenue, Hershey, PA 17033-1240, USA, www.igi-global.com. This series is composed of titles available for purchase individually; each title is edited to be contextually exclusive from any other title within the series. For pricing and ordering information please visit http://www.igi-global.com/book-series/advances-logistics-operations-management-science/37170. Postmaster: Send all address changes to above address.

Titles in this Series

For a list of additional titles in this series, please visit: www.igi-global.com/book-series/advances-logistics-operations-management-science/37170

Perspectives on Women in Management and the Global Labor Market
Elisabete S. Vieira (GOVCOPP, University of Aveiro, Portugal) Mara Madaleno (GOVCOPP, University of Aveiro, Portugal) and João Teodósio (Polytechnic Institute of Santarém, Portugal)
Business Science Reference • © 2023 • 335pp • H/C (ISBN: 9781668459812) • US $240.00

Cases on Managing Dairy Productive Chains
Eduardo Guilherme Satolo (São Paulo State University, Brazil) and Priscilla Ayllen Bustos Mac-Lean (São Paulo State University (UNESP), Brazil)
Engineering Science Reference • © 2023 • 310pp • H/C (ISBN: 9781668454725) • US $235.00

Examining the Vital Financial Role of SMEs in Achieving the Sustainable Development Goals
Dalila Taleb (University of Abou Bakr Belkaïd, Algeria) Mohammed El Amine Abdelli (University of Brest, France) Afef Khalil (University of Tunis, Carthage, Tunisia) and Asma Sghaier (University of Sousse, Tunisia)
Business Science Reference • © 2023 • 275pp • H/C (ISBN: 9781668448342) • US $250.00

Lean Thinking in Industry 4.0 and Services for Society
Katarzyna Antosz (Rzeszow University of Technology, Poland) Jose Carlos Sa (School of Engineering, ISEP, Polytechnic of Porto, Portugal) Małgorzata Jasiulewicz-Kaczmarek (Poznan University of Technology, Poland) and Jose Machado (University of Minho, Portugal)
Business Science Reference • © 2023 • 297pp • H/C (ISBN: 9781668456064) • US $250.00

Moving From R&D Development to Production and Sales in Start-Up Companies Emerging Research and Opportunities
Amiram Porath (APC, Israel)
Business Science Reference • © 2023 • 300pp • H/C (ISBN: 9781799856856) • US $215.00

Futuristic Technology Perspectives on Entrepreneurship and Sustainable Innovation
Sanjay Misra (Ostfold University, Norway) Amit Jain (Amity University, India) Manju Kaushik (Amity University, India) and Chitreshh Banerjee (Amity University, India)
Business Science Reference • © 2023 • 300pp • H/C (ISBN: 9781668458716) • US $250.00

IGI Global
PUBLISHER of TIMELY KNOWLEDGE

701 East Chocolate Avenue, Hershey, PA 17033, USA
Tel: 717-533-8845 x100 • Fax: 717-533-8661
E-Mail: cust@igi-global.com • www.igi-global.com

Table of Contents

Detailed Table of Contents

Reaching a sustainable industry is now possible through digitisation. The current era witnessed an increase in the impact of digital transformation on the economy; this encouraged various sectors to adopt Industry 4.0. Digital supply chain and Industry 4.0 are current buzzwords in all industries that can solve common drawbacks. The logistics sector in particular suffers from numerous weaknesses, one of which is cargo theft. Logistics companies started adopting technology in operations aiming to mitigate cargo thefts and reach a sustainable work environment through their digital supply chains. The Egyptian government intends to participate in the transition into a digital society. This case aims to demonstrate a best practice of digitisation in the logistics sector in the Egyptian market. Global Chains Company was one of the first logistics companies to apply a digital solution through ERP systems. Through the interviews conducted, cargo theft problems and consequences are demonstrated along with the results of applying digitisation to operations and the lessons learned.

Chapter 3
The Effects of Implementing the Advanced Cargo Information (ACI) System on Egyptian Importers 52
Farah Samir, Arab Academy for Science, Technology, and Maritime Transport, Egypt
Aya El-Garhy, Arab Academy for Science, Technology, and Maritime Transport, Egypt
Ashish Bagwari, Uttarakhand Technical University, India

Blockchain technology is gradually being applied to different customs clearance systems globally to improve the efficiency of trade transactions by digitizing customs clearance processes. This chapter explores the Advance Cargo Information (ACI) system—a blockchain-based system—implemented by the Egyptian Customs Authority (ECA) and provides recommendations for future improvements. A case study was applied on three regular importer companies in Egypt, H.B. Fuller, Ezz Steel, and Zamil Steel, to study specific customs clearance concepts related to time, documentation, and costs associated with the processes to draw a conclusion on the impacts of implementing the ACI on the import customs clearance procedures. Finally, the chapter concludes that the ACI system has had a positive impact on importers and customs employees. Nevertheless, importers still face several challenges with the customs clearance system. Therefore, recommendations are listed for the ECA to upgrade the customs clearance processes, and Misr Technology Services (MTS) to develop the ACI system's infrastructure.

Chapter 4
The Effect of Using Intelligent Transportation Systems on Transportation-Sustainable Development in Egypt 73
Ashrakat Osama, Arab Academy for Science, Technology, and Maritime Transport, Egypt
Ashish Bagwari, Uttarakhand Technical University, India
Nada Hossam, Arab Academy for Science, Technology, and Maritime Transport, Egypt

Roads have a significant positive impact on social and economic development and provide various advantages. There are several reasons why modern transportation is not sustainable. One of the most significant causes is the traffic congestion issue, since its effects severely harm both the environment and the entire community. As a technology that improves transportation quality or accomplishes other goals using programmes that watch over, manage, or enhance transportation networks, an intelligent transportation system is a crucial idea that aids in the development of sustainable transportation. Every kind of intelligent transportation used in Egypt, including the monorail, runs on electricity and requires no fuel, helping to save the environment. By encouraging people to take public transit instead of driving their own automobiles, intelligent transportation systems and methods can ease traffic congestion. This

reduces congestion and protects the environment from pollution brought on by vehicle emissions and exhaust.

Section 2
Impact of COVID-19 on Logistics and Supply Chain Management

The COVID-19 pandemic is regarded as the major disruptive event of this decade, resulting in unexpected socio-economic impacts worldwide. The COVID-19 pandemic has caused considerable damage to various industries worldwide. Availability and supply of a wide range of raw materials, intermediate goods, and finished products have been seriously disrupted. The magnitude of the COVID-19 pandemic has had an enormous impact on the health system and pharmaceutical industry in almost every country globally. This new virus has resulted in pharmaceutical organizations experiencing unprecedented logistical restrictions as a result of increasing demand and limited capacity. Accordingly, this case study assesses the impact of the COVID-19 pandemic on the supply chain (SC) integration of the pharmaceutical sector in Egypt. A case study technique was used for better understating of the situation and to analyze the industry's position and its capabilities to face the consequences of the pandemic, which hindered the integration along the supply chain.

The freight forwarding industry is an important player in the maritime transport industry that facilitates shipping processes by providing various value-added services such as securing bookings, transporting cargo, and preparing shipping documents. However, due to COVID-19 outbreak, the freight forwarding industry faced many challenges like port congestion, container shortages, and blank sailings. Therefore, this study examines COVID-19 effect on the freight forwarding industry and the challenges that the freight forwarders faced especially in Egypt, which is a logistics hub due to its strategic location. The case provides researchers and practitioners with an overview of the challenges that affected both maritime transport and freight forwarding industries in Egypt and investigates the challenges that Agility Egypt

The secret behind achieving competitive supply chains is mastering the art of finding innovative solutions to face global challenges. In a world full of significant and rapid global changes that face the supply chain industry as well as a dynamic complex environment and due to the fact of the increased number of startups that could provide innovative solutions for existing pains in the supply chain despite the existing global challenges, it becomes indispensable to study the impact of entrepreneurship on the supply chain industry to be able to adapt and survive in the market. Therefore, the primary purpose of this research is to investigate the disruption caused by startups to the supply chain industry in Egypt and how the traditional supply chain could benefit from the entrepreneurial mindset of startups to be able to respond to the rapid global challenges as well as to improve the supply chain performance.

Technology has progressed from being a supporter of the fundamental element of today's economy. The "digital economy" includes digital sectors, such as media, e-commerce, as well as traditional industries that have been touched by digitalization to varying degrees. This case study focuses on the Saudi e-commerce retail industry and how much it has grown exponentially through increased internet penetration, use of smartphones, and language diversity on e-commerce platforms. Moreover, the adoption of digital wallets is now more prevalent, supported by a general shift towards digital payments. The development of transport and logistics systems is based on digital platforms, such as Salla platform, which has a significant impact on the efficiency and competitiveness of supply chains and the logistics activities in KSA. Salla connects its sellers and customers. The platform provides companies with many advantages and tools.

Logistics in humanitarian aid is critical for effectively utilising humanitarian operations and initiatives. This chapter tries to explain the important role that humanitarian logistics plays in relief efforts. It uses the Syria crisis as an example to evaluate the performance of humanitarian logistics in Syria, especially in the healthcare sector. Over 470,000 people have died in the Syrian Civil War, and half of the country's population have been forced to leave their homes. The study determined the humanitarian logistics gaps and bottlenecks in Syria, such as physical access restrictions, a lack of logistical information, operational challenges, the need for integrated logistical coordination, and the increasing need for specialised logistical capacity-building programs. After explaining humanitarian logistics implementation in the healthcare sector in detail, the research draws on the lessons learned and drives recommendations for the future of the Syrian operation itself and identifies best practices for other operations in any humanitarian intervention.

The objectives of the case study are to highlight the possible challenges/disruptions arising from having a joint operation with multiple companies, to demonstrate operational problems encountered in the business process, and to illustrate the approach of the companies to the problems in this process and subsequent reconciliation process. Furthermore, this study aims to uncover conflict and power relations, which dominate the whole process between companies, based on some theoretical perspectives of power and conflict in distribution channels. By using a real case involving multiple players of the supply chain, this study contributes to transportation disruption and conflict management domains.

The aim of this case study is to summarize the most recent contributions by reviewing recent papers conducted on the adoption of innovative practices in the freight transport sector in addition to how their implementation in this sector will contribute to enhancing the road freight transport sector by concluding an overview of the obstacles and challenges standing against their incorporation in developing countries such as those in the Middle East. The role of the freight transport sector is increasing dramatically in most countries because most cargo is transported from point of origin to point of destination via roads.

The use of clean and renewable sources of energy is a global trend in preserving the environment. In addition, in the long run, the cost of renewable energy is lower than the energy generated by fuels. By extension, if clean energy is used in industry, it will have a very strong impact on all supply chains, both service and productivity. This case study highlighted the technical potential and economic feasibility of the activation the transformation of kinetic energy of trucks to electrical power using piezo-electric tiles, its effect in Kinda Food's warehouse, its impact on the supply chain, and the economic feasibility of its long-term application. This case explained how to convert regular warehouses into green warehouses, explained the usage of alternative energy in warehouses, explained the difference in cost of using renewable energy and fuel energy in warehouses, and obtained the benefits.

The case deals with decreasing environmental harm and pollution in all industries. The corporations have followed worldwide environmental standards to replace toxic materials with environmentally acceptable alternatives, such as lead-free glass used in producing L.E.D. lamps and Freon R410 used in the production process of air conditioners and refrigerators. ELARABY Group is one of the few enterprises in the Middle East specialized in electronics. It designed and applied a system to face the challenges, consequences, and results of replacing harmful materials with environmentally friendly ones. The case followed a qualitative approach through conducting interviews with experts in order to collect data.

Foreword

I am honoured to write the foreword for this book, which presents a comprehensive collection of case studies on logistics and supply chain management in the Middle East. The contributors have done an excellent job of bringing together a diverse range of topics, including customs and international trade, freight forwarding and logistics services, green and sustainable logistics, the impact of COVID-19, and many more. The chapters are written by experts in their respective fields, providing valuable insights and real-world examples.

One of the strengths of this book is its focus on the Middle East. The logistics and supply chain industry in this region is rapidly evolving, and this book provides a valuable resource for understanding the challenges and opportunities that it presents. The case studies in this book provide a wealth of information on logistics and supply chain management in the Middle East, and they will be of great interest to anyone working in this field.

This book is also noteworthy for its emphasis on digitalization and sustainability. These are two of the most critical trends in logistics and supply chain management today, and this book provides valuable insights into how they are being implemented in the Middle East. The case studies in this book demonstrate the importance of digitalization and sustainability in logistics and supply chain management and how to overcome the challenges in implementing these technologies.

One of the most valuable aspects of this book is the inclusion of learning goals, key information, and practical questions and answers in each chapter. These elements provide readers with an interactive and engaging learning experience, and they help to reinforce the key concepts presented in each case study. The learning goals provide a clear understanding of what the reader should expect to gain from each chapter, and the key information highlights the most important points to be considered. The practical questions and answers help to test the reader's understanding of the material and to encourage critical thinking.

The inclusion of "lessons learned" at the end of each chapter is also a significant strength of the book. The lessons learned section provides a summary of the key takeaways from each case study, and it serves as a valuable tool for readers to reflect on the material and to apply the lessons learned to their own work. This section also provides the readers with a clear understanding of the key issues and challenges that were encountered in each case, and it highlights the strategies that were used to overcome these challenges.

In conclusion, I highly recommend this book to anyone interested in logistics and supply chain management. It provides a wealth of information and insights that will be of great value to the reader. I am confident that this book will be an essential resource for anyone working in this field.

Fošner Maja
Faculty of Logistics, University of Maribor, Slovenia

Foreword

The recent COVID-19 pandemic challenges have brought the world's attention to the importance of being efficient and resilient in the highly complex global business environment. However, the scale and severity that the supply chain and logistics sector witnessed during this period have not been observed globally in the recent generation. Thus, this draws attention to the importance of a thorough understanding of the global complexities in business logistics in the post-COVID-19 era.

I am delighted to write the foreword for this book as I have been a strong advocate of disseminating the current knowledge and wisdom to the next generation of researchers, aspiring professionals, seasoned practitioners, established academics and curious forward thinkers. The book offers a brilliant collection of thoughtful and rigorous research cases addressing the business community's current challenging and complex scenarios. The range of topics covered in the book will provide readers with different perspectives on COVID-19 challenges to logistics and supply chains and the role of digital technologies in mitigating those challenges by offering cases from different sectors across the Middle Eastern region. I personally found this book very interesting and valuable, and I believe readers would equally find this a helpful resource. In addition, the book includes a collection of papers from researchers who bring their wealth of industrial and academic experience to this compelling and timely domain of international business logistics. This book includes 15 chapters addressing a range of topics around international business logistics. These chapters can be broadly classified into two themes; 1) the role of technological/digital solutions to challenging supply chain and logistics problems, and 2) highlighting the COVID-19 challenges to the supply chain and logistics operations across the sector in the Middle East. In addition, the book covers interesting and insightful cases from various sectors, such as oil and gas, freight/cargo, steel, pharmaceutical and food.

I strongly recommend this book to all practitioners, young and established researchers and students. Particularly students in their final year of undergraduate studies, MSc and MBA students in business and engineering domains, professional consultants, and mid-to-senior management would find this book an essential reference to understand the challenges businesses face in the Middle East and how these challenges could be mitigated. The solutions discussed in the book will help them understand how to become a more resilient and competitive organisation in a fast-paced global environment.

Vikas Kumar
Birmingham City University, UK

Preface

The logistics and supply chain management field are paramount in the global markets and the Middle East, particularly, where ongoing economic and political changes and the constant need to adapt to the fast-paced global business environment have presented unique challenges and opportunities for practitioners and researchers. This field in the Middle East faces a wide range of logistical challenges related to infrastructure, customs, regulations, cultural and political differences. The COVID-19 pandemic has emphasised the crucial role that logistics and supply chain management play in maintaining the resilience and sustainability of supply networks in the Middle East region.

Despite the significance of logistics and supply chain management worldwide, a limited number of case studies provide in-depth and up-to-date information on this subject, especially in the Middle East.

This book on international business logistics in the Middle East tries to bridge this knowledge gap by providing a collection of case studies that cover a wide range of topics related to logistics and supply chain management in the Middle East.

The case studies in this book are designed to provide readers with an in-depth understanding of the concepts and applications of business logistics in the Middle East through real-world examples.

This book is intended for a broad audience, including students, decision-makers, managers, executives, business owners, and researchers. It is considered to provide students, researchers, entrepreneurs, and policymakers with accurate information and possible solutions in the logistics sector. The book will also provide insights and support to executive directors and practitioners while managing their projects or making decisions according to case studies experienced by other businesses in the same field. The book will also assist executive directors and practitioners with insights and help while managing projects or making decisions based on case studies from other businesses in the same field. Additionally, it aims to allow for the international exchange of knowledge regarding business logistics between practitioners and academic scholars. It also represents a significant contribution to the applied science of logistics by providing scientific record case studies of the business environment in the Middle East.

The book is divided into five main sections, each of which covers a specific topic related to logistics and supply chain management in the Middle East. The 15 chapters, written by 35 international experts in the field, delve into areas such as inventory management, warehouse management, transportation and logistics, supply chain sustainability and the impact of technology on logistics operations. The chapters are grouped into the following categories:

Section 1: Impact of Advanced Technology on Logistics and Supply Chain Management

This section covers chapters that explore the impact of advanced technologies such as blockchain, E-commerce and online platforms, intelligent transportation systems and autonomous vehicles and robotics on logistics and supply chain management in the Middle East.

Section 2: Impact of COVID-19 on Logistics and Supply Chain Management

This section covers chapters that discuss the impact of the pandemic on logistics and supply chain management in the Middle East, with a focus on the steel and pharmaceutical industries.

Section 3: Entrepreneurial Thinking in Logistics and Supply Chain Management

This section covers chapters that examine the role of entrepreneurial thinking in improving logistics activities' performance and supply chain management in the Middle East.

Section 4: Conflicts and Challenges in Logistics and Supply Chain Management

This section covers chapters that address challenges and conflicts that arise in logistics and supply chain management in the Middle East, including cargo theft, humanitarian aids, and multi-actor logistics incidents.

Section 5: Sustainable Logistics and Supply Chain Management

This section covers chapters that discuss various aspects of sustainable logistics and supply chain management in the Middle East, including green warehouses, ecologically friendly products, and sustainable road freight transport operations.

These topics have been selected to provide a comprehensive overview of the key challenges and opportunities facing logistics and supply chain professionals in the Middle East. Each chapter includes real-life case studies that give readers an in-depth understanding of the concepts and applications.

Furthermore, the book is designed as an applied case study for learning and teaching purposes in educational institutions and training programs for the logistics and supply chain management field. The case studies are supported by lessons learned section and practice questions with their answers to help readers to study, assess, and apply the concepts and strategies presented in the case studies. This approach will assist students in gaining a deeper insight into the subject matter.

Finally, this book is an essential resource for anyone interested in logistics and supply chain management in the Middle East. It provides a broad overview of the key challenges and opportunities facing the region's logistics and supply chain professionals and offers valuable insights and practical examples that can be applied to real-world situations. We believe that this book will be a valuable resource for anyone in the field of logistics and supply chain management.

Islam Abdelbary
University of Plymouth, UK

Sandra Haddad
Arab Academy for Science, Technology, and Maritime Transport, Egypt

Ghada Elkady
Arab Academy for Science, Technology, and Maritime Transport, Egypt

Acknowledgment

We would like to express our deepest appreciation and gratitude to all the individuals and organizations who have played a vital role in making this book a reality.

First and foremost, we would like to express our sincere gratitude to the co-editors of this book, Dr. Mahmoud Ramadan, Dr Ahmed Hussein, and Dr Sama Gad, who have dedicated countless hours of hard work, patience and expertise to bring this project to fruition. Their dedication, guidance and support have been invaluable throughout the reviewing process.

We would also like to extend our heartfelt thanks to all authors and contributors who have shared their knowledge, experience and insights in this book. Their contributions have been instrumental in providing a comprehensive and in-depth understanding of logistics and supply chain management in the Middle East.

Sincere appreciation is extended to our 36 reviewers who have given their time and expertise to provide precious feedback and suggestions that have helped to improve the quality of this book: Ahmed Hafez, Ashrakat Osama, Dina Allam, Farida Abdelwahab, Gianfranco Fancello, Hany Ayad, Hebatallah ElM-esmary, Hesham Aly, Islam Saleh, Karim Soliman, Khaled Alammari, Maha Asfour, May Mohamed, Mohamed Farouk, Mohamed Kholief, Mohamed Mahallawy, Mohamed Shalaby, Mohamed Yacout, Mostafa Gad, Patrizia Serra, Rania Ghazal, Sahar El Barky, Saleh Eisa, Sama Gad, Sarah El-Gamal, Saurav Negi, Shady Nabil, Sohaila Elgazar, Tamer Roushy, and Waleed Elkhadrawy.

Also, the highest appreciation to Mrs. Hala GalalEldeen for her helpful contributions in providing proofreading for our book. Her attention to detail and dedication to ensuring the quality of our work is greatly appreciated.

We would like to express our profound gratitude to the Arab Academy for Science, Technology, and Maritime Transport (AASTMT), especially Prof. Alaa AbdelBary, Vice President of the Academy for Postgraduate Studies and Scientific Research and Prof. Yasser Gaber, Dean of Scientific Research for their encouragement, guidance, providing the necessary resources and support, without which this book would not have been possible.

We would also like to express our heartfelt appreciation to Prof. Sara Elgazar, Dean of the College of International Transport and Logistics (CITL) main branch, for hosting this project from the beginning until the final stage. Her guidance, insights and motivation have been instrumental in the development of this book. The thankful extended to Prof. Eman Ismail, CITL Dean of the Smart Village Branch, for her willingness to collaborate with us on this project. Her support has greatly contributed to the success of this book.

We would like to express our sincerest appreciation to IGI Global, for their unwavering support and publishing this book. Their guidance and expertise have been instrumental in bringing this book to the readers.

Lastly, we would like to extend our heartfelt thanks to the companies and firms who have provided the data and case studies featured in this book. Their contributions have provided real-world examples and insights into logistics and supply chain management in the Middle East.

This book would not have been possible without the contributions and support of all these individuals and organizations. We are truly grateful for their efforts, dedication, and support. They have been instrumental in bringing this book to life, and we are honoured to have had the opportunity to work with such a talented and dedicated team.

Section 1

Impact of Advanced Technology on Logistics and Supply Chain Management

Chapter 1
Impact of the Technology Revolution on the Logistics Sector:
Autonomous Vehicles and Robotics for Intelligent Supply Chain

Hesham Aly
Arab Academy for Science, Technology, and Maritime Transport-Smart Village Campus, Egypt

EXECUTIVE SUMMARY

Developing in the smart cities concept and internet of things (IoT) technologies has become more demanding for the modern governments to overcome the growth of population and monitoring and controlling of the available resources. Smart cities with the use of the latest technologies in communications and electronics, which are the heart of IoT, have been developed and branched to cover most of the daily life needs. One of these branches is the intelligent transportation system (ITS), which is the heart of several fields like the logistics sector. This chapter aims to introduce a comprehensive overview for deploying two main examples of the technology revolution, which are autonomous vehicles and robotics technologies, in the logistics sector and illustrate the effect of using current and future approaches like IoT, AI, 5G, and more in the intelligent supply chain field.

INTRODUCTION

The development in the Smart Cities concept and Internet of Things (IoT) technologies become more demanding for the modern governments to overcome the growth of population, monitoring, and controlling of the available resources (Syed et al., 2021). Smart Cities with the use of the latest technologies in the electronics and communication engineering [ECE] field are the heart of IoT have been developed and branched to cover most of the daily life needs. Several subfields have been established like Infor-

DOI: 10.4018/978-1-6684-4686-7.ch001

mation technology which merged with computer engineering and computer science fields to be named Information and Communication Technology or ICT (Merzouk et al., 2020).

The development in ECE and other technologies affects several life branches like transportation and leads to what is called the Intelligent Transportation System (ITS) (Auer et al., 2016; Hasegawa, 2015; Neuweiler & Vanessa Riedel, 2017; Sun, 2021). Nowadays, ITS become the heart of several fields like the Logistics Sector. ITS represents the effect of integrating several advanced computer processing technologies, communication transmission techniques of data, control technology of autonomous vehicles, artificial intelligence, and electronic technology into the management of transportation systems for establishing a wide range of applications.

One of the important parts of the ITS future is autonomous vehicles. This part is based on several communication technologies whether internal in the vehicle, between vehicles, or among vehicles and the network infrastructure. Autonomous vehicles (or self-driving vehicles) attract several industry leaders like Amazon, Google, Uber, Tesla and more to make a great investment in these technologies. According to some references carmakers invested around $120 billion in the field of autonomous drive development in the interval between March 2017 and March 2019 (Sun, 2021).

On the other hand, development of the Robotics field with integrating IoT techniques has become more demanding in industry as it is considered an important part in the foundation of the Industry 4.0 revolution (Calia & D'Aprile, 2020; Paksoy et al., 2021; Virbahu Nandishwar Jain, 2019). The definition of Industry 4.0 concept can be stated as the digital transformation of production, manufacturing and the related industries that symbolize a new phase in the organization and control the chain of the industrial value.

Recently, the logistic sector has become one of the most demanding fields that needs to be improved by adopting these technologies, in order to improve this sector's performance in several fields like: supply chain, logistics and operation management, etc. (Dillmann, 2016; Kersten et al., 2017; Tay & Loh, 2021; Van der Meer et al., 2018).

Integrating artificial intelligence (AI), IoT, Autonomous Vehicles (AV) and Robotics with the supply chain field leads to a new approach which is called the Intelligent Supply Chain (ISC). This approach is considered as a digital transformation of the conventional supply chain process aiming to improve the economy globally. In this chapter we will consider Egypt as a case study for illustrating the digitizing approach as an example of developing the logistic sector in the Middle East.

This chapter aims to introduce a comprehensive layout of deploying autonomous vehicle in addition to robotics technologies in the logistics sector and illustrate the effect of using current and future approaches like IoT, AI, 5G, etc.

By the end of this chapter, reader will be familiar with following:

1. General information about the current and the expected future technologies
2. The basic concepts of the autonomous vehicles and Robotics technologies
3. The impact of these technologies in the Logistic Sector in general, and especially in the field of the Intelligent Supply Chain (ISC).
4. The expected development of integrating the mentioned technologies and ISC to improve the economy in Egypt is consistent with the digital transformation vision.

This chapter contains five sections. First section shows the research scope in this chapter. Second section starts the journey of this book by showing briefly the foundation of the latest technologies and the development of these technologies. Third section discusses the smart cities concept and the merging between the technologies mentioned in section 2 and supply chain management. Fourth section describes the developing cities or what is called digital transformation with the effect of this transformation in the supply chain and focuses on Egypt which is currently considered as one of the developed countries in the Middle East. Finally, the fifth section is the conclusion of this chapter and the main outcomes from this chapter.

RESEARCH SCOPE OF THIS CHAPTER

John woke up by listening to his favorite music and the curtains was opened to enter the sunlight with a beautiful breeze getting from the air conditioning. "Good Morning John, Bathroom is ready", Alexa said. "Good morning Alexa, please prepare my breakfast quickly" John said. Alexa replied "Ok, 10 minutes' breakfast will be ready". Alexa is not his wife, it is just a smart phone App which can control all his home appliances and smart systems attached to his smart home.

While this can be categorized as a Science Fiction (Sci-Fi) movie or story from several years, it is now not considered the same. Then why? Simply, it is the technological revolution which affects our daily life and most people rely on it for most of his/her daily activities. It is very familiar these days to hear about artificial intelligence (AI), smart city, Internet of things (IoT), but what are these technologies or words? And how can these participate in the supply chain?

This chapter tries to answer these questions and more. First, it is need to understand where all these technologies start. Second, the influence of these technologies on the supply chain sector need to be explore. Finally focusing on one or two examples especially with the motivation found for most countries to make what is called "Digital transformation" to show this effect. So three steps are required to reach this chapter goals: 1) Understand basics, 2) Know the effect, and 3) Show by example.

For following this method, Figure 1 shows the research scope of this chapter. Starting from dividing the most foundations of the internet of things technology: First, the invention of the transistor then showing the developing of this invention to establish what is called sensor and actuator networks and computer network which was the milestone of IoT and the merging and applying these technologies in several fields. The main two examples mentioned in this study is Robotics technology which develops deeply in the industry sector and leads to Industry 4.0 standard that will be explained later.

The second example is the autonomous (or self-driving) vehicles, which are still in the early stages but are promising to develop the transportation sector which is one of the main fields in the supply chain management sector.

The research journey continues by explaining the effect of the previous technologies to establish smart cities concept. Smart cities concept is utilized by most of the current countries improve its service and to enhance the monitoring and controlling of their countries' resources. Hence, the intelligent transportation system (ITS) and Industry 4.0 and 5.0 standards are described in this chapter as two examples of the influence of the previous technologies on the smart cities and the supply chain management.

Digital transformation in EGYPT will be an example of employing the technologies on smart cities concept. Egypt' government is currently one of the developed governments that are starting to enhance the life quality of citizens using several of latest technologies to explore the goals of this chapter. Egypt 2030 vision is coherent with Egypt's commitment for Sustainable Development Goals (SDGs) 2035.

Figure 1. Research scope of this chapter

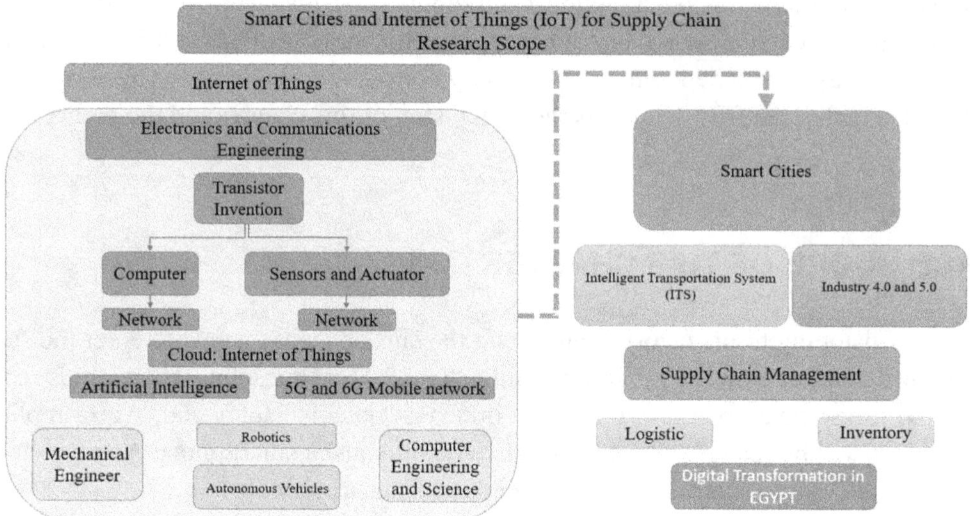

Egyptian's government has formulated an inclusive vision which contains the fundamentals related to digital transforming of Egypt society and digital economy where all technologies can be integrated in almost all life fields. For this purpose, the Government has targeted promoting and enhancing the sector of information technology and communications.

To conclude, this section explores and shows the criteria and scope of this research to explain the impact of the technologies on the supply chain management criteria. An illustration was used to explain the journey of the chapter to the reader to be familiar with the sequence of this chapter.

INTERNET OF THINGS (IoT)

As shown in Figure 1 in the previous section, the journey will start by explaining the foundation of the technology revolution which is explained in this section. While IoT can be classified or defined by several researchers based on their research background; this section explains the history timeline for the foundation of the developing current technologies which started with the transistor invention.

Transistor Invention

While there are several inventions that changed the world; transistor invention can be considered the second invention after electricity that changed the world and affects all our daily life now and is expected to extend to the future.

In the 40's at the labs of Bell, three scientists John Bardeen, Walter Brattain and William Shockley (Figure 2) developed a device that changes the world, which is called a "Transistor" (Huff, 2003). Transistor gives more control for scientists and engineers to use it in several applications like electronic switch and audio amplifiers, these words may sound like gibberish. To understand, imagine that you want to make a call with your "smartphone" then you select the number you want to dial then press on the screen

Figure 2. Bell's Lab scientists who invent transistor
Source: Ganapati, 2009

"Call button" then when you heard the voice from the other side and it was not clear then you decide to raise the volume of the sound to hear. All of these use 1000s or more transistors to make all of these steps. Actually, all of these previous steps can be considered as a logic sequence. Hence your smartphone needs to be working in logical sequence. This point is the key point of what is called a computer.

Actually, the point of start was the mathematical operations. Our daily life needs a lot of mathematical operations like purchasing, building databases and dealing with huge numbers and more. Because of these and more, scientists and engineers have always throughout history designed machines that can help them for calculating like abacus as shown in Figure 3. If we look at history, we can see that all ancient emperors like scientists at Ancient EGYPT and China era developed and designed several machines for calculating the area of the farms and use for astronomy to know the date and the year which was very essential for agriculture. However, all of these machines were based on mechanical systems, which needed maintenance and were very huge in size and took time for calculation. All of this changed after inventing the transistor.

Scientists and engineers use the transistor to build equipment based on electrical systems to compute huge numbers of mathematical operations. The main contribution of transistors is not only in its behavior but the ability to reduce its size (see Figure 4) to less than one hair diameter (17 micrometers to 181 micrometer) and the ability to connect millions of transistors in very small size packages called chips.

To understand this point; for example, the personal computers that use processors from Intel Company-Intel Core i7-1165G7 contains 8200 million transistors, the effective length of the transistor is about

Figure 3. Ancient Chinese abacus

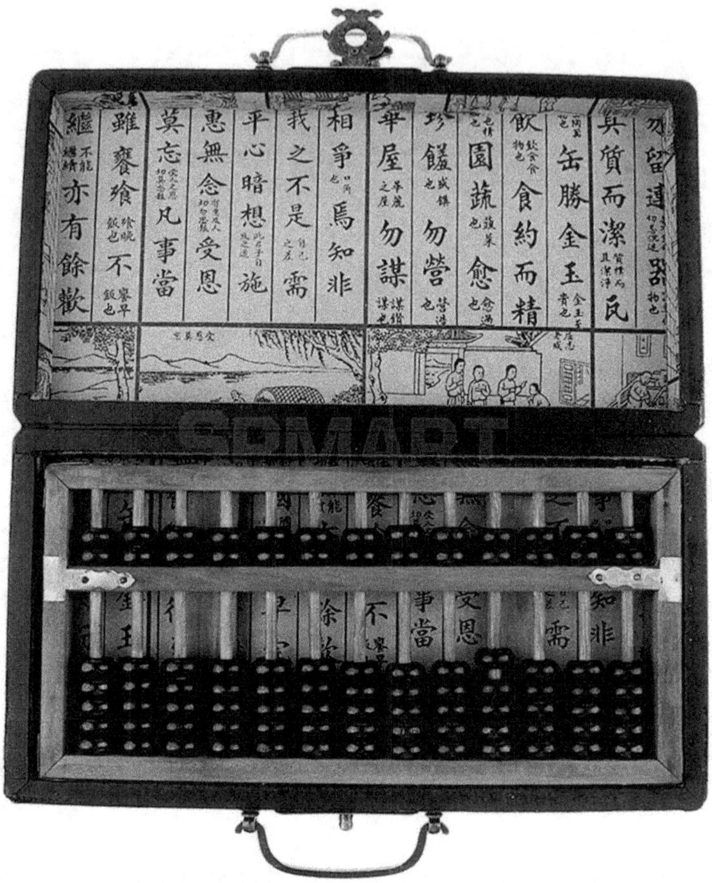

10nm working at turbo frequency 4.7GHz. The frequency means the number of times the transistor can switch OFF and ON in one second, hence the mentioned processor made of transistors can switch about 4.7×10^9 times per second. This can be translated into the ability of doing billions of operations in a few seconds. Transistor technology opened several applications that were very difficult to reach like space applications, or develop several fields like business and logistics fields. The development in electronics devices still keeps growing and the shrinking of the size of the transistors reaches nanometers and is called Nano electronics. However, this point is out of our scope in this research.

Computer and Computer Networks

The first electronic computer was named ENIAC and was used in WORLD WAR II as shown in Figure 5. ENIAC was especially designed for computing values for tables of artillery range, it missed some features which would have made it a more generally useful machine. As mentioned before, the revolution of the transistor fabrication led to designing a computer smaller in size with higher ability to process or to compute more data and numbers. Two questions were how to improve these computers' processing in

Figure 4. Revolution of transistor miniaturization

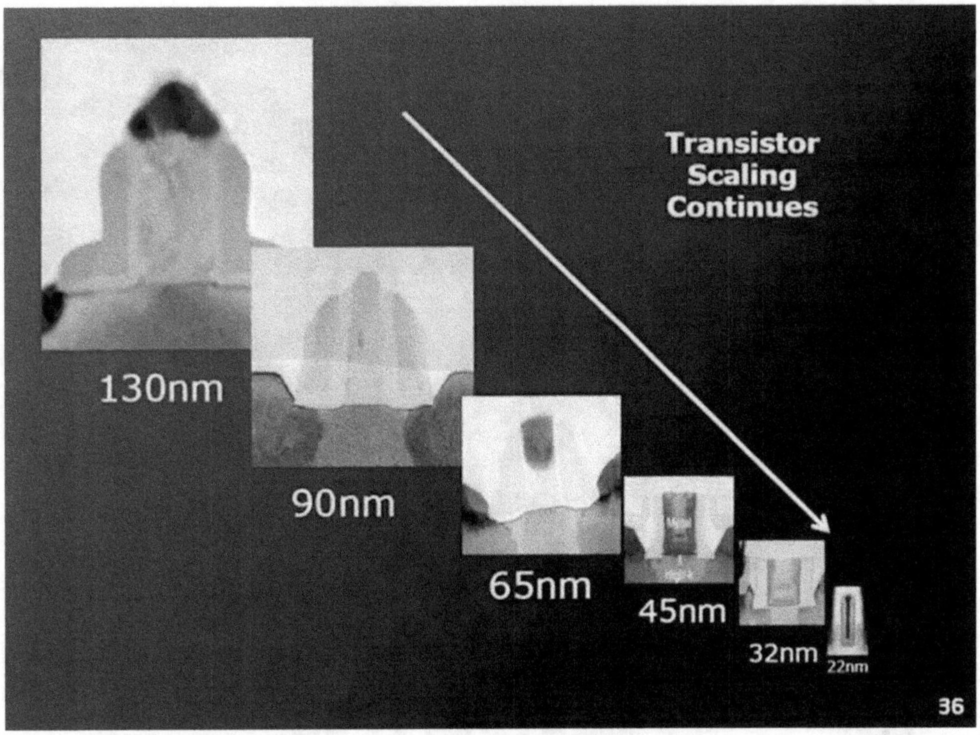

parallel with the development of the transistor fabrication and why do not these computers work together? Simply connect these computers to each other and establish what is called now "Computer networks."

In 1969, engineers in The Defense Data Network, which is a part of the Defense Department, for widespread industry use within its Advanced Research Project ARPANET (Advanced Research Projects Agency Network) communicated with two or more computers at the same time to exchange data and use it to improve mathematical processing. They invent a novel protocol of communications called Transfer Control Protocol/Internetwork Protocol (TCP/IP). This concept of connection between computers was the first step of what is now called the Internet.

Sensors and Actuator Network

Sensors are devices that convert any physical quantity like temperature, pressure, etc., to electrical signals which can be processed by transistors. Sensor signals represent these physical quantities which are called data. The sensor has the ability to work in different environments even if it was harsh environments like space, furnace, and machine.... etc. This leads to use it for collecting data in several applications. The concept of using several sensors to collect data in some applications for example collecting data about some buildings or bridges to stand on its case is called sensor network. Figure 7 shows an illustration for wireless sensor network (WSN). Electronics and Communication engineers start to attach sensors to very small computers and name it node. One node can communicate with another using a wire or wireless system. The idea is to collect data from several locations of a system for monitoring. This con-

Figure 5. ENIAC first general-purpose computer used at the World War II
Source: Burks & Davidson, 1999

Figure 6. Computer network
Source: Introduction to Computers/Networks - Wikiversity, n.d.

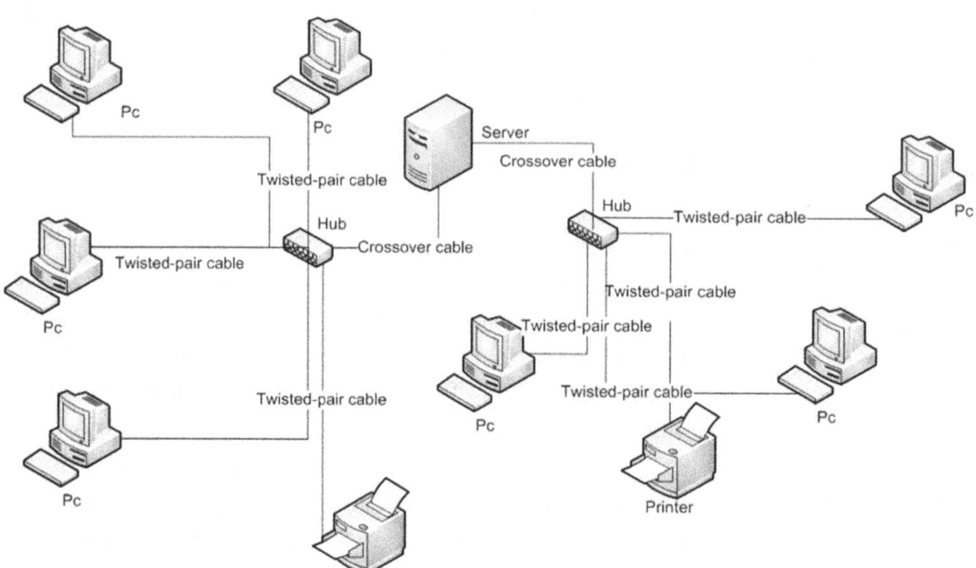

Figure 7. Wireless sensor network (WSN) example
Source: Priswanto et al., 2019

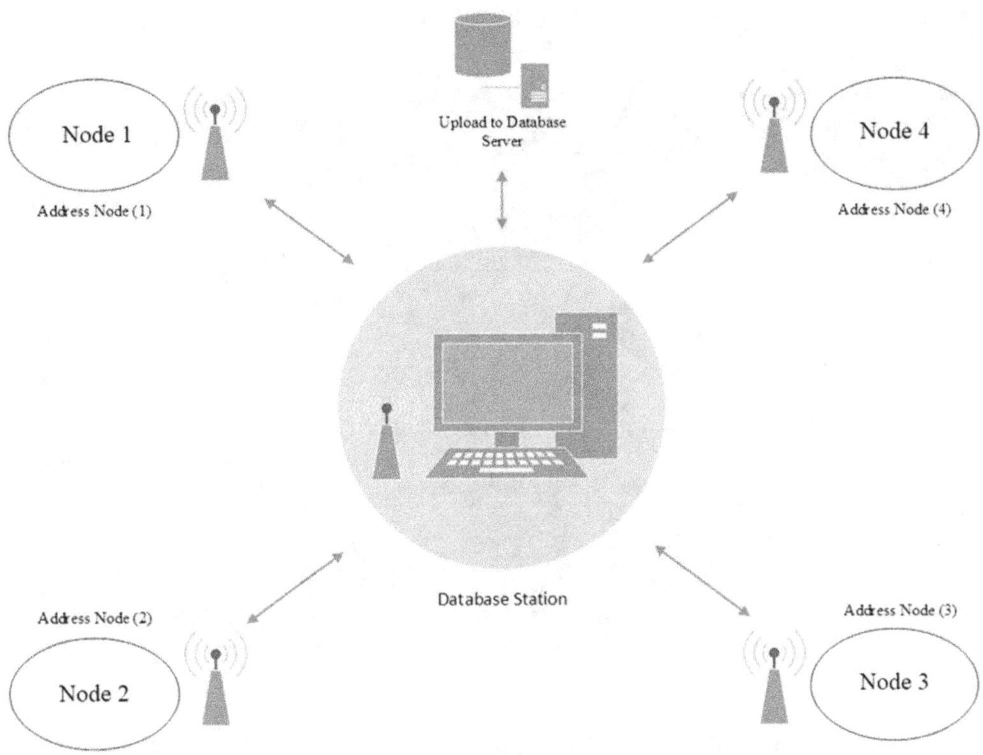

cept started to be named Wired and Wireless Sensor Network (WWSN) (Algamili et al., 2021; Gams & Kolenik, 2021; Poongodi et al., 2019).

This type of network was connected to a computer to collect all the data from several nodes and make analysis to understand the status of the system that those nodes attached to. For example, civil engineers use this concept to monitor the bridges and detect changes in structure, damage and levels of critical stress at an early stage which is called Structure Health Monitoring (SHM) see Figure 8 (Chen & Ni, 2018).

On the other hand, an actuator can be defined as a device that receives an electrical signal to convert it into mechanical motion. As sensors, actuators' fabrication technology leads to design actuators 9with a huge size to micrometers and nanometers in size (see figure 9) (Algamili et al., 2021; Charles, 2005; Kim, 2019).

The main tasks of sensors and actuators is to interact with the surroundings to receive and transmit signals for monitoring and controlling. By attaching several sensors, actuators or both to computers for controlling and analyzing the data, then Sensor and Actuator Network (SAN) (Bauer et al., 2021; Poongodi et al., 2019) is established as shown in Figure 10. SAN is the first stage of what is now called "Internet of Things".

Internet of Things and Cloud

The merge between the computer network and Internet from one side and SAN on the other side is what is called "Internet of Things (IoT)". Several definitions of IoT are exist, but one was very clear: Internet

Figure 8. Structure health monitoring
Source: Chen & Ni,2018

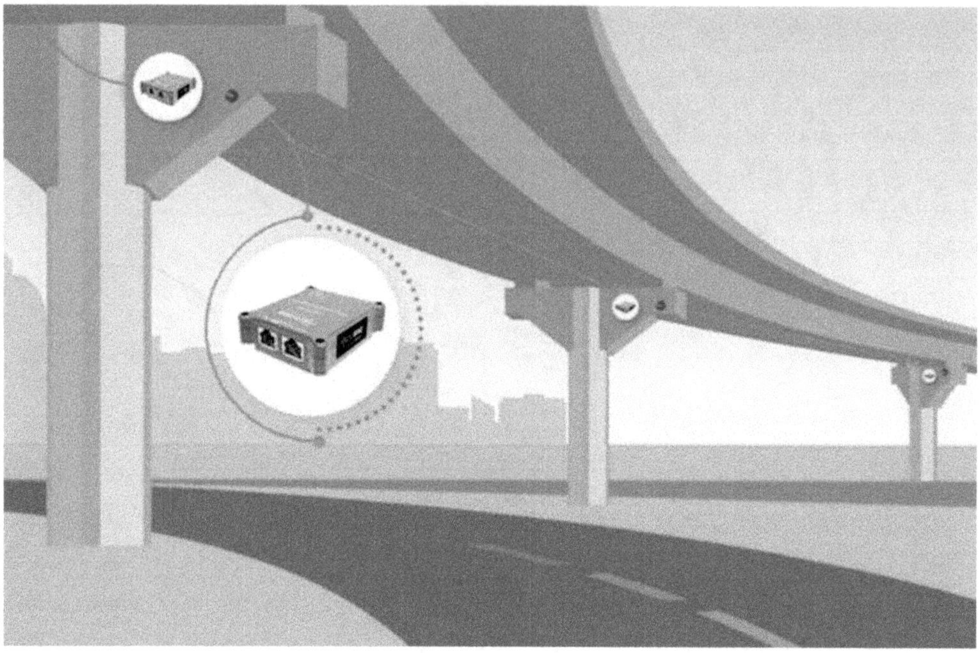

of Things = "Sensors and actuators embedded in physical objects are linked through wired and wireless networks, often using the same Internet Protocol (IP) that connects the Internet". The actual term "Internet of Things" was stated in 1999 by Kevin Ashton during the time he worked at Procter & Gamble. Ashton, who was working in optimization of the supply chain, aimed to attract attention of senior management to RFID which is a new developed technology (Alavi et al., 2018; Zambonelli, 2016). In (Poongodi et al., 2019) authors studied the IoT sensors and mentioned the spreading of the IoT sensors in many daily applications as shown in Figure 11. While Figure 11 was showing the sensors only for IoT, actuators also found for these applications. This may refer that several researchers consider SAN as sensor network and consider the connectivity between these sensors and actuators.

By increasing the data and commands from sensors and to actuators, the processing relying only on the attached computer will increase. Instead of using one computer, using computer networks will help to improve the processing. The amount of nodes (node is the sensor, actuator, or both embedded with computer or electronic control system) increased which leads to dramatically increasing the amount of data need to be processed. All of this introduce the need of using the concept of "Cloud". The cloud is a massive interconnected network of powerful servers which provides services for both businesses and people. This leads to the so called Cloud computing. it is computing services delivery including storage, networking, servers, databases, software, analytics, and intelligence—over the Internet ("the cloud") to provide rapid innovation, flexible resources, and economies of scale.

Figure 9. MEMS: micro-electro-mechanical system
Source: Kim, 2019

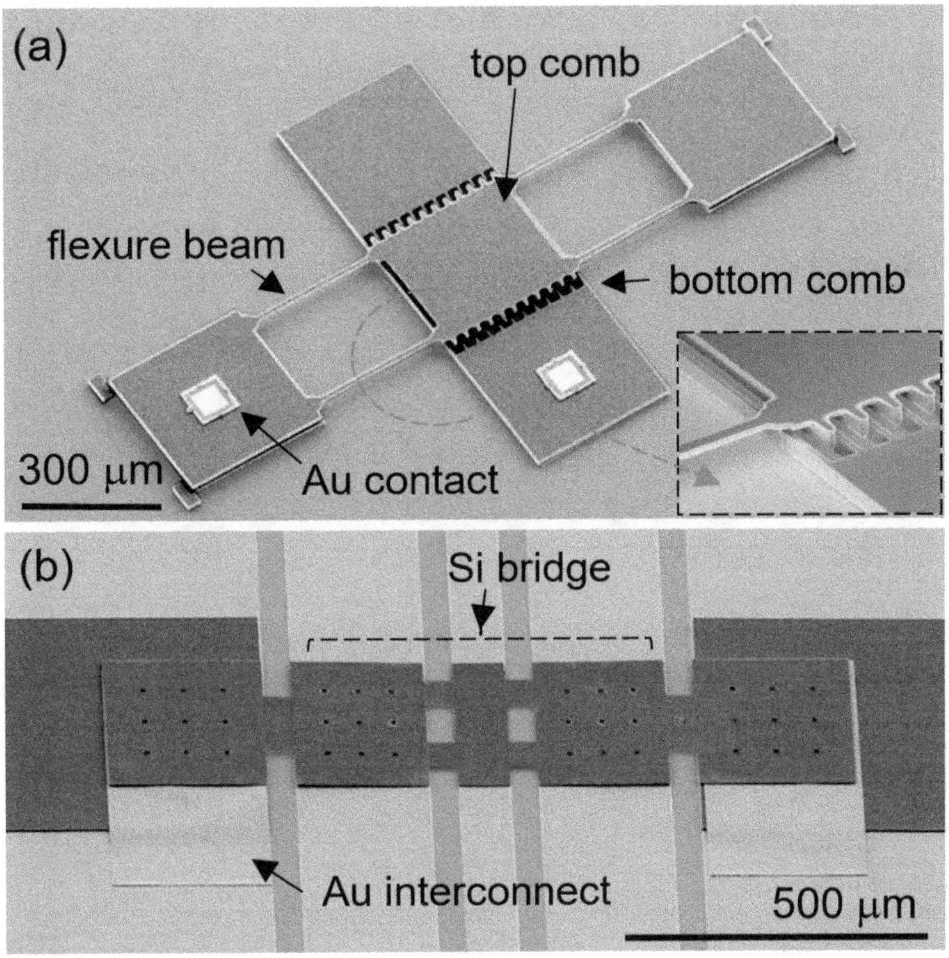

Artificial Intelligence

AI was invented in 1953 after computers started to be involved. However, it shows several challenges and was not confirmed till late 2000s with the Neural Network (NN) concept as shown in Figure 12. Neural Network is simply a trial to mimic the human brain thinking behavior. This leads scientists to study deep in the human brain and study how humans think and differentiate and make decisions (Gams & Kolenik, 2021; Sun, 2021; Taulli, 2019).

However, AI faced several challenges because of the mathematical model done by the scientist which was not sufficient to be used. In 1980, Neural networks established and was the real step to mimic the human brain structure which consists of 1000's of neurons connected to each other. Although the NN model also was not accurate because the amount of data fed to the computers programmed to analyze the data based on NN was not enough to make the computers learn and make decisions. This point was the key to explore AI, by increasing the amount of data in the way computers succeed.

Figure 10. Sensor and actuator network
Source: Al-Hammouri et al., 2007

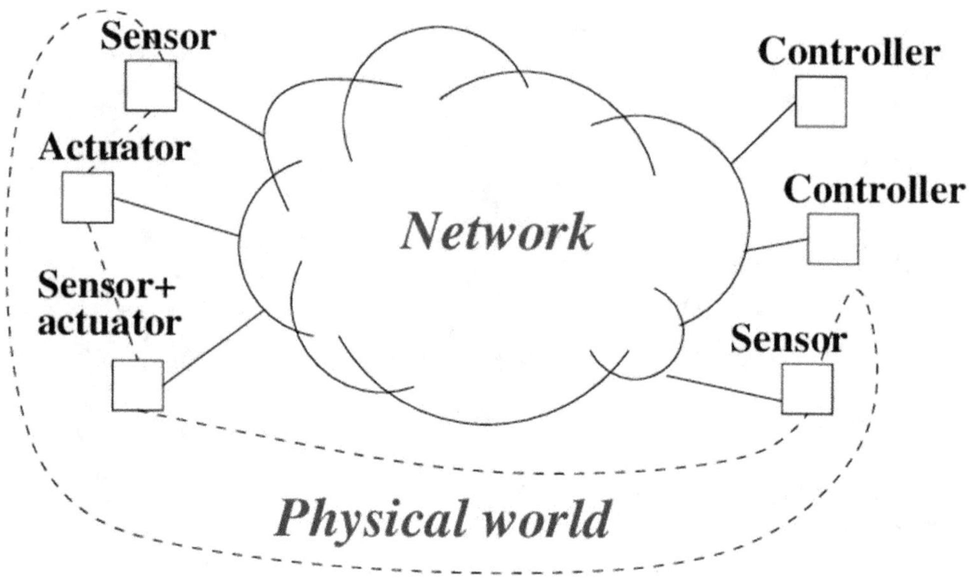

AI now has two major subfields which are: Machine Learning (ML) and Deep Learning (DL). Machine learning which mainly considers the classification between data, regression and estimation. Deep learning which is a part of machine learning dealing with predicting outcomes whenever you have a lot of data to learn from and is based on artificial neural network (ANN) theory.

Figure 11. Sensor network for IoT applications
Source: Poongodi et al., 2019

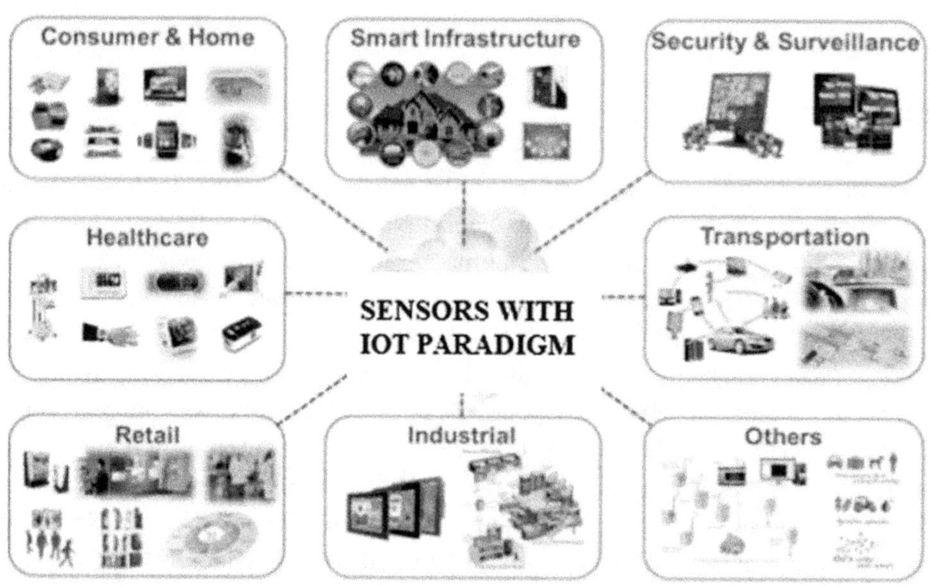

Figure 12. Artificial intelligence timeline
Source: Anyoha, 2020

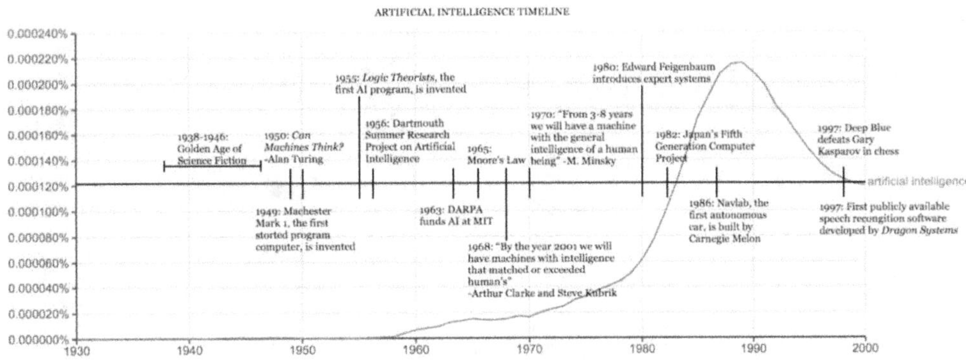

Combining IoT with AI delivers smart machines, which can directly create new products or enhance existing services by enabling the business to rapidly process & analyze the data (Aboualmal, 2018). This point is the main milestone for the future of the world.

5G and 6G

IoT is based on connecting computers and sensors and actuators attached together to process and analyze data. The technologies for establishing and developing this connection is essential. One of the challenges of the IoT is how to add more data and applications and dealing with data process in fast, reliable, low latency communications.

The communication engineering field developed rapidly especially for mobile phone networks and brings to the world communication and connection service with very high speed. The road map of the modern communication engineering starts with the revolution of cellular mobile phones. The era of mobile communication started in early 1980s, and since then, in the past few decades' mobile communication has experienced massive growth.

Mobile networks have developed from 1G to 5G and beyond (Chataut & Akl, 2020; European Commission for Industry Technologies, 2020; Sun, 2021). All mobile networks are consisting of base stations (BSs), user equipment (UE), and core networks. The developing from 1G to 6G is summarized in Figure 13. In the early 1980s, the 1G cellular networks were introduced and analog signals were used for services of voice-only. The second-generation (2G) mobile networks were reduced in the early 1990s and were generally considered digital versions of 1G networks. Along with voice services, they allowed Short Message Service (SMS) and basic email services.

In the early 2000s, 3G mobile networks were introduced and were based on Global System for Mobile communication (GSM) and Code Division Multiple Access (CDMA) systems. These systems provide web browsing on cellular phones along with voice and other services. After that in early 2010s, 4G mobile network increased the offered data rates to reach 100 Mbps and more data traffic can be handled with enhanced quality of service (QoS). This network contains applications such as video conferencing, mobile television, and online gaming. Currently, 5G cellular networks started to be implemented which is aiming to be 100 times faster than 4G networks.

Figure 13. The developing from 1G to 6G
Source: Vaigandla et al., 2021

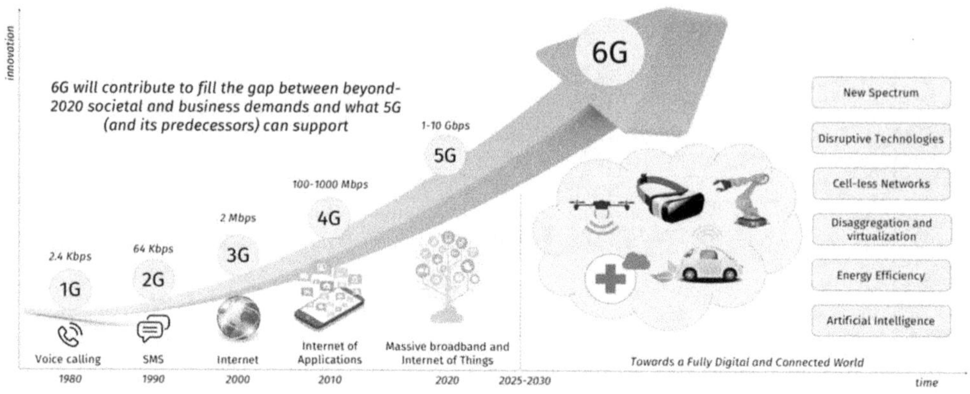

The new networks approach 6G are a complete wireless networks without limitation. Currently, the developmental stage, and it will deliver a great speed of transmission in the range of terabit. A smart antenna, large memory mobile phone and massive optical network are required for this technology. These networks will be cell-free, and it would adopt artificial AI in wireless networks (Chataut & Akl, 2020).

Robotics and Autonomous Vehicles

Merging disciplines to invent and develop products or services become more demanding for individuals and governments. The technology revolutions, and merging the previous technologies with several fields lead to big development in those fields.

Robotics

Robot may be a machine taking after a human being and able to replicate certain human developments and capacities naturally. The primary electronic independent robots (or "modern-day" robots) were made in Bristol, Britain in 1948 by William Dark Walter (Holland, 2003). There's common understanding that for a machine to be characterized as a robot by today's measures, it ought to meet the taking after criteria:

- Capable of programming electronically.
- Capable of data processing or physical receiving.
- Autonomous working.
- Mobility.
- Physical parts operation or processing.
- Environment sensing.
- Intelligent behavior similar to humans.

Robots nowadays are commonly used in the field of industry to perform tasks like manufacturing, on the other hand their usage in other purposes are increased such as medical fields like operating robots

Figure 14. Society of automotive engineers (SAE) automation levels
Source: Harrison, 2022

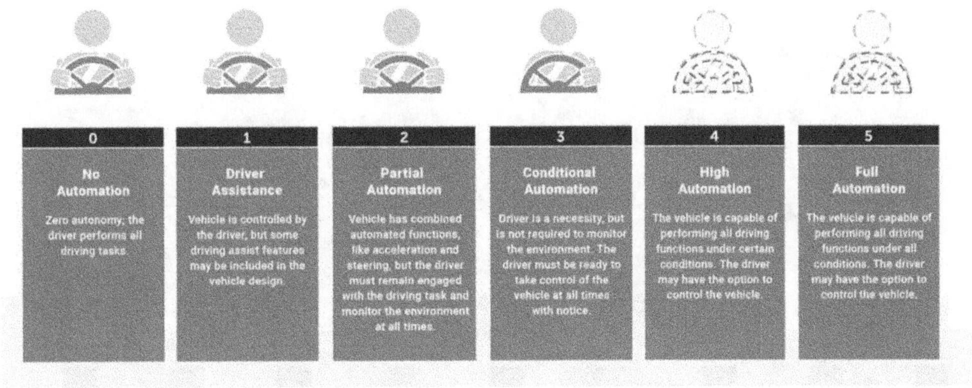

and dog therapy robots. Also, utilizing robots to perform tasks that are too dangerous for humans are increasing rapidly like using drones in military situations.

Applying AI on the Mechanical technology leads to what is called Independent robots (Paksoy et al., 2021). Independent robots are cleverly machines competent of performing assignments within the world autonomously of either coordinate human control or settled programming. Cases run from independent rambles, to mechanical generation robots, to your mechanical vacuum cleaner. They combine mastery from the areas of Fake Insights, mechanical autonomy, and data science. The independent robot must have the capacity to see its environment, analyze situational data in arrange to create choices based on what it sees, and after that adjust its activities based on these choices.

There are few autonomous robots in operation nowadays. Indeed, most modern, energetic robots such as those utilized in a car manufacturing plant perform concurring to inactive programming. Most autonomous robots are as it were semi-autonomous and will likely stay so indeed as more principal independence gets to be in fact doable.

For case, the Roomba vacuum cleaner does not move agreeing to a pre-programmed course and can adjust its course powerfully as its environment changes. Be that as it may, it encompasses an exceptionally constrained degree of flexibility that's decided by its programming.

Autonomous Vehicle

In the field of vehicle engineering or Aerospace; vehicles design is developed to what is called Autonomous vehicle or self-driving vehicle. The development of this field effects in several sectors like supply chain. Before showing this influence of AV on Supply chain, this section will bring overview on AV.

Autonomy in vehicles is often categorized in six levels, according to a system developed by Society of Automotive Engineers (SAE) (Gams & Kolenik, 2021; McKinsey, 2019). The SAE levels can be roughly understood as Level 0 - no automation; Level 1 - hands on/shared control; Level 2 - hands off; Level 3 - eyes off; Level 4 - mind off, and Level 5 - steering wheel optional as shown in Figure 14.

The autonomous vehicle has the potential to transform not only our transportation systems, but also our economies and urban planning. While the majority of the research focused on the political and regulatory context for autonomous vehicles, future implications were also explored. Policymakers must

Figure 15. Autonomous vehicle (self-driving)
Source: Thakurdesai & Aghav, 2020

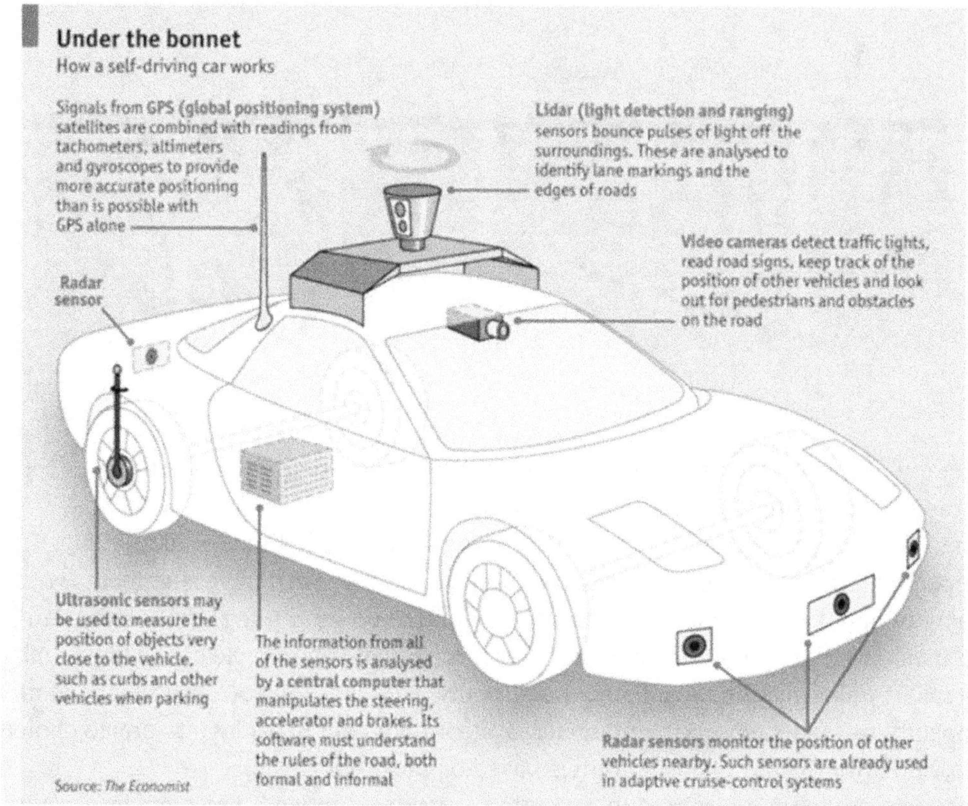

think about how to plan for future outcomes as well as how to support autonomous vehicle innovation in the existing political and regulatory context.

In common, autonomous vehicles utilize sensors and data innovation to decide their area and boundaries amid a voyage whereas keeping up security, proficiency, and availability. From checking all parts of the car for the driver to utilizing AI-based cars to form judgments and take control of the controlling wheel, the conceivable outcomes are perpetual (Anderson et al., 2014; Angerholzer III et al., 2017; European Commission for Industry Technologies, 2020; Raats et al., 2020).

The change in security that comes normally when we dispose of the root of most activity occurrences: human conduct on the street, is a remarkable advantage of AV computerization. Producers have a parcel of encounter testing non-autonomous vehicles, and the strategy involves running millions of test kilometers to settle issues. Once the parameters are set, the vehicle must be innovatively reasonable for the street and meet all appropriate rules. The same strategy applies to independent vehicles, which must follow to an assortment of laws and directions that are regularly the obligation of the driver.

Since of the different issues experienced amid testing on open roadway foundation with ordinary activity, this approach cannot be considered secure sufficient in all utility cases. As a result, test destinations and frameworks that permit independent vehicles to test in whimsical activity circumstances in practical settings are required. Moreover, a ensured environment permits for the advancement of circumstances

Figure 16. The revolution of autonomous vehicle technologies
Source: Matthews (2020)

that are troublesome to reproduce or hazardous in real-life circumstances (e.g., near-accident affairs) (Raats et al., 2020).

Meeting safety necessities and creating selections for multi-focal optimized driving are power-assisted by sensors settled within the vehicle or within the atmosphere (including alternative vehicles) see Figures 15 and 16. Furthermore, info is changed with the vehicle' Digital Twin, which can have extra information concerning traffic, roadwork, weather, and other conditions. The communication between the vehicle and other external entities is enabled by wireless communication technologies, the foremost distinguished of that is 5G, which provides end-to-end service guarantees.

Section Conclusion

To conclude, this section gives a very brief introduction on the technologies used to establish the IoT and show the future view of these technologies. It started from the transistor invention to Autonomous Vehicles. All these technologies affect directly to our current and future life. In the next section, Smart Cities concept is explained to show the influence of these technologies form the governmental point of view especially the supply chain management sector.

SMART CITIES

In the previous section of this chapter, technology's foundation of IoT was discussed briefly to make the reader familiar with the need and the impact of these technologies on the smart cities concept and especially for the Supply chain sector. This section will continue the journey by describing the Smart Cities concept and the impact of the previous technologies on it. Hence, two examples will be more focused which are the Intelligent Transportation Systems (ITS) and Industry 4.0 Concept.

ITS and Industry 4.0 were selected to demonstrate the robotics and autonomous vehicles technologies in the smart cities and Supply chain management sector. From this point this section will go through the Intelligent Supply Chain (ISC) management calls for the implementation and leveraging of modern technologies to optimize various facets of the supply chain. Supply chain has several subfields which are affected by the utilization of the new technologies in this sector. The employment of the explained technologies in this chapter on Logistic and inventory subfields will take place as two cases.

Smart cities concept has been developed in many countries and it is familiar for some countries to use this concept with the big revolution of several technologies to adapt and improve its services for its people. This improvement is called digital transformation. Nowadays, digital transformation has been demanded by several developed countries like Egypt. Egypt established a political strategy called EGYPT 2030 which is transferring all of its services to be based on digital transformation. In this chapter, EGYPT 2030 will be explored and identify the plan of this transformation especially for the Supply chain management sector.

Population in big cities and capitals started to rapidly increase after the Second World war. This leads to increased consumption of the resources without any controlling or monitoring. Therefore, governments started to use the latest technologies which developed to be IoT to establish what is called Smart Cities concept. Smart cities is a concept that the new government uses the new technologies in the ICT field not only to monitor and control but also to improve the service for their people.

The concept of "Smart City" first appeared in the 1990s. At that point in time, the focus was on the impact of new Information and Communication Technologies on modern infrastructures within cities. The California Institute for Smart Communities focused on how a city could be planned to implement information technologies and how communities could become smart (Aboualmal, 2018; Samih, 2019; Syed et al., 2021).

Some years later, the Center of Governance at the University of Ottawa started criticizing the idea of smart cities as being too technically oriented. A few years ago, researchers started asking real smart cities to stand up and illustrate the aspects that are hidden behind the term "smart city" (Alavi et al., 2018; Bauer et al., 2021; Gupta, 2019; Syed et al., 2021).

The label "smart city" is used interchangeably with similar terms like "intelligent city" or "digital city" (Albino, Berardi, & Dangelico, 2015). These variants are categorized into three dimensions (Harrison et al., 2010; Nam & Pardo, 2011): Technology, People and Community.

Smart cities applications are many and can be classified in several aspects (Aly, 2019; Gupta, 2019; Samih, 2019). Figure 17 shows the main applications of Smart Cities (Syed et al., 2021). It can be concluded from the figure, that most of the governmental services have been covered.

IoT is considered as a combination of several huge networks combined like computer, WWSN, and cellular; Smart cities architecture can be designed based on Network architecture as shown in Figure 18. Based on (Samih, 2019), Smart cities architecture is composed of 3 sections:

1. Physical layer, which considers gathering data from an object or sending information to it.
2. Network layer, which mainly focus on the communication technologies between the physical layer elements and the application layer
3. Application layer, which is dealing with the analysis of the data gathered by the physical layer and the decision need to make

The relation between IoT and Smart cities is relation needs and technology as shown in Figure19 below (Alavi et al., 2018). The cycle between needs and technology is the main foundation for sustainability of the IoT and the Smart cities.

However, Smart cities concept development faces several challenges. These challenges also can be classified in several ways as shown in Figure 18 (Bauer et al., 2021; Gupta, 2019; Syed et al., 2021). In

Figure 17. Smart city applications
Source: Syed et al., 2021

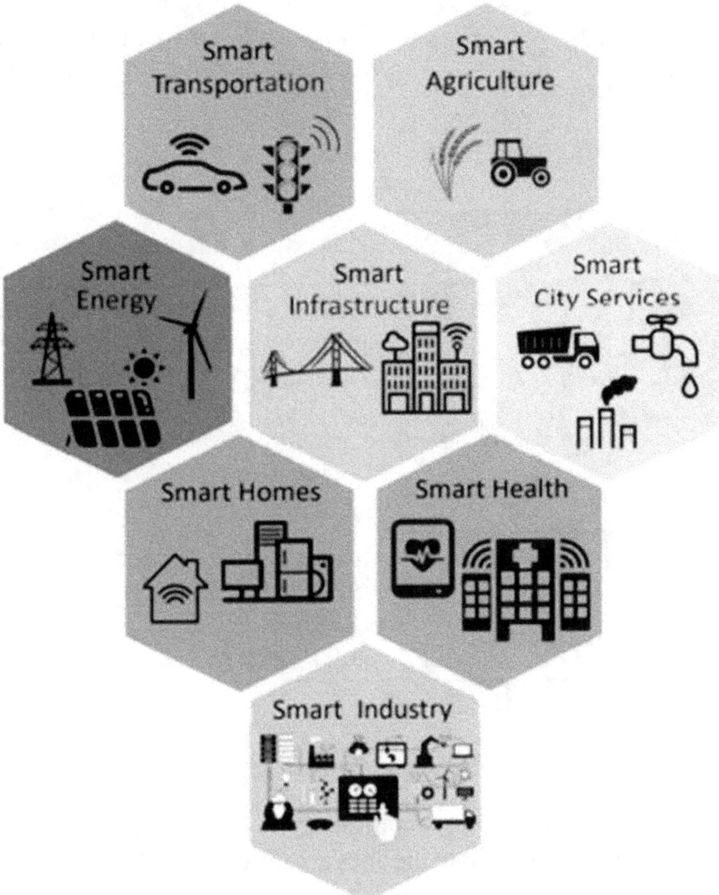

Figure 18, three different references were used to show the variation of classification. However, mainly the security issue is the main concern. This point is very essential because the value of information is invaluable. The information deal or process can affect the national security of the countries. This can be the other side of the technology. This issue and challenge fetched the nation's gigantic sums of cash to secure their individuals and resources.

While most of the applications of the smart cities are affected the Supply chain, the big demand and the revolution in the industry and transportation is very noticeable and can be considered the big impact of the supply chain development. In the contexts of the smart industry, standardization for the Industry revolutions have been commonly divided into 5 sections from Industry 1.0 till Industry 5.0 as will be shown later. While Industry 5.0 is still in the early stage, Industry 4.0 standard and concept is currently not reached to its end. Industry 4.0 deals with the using the latest technologies to reach fully automated industries. This rises by the big revolution of robotics and the merging with AI.

Figure 18. Smart cities architecture can be designed based on network architecture
Source: Samih, 2019

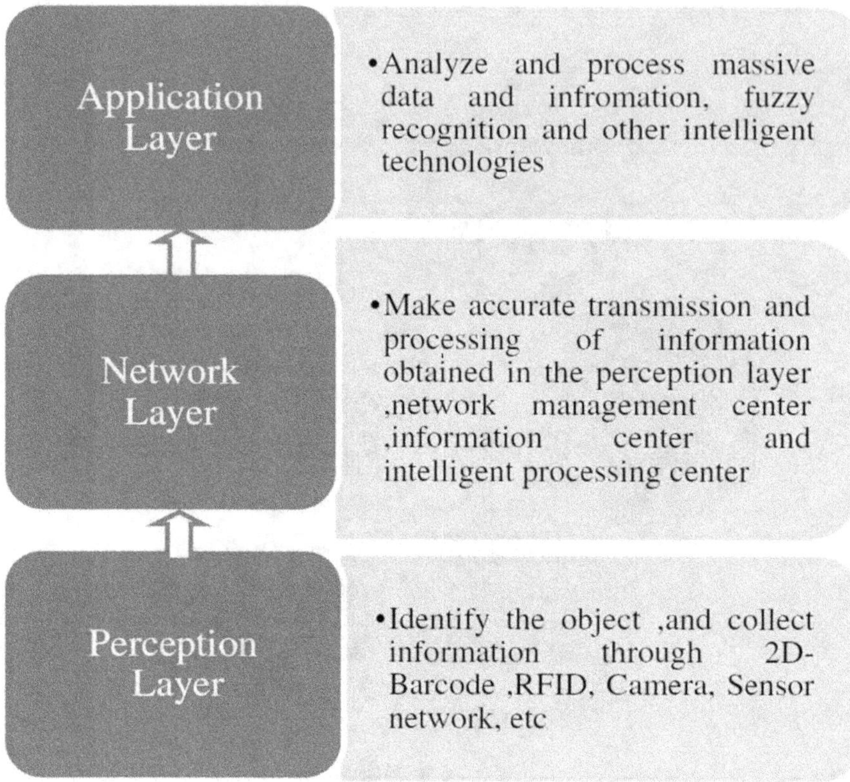

On the other hand, Smart Transportation or commonly now known as Intelligent Transportation System (ITS) is presented as a sustainable solution to the abovementioned challenge in urban and interurban areas.

Figure 19. Relation between IoT and smart cities
Source: Alavi et al., 2018

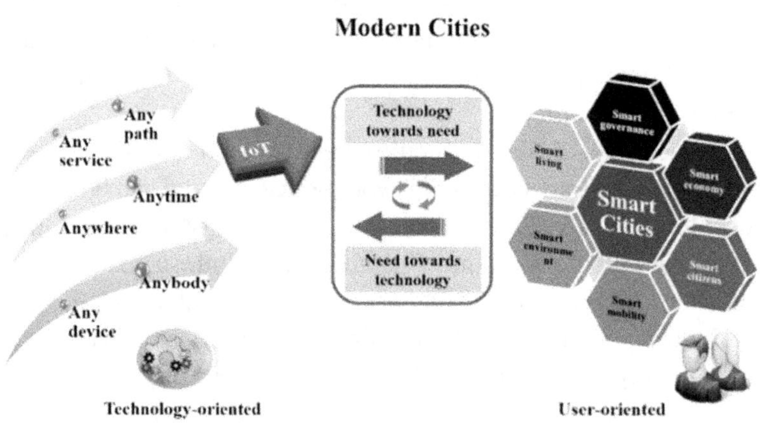

Figure 20. Different classifications for smart cities challenges
Source: Syed et al., 2021

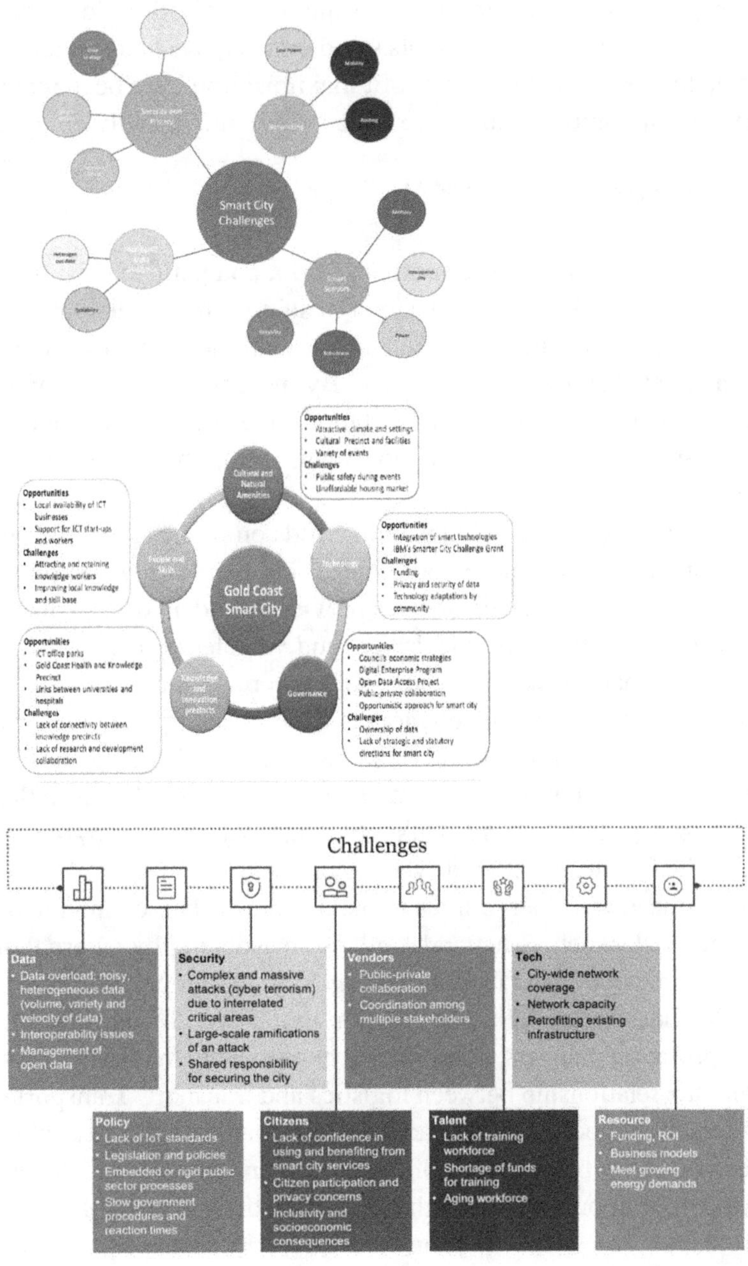

ITS is a commitment to more sustainable mobility, based on innovation and flexibility, where aspects such as the effectiveness and efficiency of transport and provision of security to users are the drivers. The ITS purpose is to develop transport systems through solutions that improve the quality, quantity, flow, and access to information related to transport and traffic, both individually and collectively. In parallel, ITS considers infrastructures and vehicles from a holistic approach that integrates all stakeholders. By merging AI and automotive engineering, autonomous vehicles (AV) open a new era in the transportation sector. While AV is still in the early stage, it is expected that development in Supply chain track.

The big development in these two sectors -Industry and transportation- leads to big development in supply chain management which accordingly put its standards that reached to what is called now Supply chain 5.0. The potentials for cost reduction and profit maximization have been realized by the involved corporations and a significant number of them are already investing heavily on the new technologies.

Intelligent Transportation System (ITS)

Transportation may be a major supply to the economy and a competitive drive in commerce. It is the action that physically interfaces the trade to its supply chain partners, such as providers and clients, and could be a major impact on the customer's fulfillment with the company. Transportation is among the more imperative financial exercises for commerce. By moving products from areas where they are sourced to areas where they are requested, transportation gives the fundamental benefit of linking a company to its providers and clients. It is a basic movement within the coordination's work, supporting the financial utilities of put and time.

Intelligent Transportation System (ITS) innovation builds on information and communication technology (ICT) to enable smarter, safer, more coordinated and increasingly automated transport. Connected sensors, cameras and other connected devices provide abundant data to distributed applications, applications which process this data to provide drivers and vehicles with actionable insights or trigger the actuation of other devices part of the ITS system, often in real time.

Manufacturing and logistics generate huge amounts of data due to its networking capabilities with different stakeholders. With the transport industry playing a major role in logistics it is only appropriate that the generated data is put to use through application of various technologies in the operations. Future research is recommended through an agent-enabled supply chain optimization by the process of simulation.

The study ponders on the fact that whether driverless cars with AI have an adverse impact on humans. Extreme automation might lead to vulnerabilities in the machines. These integrated intelligent systems are vulnerable to systemic risks such as network collapse or hacking by external agencies. The study proposes Industry 5.0 which can democratize knowledge co-production from Big Data. The improvement of transportation logistics resulting in contribution to the overall business is due to the influence of researchers and transportation planners to define and comprehend the basic views of logistics and its various applications and the relationship between logistics and transport. Transportation logistics is not only limited to the movement of goods across space and reducing time and costs along the supply chain. Its scope has expanded and it has become part of strategic management too. Hence, it is significant to integrate core business information systems with a set of modern analytical and AI tools to discover relevant knowledge from all sources. This helps in managing uncertainty and achieving competitive advantage. From all the previous, it is evident that AI plays a significant role in building efficient transport systems using data.

Industry 4.0 and 5.0

The theme of Industry 4.0 was initially introduced in 2011 at the Hannover Fair—Germany (Pfeiffer, 2017; Rojko, 2017). In the wave of Industry 4.0, several discussions and developments have been deployed through different countries and industry sectors (Araújo et al., 2021; Frederico, 2021; Kassai et

Figure 21. Industry revolutions standards
Source: Spectral Engines, 2018

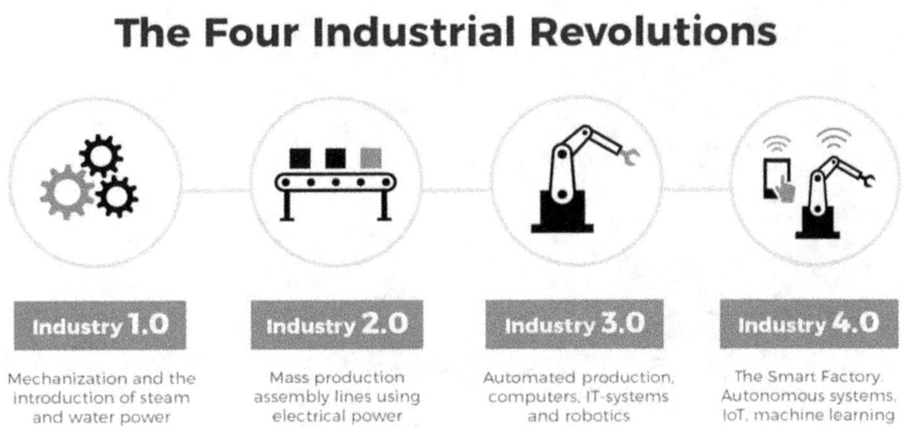

al., 2020; Kersten et al., 2017; Paksoy et al., 2021; Pfeiffer, 2017; Rojko, 2017; Shah et al., 2019; Virbahu Nandishwar Jain, 2019). Industry revolution can be classified into 4 phases as shown in the Figure 21.

First Revolution or Industry 1.0 was the starting point of using steam and water to activate mechanical systems like Steam trains as most of us can see it in several western american movies. Industry 2.0 combines the mechanical systems in industry with electrical power to move products on the production line. Combining robotics with ICT to use in some factories like car parts assembly is the Industry 3.0 phase. However, robotics in Industry 3.0 are designed to do specific actions.

By combining AI with Mechatronics systems, can robotics think? This is the foundation of Industry 4.0. While industry 4.0 still has not matured enough, researchers start to think about the Industry 5.0 scheme. Industry 5.0 complements the existing Industry 4.0 paradigm by highlighting research and innovation as drivers for a transition to a sustainable, human-centric and resilient European industry. It moves focus from shareholder to stakeholder value, with benefits for all concerned. Industry 5.0 attempts to capture the value of new technologies, providing prosperity beyond jobs and growth, while respecting planetary boundaries, and placing the wellbeing of the industry worker at the center of the production process.

The previous tier, Industry 4.0, emerged with the arrival of automation technologies, IoT and the smart factory. Industry 5.0 takes the next step, which involves leveraging the collaboration between increasingly powerful and accurate machinery and the unique creative potential of the human being.

Supply Chain

Supply chain management (SCM) is the management of a network of interconnected businesses involved in the ultimate provision of product and service packages required by end customers. Supply Chain Management spans all movement and storage of raw materials, work-in-process inventory, and finished goods from point of origin to point of consumption (supply chain).

Figure 22. Supply chain management
Source: Kerpedzhiev et al., 2017

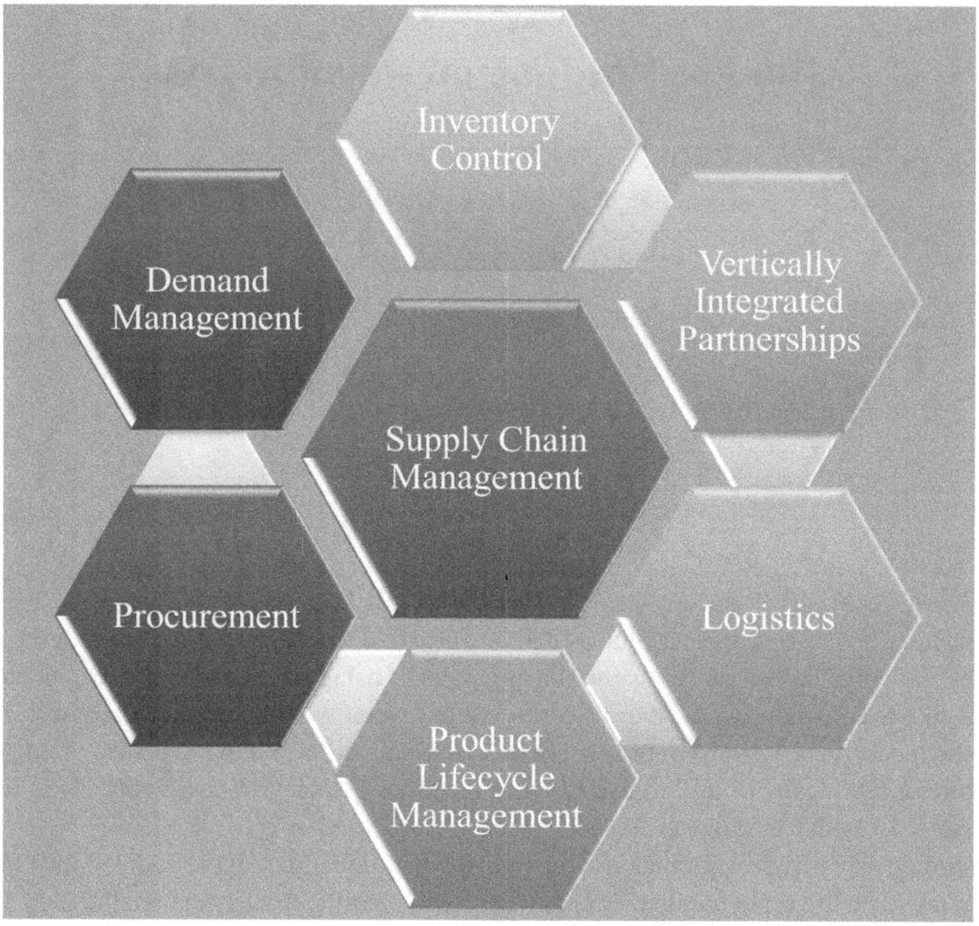

Supply chain management has several sectors as shown in Figure 22. Applying the current and the future technologies on the supply chain management spreads in all its sectors mostly with the big demand of using AI technology which has been raised lately and is promising to change the world.

In (Anca, 2019), one of the definitions for the logistics mentioned was: 'the process of strategically managing the procurement, movement and storage of materials, parts and finished inventory (and the related information flows) through the organization and its marketing channels".

Applying the robotics and AV technologies in the industry affect the supply chain and especially in logistics and inventory sectors from several side. For example, the production losses affects the delivering process, the highly reason of this losses is the human error. Using the robots reduce human error to the minimum or to zero.

In factories and warehouses, automated guided vehicles (AGVs) transport materials and inventory. A human operator can control telerobots from a distance, and they can operate in space and undersea. Walking robots (legged robots) can move by using their limbs and are useful in dangerous environments. Intelligent robots have advanced sensory feedback mechanisms and can make autonomous decisions in partially structured and unstructured environments (Bachar, 2004; Wang et al., 2012)

Figure 23. AGV in Volkswagen
Source: Volkswagen, 2019

Mobile robots can move around by using wheels, tracks, or legs. AGVs are wheeled mobile robots that are typically used in factories. AGVs can work in both an office setting and a heavy industrial setting. While most AGVs use sensors to follow guide wires attached to the floor, some can be (Bachar, 2004; Wang et al., 2012) programmed to follow a path and make decisions based on the signals they receive.

The use of AGVs is a common occurrence in flexible manufacturing systems that incorporate transport robots into their manufacturing processes. AGVs' paths are restricted to predetermined routes by incorporating magnetic stripe navigation or guide wires, and they require workplace reorganization to work efficiently (Hyams, 1999).

SEAT is one of the companies that makes extensive use of AGVs on its factory floor According to the company, 125 AGVs are in use at their Martorell facility in Spain. These robots transport nearly 24,000 parts per day, assisting 7000 employees in the manufacturing process. AGVs make workers' jobs easier and more efficient, resulting in a nearly 25% reduction in production time) as shown in Figure 23 (Ford Motor Company, 2019; Volkswagen, 2019).

Autonomous and semi-autonomous driving not only plays an important role in the design of future city logistics concepts and last-mile solutions; in long-distance transportation, autonomous concepts can solve safety issues while also addressing the driver shortage that exists in many places. Autonomous Trucks are promising to develop in logistics and supply chain management.

Digital Transformation

Because of modern digital technologies, business processes and organizational aspects are being transformed to meet market demands in the digital age, a process known as digital transformation. Several opportunities and challenges for company collaboration activities have arisen as a result of the digital transformation, which is fueled by an increase in atomization, data collection, networking, and information exchange (Tay & Loh, 2021).

Many applications of digital transformation are used, such as automation and robotics, which are used to assist workers in warehouses who perform repetitive laborious tasks such as picking and packing. Furthermore, cyber physical systems are thought to allow for synchronized decision-making during a real-time view, discussion, and analysis of dashboard critical information (Paksoy et al., 2021).

Digital transformation deploys innovative technologies for improving the business process with special focus on supply chain manufacturing, logistics, and warehousing (Kerpedzhiev et al., 2017).

Figure 24. Digital supply chain management
Source: Paksoy et al., 2021

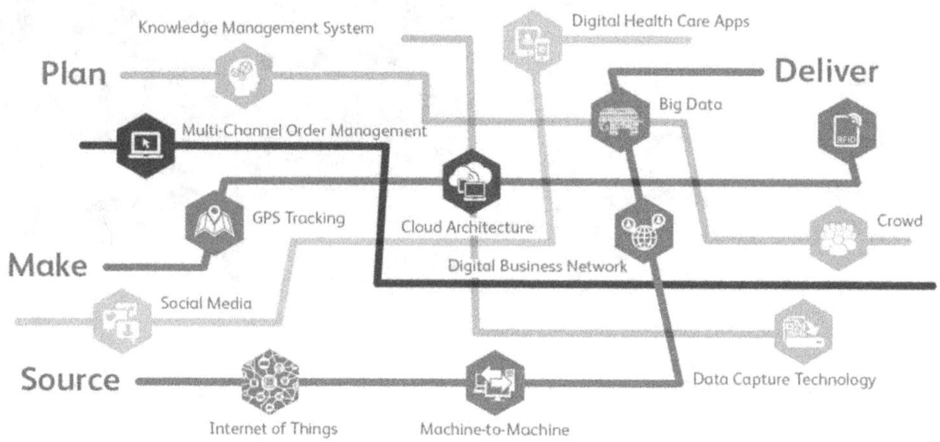

The strong adoption of the digital technologies is in the process of supply chain digitization aiming to the management of operational and strategic information and flow of materials (Cherian & SJ, 2021). Industry 4.0 revolution is linked to eight digital technologies trends in SCM which are big data analytics, social media, mobility, cloud computing, IoT, 3D printing, predictive analytics, and scanning robotics. Integration of these innovations are required to reach effective and efficient supply chains. Both Industry 4.0 and digital transformation target to enhance flexibility, productivity, and customer orientation by linking the supply chain process (Paksoy et al., 2021).

SUPPLY CHAIN MANAGEMENT AND DIGITAL TRANSFORMATION

Because of the modern digital technologies business process and organizational aspects is transformed to achieve market demands in the digital age which is called Digital transformation. Several opportunities and challenges for activities of company collaboration had been created due to the digital transformation that is driven by the increase in the atomization level, data collection, networking, and information exchange (Paksoy et al., 2021).

Digital Transformation is applied in many applications such as automation and robotics that are adopted to help workers in warehouses working on repetitive laborious tasks like picking and packing process. Also, cyber physical systems are considered to permit synchronized decision-making during a real-time view, discussion and analysis of dashboard important information (Tay & Loh, 2021).

Digital transformation deploys innovative technologies for improving the business process with special focus on supply chain manufacturing, logistics, and warehousing (Dillmann, 2016). The strong adoption of the digital technologies is in the process of supply chain digitization aiming to the management of operational and strategic information and flow of materials (Paksoy et al., 2021). Industry 4.0 revolution is linked to eight digital technologies trends in SCM which are big data analytics, social media, mobility, cloud computing, IoT, 3D printing, predictive analytics, and scanning robotics. Integration of these innovations are required to reach effective and efficient supply chains. Both Industry 4.0 and digital transformation target to enhance flexibility, productivity and customer orientation by linking the supply chain process.

Egypt and Digital Transformation

Egypt plays one of the big role in politics, economy, history and culture within the Middle East. While Egypt is considered from several years as one of the third world, it is now one of the leading developing countries. This because Egyptian government starts from few years a plan called Egyptian Vision 2030 (NMI, 2021). Egypt Vision 2030 plan in Egypt is to achieve fully digital transformation in the country.

Egypt 2030 Vision Based on Egypt's commitment to the 2035 Sustainable Development Goals (SDGs), the Government of Egypt (GoE) has developed a comprehensive vision that includes transforming Egypt into the foundations of a digital society in which virtually all technologies in all fields Al lives can be integrated (Dr. Abdel Wahab Ghoneim, 2021).

In this context, the government improve and develop communications and information technology infrastructure. This improvement includes enhance digital services at all ministries and government agencies, providing a better work environment and the necessary support to government agencies.

The vision includes the economic sector. This was in line with its valiant efforts to accelerate development and improve citizens' quality. The strategic goals of digital transformation in Egypt are primarily focused on improving the services provided to citizens through digitization (Dr. Abdel Wahab Ghoneim, 2021).

Digital transformation in Egypt include administrative work at the state level while also ensuring efficiency and effectiveness. Another strategic goal is to promote electronic governance and transparency, accountability, and monitoring principles across all government agencies.

Generally, Egyptian Vision 2030 has 17 global goals shown in the Figure 25. President Abdel Fattah El-Sisi launched the digital transformation to reengineer the processes, move governmental institutions to new business models, and provide E-services to the citizen. Hence, all of these efforts are based on using the current and future technologies as mentioned before.

The strategy of Egypt digital transformation is shown in the Figure 26. It is shown from Figure 26 that one of the milestones that are taken by the Egyptian government for digital transformation is the ICT infrastructure. The Cabinet formed a supreme committee of ministers for the digital transformation to follow up this strategy. The Egyptian government has allocated around EGP 6B to develop the technological infrastructure for several projects, such as: replacing the old copper cables using for ground line network by fiber optics cables targeting connection of around 32,000 Govt. buildings allover Egypt for providing reliable services. In 2021, the internet speed is in the range of 40 Mbps, and in the range of 100 – 200 Mbps in the new smart cities. For providing high-speed broadband internet and improving telecommunications for the E-services in Sinai, New Valley and south Egypt, Egyptian satellite "TIBA-1" (see Figure 27) was launched on 26/11/2019 and also to be used as backup and alternative network (Dr. Abdel Wahab Ghoneim, 2021; NMI, 2021).

The New 4G Smart Cities in Egypt

The Egyptian State has adopted a strategic plan for urban development in Egypt since 2014, and spend till now LE 700B, around USD 45B to build and develop smart cities like the new administrative capital,

Figure 25. Egypt Visio 2030
Source: NMI, 2021

New Alamein, New Mansoura, Galala City and Resort, with total areas around 380,000 acres, which give the chance of about 6M permanent job opportunities.

The Egyptian 4G new smart cities are distinguished by the combination of the city, industry and citizens together to improve life in urban areas, through integrated solutions more sustainable, and this includes applied innovations, better planning, a more participatory methodology, greater energy efficiency, better transportation solutions, and smart use of ICT to meet the needs of citizens in all aspects including providing online services depending on the IoT to measure a lot of information and transfer all data at the same time to the citizens or the concerned authorities, save time and effort and seek to provide an environmentally friendly digital environment that stimulates learning and creativity that contributes to providing a sustainable environment that promotes a sense of happiness, well-being and health.

Digital transformation in Egypt faces several challenges like: Cost & Budget pressures, lack of enough HR specialized in ICT, the need for big ICT investments, Cyber security & Privacy. However, Egypt government keep moving forward in its plans by several means like:• developing the online interactive education, support for creativity and innovation centers, developing Laws and legislation, supporting R&D, establish industries based on Industry 4.0.

Figure 26. Strategy of Egypt digital transformation
Source: NMI, 2021

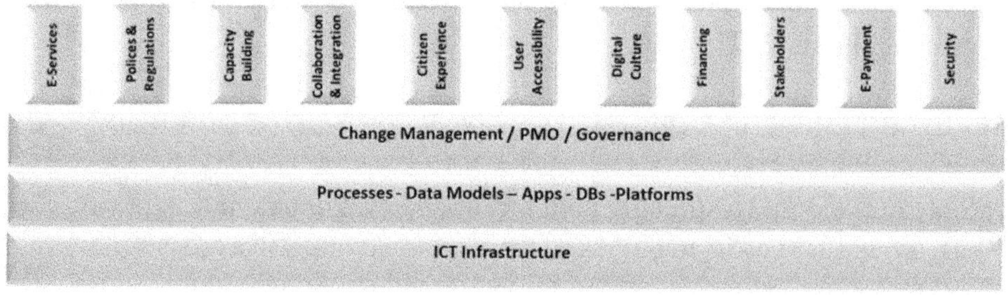

Figure 27. The Egyptian satellite TIBA-1
Source: NMI, 2021

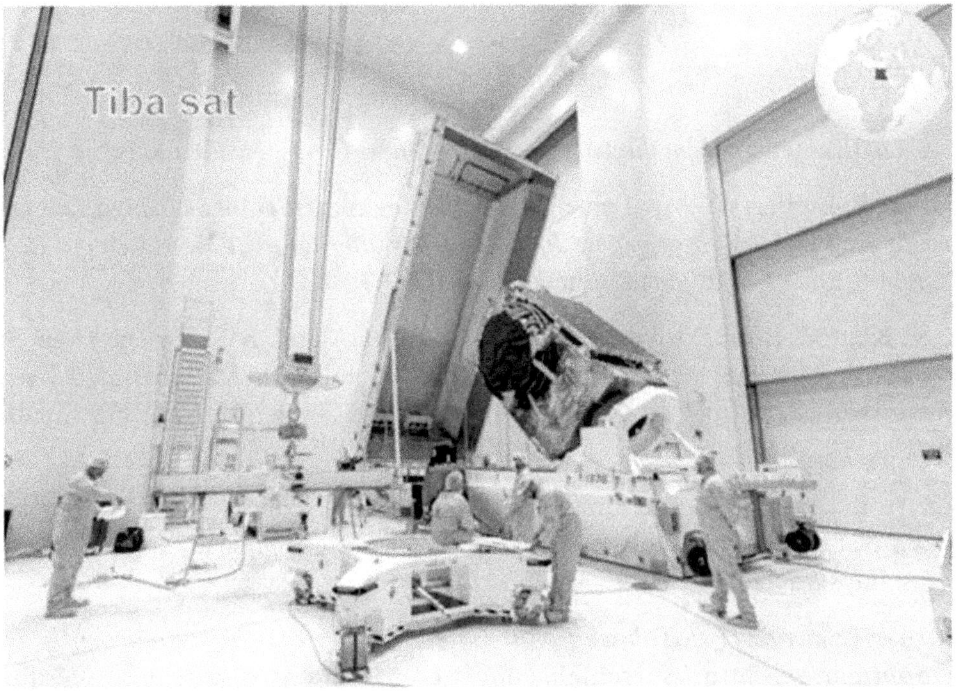

CONCLUSIONS AND DISCUSSION

The revolution of technologies affects our daily life and reshape our future. Starting from the transistor invention the world starts to be different and the revolution steps of technology evolve rapidly. This chapter show briefly the foundation of the current and future technologies and the influence of these technologies on smart cities concept. Also, this chapter focused on two applications only in smart cities which are the intelligent transportation systems and Industry 4. The discussion for these two applications was to show the impact of the current technologies on these applications which leads to improve other important section in our life which is Supply chain management.

The journey of the book did not stop at this point, but gives an example of the digital transformation which taken by several countries to reach to ideal smart cities concept for improving their citizens' life. Egypt was taken as a case study because of the big role of EGYPT in Middle East from the beginning of the history till now.

Because of the need of using the current and future technologies in several sectors of the daily life, multidisciplinary efforts is demanding pointedly. The phrase "World is a small village" become a fact. The future needs a very educated generation who have the ability to utilize these technologies to improve the people life.

While Artificial Intelligence (AI) invade all the technologies for establishing autonomous systems and relying on machines like computer to deal with most of our daily life requirements, it also need to rethink about the creativity of the humans. People are the main wealth for any society. These leads most of the current government to consider the status of the interaction between people and the new era of technologies. Hence, several standards like Society 5.0 and Industry 5.0 were established to study this interaction and reshape the future to be better and peaceful.

REFERENCES

Aboualmal, A. (2018). *Artificial Intelligence for IoT & Smart Cities*. Academic Press.

Alavi, A. H., Jiao, P., Buttlar, W. G., & Lajnef, N. (2018). Internet of Things-enabled smart cities: State-of-the-art and future trends. *Measurement: Journal of the International Measurement Confederation*, *129*(July), 589–606. doi:10.1016/j.measurement.2018.07.067

Algamili, A. S., Khir, M. H. M., Dennis, J. O., Ahmed, A. Y., Alabsi, S. S., Ba Hashwan, S. S., & Junaid, M. M. (2021). A Review of Actuation and Sensing Mechanisms in MEMS-Based Sensor Devices. *Nanoscale Research Letters*, *16*(1), 16. Advance online publication. doi:10.118611671-021-03481-7 PMID:33496852

Al-Hammouri, A. T., Liberatore, V., Al-Omari, H., Al-Qudah, Z., Branicky, M. S., & Agrawal, D. (2007). A co-simulation platform for actuator networks. International Conference on Embedded Networked Sensor Systems. https://doi.org/10.1145/1322263.1322306

Aly, H. (2019). *Low power IoT based automated manhole cover monitoring system as a smart city application*. http://search.ebscohost.com/login.aspx?direct=true&db=ddu&AN=035B68D36D29E1CB&site=ehost-live

Anca, V. (2019). Logistics and Supply Chain Management: An Overview. *Studies in Business and Economics*, *14*(2), 209–215. doi:10.2478be-2019-0035

Anderson, J. M., Kalra, N., Stanley, K. D., Sorensen, P., Samaras, C., & Oluwatola, O. A. (2014). Brief History and Current State of Autonomous Vehicles. *Autonomous Vehicle Technology: A Guide for Policymakers*, 55-74. https://www.jstor.org/stable/10.7249/j.ctt5hhwgz

Angerholzer, M., III, Mahaffee, D., Vale, M., Kitfield, J., & Renner, H. (2017). *The Autonomous Vehicle Revolution: Fostering Innovation with Smart Regulation*. http://www.thepresidency.org/sites/default/files/pdf/The Autonomous Vehicle Revolution—Fostering Innovation with Smart Regulation.compressed.pdf%0Ahttps://trid.trb.org/view/1491418

Araújo, N., Pacheco, V., & Costa, L. (2021). Smart Additive Manufacturing: The Path to the Digital Value Chain. *Technologies*, *9*(4), 88. doi:10.3390/technologies9040088

Auer, A., Feese, S., & Lockwood, S. (2016). History of Intelligent Transportation Systems. Intelligent Vehicle Systems Joint Program Office, 1–56.

Bachar, Y. (2004). Developing Controllers for Biped Humanoid Locomotion. *Science*, 1–137. http://citeseerx.ist.psu.edu/viewdoc/download?doi=10.1.1.66.2645&rep=rep1&type=pdf

Bauer, M., Sanchez, L., & Song, J. (2021). Iot-enabled smart cities: Evolution and outlook. *Sensors (Basel), 21*(13), 1–29. doi:10.339021134511 PMID:34209436

Burks, A., & Davidson, E. (1999). Introduction to "The ENIAC.". *Proceedings of the IEEE, 87*(6), 1028–1030. doi:10.1109/jproc.1999.763315

Calia, E., & D'Aprile, D. (2020). Industry 4.0. *Analytics for the Sharing Economy: Mathematics, Engineering and Business Perspectives*, 309–333. doi:10.1007/978-3-030-35032-1_18

Charles, H. K. (2005). Miniaturized electronics. *Johns Hopkins APL Technical Digest, 26*(4), 402–413.

Chataut, R., & Akl, R. (2020). Massive MIMO systems for 5G and beyond networks—Overview, recent trends, challenges, and future research direction. *Sensors (Switzerland), 20*(10), 1–35. doi:10.339020102753 PMID:32408531

Chen, H.-P., & Ni, Y.-Q. (2018). Introduction to Structural Health Monitoring. *Structural Health Monitoring of Large Civil Engineering Structures,* 1–14. doi:10.1002/9781119166641.ch1

Cherian, T. M., & SJ, C. J. A. (2021). Digital Transformation in Supply Chain Management: A conceptual framework for construction industry. *Indian Journal of Economics and Business, 20*(3), 1167–1187.

Dillmann, R. (2016). Digital Transformation in Supply Chain Management. *BearingPoint, 1*(2). https://www.onenetwork.com/supply-chain-management-solutions/digital-transformation/

European Commission for Industry Technologies. (2020). Advanced technologies for industry. In *Product watch: IoT components in connected and autonomous vehicles.* Author. doi:10.2826/70918

Ford Motor Company. (2019). *Ford - Volkswagen expand their global collaboration to advance autonomous driving, electrification and better serve customers*. Ford Media Center. https://media.ford.com/content/fordmedia/fna/us/en/news/2019/07/12/ford-vw.html

Frederico, G. F. (2021). From Supply Chain 4.0 to Supply Chain 5.0: Findings from a Systematic Literature Review and Research Directions. *Logistics, 5*(3), 49. doi:10.3390/logistics5030049

Ganapati, P. (2009, December 23). Dec. 23, 1947: Transistor Opens Door to Digital Future. WIRED. https://www.wired.com/2009/12/1223shockley-bardeen-brattain-transistor/

Gams, M., & Kolenik, T. (2021). Relations between electronics, artificial intelligence and information society through information society rules. *Electronics (Switzerland), 10*(4), 1–16. doi:10.3390/electronics10040514

Ghoneim. (2021). *Egypt Digitalization*. Academic Press.

Gupta, A. K. (2019). Creating the smart cities of the future: A three-tier development model for digital transformation of citizen services. *1PwC/World Economic Forum*, 1–16. https://www.pwc.com/gx/en/sustainability/assets/creating-the-smart-cities-of-the-future.pdf

Harrison, L. (2022, April 7). Standards And Threat Testing For Secure Autonomous Vehicles. Semiconductor Engineering. https://semiengineering.com/standards-and-threat-testing-for-secure-autonomous-vehicles/

Hasegawa, T. (2015). Chapter 5-Intelligent Transport System. *Traffic and Safety Science - Interdiciplinary Wisdom of IATSS*, 212. http://www.iatss.or.jp/en/publication/commemorative-publication/

Holland, O. (2003). The first biologically inspired robots. *Robotica, 21*(4), 351–363. doi:10.1017/S0263574703004971

Huff, H. R. (2003). *John Bardeen and transistor physics.* doi:10.1063/1.1354371

Hyams, J. (1999). *Autonomous Multi-Agent Docking using Color Segmentation.* Academic Press.

Introduction to Computers/Networks - Wikiversity. (n.d.). https://en.wikiversity.org/wiki/Introduction_to_Computers/Networks

Jain, V. N. (2019). Robotics for Supply Chain and Manufacturing Industries and Future It Holds! *International Journal of Engine Research, V8*(03), 66–79. doi:10.17577/ijertv8is030062

Karthik Kumar Vaigandla, Sandyarani Bolla & Radhakrishna Karne. A Survey on Future Generation Wireless Communications-6G: Requirements, Technologies, Challenges and Applications. (2021). *International Journal of Advanced Trends in Computer Science and Engineering, 10*(5), 3067–3076. https://doi.org/ doi:10.30534/ijatcse/2021/211052021

Kassai, E. T., Azmat, M., & Kummer, S. (2020). Scope of Using Autonomous Trucks and Lorries for Parcel Deliveries in Urban Settings. *Logistics, 4*(3), 17. doi:10.3390/logistics4030017

Kerpedzhiev, G., König, U., Röglinger, M., & Rosemann, M. (2017). Business Process Management in the Digital Age. *BPTrends, 4801*, 1–6. www.bptrends.com

Kersten, W., & Blecker, T., & M., R. C. (2017). Digitalization in supply chain management and logistics. *Proceedings of the Hamburg International Conference of Logistics (HICL).* doi:10.15480/882.1442

Kim, S. (2019). *Micro-LEGO for MEMS.* Academic Press.

Matthews, K. (2020, June 4). The 4 cities competing to fully implement autonomous vehicles. IoT Times. https://iot.eetimes.com/the-4-cities-competing-to-fully-implement-autonomous-vehicles/

McKinsey. (2019). *Industrial robotics - Insights into the sector's growth dynamics.* McKinsey & Company. https://www.mckinsey.com/industries/advanced-electronics/our-insights/growth-dynamics-in-industrial-robotics

Merzouk, S., Cherkaoui, A., Marzak, A., & Nawal, S. (2020). IoT methodologies: Comparative study. *Procedia Computer Science, 175*, 585–590. doi:10.1016/j.procs.2020.07.084

Neuweiler, L., & Vanessa Riedel, P. (2017). *Autonomous Driving in the Logistics Industry* [Thesis]. Jönköping University.

NMI. (2021). E-Governance and Digital Transformation - Egypt. NMI.

Paksoy, T., Koçhan, C., & Ali, S. S. (2021). *Logistics 4.0: Digital transformation of supply chain management*. CRC Press.

Pfeiffer, S. (2017). The Vision of "Industrie 4.0" in the Making—A Case of Future Told, Tamed, and Traded. *NanoEthics*, *11*(1), 107–121. doi:10.100711569-016-0280-3 PMID:28435474

Priswanto, A., Maryanto, S., & Santoso, R, D. (2019). Wireless sensor module for 3-axis vibration and tilt monitoring on the structural building. *Journal of Physics: Conference Series*, *1153*, 012040. doi:10.1088/1742-6596/1153/1/012040

Poongodi, T., Rathee, A., Indrakumari, R., & Suresh, P. (2019). Iot sensing capabilities: Sensor deployment and node discovery, wearable sensors, wireless body area network (WBAN), data acquisition. *Intelligent Systems Reference Library*, *174*(July), 127–151. doi:10.1007/978-3-030-33596-0_5

Raats, K., Fors, V., & Pink, S. (2020). Trusting autonomous vehicles: An interdisciplinary approach. *Transportation Research Interdisciplinary Perspectives*, *7*, 100201. doi:10.1016/j.trip.2020.100201

Rockwell Anyoha. (2020, April 23). The History of Artificial Intelligence. Science in the News. https://sitn.hms.harvard.edu/flash/2017/history-artificial-intelligence/

Rojko, A. (2017). Industry 4. 0 Concept. *Background and Overview.*, *11*(5), 77–90.

Samih, H. (2019). Smart cities and internet of things. *Journal of Information Technology Case and Application Research*, *21*(1), 3–12. doi:10.1080/15228053.2019.1587572

Shah, S., Logiotatopouloh, I., & Menon, S. (2019). Industry 4.0 and Autonomous Transportation: The Impacts on Supply Chain Management. *International Journal of Trasportation Systems*, *4*, 45–50. http://www.iaras.org/iaras/journals/ijts

Spectral Engines. 2018. Industry 4.0 and how smart sensors make the difference. https://www.spectralengines.com/articles/industry-4-0-and-how-smart-sensors-make-the-difference

Sun, N. (2021). Intelligent Transportation System Planning in the Age of Artificial Intelligence. *E3S Web of Conferences, 253*, 4–8. doi:10.1051/e3sconf/202125301036

Syed, A. S., Sierra-Sosa, D., Kumar, A., & Elmaghraby, A. (2021). Iot in smart cities: A survey of technologies, practices and challenges. *Smart Cities*, *4*(2), 429–475. doi:10.3390martcities4020024

Taulli, T. (2019). *Artificial Intelligence Basics*. Artificial Intelligence Basics. doi:10.1007/978-1-4842-5028-0

Tay, H. L., & Loh, H. S. (2021). Digital transformations and supply chain management: A Lean Six Sigma perspective. *Journal of Asia Business Studies*. doi:10.1108/JABS-10-2020-0415

The Story of the Chinese Abacus. (n.d.). http://en.chinaculture.org/classics/2010-04/20/content_383263.htm

Thakurdesai, H. M., & Aghav, J. V. (2020). Autonomous Cars: Technical Challenges and a Solution to Blind Spot. Advances in Intelligent Systems and Computing, 533–547. https://doi.org/ doi:10.1007/978-981-15-1275-9_44

Van der Meer, J. J., Hassan, S., Lofink, O., Jones, R., & Hagedorn, R. (2018). *AI and robotics automation in consumer-driven supply chains*. https://www.theconsumergoodsforum.com/wp-content/uploads/2018/04/201805-CGF-AI-Robotics-Report-with-PA-Consulting.pdf

Vasileska, D., Khan, H. R., & Ahmed, S. S. (2008). Modeling Coulomb Effects in Nanoscale Devices. *Journal of Computational and Theoretical Nanoscience*, *5*(9), 1793–1827. doi:10.1166/jctn.2008.901

Volkswagen. (2019). *Mobility for generations to come*. Volkswagen. https://www.volkswagenag.com/presence/investorrelation/publications/annual-reports/2020/volkswagen/Y_2019_e.pdf

Wang, S., Chaovalitwongse, W., & Babuška, R. (2012). Machine learning algorithms in bipedal robot control. *IEEE Transactions on Systems, Man and Cybernetics. Part C, Applications and Reviews*, *42*(5), 728–743. doi:10.1109/TSMCC.2012.2186565

Zambonelli, F. (2016). Towards a discipline of IoT-Oriented software engineering. *CEUR Workshop Proceedings*, *1664*, 1–7.

Chapter 2
Stop the Thief?
The Role of Digitalisation in Preventing Cargo Theft in the Shipping Companies

Sarah Yousry El-Gamal
College of International Transport and Logistics, Arab Academy for Science, Technology and Maritime Transport, Alexandria, Egypt

Hany Ayaad
College of International Transport and Logistics, Arab Academy for Science, Technology and Maritime Transport, Alexandria, Egypt

Rowan Hamdy Abd El-bary
College of International Transport and Logistics, Arab Academy for Science, Technology and Maritime Transport, Alexandria, Egypt

EXECUTIVE SUMMARY

Reaching a sustainable industry is now possible through digitisation. The current era witnessed an increase in the impact of digital transformation on the economy; this encouraged various sectors to adopt Industry 4.0. Digital supply chain and Industry 4.0 are current buzzwords in all industries that can solve common drawbacks. The logistics sector in particular suffers from numerous weaknesses, one of which is cargo theft. Logistics companies started adopting technology in operations aiming to mitigate cargo thefts and reach a sustainable work environment through their digital supply chains. The Egyptian government intends to participate in the transition into a digital society. This case aims to demonstrate a best practice of digitisation in the logistics sector in the Egyptian market. Global Chains Company was one of the first logistics companies to apply a digital solution through ERP systems. Through the interviews conducted, cargo theft problems and consequences are demonstrated along with the results of applying digitisation to operations and the lessons learned.

BACKGROUND

DOI: 10.4018/978-1-6684-4686-7.ch002

After 1980, as a result of globalisation, the relevance of SCM expanded significantly among scholars and practitioners. Supply chains become more robust, complicated, and expensive as a result. Today, rivalry is framed as supply chain versus supply chain rather than company versus company. As a result, top management began to see the potential for successful SCM to greatly boost an organisation's worldwide competitiveness. SCM may be considered a conduit for the efficient movement of goods or materials, services, and information from suppliers to end users (Akbari, 2018).

Logistics management is the part of supply chain management that plans, implements, and controls the efficient, adequate forward and backward flow and storage of goods, services, and associated information between the point of origin and the point of consumption in order to meet customer requirements. Logistics activities are divided into two types which are primary and secondary activities. Primary activities are setting customer service goals, transportation, inventory management and information flow, while warehousing, material handling, purchasing and packaging are considered secondary activities (Murphy and Knemeyer, 2009).

In recent years, outsourcing has evolved as a critical component of global supply chain strategy. After the mid-1990s, practitioners saw a noticeable growth in the relevance of supply chain management (SCM). As a result, the study of supply chain management and outsourcing has exploded in popularity. The supply chain is defined as a sequence of end-to-end procedures that result in the production of products or the provision of services to the final consumer. SCM is the process through which management operations and activities are planned and controlled. Outsourcing non-core business services have been a typical supply chain strategy for many enterprises and organisations in growing countries where consumer expectations are expanding. Due to the complexity and development of today's supply chains, logistics is critical to effective operations. Additionally, businesses are increasingly focusing on their core capabilities as logistics has become a popular issue for outsourcing to third-party suppliers. As a result, third-party suppliers have a unique opportunity to impact the efficiency of SCM. According to the 2016 Third-Party Logistics Study, shippers increased their use of logistics outsourcing or third-party logistics (3PL) services by 5% in 2016 (from 68 to 73 percent).

Numerous contemporary businesses have espoused outsourcing some or all of their logistics operations to enterprises known as 3PLs in order to benefit from the expertise and economies of scale provided by 3PLs, thereby reducing costs, increasing efficiency, and improving service, and allowing client businesses to focus on their core competencies. Since its origin, the term "third-party logistics" has been defined in various ways by various researchers. Third-party logistics is described as an inter-organisational interaction between shippers and logistics service providers in a supply chain.

Third-party logistics providers have established themselves as integral players in many supply chains by providing a range of services to client companies, including transportation and distribution, customer support, warehousing and distribution, information technology support, effective route planning, cost reduction, and value-added services to increase customer satisfaction. According to Hendrickx et al. (2020), despite the industry's development, transactional, operational, and repetitive operations continue to be outsourced to 3PLs at a higher rate than strategic, information technology-intensive and customer-facing activities. According to the research, domestic transportation, warehousing, international transportation, customs brokerage, and freight forwarding are the most commonly outsourced operations.

Third-Party Logistics services (3PLs) can be asset-based, in which case they have physical assets such as trucks and warehouses, or they can be non-asset-based, in which case they depend mainly on personal expertise and information systems to provide services including management-oriented solutions, subcontracting physical distribution activities to asset-based companies, and designing and reshaping the supply chain (Akbari, 2018).

Cargo theft is one of the main problems experienced by the logistics sector worldwide (BSI, 2020). Therefore, logistics companies globally started adopting more technological techniques in operations aiming to mitigate cargo thefts and their consequences and reach a more sustainable work environment. Likewise, the Egyptian logistics sector recently started following the same route to decrease cargo thefts' consequences using a digital solution. The current research demonstrates the problems experienced by Global Chains Company in mitigating cargo thefts through digital solutions implemented. The conclusions and lessons learned could provide other 3PLs in the Egyptian logistics sector an idea about the benefits of digital transformation in solving well-known industry problems.

The following sections in this study are structured as follows; Section 2 - Cargo Thefts in Supply Chain, where the types of stolen goods and methods of cargo thefts in supply chains are explained. Section 3 – Digital Transformation in Cargo theft demonstrates the concept of digital supply chain and Industry 4.0, besides the role of technology in preventing cardo theft. A best practice case study in the Egyptian logistics sector is illustrated in Section 4, where the company's background, services and methods undertook by the company to mitigate cargo theft are explained. Finally, section 5 shows the recommendations and lessons learned from the case study.

CARGO THEFTS IN THE SUPPLY CHAIN

Introduction

In today's global economy, supply chains are frequently dispersed across countries, regions, and continents. Today, many enterprises' supply chains have become more global, outsourced, and integrated than ever. Disruptions in the economy, shifting commodity prices, and a global economic crisis have raised the demand for black market commodities, so cargo theft has surged (Reidy, 2020). Many institutions, particularly freight forwarding corporations, are constantly attacked for theft, whether of cargo from warehouses or while transportation, money, or crucial documents. Cargo theft is a serious issue all over the world and is more common in transportation than money and documents thefts. Some countries have seen steady growth, like Brazil, which is one of the countries with the biggest risk to cargo security in the world. According to the Brazilian penal code, cargo theft is described as taking items for resale while they are being transported (Justus et al., 2018).

Contrary to other regions of the world, the Middle East and Africa saw cargo truck hijacking is the most common kind of theft (BSI, 2018). Due to poor security regulations in most nations and the ubiquitous availability of weapons, robbers can undertake violent cargo truck hijackings with high impunity. As shown in Figure 1, in 2018, South Africa and Egypt had the highest number of cargo truck hijackings, where Egypt and South Africa ranked first among the top 10 countries in African cargo theft with 31 theft percentage. The situation changed in 2020, where South Africa still got the highest truck hijacking records, but the good news s that Egypt records for cargo theft decreased to only 6%. This development could be due to the efforts made by the Egyptian government to mitigate cargo theft (BSI, 2020).

Cargo theft is defined as the theft of any cargo throughout the products' journey through the global supply chain. Between the place of origin and the final destination, items are vulnerable to exploitation by resourceful and highly motivated robbery gangs (Burges, 2012). This creates an entirely new and tough

Figure 1. Top countries for cargo theft in the Middle East and Africa
Source: BSI and TT Club annual report, 2018 and 2020

set of challenges for manufacturers, suppliers, terminal operators, third-party logistics providers, and logistics and transportation providers. This may also involve physical theft, cyber theft, money theft or document fraud, in which the owner, destination, or cargo shipment's contents are altered (Reidy, 2020) .

Pilferage of cargo, which costs the US economy millions, if not billions, of dollars each year, can serve as a gate crime for other, more severe kinds of cargo theft, as theft of a single piece progresses to a box, then a case, and finally a pallet. As this new source of revenue becomes ingrained in the employee's lifestyle, progression to higher objectives is frequently the obvious next step. While this is obviously not true for every employee who has ever walked out of a warehouse with stuff concealed in his lunch pail, it is true for many others (Burges, 2013).

Based on Reidy (2020), cargo theft is a \$15–30 billion-dollar problem in the United States each year, based on aggregated findings. The average lost value per occurrence was \$254,800, with food and beverage being most often targeted categories. According to a study during the first quarter of 2018, there were 159 cargo theft incidents in the United States and Canada. During the quarter, the business reports that 98 trucks and 119 trailers were declared stolen. In Quarter one of 2018, 382 cargo crimes were reported in the United Kingdom, 57 in the Netherlands, and 34 in Sweden, according to the year-on-year analysis of documented events. The crime with the biggest loss value in the first quarter of 2018 was the theft of vehicle components from a truck in Romania, which resulted in a €2,017,440 loss. This was one of the quarter's two seven-figure losses. The other incident included the theft of €1,900,000 worth of automotive parts — multimedia control units and shock absorbers – from a motorist who left his laden vehicle alone on an industrial site in the German state of North Rhine-Westphalia over a January weekend. In the first quarter of 2018, the UK, Netherlands, Russia, Sweden, Germany, France, and South Africa accounted for 572 or 92.2 percent of all cargo crimes reported in Europe, the Middle East, and Africa (EMEA) area (Reidy, 2020).

According to the Transport Asset Protection Association (TAPA), a supply chain resilience and security organisation, over €172 million worth of items were stolen during the road transport process in 2020 throughout Europe, the Middle East, and Africa (EMEA). This indicates that, on average, about €471,000 worth of products is lost during the transportation between loading and discharging locations. Surprisingly, Transport Asset Protection Association reports that 74.6 percent of all occurrences reported by Transported Asset Protection Association (TAPA) of the Europe, Middle East, and Africa (EMEA) Incident Information Service (IIS) included cargo thefts in the United Kingdom and Germany, reaching 3,100 and 1,727 offences during 12 months (Girteca, 2021).

Even so, the group estimates that recorded crimes accounted for just a small percentage of total losses. Transport Asset Protection Association said that the 2020 total loss is based on just 65.1 percent of submissions to TAPA EMEA's IIS that included financial data. The year 2020 will be remembered as unlike any other in history. At a time when the majority of enterprises were almost exclusively focused on survival, and government agencies had the additional load of police new government lockdowns, established sources of cargo crime data were also significantly damaged, as predicted (Girteca, 2021).

There has been a steady movement away from the theft of whole truckloads toward the pilferage of loaded trailers when they are at rest. Burglary and theft occurrences – most frequently, trailer break-ins and pilferages – have progressively increased each year, accounting for 22% of all recorded thefts in Quarter three of 2020 (Straight, 2020).

However, statistics indicate that cargo theft costs the global economy tens of billions of dollars, an exact amount is impossible to quantify because the majority of these crimes go undetected. When given the option of retrieving their stolen goods or being monetarily compensated, the majority of cargo theft victims will likely choose the latter to avoid quality control difficulties. Stolen food goods, perishables, or medications, for example, if stored in improperly temperature-controlled surroundings, might result in a significant health issue if sold.

Another factor that might contribute to undetected cargo theft is an unfavourable public opinion or reputation. A carrier may lose existing or prospective customers due to fears that the firm was complicit in the theft or lacked adequate security standards and practises (Reidy, 2020).

In certain instances, the difficulty in monitoring a single pallet or even a few boxes of products is since drivers may not even realise a pallet is missing from a complete truckload until the merchandise is unloaded and tallied. Often, these thefts go unreported because there is no record of when they occurred (Straight, 2020).

Types of Stolen Goods

The Most popular types of stolen goods are high-value items. While the phrase "high-value items" is wide, it refers to branded fashion clothing such as designer sweaters and shoes, cosmetics and fragrances, technological equipment such as phones, tablets, and laptops, and medicinal products. Catalytic converters, for example, might also be considered high-value commodities. Road transport businesses generally have internal regulations about what constitutes valuable cargo. A valuable shipment is defined as the entire cost of products loaded into a trailer, which can range from a five-digit figure to several million euros. Such items are desirable because they may readily be resold on underground markets or online classifieds websites. While phone manufacturers like Apple have included protections to effectively deactivate the phones in the event of theft, they remain desirable to second-hand purchasers for components. There is little chance for fashion makers to restrict the second-hand market for stolen items, so regulating the process to avoid theft is the only choice for some (Girteca, 2021).

Consumable products such as electronics, food, and drinks account for the majority of stolen cargo value, followed by domestic goods and construction supplies (Reidy, 2020).

Methods for Cargo Theft

Cargo that is at rest is cargo that is at risk. As a result, criminals target weekends and holidays when much cargo is idle and unsecured. About half of all cargo thefts occur between Friday and Sunday, with Friday being the most typical day for theft. Additionally, when businesses are most pressured to move freight off the port, Friday afternoons may provide the greatest danger of succumbing to this technique. The burglars anticipate that the pressure of transporting the freight would result in less examination of credentials upon pickup. Compared to ordinary weekends, holiday weekends saw a spike in thefts, according to Freightwatch, which states that organised criminal rings are more active during these periods (Justus et a', 2018; Palmer, 2010).

Cargo robbers choose commodities they can readily broker via a "fence" or a person who purchases stolen material with the intent of reselling it. They collect information on industrial parks and manufacturing/distribution sites where such things are manufactured or kept, and then either break into the facility or establish surveillance posts outside to observe shipping operations, particularly the utilisation of trucks. Depending on their work method, the thieves will then wait for a chance to strike. If the criminals' objective is to steal the truck, they may already have obtained a facility to temporarily store the freight, as well as a stolen vehicle to attach to the stolen trailer. They may have even obtained a second trailer for offloading the stuff.

Another option is to compensate drivers at rest areas or fuelling stations for surrendering their trucks or wait until the driver abandons the truck and trailer. The thieves are skilled and knowledgeable about accessing the truck and controlling the ignition system. They then flee with the stolen property. If a trailer is not linked to a truck – sometimes referred to as dropped or unsupervised – the criminals attach their newly obtained stolen tractor to the loaded trailer and transport it to a secure area. Alternatively, they may break into the trailer and unload the merchandise into an empty trailer, impeding law enforcement's ability to find and recover the stolen items (Reidy, 2020, Ekwall and Lantz, 2015).

Criminals with greater sophistication may take the truck and/or trailer and abandon them on the roadside or in an industrial area. They can then observe from a safe distance to see whether the vehicle and/or trailer are equipped with a tracking device and to determine whether law enforcement is tracking the stolen equipment (Reidy, 2020).

If the thieves feel no one is following the truck and/or trailer, they will transport it to a safe warehouse and begin dismantling the merchandise for resale on the black market. Preparing stolen items for resale may involve altering the packing, re-labelling the boxes, and even fabricating forged bills of lading or customs documentation to enable the removal of the stolen cargo (Girteca, 2021).

The European Commission (EC) commissioned Switzerland's Cross-Border Research Association (CBRA) and Transported Asset Protection Association (TAPA) to develop a security toolbox for Europe's road freight transport business. According to a condensed version of the paper, the danger of cargo theft was significantly increased anytime a truck was parked in an unprotected parking space. However, as the risk matrix demonstrated, simply operating the truck or loading and unloading posed hazards to the cargo's security (BSI, 2021).

DIGITAL TRANSFORMATION IN CARGO THEFT

The changes brought about by the broad adoption of digital technology, which produces, shares, and transfers data, could be referred to as 'Digital Transformation'. It is based on the development of several technologies, including computer technology, software engineering, telecommunications networks, and the effects of their use. Significant digital innovations are affecting the economies of both established and emerging nations, bringing with them both new opportunities and challenges. The contemporary period has seen a considerable increase in the impact of digital transformation on the economy, which has a big impact on the economy's growth rate, employment rate, and labour productivity, among other things. If the framework required for its implementation is not in place, it has the potential to restrict growth while also having the potential to be an engine for driving economic advancement (Khalifa et al., 2021).

Digital Transformation Overview

In order to improve communication and integration among supply chain partners, Korpela et al. (2017) define the Digital Supply Chain (DSC) as the strategic and practical flow of information that comprises financial, production, research, or design. Meanwhile, Supply Chain 4.0, the new term for the digital supply chain, is described as: "an intelligent best-fit technological system that is based on the capability of massive data disposal and excellent cooperation and communication for digital hardware, software, and networks to support and synchronise interaction between organisations by making services more valuable, accessible and affordable with consistent, agile and effective outcomes" (Queiroz, et al., 2019, p.4).

According to Maier et al. (2011), ecosystem actors (suppliers, firms, employees, and customers) can benefit from DSC's multiple advantages, such as the service's cost-effectiveness and value-creating activities. DSC also has advantages for enhancing design flexibility in SCs, lowering production costs, eliminating lead times in the supply chain, and gaining competitive advantages.

The usage of "smart technologies" including the Internet of Things, big data, autonomous control systems, and advanced analytics is crucial to DSC. The supply chain's overall performance is enhanced and improved by these cutting-edge Industry 4.0 technologies. Figure 2 demonstrates the technologies that are assumed to characterise Industry 4.0. As a result, prominent businesses are re-designing their operational models to boost product availability and responsiveness, decrease capital workforces, and double profits through the use of Digital Supply Chain Management (DSCM). Industry 4.0 and DSC are hence current buzzwords in commercial settings.

Industry 4.0, which aggregates current ideas to create new value, is the manufacturing model of the future that will be vital in transforming whole value chains across the life cycle of items to create cutting-edge services and goods. Building new sorts of useful data and systematic, high-agility value chains requires integrating and combining intelligent machines, human resources, physical things, and production procedures across organisational stages. As a result, they are able to manage and optimise resource consumption and product service requirements autonomously, hence maximising efficiency and lowering costs (Tay et al., 2018).

Industry 4.0 technologies, by relative emphasis in recent studies.

According to Kamel (2021), Egypt has the potential to become one of the manufacturing destinations in a world that may see a shift towards more local or regional sourcing and distribution logistics by providing the right incentives in an alluring legal and regulatory environment. However, Egypt's diversified economy, manufacturing base, competitively priced labour, and large human capital also

Figure 2. Industry 4.0 technologies, by relative emphasis in recent studies
Source: Ferrantino and Koten (2019)

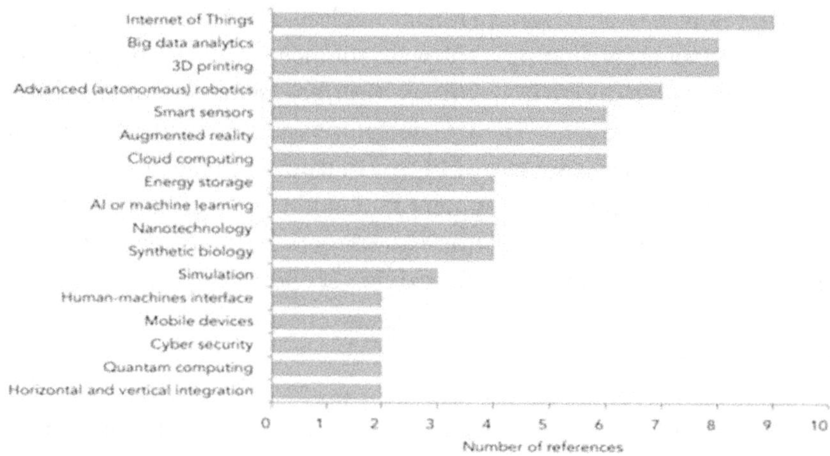

present challenges. While focusing on growth that, at its core, has the private sector as a driver, it is also important to take advantage of the opportunities made possible by accelerating digital transformation and play a significant part in realising Egypt's Vision 2030.

In order to create a Digital Egypt, the ICT 2030 plan assists in attaining the goals of Egypt's Vision 2030. These goals include strengthening the ICT infrastructure, promoting digital inclusion, achieving the shift to a knowledge-based economy, supporting innovation, boosting capacities, combating corruption, ensuring cybersecurity, and advancing Egypt's standing on the regional and global stages. The fundamentals for converting Egypt into a digital society are laid out in the comprehensive vision and strategy known as "Digital Egypt." The three primary pillars of the "Digital Egypt" strategy are digital transformation, digital skills and jobs, and digital innovation. These three pillars are supported by the legislative framework and the digital infrastructure, which are both crucial foundations (Ministry of Communication and Information Technology, 2022).

To achieve administrative reform, develop and improve government services, and combat corruption, the Egyptian government has intended to take part in the transition into a digital society. As a result, the government worked very hard to build Egypt's information infrastructure, in which the Ministry of Communications collaborates with many other departments. The presidential efforts to encourage innovation and creativity establish a fund to aid inventors with a shared contribution from the business sector and institutions of civil society. By setting up training programmes for young people in this area, the Ministry of Communications is reflecting its increased efforts on the path to the fourth industrial revolution. In addition, Egypt's Ministry of Industry and Trade has implemented a number of policies and measures to increase opportunities for sustainable industrial development in the industrial sector, focusing on: extensive use of knowledge, technology, and industrial digital transformation; utilising all of the comparative and competitive advantages of the Egyptian industry; the development of industrial zones within the framework of the Egyptian government's vision 2030; to be in line with the United Nations' Sustainable Development Goals; and utilising all of the comparative and competitive advantages of the Arab world (Institutional Development, 2022).

The Egyptian industry has potentials that qualify it to take advantage of the technologies and opportunities associated with Industry 4.0. It can benefit in a short time from the significant changes and boom in the global industrial sector. In this context, the company "Siemens," the world leader in technology and highly valued by the Egyptian industrial sector, has implemented several projects with the Egyptian government. Among the projects is the construction of three electric power stations that are highly efficient in the regions of Burullus, the New Administrative Capital, and Beni Suef at a total cost of about 6 billion euros. It will also build 12 wind farms to generate electricity. This agreement comes within the framework of the strategy launched by the ministry to promote industrial development and foreign trade for 2020. It aims to develop a digital industrial system in Egypt and adopt the latest global solutions and practices in the field of automation, remote control services, digital factory solutions, and smart manufacturing systems.

Accordingly, companies in various fields have started to take serious steps towards digitisation, one of is the logistics and supply chain sector, in which companies as 3PLs started taking serious steps. Logistics companies started to adopt different technological tools to manage their internal operations.

Role of Technology in Preventing Cargo Thefts

Reaching a more sustainable industry may be made possible through digitisation. Literature discussed the technologies used to mitigate cargo theft worldwide. Lorenc and Kuźnar (2018) mentioned some of the technologies used in the monitoring of cargo transportation; as: systems to track cargo location, which is a GPS-equipped location gadget mounted in the vehicle that gathers information on the cargo's present location and Systems to monitor cargo-specific parameters, which is a system that makes it possible not only to identify the exact location of the cargo unit, but also allows one to specify the actual parameters of the load. Song et al. (2020) discussed IT technologies, including RFID and IoT installed in port operations, which can be coupled with data analytics to achieve better insights. Installing Internet of Things (IoT) devices on trailers and cargo can aid with track-and-trace, and door sensors that record every door action can be used to provide crucial information in the event of a theft. Pallets can now be tracked using single-use tracking devices as well as radio frequency identifiers (RFID), which make the goods trackable in the event of theft. Employing a 3D interactive inventory management map that accurately depicts indoor and outdoor operations has several advantages for businesses (Bluegrace Logistics, 2022).

Blockchain-based technologies may contribute to cargo safety by tying together watchdog platforms to make it simpler for the trucking industry to report, share, and use caution. In a direct peer-to-peer transaction, where the issuer provides the recipient with an official document, and both parties can demonstrate cryptographically that they are the rightful owners, blockchain creates an encrypted digital record that is held by the recipient and co-owned by the issuer. All parties benefit from this's transparency and complete visibility, and it's practically impossible to manipulate. Blockchain can potentially be a tool for an industry that lacks openness in cargo theft incidents, mostly because brokerage businesses don't communicate with one another and only see one another as rivals (Bluegrace Logistics, 2022; Balcerzak et al, 2022).

The most commonly used technology in Egypt is Enterprise Resource Planning, which plays a vital part in managing the operations of organisations in both the public and private sectors in today's modern computer world. These integrated software solutions are designed to integrate all of an organisation's information and resources. ERP systems are meant to give benefits such as confidentiality, integrity, and visibility to an organisation's information and resources, and companies may improve their performance, efficiency, and production by utilising these features. Furthermore, ERP systems are integrated suite that controls an organisation's whole operations and procedures (Mahmood et al., 2020). Accounting and management processes are handled more efficiently and effectively using ERP systems. They are beneficial in both public and commercial sector decision-making.

Furthermore, they assist firms in improving their performance by providing various problem-solving solutions. Organisations use the ERP system to manage everyday operations, processes, and other functions, allowing them to complete tasks more efficiently and effectively. It also oversees the organisation's communication, information, and other services (Dezdar and Ainin, 2011).

The ERP system facilitates the flow of vital and critical information between departments as well as between employees in new and innovative ways. ERP systems are used to manage, maintain, run, and administrate the organisation's data and other business activities. They are highly interconnected, synchronised, and centralised. These systems are frequently recognised as a necessary tools for businesses. Furthermore, with the expanding hands of global marketplaces, they may fulfil their objectives successfully (Bawack and Kamdjoug, 2022). As a result, these systems are generating long-term competitive advantages. The need for ERP systems is skyrocketing in today's industry due to the integrated information's capability, as well as the expanded variety of solutions and administration techniques (Dezdar and Ainin, 2011).

THE CASE STUDY: GLOBAL CHAINS COMPANY FOR TRADE AND TRANSPORT

Company Background

In order to analyse the impact of digital transformation in the Egyptian logistics sector, the authors selected Global Chains Company for Trade and Transport as a best practice for digital transformation. The company is considered a best practice; since it is one of the first companies to adopt digital technologies to mitigate cargo thefts, among other problems. The authors conducted two structured interviews with the company's CEO to discover the main reasons for digital transformation, besides analysing the effects of applying digital technologies and reaching conclusions.

Global Chains Company provides logistics services such as Inland Trucking, warehousing and stevedoring. It also offers supply services for materials like Pet coke and steam coal. The company also provides consultancy services in fleet management systems and oil and gas. Global Chains for Trade and Transport was established in early 2017. The company's founders have substantial expertise in the sector of logistics. Global Chains' commitment to quality, transparency and other values resulted in quick success, with more than 1.2 million tons of bulk and bagged goods carried and distributed across the country in what many would consider a "short" period of time (Global Chains Company, 2019). In addition to effectively carrying and delivering industrial commodities, Global Chains demonstrated that it is qualified to serve as a consultant to other organisations in the market. The vast number of different goods handled by Global Chains Company also opened the door to function as mining and industrial commodities suppliers to the most well-known firms in the Egyptian market.

The mission of Global Chains is to provide flexible solutions in logistics and trading. Its customer-focused culture drives its operations; devotion and adherence to this culture enable the firm to produce dependable and personalised services that are supported by long-term relationships with the company's trusted different suppliers. Global Chains' vision is to be the obvious choice for the customer. By providing effective logistics solutions using cutting-edge technology and trusted services, the company aspires to a stable and responsible growth rate by correctly building a market position as a strong and outstanding service provider in all areas of its activity. The company's main values are transparency, mutual respect, quality, excellence, and timekeeping. Global Chains Company serves more than one sector, such as construction building materials, fast-moving consumer goods, grains, and general cargo and oil and gas products (Global Chains Company, 2019).

Elsewedy cement, The Egyptian Ferro for Alloys Company EFACO, El-Arish cement, Arabian cement, Reliance mining, Reliance investments, Reliance Logistics and Silika mining are all clients of Global Chains Company (Global Chains, 2019). Customers choose Global Chains among others companies due to various reasons. Global Chains specialises in bulk commodities; the company provides the most transparent and cost-efficient solutions for company requirements, whether inland transportation, stevedoring, or storage. The company also handles large quantities of materials supplied regularly and provides highly competitive pricing. Also via its significant organisational abilities, it serves not only as a supplier, but also as a success partner to all of its clients through its consultancy services as:

- **Fleet Management Systems (FMS):** Global Chains provides its clients with efficient and effective fleet management solutions by leveraging cutting-edge technologies and processes. Fleet Management Systems enable businesses to centralise all fleet information and records. FMS makes planning all impending maintenance and inspections easy, saving clients time and providing them control over the fleet's history and expenditures.
- **Oil and Gas:** Global Chains provides critical services and consulting to the oil and gas industry. The company provides manpower, cathodic protection services, heavy equipment, and various other services. The organisation offers highly skilled geologists for exploration as well as tank and vessel cleaning services (Global Chains Company, 2019).

The company's role is to improve the flow of products and to establish a relationship between suppliers, trade businesses, and end customers. The company strives to produce actual and long-term economic value for its clients through dependable and adaptable logistics operations. In an ongoing attempt to improve global chain status, the organisation employs cutting-edge ways to remain adaptable to the quick changes that occur in the ever-changing global logistics industry.

Company Services

Global Chains Logistics Services Includes:

- **Inland Trucking:** The company recognises that logistics entails more than just the movement of products and services. Global Chains Compan aims to create a more flexible and easy flow, opening the path for time efficiency and cost savings for all clients. It also continually monitors the source and destination to ease the loading and discharging procedure for the specified fleet. The fleet includes a wide range of machinery, including tippers, flatbeds, liquid tankers, and other heavy equipment. To provide the best quality service, the company's constantly ensures the prompt availability of both professional drivers and heavy-duty vehicles.

- **Warehousing:** The company offers a comprehensive range of warehouse services, including long-term and short-term leasing, expert manpower, and innovative handling equipment. The company's acute eye for detail contributes to the provision of clients with storage choices that are dependable, cost-effective, and safe. The company's warehouse selection is subjected to an in-depth survey. It ensures that all employees share the same beliefs and ideas in order to provide the most trustworthy and transparent service possible.
- **Stevedoring:** The company is a specialist in the loading and unloading bulk commodities and general freight. The organisation employs a highly skilled workforce that assures the safety and effectiveness of all activities. By employing existing staff talents, equipment, and facilities, the global chains team can manage a wide range of commodities, regardless of the severity of any probable situations, whether natural or unnatural (Global Chains Company, 2019).

Because the company's capabilities include managing and shipping mining products, the company was able to operate as a supplier to various market firms. Due to the large numbers that Global Chains Company handles regularly, the firm is able to offer affordable costs. Furthermore, the obvious experience in logistics and shipping assures on-time delivery.

Cement, Clinker, Gypsum, Iron Oxide, Clay, Quartz, Slag, Phosphate, and Dolomite are among the materials offered by Global Chains. Cement components like Pet coke and steam coal are considered the most transported by Global Chains Company, around 90% of its work. The company transports pet coke and steam coal as main cement components to Alexandria factories to produce Clinker, then transports Clinker from Alexandria to factories all over Egypt for energy production. Also, Tire Derived Fuel (TDF) and Refused derived Fuel (RDF) from waste recycling factories in Ismaillia City and Port Said City Egyptian factories for producing energy. The company transports coal components from Alexandria to National Cement Complex in Beni suef city and then transports clinker to Egypt or Alexandria port warehouses. This back holing activity decreases the selling price by %30. It also transports Quartz and Phosphate from quarries in Aswan to Damietta port, El Sokhna port and Suez port to be exported. Global Chains Company delivers raw sugar to factories in Al-Sharkia from Elsukhna manufactories-Savola Food Emerging Company.

When a client submits a service request, the following information about his shipment must be provided:

- What is the origin and destination? Is there just one origin and one destination, or many destinations from a single point of origin? or are there many sources to collect materials or products from and just one destination? Loading usually happens from ports, factories, warehouses or stone-pits to some destinations like: ports, factories and warehouses.
- Commodity type (chemical, building materials, cement components, others)
- Quantity of products
- Unit used (per ton, day or meter)
- Truck type (one box, two boxes, counter truck, other)
- Number of days needed by the customer
- Start and end date
- Load type (loose or on pallets)
- Cost includes expenses or not, only transportation.

DEALING WITH CARGO THEFTS

Overall Problem

Like many Egyptian 3PL provider companies, Global Chains Company suffers from transportation crimes; cargo theft, money theft, and documents theft. In order to reach the objective of having a better competitive advantage, most organisations outsource their logistical services, like transporting cargos to third-party logistics (3PL) providers. Increased flexibility, operational efficiency, higher customer service levels, and a better focus on core industries are the top benefits of using 3PL suppliers. Companies started 3PL alliances by outsourcing some or all of their transportation and distribution functions. In recent years, most 3PLs have transitioned from providing a single function to providing integrated logistics services, which include two or more tasks (GÖL and ÇATAY, 2007).

According to the company, cargo theft is more common while transferring loose or bulk cargo between two locations, such as grains. Crime can occur while in transit between two points, during loading and unloading, or at any moment during transportation. Cargo theft can be committed not only by thieves but also by trailer drivers. The trailer has a capacity of 50 tonnes while hauling grains. Any trailer driver is aware that he has a tolerance of up to 150 kg per transfer if the trailer is ost or stolen. However, after loading the items, the driver takes the tolerance for himself, causing the firm to lose money.

Money and document theft frequently occur as the company transports items between two points when a driver collects 50% of the shipping bill in advance to pay for the petrol and other shipping charges. After delivering the shipment to its destination and receiving the bill of lading. The driver stops at any broker along the road and collects the remaining 50% of his shipment price. During the preceding steps, any driver is vulnerable to theft at any time. Money, cargo, and documentation theft is a global problem affecting consumers and businesses. According to many reports, it impacts every industry, state, and mode of transportation.

Solution Provided by the Company

From the interviews conducted with the company's CEO, the authors have highlighted the leading solutions adopted along with the recommendations for other 3PLs wishing to start their digital transformation process as follows:

1. Global logistics chose to convey most commodities, such as grains, in sacks rather than bulk, so that the number of sacks transported can be accurately counted. It seals the vehicle after loading; each has a code number from 1 to 100, which matches the code on the bill of lading. Besides, there is just one employee from Global Chains Company who is authorised to remove this seal. This approach eliminates cargo theft, particularly of bulk freight.
2. The company implemented an ERP system in the form of a mobile application, so that after loading the goods on the trailer, the driver can collect 50 percent of the shipment fee at the same time on a Meeza card- it is a Prepaid card, the first national Egyptian e-payment card, and is widely regarded as one of the primary e-payment methods that people use to pay their local bills or conduct other local financial operations- or a bank account rather than cash. After delivering the shipment to its destination, the driver can use the mobile application to indicate that he has already discharged the shipment, submit the shipping document, and receive the remaining 50 percent of the shipment fee

on his bank account or Meeza Card. This technique prevents document theft by converting paper documents to digital forms. It also prevents money theft.

3. Tracking the location of each driver throughout Egypt and send a notification to nearby drivers when cargo needs to be transported elsewhere. The driver receives the order and proceeds immediately to load it, rather than to call over a thousand drivers to determine their whereabouts and setting schedules based on each driver's location and all shipments' origin and destination. This strategy saved employees time, and their extraordinary efforts also aided in promptly loading shipments rather than waiting too long for the trailer to arrive.

CONCLUSION

Recommendations

Since Global Chain was one of the first companies in the Egyptian logistics sector to apply a digital solution to mitigate cargo thefts, the following recommendations are derived that could help pave the way for other companies in digital transformation.

1. Since the loading and off-loading points are the most vulnerable to deception, implying that a truck driver using a false identity picks up a load from the sender (and then vanishes with it) or a warehouse worker using a false identity directs the truck to a fraudulent discharge point (and then steals the cargo). As a result, it is critical to ensure that the carrier selected to deliver high-value products can pass due diligence.
2. If the logistics partner outsources the transportation procedure, they must assign the actual carriage of goods to a reputable operator capable of providing proper protection to avoid cargo theft. One approach to determine whether a carrier has implemented necessary safeguards is to see whether they are a Good Distribution Practice (GDP)-certified road transport firm or have successfully completed a TAPA audit. A third-party audit not only guarantees an impartial examination of a carrier, but also demonstrates that they conform to common criteria, rather than a collection of unusual features used to evaluate logistics providers. For example, the European Medicines Agency (EMA), a decentralised commission of the European Union (EU), disregards GDP criteria, which include laws governing the pharmaceutical industry's transportation procedure.

Although digital solutions have lots of advantages for managing data in businesses (Chaffinch, 2021), it's crucial to note that using digital documents has some very significant disadvantages as follows:

- Encrypted digital data can be hacked, and
- Many consumers still prefer receiving a physical receipt or invoice rather than a digital one.

REFERENCES

Akbari, M. (2018). Logistics outsourcing: A structured literature review. *Benchmarking, 25*(5), 1548–1580. doi:10.1108/BIJ-04-2017-0066

Balcerzak, A. P., Nica, E., Rogalska, E., Poliak, M., Kliestik, T., & Sabie, O. M. (2022). Blockchain Technology and Smart Contracts in Decentralised Governance Systems. *Administrative Sciences, 12*(3), 96. doi:10.3390/admsci12030096

Bawack, R. E., & Kala Kamdjoug, J. R. (2022). (Preprint). Managing client–consultant relationships to derive benefits from ERP projects. *Information Technology & People*. Advance online publication. doi:10.1108/ITP-07-2021-0573

BSI. (2018). *BSI & TT Club Cargo Theft Report H1 2018*. Available at: https://www.ttclub.com/fileadmin/uploads/tt-club/Documents/BSI_TT_ClubCargoTheftReportH1_2018_FinalRev.pdf

BSI. (2020). *BSI and TT Club Cargo Theft Report 2020*. Available at: bsigroup.com/supplychain.

Burges, D. (2012). *Cargo Theft, Loss Prevention, and Supply Chain Security*. Available at: https://books.google.com.eg/books?hl=ar&lr=&id=Fk2AK3pAkQkC&oi=fnd&pg=PP1&dq=cargo+theft+crime+pdf+&ots=9XITY3QrO_&sig=2 4TV_SYzP53cU-0snsGDnJZQjUM&redir_esc=y#v=onepage&q&f=false

Burges, D. (2013). Truckload Theft. *Cargo Theft, Loss Prevention, and Supply Chain Security*, 17–33. . doi:10.1016/B978-0-12-416007-1.00002-9

Dezdar, S., & Ainin, S. (2011). The influence of organisational factors on successful ERP implementation. *Management Decision, 49*(6), 911–926. doi:10.1108/00251741111143603

Ekwall, D., & Lantz, B. (2015). Cargo theft at non-secure parking locations. *International Journal of Retail & Distribution Management, 43*(3), 204–220. doi:10.1108/IJRDM-06-2013-0131

Ferrantino, M., & Koten, E. E. (2019). Understanding Supply Chain 4.0 and its potential impact on global value chains. *Global Value Chain Development Report: Technological Innovation, Supply Chain Trade, and Workers in a Globalised World*. Available at: https://www.wto.org/english/res_e/booksp_e/gvc_dev_report_2019_e.pdf

Girteca. (2021). *Carrying high-value goods on the road: Challenges and requirements*. Girteka Logistics. Available at: https://www.girteka.eu/carrying-high-value-goods-on-the-road-challenges-and-requirements/

Global Chains Company. (2019). Available at: https://global-chains.com/

Göl, H., & Çatay, B. (2007). Logistics Outsourcing and 3Pl Selection :A Case Study in an Automotive Supply Chain. *Engineering*.

Hendrickx, A. (2020). *Infosys Annual Report 2020-21*. Available at: https://www.infosys.com/investors/reports-filings/annual-report/annual/documents/infosys-ar-21.pdf

Justus, M., Ceccato, V., & Kahn, T. (2018). *Crime Against Trading: The Case of Cargo Theft in São Paulo*. doi:10.1007/978-3-319-73065-3

Kamel, S. (2021). *The Potential Impact of Digital Transformation on Egypt*. https://erf.org.eg/publications/the-potential-impact-of-digital-transformation-on-egypt/

Khalifa, N., Abd Elghany, M., & Abd Elghany, M. (2021). Exploratory research on digitalisation transformation practices within supply chain management context in developing countries specifically Egypt in the MENA region. *Cogent Business and Management*, *8*(1), 1965459. doi:10.1080/23311975.2021.1965459

Korpela, K., Hallikas, J., & Dahlberg, T. (2017). Digital Supply Chain Transformation toward Blockchain Integration. *Proceedings of the 50th Hawaii International Conference on System Sciences*, 4182-4191. Available at: http://hdl.handle.net/10125/41666

Logistics, B. (2022). *3 Tips For Protecting Freight From Cargo Theft with Technology*. Available at: https://mybluegrace.com/bluegrace-logistics/protecting-freight-from-cargo-theft-with-technology/

Lorenc, A., & Kuźnar, M. (2018). An intelligent system to predict risk and costs of cargo thefts in road transport)-System for proactive management and analysis of resources View project An Intelligent System to Predict Risk and Costs of Cargo Thefts in Road Transport. *International Journal of Engineering and Technology Innovation*, *8*(4), 284–293.

Mahmood, F., Khan, A. Z., & Bokhari, R. H. (2020). ERP issues and challenges: A research synthesis. *Kybernetes*, *49*(3), 629–659. doi:10.1108/K-12-2018-0699

Maier, R., Passiante, G., & Zhang, S. (2011). 'Creating value in networks. *International Journal of Innovation and Technology Management*, *8*(3), 357–371. doi:10.1142/S0219877011002416

Ministry of Communication and Information Technology. (2022). Available at: https://mcit.gov.eg/en/ICT_Strategy

Murphy, J., Paul, R., & Knemeyer, A. M. (2009). Contemporary Logistics. Pearson.

Palmer, J. S. (2010). *The Cargo Theft Threat*. Inbound Logistics. Available at: https://www.inboundlogistics.com/cms/article/the-cargo-theft-threat/

Queiroz, M. M., Pereira, S. C. F., Telles, R., & Machado, M. C. (2019). *Industry 4.0 and digital supply chain capabilities A framework for understanding digitalisation challenges and opportunities. Benchmarking: An International Journal*. doi:10.1108/BIJ-12-2018-0435

Reidy, S. (2020). *Cargo Theft: An unavoidable problem within your supply chain*. Available at: https://arviem.com/cargo-theft-problem-supply-chain/

Song, R., Huang, L., Cui, W., Óskarsdóttir, M., & Vanthienen, J. (2020). Fraud detection of bulk cargo theft in port using bayesian network models. *Applied Sciences (Switzerland)*, *10*(3), 1056. doi:10.3390/app10031056

Straight, B. (2020). *Cargo theft on the rise*. FreightWaves. Available at: https://www.freightwaves.com/news/cargo-theft-on-the-rise

Tay, S. I., Lee, T. C., Hamid, N. A. A., & Ahmad, A. N. A. (2018). An Overview of Industry 4.0: Definition, Components, and Government Initiatives. *Journal of Advanced Research in Dynamical and Control Systems, Safety and Environmental Protection, 117*, 408–425.

Chapter 3
The Effects of Implementing the Advanced Cargo Information (ACI) System on Egyptian Importers

Farah Samir
Arab Academy for Science, Technology, and Maritime Transport, Egypt

Aya El-Garhy
Arab Academy for Science, Technology, and Maritime Transport, Egypt

Ashish Bagwari
Uttarakhand Technical University, India

EXECUTIVE SUMMARY

Blockchain technology is gradually being applied to different customs clearance systems globally to improve the efficiency of trade transactions by digitizing customs clearance processes. This chapter explores the Advance Cargo Information (ACI) system—a blockchain-based system—implemented by the Egyptian Customs Authority (ECA) and provides recommendations for future improvements. A case study was applied on three regular importer companies in Egypt, H.B. Fuller, Ezz Steel, and Zamil Steel, to study specific customs clearance concepts related to time, documentation, and costs associated with the processes to draw a conclusion on the impacts of implementing the ACI on the import customs clearance procedures. Finally, the chapter concludes that the ACI system has had a positive impact on importers and customs employees. Nevertheless, importers still face several challenges with the customs clearance system. Therefore, recommendations are listed for the ECA to upgrade the customs clearance processes, and Misr Technology Services (MTS) to develop the ACI system's infrastructure.

DOI: 10.4018/978-1-6684-4686-7.ch003

INTRODUCTION

International Trade has always been shaped by technology; however, over the last few decades, technological advancements have rapidly transformed trade, in terms of what we trade, how we trade, and who is trading. Digital technologies, such as Blockchain, has affected the efficiency of the importing and exporting industries globally (World Trade Organization, 2018).

Blockchain is a decentralized open-source platform that allows a secure flow of transactions between companies and individuals, established by Ben Reeves in 2011. The idea behind this came from wanting to create a secure mechanism for digital currencies from the risk of replication, which helped create the world's first cryptocurrency, "Bitcoin". The technology has many benefits, most significantly, is time and cost savings, and the secure documents flow through encryption and sharing within the network (Frankenfield, 2021).

The World Customs Organization (WCO) has initiated work to identify possible uses of blockchain for Customs procedures and other border agencies, looking to improve compliance, trade facilitation, and fraud detection. Hence, following the WCO's protocol, the Egyptian Customs Authority (ECA) in association with Misr Technology Services (MTS) adopted the idea of using blockchain-based applications in customs clearance procedures. In 2021, the ECA implemented a new system for customs clearance and pre-registration of sea shipments called the Advance Cargo Information (ACI) system that consisted of two blockchain-based applications; the "Nafeza platform" for Egyptian importers, and the "CargoX Platform" for foreign suppliers (Egyptian Customs Authority, 2022).

The importance of this research lies in spreading knowledge about the significance of efficient customs clearance procedures to the Egyptian import market, as trade is a major factor that determines the social and economic development of the country (Japan international cooperation agency, 2008). And importing in Egypt is usually considered a complex process, as perceived by foreign suppliers, due to the difficulties in customs clearance paperwork procedures, which include registration, certification, and legalization requirements for various documents (Swiss Embassy in Egypt, 2016). Additionally, due to the lengthy customs procedures and the high rate of cargo inspection by the Egyptian Customs Authority, therefore, Egyptian importers suffer from a time- and cost-consuming importing process (Awad, 2021).

This research aims to investigate the impact of implementing the ACI system in the Egyptian customs clearance procedures on Egyptian importers and the Egyptian importation market, and recommend further potential developments to the system, through achieving the following objectives:

- Determine the difference between the Egyptian customs clearance processes in the past and present
- Present different customs systems globally
- Assess the impact of implementing the ACI system on Egyptian importers

LITERATURE REVIEW

This section reviews the literature of previous studies related to international trade, import management, and importing in Egypt specifically. In addition to, an overview of customs clearance procedures in Egypt in terms of documentation required, time spent, and costs associated with the process. Moreover, the digitalization in trade, highlighting blockchain technology's basic concepts and the study of implementing it in customs clearance procedures are discussed, focusing on the ACI system.

International Trade

Rai Technology University (2012) defined international trade as "a vital part of development strategy and it can be an effective instrument of economic growth, employment generation, and poverty alleviation". The author further explained that international trade consists of importing and exporting goods and services, which results in the outflow and inflow of foreign exchange. Since this chapter addresses the impact on importers, imports will be the main topic reviewed.

Import Management

Several studies such as (Thapa, 2014; Dimapindan, 2014) have investigated the import management process. They defined the import process as ensuring the safety of imported goods by sharing the responsibilities with other agencies. Internal and external documented processes can become difficult when many imported products are subject to rules by multiple departments.

A study by Thapa, (2014) concluded that streaming the import management process offers some benefits, such as reducing the risk, improving productivity, and reducing shipment delays, as the import process becomes more complex and time-consuming. The authors bring up some information about the background of the problem, that global trade is full of constantly changing regulations, which tend to change the import process frequently. The different parties that are involved in the import process are important for the smooth flow of the transaction.

Olesen's research in 2015 was mainly focused on the actors engaged in the importing process (see Figure 1), which viewed the main actors as

1. The Importer, who's known as the buyer or consignee,
2. The Carriers, add value to the shipper by moving goods from the point of production to consumption,
3. The Third parties, also known as freight forwarders, may provide several value-added services, by improving the level of service, quality, cost, and time reduction.
4. The agents that are employed by the shipper/carrier; maybe chartering agents who provide market knowledge or port agents who ease the port operations, or customs agents known as customs brokers of the customs authority play a prominent role in the customs clearance of import transactions (Grainger, 2007).

Importing to Egypt

The International trade center (2018) argued that Egyptian customs clearance is the main character in the importing and exporting process management. Whereas, under the supervision of the Customs Department, the importer must provide sufficient annual inventory to display items cleared. Also, the author added, that if the Egyptian Customs Department is motivated to doubt the accuracy of any document, the customs officer may apply for additional documents proving the value of the total amount paid, through the request for additional written documents and give them 15 days to respond. Alternatively, the Customs Department must clarify the reasons for the doubt and the final decision and its justifications and it must be written.

Figure 1. Maritime chain of transportation actors
Source: Olesen (2015)

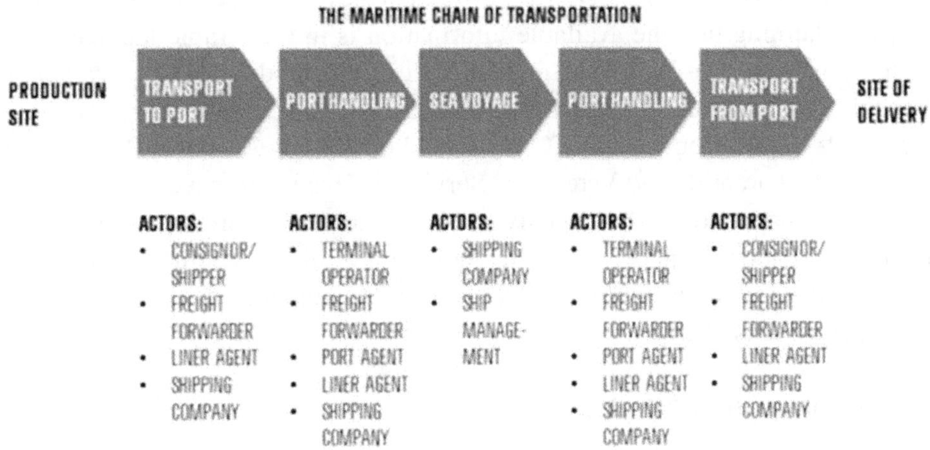

A comprehensive description of the import process in Egypt can be found in (European Union, 2019), where they discussed that if the importer wants to release the imported goods, it must be accompanied by an invoice containing the producer's name and the trademark. Additionally, the certificate of origin or other documents establishing the origin and their accompanying documents shall be submitted after being authenticated by the Egyptian Embassy or Consulate in the exporting country. Furthermore, the Embassy of Switzerland in Egypt (2016) discussed the latest import procedure changes in Egypt, which are mainly in the customs clearance processes, "These new measures include registration and certification requirements, the requirement to legalize various documents, restriction of the free flow of payments as well as increased customs tariffs. These new measures represent serious difficulties for Swiss companies exporting to Egypt".

Customs Clearance

The World Customs Organization (2018) described customs clearance as two separate words; where's the author-defined Customs as Government Service responsible for administrating Customs law and for the application of other laws and regulations relating to the importation, exportation, movement, or storage of goods, in addition to the collection of customs duties and taxes. While the term "Clearance" was defined as the accomplishment of the customs formalities necessary to allow goods to be imported or exported. Moreover, the Ministry of Commerce People's Republic of China (2021) described customs procedures as the measures applied by the customs authority to imported or exported goods subject to customs laws and regulations.

Several previous studies by (Japan International Cooperation Agency, 2008; Embassy of Switzerland in Egypt, 2016; Shahin, 2021) suggested that customs clearance procedures in Egypt were considered a bottleneck when trading, before implementing the automated system in 2021. Shahin (2016) argued that outdated and overly bureaucratic customs clearance processes imposed by governmental authorities are considered a great barrier to trade, leading to increased costs and time spent, primarily due to the documentation process.

Documentation for Clearing Customs in Egypt

The documentation needed is also considered a constraint in the Egyptian customs procedures, as reported by Shahin (2021). Claiming that the available information is in the Arabic language only; moreover, the information available varies since trade regulations come from different government agencies with different information and policies (e.g., Customs, Ministry of Finance, Ministry of Trade, General Organization for Export & Import Control/GOEIC, National Food Safety Authority/NFSA, and the Ministry of Agriculture's Plant Quarantine and Veterinary Services). This leads to a complicated documentation process with unknown paperwork. Additionally, according to the Egyptian Customs Authority (2022), all the documentation had to be paper-based, including an original document along with at least one copy, all stamped. Also, some documentation issued by the customs authorities had to be manually handwritten, requiring loads of time.

Time Spent Clearing Customs in Egypt

As reported by the Egyptian customs authority (2022) to clear customs for imported goods, there were multiple administrative offices under the ECA in addition to other government agencies that are involved in the clearing process; including the customer service center, the bank, the general organization for export and import control, customs windows one and two, information center, examination, and inspection areas, and other authorities, thus leading to a time-consuming customs process. The Federation of Egyptian Industries (2021) argued that the process of clearing customs could take between two weeks and five weeks, specifying the causes of delay; including the length of inspection procedures, the non-fixed expenses, the failure to generalize the electronic link between the different customs administrations, and the lack of coordination in the policies between different authorities, increasing the overall cost of the process.

Costs of Clearing Customs in Egypt

The following studies (Shahin, 2021; Japan International Cooperation Agency, 2008) well acknowledged that Egypt has the highest number of non-tariff barriers imposed on trade, particularly administrative barriers, to compensate for tariff reduction. Likewise, Shahin (2021) suggested that the highly inflexible and outdated customs administration may be the main reason for causing increased costs, as the government continues to believe that tariffs are a revenue source, therefore, the costs of clearing customs vary and weren't clearly declared. Furthermore, a study by Mahmoud in 2021 claimed that expenses paid by importers to comply with customs procedures in Egypt are estimated to range from 457 to 7,962 USD.

On the contrary, the Ministry of finance in 2013, asserted that customs laws, executive regulations, and importing regulations are all applied in the field of customs clearance, especially when importing, which are a part of the efforts in the framework of achieving justice in the field of customs tax collection, however, it shall be taken in consideration that the needed documentation should be issued correctly for the fees to be calculated accurately. Furthermore, Shahin (2021) added, that the WTO prohibits customs clearance charges from being overvalued.

The inefficient customs procedures encouraged the country to adopt digital technologies in trading to make the process more effective. Therefore, the following sections will review the technological advancements in the international trade industry, focusing on Blockchain technology and its adoption in customs procedures.

Digitalization in Trade

Blockchain Technology

Previous studies (Sadouskaya, 2017; Ewald, Hjortstam, and Wilén, 2021; Li and Zhou, 2020; Tsiulin et al., 2020; Vorotyntseva, Nemirova, and Vinichenko, 2019; Yang, 2019) defined Blockchain technology as a distributed, shared, and encrypted database that is tightly connected to computer science considered as a decentralized technology. It is also a public network distributed among participant computers around the world, thus, there is no need for intermediates such as a central database. Moreover, Ewald et al. (2021) discussed that "the blockchain system is very secure due to encryption and its structure of permanent information storage. Information is stored in chains of digital blocks that are distributed throughout the network". In addition, Li and Zhou (2020), and Vorotyntseva, et al. (2019) added that it's nearly impossible to change, add, or remove information on a blockchain without causing other users to notice.

Research by Li and Zhou (2020) showed that the use of blockchain technology in marine and shipping transactions can revolutionize the industry, as Blockchain combines the openness of the internet with cryptography's security function to give marine enterprises and shipping agents a safer and faster solution to authenticate crucial transaction information and create supply chain trust. Blockchain technology is gradually being applied to the global logistics of international trade to improve the efficiency of transactions by digitizing maritime shipping records, such as keeping real-time track of cargo status, improving visibility in the global supply chain, and contributing positively to customs clearance time, costs, and risks. (Ewald et al., 2021; Yang, 2019).

Blockchain Technology in Global Customs Clearance: NACCS, ABI, and ICS

According to these studies (Belu, 2020; Angert, 2019; Sturmanis, et al. 2020) blockchain technology integration in customs clearance procedures reduces goods' delivery time and provides transparency and confidence to foreign trade participants. The most efficient E-customs systems for pre-register filling of customs documentation that is implemented globally in the customs processes by different countries' governments, especially in the importation, include; 1) the Nippon Automated Cargo and Port Consolidated System (NACCS) in Japan, 2) the Automated Broker Interface (ABI) program in the United States of America, and 3) the Import Control System (ICS) in the European union member states.

ESCAP (2019) reviewed the Japanese customs clearance-automated system, known as the Nippon Automated Cargo and Port Consolidated System "NACCS", Japan was one of the first countries to adopt this system in its customs clearance procedures for imports and transit shipments. According to the Ministry of Finance in 2013, it was discussed how Japan's customs authority required a detailed filling about the cargo's information at the earliest time accepted by the "SAFE Framework" or not later than 24 hours before loading the cargo at the ports of departure. Moreover, the WCO (2018) stated that Advance Filing Rules on Maritime Container Cargo Information oblige the traders to electronically file cargo information through the NACCS, whenever importing or exporting goods from or to Japanese ports. This results in a Single Window system, thus an efficient paperless trading facility and a cost and time-efficient customs clearance process.

Another real-world example of an automated customs clearance procedure is being implemented in the United States, explains Angert (2019), by conducting an interview approach with subject-matter experts. The U.S. customs and border protection (CBP) 2022, discusses the implementation of the Automated Broker Interface (ABI) program by the government in its customs procedures, for the importers to file the documents necessary to determine whether merchandise may be released from the CBP's custody, and file the documents that contain information for duty assessment and statistical purposes, electronically. Furthermore, (Angert, 2019) discussed the success observed, whereas the ABI program improved the processing and tracking of trade documents, facilitating interaction with multiple entities, enabled better audibility, expedited processing, encouraged global standards, and promoted economic growth and fair trade practices.

Finally, the third example of electronic system implementation in customs clearance procedures is the Import Control System (ICS) developed by the European Commission for the European Union member states. According to the Irish tax and customs (2021), the ICS is an electronic data exchange between customs administrations, traders, and the European Commission. (Irish tax and customs, 2021; European Commission, 2021) emphasized the benefits of the ICS implementation, which affected the efficiency of these countries' import processes, facilitated communications between traders and customs administrations of Member States, created security against the threats posed by the trafficking of goods that happen outside the borders and ensured that the customs office could carry out risk analysis on the goods prior to them entering the territory of the European Community.

Although there are many studies reviewing the successful implementations of the NACCS, the ABI, and the ICS in the customs clearance procedures, yet, the challenges that the importers may have faced in the process of using these automated systems are rarely analyzed in the literature because there are hardly any.

Blockchain Technology in Egyptian Customs Clearance: ACI System

According to these studies (Belu, 2020; Angert, 2019), blockchain technology integration in customs clearance procedures reduces goods' delivery time and provides transparency and confidence to foreign trade participants globally.

The ACI system was defined by recent research (Shahin, 2021; WCO, 2018) as a system that uses blockchain technology to deliver real-time information on transactions and operations before, during, and after the delivery of cargo. The ACI system operates under the WCO protocol following the WCO SAFE Framework of Standards to Secure and Facilitate Global Trade (USDA, 2021; WCO, 2018).

Shahin (2021) explained that this newly implemented system would increase customs officials' capacity to deal efficiently with shipments, thus increasing the confidentiality between importers/exporters and customs authorities. Additionally, the ACI system will indirectly lead to the expanding use of information technology, allowing traders and governmental authorities to deal less with paper documentation.

The MTS published clear steps (see Figure 2) and instructions that an importer needs to follow to prepare and register for using the ACI system, along with the needed documents. Additionally, provided further information about the certified Block-chain Service Provider, which is CargoX, an open system that enables the creation and exchange of information and documents by using Blockchain technology and decentralized, encrypted data storage, a platform with a variety of applications, the most prominent of which is providing Smart contracts, such as bill of lading (Nafeza, 2021).

Figure 2. ACI system procedure
Source: Nafeza (2021)

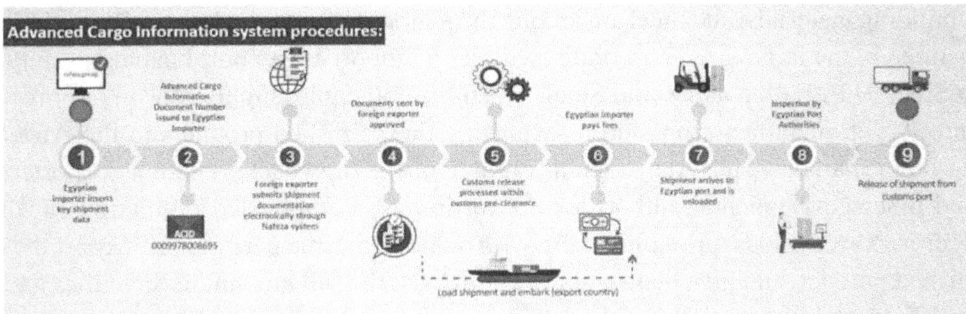

Research Gap

Based on the above literature, previous research can only be considered as the first step toward a more profound understanding of the impact of implementing the ACI system in Egyptian customs procedures on importers. Prior Papers discussed the topic from the government's point of view of the expected benefits of implementing the system; however, this chapter considers the topic from the Importer's point of view to prove whether the ACI system has impacted their trade transactions, through applying a case study.

RESEARCH METHODOLOGY

This research follows an inductive research approach with an exploratory nature. The data collected in this research are secondary and primary sources analyzed qualitatively to answer research questions.

Research Methods

It is qualitative research that seeks an understanding of the ACI system's implementation in Egyptian customs clearance, by following an inductive research approach, which first observed the problem of the customs procedures inefficiency, then seeks to find patterns from the collected data, to finally reach a theory concluding the impact of ACI on the importers.

In addition to primary sources, through conducting semi-structured interviews, by interviewing three candidates in-person: Ezz Steel's Import Manager, HB Fuller's Logistics supervisor, and Zamil Steel's Import Specialist. These interviewees were chosen due to their extensive experience in the field, besides working in some of the major importing companies in Egypt, making them most aware of the topic discussed.

Moreover, after collecting all the data, to gain meaningful results, the data will be analyzed qualitatively, by organizing, connecting, and summarizing it. Finally, the research's design is exploratory, as it applies qualitative methods, and relies on case studies of E-customs from different countries globally, as a source of data, which will help in the application of a case study on the Egyptian E-customs, and recommend further solutions for developing the ACI.

Organizations' Background

Chemicals, building materials, and Steel are among the major imported products in Egypt. Therefore, this case studies three of the large-sized corporates with large import and export businesses in the Egyptian market, Ezz Steel, H.B. Fuller, and Zamil Steel. The three companies highly rely on importing their raw materials into Egypt, manufacturing, and re-exporting their finished products to the African, Middle Eastern, and other markets. Thus, they take advantage of the drawback system as exporters, in which the ECA and other governmental authorities do not impose complicated regulations in the customs procedures for imported goods, providing them with a one-year time permit to re-export these goods as part of a finished product, and give them right to claim back the full amount of the duties and taxes paid (International Trade Administration, 2021).

Ezz Steel Company

Ezz steel Co. was established in 1959 in Egypt by Ahmed Ezz, an Egyptian businessman. The company grew rapidly to become the largest steel producer in Egypt, the Middle East, and the North African Region and one of the world's fastest-growing and most technically advanced steel producers. The company produces 4.7 million tons of rebar, wire rod, and 2.3 million tons of flat steel and welded steel fabric every year to meet challenging international standards considering quality, integrity, reliability, flexible production capabilities, and competitive prices (Ezzsteel, 2022). The company's products are distributed to customers in Africa, Asia, Europe, and North America, where it makes a significant contribution to major construction, engineering, and infrastructure projects.

Ezz steel aims to be Egypt's key importer of rebars (steel bars). Therefore, to meet these high demands, they import a volume of 4 million tons of steel raw materials and spare parts every year, to produce long and flat steel, and re-export to their customers in four continents.

H.B. Fuller Company

H.B. Fuller is a global adhesives manufacturing and supplying company. It was founded by Harvey Benjamin Fuller in 1887, initially in the United States of America, and later, the company expanded into international markets in South America, Europe, Africa, and Asia, with 55 manufacturing sites in 42 countries (H.B. Fuller Company, 2022). The Company's site in Egypt, since 2008, is amongst H.B. Fuller's most important manufacturing sites worldwide, due to its high efficiency and high production capacity, which serves the Egyptian, Turkish, Middle Eastern, and African markets.

H.B. Fuller's products are an integral part of almost every finished good available in the market, providing adhesive solutions for industries such as automotive and transportation, building and construction, industrial assembly and manufacturing, electronics, hygiene, packaging and labeling, wood and composites, and others (H.B. Fuller, 2022). However, the company in Egypt is focused more on supplying adhesives specialized for packaging, labeling, and disposable hygiene, with annual revenue growth of 17.5% in 2021, than the preceding year, and an average of 600 import transactions of chemicals yearly.

Zamil Steel Company

Zamil Steel Holding was established in 1977 in Saudi Arabia and specialized in the design, manufacture, and supply of steel. The company expanded its factories to Egypt, India, United Arab Emirates, and Vietnam, with a total production capacity of more than 6,000,000 m^2 annually (Zamil Steel, 2022). Zamil Steel pre-engineered buildings is a subsidiary of Zamil Steel Holding and are considered the largest manufacturer and supplier of steel for pre-engineered buildings in Asia and Africa, supplying to more than 95 countries worldwide.

Egypt's factory is a leading supplier of pre-engineered buildings in Africa, exporting to more than 30 African nations and owning more than 50% of the Egyptian market's steel supply. Thus, to meet high market demands, their importing business in Egypt is focused on steel raw materials and semi-finished products to use in their construction projects, with about 5,000 tons of imported steel per year.

The company aims to be the world's most reliable and innovative manufacturer in the steel industry, by supplying high-quality steel products, and providing ultimate solutions worldwide, while utilizing innovative technologies focused on continuous improvement, to add value for their customers and sustain the return on investment to their shareholders.

CASE STUDY ANALYSIS

The following findings presented are primarily based on the data collected through the interviews conducted with Ezz Steel's Import Manager, HB Fuller's Logistics supervisor, and Zamil Steel's Import Specialist, on the Egyptian market, the customs processes before the system's implementation, and the impact of the ACI system on their importing business.

Import and Export Markets in Egypt

Egypt is a country that highly relies on imported products, yet, importing in Egypt is usually considered a complex process, due to the difficulties in customs clearance paperwork procedures, which acts as a non-tariff barrier to trade. Additionally, due to the lengthy customs procedures, Egyptian importers suffer from a time and cost-consuming importing process (Awad, 2021).

The geographic location of Egypt makes it a trade hub, connecting continents to the rest of Africa. According to the General Organization for Export and Import Control, Egyptian total exports for 2020 were equivalent to $25.295 billion, while an equivalent of 63,563,587 billion dollars' worth of cargo was imported to Egypt in the year 2020. Its largest export markets are the United Arab Emirates, Saudi Arabia, Turkey, the United States of America, and Italy. However, the largest Egyptian import markets are China, the United States of America, Germany, Italy, and Turkey, importing products such as chemicals and fertilizers, building materials and steel, food and beverages, agricultural crops, furniture, textiles, and leather.

Although trade is unrestricted, importers are discouraged in their trade transactions through various measures relating to documentation, testing, inspection, and certifications established by the Government to enhance economic development and increase exports, anticipating for Egypt to become a key player in the global economy and adjust to international developments. The following graph illustrates the time spent and costs associated with the import and export transactions:

Figure 3. Time and cost for imports/exports compliance in Egypt 2020
Source Awad (2021)

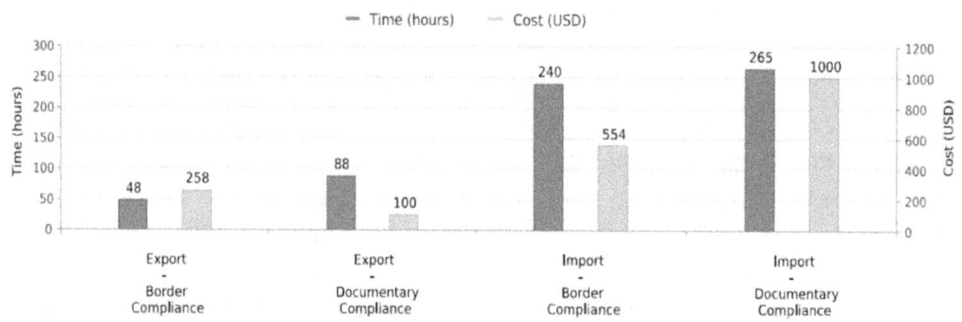

Importing Before ACI Implementation

Prior to the ACI system implementation, Ezz steel company used to consume loads of time and costs in the customs clearance procedures, due to a large amount of paper documentation, and the different parties that had to be dealt with. Similarly, H.B. Fuller and Zamil Steel's documentation process was considered complex and time-consuming, due to the authentications needed from different authorities at the shipment's origin, such as; some documents needed to be stamped by the chamber of commerce and the Egyptian Embassy at the supplier's country to be accepted by the ECA. Additionally, clearance procedures highly varied in time, and different authorities were included throughout the process, which led to increased overall customs clearance fees and the incapability to keep the costs under control.

The Customs clearance procedures were as follows: once the shipment has been discharged and received by the customs authority in the Customs Warehouse, the clearance agent's role starts here. First, the agent receives all the shipment documents in hard copies, to obtain a delivery order from the shipping line against handing in an original Bill of lading. Then opens a customs certificate, also known as the "customs declaration", at the customs authority, by providing all the original documents of the shipment. Moreover, the clearance procedures are as follows:

1. The relevant inspection authority undertakes cargo inspection processes to match the shipment with the documents provided.
2. Followed by the valuation processes to determine the shipment's customs duties and Value Added Taxes (VAT), done by the Customs authority's valuation department.
3. The agent then pays all the relevant customs clearance fees at the bank and acquires a document as proof of payment for the customs authority to obtain a final release report in exchange.

At the same time, Ezz Steel's, HB fuller's, and Zamil Steel's import managers along with their teams are responsible for filing all the necessary paperwork throughout the whole customs process. For instance, each inspection authority requires a different set of documents to be able to start the inspection procedures, in addition to the forms required by the bank to obtain the final release permission accordingly.

Hence, the old customs clearance system has had several disadvantages. First, before starting any clearance step, the companies had to yearly permit a customs agent to be able to perform the clearance procedures on their behalf, in an official letter, which was time and cost-consuming. Since the clearance procedures started after discharging, and as every step in the process required paper documentation, shipments used to spend loads of time stored at the port, which led to arising storage and demurrage fees. The minimum time of customs procedures at the port took an average of 7 to 10 days for the cargo that doesn't need special conformity, in addition to the 7- 10 days of pre-clearance time needed for documents' preparations. Also, the only backup of documents was paper-based, held in the archive department, which would take months to find the needed documents. Moreover, there wasn't any integration between different customs authorities, regulatory authorities, shipping lines, the bank, importers, and exporters; making the process hard to follow up on. Finally, it was an uncontrolled and corrupted overall system, because of the manual processes that allowed bribery and fraud.

Given the previous customs clearance inefficiency, the government decided to introduce the ACI system.

The Concept of ACI System

According to Mele (2021), the ACI system consists of two blockchain-based applications; the "Nafeza Platform" for Egyptian importers, and the "CargoX Platform" for foreign suppliers, under which the trading partners are required to declare full information about goods that will be shipped to Egypt before actual loading from the exporting country electronically. Moreover, the Nafeza platform issues an Advanced Cargo Information Declaration Number (ACID) to the importer and the exporter once a shipment is registered. ACID is an initial customs registration 19-digit number that identifies every single shipment, included on all shipment documents (Nafeza, 2021).

The system was implemented through two stages; the first launched as an initial phase for trial on April 1, 2021, and was later mandatory applied on all Egyptian seaports in its second stage. According to the World Trade Organization (2018) and Shahin (2021), the ACI system aims to:

1. **Reduce clearance time:** By using blockchain technology to deliver real-time information on transactions and operations before, during, and after the delivery of cargo, therefore, clearance will take less time to be released from the customs authority, facilitating trade and foreign direct investments.
2. **Increased integration between authorities:** The system seeks to achieve integration and coordination between all parties involved in the trade transaction, including customs authorities, banks, importers, and exporters.
3. **Better risk management:** The risk-based system identifies security risks before cargo arrival, indicates whether it requires sampling and inspection, and eliminates harmful or unidentified goods that may cause damage. Thus, protecting Egyptian citizens and ports.
4. **Standardized procedures without paper documents:** ACI allows the trade community to submit all documents and transactions electronically on a single platform while maintaining the confidentiality of documents between the importers/exporters and the customs authority.
5. **Decreased prices of goods and services in the Egyptian market:** Efficient customs clearance procedures will allow fewer storage costs leading to an overall reduced cost of releasing goods, in addition, to helping in a better customs valuation of goods.

The Impacts of ACI System

The following shows the impact of implementing the ACI system on each company. Although the case studies cover the same topics, they slightly differ in their outcome.

Ezz Steel Company's Case

The ACI system implementation has had a noticeable impact on all import transactions' customs clearance procedures, in terms of the time spent, expenses paid, and paper documentation required.

Starting with the system's initial phase, according to Ezz Steel's Import manager, they used the NAFEZA platform and demanded their supplier to use CargoX, aiming to get used to the system and be as efficient as possible before its final implementation phase. Throughout the stage, they faced numerous challenges and obstacles in the system, as it was very complicated, unprofessional, and time-consuming. For instance, the poor communication with the customer service agents, due to their lack of knowledge of the system, the continuous system failures, and the long and complicated steps to request an ACID number for a shipment that could take as long as 10 days. Nonetheless, the ECA and MTS have detected these system drawbacks and solved them by the final implementation phase. And by the time of the final implementation phase, Ezz steel's import department had mastered using the new customs system, the "Nafeza platform".

The customs clearance procedures vary slightly from the old system, whereas the process starts before the shipment arrives at the port. First, one of Ezz steel's import department employees uploads the shipment's initial documents and registers the importer and exporter's information on NAFEZA to request an ACID number for the shipment(s). The customs authority revises and verifies all the information electronically, and creates an ACID number for the shipment within a few hours. After obtaining an ACID number, they require the supplier to upload the shipment's final documents with the ACID number on them on the CARGOX platform.

Once the shipment arrives, the importer issues a customs certificate on the NAFEZA platform, and the delivery order is uploaded on the NAFEZA platform by the shipping line. Moreover, all the proceeding steps aren't fully electronic yet, and still require some paperwork, including the inspection, valuation, and bank processes. Nonetheless, the partial paperwork elimination decreased the customs clearance procedures' overall time spent at ports, thus a decreased storage and demurrage costs on each shipment. Additionally, fewer efforts are required by Ezz Steel's employees to track the shipment's status, as tracking every step and report of the clearing process became electronic through NAFEZA. Finally, the system allowed them to easily review past shipments' information.

H.B. Fuller Company's Case

On the contrary, HB Fuller's imports weren't highly affected by the ACI system's implementation until the present time. The shipments' time spent at the ports and the related costs remained the same, but the efforts required throughout the procedures slightly increased.

At the time of the ACI system's pilot phase launching in April 2021, the company's employees weren't regular users of the system in all of their import transactions, due to the obstacles that occurred. Facing these challenges such as the constant system failures, the extremely slow loading, and most importantly, the unfamiliarity and lack of training on a newly implemented system, along with NAFEZA and CAR-

GOX's high registration and operation fees, HB Fuller didn't view the system as efficient to be used in its initial phase and could've caused them unwanted delay in their transactions. Nevertheless, after the final implementation stage, the ECA obligatory the ACI system for all import transactions in Egypt.

For HB Fuller, the time spent clearing customs did not change. All the paperwork required remained the same, in addition, all documents of every step must be uploaded on NAFEZA now, which requires extra effort.

The clearance procedure became divided into two phases. The first phase is before the shipments' arrival, where the importer and exporter must upload the shipment documents on NAFEZA and CARGOX to receive approval for importing by obtaining an ACID number from the ECA. Afterwards, the second phase starts when the cargo is discharged in the Customs warehouse at the port; a customs certificate is opened electronically after the shipping line has uploaded the delivery order on NAFEZA. Subsequently, all the inspection and valuation processes take place physically, demanding original shipment documents as hard copies, as well as providing all the reports manually besides uploading them on NAFEZA. Finally, the final release report and bank forms are issued manually without their integration into the system until the present time.

Similarly, the costs of clearing customs have either remained the same for some shipments or increased for others. Beginning with the costs of document issuance since all the documents required remained the same as pre-system implementation, costs haven't changed as well. Furthermore, registration and document upload fees for foreign suppliers are relatively high, thus, some suppliers demand HB Fuller bear these expenses. Finally, storage and demurrage fees usually remain the same, except otherwise, when any step is delayed due to a late upload of documents on NAFEZA or CargoX, the fees increase on the importer.

The advantages of implementing the ACI system are very limited from HB Fuller's perspective. Summarized in the easy tracking of the clearance process and expenses, which earlier had to be followed up by physically approaching the different authorities involved in the process. In addition to the effortless process of delegating a clearance agent on their behalf through simple steps on the NAFEZA platform. Furthermore, the company now ensures the authenticity of the shipment documents uploaded by the supplier, the validity of the inspection necessary by the relevant authorities and the originality of their reports, and finally the accuracy of the customs valuation documents.

Zamil Steel Company's Case

In Zamil Steel, the implementation of the ACI system in Egyptian customs clearance was highly impactful on their import business. Even though their import frequency decreased in the number of transactions monthly, yet each transaction became much more efficient than in the past, in terms of costs and time spent throughout the process.

The initial ACI system implementation phase fairly benefited the company's employees. The MTS offered training courses to help the employees get familiar with the ACI system, therefore, they insisted on using it in their trade transactions to master the system and tackle any challenges faced before its mandatory phase. So far, during the 7 months of the pilot phase, the only challenge faced was the slow system that logged out a lot. Nevertheless, by the final phase, the MTS did solve a lot of issues that were addressed in the system.

In October 2021, the system was obligatory on all importers, as a result, Zamil Steel started noticing the impact of its implementation on their import procedures. Starting with the documentation process, all the needed documentation became uploaded on NAFEZA before trading, which decreased the time needed for paperwork preparation before importing. Additionally, the importers are notified of every step of the clearing process, meaning they don't have to follow up with the port customs authority physically. Furthermore, the inspection process became more organized, in terms of getting the inspection time and date electronically through NAFEZA, which eliminated the delay that used to happen due to waiting for the inspection time in a disorganized system. Consequently, the inspection of cargo could take from one to 2 days, and in some cases, can be on the same day.

Simultaneously, the costs associated with the customs procedures have noticeably decreased. Considering the storage and demurrage costs, the system's implementation has impacted them because of the time reduction. Furthermore, the costs of the customs brokers were decreased, as their role became limited within the ACI system, starting at the inspection and valuation processes.

The ACI system has overcome many hurdles that came along with the old customs system. For instance, it relatively excluded dealing with hard copies of shipment documents, prevented illegal activities throughout the clearance process, and positively affected the time and costs associated related to the process. Still, there are several challenges the company faces with the new system that need to be addressed, for improved system performance.

Challenges Facing the Organizations

Like any newly implemented system, users might face several hurdles when using the system. Even though there are many benefits to the ACI system implementation within the Egyptian import customs clearance procedures, there are still some challenges facing the organizations today, as the system is still developing.

Firstly, the system obligates exporters to register on CargoX to be able to trade with any Egyptian importer, with an increased number of steps, and relatively high fees for registration and submission of any documents. Meanwhile, not all foreign exporters are qualified or willing to pay these fees, leading to the turndown of some exporters. Besides the high amount of time required for the Egyptian importer to guide the foreign exporter in using the platform, due to the lack of resources provided by the ECA and MTS regarding this topic.

Secondly, the partial paperwork inclusion leads to double work in the documentation, where the exporter must upload the shipment's documents electronically on CargoX and send them as hard copies to the importer to use throughout the clearance process, which incurs double transfer fees.

Thirdly, not all customs employees are trained enough to be able to use the system efficiently, which delays some confirmation and uploading processes. Besides, only about 50% of the authorities that are dealt with throughout the clearance procedures are present in the system, which leads to increased efforts in the remaining authorities' transactions that carried out manually.

Finally, the weak system infrastructure operating with a few servers leads to system failures at high-demand periods, resulting in increased time and costs due to the delay of some processes. Additionally, the ECA restricts changing any information related to the shipment once an ACID is acquired and the shipment documents are uploaded, leading to a long and complex process to amend any incorrect documents uploaded by any party on the system.

Nonetheless, according to the General Manager of the customs authority at an Egyptian port, the ECA, and the MTS are putting continuous efforts into monitoring and tracking down all the arising problems within the system, to solve and enhance the system over time. "Egypt is developing toward a new republic by the strategic direction of digital transformation and by applying new technological solutions (e.g., the ACI system) in all sectors", he affirmed.

CONCLUSION AND MAIN FINDINGS

Efficient customs clearance procedures on country borders facilitate international trade and increase the development of countries. Egyptian importers have always complained about how complex the importing procedures were in Egypt, due to the difficulties they faced in the customs clearance processes. Therefore, the importers have suffered from the time and cost-consuming importing process. As a result, according to the Egyptian Customs Authority (2022), the ECA in association with the MTS implemented the blockchain-based system, the ACI, in the customs clearance procedures in October 2021.

Blockchain technology revolutionized the Egyptian import industry by partially digitizing the customs clearance procedures (refer to Figure 4) whereas the first four steps documentation process varied before and after implementing the ACI system.

The system's implementation enhanced the Egyptian customs clearance procedures compared to the old customs system. Where the procedures became effortless to some extent, in terms of the automated steps of the process, and the partial elimination of paperwork as a result of electronic data exchange. Furthermore, as the customs clearance processes are constantly developing, the future of the ACI system is perceived to be outstanding when it is fully implemented according to the WCO principles.

The ACI system is beneficial to the importers as well as the customs authority in multiple aspects. The importers benefited in terms of the electronic documentation and the tracking of customs clearance procedures electronically, meanwhile, the customs employees gained the advantage of an enhanced work experience and more control over the imported goods, leading to improved fraud detection, and elimination of unidentified imports.

Compared to other efficient E-Customs, such as NACCS, ICS, and ABI, the ACI system is almost as advantageous as the other systems; however, the ACI system implementation incorporates more challenges than the other systems, which hardly has any challenges. The most significant challenges the Egyptian importers face are system failures, double documentation and inspection, and inexperienced users leading to struggles in using the system.

Nevertheless, since the system is still developing, the challenges importers face outweigh the benefits at present, resulting in either a decreased import frequency by some importers or an unchanged importing frequency by others and unchanged process costs.

RECOMMENDATIONS

Therefore, and in light of the ongoing efforts by the Egyptian government to enhance international trade in Egypt, several recommendations are presented to the ECA and MTS for improving the current customs system and overcoming the challenges facing Egyptian importers.

- Invest in additional servers to minimize or prevent system failures.
- Implement an e-payment system in the ACI, by integrating the bank system with the customs clearance system, to enable importers to pay all the customs clearance and related fees electronically.

Figure 4. Customs clearance process before and after ACI

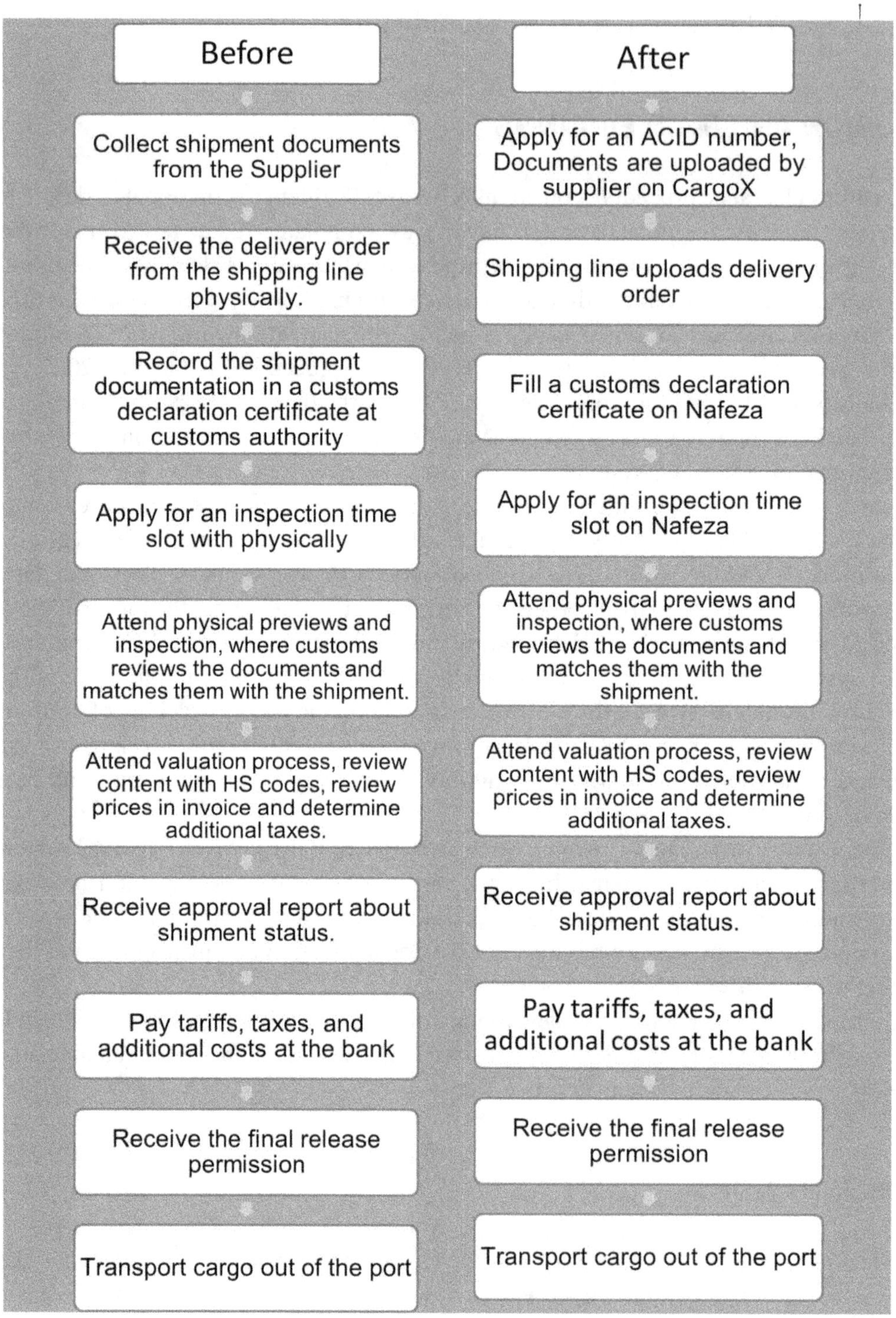

- Provide consistent training for all system users; importers, customs authority employees, and the relevant parties. Along with providing sufficient instructional materials for first-time users, such as foreign exporters registering on the system for the first time.

- Integrate all the related entities on the system, the Inspection Department, the Valuation Department, the Bank, and other related parties, to eliminate any inefficiency throughout the process. In addition to issuing an E-signature for the customs employees to sign and approve all the reports electronically.
- Administer a technical support system, by employing a sufficient number of customer service representatives for immediate response to inquiries around the clock.
- Fully eliminate paper documentation; even though the ACI system's main goal was to automate the whole process, customs authority still partially requires some paperwork. Thus, the process should be more digitalized by excluding all paper documents.

RESEARCH LIMITATIONS AND RECOMMENDATIONS FOR FUTURE STUDIES

This study's importance is to highlight the impact of the ACI system on the import industry in Egypt, regarding the efficiency of customs clearance procedures. However, this study has possible limitations that arose from the limited time, materials, and scope, which may have influenced the interpretation of research findings.

The authors have identified several recommendations for future researchers to overcome these limitations for more profound results on the topic, including:

- A further extended and deeper analysis of various case studies, since this research was limited to only three case study applications.
- Hopefully, the increasing findings on the ACI system will be available over the next few years, as it will be an important topic to research over time.
- Investigating the further enhancements of the system and its application on the customs procedures transformation.

ACKNOWLEDGMENT

The authors are thankful to Dr. Rabab Sobhi and Mr. Amr ElSayed for their comments and feedback that greatly improved the manuscript. The authors highly appreciate the hard work of data collection carried out by Yara Ayman, Ola Mohamed, Mohamed Tarek, and Ali Mohamed. Finally would also like to thank the interviewees for their time and effort in answering all the authors' questions.

REFERENCES

Angert, S. (2019). *Blockchain technology implementation in the US customs environment.* Naval Postgraduate School. Retrieved from apps.dtic.mil/sti/pdfs/AD1086921.pdf

ASI Sealants and Adhesives Industry. (2021). *H.B. Fuller to Build New Facility in Egypt*. Retrieved from: www.adhesivesmag.com/articles/98765-hb-fuller-to-build-new-facility-in-egypt

Awad, E. (2021). *Measuring logistics performance in ports: a case of Alexandria in Egypt*. World Maritime University Dissertations. 1678. Retrieved from https://commons.wmu.se/all_dissertations/1678

Bavassano, G., Ferrari, C., & Tei, A. (2020). Blockchain: How the shipping industry is dealing with the ultimate technological leap. *Research in Transportation Business & Management, 34*. doi:10.1016/j.rtbm.2020.100428

Belu, M. G. (2020). Blockchain Technology and Customs Procedures. *Romanian Economic Journal, 23*(78), 13–26.

CBP. (2022). *ACE Automated Broker Interface (ABI)*. CBP and Trade Automated Interface Requirements (CATAIR). Retrieved from www.cbp.gov/trade/ace/catair

Dimapindan, P. R. (2014). *An Integrated Framework to Evaluate Customer Service Delivery: A Study of Electronic Systems at FDA's Los Angeles Import Operations Branch*. University of Southern California.

Egyptian Customs Authority. (2022). *Advance Cargo Information*. Retrieved from www.customs.gov.eg/Services/Customs_Clearance/ACI

ESCAP. (2017). Cross-border paperless trade and single window in East and North-. *East Asia*.

European Commission. (2021). *Import Control System Trader Guide*. Retrieved from www.revenue.ie/en/customs-traders-and-agents/documents/electronic/ics-trade-guide.pdf

European Union. (2019). *The Food and Beverage Market Entry Handbook: Egypt. A Practical Guide to the Market in Egypt for European Agri-food Products and Products with Geographical Indications*. doi:10.2818/256126

Ewald, L., Hjortstam, A., & Wilén, J. (2021). *Blockchain Technology in Transportation Management - A case study with Rhenus Logistics AB (Undergraduate)*. Linnaeus University, School of Business and Economics, Department of Management Accounting and Logistics.

Ezz Steel. (2022). *About Ezz Steel*. Retrieved from: www.ezzsteel.com/about-ezz-steel

Frankenfield, J. (2021). *Cryptocurrency*. Retrieved from: www.investopedia.com/terms/c/cryptocurrency.asp

FullerH. B. (2022). *About us*. Retrieved from: www.hbfuller.com/en/north-america/about-us/

Grainger, A. (2007). Government Actors in international supply chain operations: Assessing requirements for skills and capabilities. In *Logistics research network conference proceedings* (pp. 293-298). Doi:10.1.1.621.1935

International Trade Administration. (2021). *Import Requirements & Documentation*. Retrieved from www.trade.gov/country-commercial-guides/egypt-import-requirements-documentation

International Trade Center. (2018). *Customs procedures guide to import and export in Egypt*. Retrieved from euromed.tradehelpdesk.org/euromed/ar/market-access-info/customs-procedures-guides/download?reporter=818

Irish Tax and Customs. (2021). *Import Control System (ICS)*. Retrieved from www.revenue.ie/en/customs/businesses/electronic-systems/import-control-system.aspx

Japan International Cooperation Agency. (2008). *The study on multimodal transport and logistics system of the eastern Mediterranean region and master plan in the Arab Republic of Egypt*. Retrieved from openjicareport.jica.go.jp/pdf/11893450_01.pdf

Li, L., & Zhou, H. (2020). A survey of blockchain with applications in maritime and shipping industry. *Information Systems and e-Business Management, 19*(3), 789–807. doi:10.100710257-020-00480-6

Mele, J. (2021). *What is ACI?* Retrieved from cargox-help.zendesk.com/hc/en-us/articles/360018855758-What-is-ACI-

Meltzer, J. P. (2018). *The impact of artificial intelligence on international trade*. Brookings Institution.

Ministry of Commerce People's Republic of China. (2021). *Customs Clearance Procedures*. Retrieved from: http://english.mofcom.gov.cn/

Ministry of Finance. (2013). *Introduction of the Advance Filing Rules on Maritime Container Cargo Information Guidance*. Customs and Tariff Bureau Ministry of Finance. Retrieved from www.wcoomd.org/-/media/wco/public/global/pdf/topics/wto-atf/dev/japan-_-advance.pdf?la=en

NAFEZA. (2021). *Your Comprehensive (ACI) Guide*. Retrieved from www.nafeza.gov.eg/en

Olesen, T. R. (2015). Value Creation in the Maritime Chain of Transportation: The Role of Carriers, Ports and Third Parties in Liner and Bulk Shipping (2nd ed.). CBS Maritime.

Qiuxia, H., & Yujie, H. (2022). The Application of Internet of Things Data Analysis in the Development of International Trade. *Computational Intelligence and Neuroscience, 2022*, 1–8. Advance online publication. doi:10.1155/2022/5507951 PMID:35769269

Rai Technology University. (2012). *Import-Export Management*. Retrieved from www.raitechuniversity.in

Sadouskaya, K. (2017). *Adoption of Blockchain Technology in Supply Chain and Logistics*. Retrieved from www.semanticscholar.org/paper/Adoption-of-Blockchain-Technologyin-Supply-Chain-Sadouskaya/2ed7baf04dc202f1e

Shahin, M. (2021). *Trade Facilitation Profile*. Retrieved from www.idsc.gov.eg/

Sturmanis, A., Hudenko, J. & Jurušs, M. (2020). *The Application of Blockchain Technologies for Rail Transit Customs Procedures*. . doi:10.1007/978-3-030-44610-9_26

Swiss Embassy in Egypt. (2016). *Egypt: New Import Procedures/Measures. Cairo: State Secretariat for Economic Affairs SECO*. Retrieved from www.sage.com/sites/default/files/mig/sites/default/files/EGYPT-Import_April.pdf

Thapa, B. (2014). *Adoption of new technology in supply chain management: A survey of Nepalese organizations*. Academic Press.

Tsiulin, S., Reinau, K., Hilmola, O., Goryaev, N., & Karam, A. (2020). Blockchain-based applications in shipping and port management: A literature review towards defining key conceptual frameworks. *Review of International Business and Strategy*, *30*(2), 201–224. doi:10.1108/RIBS-04-2019-0051

USDA. (2021). *Egypt Postpones Launch of the Advanced Cargo Information System to Oct 1*. Global Agriculture Information Trade. Retrieved from www.fas.usda.gov/

Vorotyntseva, T., Nemirova, G., & Vinichenko, A. (2020). Problems of application of digital technologies in international trade. In New Silk Road: Business Cooperation and Prospective of Economic Development (NSRBCPED 2019) (pp. 452-456). Atlantis Press. doi:10.2991/aebmr.k.200324.085

Wang, Y. (2022). Optimal Design of International Trade Logistics Based on Internet of Things Technology. *Computational Intelligence and Neuroscience*, *2022*. Advance online publication. doi:10.1155/2022/8781095 PMID:35479599

World Customs Organization. (2018). *Advance Cargo Information (ACI) Implementation Guidelines*. Retrieved from www.wcoomd.org/

World Trade Organization. (2018). The future of world trade: How digital technologies are transforming global commerce. *World Trade Review*, *17*(4), 707–709. doi:10.10171474745618000289

Yang, C. (2019). Maritime shipping digitalization: Blockchain-based technology applications, future improvements, and intention to use. *Transportation Research Part E, Logistics and Transportation Review*, *131*, 108–117. doi:10.1016/j.tre.2019.09.020

Zamil Steel. (2022). *About the company*. Retrieved from www.zamilsteel.com/peb/en/the-company

Chapter 4
The Effect of Using Intelligent Transportation Systems on Transportation-Sustainable Development in Egypt

Ashrakat Osama
Arab Academy for Science, Technology, and Maritime Transport, Egypt

Ashish Bagwari
https://orcid.org/0000-0002-6232-2772
Uttarakhand Technical University, India

Nada Hossam
Arab Academy for Science, Technology, and Maritime Transport, Egypt

EXECUTIVE SUMMARY

Roads have a significant positive impact on social and economic development and provide various advantages. There are several reasons why modern transportation is not sustainable. One of the most significant causes is the traffic congestion issue, since its effects severely harm both the environment and the entire community. As a technology that improves transportation quality or accomplishes other goals using programmes that watch over, manage, or enhance transportation networks, an intelligent transportation system is a crucial idea that aids in the development of sustainable transportation. Every kind of intelligent transportation used in Egypt, including the monorail, runs on electricity and requires no fuel, helping to save the environment. By encouraging people to take public transit instead of driving their own automobiles, intelligent transportation systems and methods can ease traffic congestion. This reduces congestion and protects the environment from pollution brought on by vehicle emissions and exhaust.

DOI: 10.4018/978-1-6684-4686-7.ch004

Figure 1. The number of injuries in road accidents during the period (2017-2021)
Source: CAPMAS (2021)

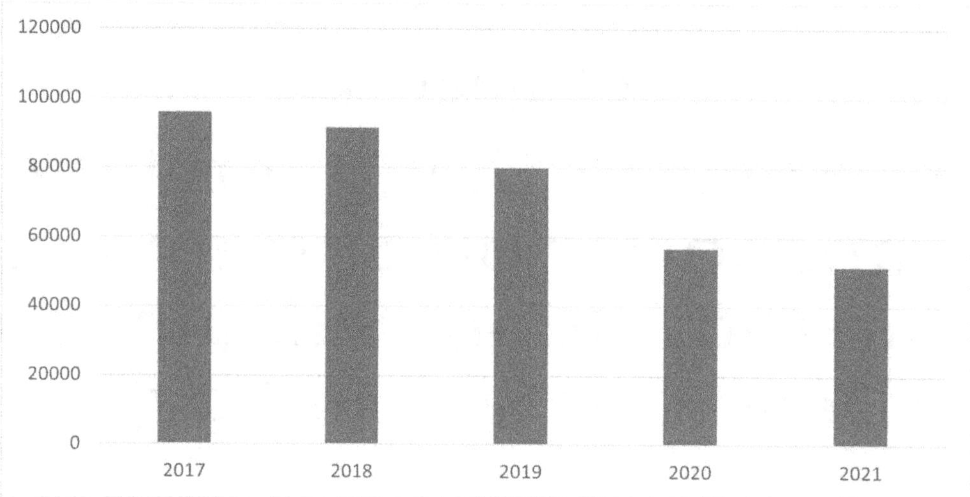

INTRODUCTION

What is facing road development in this period is not limited to an expansion only, but also to find a solution to the traffic crisis and the disasters and damages caused. Because roads contribute decisively to growth, economic, environmental, and social development and achieve many countless benefits. According to (youmatter, 2021), sustainability also plays an important role alongside technology, as sustainable development is an organizing principle to achieve human development goals while preserving the ability of natural systems to provide natural resources and ecosystem services. Many causes lead to Transportation unsustainability, including road congestion and road accidents, as their consequences are harmful.

Most of the causes of traffic congestion are accidents that occur on the roads as a result of the collision and the presence of unqualified roads. In addition, the aggressive behavior of some drivers leads to a traffic crisis. Road safety is a measure to reduce the risk of road accidents and roadside injuries due to people's driving mistakes. Traffic accidents cost Egypt more than thirty billion pounds ($1.82 billion) each year and a large number of injured people as shown in figure one. The deployment of traffic laws and monitoring systems on new roads and axes has minimized the human factor as one of the key causes of accidents. Hisham Hassan explained that applying advanced technology, such as intelligent transportation systems, has an effective role and will help solve this crisis (Essam, 2020).

As well as dealing with a transportation network that respects humanity, preserves life, attracts national, and foreign investments, and reconstructs the country. From an economic perspective, the injured people cost medication, salaries, repairing cars, repairing roads, and other related costs. While from a social perspective, drivers make unethical behaviors by driving or taking medications to stay awake and drive for a long journey, which also decreases their focus on the roads .From the environmental perspective, trucks mainly use diesel as a fuel source which harms the environment and causes emissions, besides the danger of the movement of gas cars that, their accidents cause serious and catastrophic damage to people and roads (Osama, et al 2022).

Therefore, one of the methods that can decrease transportation unsustainability, including traffic crisis, traffic congestion, and road accidents, is about applying intelligent transportation systems, an advanced technology. Intelligent transportation systems on highways work to reduce traffic accidents by managing the road network and essential hubs following the highest international standards. In addition to the main control center, computers, communication technologies, and electronics are used, which include a traffic management system and fee collection system. That will ensure the security and safety of citizens' movement, besides enhancing road sustainability.

Through the application of a modern technological system to manage the road network and hubs that connect cities and logistic areas with commercial ports on the Mediterranean and the Red Sea. Thus, opening new economic horizons and maximizing the state's benefit from linking and integrating its infrastructure. The new intelligent transportation organization also relies on advanced electronic systems and communications to manage and operate traffic, monitor lanes, collect information, locate traffic jams, monitor accidents, direct motorists, and collect transit tolls electronically without stopping. Which works to control traffic behavior and thus reduce accidents on the roads and solve the traffic crisis (Al-Badri, 2021).

Therefore, traffic congestion is one of the biggest obstacles that affect the movement of the road and traffic. Causing a waste of time, effort and an increase in spending on fuel. Moreover, the poor engineering design and intersections cause many traffic accidents. As well as the lack of dedicated roads for heavy transport vehicles which results in a sudden drop in the road due to increased loads. In addition to the poor condition of the infrastructure, all of this leads to a state of traffic chaos and congestion and the lack of prior notification to road users of the traffic situation. Besides, driving style and lack of awareness among some drivers and road users are among the biggest factors leading to traffic congestion. In addition, traffic congestion stops the road for long periods, which leads to the consumption of a large amount of fuel, which emits a lot of exhaust, negatively affecting environmental stability. The efforts of the state appear in establishing and using modern means that depend on technology and development. These are represented in intelligent transportation systems and means, and these systems and means will have beneficial returns on society, the economy, and the environment. The reason for its establishment is due in the beginning to reduce the rate of accidents and traffic congestion, in addition to that, it plays an essential role in preserving the environment by using clean energy that is free of emissions. Unlike all normal means, the trend toward using intelligent transportation means and systems will reduce the individual's use of fuel-powered cars and hence the beginning to achieve sustainability on the road.

Therefore, this research aimed to fulfill the following objectives:

- To highlight the main problems that lead to the unsustainability of transportation
- To observe the effects of an unsustainable transportation system
- To identify the intelligent transportation system
- To emphasize the effect of using intelligent transportation systems on sustainable transportation development.

From the research problem and the research objectives stated above, the following research questions will be explored:

RQ1: What are the major problems of the transportation sector?

RQ2: How to improve road conditions and achieve sustainability by applying intelligent transportation systems?

RQ3: What are the current and future efforts the Egyptian government is taking to achieve sustainable development targets, especially in transportation?

As there are many problems related to transportation sustainability, including traffic congestion, problems in roads beside the bad behavior of drivers, which leads to an increasing number of accidents, moreover the harmful emissions due to the large amount of fuel consumed.

This research will secondly discuss literature about the main transportation problems in Egypt and the intelligent transportation system tools that can be applied, then the research methodology, after that the case study will be discussed with its main results s and analysis, and finally, the conclusion, recommendation, and the limitation of the study.

LITERATURE REVIEW

Transportation Sustainability Impacts

One of the biggest problems that affect transportation sustainability is traffic congestion. Different researchers have provided alternative definitions of traffic congestion. At its most fundamental level, traffic congestion occurs when road speeds decrease, and vehicle lines form because of interactions between vehicles on the road. Economists define congestion as the presence of interactions among vehicles on the route. In practice, all highways with significant traffic volumes are congested to some degree. When speeds fall below an acceptable level, users perceive roadways to be congested, varying from person to person, region, and time. Engineers classify congestion as more vehicles attempting to utilize a road than it can handle (Wallis & Lupton, 2019). Traffic congestion can be described in this way vehicles interact to obstruct each other's movement. These interactions and their impact on individual travel typically rise as demand for available road space approaches capacity or as capacity is restricted due to road construction or closures. Furthermore, one-time events such as bad weather or traffic accidents can considerably impact traffic congestion (Bull, 2017).

There are many causes for Congestion in Greater Cairo, which is caused by a rise in car ownership because of the increasing population, as some people believe that urbanization and sophistication entail having their car. In addition, there is a lack of information regarding the road conditions and traffic situation as well as the existence of inappropriate modes of transportation such as tuk-tuks and carts (carriages pulled by a horse). People also show a lack of respect for the law by not strolling in the pedestrian lanes and violating traffic lights and the presence of many street merchants on both sides of the road. The intricate network of streets, whether on main roads, side streets, or U-turns, causes frequent accidents and road closures for lengthy periods, resulting in lost time, increased fuel costs, and increased pollution due to car exhaust and high temperatures. Parking lots are haphazard, attracting hawkers and leading to increased crowding and waste accumulation in collective vehicle parks used to transport passengers, employees, and workers, all of which contribute to increased pollution levels (El-Kadi, 2013). Therefore, there are two main problems related to the Egyptian road in terms of road conditions and drivers' habits. The first problem is Road conditions due to the defects and problems of the roads are many and different, the most important of which is the design and maintenance problems which are represented in the occurrence of a sudden drop which is the descent of the road base layers under the asphalt layer because of the effect of excessive loads. The lack of bonding between the asphalt layers is because of the loss of fine materials, a large number of coarse materials, and sometimes the lack of cleanliness of the materials, which weakens the bonding between the materials and sometimes the asphalt is damaged because of the high temperature inside Lab and bad mix design. Besides the presence of cracks and potholes along the roads, which puts the road surface in poor condition, in addition to the poor engineering planning of intersections, all these problems lead to traffic congestion and then many accidents. The second problem is about driving habits, as Some driving habits cause congestion. Some drivers show no respect for others road users. In other words, some drivers want to reach their locations or destinations faster, so they do inappropriate actions on the road, such as blocking the road to other cars without warning. This is considered uncivil behavior and causes a lot of traffic because it results in car collisions and wasted time (GOV.UK, 2022). Therefore, the effects of increased congestion include slower velocities, longer route times, more queuing at intersections or bottlenecks, more stopping and starting, more time spent motionless, and increased fuel consumption.

According to (WHO, 2022) The lives of almost 1.3 million individuals are cut short annually as a result of traffic accidents. There are an additional 20 to 50 million people who sustain non-fatal injuries, many of whom go on to develop disabilities. Road traffic accidents result in significant economic damage for victims, their families, and whole countries. These costs result from the price of medical care, lost wages for individuals who are killed or rendered incapacitated by their injuries, and caregiving expenses for family members who must take time off from work or school to look after the injured. Most nations incur a 3% loss in the gross domestic product as a result of traffic accidents.

Moreover, there are economic and environmental consequences of traffic congestion. Although economic progress can frequently fuel higher demand for the road network, congestion can also stifle further expansion because more time is spent traveling at the expense of other productive activities. Furthermore, the inability to precisely forecast route times due to congestion can result in lost time as people either come late for appointments or arrive early by giving themselves too much time. However, Increased congestion can result in more pollution and carbon emissions because vehicles spend more time immobile or at very low speeds, reducing engine efficiency. Furthermore, increasing traffic congestion can cause increased vehicle wear and tear due to frequent stopping and accelerating in slow-moving traffic. Therefore, they strive to reach sustainability (GOV.UK, 2022).

Environmentally the road sector is the source of the most greenhouse gas emissions, directly from fossil energy used in mining, transportation, and paving and indirectly from car emissions. Indeed, the steady expansion in the number of road vehicles and, as a result, traffic causes significant pollution and noise disruptions. The road construction sector needs to face the challenge of sustainability. The ability to meet current demands without jeopardizing the ability of future generations to meet theirs is called sustainability. This notion combines economic, societal, and environmental considerations. Sustainability may also be described as using a resource without depleting or permanently damaging it.

Want sustainability for obvious reasons, the global population is growing by 2050. The UN predicts a population of 9.7 billion, while Egypt's population will grow from 102 million in 2020 to just under 160 million in 2050. It is projected that in the last ten years, the population has expanded by twenty million (Assaad, 2020), and natural resources such as crude oil, aggregates, and iron core are scarce. In this perspective, achieving sustainability in highway construction appears to be quite a problem, given that the latter by its very nature, creates a lot of energy and consumes a lot of fossil resources. The road construction industry, like many others, is subject to many rating systems that evaluate its efforts to achieve sustainability in the road sector. Intelligent transportation systems are one of Egypt's most important ways to reach road sustainability (world highways, 2015).

From a social perspective, the direct participants in traffic accidents and their families are the group most impacted by the consequences of traffic accidents. In particular, road traffic accidents direct participants to experience adverse health effects. Road traffic accidents result in a significant number of fatal incapacitating injuries; therefore, the effects of these incidents are profoundly reflected in society. Losses of employment and the ensuing financial hardships, loss of amenities, and a devastating impact on the functioning of the entire family are all addressed here. Along with the psychological effects, road traffic accidents have other long-term effects that affect not only the direct victims but also their families. The entire society is liable for the costs incurred as a result of traffic accidents (Másilková, 2017).

Intelligent Transportation Systems in Transportation

Intelligent Transportation Systems are a set of cutting-edge information and communication technologies that are used in transportation and traffic management systems to improve safety, efficiency, and sustainability according to (Lishchenko, 2021). Date uploaded refers to the procedures and actions humans use to avoid depletion of natural resources and maintain an ecological balance that does not degrade the quality of life in modern transportation networks, as well as to reduce traffic congestion and improve driver's experiences.

An intelligent transportation system is a technology, application, or platform that enhances transportation quality or achieves other goals using applications that monitor, manage, or improve transportation networks. Data gathering and analysis are critical components of the Intelligent Transportation System. The data collection and analysis outcomes are then used to control, manage, and plan transportation. In data collecting, sensors play a crucial role. Many benefits of using ITS positively affect traffic and traffic congestion accordingly, there will be fewer stops and delays at intersections, improved speed control, reduced travel time, capacity management, and accident management (Labs, 2019). Furthermore, the internet plays an important role in providing information and data around the clock, as well as improving the quality of protection in real-time, generating the most relevant information and promotional offers, improving the quality of program operation, detecting and correcting errors associated with the installation mechanism on time, removing and updating the program.

Role of Intelligent Transportation Systems in Enhancing the Road Transport Sector

Intelligent transportation systems play an important role in enhancing sustainability and increasing road safety and traffic flow. These fundamental studies were conducted to prevent and reduce road accidents and enjoy a more sustainable environment. According to the World Road Safety Commission, nearly 1.25 million people die yearly from traffic accidents. In 1999, the World Health Organization (WHO) report revealed that traffic accidents were the leading cause of death (Mathew & Bombay, 2014). The effects of using and applying intelligent transportation systems on roads. According to (Benevolo, et al., 2016) technical advances have enabled the creation of hybrid cars and car-sharing as examples of smart mobility for modern cities. A basic underlying value of intelligent transportation, hybrid vehicles that use electricity in addition to gasoline would result in lower emissions from motor vehicles. Furthermore, the car-sharing social platform works by allowing residents of modern cities to reserve automobiles of their choosing, drive them, and return them from the place of pick-up while incurring a modest service fee. Concluded that this type of intelligent transportation kills two birds with one stone by reducing traffic congestion in modern cities while also cutting emissions.

Role of Intelligent Transportation Systems in Enhancing the Road Transport Sector

Smartphone applications could be used as a communication platform to educate pedestrians and vulnerable road users on public transportation systems about their destinations, hence reducing dangers (Olaverri & Monreal, 2016). Went on to say that vehicle-to-pedestrian and pedestrian-to-vehicle information systems are ultimately geared at increasing road safety by alerting app users to impending collision hazards. This type of road safety campaign has been thoroughly investigated in this case, with most modern cars equipped with motion-detecting software and automatic stopping systems.

A traffic control system is a system that handles traffic problems by continuously monitoring and adapting, and an Intelligent Traffic Control System is a system that adjusts the timing of traffic lights to the actual traffic load. The benefits of deploying Intelligent Traffic Control Systems include reduced congestion, lower costs, the availability of alternate routes for commuters, and increased infrastructure efficiency. Image processing techniques such as edge detection can be used to identify the traffic density in one such traffic management system, and systems based on traffic density can regulate traffic light signals. Encryption of images An RGB (Red, blue, and green) image is converted to a grey image using an image encryption algorithm. The term "cipher picture" refers to an encrypted image. The image was captured in RGB format. That RGB image must be converted to a grayscale image. To do this, precise thresholding during binary conversion is required to exhibit the image in contrast to its background. This is referred to as image enhancement. Image enhancement techniques aim to process an image so that the processed image is better suited for the application than the original image (Al-Abaid, 2020).

According to (Torbaghan, et al., 2022) they started using a range of innovations to reach the possibility of providing, collecting, and analyzing data more comprehensively and effectively to improve road safety. These are digital technologies to collect and monitor information related to the road and the factors contributing to accidents. They used state-of-the-art digital technologies, artificial intelligence, machine learning, image processing, the internet of things, smartphone applications, geographic information system, virtual location, radar, and sensing. All to determine and provide information about road safety factors. Road user behavior, characteristics, and operating environment include weather and traffic congestion. By using digital technology, they were able to reduce the rate of road accidents and traffic congestion.

According to (Alyavina, et al., 2020) the Maas model (Mobility as a Service) is a new mode of transportation that aims to replace private cars with customized multimodal mobility packages facilitated by a digital platform that integrates travel planning, reservation, and ticketing, as well as real-time information services. It is an intervention that aims to encourage and enhance the shift to a more sustainable mobility model through digitization, networking, information, and participation. People's perceptions of private cars must change for Maas to succeed (which is very difficult). Maas is a unique concept that can help people avoid relying on private cars for transportation. Customized multimedia mobility service packages will replace privately owned cars on a contract or "pay-as-you-go" basis.

According to (Dia &Panwai, 2014) traffic congestion costs 1–3% of a country's GDP on average, while global road death rates are around 1.2 million and cost $100 billion yearly. Modern cities have gone above and beyond to build intelligent transportation systems that improve the flow of urban traffic while also increasing the mobility of their residents. Many modern cities have recently adopted a tendency to purposefully integrate information and communication technologies into transportation and administration to adapt to the digital age. Are attempting to develop a smart traffic control system using simple approaches mixed with image processing in this system. It will need to get some photographs of busy roadways to determine the traffic density; these photos are analyzed using MATLAB code. The system generates commands based on the processed image and traffic density, which indicate the duration of the traffic light signal. Depending on the traffic congestion on the route, the duration of this signal may be raised or lowered. This system is implemented by performing image acquisition, then image encryption, which entails RGB to grey conversion. After that, picture augmentation is carried out. The quality of the image is improved by better image restructuring. The match to the original image is improved by better restructuring the image.

According to (Dawood & Wang, 2013) the Efficient Emergency Message Broadcasting routing mechanism was presented as an accident-avoidance scheme. The goal was to alleviate traffic bottlenecks and avoid several road accidents by transmitting emergency alerts at fast speeds with minimum overheads. Following a collision between two vehicles, the affected vehicle will choose the best forwarder and broadcast the emergency message until the entire risk zone has been covered. By utilizing the early prediction system, the forwarding technique achieved the lowest possible overhead caused by the beacon message. Proposed a routing strategy based on distance. The primary idea behind this routing plan is to avoid an accident at the intersection, as anonymous vehicles frequently emerge from the opposite side of the road and cause accidents at the crossing. This accident-prevention technique begins by determining the vehicle's location and estimating the distance between vehicles approaching the intersection. Following the calculation of each vehicle's location, all vehicles will receive information on the location of other vehicles approaching the intersection. The car with the shortest distance will issue a distance and location notice to other vehicles. Less traffic congestion was obtained because of the suggested strategy, which helps to prevent or decrease traffic accidents.

According to (Akinboro S, et al., 2017) the technology was able to give road users real-time traffic information on their mobile devices, as well as alternate routes. This will equip road users with the necessary traffic data to make informed decisions for a safe, faster, and more convenient journey. Weighted sensors, a global positioning system, VSAT (Very Small Aperture Terminal) a control room, and mobile devices are all part of the proposed architecture. It shows how data from road sensors reach the control room and is shown on mobile devices using Google Maps. When a certain location is crowded, road users will be notified via their mobile devices about the traffic situation and given alternate routes. Weighted Sensors are used in a mobile road traffic management system. Intelligent traffic control system model architecture weighted sensors are installed on roads that are a significant distance from traffic signal junctions and assist in obtaining information on the number of automobiles on the road. When the number of cars on the road reaches the threshold, the road sensors send signals to the road VSAT. The received signal is sent to the control room via the control room VSAT by the VSAT on the road. Google map receives road updates from a GPS satellite orbiting the earth. An application server, database server, and system administrators make up the control room, which keeps track of traffic statistics. The data collected in the control room is used to send traffic updates to mobile devices. The sensor signal is processed in the control room, which then checks its database to see if sensor signal is processed in the control room, which then checks its database to see if any alternate routes are available. If alternative routes are discovered in the database, the control room connects to the internet through a gateway.

Then, uses the Google Map application on the mobile device to relay the information in the form of a notification with the message Road is congested, please take the alternative route. The system provides a list of alternate routes.

According to (Shigehiro, et al., 2012) it is challenging to reduce traffic congestion in densely populated areas. Offered cooperative car navigation as a possible solution to this problem. The route information server predicts future congestion based on the intended route of each vehicle and drivers use this knowledge to adjust their lanes independently to avoid congestion. The sound performance and feasibility of the system are assessed using three adoption rate criteria (initial use incentive, continued use incentive, and social acceptance). (Vehicle Information and Communication System) is another practical tool for reducing traffic congestion. VICS is a traffic information and communication system that regularly sends traffic data such as congestion levels and traffic regulations. Drivers can avoid traffic jams and other problems using this information. If many vehicles can avoid busy sections of the road, traffic in these areas is likely to decrease. They developed methods and theories to reduce traffic congestion, such as how road conditions change, the traffic situation should be constantly monitored in the traffic control center, and the improved traffic smoothing methods should be dispersed among all cars. In addition, by selecting from a variety of boundaries, one can track how the car is moving. They devised a strategy and algorithm to determine how to alleviate traffic congestion. They used numerical experiments to test the efficiency of the proposed method. They used a simulator to analyze the groups of vehicles that were designed, as well as route searches for this purpose. They used the same simulations for realistic group vehicle and dropped car simulations. Were able to construct a model and an application called "Mobile Route" because of our research, which allows us to simulate and show multiple accessible routes ranked by their likelihood of being traffic-free. By reducing road congestion, long hours spent on the road, and creating more access routes at intervals when the road network is congested, a traffic management system in which traffic updates are received on mobile devices based on information obtained from weighted sensors can provide a viable alternative to the existing predetermined fixed-based traffic control system, especially in developing countries. Congestion reduction or elimination will improve work-life balance, human productivity, and economic growth.

Reduce traffic congestion with apps and caution messages. Proposed the warning message technique to avoid vehicle-to-vehicle collisions by delivering a warning message to inform drivers of the current accident's status. The timing of the vehicle's reaction after the accident was calculated to prevent further traffic accidents. A warning message dissemination method has been implemented for low-priority connections to maximise bandwidth consumption. The proposed routing method obtained the best high and low-priority message delivery in extreme weather circumstances such as rain, sun, and snow. Furthermore, the routing strategy demonstrated lower latency and more efficient bandwidth consumption in various traffic situations (Garcia-Lozano, et al., 2013).

The lives of Cairo residents appear to be defined by traffic difficulties. This metropolis has a population of over twenty million people, the majority of whom spend an excessive amount of time stuck in traffic in over two million cars. The city has a total roadway length of almost ten thousand kilometers. Long traffic lanes have given rise to a new social life in Cairo streets, where individuals socialize and communicate with one another while trapped in traffic. More citizens own personal vehicles, poor traffic administration, traffic jams, poor compliance with regulations, unsuitable modes of public transportation, causing people to shift to personal vehicles, and centralization of services in Cairo, which causes all suburban residents to travel to Cairo to get their services done, causing mass congestion in Cairo. The main traffic congestion reasons in Cairo to solve this problem by using intelligent transportation systems (A set of cutting-edge information and communication technologies used in transportation and traffic management systems to improve the safety, efficiency, and long-term viability of transportation networks, as well as to minimize traffic congestion and improve driver experiences) (Lishchenko, 2021). The problems caused by traffic bottlenecks and rapid growth in modern communication and simulation networks were the driving forces behind ITS. As the world's population grows exponentially, the increased number of people living in cities has resulted in increased traffic density and difficulties. ITS can play a critical role in mass commuter evacuations during times of danger, such as natural disasters or conflicts (Radwan, 2015).

RESEARCH METHODOLOGY

To achieve the objectives of the research, the research follows qualitative research to be able to know how the use of the application of intelligent transportation systems will help reduce traffic congestion and accidents and know the effects of its application on the sustainability of transportation, in addition to knowing the challenges facing the state in the road sector in the coming period. This research type is based on a Deductive Approach as its main goal is to understand how the application of intelligent transportation systems will affect reducing traffic accidents and achieving sustainability. This research will use primary and secondary data collection. Primary data such as semi-structured interviews, is a face-to-face discussion to obtain information from a person using oral responses to oral questions, and secondary data from papers and books.

In order to obtain data related to the research, face-to-face interviews are conducted with the transportation sector in Egypt, a sample of three representatives from transportation sectors has been chosen, and the Ministry of Transport, a sample includes the President of the Public Authority for Roads and Bridges, the Vice President of the Roads and Bridges Authority, and the Chairman of the Board of Directors of the Roads, Bridges, and Rail Contracting Company. Three face-to-face interviews were conducted, including a detailed list containing semi-structured questions that has been prepared for use in interviews, as it covers all the information required for the evaluation and then to apply to answer it directly.

EMPIRICAL WORK

Data Analysis

The questions covered all aspects in terms of defining these projects and to what extent they will contribute to solving the traffic congestion problem and reducing accidents, environmental pollution, and fuel consumption, which in turn will develop transportation sustainability. The first thing discussed was regarding the government's efforts to establish mega projects in all governorates of Egypt, which have tangible effects, and watch their establishment constantly. For instance, the reason for establishing the monorail is traffic congestion, moreover, trains suspended on concrete pillars to avoid the problem of congestion and are part of mass transportation to transport citizens and take advantage of other places and it is considered one of the means of transportation that keeps pace with the development of the new cities. The maximum capacity of the modern monorail is about one million passengers per day, and it achieves a journey time equivalent to the time of a non-stop car journey. It also contributes to financial savings as a result of lost time and spent fuel. Moreover, using electricity in a monorail will lead to a clean environment as the electricity used is not produced by diesel but is produced by gas. The state is now on its way to becoming green and clean from pollution. Green energy is the main source of operating electricity and of course, this leads to preserving the environment because working to reduce the use of cars in the coming period and therefore the percentage of fuel will decrease. This results in fewer emissions and pollution, then becomes a clean and green environment.

Therefore, the number of passengers transported at the start of operation will be about a quarter of a million passengers per day, and the number will gradually increase. This will reduce congestion on the road as a result of reducing the number of road users and thus reducing environmental pollution resulting from emissions and exhausts of private cars and alternative fuel-powered transportation, in contrast to smart and electric transportation to preserve the environment, where its ultimate goal is to reduce congestion and environmental pollution to achieve sustainability. There are also other projects such electric train LRT, which contributes to maximizing the mass transportation system in Egypt and facilitating the movement of citizens. And the express train is also a fast, modern, and safe means of transportation, with the train's speed being 250 km/h.

Using intelligent transportation means and systems to reduce accidents and congestion in the first place, because the cause of congestion is high speed and intersections, in addition to the wrong behavior of drivers or pedestrians. employing transportation technology and services and applying intelligent transportation systems will achieve the integration of the management of transportation networks, maximizing their benefit from them to reduce fuel consumption, preserve public health and reduce harmful emissions, which means a development in transportation sustainability.

The internet plays a vital role in providing information and data, in addition to improving the quality of protection in real-time, generating the most appropriate information and advertising offers, and improving the quality of running the program, timely detecting, and correcting errors associated with the installation mechanism, remove, and update the program, count the number of users. It represents a strong and effective role in tracking, for example, the monorail works without a driver, as it works at main control stations, and this shows that it is of a high degree of safety. All these means have been linked together, meaning that the monorail is connected to the LRT train and the express train, and all of this is linked to the subway and regular railway stations as well, this requires the presence of very high technology, this link aims to facilitate and ease transportation and reduce accidents. All of these systems are linked together, where there is a complete electronic link; for example, if anyone wants to know information about a person or track goods without direct contact with the person, but this is done within any of the modern means can know all the details indirectly by tracking through the number of the train or wagon via the internet, because it uses systems capable of providing all the necessary information on time.

Therefore, intelligent transportation systems are being applied and used in the name of the green transportation journey, which is the beginning of preserving the environment using the latest technological means in transportation. It contributes to increasing the operational efficiency of the transportation system, increasing speeds, reducing stops, reducing operational costs of infrastructure, and increasing the use of public transportation, by relying on a set of electronic systems for transportation services, such as (the Global Positioning System GPS - traffic control and smart parking of vehicles - relying on Passenger information systems to encourage transportation by more environmentally friendly modes of transport - Exhaust Gas Environmental Monitoring System).

In addition, a plan to use clean fuel buses (use of gas and electric buses and BRT rapid bus systems). Using a private car compared to BRT buses, including the savings in fuel and emissions, leads to saving fuel, reducing harmful emissions, and reducing congestion. The world has developed a plan for zero emissions, and zero accidents in 2050 and the Ministry of Transport's strategy is based on insisting on achieving the planned goals until 2030 and looking forward to everything new in the future.

Then the interviewees talked about the completed components of intelligent transportation systems, and they said that intelligent transportation systems consist of many things.

First: Data collection includes the various devices responsible for collecting data related to traffic, capacity, and speed, which are mainly represented in census cameras, photographing vehicles on the roads, parking monitoring cameras, and public transportation as well as sensors.

Second: Data processing techniques, which are software and hardware that process the data collected to manage transport systems in a way that responds to changes that occur in these systems and is compatible with reality and then provides various information to users of these systems in a way that achieves safety and effectiveness in their use of various means of transport.

Third: Techniques of control and information transfer include the various techniques responsible for transferring information extracted from the decomposition of the data collected at the Traffic Department to the ground. Traffic and transport control rooms and data banks and means of transmitting information to the users of the transport system such as technologies for communicating information to the user during the trip such as radio and mobile phone.

All agreed that there are dedicated spaces for persons with special needs, with the presence of stairs designated for their use on the most recent systems, in terms of providing all means of safety for the user of modern systems with special requirements. Completing the interview, a question of great importance was answered: the difference between the old roads and the modern roads in which the use of an intelligent transportation system is applied. The response came unanimously on the Cairo-Alexandria Desert Road. At first, the road was only one way, then two directions were made, after this expanded further as a result of a large number of accidents, and one of the causes of this was heavy transport vehicles, so they were separated in a road designated for them only, then monitored the road with cameras. Currently. The cameras did not cover the entire road, but the target is that the road is covered with cameras by the end of 2025, in addition to other major roads.

DISCUSSION AND FINDINGS

Through the answers, researchers can analyze the causes of the traffic congestion problem facing the country and the means and regulations the state applies to overcome the traffic congestion crisis to avoid obstacles as much as possible, achieve sustainability and keep the environment clean. Starting with the state's efforts to establish mega projects and the continuous development processes witnessed in all governorates of Egypt that suffer from a traffic congestion crisis resulting from population increase, and about issues of environmental pollution and how to reduce fuel consumption, as indicated by interviewees the direction of the state in the coming period depends on the use of electricity as an alternative to fuel, as all means of intelligent transportation systems is powered by electricity, and this will lead to a green environment free of emissions and pollution, and a trend towards creating a clean green society, the use of solar panels in parking spaces to shade cars and also use them as clean energy to reduce the use of ordinary energy, such as gasoline and diesel power plants. Everyone pointed out the importance of establishing the monorail and all other means, not only to reduce traffic congestion and road accidents but also because it uses electricity and thus reduces environmental pollution. It can be concluded that applying the intelligent transportation system enhances transportation sustainability.

The roads contribute decisively to growth, economic, environmental, and social development and achieve countless benefits; nowadays, transportation is unsustainable for many reasons, as mentioned before. One of the most important reasons is the traffic congestion problem as its consequences represent severe damage to the entire community and the environment. An intelligent transportation system is an important concept that helps in developing transportation sustainability as it is a technology that enhances transportation quality or achieves other goals using applications that monitor, manage, or improve transportation networks. all intelligent transportation that Egypt applies, such as the monorail, works with electricity and is far from fuel, which leads to Preserving the environment. Intelligent transportation systems and means can help reduce traffic congestion, which encourages the use of public transportation instead of private cars, which leads to reducing congestion and preserving the environment from pollution caused by emissions and vehicle exhaust.

It became clear that there are many different reasons for traffic congestion, including driver's behavior, lack of respect for laws and the condition of the road itself from poor design and intersections as well as a misunderstanding of the concept of owning cars. The answers obtained by the researchers agreed with the literature that there are severe consequences resulting from the effects of increased traffic congestion economically, socially, and environmentally and which affects transportation sustainability. It also became clear through the literature and the answers obtained by the researchers that the solution lies in the application and use of the means and systems of intelligent transportation. After all, it will positively affect traffic congestion and eliminate it because it improves safety, reduces congestion, and increases road efficiency. Because it is the system through which data and information are collected, and the results are used to control the movement of transport and roads and thus reduce the percentage of accidents on the road, intelligent transportation systems and means maintain the ecological balance. Because they operate on electricity, which leads to reduced fuel consumption and thus reduced harmful emissions to the environment, individuals, and society. Hence, intelligent transportation systems and means are on the right track to make the environment clean and free from pollution resulting from car exhaust and reduce congestion, achieving sustainability on the road.

Therefore the implementation of intelligent transportation systems will enhance the transportation sustainability development in Egypt, economically, environmentally, and socially as the congestion and number of traffic accidents will decrease as the number of cars will be decreased, for the usage of new means that the government implements. Moreover, the tracking systems and radars allows good monitoring for the roads to reduce the accidents and it's compatible with the results that are indicated by (Hosny, 2021) that revealed The number of injuries reached approximately 56,789 accidents, compared to about 79,904 accidents in 2019, with a fall of around 29%, according to current statistics, which indicated a considerable decline in the number of road accidents in Egypt by the end of 2020 according to CAPMAS report.

CONCLUSION

In conclusion, the answers point to the importance of establishing and using intelligent transportation means and systems in all governorates of Egypt, which have overcrowding and population density, and not only in Cairo. The traffic congestion problem and its consequences severely damage the entire community and the environment. It was previously discussed that the state's tendency toward transport sustainability is hampered by the problem of traffic congestion and pollution caused by fuel-powered cars. To clarify more, the means and services of intelligent transportation systems can be interpreted from the perspective of their user groups, and the use of intelligent transportation means and services falls into three different groups. The first group is road operators, the entity that manages the road to achieve the required goals, which are the flow of traffic and responding as quickly as possible in the event of an accident to avoid parking and obstruction of the road and the lack of traffic flow. Road operators monitor the condition of the road and provide information to road users. The second group, road users, is represented by drivers who use intelligent transportation services and systems to collect and know data to reach their destinations on less crowded roads. The third group of users are passengers or pedestrians who use the services and means of intelligent transportation systems to obtain traffic information, plan trips, and use transit services or request assistance in emergencies.

As discussed in the previous literature as well, the importance of using the means and application of intelligent transportation systems is safe for road users, managing evidence, providing permanent support, managing traffic, and knowing the weather, in addition to tracking goods of these is provided by intelligent transportation systems and means. The services of intelligent transportation systems can be categorized into safety, whether on the road or in cars, electronic toll collection, emergency calls, and the provision of information on traffic movement. The application of the use of intelligent transportation systems and means is critical to solving the traffic congestion crisis and overcoming it permanently.

This leads to green growth and the sustainability of roads in Egypt. Moreover, achieving the main objectives of this research, which is to highlight and clarify road problems to find solutions and reach sustainability in the field of roads, required identifying the causes, risks, and obstacles guiding the state. Moreover, the road sector and the environment, which were found from a review of previous literature and interviews, and then the use of intelligent transportation means and systems to respond and solve the traffic congestion crisis and reduce accidents, which was the goal of the second research, this will be explained further by providing many recommendations.

This chapter concludes with the results of this research by achieving the research objectives, followed by a recommendation. Based on the literature review and empirical work conducted, the conclusion will be discussed, and the research questions answered. The causes of traffic congestion were known through the interviews conducted by the researchers and through the results, according to the responses of the officials. The research has shown special importance when it comes to clarifying the causes of traffic congestion and the extent to which traffic congestion affects the environment, the individual, and society. The causes of traffic congestion are multiple, including the increase in the number of cars on the road as a result of the population increase, narrow streets and poor infrastructure, poor engineering design of roads, and buildings that intersect with streets. Emergency reasons occur because of cars being disabled on the streets and the poor transportation network. In addition, the lack of security oversight is one of the causes of traffic congestion, uncivilized drivers' behavior, and non-compliance with rules, laws, and regulations, as well as people's lack of commitment to walking in pedestrian lanes and heading to cut off the road.

This chapter proved the importance of applying intelligent transportation systems and means in all governorates that are overcrowded and have a high population density, because they achieve sustainability in the end by preserving the environment from pollution, as all intelligent transportation works with electricity and is far from fuel, which leads to Preserving the environment, in addition to the fact that the systems and means of intelligent transportation provide all means of safety for users and link all governorates to each other. To know the condition of the road and crowded places, and to track people and goods as well, because intelligent transportation systems depend on many technological fields such as wireless communications, computer technologies, software, databases, remote sensing technologies, sensors, video detection of cars, analytical examination of the system and automated periodic reports. Intelligent transportation systems and means can help reduce traffic congestion, which encourages the use of public transportation instead of private cars, which leads to reducing congestion and preserving the environment from pollution caused by emissions and vehicle exhaust. In addition, smart transportation systems will contribute to the rapid response to emergencies on the roads, in addition to achieving a comprehensive and continuous view of the movements of cars and the accuracy of recording violations.

Through this chapter, it became clear to us the efforts of the government regarding the use and application of smart transportation systems and means in Egypt. The Egyptian government is interested in the application of smart transportation systems and the use of modern technology, Through the research, it became clear that the state and the government work in two directions: The first trend is the development of roads and attention to road quality, and this is done through the application of smart transportation systems, this is evident in new projects such as the monorail project and the electric light rail project LRT. The second trend is to use electricity and solar energy as fuel alternatives to preserve the environment and achieve sustainability on the road.

Research Limitations

It is important to realize that this research is to know the extent to which smart transport systems and means affect the problem of traffic congestion and access to sustainability on the road by supply. The researchers show the negative impact of traffic congestion on the road, the environment, and the entire community. In this research, the researchers try to help the state and the government to know the causes of congestion and its impact and present the solution using and applying smart transportation methods and systems. In addition, some of the recommendations will help to manage and resolve the crisis from its roots. Since smart transportation methods and systems are a key element to sustainability on the road and getting rid of the traffic crisis that hinders the movement of the Egyptian road, a lot of research and questions have been raised. Moreover, the research focuses on the most important aspect of the serious consequences of traffic congestion, whether on the individual or the environment and that aspect is unknown to most people. Some believe that development and sophistication are limited to owning private cars only, regardless of the consequences of traffic congestion. The data and information collected in this research focus mainly on the total causes and risks caused by congestion, as discussed and how to solve them using smart transportation methods and systems.

- The main limitation of the research is only semi-structured interviews used by researchers as a tool, this method is accurate for the research, but it also involves many processes of imitation.
- The researchers tried to obtain accurate information from more than one office in the Public Authority for Roads and Bridges, in the Ministry of Transport, and from a general contracting company due to the lack of time for the officials, there were many problems collecting all the required data.
- The lack of enough graphics and tables that explain the research better because the research is qualitative and does not depend on evidence and numbers

- The researchers presented some, but not all, of ITS, a limited scope of study that did not cover all aspects of ITS.

Recommendations

Causes of congestion are many and different, and their impact represents a danger to the environment and society, as the researchers mentioned before, and with the presence of the traffic congestion crisis in all governorates of Egypt. Therefore, crisis management is a must as discussed in the research. Traffic congestion management strategy drives the ability of institutions to respond effectively to today's advanced world toward green growth, so any institution must be mature enough to face all these problems and maintain its image to achieve sustainability in the field of roads. After the evaluation, there are some recommendations that institutions, must follow to be more flexible in facing different types of risks:

- The research recommends using more tools from the ITS discussed in the literature to improve the development of the road system in Egypt.
- Everyone should be aware of the importance of improving road quality, achieving sustainability, and spreading the culture of using mass transportation. Cultivating a culture of using public transportation through social media to encourage environmental preservation, and that is by directing our message in the form of advertising campaigns that occur on the road and television as well as on all social media platforms to educate people and to know the importance of what the state offers.
- Recommend the widespread use of bikes instead of cars and encourage walking to work and commercial markets at close distances instead of relying on personal cars for everything.
- Despite the developments that the country is witnessing in terms of construction and expansion in the field of roads, the problem of traffic congestion still exists so far This shows that people are not aware of the seriousness of this problem, Therefore, awareness must be raised, increasing awareness and sustainable human development to provide people with the skills that enable them to deal with intelligent transportation systems.
- The inevitability of moving towards the introduction of intelligent transportation systems in the current and future transportation systems in the transportation networks scheme in the urban development strategy in the long term, to contribute to the treatment of transportation and traffic safety problems, and coordination and integration between the multiple means and modes of transportation, whether for the movement of passengers or goods.
- Benefit from e-government services and increase citizens' awareness of using smart transportation systems and modern technology in transport networks in Egypt, to contribute to reducing traffic accidents that cause huge human and material losses.

ACKNOWLEDGMENT

The authors thank Dr. Eman Ismail and Dr. Hossam Tawfik for their continuing support and professional guidance. The authors highly appreciated the hard work of data collection carried out by the undergraduate final-year students; Mahmoud Elshazle, Khaled Hashim, Ali Mohsen, and Fares Tarek.

REFERENCES

Akinboro, S., Adeyiga, J., Omotosho, A., & Akinwunmi, A. (2017). Mobile road traffic management system using weighted sensors. *International Journal of Interactive Mobile Technologies, 11*(5), 147–160. doi:10.3991/ijim.v11i5.6745

Al-Abaid, S. A. F. (2020). A Smart Traffic Control System Using Image Processing: A Review. *Journal of Southwest Jiaotong University, 55*(1), 31. doi:10.35741/issn.0258-2724.55.1.31

Al-Badri, I. (2021). *alahramgate*. https://gate.ahram.org.eg/News/2807065.aspx

Alyavina, E., Nikitas, A., & Tchouamou Njoya, E. (2020). Mobility as a service and sustainable travel behavior: A thematic analysis study. s.l. *Transportation Research Part F: Traffic Psychology and Behaviour, 73*, 362–381. doi:10.1016/j.trf.2020.07.004

Assaad, R. (2020). *Prospects for Egypt's Population and Labor Force: 2000 to 2050*. Economic Research Forum.

Benevolo, C., Dameri, R., & D'auria, B. (2016). Smart mobility in a smart city. In Empowering organizations. doi:10.1007/978-3-319-23784-8_2

Bezerra, B. (2019). Road Safety and Sustainable Development. *CHAP*, 1-13.

Bull. (2017). *Traffic congestion: the problem and how to deal with it*. ECLAC.

CAPMAS. (2021). *The annual bulletin results of car and train accidents*. Central Agency for Public Mobilization and Statistics.

Dawood, H., & Wang, Y. (2013). An efficient emergency message broadcasting scheme in vehicular ad hoc networks. *International Journal of Distributed Sensor Networks, 9*(11), 232916. doi:10.1155/2013/232916

Dia, H., & Panwai, S. (2014). December. Intelligent Mobility for Smart Cities: Driver Behavior Models for Assessment of Sustainable Transport. *IEEE Fourth International Conference on Big Data and Cloud Computing*, 625-632.

El-Kadi, A.-W. (2013). Suggested Solutions for Traffic Congestion in Greater Cairo. *Journal of Sustainable Development, 6*, 106-107.

Essam, M. (2020). *A boom in the road network. and experts: Egypt built 250 new bridges and accidents decreased*. https://akhbarelyom.com/news/newdetails/3172829/1/%D8%B7%D9%81%D8%B1%D8%A9-%D9%81%D9%8A-%D8%B4%D8%A8%D9%83%D8%A9-%D8%A7%D9%84%D8%B7%D8%B1%D9%82-%D9%88%D8%AE%D8%A8%D8%B1%D8%A7%D8%A1-%D9%85%D8%B5%D8%B1-%D8%B4%D9%8A%D8%AF%D8%AA-250-%D8%AC

Garcia-Lozano, E., Barba, C., Igartua, M., & Campo, C. (2013). *A distributed, bandwidth-efficient accident prevention system for interurban VANETs*. IEEE. doi:10.1109/SaCoNeT.2013.6654564

gov.uk. (2022). https://www.gov.uk/government/publications/road-congestion-and-travel-times-statistics-guidance/travel-time-statistics-background-quality-report

Hosny, K. (2021). *How did Egypt succeed in reducing the number of accidents by 29% in 2020? - 4500 km of roads were built*. Alarabiya. Retrieved from https://www.alarabiya.net/aswaq/economy/2021/11/05/%D9%83%D9%8A%D9%81-%D9%86%D8%AC%D8%AD%D8%AA-%D9%85%D8%B5%D8%B1-%D9%81%D9%8A-%D8%AE%D9%81%D8%B6-%D8%B9%D8%AF%D8%AF-%D8%A7%D9%84%D8%AD%D9%88%D8%A7%D8%AF%D8%AB-29-%D9%81%D9%8A-2020%D8%9F

Másilková, M. (2017). Health and social consequences of road traffic accidents. *Kontakt*, 43-47.

Mathew & Bombay. (2014). Intelligent Transportation Systems. In Transportation System Engineering. Indian Institute of Technology Bombay.

Olaverri & Monreal. (2016). Intelligent technologies for mobility in smart cities. *Hiradastechnika, 71*, 29–34.

Osama, A., Elgarhy, A., & Elseddawy, A. (2022). *A Proposed Framework for Enhancing the transportation systems based on the physical internet and data science techniques. In Proceedings of the Future Technologies Conference (FTC) 2022*. Springer. Retrieved from https://link.springer.com/chapter/10.1007/978-3-031-18461-1_38

Radwan, A. (2015). *Intelligent transportation system as a tool in solving Cairo's transportation problems*. Academic Press.

Shigehiro, M., Miyakawa, T., & Masuda, T. (2012). Road traffic control is based on a genetic algorithm for reducing traffic congestion. *Electronics and Communications in Japan*, *95*(4), 11–19. doi:10.1002/ecj.10421

StanczykA. (2022). https://link.springer.com/article/10.1057/s41301-022-00335-2

Wallis & Lupton. (2019). *The Problem with Congestion*. World Highways. https://www.transport.govt.nz/assets/Uploads/Paper/DefiningCongestion.pdf

WHO. (2022). *Road traffic injuries*. Retrieved from https://www.who.int/news-room/fact-sheets/detail/road-traffic-injuries

youmatter. (2021). https://youmatter.world/en/definition/definitions-sustainability-definition-examples-principles

Section 2

Impact of COVID-19 on Logistics and Supply Chain Management

Chapter 5
The Impact of COVID-19 on the Pharmaceutical Supply Chain in Egypt:
The Case of Pharco Group

Sandra Samy Haddad
Arab Academy for Science, Technology, and Maritime Transport, Egypt

Zeina Ibrahem El-Desouky
Arab Academy for Science, Technology, and Maritime Transport, Egypt

Ahmed Saed Ahmed
Sedico Pharmaceutical Company, Egypt

Saurav Negi
Modern College of Business and Science, Oman

EXECUTIVE SUMMARY

The COVID-19 pandemic is regarded as the major disruptive event of this decade, resulting in unexpected socio-economic impacts worldwide. The COVID-19 pandemic has caused considerable damage to various industries worldwide. Availability and supply of a wide range of raw materials, intermediate goods, and finished products have been seriously disrupted. The magnitude of the COVID-19 pandemic has had an enormous impact on the health system and pharmaceutical industry in almost every country globally. This new virus has resulted in pharmaceutical organizations experiencing unprecedented logistical restrictions as a result of increasing demand and limited capacity. Accordingly, this case study assesses the impact of the COVID-19 pandemic on the supply chain (SC) integration of the pharmaceutical sector in Egypt. A case study technique was used for better understating of the situation and to analyze the industry's position and its capabilities to face the consequences of the pandemic, which hindered the integration along the supply chain.

DOI: 10.4018/978-1-6684-4686-7.ch005

BACKGROUND

The novel coronavirus disease (COVID-19) was discovered and diagnosed in Wuhan, China, in December 2019. The World Health Organization declared the COVID-19 outbreak a global pandemic on March 11th (WHO). Approximately the next two months, COVID-19 spread fast, infecting over 2.5 million people by April 23, 2020. The COVID-19 epidemic wreaked havoc on the global economy, particularly in the pharmaceutical business. While there is currently no cure for this unique infectious disease, the pharmaceutical sector is aiding governments in meeting unmet COVID-19 needs, which range from research and development on prospective treatment options to balancing the medications supply chain in times of crisis. In addition, pharmaceutical companies are fighting to maintain natural market flow, as the current pandemic has hurt access to important pharmaceuticals at reasonable prices, which is the basic purpose of any pharmaceutical system (Ayati et al., 2020).

For a developing nation such as Egypt, precautionary measures to control and limit the consequences of the pandemic were essential. Following the announcement of the virus's arrival, the Egyptian government has taken a number of precautionary measures to limit its spread, including enforcing a shutdown during certain hours and imposing limited partial isolation of certain areas that have seen an increase in the number of infections, in addition to a reasonably extensive examination of reported cases' contacts (Raslan, 2021).

The impact of COVID-19 on the Egyptian pharmaceutical sector was clear in several points, when Egypt put restrictions on the exportation and also when China as a main supplier of APIs stopped exporting the raw materials and APIs, which of course had a directly negative impact on the supply chain of the companies, also marketing strategies and sales of the pharmaceutical companies which mainly depends on the medical Reps and meetings with the doctors and patients which impacted by the quarantine policies which adopted by the government, Supplies were further impacted by the disruption of logistics and transportation systems, restricting access and movement of products to and from ports - all these points had a direct negative impact on the companies' business and their profits (Pharco records, 2021).

COVID-19 may be viewed by some pharmaceutical corporations as a once-in-a-century opportunity, as it increases demand for prescription drugs, vaccinations, and medical devices. One of these companies, Pharco, was instrumental in combating the coronavirus pandemic. Pharco is one of the most well-known private and local Egyptian pharmaceutical enterprises, and it is the largest pharmaceutical manufacturer in the MENA region, focusing on research, formulation, manufacturing, and commercialization of pharmaceutical goods. Its position as the market leader in Egypt's pharmaceutical sector is based on a single goal: to supply patients with highly effective and safe pharmaceutical goods at a reasonable cost.

IMPACT OF COVID-19 ON THE SUPPLY CHAIN OF THE PHARMACEUTICAL SECTOR

Prior to the Covid-19 outbreak, several pharmaceutical companies faced insufficient active pharmaceutical ingredients (APIs) supply, resulting in some essential drug shortages, while others had a stockpile of APIs; the companies either sold these supplies at exorbitant prices or refused to sell them due to insufficient amounts in their stockpile. Due to China's monopoly in API manufacturing and export, Indian pharmaceutical companies are the main importers of APIs created in China for use in their drugs. The international community relies on India for generic medications because there are no other reputable active ingredient suppliers or big drug manufacturers accessible. Furthermore, before the international community, national medication producers would respond to their own requests. As a result, multiple talks between the Indian government and key industry partners were conducted to raise the national manufacturing volume of APIs. Due to measures designed to prevent the spread of the Covid-19 epidemic, the capacity to procure raw materials, make, and supply medications has been restricted.

In developing and poor countries without national production capacities, this is a big difficulty. This reliance on imports places a significant burden on these countries when it comes to negotiating treatment prices for individuals in need. Prioritizing the development of COVID19-targeted medications and equipment leaves a gap in the development of treatments for other chronic conditions. Insufficient medicine supply, lack of vaccination therapy choices, poor hospital treatment capacity, and a lack of quarantine facilities to address escalating COVID19 infections were all effects of the outbreak on the health sector (Almurisi et al., 2020).

Obviously, Covid-19 will have a huge influence on the supply chain globally, due to lockdown circumstances in several countries and a low workforce at the operational level, which will hinder production. Similarly, the impact on transportation and shipping operations has caused significant delays in supply. In terms of time and product availability, the New Normal in operations slowed down the activities. Even so, pharmaceutical companies throughout the world are trying their best to maintain drug supply while simultaneously working around the clock in research and development for vaccine development. As the lockdown is lifted, the situation will improve even more. Despite the expected cost increases, the increasing focus on risk management across networks and supply chains is likely to persist. With diverse end points of distribution and information, supply chains might become patient-centric, causing fresh technologies to develop and transform the broader sector (Barshikar, 2020).

Besides that, the disease has stopped movement, leading to lower productivity as individuals are unable to work at their jobs. After the epidemic in china began and lockdowns were implemented, supply from their factories' plants has decreased, and if people in china are unable to return to work as quickly as possible, a supply chain shortage will eventually disrupt everybody in Europe, as they depend heavily on drug imports (Selby et al., 2021). Difficulties in trade and travel disrupted the movement of goods and services, having a cascading effect on industries that rely heavily on Chinese supplies. COVID-19 is causing delays in the production of new pharmaceutical drugs due to substance shortages, clinical trial delays, and outbreaks in China and India, which have affected the supply of active pharmaceutical imports (APIs). Since active pharmaceutical imports are so important in processing, Global Data discovered that more than 50 drugs are at risk of negative manufacturing consequences. Approvals of less important medications will likely be postponed as a result of the importance given to producing drugs that help in the cure of the epidemic and other diseases. As a result, the time it takes for new medicines to enter the market will be extended (Thompson et al., 2021).

As the COVID-19 epidemic spreads, supply chains and logistics are becoming increasingly vulnerable. It has wreaked havoc on the healthcare supply chain, hurting active pharmaceutical ingredients, transportation, procurements, and completed healthcare items, among other things (European Pharmaceutical Review, 2020). The logistics supply chain encompasses much more than the transportation of drugs and other goods across borders. It clearly addresses issues at the grassroots level, such as the migration of workers in industrial units, the prohibition of transportation activities, particularly trucks, the lack of coordination between different administrations, and the failure of transporters and couriers to operate on time. All of these causes generate supply chain disruptions, resulting in shortages of vaccines, hand sanitizers, testing kits, personal protective equipment (PPE), pharmaceuticals, medical equipment, raw materials, and much more.(The Economic Times, 2020). Based on that there are 3 variables that are claimed to affect the supply chains of the pharmaceutical industry during covid-19 and they are the raw materials, uncertainty, logistics, and transportation. According to the first variable, It found that the deficiency of raw materials during the pandemic affects the recourse allocation of the pharmaceutical companies, while the shortage that occurred during the pandemic in the raw materials affects the capacity of the industries, the shortage of raw materials it affects the distribution process and how to evaluate the resilience of pharmaceutical supply chain. For the second variable it found that the supply chain is affected by the appearance and spreading of epidemics and it affects the demand forecasting, while the shortage of medicines affects the suppliers deal with market reaction at inopportune times of orders, also the sensitivity of the supply chain affected by simple conditions, all these fall under the term of uncertainty variable. According to the third variable it found that COVID-19 affects the transportation process in the supply chains and faced many transport issues, and mainly the logistics activities it affected by COVID-19 and there are many issues happened and this lead to:

Drag Shortage

The lack of testing, gloves, and other personal safety devices, as well as ventilators, continues to exacerbate the situation. Unfortunately, the world is still dealing with another crippling issue: a lack of vital drugs for the treatment of COVID-19. Patients with COVID-19 are negatively affected by medication shortages, which are expected to escalate over time, but they also pose a threat to the health and welfare of patients with other diseases that do not have COVID-19. Medications that have been hailed as potential COVID-19 treatments are in short supply. Hydroxychloroquine is becoming more difficult to purchase for patients without COVID-19 who use it to treat rheumatoid arthritis and other autoimmune disorders. Many widely used drugs contain active pharmaceutical ingredients from China, and many of our generics are processed and shipped from other nations, including India. As the pandemic has affected global production and exports, shortages of antimicrobials and sedatives will soon threaten a broad range of drugs not related to COVID-19 care (Choo et al., 2020).

Logistics Challenges

In the pharmaceutical supply chain, logistics is also a significant challenge. Many people's lives are dependent on pharmaceutical drugs, so ensuring the medicines are distributed safely and on schedule is important. The supply chain must be managed in order to make decisions about shortages, product checks, and consumer needs. Some Hospitals may not treat a patient until they are confident that they have all of the appropriate drugs on hand; others will initiate therapy ensuring that the prescription will be administered shortly. As a result, shortages and delays in the prescription supply chain are unacceptable (Strong et al., 2020).

Distributor and Pharmaceutical Industry

The pharmaceutical supply chain's distribution and retail markets seem to have problems. Since the epidemic prevented many people from going to work and prevented some from returning to work despite their overall good health, transportation companies suffered a significant blow to their employees. Drugs cannot be delivered to hospitals without these transportation operators. Even so, pharmacies are working to build and introduce safe distribution strategies for their clients (Strong et al., 2020).

THE SERVICES AND INDUSTRIES THAT HAVE BEEN AFFECTED BY COVID-19 IN EGYPT

Egypt was one of the first countries to respond to the outbreak of the pandemic. To combat the spread of COVID-19, the government enacted a number of restrictions in mid-March, including travel bans on international commercial passenger flights, a nighttime curfew from 8 p.m. to 6 a.m., gathering bans, and the closure of schools and religious organizations. While many factories continue to operate, labour hours and shifts are frequently decreased. The partial lockdown of the Egyptian economy attempts to achieve a compromise between public health and economic reasons, therefore these local anti-COVID-19 measures are moderate by international standards. As a result, the country has managed to maintain a reduced pace of economic activity while avoiding a complete shutdown (Breisinger et al., 2020).

Services Like

Information and communication technologies: The use of the internet and other information sector related services has increased dramatically as a result of home offices, e-learning, shopping online, and other internet-based activities. For example, the Minister of ICT recently stated that internet service use has surged by roughly 50%.

Transportation: Air travel has declined substantially and is now primarily used for freight. The demand for land transportation, such as taxis, ride-hailing firms, buses, and metro, has decreased as a result of home office work and the partial curfew. We estimate that air travel will be cut by 90% and land travel would be reduced by 30%.

Wholesale, retail, and trade: The productivity of trading establishments is reduced when they are partially closed during the curfew. Thousands of businesses have been forced to close, including coffee shops and commercial establishments. We project a 15% reduction in the wholesale and retail trade sectors as a result of the trade restrictions.

Industries Like

Durable and consumer products, such as metals and machinery: We anticipate a large drop in output of these items. The cause is a mix of lower demand and supply limitations for intermediate inputs. We project a 20% drop in metals and machines, as well as a 20% drop in other manufacturing activities.

Chemical and pharmaceutical items: Because of the severity of the health crisis, there is a stronger demand for medical supplies, sanitizers, and other chemical industry products. We anticipate a 30% rise in demand for such products as a result of COVID-19. (Breisinger et al., 2020). And the next parts will talk in details about the pharmaceutical sector that has been influenced by the country's economic position, which has come from the COVID-19 pandemic scenario since the World Health Organization labeled the outbreak a worldwide emergency.

EGYPT'S CHALLENGES

Despite the multiple policies and tools Egypt has adopted and used to curb the spread of the COVID-19 pandemic, numerous challenges have emerged, such as:

Reluctance to Receive Vaccines: Egypt engaged in serious negotiations with the three firms that produce coronavirus vaccines, China's Sinopharm, the United States' Pfizer, and the United Kingdom's AstraZeneca to obtain enough vaccines to vaccinate 40% of Egypt's 100 million populations by the end of 2021. In reaction to COVID-19, Egypt has not depended on a single vaccination. The negotiations necessitated meetings with Pfizer representatives from the United States, the United Arab Emirates, and Egypt, as well as representatives from the Unified Procurement Authority and the Egyptian Drug Authority, to consult on the supply of the company's vaccines after the company presented its financial offer. It also needed to be approved by the Egyptian Drug Authority, which had already approved the license of the Sinopharm vaccine of China for emergency use. Even though the state developed a website to register the data of people who wish to obtain the available anti-COVID-19 vaccinations, there has been a reluctance to register among both doctors, despite the fact that they are the most in need of vaccination, and citizens. According to Minister of Health Hala Zayed, just 50% of medical professionals registered for the anti-COVID-19 vaccination, despite the fact that 100% were targeted, and 40% of registered medical staff failed to show (Elbahy, 2021). Undoubtedly, individuals' unwillingness to obtain the vaccination occurred not just in Egypt, but in most countries throughout the world. This was ascribed to social media, the anxiety of negative effects and long-term implications of the vaccination, particularly in light of limited studies, and the AstraZeneca vaccine being connected to blood clots.

The Private Sector: There have been negotiations concerning the participation of the private sector in the COVID-19 vaccination campaign. The Proposals and Complaints Committee of the House of Representatives has approved a proposal on private sector participation in the vaccination system, provided that private sector institutions receive the approval of the Egyptian Drug Authority. A senior executive of the Ministry of Health confirmed in a statement that some steps are being taken by the Ministry in this direction. There are procedures currently taking place for contracting with two companies to provide the vaccine to citizens, as there is room for any company to apply to participate under the standards of the Ministry of Health. There is no doubt that this step requires precise study. It is well-known that vaccines and treatments are provided free of charge in times of pandemics and health epidemics under the supervision of the Health Ministry. So, opening the door to the private sector will thus create inequality and commodification at a time of the global pandemic. There will be two vaccination systems, one free of charge with a waiting list for those who want to get it through government outlets, and the other is with fees for those who want to be vaccinated quickly (Elbahy, 2021).

Economic Considerations: Egypt faced a challenge in terms of providing strategic stocks of certain food commodities, particularly as some consumption patterns changed with the spread of COVID-19. This has required strenuous efforts on the part of the Ministry of Supply and Internal Trade, represented by the General Authority for Supply Commodities and the Ministry of Agriculture and Land Reclamation, to expand wheat cultivation through; the contract farming system, procedures for early contracting with external actors to ensure the supply of appropriate quantities, provision of appropriate import ports and wheat collecting centers, in particular the establishment of modern metal silos and the development and upgrading of the list, and ensuring a strategic stockpile that meets the demand of some 70 million citizens on an estimated 128 billion loaves (5 loaves per person per day) (Elbahy, 2021).

Reforming the Health Sector: Most world countries, including Egypt, have embarked on a serious scheme to reform the health sector. It is a serious challenge, especially since it requires progressive reform in partnership with various bodies in the governmental, non-governmental and private sectors to provide Egyptians with quality services. There is a need to improve the mental image of all healthcare providers, continue medical training, promote a positive working environment, and scientifically develop medical and nursing staff accommodation in government hospitals to attain this goal. There is no doubt that special legislation is required to prepare for the launch of The National Project for Model Hospitals in all governorates of the Republic in conjunction with implementing the National Project for the Unified Health Insurance (Elbahy, 2021).

EGYPT'S TOOLS TO FIGHT COVID-19

High-Tech Tools: Egypt brought its high-tech solutions to the front lines of the coronavirus battle, combining the efforts of the Ministry of Communications and Information Technology (MCIT), the private sector, and innovators, giving rise to a number of innovative robots, novel initiatives, e-applications, and thermal imaging infrared cameras, etc. On 10 June 2020, Mansoura University launched its first domestically manufactured robot designed to provide food and medical supplies to coronavirus patients in isolation hospitals. High-resolution thermal imaging infrared cameras were used in airports for the early detection of suspected cases of COVID-19. As of 5 June 2020, the Egyptian Holding Company for Airport and Air Navigation started installing thermographic cameras in arrival halls at Cairo International Airport. Additionally, Egypt launched the Sehat Misr [Egypt's Health] mobile app dedicated to COVID-19 resources and inquiries. The app was introduced to replace the hotline 105 established by the Ministry of Health for the same purpose. The app includes COVID-19 related questions and guidance. Through the app, users can report suspected cases of COVID-19 by clicking the "Report" button and entering the patient's name and national ID number (Elbahy, 2021).

Egypt's Foreign Assistance: On 10 May 2021, three military transport aircraft took off from the East Cairo Air Base carrying large quantities of medical aid provided by the Ministry of Health to India. This step came to alleviate the burden on the Indian people due to the rapid spread of the coronavirus and the high rate of infections and deaths amid a severe shortage of medication, medical supplies, and protective equipment (Othman, 2021). In addition, Egypt built an air bridge for medical supplies and treatment to victims of the Beirut Port explosion of August 2020. In October 2020, Egypt sent tons of milk and medication to Iraq. Egypt also sent medical aid to the Jordanian people in December 2020. Moreover, three aircrafts loaded with large quantities of medical supplies, equipment, and 477 International Organizations and States' Response to Covid-19 milk were sent to Lebanon in the face of the spread of the second wave of the coronavirus. In May 2020, Egypt sent a large virus-aid shipment of sterilization tools to the United States of America following a surge in death rates. The shipment, which consisted of tons of medical devices, carried the label, "From the Egyptian People to the American People", an initiative that was later extended to include other countries. In April 2020, a time when Italy was one of the first hotspots of the pandemic in Europe, Dr Hala Zayed, Egypt's Minister of Health, visited Italy to personally deliver the Egyptian aid, which included protective masks and gloves, to the Italian Minister of Foreign Affairs, Luigi Di Maio (Elbahy, 2021).

PHARMACEUTICAL SECTOR IN EGYPT

The pharmaceutical industry in Egypt has gone to unprecedented heights and is estimated to be one of the most valuable sectors in the country. The value of the global pharmaceutical industry is anticipated to be about $1.42 trillion by the end of 2020. With the rising need of developing drugs to satisfy the ever-increasing demand, the pharmaceutical companies are working tirelessly to come up with cutting-edge and innovative treatments for patients. The pharmaceutical sector is one of the major global marketplaces, each with its unique set of circumstances. Egypt is a key pharmaceutical rising market in the Middle East area, with a geographical, historical, and political effective leadership position among Arab nations. As a result, this market has a high economic worth (Egypt Pharmaceuticals & Healthcare Report, 2019).

Egypt's pharmaceutical business is the largest in the MENA area, accounting for 30% of market supply. Enterprises in the Egyptian pharmaceutical market are divided into three categories: public sector companies, which include the Drugs Holding Company's eight companies, international companies, and domestic private companies. By the end of 2009, retail pharmaceutical consumption had reached US$2.48 billion; nonetheless, per capita spending was among the lowest in the area.

Despite the government's commitment to stimulate foreign investment and set a target of US$10 billion by June 2010, just US$2.6 billion had been reached by April. The majority of market forecasts are positive, indicating that the pharmaceutical industry in Egypt will grow further. This is due to the expansion of the domestic industry and increased exports, as well as the government's attempts to reform the registration and pricing process and intellectual property rights. (Abd Elsalam, 2021).

Egypt's indigenous pharmaceutical sector is strong, with roughly 120 pharmaceutical firms present, less than ten of which are multinationals with local production divisions. In the industry, there are 17 private sector enterprises and 9 multinational pharmaceutical players. There are three types of pharmaceutical firms in Egypt: public sector firms, private sector Egyptian firms, and multinational corporations. Pharmaceutical items sold include generic drugs, over-the-counter (OTC) medications, and patented treatments. Despite the fact that Egypt is the middle east and Africa region's largest pharmaceutical producer and consumer in terms of volume, the market is fragmented, and distribution is unplanned and scattered, as a result of inadequate supply chain management procedures. The private sector controls more than three-quarters of the local market. The five largest pharmaceutical companies control one-third of the market (Haddad, 2020). Pharmaceutical sales in Egypt are expected to increase from EGP38.3 billion (USD2.1 billion) in 2017 to EGP56.6 billion (USD2.9 billion) by 2022, with a CAGR of 8.1 percent in local currency and 6.5 percent in US dollar terms. Annual growth rates are predicted to stay consistent in the second half of the 10-year forecast period, with sales reaching EGP85.5bn (USD3.9bn) by 2027(Egypt Pharmaceuticals & Healthcare Report, 2019).

The public sector contributes a very small percentage to Egypt's pharmaceutical industry, amounting to only 6%, through 11 companies involved in the manufacture, export, and import of medicines and medical supplies, and it is affiliated with the Holding Company for Medicines, Chemicals, and Medical Supplies. While the private sector controls 94 percent of the market. As a result, the government sector's production of medicines does not surpass 20% of overall production, while the private sector generates around 80% of Egypt's medications. As a result, the private sector's domination of the medicine market, whether local or international, becomes clear, with the second accounting for 69 percent, whereas the first accounted for 31% of the drug's market share in 2019 (The Egyptian Centre for economic studies, 2019). In terms of pharmaceutical firms in Egypt, Novartis, Sanofi, and GlaxoSmithKline rank first and second, respectively, in terms of the relative weight of their sales in the Egyptian market in the first quarter of 2020, while Amon, Eva, and Pharco are at the forefront of local pharmaceutical firms according to (The Egyptian Centre for economic studies, 2019).

Egyptian Pharmaceutical Sector During COVID-19 Pandemic

The pharmaceutical sector is critical in providing society with life-saving products and services. Several obstacles faced by the pharmaceutical business in managing the pandemic were recognised, including difficulty meeting demand for protective gear and diagnostic testing facilities. Pharmaceutical businesses rely largely on compounds produced in China, which has a monopoly on the world's active ingredient manufacturing (up to 60% of China's production). Due to factory closures, notably in China, where most medication goods are made, the Covid-19 problem has had a direct impact on medical supply shortages, supply chain uncertainties, logistics, and transportation. The real economy was threatened by the barriers encountered in commercial transactions and the transportation of products and resources (Almurisi et al., 2020).

COVID- The outbreak of 19 had a significant impact on the pharmaceutical industry. On the one hand, money would be lost due to manufacturing delays and supply constraints. Revenue growth in 2020 will be hampered by supply chain deficiencies and the deferral of all improvement plans in order to focus resources on ensuring the delivery of vital products. In reaction to the pandemic, which revealed gaps and threats of supply chain weak points, massive changes in supply model and supply chain design are expected to be proposed. On the other side, any corporation working on vaccine and medicine development, or planning to develop a cure or vaccination, has an opportunity (Nicola, 2020). An investigational COVID-19 vaccine is now being tested in clinical studies. Nonetheless, demand for goods associated to the treatment of COVID-19 and its symptoms or a consequence has risen dramatically. As in the case of Dexamethasone, demand has increased after the preprint of the RECOVERY study at Oxford University was published, as reported in a BMJ article (Mahase, 2020).

According to a study released on March 20th, there were 769 reported cases of COVID-19 in 37 African countries, with 15 deaths. The first appearance of Covid-19 in Egypt was in the first week of March 2020. Egypt was ranked 50th out of 212 areas and countries in terms of the number of patients infected as of the evening of April 21, 2020. 147th out of all regions and countries reporting infections in terms of the overall number of infected individuals (36 infections per one million population), 106th in terms of infection recovery rate (26.6 percent infection recovery), and 34th in terms of deaths per total infected individuals (7.5%). Egypt had 3659 infected people, 935 recovering people, 1270 negative test outcomes, and 276 deaths as of April 21st (Bahlola & Dewey, 2020).

Despite the fact that the COVID-19 pandemic's human costs and economic disruptions have sent shockwaves throughout the world, pharma executives have been focused on assuring a steady supply of vital medications and on innovation. Most industries have taken a financial impact, however, the pharmaceutical industry's issues are pressing, such as ensuring that supply chains operate so that patients can fill prescriptions and continue to get important medicines. With so much at risk, pharmaceutical companies are working feverishly to safeguard patients' health, manage delays, and produce a COVID-19 vaccine, antiviral, or other cure (Bahlola & Dewey, 2020).

By assessing the capabilities of the Pharmaceutical companies, we will find a clear weakness needs to be developed to help the companies overcome this negative impact the main of this weakness are in the digital technology using and in the environmental sustainability which have a direct impact on the efficiency, material consumption and quality. In this case the information will illustrate that it is very

Figure 1. Illustrates the weekly COVID-19 cases reported in Egypt
Source: WHO (2020)

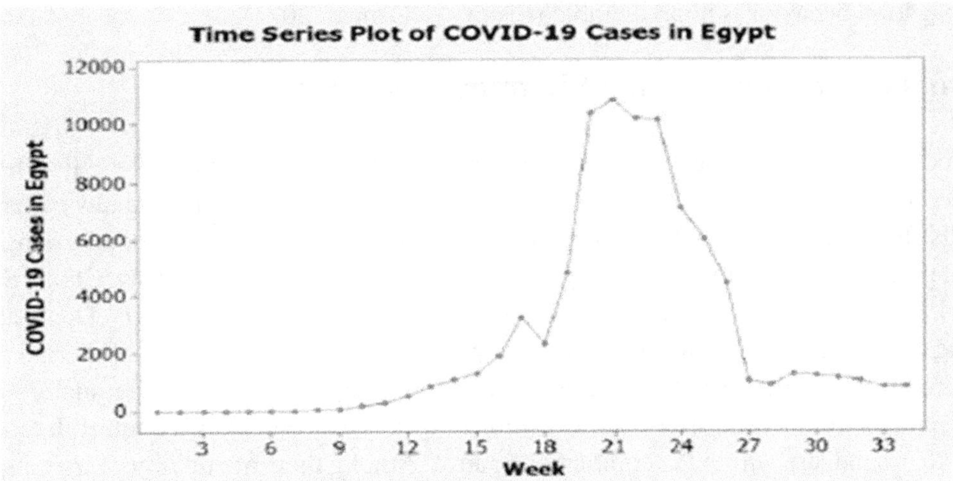

important that companies determine the digital transformation and environmental sustainability in their strategies and processes described by (Pharco records, 2020).

External Environment of the Pharmaceutical Firms

Egyptian authorities have adopted a number of preventive measures to restrict the virus's spread at the macroeconomic level. These limitations included a nightly curfew, a total lockdown of commercial malls, and the closure of all leisure facilities and places of worship, such as mosques and churches. The Ministry of Health then announced incremental relaxations, implementing a three-stage strategy to return to regular working practices. According to the International Monetary Fund study 'Policy responses to COVID-19' (IMF, 2020), it is predictable that the pandemic would have an impact on the Egyptian economy since the WHO reported the first case in Egypt on February 14th, 2020. Travel and tourist activities are dropping, local business activities are slowing due to the lockdown and the related global recession, and exports are being reduced due to poor demand, to name a few causes that justify the impact (Elsafty & Osman, 2021).

People are in a state of panic as a result of the outbreak's declaration. Fear drove customers to stock up on basics in order to prevent the predicted stock-outs of pharmaceuticals and supplies. In the media, there has been a significant increase in the consumption of food, sanitizers, and cleaning goods. Medication, on the other hand, had a similar effect. Similarly, increased purchasing of chronic illness medications was reported at pharmacies. Some insurance providers let you double the monthly required amount. COVID-19-related medications saw significant demand fluctuation, notably in the Egyptian market, where the prescription practice is not well followed (Elsafty & Osman, 2021).

The use of technology is assisting in the management of the crisis. Data analysis and statistical models are commonly utilized to anticipate infection and mortality rates and take proactive determined steps to control them. Telecommunications is one of the areas that has thrived since it offered the primary means of contact during times of lockdown and is still giving solutions to run businesses, schools, and institutions remotely. There is no evidence that climate change will affect disease spreading. Summer has come and gone, with only a few new recorded cases and deaths. However, winter is coming, and the virus's propagation behavior is unpredictable (Elsafty & Osman, 2021).

The Internal Environment of the Pharmaceutical Firms

Suppliers and customers must be identified in order to demonstrate the internal environment of pharmaceutical companies. In general, Egypt's pharmaceutical sector heavily relies on raw material exports, notably APIs. Egypt imports around 90% of its chemical needs for pharmaceuticals. This is due to a lack of local production capacity. According to (Elsafty & Osman, 2021) Germany, China, Switzerland, the United States, and India account for many raw and packaging material imports. Domestic suppliers of packaging components or chemicals, in turn, rely on imports of raw materials. External and internal customers are the two types of process customers. External customers include regulatory authorities, distributors, and, of course, end-user patients, who are beyond the company's control. Internal customers, on the other hand, are within the company's control. Among them are quality, warehouse, and asset planners. Employees are well-trained and subjected to critical qualifying standards before being allowed to work autonomously. Both firms under consideration are among the highest paying in the industry. One of them has been named Egypt's greatest place to work. The production process begins with the dispensing of supplies for preparation, followed by processing and formulation steps to generate homogeneous product granules. Tablet compression machines next compress the granules into tablets. The final phase in the in-house production process of pharmaceutical items is packaging, which involves filling tablets into prepared blisters, sealing them, and packing them. However, it is a vital unit process that offers the necessary protection for pharmaceutical items during transit, handling, and storage.

PHARCO PHARMACEUTICALS COMPANY

One of the biggest pharmaceutical companies operating in Egypt is Pharco Company. Dr. Hassan Abbas Helmy formed Pharco Corporation in 1987, it began operations in 1988 and began producing, formulating, and marketing a broad range of generics, brands, and licensed pharmaceutical products. It considered a dominant player in the pharmaceutical industry in Egypt, the Middle East, and Africa, offering an unrivaled range of pharmaceutical generics and branded generics, as well as nutritional and vitamin products for disease treatment and prevention to improve the quality of life of every patient (Pharco records, 2021). Pharco Corporation maintains the most modern and advanced pharmaceutical facilities in Egypt and the Middle East since up-to-date technology and cGMP (current good manufacturing practice) are the company's cornerstones (Saed, 2021). According to (Pharco records, 2021) there are $ 320 Million in Sales 2020, more than 7800 employees, more than 800 production a variety of dosage forms, covering most of the therapeutic groups. Egypt market leader accounting for 6% of the Egyptian Market's volume sales and 9.6% of volume units, 16% annual growth in value, exports to 57 countries around the world, before 2019 by 29$ million and after 2020 increase to 43$ million, and over 13% of sales are generated from export to regional and international markets comprising $ 35 million with plans to increase export sales to more than 30% in the next five years. Pharco Company has a well-established Sales & Marketing department devoted to fulfilling the company's goals through a skilled Sales and Marketing staff that collaborates closely with health care experts to address and anticipate client demands. We want to become real partners in healthcare by building strong connections with healthcare professionals and delivering tools for continually evolving healthcare concerns (Heidar, 2021). At pharco's supply chain network the pharmacy distributors have extensive distribution networks that cover the world, selling and distributing medications to retail pharmacies, clinics, and hospitals. And there are a large range of intermediaries, pharco sells 237 products, generics, branded generics, and approved products to over a dozen large authorized distributors as well as a large number of smaller distributors. There is High fragmentation also, the supply chain members work independently of each other, limiting the capacity for concerted activities. The goods are moved down the supply chain, and manufacturer and distributor sales forces are rewarded depending on their annual sales goals. These factors lead to higher stock levels and a greater risk of expiration at the retail level. Furthermore, upstream representatives are unwilling to consider any expired drug returns, resulting in expired items staying on the store shelves. Drug information is lost as products pass downstream due to various coding systems used by members of the supply chain, rendering it difficult for pharco to trace its products to the point of sale. As a result, the process's absolute traceability cannot be achieved across the supply chain. Furthermore, some pharmacies and warehouses do use paper to keep track of product. (Saed, 2021)

Pharco's mission is to Providing safe, effective pharmaceutical products that are affordable and available for every patient all over the globe and providing patients with the latest up to date, affordable treatments for chronic diseases (HCV, Diabetes, Hypertension ...etc.), pharco Corporation's vision is strives to improve health and well- being of patients at every stage of life through providing high quality, safe, effective pharmaceutical products at affordable prices, and unraveling major health challenges via innovation and sharing success with partners all around the globe with everlasting relationships built on trust, and pharco Company's CSR is continues to serve the community through corporate and individual ventures in terms of direct monetary donations, participation in charity programs for the underprivileged, charitable contributions for educational programs and youth initiatives. Pharco has taken initiatives in Nigeria, Chad and other nations in need of support of underprivileged children who do not have the means to obtain medications. Besides donating medicine, Pharco has worked hard in the eradication of famine in countries such as Lebanon, Palestine and Iraq (Pharco records, 2020).

Pharco Company During COVID-19

Pharco is a player in different international pharmaceutical markets besides the country of origin market (Egypt), as we export pharmaceutical and nutraceutical products (Saed, 2022). Before covid-19 Pharco could take manual approvals from The Egyptian Ministry of Health to export abroad but the social distances restricted them and delay the response so they made a new website take one month to convert all the activities into digitalization so that they can communicate with each other during the pandemic without any barriers (Saed, 2022).

In Egypt, Pharco pharmaceutical company announced that it had acquired the rights to produce the Russian vaccine Sputnik V and that the production should begin before the end of 2021. This move coincided with the local production of the Chinese Sinovac vaccine in Egypt, alongside plans of the Egyptian Ministry of Health to produce the European AstraZeneca vaccine later, as well as the ongoing research on a 100% Egyptian vaccine for its manufacture in the country. Egypt aims to produce a variety of foreign and local vaccines to reach "self-sufficiency", meet the needs of the citizens, start exporting abroad, provide the largest quantity of vaccines, and vaccinate 70% of the population. The Egyptian Ministry of Health recently announced the beginning of the production of Sinovac in Egypt, the first dose of which will be produced within factories of the company holding biologics and vaccines VACSERA. Egypt aspires to produce 40 million doses of that vaccine by the end of 2021, to transfer the entirety of its manufacturing technology to Egypt, invest in this production to achieve self-sufficiency in vaccines, and export the surplus and manufacturing technology to Arab and African countries. With Egypt's success in producing Sinovac, it will become the first African country to produce an anti-coronavirus vaccine locally (Elbahy, 2021).

Pharco pharmaceuticals, with its great experience in the pharmaceutical industry in Egypt, the Arab world and Africa, attaches great importance to finding quick and effective treatments to confront the emerging coronavirus disease Covid-19, and this is a national mission that requires cooperation with all research agencies and with the Ministry of Health To find effective, safe and moderate value treatments for patients with the emerging coronavirus. Therefore, the company submitted to the Scientific Research Ethics Committee three clinical studies for the use of some of its antiviral drugs circulating in the Egyptian and African markets to treat patients with the emerging coronavirus. The committee agreed to start the application of one of the clinical studies using the antiviral drugs registered by the company, and the study has actually begun, and the rest of the studies are awaiting approval by the Scientific Research Ethics Committee on the protocols submitted to it so that the company can actually start these studies (Saed, 2022)

The company is also carrying out advanced research that was carried out in a laboratory (In Vitro) on a new compound and has given promising results that will achieve a major leap in the treatment of patients with the emerging coronavirus, and the study protocol is currently being submitted to the Ministry of Health so that it can be completed and clinical studies conducted (Saed, 2022).

The company is also cooperating with the Ministry of Health to find quick diagnostic tools at a moderate cost so that a general examination can be carried out on all citizens, similar to what happened in the One Hundred Million Health Initiative in order to ensure the speedy control of this disease at a low cost that the state can afford (Pharco records, 2021).

The company also produces Dexamethasone, which scientific studies have proven successful in implementing many critical cases, and the Scientific Committee to combat the emerging coronavirus at the Ministry of Health was the first to include it in the treatment protocols for critical cases in intensive care in Egypt (Pharco records, 2021).

Pharco has more than ten pharmaceutical products that are described within the approved treatment protocols for the emerging coronavirus disease. The company provides them in appropriate quantities and puts them at the disposal of the Ministry of Health to serve the citizens' patients who need those (Pharco records, 2021).

The company also made a quick registration for the production of gelatin capsules of vitamin D, vitamin C and zinc capsules, in order to fill the shortage in the drug market needs of these vitamins and important elements that have a major role in strengthening immunity to resist viral diseases (Saed, 2021).

The company continues to work and cooperate with all scientific and research bodies in order to reach the best treatments and in order to produce an effective, safe and affordable Egyptian medicine at an affordable cost for the Egyptian patient so that it can be made available without adding significant burdens to the state or the citizen, and Pharco confirms its continuous mission to provide treatment Effective and safe for all citizens (Heiadr, 2021).

The European company, affiliated with the Pharco Pharmaceutical Group, launched a press conference at Thursday, March 18 in Cairo, under the slogan "Yourself in the World" to announce the launch of the drug "Molnupiravir", the latest new oral treatment for the treatment of Corona virus, for the treatment of mild and moderate cases of Corona. And all procedures were done and obtained the approval of the Egyptian Medicines Authority, and currently it is provided in government and private hospitals, and after all steps are completed, it will be provided in pharmacies, which is 4 capsules taken every 12 hours for 5 days, stressing that trying the drug in severe cases was ineffective, but It has proven its effectiveness in medium and simple cases, stressing that 85% of cases were simple, and they are treated at home, and its effect is positive in simple and medium cases. Said that its price for the public is 625 pounds, and it is freely given to those who are unable in government hospitals at a cheaper price than that (Pharco records, 2022).

Pharco's SWOT Analysis

The Egyptian market was affected by the shortage of raw materials at the time of the Corona virus, and thus affected the expectation of production and the increase in demand for products and the lack of demand for other products, and thus the effect of this on the lack of knowledge of the required quantity to purchase and its direction, and it was an opportunity for companies that were able to overcome it, such as Pharco, the company was able to cover the production plan with the requirements in the market, as it owns 6 factories that contain a production line in European and Amreya.

COVID-19 may be seen as a century's opportunity for pharmaceutical industry; as it increases the demand for prescription medicines, vaccines and medical devices. The period of exacerbation of the crisis witnessed a shortage of certain types of medicines and vitamins and the complete disappearance of some of them, which led to a clear increase in their prices, and a scarcity of protective equipment like masks, medical gloves and sterilization preparations such as alcohol and others, which led to a high rise in its prices, and this resulted in decisions from the Ministry Commerce and Industry to stop the export of alcohol of all kinds and its derivatives and surgical masks, and companies were obligated to supply their stock and production to the Unified Purchase and Medical Supply Authority. All of these are considered an opportunity to some companies, such as Pharco, which was for it an opportunity, as it was able to overcome the shortage of raw materials through the assistance of the Egyptian Ministry of Health, which has increased the number of suppliers to pharmaceutical companies from 3 to 5, and Pharco used an action plan to search for suppliers in other countries without any restriction.

The lockdown of countries led to an impact on transportation and logistics in terms of stopping the import and export of medical raw materials, and in turn, the impact on the Egyptian pharmaceutical market and delaying the arrival of medical raw materials needed for suppliers. This had an impact on Pharco so, the company had to re-scheduling the allocation of the resources and resorted to the export department to find an opportunity in other countries to sell these products and start making offers and discounts.

Through the SWOT analysis that applied to know how covid-19 impact the Egyptian pharmaceutical supply chain, founding that there is forecasting about the demand of pharmaceuticals and all raw materials are available from china and India and the safety stock was for 3 months, in addition to there are some of products that not always be required like antibiotics and some of medicines that have low demand like vitamin-c and zinc. But after covid-19 there are high shortages in supply chain in raw materials and high demand on some products like antibiotics and medicines that entered in the treatment protocol of covid-19 pandemic, and there is high demand for vitamin-c and zinc. Although there is shortages in raw material but there is strong threats on some companies that cannot provide medicines for patients and raw materials for suppliers on another hand there is an opportunities for other companies that have the ability to provide this raw materials like pharco company in Egypt which achieved highest export rate in 2020 unlike other companies and it has the potential to use new suppliers from Egypt because of the lockdown of import and export process and the restrictions that imposed.

Due to the proactivity in facing the challenges of COVID-19 and measures taken to confront the pandemic (multiple supplier strategy, increase of safety stocks, digitization, and cooperation with the Egyptian Ministry of Health), during 2021 Pharco B International was able to increase its local sales by 18% and its exports by 48% as it substituted other exporters in the region who were not able to sustain their operations. Instead of China Pharco imported its raw materials from France, England, Korea, and Mexico. The companies in these countries were eager to enter new markets and grasp the opportunity which made them propose win-win deals (Saed, 2022).

So, based on all of the above, the records, the interviews applied in pharco company in which it was discussed the questions to define the impact of COVID-19 on supply chain in pharmaceutical sector in Egypt specifically in pharco, and also the information collected about the company and how it faced the coronavirus pandemic in different way, The SWOT analysis will be:

Strengths

- Following the safety stock system for raw materials, so it was not greatly affected by waiting to import new materials.
- The company had an efficient supply chain team who were able to quickly make an action plan and new forecasting plan to deal with the new situation during the crisis.
- Pharco has an efficient foreign procurement team that has a strong network and database for the foreign suppliers even if they did not deal with them before.
- The company had a large capacity and space in warehouses to accept the pressure of demand for the medicines they manufactured due to its entry into the protocol.

Weakness (Areas of Development)

- Training employees to cope with digital transformation.
- Implement digital infrastructure because the company reduces physical transaction

Opportunities

- The Egyptian Ministry of Health launched a decision to allow a maximum of 5 suppliers for each product instead of 3.
- The company resorted to changing its production plan based on changing the forecasting plan in terms of placing certain medicines as the priority of production.
- Pharco contracted with a Russian company to produce the Russian vaccine in Egypt, and this gave Pharco an opportunity to obtain a distinguished position in the pharmaceutical industry.
- The Egyptian Ministry of Health's approval of Pharco's medicines to treat corona patients in government hospitals.

Threats

- Shortage of raw materials as a result of the lack of the company's main suppliers, like China and India, when the lockdown occurred.

RECOMMENDATIONS

To overcome the challenges facing the Egyptian pharmaceutical supply chain, as enumerated earlier; concrete steps to meet obstacles and challenges and enhance efficiency should be carried out. Some of the recommended changes are summarized below:

- The pharmaceutical industry's companies should increase the use of digitalization.
- Assess timely and transparent communication in order to avoid unnecessary panic and develop a backup plan.
- Implement the methods and variables used in this research to be used in other companies or in other industries.
- Collaborate closely with partners to identify and resolve critical supply chain challenges.
- Pharmaceutical companies can implement the use of technology more widely in the field of sales to develop in the pharmaceutical supply chain industry by giving smart devices like tablets to their customers to communicate with them and present offers to them and apply this idea to help them implement social distancing and on the other hand reduce the number of individuals working in the field of sales and dealing in a more time-efficient manner.
- Use of technology to promote digitalization along the supply chain to enhance efficiency and sustainability.
- Frequent collaboration with the ministry of health and governmental bodies is essential for facing challenges and overcoming them.

REFERENCES

Abd Elsalam, S. R. (2021). *Measuring transparency in the Egyptian pharmaceutical system*. Academic Press.

Almurisi, S. H., Al Khalidi, D., Al-Japairai, K. A., Mahmood, S., Chilakamarry, C. R., Kadiyala, C. B. N., & Mohananaidu, K. (2020). *Impact of COVID 19 Pandemic Crisis on the Health System and Pharmaceutical Industry*. Academic Press.

Ayati, N., Saiyarsarai, P., & Nikfar, S. (2020). Short and long term impacts of COVID-19 on the pharmaceutical sector. *Daru: Journal of Faculty of Pharmacy, Tehran University of Medical Sciences*, *28*(2), 799–805. doi:10.100740199-020-00358-5 PMID:32617864

Bahlol, M., & Dewey, R. S. (2021). Pandemic preparedness of community pharmacies for COVID-19. *Research in Social & Administrative Pharmacy*, *17*(1), 1888–1896. doi:10.1016/j.sapharm.2020.05.009 PMID:32417070

Bahlol, M. M., & Lagutkina, T. P. (2016). Pharmaceutical marketing communication tools and company activities orientation. In Актуальные вопросы медицины в современных условиях (pp. 179-182). Academic Press.

Barshikar, R. (2020). Covid 19–Impact and new normal for pharmaceutical industry (Part–I). *Journal of Genetic Medicine*, *16*(3), 112–119.

BMI Research. (2019). *Egypt Pharmaceuticals and Healthcare Report*. https://nationsemergentes.org/wp-content/uploads/2019/02/egypt-pharmaceutical

Breisinger, C., Raouf, M., Wiebelt, M., Kamaly, A., & Karara, M. (2020). *Impact of COVID-19 on the Egyptian economy: Economic sectors, jobs, and households* (Vol. 6). Intl Food Policy Res Inst.

Choo, E. K., & Rajkumar, S. V. (2020, June). Medication shortages during the COVID-19 crisis: What we must do. *Mayo Clinic Proceedings*, *95*(6), 1112–1115. doi:10.1016/j.mayocp.2020.04.001 PMID:32312491

Economics, C. (2020). *Economic consequences of the COVID-19 Pandemic*. https://copenhageneconomics.com/publication/economic-consequences-of-the-covid-19-pandemic

Elbahy, R. (2021). *The Egyptian battle against the coronaviruses: policies and tools*. Institute of International Politics and Economics.

Elsafty, A., & Osman, M. (2021). The Impact of COVID-19 on the Efficiency of Packing Lines in Pharmaceutical Manufacturing Sites in Egypt. *International Journal of Business and Management*, *16*(7), 57–72. doi:10.5539/ijbm.v16n7p57

European Pharmaceutical Review. (2020). COVID-19 update: Coronavirus and the pharmaceutical supply chain. *European Pharmaceutical Review*. https://www.europeanpharmaceuticalreview.com/article/116145/covid-19- update-coronavirus-and-the-pharmaceutical-supply-chain/

Haddad, S. (2020). Developing an e-business system to improve the downstream Pharmaceutical supply chain (a study on the Egyptian market. *Proceedings of the 8th International Conference on Advanced Materials and Systems (ICAMS)*. 10.24264/icams-2020.III.7

Mahase, E. (2020). Covid-19: *Demand for dexamethasone surges as RECOVERY trial publishes* preprint. *BMJ*, *369*, 2512. doi:10.1136/bmj.m2512 PMID:32576548

Medhat, M. A., & El Kassas, M. (2020). COVID-19 in Egypt: Uncovered figures or a different situation? *Journal of Global Health*, *10*(1), 010368. doi:10.7189/jogh.10.010368 PMID:32566159

Nicola, M. E., Alsafi, Z., Sohrabi, C., Kerwan, A., Al-Jabir, A., Iosifidis, C., Agha, M., & Agha, R. (2020). The socio-economic implications of the coronavirus pandemic (COVID-19): *A Review. International Journal of Surgery*, *78*, 185–193. doi:10.1016/j.ijsu.2020.04.018 PMID:32305533

Pharco. (2021). *Pharco Reports*. Pharco Corporation in Egypt.

Raslan, W. E. (2021). Fractional mathematical modeling for epidemic prediction of COVID-19 in Egypt. *Ain Shams Engineering Journal, 12*(3), 3057–3062. doi:10.1016/j.asej.2020.10.027

Selby, L. M., Hewlett, A. L., Cawcutt, K. A., Wood, M. G., Balfour, T. L., Rupp, M. E., & Starlin, R. C. (2021). Effect of severe acute respiratory coronavirus virus 2 (SARS-CoV-2) mRNA vaccinations in healthcare workers with high-risk coronavirus disease 2019 (COVID-19) exposure. *Infection Control and Hospital Epidemiology, 42*(10), 1281–1282. doi:10.1017/ice.2021.193 PMID:33934742

Strong, S., Delzell, P., Trygstad, W., Fitzpatrick, G., Haley-Hyer, P., Bates, A., & Awwad, M. (2020, January). The impact of covid-19 on the pharmaceutical supply chain. In *2nd African International Conference on Industrial Engineering and Operations Management* (pp. 565-572). IEOM.

The Economic Times. (2020a). COVID-19 impact: Drugs essential, ancillaries not so, means supplies take a hit. *The Economic Times*. https://economictimes.indiatimes.com/industry/healthcare/biotech/pharmaceuticals/drugsessential-ancillaries-not-so-means-supplies-take-a-hit/articleshow/75038462.cms?from=mdr

The Egyptian Centre for Economic Studies. (2019). *Egypt Pharmaceuticals and Healthcare Report*. https://nations-emergentes.org/wp-content/uploads/2019/02/egypt-pharmaceutical-survey.pdf

The World Bank for Egypt's Economic Update. (2020). *Impact of Covid-19 on Egypt's Economy*. https://www.worldbank.org/en/country/egypt/publication/economic-update-october-2020

Thompson, D. D., & Anderson, R. (2021). The COVID-19 response: Considerations for future humanitarian supply chain and logistics management research. *Journal of Humanitarian Logistics and Supply Chain Management, 11*(2), 157–175. doi:10.1108/JHLSCM-01-2021-0006

World Health Organization. (2020). *Impact of Coronavirus disease (COVID-19) on pharmaceutical sector*. https://www.who.int/emergencies/diseases/novel-coronavirus-2019

Chapter 6
Effect of COVID-19 on the Freight Forwarding Industry in Egypt:
An Empirical Study on Agility Egypt

Rawan Hisham El Haddad
Arab Academy for Science, Technology, and Maritime Transport, Egypt

Sara Hassan El-Gazzar
Arab Academy for Science, Technology, and Maritime Transport, Egypt

May Salah El-Dine Mohamed
Arab Academy for Science, Technology, and Maritime Transport, Egypt

Bojan Rosi
University of Maribor, Slovenia

EXECUTIVE SUMMARY

The freight forwarding industry is an important player in the maritime transport industry that facilitates shipping processes by providing various value-added services such as securing bookings, transporting cargo, and preparing shipping documents. However, due to COVID-19 outbreak, the freight forwarding industry faced many challenges like port congestion, container shortages, and blank sailings. Therefore, this study examines COVID-19 effect on the freight forwarding industry and the challenges that the freight forwarders faced especially in Egypt, which is a logistics hub due to its strategic location. The case provides researchers and practitioners with an overview of the challenges that affected both maritime transport and freight forwarding industries in Egypt and investigates the challenges that Agility Egypt encountered due to COVID-19 restrictive safety measures. Also, it presents the solutions undertaken to deal with those challenges. Data were collected through interviews with various operation managers, executives, and specialists in Agility Egypt for shipping and freight.

DOI: 10.4018/978-1-6684-4686-7.ch006

INTRODUCTION

According to the United Nations Conference on Trade and Development (UNCTAD), the maritime transport industry is considered the heart of global trade (UNCTAD, 2017) since it handles about 90% of total international trade volume (Phuong Vu et al., 2020) transported at competitive prices (UNCTAD, 2017). It plays a significant role in delivering all resources efficiently and effectively especially critical ones such as medical and food supplies to cover rising global market demands through the support of the freight forwarding industry (Asariotis et al., 2020). Maritime industry parties need the assistance of the freight forwarding industry to arrange shipments and transport huge freight volumes globally (Caliskan & Ozturkoglu, 2016). The freight forwarding industry is an important player in the maritime transport industry in terms of shipping cargo despite any obstacles (Stojanović & Velickovic, 2019).

According to Shang & Lu (2012) in Christopher & Fredrick (2019), the freight forwarding industry is a customer-intensive service sector that connects buyers and sellers as well as creates economic value through the effective delivery of goods. It assists in delivering safe, cost-effective, and environmentally friendly activities, as stated by the International Federation of Freight Forwarders Association (FIATA) through flexible coordination of value-added logistics services (Stojanović & Velickovic, 2019). Freight forwarders provide resources, technologies, and entrance to global markets, which significantly affect countries' economic activity (Kherbash & Mocan, 2015). They provide high-quality services and flexible, customised solutions to meet customers' demands to be able to survive fierce market competition (Caliskan & Ozturkoglu, 2016).

As acknowledged by the FIATA, forwarders act on behalf of their customers to provide main logistics activities such as handling, distribution, consolidation, de-consolidation, and customs clearance (FIATA, 2021). Also, they assist in securing vessel bookings, issuing bills of lading, freight invoices, arrival and delay notices of shipments, and other shipping documents as well as supporting logistics activities such as inventory management, packaging, packing, and warehousing (Caliskan & Ozturkoglu, 2016). Other activities added by Subhashini & Preetha (2018) are labelling goods and updating customers with shipping regulations.

As providers of logistics services, freight forwarders support trade processes in many countries such as Egypt, which is developing into one of the key trade nations as the government aims to transform it into a production and distribution hub for the Middle East and Africa as well as Europe. Egypt is a major freight hub and is responsible for arranging international shipping services where the Egyptian freight forwarders are concerned with coordinating shipping procedures, issuing shipping documents, packing and freight delivery reliably and safely (Samir, 2022). Freight forwarders in Egypt organize and handle all shipping procedures for their customers since shipping process requires multiple documents and approvals which are difficult for the involved parties to complete without the assistance of a freight forwarder because of lacking the necessary expertise and knowledge to finalise the documents and to arrange the shipping process (Moneim, 2021). Egypt's strategic location between global trade routes makes it a global logistics center and a gateway to the African continent (Samir, 2022). Egypt's unique geographical location at the crossroads of global trade between Europe, the Middle East, Africa, and Asia allows it to strategically link international trade flow through Mediterranean and Red Sea ports (Elzarka, 2019). Especially since the Suez Canal connects the Mediterranean and the Red Sea in north-eastern Egypt, allowing ships to transit between Europe and Asia (Moneim, 2021).

However, the coronavirus (COVID-19) pandemic in first quarter of 2020 disrupted the economic growth across the country, especially in Egypt's freight forwarding industry as well as the global supply chain and trade process (CEIC, 2020). The Egyptian freight forwarding industry faced several difficulties, including port congestion, lack of containers, and blank sailings due to COVID-19 (CEIC, 2020). The uncertainty of the ocean freight and transportation sector was rising because of decreased manufacturing and low demand for raw materials and commodities (Mordor intelligence, 2022). Also, decreased cargo volumes and trade across the Egyptian seaports were due to the strict containment restrictions enforced by governments throughout the world and the precautionary measures undertaken to limit the impact of the COVID-19 outbreak (Mordor intelligence, 2022). UNCTAD reported that Egypt's container port throughput had faced a reduction from 6,306,865.638 twenty equivalent unit (TEU) in December 2019 to 5,928,454.000 TEU in December 2020 (CEIC, 2020).

Such disruptions had an impact on the freight forwarding industry as it plays an important role in shipping and trade processes. Therefore, this study examines the COVID-19 effect on maritime transport and freight forwarding industries to provide researchers and practitioners with an overview of the challenges faced in both industries. It follows an interpretivism research philosophy and uses an inductive research approach as qualitative data is collected through semi-structured interviews based on observations, human perceptions, and interpretations of several shipping and freight operators from the freight forwarding industry.

Further, this study uses Agility Egypt for shipping and freight as a case study to formulate this research. It assesses the difficulties that Agility Egypt faced because of COVID-19's severe global safety regulations based on the collected data from semi-structured interviews with operation managers, seniors, and executives at Agility Egypt. Also, it investigates the challenges that Agility Egypt faced in providing value-added services such as pricing shipments, securing bookings, transporting containers, preparing shipping documents, getting containers onboard, tracking and tracing, and releasing containers. Finally, it presents the solutions and digital tools that Agility Egypt used to mitigate those challenges and satisfy its customers.

COVID-19 EFFECT ON MARITIME TRANSPORT

The maritime transport industry was globally affected by the pandemic due to social restrictions, lockdowns, safety measures and regulations taken by the authorities and the governments to contain the dynamic spread of the virus (UNCTAD, 2020). Especially that COVID-19 cases were first reported in China, which is recognised as a logistics hub for the ten busiest container ports worldwide, such as the Port of Shanghai, Port of Shenzhen, Port of Guangzhou, and Port of Ningbo-Zhoushan and many others (Menon, 2021). As per the American Chamber of Commerce in Egypt, the pandemic outbreak coincided as well with the Chinese Lunar New Year, when the factories in all the Chinese cities were closed for the holidays, which caused a significant drop in the number of vessels calling at the seaports as well as fluctuations of supply due to halt of production and lower demand of Chinese products because the importing countries were afraid of being infected from the coronavirus (AmCham Egypt, 2020).

Moreover, the decrease of merchandise trade in the United States in the first half of 2020 and the slowdown of manufacturing in China forced the shipping lines to cancel about a thousand voyages and consolidate their shipping routes on the main ports only (USITC, 2020). Seaports around the world started to notice fewer cargo volumes which caused freight rates to fall dramatically because of lower transported volumes and reduced demand due to COVID-19 restrictions and lockdowns of countries (AmCham Egypt, 2020). As the coronavirus rapidly spread across the countries, the demand for freight shipping declined globally, leading to a rise in blank sailings in vessels' schedules where the shipping lines cancelled some planned port stops or entire vessel itineraries, which negatively affected all the parties of the maritime transport industry (AmCham Egypt, 2020). The ocean carriers consolidated their shipping routes to only major seaports in the first half of 2020 (USITC, 2020). The three main ocean carrier alliances in the industry are THE Alliance (Hapag-LIoyd, Ocean Network Express (ONE), Hyundai Merchant Marine (HMM) and Yang Ming), 2M Alliance (Mediterranean Shipping Company (MSC) and Maersk line), and Ocean Alliance (China Cosco Shipping, Orient Overseas Container Line (OOCL), CMA-CGM, and Evergreen) cancelled almost 1,000 voyages in the first six months of 2020 that were mostly scheduled sailings between Asia and North America and between Asia and Europe (USITC, 2020). The surge in the number of blank sailings in the first half of 2020 reached about 221 blank sailings globally in February 2020 and 263 approximately in May 2020 (Statista, 2022).

Although the maritime transport industry's situation slightly improved after the Chinese holidays and the resumption of the production of the Chinese factories, the exported volumes from China remained low and the deliveries were slow because of some Chinese ports' closure, especially since the freight rates were still not generating profits (AmCham Egypt, 2020). According to the International Finance Corporation report, total container volumes handled of ocean freight at Chinese ports fell by 10.1 percent in the first months of 2020, affecting both significant exporters such as Brazil, China, India, and Mexico and importers such as European Union (Logfret, 2021). Also, Covid-related port closures caused delays and queues at terminals worldwide, resulting in port congestions of thousands of containers for days or weeks (Merwe, 2021). Such case happened at Port of Ningbo-Zhushan in China where it had been closed several times due to Covid-19 outbreaks (Merwe, 2021).

Furthermore, COVID-19 affected Chinese ports where by April 11, 2022, bulkers were waiting in Shanghai as per Bloomberg data records, resulting in a 15% increase from the prior month due to a lack of port personnel, which delayed delivery of shipping documents required to discharge cargo and shortage of truckers (Varley & Koh, 2022). Therefore, ship owners and traders rapidly rerouted vessels to other ports around the country to avoid delays and trucker shortages (Varley & Koh, 2022). This resulted in heavy congestion in other ports like Rizhao, Dongjiakou, and Qingdao, encountering an increase of 33%, up to 121 vessels awaiting at those ports (Varley & Koh, 2022). Additionally, the combined anchorage of Shanghai and Ningbo had 197 container ships either loading or waiting to load, an increase of 17% from March (Varley & Koh, 2022). As for Tianjin where transportation services haven't been as negatively disrupted, 54 ships were waiting on April 11, a 29% increase in a month (Varley & Koh, 2022).

However, before the holidays and COVID-19 crisis, China had already exported huge volumes of cargo to both the European Union and the United States, which resulted in tremendous trade imbalances and the stacking of the empty containers in both European and North American seaports because of the lockdown measures taken to prevent COVID-19 from spreading across the world (Merwe, 2021). Later, when China's exports increased remarkably in July 2020, European and North American ports gathered massive numbers of containers which caused a global container shortage issue in the maritime transport industry as well as severe port congestions at both Europe and the United States, especially that the shipping lines did not send the empty containers back to China (Merwe, 2021). It was explained that the misallocation of containers caused the severe situation of global container shortage (USITC, 2020).

By mid-2020, customers' demands and the countries' economic activity significantly increased, resulting in a boom in merchandise trade but creating capacity shortages in the maritime transport industry (USITC, 2020). Also, container shipping freight rates increased remarkably especially from Northeast Asia while the container shortages situation remained the same (USITC, 2020). Even though the shipping lines operated at almost full capacity by the fourth quarter of 2020, the container supply was still inadequate to cover the global rising demand (USITC, 2020).

Furthermore, the effect of the lockdown situation that happened in China at the beginning of March 2020, due to COVID-19 started to reflect and have an impact on Egypt since China was reported as Egypt's top importing market in 2020 (UN Comtrade, 2021). The COVID-19 outbreak had the most direct and immediate impact on Egypt's maritime transport industry (USITC, 2020). This is because the country relies on international trade flows, which have been severely harmed by the prolonged pandemic situation (Omran, 2020). However, curfew exemptions have been permitted by the Egyptian government for the transportation of food and other vital commodities required to serve manufacturers, distributors, wholesalers, and retailers. (Omran, 2020). As authorised by Vice Admiral Kamel Elwazir, the Minister of Transport of Egypt, all transportation processes, including maritime transport in Egypt, shall continue to proceed despite the COVID-19 pandemic and operators in the field like freight forwarders can operate freely to deliver cargo worldwide while following the safety measures strictly set by the official responsible authorities to contain the virus and to avoid infections (EIFFA, 2020).

As per Tarek Fahmy, the CEO of Mediterranean Shipping Co. Egypt (MSC), Egypt's maritime transport industry faced many challenges as the cargo volumes imported from the Chinese ports to the Egyptian ports decreased for several weeks, the lockdown imposed on Italy which is one of Egypt's top export markets caused the rerouting of freight to other countries like Germany, Spain, Austria, and other European countries, India's lockdown on March 25 in 2020 for more than a month led to imbalances of supply in Egypt's maritime transport industry since India utilises the services of the ports in Egypt on its shipping routes to Europe and the United States, and the decrease of Egypt's shipping market capacity because of the multiple blank sailings schedules and that also affected the balance sheets of shipping lines operating in Egypt (AmCham Egypt, 2020). Marwan El Sammak, Chairman and CEO of Ship & Crew Egypt added that the negative fluctuations in supply and demand in terms of the drastic decrease in the cargo volumes loaded on vessels have increased the cost per unit, which in turn changed the cost structures of shipping lines (AmCham Egypt, 2020).

Although, the East Port Said terminal in Port of Port Said in Egypt was shut down completely, Egyptian port authorities avoided full closure of seaports by strictly setting precautionary and virus-containment procedures, stringent inspections, and disinfection procedures as well as limiting the operations at all the ports such as at West Port Said terminal at Port of Port Said, while the Ports of Alexandria only accepted vessels for cargo discharging, and the Port of Damietta only accepted container ships (AmCham Egypt, 2020). Egypt's situation improved during Egypt's agricultural export season and when Wuhan city in China removed its seventy-seven-day lockdown from January 23 to April 8 in 2020 resulting in increased shipping operations but with significant operational issues, shortages in labour, and port congestions (AmCham Egypt, 2020).

All those challenges in the maritime transport industry caused freight forwarders to struggle in securing bookings, handling shipments, operating, competing in markets, and satisfying customers due to the limited capacity of operating vessels, unavailability of schedules due to blank sailings, container shortages, abandoned cargo, and ports and terminals congestions (FIATA, 2021).

COVID-19 EFFECT ON THE FREIGHT FORWARDING INDUSTRY

As stated by the British International Freight Association (BIFA) director general Robert Keen, the Covid-19 world crisis shed light on the importance of the role of freight forwarders in supporting the shipping industry by delivering freight globally by providing various logistics services (Keen, 2020). The freight forwarders are considered trade architects as they have an essential role in facilitating freight transportation and shipping processes despite the complex situations and challenges faced in the global trade environment and the related trade laws and regulations (FIATA, 2021). Moreover, COVID-19 demonstrated the significant role of freight forwarders as they act as a major intermediary between all modes of transport and a connection medium for all the parties involved to ensure successful freight delivery, allowing the freight forwarders to be an integral part of any supply chain in all the sectors (FIATA, 2021).

Nevertheless, the COVID-19 situation and safety measures taken by the authorities caused plenty of complicated challenges to the freight forwarding industry, which affected the delivery as well as the quality of the freight forwarding industry services provided to the customers; COVID-19 had a significant impact on the global freight forwarding sector (Mazareanu, 2021a). The pandemic has put shippers, freight forwarders, and other logistics service providers in an unusual position in the shipping market (Clover, 2021). As reported by FIATA, ocean freight shipping faced complex challenges such as container imbalances, blank sailings, abandoned cargo and ports and terminals congestion that severely affected the shipping process flow as well as the performance of the freight forwarding industry in terms of services delivery to its customers (FIATA, 2021).

Moreover, the freight forwarding industry had to cope with those dynamic market changes due to the pandemic crisis by utilising its resources and investing in digital technologies to adapt to the drastic changes that occurred to all its supply chain stakeholders and to find optimal solutions to balance trade-offs such as cost, quality, and revenue to manage supply chain risks and ensure business continuity (SHIPA, 2022). The pandemic showed the urgency to shift to digitalization where all processes had to be coordinated online using technological solutions depending vastly on IT infrastructure, networking, and communication to keep all parties connected and business secured. Therefore, this study examines the challenges caused by COVID-19 on the freight forwarding industry in Egypt and how Agility Egypt dealt with such complications using digital tools and technologies.

AGILITY BACKGROUND

One of the most important freight forwarding companies in the freight forwarding industry is Agility Global Integrated Logistics (GIL) as according to Mazareanu (2021), it ranked the 15th among the world's top ocean freight forwarders ranking in 2020 based on ocean freight TEU handled (in thousands). In terms of infrastructure, innovation, and supply chain services, Agility is a world leader (Agility, 2022b). The company runs multiple businesses and long-term investments (Agility, 2022a). They invest in the technology and innovation that are altering the future and provide the supply chain expertise that connects companies to international markets (Agility, 2022b). The study focuses on the case of Agility, specifically its branch in Egypt named Agility Egypt for shipping and freight to present the challenges faced due to the COVID-19 crisis and how that impacted Agility Egypt's performance in the Egyptian freight forwarding industry as well as how it adapted to the crisis and managed to operate and to survive in the fierce market situation along with the complexity of the challenges faced.

The rise of emerging markets in the global economy ignited Agility's journey at the year 1979. The company began as a local warehouse provider in Kuwait and has grown since then to be a popular huge logistics company in the Middle East (Goodfirms, 2022). It invested in entities around the world by acquiring more than forty logistics brands some of which had been operating since the mid-1800s; Agility Global Integrated Logistics (GIL) has become one of the world's top integrated logistics providers as well as the Middle East and North Africa's largest private owner and developer of industrial real estate (Goodfirms, 2022). Agility GIL is one of the Middle East, Africa, and Asia's major private owners and developers of warehouse and light industrial parks (Agility, 2022a). In the world's quickest developing markets, Agility's subsidiary firms provide airport services, e-commerce enablement, customs digitization, remote infrastructure services, fuel logistics, and commercial real estate and facilities management (Agility, 2022a).

Agility Egypt for shipping and freight plays a significant role in the Egyptian market and is a market leader in freight forwarding services as well as in contract logistics, and customs clearance (Agility, 2022a). It has four facilities in Egypt and offers online cargo tracking for land, air, and sea freight shipments as well as handles time-sensitive cargo professionally and with great care and sense of urgency to gain customers' satisfaction as well as reliability in managing the complicated laws related to the freight forwarding industry (Agility, 2022a). Also, Agility Egypt provides customs clearance services to all its customers based on their request at all Egyptian ports and at dedicated branches with more than twenty brokers and outsourced organizations. These customs brokerage teams develop standard operating procedures and service level agreements (SLAs) for their customers, obtain clearance at bonded warehouses, dry ports, and free zones, and lead market research in customs processes. Agility Egypt provides extensive logistics services such as Air Freight, Ocean Freight, Road Freight, Warehousing & Distribution, Customs Clearance, Project Logistics, Chemical Logistics and Fairs & Events Logistics (Agility, 2022a). Agility Egypt also supported the Egyptian government by handling, managing, and coordinating projects such as the Gosoor project in 2019 for the Egyptian ministry of the public business sector (ZAID, 2020). For Ocean freight services, Agility Egypt manages to comply with all transportation documentation whether import or export, import licenses requirements, regulations, country-specific compliance, local requirements, and customs clearance to smoothly transfer and dispatch freight to its destination as per customers' requirements (Agility, 2022a).

COVID-19 CHALLENGES

The effect of COVID-19 is presented in this section by analysing the challenges faced by Agility Egypt for shipping and freight in coordinating and handling shipments and how such challenges affected its performance based on the conducted semi-structured interviews with Agility Egypt operation managers, seniors, and executives.

Securing Bookings

The unreliable sailing schedules of shipping lines put great pressure on the freight forwarding industry to satisfy customers as securing bookings was no longer easy with shipping market changes and COVID-19 protective safety procedures and restrictive measures. The issue started when shipping lines scheduled blank sailings, which limited the available vessels' timings and routings, which in turn complicated the booking processes. Agility Egypt's operators faced difficulty in finding cargo spaces on available vessels to secure bookings for its customers especially since most vessels were fully booked due to the high demand and the peak season of freight shipping worldwide as well as the limitations in the capacity of vessels due to the cancelled voyages by ocean carriers.

Agility Egypt's operators were striving to continue their freight forwarding operations despite the blank sailings. However, the challenges got extremely complicated as securing bookings from shipping lines was not possible for weeks due to container shortages which complicated the freight forwarding process even further. Container shortages were another challenge because of the worldwide lockdowns due to COVID-19 rapid infection spread and port congestions globally. High container shortages were mostly in the 40ft standard height container referred to as (40 DC), and the 40ft high cube container referred to as (40 HQ). This was one of the global issues that severely affected the shipping and freight forwarding industries. Agility Egypt was significantly affected by those circumstances as its operators faced difficulties in securing bookings and delivering cargo to planned destinations since the empty containers were not available, especially for Agility's customers that were importing cargo from the far east like China, Hong Kong, Taiwan, Singapore, Thailand, Vietnam, and Malaysia. Seaports in Asia were facing high container shortages, which affected the booking process and securing spaces on vessels.

Also, Agility Egypt faced difficulties with its global offices in securing bookings due to temporary closures of some offices, such as Agility Italy, Agility Germany, Agility Morocco, and Agility Saudi Arabia, due to lockdowns and strict governmental restrictions in some countries, which led to a shortage in staff due to rotational shifts and working from home strategies. All the above-mentioned challenges pressured Agility's operators in Egypt with plenty of tasks and obstacles to satisfy customers by securing bookings and handling shipments.

Transporting Containers by Other Modes

After securing bookings, Agility operators used to coordinate normally with trucking agents to withdraw empty containers and to arrange the stuffing procedures by transporting those withdrawn empty containers to the shipper's premises, like the factory's warehouse then transporting them back to the seaport to be loaded on board before the agreed cut-off date of the vessel's departure. However, Agility Egypt was exposed to various obstacles in the delivery of containers to and from seaports because of multiple constraints set by the Egyptian authorities in response to COVID-19 protection measures, such as limited working hours of Egyptian ports' operations resulting in time limitations of the process of withdrawing empty containers and transportation limitations by roads due to strict curfew timings as well as labour shortages of port operators and truck drivers.

Operators at Agility Egypt struggled to coordinate with all the parties involved in the shipping process as shippers, truckers, and customers to catch the vessels not to miss the secured spaces booked, to avoid any extra trucking fees incurred due to delays or waiting times of drivers at ports, and to deliver cargo to its customers the soonest to ensure their satisfaction and loyalty. Nevertheless, extra trucking fees were incurred for many shipments, so Agility Egypt had to pay the required fees to the trucking agents, causing losses on some of its handled shipments. Also, some vessels were missed, which caused shipments to be postponed and led to customers' dissatisfaction.

Preparing Shipping Documents

An integral part of freight forwarding services is the preparation and issuance of shipping documents of the cargo on behalf of its customers like Certificate of Origin (CO), EUR1 certificate issued when cargo is imported from Europe, Bills of lading like seaway bill, packing lists, commercial invoices, insurance certificates and so forth depending on the country that the cargo is imported from or exported to.

However, because of COVID-19 restrictions in Egypt like partial lockdowns, quarantine periods, and curfew hours in addition to preventative measures like working from home and rotating shifts of employees, Agility Egypt faced delays and inconveniences in preparation and issuance of shipping documents regarding getting official stamped documents and authorised signatures from the responsible authorities like Chamber of Commerce and Embassies of the countries that cargo is being exported to or receiving Original official shipping documents from abroad by courier to finalise customs clearance processes and release the imported cargo to Egypt. Such a situation was faced by Agility Egypt when it was exporting cargo to Iraq on behalf of one of its customers, but the Embassy of Iraq in Egypt was closed, which caused a major issue and a delay in certifying the shipping documents and proceeding with the delivery process. In addition to not being able to receive original shipping documents in the hard copy sent by courier from some global Agility offices to Agility Egypt due to temporary closure because of lockdown restrictions and shortage of operators.

Getting Containers Onboard

Since sailing schedules were unreliable due to COVID-19 outbreak, one of the issues that extremely challenged freight forwarders were the sudden notifications sent by the shipping lines to the forwarding operators informing them that the already secured bookings were altered. The reasons behind that change were either vessel rollover, vessel delay, or Port omitting situations which happened even after securing the booking and transporting the containers to the port already. Consequently, the freight forwarders were placed in a very critical situation.

Agility Egypt encountered such issues with many shipments. One of which was when handling an ocean import shipment from Italy to Egypt where the booking was secured, and the containers were already transported to the Port of Genoa before the vessel's cut-off date to be shipped to the Port of Alexandria. Nevertheless, Agility Egypt was notified by the shipping line on the vessel's departure date that the sailing schedule has changed due to a Port omitting situation where the vessel was no longer calling at Port of Genoa and so the booking was to be rolled over to the first available vessel. Moreover, the operators were informed by the shipping line that the booking was postponed to the next vessel's departure date which was after two weeks. Agility Egypt was left with an obstacle to deliver cargo as planned and an enraged dissatisfied customer as shipment was urgent and had to be quickly delivered to avoid supply chain disruptions.

Releasing Containers

Agility Egypt experienced a cut-and-run situation in one of its imported shipments from the Port of Hamburg in Germany to the Port of Alexandria in Egypt where the shipment contained two containers 20-foot (20 DC) and 40-foot (40 HC) cargo containers. However, when the vessel arrived at the Port of Alexandria in Egypt, it only discharged the 40 HC container then continued sailing up to the Port of

Damietta. Afterwards, the vessel returned to the Port of Alexandria after a week and discharged the 20 DC container.

The vessel's cut-and-run situation caused various complications, such as that the customer could not release the 40 HC container from the shipping line upon its arrival since both containers were shipped together on the same bill of lading (sea waybill), and so waiting the 20 DC container to return was a must for the customer to receive the cargo. Another hurdle was that the port authorities charged the shipping line with both storage and demurrage fees for the 40 HC container that stayed on the container yard inside the port premises which forced the customer to pay the accumulated charges for the whole week of delay to the shipping line to be able to release the cargo. Agility Egypt was neither able to get the 20 DC container earlier from Port of Damietta nor was it able to stop the port authorities from charging the fees. The customer was annoyed by the complexity of the situation and unsatisfied with the delay of the shipment and the extra costs incurred.

Tracking and Tracing Containers

Agility Egypt faced an issue as the shipping lines' websites were not always updated with accurate timings of vessels' departure and arrival due to technical issues that made Agility Egypt and its customers dissatisfied and confused.

Pricing Shipments

Fluctuations in freight rates and surcharges of the shipping market created a great challenge to Agility (GIL) regarding pricing shipments to customers and generating profits. Agility's tender agreements with its global customers, restricted annual fixed prices for shipments from and to certain origins and destinations. Thus, Agility Egypt was severely affected due to the surge in freight rates that decreased its revenues, significantly reduced its profit margins, and, even worse, some handled shipments were causing losses.

Another issue that affected pricing shipments was that requesting quotations for freight shipping and receiving freight contract rates from shipping lines was difficult as there were high fluctuations in freight rates as well as container shortages. On the other hand, Spot rates were advised by the shipping lines for the freight forwarders to secure bookings instantly. However, since each spot rate lasted only for twenty-four hours, Agility Egypt and its customers were pressured to take immediate decisions.

AGILITY EGYPT SOLUTIONS

This section tackles the solutions that Agility Egypt undertook to deal with the challenges explained above in detail, which were encountered due to COVID-19's global impact. This part covers the issues of securing bookings, transporting containers by other modes, preparing shipping documents, getting containers onboard, releasing containers, tracking containers, and pricing shipments based on the data collected from the semi-structured interviews that were conducted with Agility Egypt's managers and operators.

Securing Bookings Solutions

Agility Egypt urged its pricing and sales teams to provide multiple quotations of freight rates from different shipping lines for each shipment to its operational teams to ease finding available cargo spaces on vessels, to solve securing bookings challenge by avoiding blank sailings and container shortages of some shipping lines as well as to quicken the process to satisfy customers.

Furthermore, the freight forwarding industry started depending more on digital tools, especially since shipping lines converted their manual operational systems such as container booking, freight quotations, demurrage calculations, and issuance of documents such as freight invoices and bills of lading to digital platforms to exploit the benefits of digitalization (Zeng et al., 2020 in Balci, 2021). This helped Agility Egypt during the period of lockdowns and the temporarily closure of multiple Agility global offices in some countries, where operators managed to continue their business online by depending on digital tools and technologies to handle shipments and to coordinate with Agility teams smoothly.

Transporting Containers by Other Modes Solutions

Rerouting shipments using alternative modes of transport such as rail and road to transport cargo from one seaport to another was one of the solutions that Agility Egypt depended on to ship cargo based on shipping lines' space availability on vessels and suitable possible sailing schedules to deliver shipments to its customers on time and to avoid challenges such as blank sailings, port omitting, or congestions. Agility Egypt flexibly rerouted some of its shipments in coordination with shipping lines and trucking agents to ship the cargo to its customers without delays or inconveniences. For example, Agility Egypt assisted in shipping cargo from the Port of Rizhao in China to the Port of El-Adabiya in Egypt, then transported the cargo by trucks to Alexandria in Egypt.

Another case that Agility Egypt faced was related to extra trucking fees incurred when transporting containers to and from ports due to the strict transportation limitations of roads which Agility handled by charging the fees to customers' invoices upon agreement or paying part of it with its customers to avoid handling shipments on loss basis and customers' dissatisfaction.

Finally, some shipments were transferred to Agility Egypt's air team to be quickly delivered to customers by air instead of the ocean in case of urgent cargo deliveries according to the requirements of customers to avoid delays due to issues like blank sailings, port congestions and container shortages in ocean shipping.

Preparing Shipping Documents Solutions

Agility Egypt mitigated the challenges related to the issuance and the preparation of the shipping documents by relying on using Express or Telex release bills of lading (sea waybill) to quicken the shipping processes and releasing of cargo. For example, Agility Egypt used that approach when exporting on behalf of its customers to Saudi Arabia and needed official shipping documents to finalize customs clearance procedures and deliver shipments to customers successfully. The situation was solved when the involved parties and the responsible authorities allowed usage of scanned copies until the arrival of official original shipping documents were sent by couriers such as Aramex and DHL from and to Agility offices worldwide or outsourced agencies to save time and quicken the release of shipment.

Another challenging situation was due to the closure of the Embassy of Iraq; where Agility Egypt overcame that issue by coordinating with Agility Bahrain to send the shipping documents to them by courier for certifying the documents from the Embassy of Iraq in Bahrain. Agility Bahrain then sent the official shipping documents stamped and signed back to Agility Egypt to proceed with the shipment and deliver it to Iraq smoothly without any drawbacks.

Getting Containers Onboard Solutions

Agility Egypt's operators had to calm down enraged customers due to the change of sailing schedule because of port omitting as well as push shipping lines to revert with the updated booking on the first available vessel to deliver cargo to customers as soon as possible. Agility Egypt had to coordinate with Agility Italy and the shipping line to rollover to the next vessel immediately to avoid further delays. However, since the first available vessel's departure date was after two weeks and the shipment was urgent to the customer, Agility Egypt managed to transfer the shipment to another port in Italy through road transport by coordinating with a trucking agent to catch an earlier vessel as per the routing schedule of the shipping line. The customer was satisfied as the cargo reached the planned time to Egypt with no delays, and the customer's supply chain was not interrupted. Agility Egypt handled the situation through a customised solution that satisfied its customer by communicating directly with shipping line operators.

Releasing Containers Solutions

Agility Egypt with its strong connections and long-term relationship with one of the shipping lines was able to get approval to refund the full amount paid by the customer for the storage and the demurrage fees of the 40 HC container that stayed in Port of Alexandria due to the cut and run situation that occurred. Although the cut and run of a vessel is out of Agility Egypt's control, they are considered responsible for the shipment on behalf of the customer. As per the operators and managers at Agility Egypt, all their resources and connections with the related parties in the maritime transport industry are being used for the best interest of their customers.

Tracking and Tracing Containers Solutions

Directly contacting operators in shipping lines through phone or email instead of only depending on data on websites was the solution undertaken by Agility Egypt operators to get accurate data to update their customers and avoid errors.

Pricing Shipments Solutions

Pricing shipments was very challenging due to the high freight rates in markets due to container shortages and vessel space limitations, but Agility Egypt managed to handle and continue business with its customers. Operators of Agility Egypt quickly coordinated with their customers to secure bookings under a spot rates basis to catch spaces on vessels and ship cargo with best prices. Also, any extra surcharges or differences in freight rates charged by shipping lines after shipment arrival were charged to customers' freight invoices upon agreement to avoid handling shipments on a loss basis.

AGILITY DIGITALIZATION

Agility Global Integrated Logistics (GIL) invested in digital technologies like Blockchain and IOT to handle and track shipments (Kewalram, 2020a). Essa Al-Saleh, the former CEO of GIL, discussed that exploiting those technologies decrease costs, maximise operational efficiency, eliminates paperwork, reduces errors, shortens transit and clearance times, and allows real-time visibility and integration of data about shipments onto a secure platform that is available to all stakeholders (Agility, 2018).

Due to the COVID-19 outbreak, Agility Egypt depended more on digital solutions and invested to improve its operations and to survive the complex market situation. Digitalization's booming allowed it to participate in online tenders to win freight forwarding contracts and secure global business opportunities. It created and depended on many in-house ERP systems such as Control, Focis, Transfora, and Shipa freight. The usage of those digital applications by Agility Egypt kept all its shipments and customers' data organised and secured.

Agility exploits digitalization to automate its services and improves its performance in the freight forwarding industry, where it uses **Control** which is an essential digital tool for operators of Agility Egypt to update shipments' data as cargo receipt, vessels' departure and arrival dates, and cargo release and delivery dates to customers. As for **Focis,** it is used by Agility Egypt's operators to scan and upload shipping documents on it such as Bills of lading, EUR1, Certificates of Origin, Commercial invoices, packing lists and other related documents. Operators use **Transfora** to contact Quality or IT teams to report any operational issues faced or ask for assistance as well as submit sick leaves and holidays and receive permissions, salary reports and performance appraisals from HR teams. Lastly, **Shipa freight** is a digital system for freight forwarding services that notifies Agility's operators with customers' requests for freight quotations and offers a complete digital end-to-end experience to customers as it allows online booking processes, provides online freight quotations instantly to customers and real-time tracking of shipments, in addition to automatic issuance of invoices and payment process' facilitation.

Further, Agility Egypt reached an agreement with its global customers like ABB and General Electric (GE) to use a unified system for sharing shipments' details, such as updates of shipments' departures and arrivals, to avoid any confusion, save time, and increase operational efficiency. Also, Agility Egypt coordinated with the shipping lines through emails and phone calls for tracking and tracing containers to get accurate data and to avoid any hassles or sudden technical issues of shipping lines' websites while updating its customers. In addition to online payments and bank transfers that became possible either for paying the agreed freight rates to the shipping lines upon shipments' arrival or at customs clearance premises to release shipments which allowed eased processes and quickened shipping-related transactions. Agility Egypt relied greatly on online payments and bank transfer processes to save time and facilitate procedures to increase its customers' satisfaction.

Moreover, shipping documents were digitised and shared online to secure and organise data for easier coordination and management of shipments details with Agility teams especially during working from home and rotational shifts due to social distancing preventative measures and strict safety procedures taken in response to the COVID-19 pandemic by the responsible authorities. Agility Egypt depended on digital applications like Google Drive, Microsoft Office's word documents, and excel sheets for saving and organising data and Outlook application for receiving and sending emails. This reduced the usage of hard papers for documentation and archiving processes, which saved resources and time and helped Agility Egypt's operators to work from home and on rotational shifts to stay safe from COVID-19 infections. Other digital applications used by Agility Egypt were Zoom and Microsoft teams videoconferencing for conducting online meetings with its customers and coordinating shipments with Agility offices worldwide. As discussed by Biju Kewalram, chief digital officer, the usage of digitalization increased productivity and enhanced interaction and collaboration between team members (Kewalram, 2020b).

Currently, after COVID-19, the freight forwarding industry is depending greatly on digital technologies and tools as digitalization helps freight forwarders to facilitate communication and to provide status updates on each shipment promptly to their customers. It also helps save time and increase the operational efficiency of operators by eliminating paperwork by creating, uploading, and sharing all documents online for stakeholders to access them easily. Freight forwarders will keep investing in digital technologies and tools, especially regarding financial transactions and exchanging shipping documents, as it is a necessity for the forwarding industry's future to ensure continued business and success in global markets. For the case of Agility, it was acquired by global freight forwarder DSV to create a further integration of digital solutions and tools to increase the value and widen the scope of their freight forwarding services offered to the customers.

Finally, the above sections clearly showed that Covid-19 significantly impacted the freight forwarding industry's ability to deliver services such as securing bookings, transporting containers, preparing shipping documents, loading, releasing containers, tracking containers, and pricing shipments. Although several challenges hampered the shipping and delivery of cargo to customers due to the Covid-19 outbreak, including port congestions, cut-and-run situations, rollovers, blank sailings, and delays in the vessels, Agility Egypt responded to the crisis with a variety of strategies and solutions. Most cases were solved by relying on digital tools, alternate plans for rerouting shipments, and the exploitation of multiple modes of transportation. The use of digitalization in the freight forwarding industry greatly helped operators solve most challenges and enhanced the performance of the freight forwarding industry in satisfying customers.

Further, Agility Egypt managed the continuation and success of the business by mainly being concerned by satisfying its customers and maintaining strong long-term relationships with them. Also, it focused on investing in training the operators to build skills like problem-solving, decision making, creative thinking, crisis management, and working remotely as a team to be more innovative in providing customised solutions to handle shipments in the best interest of the customer.

RECOMMENDATIONS

Further suggestions that were collected from the semi-structured interviews regarding the actions that Agility Egypt could have implemented to deal better with the challenges faced during COVID-19 are summarised below.

- Using the services of trucking agents that use GPS technology in the trucks for Agility Egypt's operators to be able to track shipments, provide real-time updates to its customers, and ensure that the incurred extra trucking fees claimed by truck drivers are charged correctly.
- Implementing authorised electronic signatures for the responsible Agility Egypt's employees to sign and deliver surrender letters electronically to customers after online payment and for Agility employees to be able to work from home fully instead of working on a rotational shifts basis.
- Training and empowering Agility Egypt's operators to deal with sudden situations or crises through creating multiple contingency plans and taking efficient re-routing decisions when needed.

- Investing more in building strong relationships with shipping lines by communicating and networking

REFERENCES

Agility. (2018). *Agility is First Forwarder to Work with Maersk IBM on Blockchain Solution*. Agility. https://www.agility.com/en/agility-first-forwarder-work-maersk-ibm-blockchain-solution/

Agility. (2022a). *About Us*. Agility Logistics. https://www.agility.com/en/about-agility-3pl-company/

Agility. (2022b). *Supply Chain Services and Innovation*. Agility. https://www.agility.com/en/

AmCham Egypt. (2020). *COVID-19 Impacts on Egypt's Transportation Sector*. AmCham Egypt. https://www.amcham.org.eg/information-resources/covid-19-response/covid-19-impacts-on-egypts-transportation-sector

Asariotis, W. J. R., Assaf, M., Ayala, G., Ayoub, A., Benamara, H., Chantrel, D., Hoffmann, J., Larouche-Maltais, A., Premti, A., Rodríguez, L., Sun, S., Youssef, F., Abbas, H., Bradford, G., Cariou, P., Crowe, T., Davidson, N., Manuel, J., Orejas, D., … Verhoeven, P. (2020). *Review of Maritime Transport 2020*. Academic Press.

Balci, G. (2021). Digitalization in container shipping: Do perception and satisfaction regarding digital products in a non-technology industry affect overall customer loyalty? *Technological Forecasting and Social Change*, *172*, 121016. doi:10.1016/j.techfore.2021.121016

Caliskan, A., & Ozturkoglu, Y. (2016). Maritime logistics. In Handbook of Research on Military, Aeronautical, and Maritime Logistics and Operations (pp. 361–384). IGI Global. doi:10.4018/978-1-4666-9779-9.ch019

CEIC. (2020). *Egypt Container Port Throughput, 2008 – 2022*. CEIC Data. https://www.ceicdata.com/en/indicator/egypt/container-port-throughput

Christopher, D., & Fredrick, K. (2019). *Investigative analysis of CRM system implementation and the challenges attached to its integration into the existing ERP system From an organization perspective: A case study of a Freight Forwarding Company in Sweden*. Academic Press.

Clover, M. (2021). *The Future Of Freight Forwarding In A Post-Covid World Survey*. Bolloré Logistics.

EIFFA. (2020). https://www.eiffa.com/april-2020/

Elzarka, S. (2019). *A study on logistics risk assessment: The case of container shipping in Egypt*. Research Gate. https://www.researchgate.net/publication/354423556_A_STUDY_ON_LOGISTICS_RISK_ASSESSMENT_THE_CASE_OF_CONTAINER_SHIPPING_IN_EGYPT

FIATA. (2021). *International Federation of Freight Forwarders Associations (FIATA) Digitalization and logistics resilience: lessons learned from COVID-19 and challenges ahead.* FIATA.

GoodFirms. (2022). *Agility Reviews & Profile.* GoodFirms. https://www.goodfirms.co/company/agility

Keen, R. (2020). *Covid-19 crisis emphasises the key role of freight forwarders, says logistics association.* BIFA. https://bifa.org/news/articles/2020/mar/covid-19-crisis-emphasises-the-key-role-of-freight-forwarders-says-logistics-association

Kewalram, B. (2020a). *Data-Driven Decision Making and How to Get There.* Agility Logistics. https://www.agility.com/en/blog/data-driven-decision-making-and-how-to-get-there/

Kewalram, B. (2020b). *Part 1: A Conversation with the Chief Digital Officer.* Agility. https://www.agility.com/en/a-conversation-with-biju-kewalram-chief-digital-officer-of-agility-gil-part-one/

Kherbash, O., & Mocan, M. L. (2015). A Review of Logistics and Transport Sector as a Factor of Globalization. *Procedia Economics and Finance, 27*, 42–47. doi:10.1016/S2212-5671(15)00969-7

Logfret. (2021). *How is technology changing the future of freight forwarders?* Logfret. https://logfret.com/how-is-technology-changing-the-future-of-freight-forwarders/

Mazareanu, E. (2021b, April 6). *Logistics - Leading ocean freight forwarders worldwide 2020.* Statista. https://www.statista.com/statistics/254936/leading-ocean-freight-forwarders-worldwide-based-on-market-share/

Mazareanu. (2021a). *COVID-19 impact on the global freight forwarding market.* Statista. https://www.statista.com/statistics/1115277/year-on-year-change-freight-forwarding-market-worldwide/

Menon, A. (2021). *10 Major Ports in China.* https://www.marineinsight.com/know-more/10-major-ports-in-china/

Moneim, D. (2021). *Egypt aims to be logistics hub for global trade flow: ETA head.* https://english.ahram.org.eg/NewsContent/3/12/413251/Business/Economy/Egypt-aims-to-be-logistics-hub-for-global-trade-fl.aspx

Mordor Intelligence. (2022). *Egypt Freight and Logistics Market Size, Share, Trends (2022 - 27).* https://www.mordorintelligence.com/industry-reports/egypt-freight-logistics-market-study

Omran, H. (2020). *Egypt's maritime, air freight sectors hit by COVID-19: AmCham.* Daily News Egypt. https://dailynewsegypt.com/2020/04/29/egypts-maritime-air-freight-sectors-hit-by-covid-19-amcham/

Phuong Vu, T., Grant, D. B., & Menachof, D. A. (2020). Exploring logistics service quality in Hai Phong, Vietnam. *The Asian Journal of Shipping and Logistics*, *36*(2), 54–64. doi:10.1016/j.ajsl.2019.12.001

Samir, N. (2022). *Egypt acts as hub for global trade routes: South Korean Ambassador.* Daily News Egypt. https://dailynewsegypt.com/2022/05/31/egypt-acts-as-hub-for-global-trade-routes-south-korean-ambassador/

SHIPA. (2022). *About Us*. https://www.shipafreight.com/about-us/

Statista. (2022). *Blank and skipped sailings worldwide*. Statista. https://www.statista.com/statistics/1223853/blank-and-skipped-sailings-worldwide/

Stojanović, D. M., & Velickovic, M. (2019). *Freight forwarding industry-The contemporary role and development trends in Serbia*. https://www.researchgate.net/publication/340446983

Subhashini, S., & Preetha, S. (2018). An empirical analysis of service quality factors pertaining to ocean freight forwarding services. *Maritime Business Review*, *3*(3), 276–289. doi:10.1108/MABR-01-2018-0004

UN Comtrade. (2021). *Egypt | Imports and Exports | World | ALL COMMODITIES | Value (US$) and Value Growth, YoY (%) | 2009 - 2020*. https://trendeconomy.com/data/h2/Egypt/TOTAL

UNCTAD. (2020). *COVID-19 and maritime transport: Impact and responses*. UNCTAD.

UNCTAD. (2017). *Review of Maritime Transport*. https://unctad.org/system/files/official-document/rmt2017_en.pdf

USITC. (2020). *The Impact of the COVID-19 Pandemic on Freight Transportation Services and U.S. Merchandise Imports*. https://www.usitc.gov/research_and_analysis/tradeshifts/2020/special_topic.html

van der Merwe, B. (2021). *How Covid created shipping's container shortage*. Investment Monitor. https://www.investmentmonitor.ai/analysis/covid-global-shipping-container-shortage

Varley, K., & Koh, A. (2022). *Supply-Chain: China Port Congestion Worsens as 477 Bulk Ships Waiting to Berth*. https://www.bloomberg.com/news/articles/2022-04-11/477-bulk-ships-wait-off-east-china-s-ports-amid-virus-lockdowns

Zaid, M. A. (2020). *Kuwait's Agility signs contract to operate Egypt's Gosoor Project.* Arab News. https://www.arabnews.com/node/1780871/business-economy

KEY TERMS AND DEFINITIONS

Blank Sailings: Blank sailing, also known as void sailing, is when a shipping line or carrier chooses to skip a certain port or an entire trip on a planned sailing route.

Cut and Run: When a vessel decides to cut and run, it abruptly transports its cargo to a different port than intended, requiring subsequent travels to be arranged from the new site, which can result in weeks of delays in expected delivery timeframes. Ships may only dump a portion of their cargo before 'cutting and running' to their next destination to avoid losing berthing slots elsewhere.

Demurrage: Demurrage is a cost levied by a carrier on a consignee if rented containers are not cleared at the port or terminal and returned to the carrier's designated location. Typically, the consignee is provided with laytime (free time). The consignee must clear and return the container within this period. Otherwise, he will be charged a fee for exceeding his time at the port. Demurrage is the charge that the merchant pays for the use of the container within the terminal after the free time has expired.

Detention: After a ship has been emptied, a consignee has a certain amount of time to unload his products from a container and then return the container to the shipping firm. If the free time allotted expires and the container is not returned, the consignee will be charged a detention cost. A detention fee is a cost paid by a shipper for holding on to a container after leaving the port/terminal to load or unload the container for an extended period. Detention is the fee paid by the merchant for using the container outside of the port or depot after the free time has expired.

Port Congestions: The containers are piled high in the port's yard, waiting to be collected and transported to their destination.

Port Omitting: Port omitting is a change in the shipping line's routing of the vessel in which the vessel bypasses a specific port calling and thus the secured booking is delayed to the following vessel.

Securing Bookings: Declaring the exact date of the vessel's departure and the projected date of the vessel's arrival, as well as declaring the availability of spaces and an unbroken seaworthy container for shipment.

Storage: Storage is a fee paid to the port authority by a shipping line if their container stays in the port or terminal after the allowable laytime to clear them. Simply explained, storage is a fee charged for each container that is not transported from the storage space/terminal when it is ready to be loaded onto a truck or a vessel.

Vessel Roll Over: If reported congestion levels are excessively high, ships may avoid a scheduled port entirely.

Chapter 7
Investigating the Impact of COVID-19 on the Oil and Gas Supply Chain in the Middle East:
A Case Study of Egypt

Amr Ekram
Arab Academy for Science, Technology, and Maritime Transport, Egypt

Sara El-Gazzar
Arab Academy for Science, Technology, and Maritime Transport, Egypt

Hebatallah El Mesmary
Arab Academy for Science, Technology, and Maritime Transport, Egypt

EXECUTIVE SUMMARY

The oil and gas supply chain (OGSC) significantly impacts numerous operations in multiple industries. However, lately, it encountered myriad disruptions like global oil supply and demand mismatch due to COVID-19. Therefore, the case studies the oil and gas supply chain in Egypt during COVID-19 as Egypt is Africa's largest oil exporter outside of the Organization of Petroleum Exporting Countries (OPEC) and the continent's third-largest natural gas exporter, and its economy is heavily reliant on the oil industry. The unique organizational structure that makes up the OGSC in Egypt is fully controlled by the Egyptian Ministry of Petroleum, which deals with all the disruptions that occur in the Egyptian petroleum sector differently. The case investigates the disruptions that OGSC faced in Egypt due to the pandemic and provides researchers with an understanding of the challenges in the sector and the proposed solutions by the sector in Egypt, in addition to the recommendations provided by experts in the sector.

INTRODUCTION

The oil and gas industry is one of the key industries in the energy market that significantly impacts the

DOI: 10.4018/978-1-6684-4686-7.ch007

global economy as the world's primary fuel source. Oil and gas production and distribution processes and chains are very complicated, capital-intensive, and need advanced technology. OGSC has different characteristics from the regularly known supply chain. The oil and gas sector is to an extent distinguished with some features from other sectors in terms of its supply chain. These are some distinctive features of OGSC: long product life cycle, non-perishable products, less unsteady demand, static product mix, methods of valid transport are limited, inventory is mutually interchangeable, discontinuous supply chain, bulk inventory that is process-based, reversed production flow, legal and environmental regulations, inflexible assets, cost-effective transportation (Wan Ahmad et al., 2016). The oil and gas supply chain (OGSC) has more obstacles, uncertainties, and hazards than any other industry, particularly in the supply chain management area. Supply chain disruption is one of the most critical problems in OGSC. (Queiroz et al., 2020). Therefore, it is important to investigate and thoroughly understand the disruptions that disturb the streamlined flow of the oil and gas supply chain and how the oil and gas businesses are dealing with these disruptions through supply chain strategies. Lately, Oil and gas supply chains encountered a myriad of disruptions including operational instability, political upheavals, lack of organizational support, poor route selection, and a pandemic that adversely affect the streaming of oil and gas supply chain activities (Sakib et al., 2021).

EFFECT OF COVID-19 ON THE OIL AND GAS INDUSTRY GLOBALLY

The oil and gas industry has faced a two-pronged crisis: the oil price war between Russia and Saudi Arabia and the impact of COVID-19 that caused a dramatic drop in worldwide demand. The oil price war occurred when "Organization of Petroleum Exporting Countries" (OPEC) and Russia failed to reach an agreement on output cutbacks, which was reached in an attempt to stabilize sliding prices. To stabilize sliding prices, OPEC, and its partners (OPEC+) decided to reduce its combined output by 9.7 million barrels per day in May and June from the agreed baseline (OPEC, 2020). The arrangement comes at a time when the global crude oil market has cruder than it can utilize or potentially store. Moreover, as a result of the industrial slowdowns and the travel restrictions set due to the COVID-19 crisis, the global oil supply, and demand mismatch was developing in tandem with the reduced demand for chemicals and refined products (Abegunde, 2020).

The viral COVID-19 pandemic was first reported in December 2019 in Wuhan City, Hubei Province, People's Republic of China (WHO, 2020). Covid-19 had already spread beyond China's borders by the beginning of 2020. It was declared a public health emergency of worldwide concern by the World Health Organization on the 30th of January 2020, and a global pandemic on the 11th of March 2020 (WHO, 2020). The virus eventually spread to a reported all nations and territories throughout the world. COVID-19 has caused widespread disruption in all economic sectors and businesses throughout the world. Lockdown procedures are executed throughout the world as a health policy to reduce the impact of the pandemic's spread because of the disruptions (El Baz & Ruel, 2021).

The pandemic has put pressure on the international oil sector in a multitude of ways. Oil prices plunged during the onset of the pandemic due to a dramatic drop in worldwide demand, particularly due to the effect of COVID-19 on the economy of key crude users: the EU, China, and the US. Consequently, on Sunday, the 12th of April 2020, the 10th (Extraordinary) OPEC and non-OPEC Ministerial Meeting was conducted via videoconference (OPEC, 2020). All the countries that took part in the event agreed to adjust their entire crude oil production by 9.7 million barrels per day beginning the 1st of May

2020, for two months ending the 30th of June 2020. The entire adjustment agreed upon over the next six-month period, from the 1st of July 2020 to the 31st of December 2020, will be 7.7 mb/d. It will be followed by a 5.8 mb/d adjustment for 16 months, from the 1st of January 2021 until the 30th of April 2022 (OPEC, 2020; WEF, 2021).

On the demand side, containment measures for the COVID-19 pandemic, as well as economic disruptions have caused a global halt in output and transportation, resulting in a significant drop in global oil demand. The major factor contributing to the decline in demand was the huge drop in demand from China as authorities stopped industrial facilities as part of their attempts to restrict the virus's spread (WEF, 2021). According to the International Energy Agency's (IEA) February Oil Market Report, China's oil demand presently accounts for 14% of world demand (IEA, 2021).

The transportation sector accounts for most of the oil demand after industry usage. For OECD member nations, nearly half of the demand comes from road transportation, 8% from aviation, 14% from petrochemicals, and 9% from the residential, commercial, and agricultural sectors. Approximately 15% is derived from various industrial activities (Jefferson, 2020).

On the supply side, the members of the OPEC+ alliance failed to renew their agreement to limit production just as the worldwide effect of the COVID-19 problem was becoming obvious in March 2020, resulting in certain producers, notably Saudi Arabia and Russia, momentarily flooding the market. With oil demand starting to dwindle as lockdowns took effect, OPEC+ ultimately agreed to limit output on the 12th of April 2020. The accord, which required decreasing these nations' aggregate daily output by over a fifth for the following two months, was the greatest reduction in the producer cartel's history (OECD, 2020b).

To compensate for weaker demand, global oil output has been reduced by 2%, from 101.89 million barrels per day in November 2019 to 99.96 million barrels per day in February 2020. Global oil investments have also plummeted; more than 21 international oil firms have planned 20–50 percent capital reductions by 2020 (IEA, 2021).

Brent crude oil fell below $20 per barrel, the lowest level since the 1991 Gulf War. Brent crude prices have roughly an average of 63 dollars per barrel before the pandemic (Stevens, 2020).

EFFECT OF COVID-19 ON THE OIL AND GAS INDUSTRY IN THE MENA REGION

According to the Organization for Economic Cooperation and Development, lower oil prices have immediately impacted the fortunes of producing economies in the Middle East and North Africa. Oil and gas revenues in production countries such as Iraq, Algeria, and Oman might plummet by up to 80% by 2020 (OECD, 2020a). In Saudi Arabia, oil income plummeted by 24% year on year in the first quarter (Arabia, 2020). In the first quarter, non-oil revenue fell by roughly 17% (Blunt et al., 2020). The government responded to the income decrease by asking government departments to cut their expenditures by 20-30%, but this did not occur quickly enough to balance the revenue decline, and the quarterly budget slid into a deficit equivalent to roughly USD 9 billion (OECD, 2020a).

The American Chamber of Commerce in Egypt reported that locally, the impact of the COVID-19 pandemic on the oil industry has varied depending on the importance of the sector economically for a country and whether the country was a net exporter or importer of oil. Lower prices are favorable for oil-importing countries but negative for oil-exporting countries in the Middle East and North Africa (MENA) (AmCham, 2020a). Multiplying the difference between production and consumption (net oil export) as a share of GDP by the percentage point change in the oil price is a straightforward technique to get an idea of the extent of the real income effect of an oil price shift. For example, if oil prices remain 48 percent below their 2019 levels, Kuwait, whose net oil exports contribute for 43 percent of GDP, would see a 20 percent drop in real income, while importer Morocco would see an increase in real income equivalent to 3% of the gross domestic production (Ashraf et al., 2020). On the other hand, lower oil prices harm both importers and exporters in the Middle East and North Africa (MENA), with exporters suffering directly and importers suffering indirectly from reduced foreign direct investment, remittances, tourism, and exporter grants (Arezki & Nguyen Ha, 2020). Since Egypt is one of the most important countries in the MENA region in terms of the oil and gas industry, the study will focus on the disruptions that affected the oil and gas industry, specifically the COVID-19 pandemic in Egypt.

THE EGYPTIAN OIL AND GAS SECTOR

According to the U.S. Energy Information Administration (2018), since 1974, Egypt has relied heavily on four external demand-driven sectors: tourism, labor remittances, the Suez Canal, and the oil sector, leaving the country exposed to disruptions (Mabrouk, 2020). According to the International Trade Administration 2020, oil and gas are two of Egypt's most dynamic businesses, and petroleum production has been the country's largest industrial activity, accounting for approximately 13.6 percent of the GDP in 2018 (ITA, 2020). Egypt is Africa's largest oil exporter outside of the Organization of Petroleum Exporting Countries (OPEC) and the continent's third-largest natural gas exporter after Algeria and Nigeria. Egypt's operation of the Suez Canal and the Suez-Mediterranean (SUMED) Pipeline plays a critical role in worldwide energy markets. Oil and liquefied natural gas (LNG) shipments moving northbound from the Persian Gulf to Europe and North America, as well as shipments traveling southward from North Africa and nations bordering the Mediterranean Sea to Asia, are using the Suez Canal. The Egyptian government earns a large amount of money from the fees collected at these two transit hubs (US EIA, 2018).

The Egyptian economy is heavily reliant on the oil and gas industry. In 2019, the Egyptian petroleum sector contributed roughly 11% of GDP, with exploration activities accounting for about half of it (AbdelMaksoud et al., 2021). The petroleum sector attracts most of the foreign direct investment (FDI) in Egypt, accounting for 74.3 percent of total FDI inflows (above $10 billion) in 2018/2019, in addition to transferring technology from international oil companies (IOCs), which led to the establishment of national oil companies (NOC) in the 1970s. Therefore, Egypt's economy has traditionally relied on capital-intensive industries such as oil and mineral extraction (Mabrouk, 2020).

Egypt's consumption is rising in tandem with its oil output. Egypt is Africa's greatest energy consumer, with an annual consumption of more than 4 trillion BTU. This is attributable, in part, to Egypt's unusually strong production and rapid population expansion. Despite a recent narrowing of the difference between crude oil exports and imports due to a strong rise in oil product exports, Egypt is regarded as a net importer of oil (AbdelMaksoud et al., 2021).

Despite recent oil and gas discoveries, Egypt cannot be called a significant oil exporter and remains a net importer of oil and gases, as Egypt didn't achieve self-sufficiency from refined oil products. This explains why Egypt's economy has seen both good and bad impacts as a result of the COVID-19 outbreak. As an exporter of natural gas, Egypt loses directly, and as an importer, it suffers indirectly as a result of lower foreign direct investments (IEA, 2021).

An international supply disruption caused by the "oil price war" between Saudi Arabia and Russia had a beneficial influence on the Egyptian oil sector at the start of 2020 (Mabrouk, 2020).

Oil transported through the SUMED pipelines increased by 33% at the start of 2020 compared to the same period in 2019, amounting to 1.1 million bbl./day in January 2020. Concurrently, Egypt's oil imports fell significantly, despite a 23 percent increase in the volume of oil imports compared to December 2019. During the same time. With only a minor decline in production, both oil production and exports remained unchanged (AbdelMaksoud et al., 2021).

According to the Central Agency for Public Mobilization and Statistics in Egypt, oil consumption fell in March 2020 in comparison to March 2019 by 9% due to lower industrial activity levels. Later in April, oil imports decreased by 37.3 percent. Although, it was increasing slowly in March 2020 and reached the highest level since 2017, 318.5 bbl./day.

Despite falling oil prices, the industry's inability to store or refine bigger amounts of imported oil was to blame for the decline in imports. By May 2020, though, there was enough storage room to resume oil imports, albeit at a slower rate of 260 000 barrels per day. Egyptian oil exports also saw ups and downs at the same time. Exports reached their lowest point in March 2020, but they quickly recovered. Between March and May, they increased by 62 percent, and between May and July, they increased by 35.5 percent (Capmas, 2020). A new subsidy package approved by the Egyptian parliament decreased oil subsidies by 47% from 2019 levels. In May 2020, oil flow through the SUMED pipelines decreased by 42% to 1.2 million barrels per day as a result of the OPEC deal to reduce global oil output. Following that, production fell by 57 percent (to 0.5 million bbl/day) by July 2020 (AbdelMaksoud et al., 2021).

The Egyptian economy has overall benefited from lower oil prices, resulting in an estimated decrease in the overall trade imbalance. The price of imported oil has decreased as a result of the drop in oil prices. From 12.1 billion dollars in the fiscal year 2018/2019 to almost 6 billion in the following year, the price of oil imports decreased. As a result, Egypt's overall trade deficit has decreased. The public spending on petroleum products has reduced as a result of the decline in oil prices, which has also allowed for a reduction in the national budget deficit and the mobilization of funds for the economy to support both investments and social expenditures (AbdelMaksoud et al., 2021).

The drop in oil and gas prices is impacted by the profitability of upstream activity, the valuation of its assets, its ability to produce cash, and its investment plans (Repsol, 2020).

Another situation that faced Egypt was that the foreign direct investments in the exploration operations were on hold by the foreign investors and the tenders for utilizing concessions were postponed, which led to a loss of investment opportunities.

AN OVERVIEW OF THE ORGANIZATIONAL STRUCTURE OF THE OIL AND GAS SECTOR IN EGYPT:

According to Egypt's Ministry of Petroleum, the petroleum sector is overseen and managed by the following five state-owned organizations (SOEs):

- Egyptian General Petroleum Corporation (EGPC)
- Egyptian Natural Gas Holding Company (EGAS)
- Egyptian Petrochemicals Holding Company (ECHEM)
- Egyptian Mineral Resources Authority (EMRA)

- Ganoub El-Wadi Holding Company (Ganope)

EGPC is a state-owned enterprise linked to the Ministry of Petroleum.

Its primary objectives are to increase exploration efforts and hunt for further oil potentialities, increase oil production and reserve development, increase petroleum export profits, and implement worldwide HSE standards. Among the operating companies in the sector. 12 public sector entities, 41 joint venture companies, and 87 investment law firms are among the EGPC-connected organizations in whom EGPC is a shareholder with at least 51% of the shares, either directly or indirectly through other associated companies. The primary operations of these related firms include exploration, development, production, refining, processing, transportation, distribution, drilling, engineering, construction, fabrication, maintenance, and training (EGPC, 2021). ECHEM is in charge of the petrochemical industry. In contrast, EMRA is in charge of the country's mineral resources evaluation and geological mapping. Both EGPC and Ganope oversee upstream oil activity and are responsible for issuing upstream licensing. Ganope emphasizes southern activities, whilst EGPC focuses on the remainder of the country. EGAS oversees natural gas development, production, and marketing, as well as conducting international exploration bid rounds and granting natural gas exploration licenses. To develop and operate oil and natural gas resources, EGAS and EGPC collaborate with international corporations.

International oil companies (IOCs) play a significant role in Egypt's upstream oil sector, investing in producing assets in collaboration with EGPC. The biggest oil and gas companies operating in Egypt include BP, Eni, Royal Dutch Shell, and Apache. Except for marketing and storage activities, the downstream industry is state-controlled and lacks private investment, leaving EGPC and its subsidiaries as the sole participants (EGPC, 2021).

ANALYSIS OF THE MAIN DISRUPTIONS IN THE EGYPTIAN OGSC DURING PANDEMIC

At the start of the disruptions created by the pandemic, executives in the oil and gas sector were concerned about the situation, prompting queries like "How should labor safety be prioritized?" How can assets (such as oilfields, chemical plants, LNG platforms, and refineries) continue to operate in an environment where everyone feels threatened? How can we assess and mitigate supply chain risk, including cross-border risk? How can the sector attract more foreign direct investment? How can we ensure the long-term viability of existing and future revenue streams? (Abegunde, 2020).

Interviews had been conducted to provide access to a deeper level of understanding of the impact of COVID-19 on OGSC in Egypt and the challenges in the industry in the COVID-19 era. The interviews had been arranged with a variety of experts in different areas in the sector (such as project managers, laboratory managers, operation managers, and representatives of the general syndicate of engineers) representing multiple companies with different business scopes operating in the Egyptian oil and gas sector. Each interview was of a duration of an average of twelve minutes. The interviews revealed multiple challenges and disruptions to the OGSC and likewise, the counteraction procedures were taken by the ministry to mitigate the disruptions.

MAIN CHALLENGES FACED BY THE EGYPTIAN OIL AND GAS SECTOR DURING COVID-19

Labor

The reduction in oil prices and the global lockdowns appear to have had an impact on Egypt's oil production processes. Due to lockdown protocols that have made it difficult to get to production facilities, a decrease in the workforce brought on by the pandemic, and/or a cap on the number of hours that can be worked, national oil corporations have experienced a decline in the workflow (AbdelMaksoud et al., 2021). Also, due to quarantine procedures, a shortage of on-site employees caused delays and interruptions in supply and service delivery, as well as platform operations (Stewart et al., 2020).

The labor disruption can be elaborated as follows: directly because workers became sick as a result of COVID-19. All the workers who were infected or showed any symptoms that have been declared by the World Health Organization were quarantined, whether in their homes or the specialized hospitals, and indirectly as a result of travel restrictions, curfew, quarantine attempts, and workers remaining at home to care for sick family members or children. Also, the sector greatly depends on foreign experts who used to travel to and from Egypt but were restricted due to the pandemic's disruption of transportation. As moving personnel from and to sites was exceedingly difficult due to the disruptions that occurred to all transport modes, where travel disruptions, border closures, and supply chain disruptions caused delays in personnel rotations or supply delivery at remote sites (Arezki & Nguyen Ha, 2020).

A lot of units and machines in the sector are imported from outside; therefore, any maintenance work in case of failure is meant to be done by an agency from outside Egypt, which requires experts for travelling to Egypt to provide technical support, and due to the lockdown worldwide these experts couldn't travel which led to the stoppage of machines and so production disruption.

Another issue that was faced was that after establishing a new project and purchasing all the needed machines and units to operate, operations couldn't start due to the lockdown and the travel restrictions on foreign experts coming to Egypt to set the machines in place and test their operation in the facility. Due to this issue, various machine operations and new projects were on hold.

According to a specialized company in operations and maintenance in the Egyptian oil and gas sector, the company's most important asset is skilled labor. Due to the pandemic-related protective measures of reducing the workforce by up to fifty percent, there was a risk of not complying with the agreed levels of production.

Excess of Oil Supply

Normally, supply shortages are the main issue in supply chains, but on the other hand, excess supply represents an issue in any supply chain. Despite decreased oil costs, the sector was unable to refine or store greater amounts of imported oil, which led to a decrease in imports. However, storage space opened up in May 2020, which led to the return of oil imports—although at a lesser rate of 260 thousand barrels per day.

Shortage of Material Supply

The sector of oil and gas is heavily reliant on equipment, spare parts, chemicals, and lubricants that are imported from outside Egypt. The oil industry was directly impacted by the pandemic's effects on transportation. Due to disruptions in transportation and business in MENA countries, supply has been affected by a reduction in materials, capital, and intermediate resources. for example, the shipping sector was hugely disrupted due to limitations in spaces on vessels and shortages of equipment. Also, the lead time to release and clear the imported shipments from the seaports increased because of a reduction in labor, work rotation, lockdown, and changes in the working hours due to curfew and other protective measures taken by the Egyptian government for protection from the pandemic. All these factors have led to production disruptions in terms of produced quantities, causing an imbalance in supply and demand in the Egyptian market.

Communication

Communication is important to the success of businesses in all sectors, whether internally or externally. In the oil and gas sector, communication internally occurs between the same department or different departments of a company to manage the daily operations or to report updates, and communication occurs between the Ministry of Petroleum and the top management of the companies to strategically plan or to agree on decisions, as well as between companies in the sector to coordinate their work together. All this communication happens through live meetings. Due to COVID-19's social distancing procedures, there were plenty of constraints and challenges that hindered such meetings to be conducted effectively and efficiently, which posed a challenge for all the top management and decision-makers throughout the petroleum industry. Moreover, some of the laborers were not familiar enough with the technological platforms needed to solve the communication problem.

Another issue faced was the necessity of having an external witness to inspect the petroleum products to ensure that the specifications and standards declared are followed and by issuing a certificate to allow transport of the products from and to the facilities.

Additionally, the process of loading and unloading petroleum products in seaport terminals for exporting and importing petroleum products requires having an external representative from the company on board the ship for mandatory technical reasons like communicating some important readings (pressure, heat, flow rate, levels of inventory). However, due to the restrictions imposed by the vessels' management of not having any foreign personnel from the country onboard to avoid the infection of covid-19, there was a massive issue in figuring it out, and delays occurred as the parties could not reach an agreement and a suitable way of proceeding in loading and unloading processes.

Lack of Foreign Investments

The exploration and production activities in the Egyptian petroleum sector depend largely on foreign partners to pump investments that help in the exploration and production of oil. The exploration and production operations need a lot of investment to be conducted as it has high-end technology and high risk, which makes the existence of foreign investments and international oil companies necessary to run the operations. According to International Trade Administration 2020, the Egyptian government supports international oil corporations (IOCs) to invest in the petroleum sector. There are already more than fifty

IOCs working in Egypt (ITA, 2020). But the Covid-19 period and the collapse of the oil prices led to the collapse of the return on investment in the sector, which led to the decline of many international oil companies (IOCs) investing in Egypt. This caused the Ministry to postpone offering some concessions to auctions.

SOLUTIONS

Labor

To maintain production levels, Ministry of Petroleum and Mineral Resources (MPMR) facilities have decreased their workforces by rotating staff at field and production sites in shifts. All the sector workers have been exempted and excluded from the curfew procedures so that they can go to their work sites. Furthermore, on April 1, 2020, the ministry published a Local Emergency Response Plan (ERP) if COVID-19 is identified in any Egyptian oil and gas business. This ERP is to be implemented based on information provided by the WHO and Egypt's Ministry of Health. The goal of this ERP is for Egyptian oil and gas firms to coordinate and define clear methods for limiting the spread of the virus to keep personnel working in the sector and their families safe. To prevent the virus from spreading by establishing preventative measures and mitigating the impact if employees become infected with the virus to prevent future transmission. The ERP also contains a fatigue management plan in case of extended rotations for workers. In addition to all the procedures related to site preparedness and medical facilities, evacuation routes, and medical/ isolation/ testing requirements. Furthermore, the ministry reserved hotel rooms for most foreign experts and consultants supporting the sector's operations. Also, the companies dealt with maintenance and labor disruptions by conducting online meetings with the experts through the Zoom platform and following all the instructions to solve the issue.

According to the specialized company in operations and maintenance in Egypt, the company relied on overloading the engineers and labor to perform extra work on the different operating units. It was a successful practice due to the comprehensive and diverse training that the labor had had previously as a planned measure for such disruption in the workforce. The company was able to meet all the production levels agreed upon in the contract.

Excess of Oil Supply

On the 10th of June 2021, Petrojet, the EPC contractor (Engineering, Procurement, and Construction), and the executive arm of the petroleum sector was awarded a Guinness World Records certificate for constructing the world's largest floating roof tank in Ras Badran. The tank has been built with a capacity of 175,000 m3, equivalent to about 1.1 million barrels of crude oil; this is in addition to employing unprecedented techniques and methods, which are considered the first of their kind in the implementation of storage warehouses work worldwide (Guinnessworld, 2021).

According to the Ministry of Petroleum and Mineral Resources, there are around 24 gigantic strategic tanks that have been built and are currently undergoing final testing before actual operation and crude oil loading. The tanks are in the "Ajrud - Ras Badran - Ras Ghareb - Ras Shukair" areas. This project is part of a national plan to build 29 crude oil reservoirs across the country, each with a large storage capacity and trading facility, using innovative operational procedures, this project is aligned with the strategic vision of the ministry to improve the sector's infrastructure and turn Egypt into a regional hub for oil and gas commerce. The project will allow Egypt to store oil in the largest possible quantities.

Shortage of Material Supply

The strategy of the ministry to tackle this problem relied mainly on three pillars.

First, ***reallocation of the resources:*** since EGPC is a shareholder with at least 51% of the shares of any operating company in the sector, which enables the ministry to have visibility through each company's minimum and maximum (minimax) levels of stocks, such as (equipment, spare parts, chemicals, and lubricants). EGPC has the power and the authority to reallocate the resources of any stocks held by a company that has a surplus to cover any shortage that may face other operating companies which helps in optimizing the supply chain processes of the oil and gas sector in Egypt.

Second, the ***flexibility of sourcing:*** by importing needed raw materials for production from India, with accepted quality standards, not only from Europe, as the sector was mainly reliant on Europe in importing the raw materials, to cover the demand and to reduce the uncertainty and the risk of disruption. Furthermore, some companies relied on direct orders instead of tenders when sourcing their materials to avoid delays. In addition to creating agreements with various carriers to ship the needed raw materials, to create diversity and reduce risks of delays, space unavailability, and container shortages. Besides, the ministry directed all the companies in the sector to depend on local suppliers of lubricants, chemicals, and spare parts. Also, they helped the local supplier level up their production according to the sector's requirements.

Third, ***production management*** through instructing the refineries to produce specific quantities of some products to balance the market's supply and demand in Egypt. This requires continuous supervision and constant planning to overcome the rapid fluctuations and disruptions that occurred due to the pandemic.

Communication

The sector overcame the problem by activating all possible means of online communication that enabled all the sector's personnel and decision-makers to communicate and to support all the business functions to complete tasks. They also provided training for the employees to be familiar with and use the technology needed for communicating effectively. For example, by using online video conference platforms like Zoom or Microsoft teams without the need to physically meet as well as other media platforms such as emails and WhatsApp to communicate through it and to share the needed documents and certifications. The companies also bought all the licenses needed for these applications to run it safely inside the company and among the labor. Regarding the importing and exporting terminals issue, some companies started to adapt by providing their representatives with isolated suits and wireless devices and smartphones for communicating all the necessary readings.

Lack of Foreign Investments

To attract and facilitate more investments in the sector in Egypt the ministry has developed Egypt's upstream gateway EUG with a vision of optimizing the value of exploration and production by attracting global investment to the upstream sector to boost production. According to Egypt Upstream Gateway (EUG), EUG is a national data repository that went live in February 2021 and has since been a critical instrument for E&P data preservation, active data management, and upstream opportunity promotion through international bidding rounds. EUG was created to effectively handle the massive amounts of data generated by exploration and production activities, as well as to make selected information readily available and accessible. Users will also receive data of recognized quality in forms that have been agreed upon. Having EUG operational will improve petroleum exploration prospects and make bidding rounds easier by increasing the availability of high-quality data throughout the year. The EUG portal will digitally promote Egypt's oil and gas bid rounds (EUG, 2021). This project will positively impact investment in the field of research and exploration in Egypt and will maximize the chances of increasing it, attracting new international companies that have not worked in Egypt before and enhancing the investments of existing companies. The ministry worked on signing contracts with major international banks and financial institutions to ensure and hedge against the rise in the price of a barrel of oil, which will make these institutions commit to paying the value of the price increase if it exceeds a specific limit (EUG, 2021).

EXTRA MEASURES TAKEN BY THE MINISTRY TO MITIGATE THE COVID-19 DISRUPTION

In addition, some general measures were taken by the Egyptian government to resolve the problem, where they implemented quick investment policy solutions, gave specialized sectoral assistance, and promoted relocating production, particularly in free zones. They adopted fiscal and budgetary measures to relieve pressure on some industries and boosted contractual economic activities, as well as improved foreign investors, access to their local market (OECD, 2020). The Egyptian government's procedures to mitigate the impact of COVID-19 on the Oil and Gas sector: The government has reduced industrial natural gas costs to $4.50 per million British thermal units (BTUs),15 down from $5 to $6 per million BTUs previously;16 and the price of electricity for heavy and medium-sized businesses during peak and off-peak hours has been reduced to EGP 0.10 per kilowatt-hour, down from EGP 1.10.17 (AmCham, 2020b; Blunt et al., 2020). Due to travel constraints, the MPMR has built an online platform for overseas enterprises to compete in its gold exploration tender. The government has slashed rent costs on gold exploration regions by 80% to entice international firms. In the mining business, manufacturing lines have been in limited supply (OECD, 2020). Rescheduling maintenance to take advantage of lower demand and perform necessary repairs on the units.

Finally, the measures taken by the Egyptian government have had a positive impact on mitigating the disruption caused by the pandemic. According to EGPC's CEO, Abed Ezz El Regal, Low oil prices were used to accumulate reserves and keep corporate operations functioning despite pandemic-related obstacles. Despite COVID 19, a significant increase in revenue was realized when compared to the previous year. In addition, Egypt maintained positive GDP growth in 2019-20 and 2020-21 (IMF, 2021).

The latest new oil and gas discoveries in the country have provided plenty of opportunities for the production market. In the year 2021, Egypt's upstream firms made 52 discoveries in the Western Desert, the Mediterranean, the Gulf of Suez, Sinai, and the Eastern Desert, comprising 39 crude oil and 13 gas discoveries (EGPC, 2021). The value of crude oil, natural gas, petroleum products, and petrochemicals exports all surged in 2021, increasing Egypt's petroleum sector's export earnings by 84.3 percent to $12.9 billion. Egypt's natural and liquefied gas export earnings increased by more than fivefold to $3.9 billion. Crude oil shipments increased by 32% to $3.3 billion (Reuters, 2022).

RECOMMENDATIONS

The study presents a wide range of recommendations, as follows:

- All the companies in the sector should apply a strategy for training and rotation of employees between units and departments to make them ready to face any assigned task inside the company in case of any disruption, (capacity building training for the staff). Moreover, providing employees with training helps to improve their skills in using the communication technology needed in the sector. In addition to raising medical awareness among the employees as a precautionary measure.
- Organizations in the oil and gas sector execute export or import processes of petroleum material to conduct the communication protocol that includes sharing information regarding the needed requirements for loading and unloading processes before the Vessel's arrival. This will help the companies operating in the sector to be able to act quickly and save time as well as mitigate any risks or disruptions due to the lack of communication between the parties involved in the import and export process in the sector.
- Companies operating in the oil and gas sector follow a legally binding set of terms and conditions when buying a machine from any vendor. These terms and conditions state that when buying a new machine, instrument, unit, a full contract to be agreed on not only includes the warranty for fixing the machine in case of failure but also should include training of the personnel on both operations and maintenance of the machine, not only operating it. This will help to avoid full dependency on foreign technical experts from the vendor side, which may lead to disruptions in the supply chain flow.
- The decision-makers in the oil and gas sector should consider when making a new project to make them in complex form or integrated oil and gas companies instead of separate companies, which will help minimize transportation costs, employment costs, and time. It will also enhance the quality of the product due to less transportation it is exposed to. One of the opponents to the suggestion was the argument of the risk-sharing concept, which means in the petroleum complex, any environmental pollution or explosion, or serious technical problem will affect the whole complex.
- The Egyptian ministry of petroleum and mineral resources should annually gather all the related data of the purchased material for all the companies operating in Egypt in the oil and gas sector. Afterward, to sort and identify the most frequent items imported to these companies to propose a plan to construct and subside factories that supply these needed materials for the oil and gas sector companies. This will allow the sector to have the freedom to operate with minimum dependency on foreign imported materials such as valves, lubricants, and packaging.
- Implementation of a new system that connects and controls all the facilities and companies operating in Egypt's oil and gas sector. This will enable and ensure successful and efficient collaboration among these companies in terms of sharing information instantly about the stocks without the need for EGPC. Such direct communication and visibility among the different corporates in the sector will minimize many procedures and will help to apply effective reallocation of resources.
- The researcher recommends that the Ministry of Petroleum and Mineral Resources in Egypt create an external unit inside the EGPC to be responsible for all the laboratory measurements and analysis for all the Egyptian oil and gas sector companies. Outsourcing laboratory measurements and analysis services will help the companies save time and reduce procedures needed for the

transaction of delivery and receiving of petroleum products, which will allow a better streamlining of the supply chain flow.

REFERENCES

Abegunde, O. (2020). *Understanding the sector impact of COVID-19 Oil and Gas.* www.deloitte.com.ng

AmCham. (2020a). *COVID-19 Impacts on Egypt's Petroleum Sector.* AmCham Egypt. https://www.amcham.org.eg/information-resources/covid-19-response/impacts-of-covid-19-pandemic-on-egypts-petroleum-sector

AmCham. (2020b). *Impacts of COVID-19 Pandemic on Egypt's Petroleum Sector.* Author.

Arabia, S. (2020). *The Impact of COVID-19 on Natural Gas Markets.* Academic Press.

Ashraf, M., Caruso, P., & Pensado, P. G. G. (2020). *Reinventing the oil and gas industry: compounded disruption.* World Economic Forum. https://www.weforum.org/agenda/2020/09/reinventing-the-oil-and-gas-industry-compounded-disruption/

Blunt, R., Thomson, P., & Bory, O. (2020). *International: The Impact of COVID-19 on the Oil & Gas Industry.* Baker McKenzie InsightPlus. https://insightplus.bakermckenzie.com/bm/energy-mining-infrastructure_1/international-the-impact-of-covid-19-on-the-oil-gas-industry_2

Capmas. (2020). *Central Agency for Public Mobilization and Statistics.* https://www.capmas.gov.eg/

EGPC. (2021). http://www.egpc.com.eg/About_EGPC.aspx

El Baz, J., & Ruel, S. (2021). Can supply chain risk management practices mitigate the disruption impacts on supply chains' resilience and robustness? Evidence from an empirical survey in a COVID-19 outbreak era. *International Journal of Production Economics, 233.* doi:10.1016/j.ijpe.2020.107972

Guinness World. (2021). *Largest floating roof tank.* Guinness World Records. https://www.guinnessworldrecords.com/world-records/631865-largest-floating-roof-tank?fbclid=IwAR3In9XVH1YefZNsSWhHNQOiTU4og-4ZwP6Cmp9wCevLtHp-dye-mSywEkw

IEA. (2021). *Oil 2021.* International Energy Agency. www.iea.org

IMF. (2021). *Egypt: Overcoming the COVID Shock and Maintaining Growth.* https://www.imf.org/en/News/Articles/2021/07/14/na070621-egypt-overcoming-the-covid-shock-and-maintaining-growth

ITA. (2020). *Energy Resource Guide - Egypt - Oil and Gas.* https://www.trade.gov/energy-resource-guide-egypt-oil-and-gas

OECD. (2020a). *COVID-19 crisis response in MENA countries*. OECD. https://read.oecd-ilibrary.org/view/?ref=129_129919-4li7bq8asv&title=COVID-19-Crisis-Response-in-MENA-Countries&_ga=2.27386362.736981282.1637125248-1008574582.1623229278

OECD. (2020b). *The impact of Coronavirus (COVID-19) and the global oil price shock on the fiscal position of oil-exporting developing countries*. OECD. https://read.oecd-ilibrary.org/view/?ref=136_136801-aw9nps8afk&title=The-impact-of-Coronavirus-COVID-19-and-the-global-oil-price-shock-on-the-fiscal-position-of-oil-exporting-developing-countries&_ga=2.2246262.736981282.1637125248-1008574582.1623229278

OPEC. (2020). *OPEC: The 10th (Extraordinary) OPEC and non-OPEC Ministerial Meeting concludes*. https://www.opec.org/opec_web/en/press_room/5891.htm

Queiroz, M. M., Ivanov, D., Dolgui, A., & Fosso Wamba, S. (2020). Impacts of epidemic outbreaks on supply chains: mapping a research agenda amid the COVID-19 pandemic through a structured literature review. In Annals of Operations Research. Springer US. doi:10.100710479-020-03685-7

Reuters. (2022). *Egypt's 2021 petroleum exports revenue up 84.3% to $12.9 bln -minister*. Reuters. https://www.reuters.com/article/egypt-petroleum-exports-idUSS8N2SK06R

Stevens, P. (2020). *Oil plunges 24% for worst day since 1991 after OPEC deal failure sparks price war*. https://www.cnbc.com/2020/03/08/oil-plummets-30percent-as-opec-deal-failure-sparks-price-war-fears.html

Stewart, P., Broom, R., & Ahmed, N. (2020). *How Can the Oil and Gas Industry Prepare to Deal With the Impact of COVID-19?* https://www.eia.gov/beta/international/analysis_includes/countries_long/United_Arab_Emirates/uae.pdf

WEF. (2021). *The Global Risks Report 2021: 16th Edition*. https://www3.weforum.org/docs/WEF_The_Global_Risks_Report_2021.pdf

WHO. (2020). *Archived: WHO Timeline - COVID-19*. https://www.who.int/news/item/27-04-2020-who-timeline---covid-19

KEY TERMS AND DEFINITIONS

Brent Crude: Brent crude is the most traded oil benchmark, and it is defined as crude primarily drilled from North Sea oilfields. This oil is commonly used because it is sweet and light, making it simple to convert into diesel fuel and gasoline. This, combined with the relative simplicity of transporting it due to its production at sea, explains why it is so widely trafficked.

Concession: A government grant that allows a corporation to explore for and develop oil, gas, or mineral resources within a strictly specified geographic region, usually beneath government-owned lands or lands where the government holds the rights to produce oil, gas, or minerals. The grant is usually given to a corporation in exchange for a bonus, license fee, royalty, or production sharing supplied to the host government for a set period.

Downstream: The procedures involved in transforming oil and gas into final products are referred to as downstream operations. Refining crude oil into gasoline, natural gas liquids, diesel, and several other energy sources is one of them.

Integrated Oil and Gas Company or Petroleum Complex: In contrast to organizations that specialize in just one phase, an integrated oil, and gas company is a commercial entity that engages in the exploration, production, refining, and distribution of oil and gas.

LNG: Liquefied natural gas (LNG) is natural gas that has been transformed into a liquid state for ease and safety of transportation. Natural gas is cooled to around -260 degrees Fahrenheit, resulting in a transparent, colorless, and non-toxic liquid that may be transferred from locations with a substantial supply of natural gas to areas where there is a greater demand for natural gas. Natural gas takes up 1/600th of the space in its liquid condition, which means it is shrunk 600 times, making it considerably easier to ship and store when pipeline transport is not possible.

Oil and Gas Supply Chain: The oil and gas industry is supported by a global supply chain that comprises local and international transportation, trading, shipping, ordering, and inventory visibility and management. Material handling, import/export facilities, and the distribution of refined energy products from points of origin to market are other supply chain components. The supply chain is typically separated into three segments. The upstream division is responsible for the discovery and production of crude petroleum. The midstream section is in charge of energy commodity processing, storage, and transportation. In addition, the downstream category includes oil refineries, retail shops, and natural gas transportation firms.

OPEC: According to OPEC The Organization of the Petroleum Exporting Countries (OPEC) is a permanent, intergovernmental Organization, founded at the Baghdad Conference on September 10–14, 1960, by Iran, Iraq, Kuwait, Saudi Arabia, and Venezuela.

Upstream: Upstream refers to the stages of activities in the oil and gas industry that entail exploration and production.

Chapter 8
Investigating the Impact of the COVID-19 Pandemic on Supply Chain Performance:
A Case Study on Ghazala Steel Fabrication, Steel Industry

Gamal Haikal
Arab Academy for Science, Technology, and Maritime Transport, Egypt

Islam Abdelbary
https://orcid.org/0000-0003-1727-9071
Arab Academy for Science, Technology, and Maritime Transport, Egypt

Karim Soliman
https://orcid.org/0000-0002-9216-6360
Arab Academy for Science, Technology, and Maritime Transport, Egypt

EXECUTIVE SUMMARY

Organizations confront falling demand and, as a result, operational and financial restrictions during difficult economic times. The purpose of this case study is to examine the influence of COVID-19 on the SC of a steel fabrication manufacturer in Egypt, named Ghazala Steel Fabrication Company, as the massive dispersion of COVID-19 is seen as a global shock. Furthermore, the pandemic effects are being felt globally in various ways, including all SC operations, manufacturing costs, and logistical activities. The case study used primary data collection methods to investigate and analyze the impact of COVID-19 on SC performance on Ghazala's SC performance. Semi-structured interviews and site observations were used to analyze and discuss the impact of COVID-19 on the steel industry SCs and how it affected all relevant stakeholders.

DOI: 10.4018/978-1-6684-4686-7.ch008

INTRODUCTION

Businesses are more vulnerable to supply chain interruptions as globalization grows. Changes in the business environment throughout the whole supply chain can lead to unforeseen business situations like inaccurate demand estimates, faulty or broken products, and late deliveries, which can cause unpremeditated consequences and make the supply chain more vulnerable (Oh et al., 2020). Companies are looking for innovative approaches to improve supply chain management flexibility, efficiency, and reliability in light of globalization, market unpredictability, and intense competition, where supply chain management success needs companies to divert their focus from organizational improvement to the entire supply chain, which enables firms to concentrate on the entire supply chain (Duong et al., 2022).

Throughout recent years, the most challenging problem facing supply chains has been dealing with unplanned incidents. Unforeseen incidents like the COVID-19 epidemic have impeded global supply systems. Meanwhile, reprised lockdowns have triggered rushed purchases and substantial demand variations, resulting in significant paradigm shifts in how people shop, with millions of workers forced to stay home. Supply chain delays worldwide were caused by unanticipated supply and demand fluctuations and border restrictions. Moreover, the pandemic has impacted different aspects of the supply chain, including finances, time, demand, and performance (Chowdhury et al., 2021). The pandemic effects were felt globally; they affected operations, manufacturing costs, and logistical activities. In light of these wretched developments, supply chain managers were in a difficult situation to find ways to fix and ensure the sustainability of the business (Dodd & Yengin, 2021).

Previous studies have identified structural and operational recovery measures (e.g., additional inventory prepositioning) as significant measures to mitigate supply chain risks (Hosseini & Ivanov, 2019). Unlike instantaneous disasters, COVID-19 was a substantial disruption with an unpredictable time interval, damaging the supply chain ecosystem. Likewise, healing happens in a unique scenario where the disruption stays due to unpredictability. As a result, the pandemic dynamics could be viewed as a separate element that interacts with the supply chain ecosystem and simultaneously changes and influences all of the supply chain's capabilities and routine operations (Queiroz et al., 2020).

The objective of the case is to examine the impact of the COVID-19 pandemic on the steel fabrication industry, and the challenges companies face concerning supply chain disruptions. Specifically, the case focuses on GSF, a company that has implemented a zero-inventory policy, and how this policy has affected the company's ability to handle supply chain disruptions caused by the pandemic. Therefore, this study aims to present the challenges faced by companies in the steel fabrication industry due to the COVID-19 pandemic and the impact of zero-inventory policies on their ability to handle supply chain disruptions. It also highlights the importance of having contingency plans, diversifying the supplier base, and investing in technology and automation for supply chain management to mitigate the risks associated with supply chain disruptions.

The research's importance is based on providing valuable insights into the challenges faced by companies in the steel fabrication industry during the COVID-19 pandemic, which can help other companies in this industry prepare for and handle similar disruptions in the future. Additionally, the case highlights the importance of supply chain management in ensuring the continuity of business operations and the critical role of technology and automation in reducing costs and managing risks.

LITERATURE REVIEW

Supply chain discrepancies can significantly impact economic productivity and growth (Salvatore, 2020), which is why supply chain performance is critical. Moreover, supply chain management is often regarded as a critical asset for promoting customer satisfaction and enhancing a company's productivity and competitiveness (Hadrawi, 2019). It has many diverse parts that should all transpire to ensure that customers get their products on time and that businesses get the needed materials (Haffajee & Mello, 2020). Furthermore, supply chain management holds distinctive perspectives and objectives that must be achieved by properly managing the different supply chain processes (Panigrahi et al., 2018).

The dilemma facing supply chains is managing and reducing the risks inherent to any business situation. Nevertheless, building supply chain strategies in isolation is challenging since supply chains are directly influenced by other stakeholders in the supply chain (Chopra & Meindl, 2007; Ghadge et al., 2021). This is because diverse entities within the supply chain regularly pursue contradictory aims. For example, suppliers always want manufacturers to buy large fixed quantities, which contradicts cost optimization goals. Similarly, mass production for manufacturing firms contradicts the goal of inventory reduction for distribution centers (Tang, 2006). So, to achieve the goal of lowering inventory levels, transportation costs must increase, which will cause the total supply chain cost to rise (Kumar & Anbanandam, 2020; Crona & Parker, 2012).

Li et al. (2020) found that supply chain disruptions can significantly impact a company's operations and financial performance. The study suggests that companies should have a contingency plan to handle unexpected disruptions and proactively monitor market conditions to anticipate potential risks. Additionally, the study highlights the importance of investing in technology and automation for supply chain management to improve efficiency and reduce costs. Moreover, Zsidisin et al.,(2008) found that supplier relationships are essential for managing supply chain risks. The study suggests that companies should foster good supplier relationships by regularly reviewing contracts and investing in training and support. Additionally, the study highlights the importance of integrating suppliers into the company's enterprise resource planning (ERP) system to improve communication and collaboration. Furthermore, a study by (Zhang et al., 2019) found that companies can reduce the impact of supply chain disruptions by diversifying their product range and markets. The study suggests that companies should consider diversifying their product offerings and expanding into new markets to reduce dependence on a single product or market.

On the other hand, Lee et al. (2018) found that emerging technologies such as blockchain, artificial intelligence, and the Internet of Things can help companies improve supply chain transparency, traceability, and efficiency. The study suggests that companies should consider investing in these technologies to improve supply chain management and reduce risks.

The outbreak of the COVID-19 pandemic has caused server changes to the global economy. Some argue that we can track two economies before and post the pandemic global economy (Zhang et al., 2020) . Recessionary economic characteristics impact the capacity to function successfully. Luke, (2020) has introduced an unexplored area of supply chain adaptability, such as investigating supply chain operations and performance during severe circumstances (Rozhkov et al., 2022). Various performance measuring systems with distinct approaches and objectives have recently been established, including developments in risk mitigation, inventory planning, subcontracting capabilities, alternative supply, transportation capabilities, data-driven, real-time surveillance, and transparency systems have strengthened supply chain resistance (Ivanov & Das, 2020).

Likewise, the pandemic outbreak raised the importance of studying supply chain risk. This notion of risk may be summarized this way: the possibility of vulnerability to any uncertainty that could lead to a hazard can be defined as a risk (Jemaa, 2022). The goal of gaining an edge by profiting from risks that rivals cannot avoid has been shaded in some definitions (Cheese & Cheese, 2016) by certain positive qualities of risks (Kim et al., 2015). As the pandemic end is on-site due to the significant decline in weekly reported deaths since March 2020. The continuing effect of the supply chain disruptions shows that any disruptions have a long-term effect on economic growth and cause prolonged problems. On the other hand, supply chain drawbacks can considerably impact business productivity and competitiveness, and can considerably impact business productivity and competitiveness, which raises the supply chain performance significance (Salvatore, 2020).

The asset management efficiency characteristics indicate the capacity to maximize the use of the company's capital resources. In managing the supply chain asset, inventory reduction and insourcing vs. outsourcing are two of the most common approaches. Nonetheless, the goal of decreasing inventory levels necessitates a rise in transport costs, which, in turn, will result in a significant increase in the total cost of managing the supply chain operations (Crona & Parker, 2012). Just-in-time (JIT) or zero-inventory policies have been widely studied and acknowledged in materials planning models that have been effectively implemented in Japanese industrial circumstances. This is considered one of the variables contributing to the higher competitive advantage of Japanese manufacturing systems. One way that companies have tried to mitigate the risks associated with supply chain disruptions is through the implementation of zero-inventory policies. Zero-inventory policies aim to reduce operational costs by eliminating the need for warehousing and idle funds invested in inventory.

A study by (Zhang, et al., 2020) found that the COVID-19 pandemic has further highlighted the weaknesses of zero-inventory policies and the need for companies to have contingency plans to handle unexpected disruptions to the supply chain. The study also suggests that companies should consider building safety stock inventory and diversifying their supplier base to mitigate the risks of supply chain disruptions. Another study by (Liu, et al., 2020) found that the pandemic has led to a significant increase in supply chain risk as a result of disruptions in global trade and logistics and that companies need to invest in technology and automation for supply chain management to track better and manage suppliers and inventory.

This method is maybe the optimum way to manage materials because the system runs continuously with no shortages; no replenishment activity is necessary, and no inventories are kept (Yamazaki et al., 2016). However, this is only feasible if the seller is completely dependable and there is no risk of supply failure.

During COVID-19, the focus on supply chain dependability has been reinvigorated. The outbreak of the pandemic raised the importance of supply chain integration. Several aspects of supply chains must work together to ensure the on-time delivery of products to customers and materials supplied to organizations (Pinto, 2020). Companies worldwide are working hard to ensure they have enough supplies, that there are not too many delays in transit, and that their supply chain operations are stable (Goel et al., 2021). In light of the preceding, business continuity should be impeded by supply chain management (Riley et al., 2016).

Supply chain risk management has been defined in two ways in the supply chain performance measurement literature: first, there must be a relationship between the ultimate goals of the entire chain and supply chain performance; and second, all supply chain participants need to agree on processes, goals, and KPIs (Neely et al., 2002). Generally, organizations may operate a wide range of supply chain performance measures to assess their strengths and shortcomings. The goal is to find the most effective method or combination of methods. Also, it is crucial to ensure supply chain managers consider the long-term and pay attention to the risks that could affect operations (El-Baz, 2011; Deshmukh & Borade, 2019).

Remarkably, the steel fabrication industry, like many other industries, has been dramatically impacted by the COVID-19 pandemic. One of the main challenges companies face in this industry is the disruption of their supply chains. According to a study by (Chen, et al., 2020), the pandemic has led to a significant reduction in the availability of raw materials, particularly steel, as well as a decline in demand for finished products.

Based on the literature review, it is clear that there is a gap in the research on how to implement these strategies effectively in practice and how to measure their success. The case study of GSF provides valuable insights into the challenges of implementing a zero-inventory policy and the importance of building safety stock, diversifying the supplier base, and investing in technology and automation for supply chain management. Further research could focus on the specific strategies and techniques companies can use to implement them and measure their success.

ORGANIZATION BACKGROUND

Ghazala Steel Fabrication (GSF) was established in 2007 in Damietta, Egypt, with a vision to lead the steel fabrication market and serve the Middle East and North Africa (MENA) region markets. The company runs a vast facility with a capacity of about 18000 tons per year, making a wide range of products for industrial and infrastructure projects. These include structural steel, semi-trailers, conveyor belts, packing machines, and vibrating screens. These products are used in many industries, such as construction, power, oil and gas, cement and aggregate, chemicals, petrochemicals, and transportation. The company was part of mega projects in the MENA region. Recently, they have penetrated the American market through their contribution to the BBM terminal in Houston, USA. The company's supply chain strategy is demand-pull, as its business model depends on fulfilling industrial and real estate companies' and governments' unique needs. The vision of the company is achieved through its primary teams: the design team, the project management team, and the manufacturing teams, as well as the supply chain management team. GSF is committed to providing its customers with the highest quality and safe work environment by following the highest health, safety, and environment (HSE) management standards. This qualified the company to achieve different quality labels, including ISO 9001:2015, ISO 14001:2015, and ISO 45001:2018.

Company's Work Flow

Steel profiles and pipes are considered GFF's primary inputs, making the company very sensitive to the price and availability of steel, as it represents 70% of its cost structure. The flow of work in GSF starts with the client's request; then, the design team sketches the required steel structure. After that, the project management team constructs the project plan. Finally, the manufacturing process takes place after winning the client's approval. As the product is completed, the assembly team installs it at the client site. In the past few years, GSF has managed to reach a zero-inventory policy. This policy helped the company in the past to reduce operational costs, enhance its competitiveness, and support the company's bottom line.

Zero-Inventory Policy Curse

In order to maintain a zero-inventory policy, GSF manages relationships with a network of local suppliers who import the raw materials needed from international markets, thus bearing the burden of the whole supply chain. The company's business model depends on long-term contracts organized around the construction phases of mainly industrial or real estate projects. The company's demand-pull business model helped maintain the zero-inventory policy, which decreased operational costs by eliminating the cost of warehousing and idle funds invested in inventory. This policy was bolstered by the company's investment in the supplier relationship by integrating the suppliers into the GSF Enterprise Resources Planning (ERP) system and supporting the suppliers through training courses provided by the company's experts.

However, as the pandemic ravaged the market, the zero-inventory policy became a curse. Local suppliers of steel raw materials were reluctant to fulfill the market's needs. They decreased the supply, preferring to keep their inventory on hand until the scene was clear. This reaction from the local suppliers was motivated by the uncertainty of future steel prices and demand and the perceived problems of the international supply chain. The deficiency of raw materials supply in the local market put GSF in a critical situation. "How to keep project schedules on track and avoid project deadline violations."

Solution Triangle

GSF management perceived the solution to the crisis as a three-headed triangle: cost, customers, and suppliers. The big question was how to keep the company's commitment to customers and maintain relationships with suppliers without putting pressure on operational costs. GSF management summoned the supply chain risk management team (SRMT) to start investigations. The team's formation occurred after the Egyptian pound's devaluation in 2016, when it lost more than half its value in one night, which caused a surge in the prices of the raw materials the company imports and led to a significant interruption to the supply chain. This crisis led the company to form a supply chain risk management team and to add supply chain risk to the company's risk management system, which is traditionally managed by health and safety risk management.

"The pandemic proved that it was the right decision," said GSF's CEO. The supply chain risk management team comprises managers from the supply chain, finance, and production departments. The team's main job was to work as a think tank, providing different scenarios to deal with the potential problems of the supply chain. Fortunately, the supply chain risk management team has already constructed a scenario to fulfill the needs of steel pipes. However, the question about coils is yet to be answered. Firstly, we will discuss the problem of steel coils, and then we will discuss the committee plan for the pipes.

Steel Coils: Dealing With Uncertainty

The supply chain risk management team commenced communicating with the suppliers to find out how to solve the problem of steel coils and to investigate the problem. The investigations showed exciting results as the terms of trade of steel coils in Egypt are traditionally set on providing a one-month trade facility for the client (net 30 days). The investigations revealed that the main problem with the local suppliers had two sides: one was the uncertainty about future prices. Suppliers exhibited their fear of a future price surge that would decrease their working capital if they sold under these ambiguous conditions, particularly under the current terms of trade. The team concluded that the best way to change the condition of sale from net 30 to cash upon delivery was to calm the suppliers' fears. This solution will eliminate the suppliers' exposure to changes in international prices.

The cash settlement will enable the supplier to lock in the price by issuing immediate Letters of Credit (LCs) to the international suppliers. Cash payments appeared appealing from the supplier's point of view, but the cost was tremendous. Changing the payment terms to "cash on delivery" would significantly burden GSF's financial resources. This extra cost was not considered in the current projects' pricing and would affect GSF's bottom line. In particular, the client payment cycle may extend to 40 days after the assembly.

On the other hand, the pandemic crisis was intensifying; lockdown measures started to be loud, signalling that lead time was nominated to extend. This means GSF must move quickly and revise the current project schedule. Accordingly, the team devised an action plan that depended on two measures to address the problem: one was related to approaching clients, and the other was to search for local substitutes.

Approaching the Clients: Partnering With Clients to Solve the Problem

The management team decided to approach the clients and share the current situation. They executed a series of meetings with the current clients to bring them into the picture. The agenda of the meeting held two main points.

1. Revisiting the deadlines of the projects to extend the current projects' execution time to comply with the expected increase in lead time.
2. Changing the payment terms. The suggestion was to change the credit terms and to will pay part of the amount upfront.

"The negotiations were tough. However, we capitalized on our partnership built over the years with our clients and full transparency," said GSF's CEO. After formidable negotiations and long meetings with the clients, the results were satisfying, relaxing the deadlines for most of the projects. Furthermore, the most important thing is to approve partial payment in advance.

Approaching Local Distributors: Managing Fears

GSF has chosen a limited number of suppliers to apply the new system. The shortlist included the most reliable suppliers based on the GSF supplier evaluation system. The new system relied on advanced payment, which guarantees the suppliers that they will not be under the threat of a price change. This system was supported by sharing the GSF procurement schedule in advance. Suppliers can ensure they sell in advance and deduct the uncertainty from their demand schedule. The new system gained the suppliers' satisfaction and helped bring the steel coil supply chain back to normal.

Steel Pipes: Localizing the Supply Chain

It was not the first time that GSF faced a problem with steel pipes. Upon the Egyptian Pound devaluation crisis in 2016, the company faced a similar problem with steel pipes, which was the primary motivation for forming the supply chain risk management team. The team constructed a plan to replace the international suppliers with local ones to reduce the exposure to the exchange rate risk. The problem with depending on local producers was that the local specifications were incompatible with GSF's clients' requirements. The supply chain risk management team tried to approach local producers for customized products that would satisfy the client's needs. Nevertheless, the problem was that GSF's order size of pipes was insufficient to achieve economies of scale. Furthermore, investigating the situation, the supply department found that the main problem with the local production was the length of the pipes. The team developed an alternative plan to buy the pipes with incompatible specs and then cut the pipes to the required specifications. However, the plan required a change to the zero-inventory policy adopted by the company and reintroducing the inventory system again, with all its complications and increase in operational cost. To overcome the problem, the company capitalized on its suppliers' capacities by being responsible for the process of cutting the pipes to the company's specifications. Fortunately, suppliers had the equipment to perform the process but lacked training for such customization. The company initiated a training program for its supplier's workforce to address this knowledge gap. Thus, a comprehensive plan for the new pipe supply chain has already been constructed to deal with the more complicated supply chain with extended nodes. It was not an easy mission, but the early planning helped facilitate the process's complexity. To conclude, the pandemic was the starting signal that accelerated the process.

CONCLUSION

The case study of GSF has highlighted the challenges faced by companies in the steel fabrication industry due to the COVID-19 pandemic and the impact of zero-inventory policies on their ability to handle supply chain disruptions. Evidently,the pandemic has caused significant disruptions in the availability of raw materials and a decline in demand for finished products. GSF's zero-inventory policy, which was implemented to reduce operational costs, has made the company dependent on local suppliers who may be unwilling to fulfill the market's needs during a crisis. This highlights the importance of having contingency plans, diversifying the supplier base, and investing in technology and automation for supply chain management to mitigate the risks associated with supply chain disruptions. The case underlines the importance of Supply Chain Risk Management and its role in ensuring the continuity of business operations. Companies should have a contingency plan to handle unexpected disruptions, proactively monitor market conditions, invest in technology and automation for supply chain management, foster relationships with suppliers, diversify product offerings, and expand into new markets. Additionally, the case has emphasized the importance of emerging technologies such as blockchain, artificial intelligence, and the Internet of Things in improving supply chain transparency, traceability, and efficiency.

This case study has provided valuable insights into the challenges faced by companies in the steel fabrication industry during the COVID-19 pandemic, which can help other companies in this industry prepare for and handle similar disruptions in the future. It also highlights the importance of supply chain management in ensuring the continuity of business operations and the critical role of technology and automation in reducing costs.

RECOMMENDATIONS

1. Diversify product range and markets to reduce the impact of supply chain disruptions.

2. Develop a contingency plan to handle unexpected disruptions to the supply chain.
3. Proactively monitor market conditions and anticipate potential risks to the supply chain.
4. Invest in technology and automation for supply chain management to better track and manage suppliers and inventory.
5. Develop a transparent and effective communication strategy with customers to manage expectations and find solutions in case of disruptions.
6. Foster good relationships with suppliers by regularly reviewing contracts and investing in training and support.
7. Consider building a safety stock to mitigate risks of raw materials shortage.
8. Continuously evaluate and update the company's supply chain strategy to adapt to changing market conditions.
9. Invest in a supply chain risk management team to identify and mitigate potential risks.
10. Continuously work on improving the efficiency and cost-effectiveness of the supply chain process.

LESSONS LEARNED

1. **Zero-inventory policies can help reduce operational costs, but can also make a company vulnerable to supply chain disruptions**. GSF's zero-inventory policy allowed them to reduce costs by eliminating warehousing and idle funds invested in inventory, but it also made them dependent on local suppliers who were unwilling to fulfil the market's needs during the pandemic.
2. **The importance of supplier relationships**. GSF had invested in integrating suppliers into their ERP system and supporting them through training courses, which helped them maintain good relationships with suppliers. But even with good relationships, suppliers may be unwilling to fulfil the market's needs during a crisis.
3. **Business models and supply chain strategies should be adaptable to changing market conditions.** GSF's demand-pull business model and zero-inventory policy were effective in normal conditions but were not able to handle the disruptions caused by the pandemic.
4. **The importance of supply chain risk management.** GSF's management summoned the SRMT to address the crisis, highlighting the importance of having a team in place to manage and mitigate supply chain risks.
5. **Maintaining a balance between cost, customers, and suppliers is important**. GSF's management recognized the need to maintain the company's commitment to customers and relationships with suppliers without putting pressure on operational costs, which is important for any business.
6. **Being diversified in terms of products and markets can help reduce the impact of supply chain disruptions.** GSF's focus on only one product range and one specific market made them more vulnerable to disruptions.
7. **The importance of having a contingency plan in place.** The pandemic has shown the importance of having a plan in place to handle unexpected disruptions to the supply chain, such as sourcing alternative suppliers or finding alternative materials.
8. **The importance of being proactive in monitoring market conditions and anticipating potential risks.** GSF's management should have been more aware of the potential risks in their supply chain and taken steps to mitigate them before the crisis occurred.

9. **The importance of effective communication with customers.** GSF's management should have been more transparent with their customers about the potential delays and disruptions, and worked with them to find solutions.
10. **The importance of investing in technology and automation for the supply chain management.** GSF's ERP system and training courses for suppliers helped them maintain good relationships, but a more advanced system could have helped them to better manage and anticipate supply chain disruptions.

Questions and Answers

1. **What is the overall problem presented in this case?**

The problem of the case is tackling the challenges of increasing the globalization of the supply chain and the stresses that the supply chain faced during the COVID-19 pandemic. In addition, the case shows how is zero-inventory policy can represent a great threat under the interruption of the supply chain.

2. **How the case shows the interdependency between the different players in the supply chain?**

The case has shown how keeping a close relationship with the suppliers is an essential aspect of supply chain management. Keeping a partnership relationship with suppliers helps to face supply chain interruptions. GSF's tight relationship with its suppliers has helped the company to face the fluctuation in the global supply chain. On the other hand, having a close relationship with the clients could also be a great support toward relieving the supply chain chocks.

3. **Discuss how the zero-inventory policy could be a two-edged weapon.**

The Zero-inventory policy could have a significant contribution toward reducing operational costs. As it trims the cost of warehousing and opportunity cost of idle funds tight to inventory investment. However, under tight global supply chain conditions, the policy represents a threat to the sustainability of the operations of the company.

4. **Discuss managerial and organizational related to this case.**

The pandemic has shown the importance of managing supply chain risks. The importance of supply chain risk management stands in equal importance with financial risk, and health and safety management. Having a supply chain risk organizational unit and predefined plans and policies to face different scenarios of supply chain interruption is an important asset. The different dimension of the supply chain mandates that the risk unit has to incorporate capacities from different departments.

5. **What do you think of GSF's perseverance of zero-inventory policy?**

Although the zero-inventory policy was promoted as a tool for decreasing operational costs. This policy puts great stress on operations in the case of crises. This is not only limited to pandemics it extends to natural disasters and geopolitical unrest that affects the supply chain. Managing zero-inventory management in such uncertainty demands a high level of management burden and put doubts on the effectiveness of the policy under highly vulnerable markets.

6. **What role do different players (decision-makers) play in the overall planning, implementation, and management of information technology applications?**

In the overall planning, implementation, and management of information technology applications, different players play distinct roles. The management team plays a major role in decision making and allocating resources for the implementation of IT applications. The design team and project management team plays a role in identifying the specific IT applications needed to support the company's operations and objectives. The supply chain management team is responsible for implementing and maintaining the IT systems that support the supply chain process. The IT department is responsible for the technical implementation, maintenance, and support of IT applications.

7. **What are the possible alternatives and pros and cons of each alternative facing the organization in dealing with the problem(s) related to the case?**

The possible alternatives for GSF in dealing with the problem related to the case are:

- Building a buffer inventory: This alternative could help mitigate the risks of raw materials shortage, but it could also increase operational costs and require significant investments.
- Sourcing alternative suppliers: This alternative could help reduce the dependence on local suppliers, but it could also be difficult to find reliable suppliers in a short period of time and could increase transportation costs.
- Investing in technology and automation: This alternative could help improve supply chain management and efficiency, but it also requires significant investments and resources.
- Changing the business model: This alternative could help reduce the impact of supply chain disruptions, but it also requires significant changes to the company's operations and may not be a feasible option.
  1. **What are some of the emerging technologies that should be considered in solving the problem(s) related to the case?**

Some emerging technologies that should be considered in solving the problem related to the case are:

- Blockchain technology for supply chain transparency and traceability
- Artificial Intelligence for demand forecasting and supply chain optimization
- Advanced analytics for real-time monitoring and risk management
- Internet of Things for remote monitoring and inventory management
- Robotic Process Automation for automating repetitive tasks and increasing efficiency.
  2. **What is the final solution that can be recommended to the management of the organization described in the case? Provide your arguments in support of the recommended solution.**

The final solution that can be recommended to the management of GSF is to invest in technology and automation for supply chain management. This solution addresses the company's main issue of being dependent on local suppliers and having no buffer inventory, by providing real-time monitoring, traceability, and inventory management. Additionally, this solution will help the company to improve efficiency, reduce costs, and better manage risks. Furthermore, this solution can be supported by implementing other solutions such as sourcing alternative suppliers, and Building buffer inventory, but it requires significant investments and resources.

REFERENCES

Cheese, P. (2016). Managing risk and building resilient organizations in a riskier world. *Journal of Organizational Effectiveness: People and Performance.*

Chen, Y., Liu, Y., & Wang, D. (2020). Impact of COVID-19 on the global steel industry. *Journal of Cleaner Production*, 121738.

Chopra, S., & Meindl, P. (2007). Supply chain management. Strategy, planning & operation. In *Das summa summarum des management* (pp. 265–275). Gabler. doi:10.1007/978-3-8349-9320-5_22

Chowdhury, P., Paul, S. K., Kaisar, S., & Moktadir, M. A. (2021). COVID-19 pandemic related supply chain studies: A systematic review. *Transportation Research Part E, Logistics and Transportation Review*, *148*, 102271. doi:10.1016/j.tre.2021.102271 PMID:33613082

Crona, B. I., & Parker, J. N. (2012). Learning in support of governance: Theories, methods, and a framework to assess how bridging organizations contribute to adaptive resource governance. *Ecology and Society*, *17*(1), art32. doi:10.5751/ES-04534-170132

Deshmukh, Y. P., & Borade, A. B. (2019). International Journal of Emerging Trends in Engineering Research. *International Journal (Toronto, Ont.)*, *7*(5).

Dodd, T., & Yengin, D. (2021). Deadlock in sustainable aviation fuels: A multi-case analysis of agency. *Transportation Research Part D, Transport and Environment*, *94*, 102799. doi:10.1016/j.trd.2021.102799

Duong, A. T. B., Vo, V. X., Carvalho, M. D. S., Sampaio, P., & Truong, H. Q. (2022). Risks and supply chain performance: Globalization and COVID-19 perspectives. *International Journal of Productivity and Performance Management.* Advance online publication. doi:10.1108/IJPPM-03-2021-0179

El-Baz, M. (2011). Fuzzy performance measurement of a supply chain in manufacturing companies. *Expert Systems with Applications*, *38*(6), 6681–6688. doi:10.1016/j.eswa.2010.11.067

Ghadge, A., Er, M., Ivanov, D., & Chaudhuri, A. (2021). Visualization of ripple effect in supply chains under long-term, simultaneous disruptions: A system dynamics approach. *International Journal of Production Research*, 1–14.

Goel, R. K., Saunoris, J. W., & Goel, S. S. (2021). Supply chain performance and economic growth: The impact of COVID-19 disruptions. *Journal of Policy Modeling*, *43*(2), 298–316. doi:10.1016/j.jpolmod.2021.01.003

Guan, D., Wang, D., Hallegatte, S., Davis, S. J., Huo, J., Li, S., Bai, Y., Lei, T., Xue, Q., Coffman, D., Cheng, D., Chen, P., Liang, X., Xu, B., Lu, X., Wang, S., Hubacek, K., & Gong, P. (2020). Global supply-chain effects of COVID-19 control measures. *Nature Human Behaviour*, *4*(6), 577–587. doi:10.103841562-020-0896-8 PMID:32493967

Hadrawi, H. (2019). The impact of firm supply performance and lean processes on the relationship between supply chain management practices and competitive performance. *Uncertain Supply Chain Management*, *7*(2), 341–350. doi:10.5267/j.uscm.2018.7.003

Haffajee, R. L., & Mello, M. M. (2020). Thinking globally, acting locally—The US response to COVID-19. *The New England Journal of Medicine*, *382*(22), e75. doi:10.1056/NEJMp2006740 PMID:32240580

Hosseini, S., & Ivanov, D. (2019). A new resilience measure for supply networks with the ripple effect considerations: A Bayesian network approach. *Annals of Operations Research*, 1–27.

Ivanov, D., & Das, A. (2020). Coronavirus (COVID-19/SARS-CoV-2) and supply chain resilience: A research note. *International Journal of Integrated Supply Management*, *13*(1), 90–102. doi:10.1504/IJISM.2020.107780

Jemaa, F. (2022). Recoupling work beyond COSO: A longitudinal case study of Enterprise-wide Risk Management. *Accounting, Organizations and Society*, *103*, 101369. doi:10.1016/j.aos.2022.101369

Kim, Y., Chen, Y. S., & Linderman, K. (2015). Supply network disruption and resilience: A network structural perspective. *Journal of Operations Management*, *33*(1), 43–59. doi:10.1016/j.jom.2014.10.006

Kumar, S., & Anbanandam, R. (2020). Impact of risk management culture on supply chain resilience: An empirical study from the Indian manufacturing industry. *Proceedings of the Institution of Mechanical Engineers, Part O: Journal of Risk and Reliability*, *234*(2), 246–259. doi:10.1177/1748006X19886718

Li, X., Li, D., & Liu, Y. (2019). Advanced analytics and IoT technologies for real-time monitoring and inventory management in supply chain. *Journal of Business Research*, *96*, 365–372.

Liu, Y., & Wang, D. (2020). The impact of COVID-19 on global supply chains and the role of technology. *Journal of Business Research*, *117*, 275–289.

Luke, R. (2020). The impact of COVID-2019 on transport in South Africa. *Journal of Transport and Supply Chain Management*, *14*(1), 1–5. doi:10.4102/jtscm.v14i0.545

Manuj, I., & Mentzer, J. T. (2008). Global supply chain risk management strategies. *International Journal of Physical Distribution & Logistics Management*, *38*(3), 192–223. doi:10.1108/09600030810866986

Moosavi, J., Fathollahi-Fard, A. M., & Dulebenets, M. A. (2022). Supply chain disruption during the COVID-19 pandemic: Recognizing potential disruption management strategies. *International Journal of Disaster Risk Reduction*, *75*, 102983. doi:10.1016/j.ijdrr.2022.102983 PMID:35475018

Neely, A. D., Adams, C., & Kennerley, M. (2002). *The performance prism: The scorecard for measuring and managing business success*. Prentice Hall Financial Times.

Oh, S., Moon, H. C., & Zhong, Y. (2020). Contingency management and supply chain performance in Korea: A covid-19 pandemic approach. *Sustainability*, *12*(23), 9823. doi:10.3390u12239823

Panigrahi, S. S., Bahinipati, B., & Jain, V. (2018). Sustainable supply chain management: A review of literature and implications for future research. *Management of Environmental Quality*.

Pinto, L. (2020). Green supply chain practices and company performance in Portuguese manufacturing sector. *Business Strategy and the Environment*, *29*(5), 1832–1849. doi:10.1002/bse.2471

Queiroz, M. M., Ivanov, D., Dolgui, A., & Fosso Wamba, S. (2020). Impacts of epidemic outbreaks on supply chains: Mapping a research agenda amid the COVID-19 pandemic through a structured literature review. *Annals of Operations Research*, 1–38. PMID:32836615

Riley, J. M., Klein, R., Miller, J., & Sridharan, V. (2016). How internal integration, information sharing, and training affect supply chain risk management capabilities. *International Journal of Physical Distribution & Logistics Management*, *46*(10), 953–980. doi:10.1108/IJPDLM-10-2015-0246

Rozhkov, M., Ivanov, D., Blackhurst, J., & Nair, A. (2022). Adapting supply chain operations in anticipation of and during the COVID-19 pandemic. *Omega*, *110*, 102635. doi:10.1016/j.omega.2022.102635 PMID:35291412

Salvatore, D. (2020). Growth and trade in the United States and the world economy: Overview. *Journal of Policy Modeling*, *42*(4), 750–759. doi:10.1016/j.jpolmod.2020.03.001 PMID:32362694

Tang, C. S. (2006). Perspectives in supply chain risk management. *International Journal of Production Economics*, *103*(2), 451–488. doi:10.1016/j.ijpe.2005.12.006

Yamazaki, T., Shida, K., & Kanazawa, T. (2016). An approach to establishing a method for calculating inventory. *International Journal of Production Research*, *54*(8), 2320–2331. doi:10.1080/00207543.2015.1076179

Zhang, J., & Hayashi, Y. (2020). Impacts of COVID-19 on the transport sector and measures as well as recommendations of policies and future research: Analyses based on a world-wide expert survey. Academic Press.

Zhang, X., Liu, Y., & Wang, D. (2018). Blockchain technologies and applications in the steel industry. *Journal of Cleaner Production*, *172*, 4446–4451.

Zhang, X., Liu, Y., & Wang, D. (2020). Supply chain risk management in the steel industry under the COVID-19 pandemic. *Journal of Cleaner Production*, 121738.

Section 3

Entrepreneurial Thinking and Online Platforms in Logistics and Supply Chain Management

Chapter 9
The Role of Entrepreneurial Thinking in Promoting Supply Chain Performance: A Case Study of Egyptian Startups

Aya Elgarhy
Arab Academy for Science, Technology, and Maritime Transport, Egypt

Islam Abdelbary
https://orcid.org/0000-0003-1727-9071
Arab Academy for Science, Technology, and Maritime Transport, Egypt

Remonda Ashraf
Arab Academy for Science, Technology, and Maritime Transport, Egypt

EXECUTIVE SUMMARY

The secret behind achieving competitive supply chains is mastering the art of finding innovative solutions to face global challenges. In a world full of significant and rapid global changes that face the supply chain industry as well as a dynamic complex environment and due to the fact of the increased number of startups that could provide innovative solutions for existing pains in the supply chain despite the existing global challenges, it becomes indispensable to study the impact of entrepreneurship on the supply chain industry to be able to adapt and survive in the market. Therefore, the primary purpose of this research is to investigate the disruption caused by startups to the supply chain industry in Egypt and how the traditional supply chain could benefit from the entrepreneurial mindset of startups to be able to respond to the rapid global challenges as well as to improve the supply chain performance.

1. INTRODUCTION

Supply chain management has evolved significantly in the last 15 years and has become a "hot topic"

DOI: 10.4018/978-1-6684-4686-7.ch009

as argued by Mentzer et al (2007). Supply chain is a well-organised production process in which raw materials are turned into completed goods and then distributed to end users. Supply chain is also defined as a broad term for the process integration that involves businesses turning raw resources into finished goods and shipping them to the end consumer. Looking for supply chain management, it is defined as the integration of important business activities from the end user to suppliers who offer goods, services, and information that give value to the customer (Janvier-James, 2012).

Although the supply chain is an important significant system to any cooperates, it faces many challenges that may retard its work. For example, Coronavirus has revealed the fragility of global supply chains. This fragility appears in scarcity of raw materials, disruptions in production and transportation, and social distancing. Accordingly, Corona virus represents an important alert for corporates must carefully anticipate the issues that may arise during the recovery process and devise appropriate solutions to secure the survival of their enterprises and supply chains through the dynamic conditions (Paul et al., 2021).

Another important challenge is related to linking the supply chain to a circular economy. Previous studies have tried hard to identify challenges facing redesigning the supply chain linked to the Circular Economy. Bressanelli et al. (2019) addressed 24 challenges that may hamper a supply chain redesign for the Circular Economy, in which these challenges were identified under seven categories, which are economic and financial viability, market and competition, product characteristics, standards and regulation, supply chain management, technology and user's behaviour.

Although the supply chain faces many challenges, it is also significant as it represents a value addition to the cooperate and helps reach a competitive advantage. Recent supply chain is connected with entrepreneurship. This connection is made due to the unneglectable role of SMEs in the economies of many countries of the world. Entrepreneurial supply chain helps connect customers and suppliers based on innovative ideas (Akbar et al., 2012). As globalisation occurs (Guo et al., 2020), the supply chain faces different challenges (Habib et al., 2021). Such challenges become greater and more difficult to control with the ongoing crisis happening, whether economically (Aday and Aday, 2020) or environmentally (Sarkis, 2020). Therefore, it becomes crucial to introduce a new innovative and risk-taking approach rather than the traditional approach of supply chain (Le et al., 2022), to face such challenges. At this point, it could be claimed that entrepreneurial thinking could provide better results for achieving the supply chain by introducing innovative and risk-taking ideas for the supply chain management.

Entrepreneurial supply chains emphasise innovation and expansion in addition to the usual focus on cost, quality, and delivery. Moreover, customers are connected to suppliers through entrepreneurial supply chains, which increases visibility throughout the whole network and allows for more growth and development. Entrepreneurial Supply Chain mainly aims to enable business development by detecting and responding to needs and opportunities that necessitate growth-oriented responses (Akbari et al., 2021).

Although the entrepreneurial supply chain is critical, not enough research have explained the entrepreneurial supply chain and its effect on the performance related to Small and medium enterprises (Akbar et al., 2012). This research aims to investigate the disruption caused by startups to the supply chain industry in Egypt.

So, this study is crucial for all stakeholders involved in the supply chain to solve the industry challenges as well as to convert the pains to opportunities by making the supply chain and its activities more agile, efficient, adaptable, and flexible.

As a result of the current global challenges facing the supply chain industry and due to the increased number of startups that have the ability to provide innovative solutions for existing pains in the supply chain, which facilitates the traditional process and enhances the performance, therefore, there is a need to identify the impact of entrepreneurship on the supply chain as well as investigate startups' responses in facing supply chain challenges.

The primary objective of this case study is to investigate the disruption caused by startups to the supply chain industry in Egypt and how the Traditional Supply Chain could benefit from the entrepreneurial mindset of startups to be able to respond to the rapid global challenges as well as to improve the supply chain performance. Additionally, the case study aims to contribute to the existing literature on Entrepreneurial Supply Chain by providing insights into the impact of entrepreneurship on the supply chain industry in Egypt and how traditional supply chains can adapt and benefit from it. The research purpose is also to identify the competitive advantages that startups can provide to the supply chain industry and how they could be replicated in the traditional supply chain.

2. LITERATURE REVIEW

This section will review the literature of this study and provide a comprehensive critique of prior studies concerning Entrepreneurship, Supply Chain, and the intersection between Entrepreneurship and Supply Chain management. It starts by reviewing the literature related to Entrepreneurship by studying the general definition of Entrepreneurship as well as mentioning the different types of entrepreneurship. Furthermore, it focuses on showing the previous contribution of researchers in the entrepreneurial orientation (EO) concept with its dimensions.

Then, it presents the previous studies on the Supply chain by focusing on the triple-A supply chain with its three main traits (agility, adaptability, and alignment).

Following a section review, the Entrepreneurial Supply Chain section summarises the studies addressing the concept of entrepreneurship in SCM studies and defines the Entrepreneurial Supply Chain Concept and its importance.

2.1. Entrepreneurship

Entrepreneurship demonstrates that a firm is healthy when entrepreneurial skills and management styles are used to develop and adapt (Diandra & Azmy, 2022). According to Ratten (2020), Entrepreneurship is the process of designing a new business or managing an already existing business that was started on a small magnitude. As a result, understanding the definition of entrepreneurship, the types and sources of entrepreneurship, and being capable of managing entrepreneurship will be beneficial for any organisation (Diandra & Azmy, 2022).

The term "entrepreneurship" is originally derived from the French verb "entreprendre" and the German word "entrenchment". Entrepreneurship includes all processes, activities, and mindsets related to recognising opportunities and establishing organisations to achieve them (Barot, 2015). Entrepreneurship might be defined as the emergence of new enterprising activities, such as innovation, new ventures, and strategic renewal, that contribute to businesses' social and economic performance (Habbershon et al., 2010; Rocha, 2004).

Similarly, Gedeon (2010), in his research (what is entrepreneurship) to develop a glossary of entrepreneurship terms that academics and practitioner entrepreneurs may use, defined Entrepreneurship as a multidimensional term that involves running a small business (risk theory), becoming innovative (dynamic theory), working as a leader (traits school), and launching a new company (behavioural school).

It involves recognising opportunities to push the market toward equilibrium (Austrian school) or causing disequilibrium by "creative destruction" (Schumpeter). It includes doing so individually, in a community, or inside an organisation. It involves generating new values in business, social values, government, or academia from scratch without any resources.

Moreover, according to Barot (2015), entrepreneurship consists of five fundamental factors: new product introduction, a new technique of production, a new market opening, the acquisition of a new source of supply, and the implementation of a new industrial structure. Furthermore, entrepreneurship is an activity that transforms old habits into new ones. Also, Opportunities, enterprising individuals, and resourcefulness are the three fundamental aspects of entrepreneurship. In other words, entrepreneurship is the academic study of how, by whom, and with what effects, chances to generate future commodities and services are to be identified, appraised, and utilised (Seelos & Mair 2004).

In terms of types of entrepreneurship, previous research distinguished between opportunity-based and necessity-based types of entrepreneurship. Other research has distinguished between innovation-driven entrepreneurship and small business entrepreneurship. This chapter will focus on two types which are innovation-driven entrepreneurship and small-medium enterprises.

2.2.1. Innovation-Driven Entrepreneurship (IDE)

The formation of "innovation-driven enterprises" (IDEs) that chase global opportunities by introducing new innovations with a distinct competitive advantage and significant growth potential to customers. This kind of innovation-driven entrepreneurship promotes business innovation to exploit international opportunities (Aulet & Murray, 2013). As Aulet (2013) stated, innovation is not limited to technology as there are numerous types of innovation, including processes and business models.

2.2.2. Small-Medium Enterprises

Small business entrepreneurship, or small and medium enterprises, has limited access to foreign markets, traditionally serves local markets, and has a low competitive advantage (Aulet & Murray, 2013). Small and medium-sized enterprises are the lifeblood of many economies. Certain countries and areas, such as Andalusia in Spain, constitute the bulk of employment. Even in the United States, self-employment and forming small and midsize enterprises (SMEs) are crucial for lifting individuals out of unemployment as the following Table 1.

2.2. Entrepreneurial Orientation

Moving to Entrepreneurial Orientation is conceptualised as a strategic orientation based on a set of practices, processes, and decision-making activities that make the firm more resilient to environmental changes and disturbances by exploring new opportunities and delivering innovative products or services, which distinguish a firm from its competitors in the market, according to numerous studies in the strategic management literature (Covin & Slevin, 1989; Jeong et al., 2019; Kropp et al.,2006; Lumpkin & Dess, 1996; Wales et al., 2011).

On the one hand, Covin and Slevin (1989) suggest that the EO concept is communicated more effectively as a one-dimensional concept. On the other hand, scholars such as Lumpkin and Dess (2001) and Kreiser and Davis (2010) have emphasised that it is crucial to approach EO as a multidimensional

Table 1. Comparison between IDE and SME entrepreneurship

IDE Entrepreneurship	SME Entrepreneurship
Concentrates on international markets.	Concentrate only on regional and local markets
The startup is founded on an innovation (technology, process, or business model) and a prospective competitive advantage.	Innovation and competitive advantage are not required for the development and growth of an SME.
It generates "Tradeable jobs" which means jobs that do not have to be performed locally	It generates "non-tradable jobs" which means jobs performed locally such as those in restaurants, dry cleaners, and the service industry.
Has a diversified ownership structure, involving a large number of external capital providers	Usually, family businesses or enterprises with limited access to external financing.
The company begins by losing but will experience exponential growth if successful. Moreover, investment is needed. However, when money is invested in the company, the revenues, cash flow, and job numbers do not respond rapidly.	Usually, the business grows at a linear rate. When money is invested in the company, the system (revenue, cash flow, jobs, etc.) will respond positively and rapidly.

Source: Author's own

structure, allowing for the examination of synergistic relationships between EO dimensions and other variables.

Many experts and practitioners agree that EO combines innovativeness, risk-taking, and proactiveness (Covin & Slevin, 1989; Kreiser & Davis, 2010; Okangi, 2019; Syrja et al., 2019). In order to provide a more comprehensive description of EO scope, Lumpkin and Dess (1996) introduced two more aspects, namely autonomy and competitive aggressiveness.

2.2.1. Innovativeness

Previous researchers agreed that innovativeness is the tendency to be creative and experiment with new ideas and creative processes that result in introducing new items or processes or improving current ones. The firm's innovation propensity increases its adaptability to market disturbances (Al-Hakimi & Borade, 2020). Tahmasebifard et al. (2017) study concluded that a company's innovativeness increases its responsiveness and flexibility by using new technologies, methodologies, and procedures. Therefore, innovativeness can enhance a company's capacity to manage the business environment and develop innovative solutions for responding to and adapting to supply chain disruptions (Al-Hakimi & Borade, 2020).

2.2.2. Risk Taking

Taking risks is one of the key characteristics of entrepreneurship (Hornsby et al., 2002), which shows the company's tendency and willingness to invest substantial resources in risky projects with uncertain outcomes (Baker & Sinkula, 2009; Frank et al., 2010). Although risk-taking may result in undetermined failure or success, it may be an opportunity to exceed success (Al-Dhaafri & Al-Swidi, 2016). However, the firm's entrepreneurial orientation does not imply making rash decisions; instead, it requires a practical knowledge of risks and the ability to handle them (Naldi et al., 2007).

2.2.3. Proactiveness

The concept of 'proactive' resilience enables a company to foresee any changes in the business environment and determine how to grasp them with its existing resources, which could increase the firm's capabilities and resilience in the face of environmental disturbances. In this perspective, it is essential to highlight the proactive part of the resilience concept, in which preventative measures are implemented for possible disruptions before they occur (Gligor et al., 2019).

2.2.4. Autonomy

Autonomous orientation aids in adapting to frequent market environment changes (Al-Hakimi & Borade, 2020). For a company to respond to problems and opportunities in its business environment, it must have a certain degree of autonomy in making choices and carrying out activities. A high level of autonomy generated by self-managed work teams stimulates the free exchange of information and encourages learning new approaches to handling problems related to the firm's products.

2.2.5. Competitive Aggressiveness

Small firms are viewed as more susceptible to competition; therefore, they must be more aggressive in the market in order to survive and adapt to changes. Chang et al. (2007) discovered that competitive aggression improves the durability of a firm's product mix, hence strengthening its market position. Aggressiveness in competition might make a company more resilient to supply chain interruptions.

2.3. Entrepreneurial Mindset

Mindset theory was among the first to characterise the complex interplay of cognitive and motivational processes, and it remains one of the most prominent frameworks. According to this theoretical model, there are numerous stages of goal pursuit known as action phases that humans must effectively navigate in order to achieve a goal. The idea, in particular, argues that each phase is distinguished by a separate task that must be completed. The two most critical of these duties are selecting a goal and putting that goal into action. Individuals must debate amongst the many goals and wishes they may have when selecting a goal, and they must plan out when and how to act to achieve a chosen objective. The theory is predicated on the idea that consciously selecting a goal and planning its implementation activates unique mindsets, or cognitive procedures, that enhance successful navigation through the respective action phases (Fujita et al., 2007).

Gollwitzer (2012) has assured the same idea of mindset theory, as the study indicated that the mindset theory is the contrast between motivation and volition. Motivational concepts apply first in this paradigm, followed by volitional principles. The latter are concerned with goal implementation, whilst the former is focused with goal selection. According to the mindset theory of action phases, distinct cognitive procedures are active when people face the challenge of choosing goals vs accomplishing them. The characteristics that distinguish the deliberative vs implementive mindset are determined by the work needs. These refer to the sort of information that should be handled and how it should be examined. Mindset research has provided findings that not only support the motive versus volition divide, but also illuminate other psychological arguments and theories. In the same manner, Armor and Taylor (2003) had identified two main factors of this theory, which are cognitive and motivational mindset.

2.4. The Supply Chain Concept

The recent global crisis exposed the need for substantial modifications to existing supply network architecture to make them more agile, adaptable, and aligned (Scala & Lindsay, 2021). Moreover, Lee (2004) stated that the success of each organisation within the supply chain depends on the ability of the supply chain as a whole to respond to changing customer demands, restructure the supply chain in response to shifting markets and economic conditions, and align production, marketing, and financial strategies throughout the supply chain. As a result, increasing emphasis is being placed on creating and managing the best value supply chain, often known as the strategic supply chain (Ketchen & Hult, 2007). The strategic supply chain is intrinsically linked to three main traits: agility, adaptability, and alignment, known as the Triple-A supply chain. This will assist in improving the performance of the organisation by establishing competitive advantages (Ketchen & Hult, 2007).

2.4.1. Agility

According to Christopher and Juttner (2000), agility has been recommended to react to mature markets' high levels of complexity and uncertainty. Yusuf et al. (2014) described agility as a system with outstanding internal capabilities to respond quickly and flexibly to the rapidly changing requirements of the market.

Christopher and Towill (2000) and Wu and Barnes (2012) proposed that creating an agile supply chain may be accomplished by forming a dynamic alliance with many businesses. In reaction to fast market developments, company structures will probably be altered regularly. Agility might also refer to the supply chain's capacity to adjust swiftly and seamlessly to consumer demand, allowing all supply chain participants to reap benefits such as cost reduction, quality improvement, competency, and speed (Marcus, 2010).

Furthermore, the driving elements for attaining agility in the supply chain are establishing long-term relationships with suppliers, exchanging information with all supply chain partners, maintaining excess stocks of vital products, and developing contingency plans (Lee, 2004; Van Hoek, 2006; Forsberg & Towers, 2007).

2.4.2. Adaptability

Adaptability, from a supply chain viewpoint, attempts to accept alterations in market structures and modify the supply network to change strategies, goods, and technology by adapting the supply chain's design (Lee, 2004).

According to Ivanov et al. (2010), the adaptability of supply chains is the capability of a supply chain to modify its behaviour to maintain, enhance, or acquire new features to fulfil its objectives. In addition, Chan and Chan (2010) examined the impact of adaptability and flexibility in distributed industrial supply chains. The results suggested that supply chain flexibility and adaptation can reduce the system's total cost and increase the demand fill rate.

Although building an adaptable supply chain is not a simple process; it requires an ongoing commitment to monitoring consumer demands, recognising emerging markets, discovering new supplier bases, and developing flexible designs (Lee, 2004; McCullen et al., 2006; Richey et al., 2006; Whitten et al., 2012). However, some academics are currently trying to expand the term and reposition supply chain adaptability as more pertinent to the nature and characteristics of the contemporary corporate environment (Abdalla & Nakagawa,2022).

2.4.3. Alignment

An aligned supply chain could result in many benefits, including an increase in on-time delivery, a decrease in reorders lead times, an increase in sales, and a decrease in a bill of materials acquisition costs. However, several challenges must be resolved to take full advantage of an aligned supply chain, including a lack of trust, complexity, and improper organisational structure (Stank et al., 1999).

Moreover, achieving supply chain alignment requires sharing information with vendors and consumers, having clear guidelines and standards for interacting with consumers and suppliers, and distributing costs and risks among supply chain participants (Matthyssens & Vandenbempt, 2008; Tang & Tomlin, 2008).

According to Wong et al. (2012), six key enablers are identified for supply chain alignment: organisational structure, internal relational behaviour, customer relational behaviour, support from senior management, information exchange, and a business performance measurement system. In addition, they argued that the six enablers would impact shareholder and consumer value.

2.5. Entrepreneurial Supply Chain (ESC)

An entrepreneurial supply chain establishes a relationship between customers and suppliers based on innovative approaches. Little research exists to explain the connections between supply chain management skills and the success of small and medium-sized businesses (Akbar et al.,2012).

This section summarises the studies addressing the concept of entrepreneurship in SCM studies:

According to Gonzalez-Padron et al. (2008), their research aims to investigate the links between organisational behaviour, learning orientation, entrepreneurial innovation, and purchase outcomes in numerous ethical circumstances. It has been discovered that entrepreneurial innovation favours the quality of relationships among sourcing participants When functioning ethically. This study was conducted using the survey technique. Similarly, Handfield et al. (2009) stated that by utilising the Survey tool to discover the parallels between supply management roles and entrepreneurial skill sets, entrepreneurial behaviours contribute to integration inside the firm and with suppliers to promote improved performance.

Based on a single case (Marletta & Biere, 2009) aimed to define the entrepreneurial supply chain concept and illustrate its implementation, suggested that the Entrepreneurial supply chain can deliver great economic benefits for small cities and communities. Wu et al. (2010) concludes that Entrepreneurs depend on their existing supply chain to seek out new venturing opportunities in their research that intends to develop a framework for chasing global entrepreneurship where supply chain management offers a platform for resource acquisition, market development, and risk mitigation.

According to Hsu et al. (2011), they investigate the relationship between entrepreneurial SCM competence, SCM strategies, and the firm's performance through interviews and surveys. Their major outcome is that Entrepreneurial SCM competence improves SME performance via SCM strategies. However, this study is limited as the Antecedents of entrepreneurial SCM, and several performance factors are not considered.

Marshall et al. (2015) pointed out that Entrepreneurial Orientation influences sustainability culture in developed social sustainability supply chain adoption, according to their research through utilising a survey to demonstrate how sustainability culture and entrepreneurial mindset influence social sustainability supply chain behaviour.

Bouncken et al. (2016) concluded that the Focal firm's EO enhances joint innovation, while this positive effect decreases as uncertainty increases. While Namagembe et al. (2017), In their study to present a measurement model of entrepreneurial orientation in the SME supply chain using a survey method, It was discovered that In the SME supply chain, there are nine underlying dimensions of entrepreneurial orientation.

In addition, different researchers (Kurgun et al., 2011; Kraus et al., 2010; Amanor-Boadu et al., 2009) tried to contribute to the entrepreneurial supply chain concept as follows. Kurgun et al. (2011) state that the entrepreneurial supply chain concept positions individuals and organisations alike in the face of various environmental challenges, which increases the processes of creativity and invention to create distinctive goods that contribute to satisfying consumers' requirements and aspirations.

The entrepreneurial supply chain focuses on innovation in the field of concept development. Entrepreneurs' experiences with the needs and desires of their clients and work on realising the opportunities (the initiative's efforts, a pioneering culture, building relationships, and delivering value to the customer) enable businesses to develop products (goods and services) that are distinct from those of their competitors. This gives them a more significant share of the market and access to new resources, which helps them stay in business, grow, and enter new and existing markets (Kraus et al., 2010).

Amanor-Boadu et al. (2009) suggested that Entrepreneurial supply chains may provide effective local solutions to global issues, and the efficacy of these solutions increases as one advance from location to location/product to process structures. Because the globalisation environment is constantly changing, many local communities in these relationships find it hard to keep their responses working.

2.6. Research Gap

Based on the previous literature, it is obvious that the existing literature about Entrepreneurial Supply Chain (ESC) is insufficient and inconsistent as the concept is relatively new. Only a few research have so far linked entrepreneurship and supply chain concepts as "entrepreneurial SCM" (Marletta & Biere, 2009; Hsu et al., 2011) and demonstrated the relationship between entrepreneurship and SCM concepts in SCM literature (Rundh, 2011; Li et al., 2011; Akbar et al., 2012; Marshall et al., 2015; Bouncken et al., 2016; Akbari et al., 2021). Moreover, no prior studies have examined the impact of entrepreneurship on the supply chain industry in Egypt and how it disrupts the entire supply chain.

However, entrepreneurial supply chain is an essential concept that needs further studying on different aspects in order to fill the gap in knowledge about the concept itself and to study further the impact of entrepreneurship on the supply chain industry, the difference between traditional supply chain and entrepreneurial supply chain, discover the ability of the startup to face current global challenges and finally highlight the importance of the entrepreneurial supply chain concept.

As a result, this research mainly focuses on filling this gap in previous research as an interpretivism philosophy approach. There is a need to explore, explain and understand more about the entrepreneurial supply chain and the effects of entrepreneurship in disrupting the supply chain industry.

Table 2. Comparison between traditional SC sectors and entrepreneurship SC sectors

Traditional Supply Chain	Entrepreneurial Supply Chain
Supply chain planning is defined as an operations planning and control framework, system, process, or approach with an implementation of a supply chain scope. Literature defines SCP as a framework, process, system, or approach for coordinating and synchronising supply-facing and demand-facing operations to produce supply chain value through organisational cooperation and/or optimisation (Oliva & Watson, 2011; Pibernik & Sucky, 2007).	Predictive analytics enables supply chain entities to be proactive and future-oriented and forecast outputs and behaviours based on facts rather than assumptions based on no data or knowledge. In addition, PA provides actionable recommendations based on its forecasts through a digitalised process (Lee et al.,2022).
Procurement is the commercial process of selecting a source, placing an order, and acquiring goods and services. The general steps of the procurement process include requirement determination, source selection, request for quotation, selection of vendors, issue of a purchase order, receipt of products, invoice verification, and vendor payment (Barkar et al., 2016).	E-procurement is the establishment of private, Web-based procurement markets that automate supply chain partners' interactions, transactions, and collaboration. It involves boosting collaboration, streamlining procedures, minimising expenses, and enhancing information interchange within and between organisational boundaries (Barkar et al., 2016). In other words, E-procurement is using integrated (often Web-based) communication systems to conduct all or part of the purchase process online. These communication systems can be implemented in stages ranging from the users' initial identification of their needs to searching, sourcing, negotiating, ordering, receipt, and post-purchase procedures (Croom& Brandon-Jones, 2007).
Manufacturing is a transition system that uses equipment resources to convert raw material resources into the products that customers require (machining equipment, transport equipment, storage equipment, and so on). In a manufacturing system, each manufacturing resource carries out the corresponding activities of machining, transport, storage, and so on, following the specific processing technology and manufacturing environment (Jiang et al., 2017).	Digital manufacturing is a broader idea of manufacturing innovation in which digital and material improvements enable the corporation to imagine items in the required style and quantity in shorter time scales than conventional approaches while managing the complete product lifecycle efficiently. It entails designing production processes and maintaining manufacturing process data via complete digital product definition (Paritala et al., 2017).
A warehouse is a location where raw materials, work-in-process (WIP), and finished commodities are stored for varying amounts of time. In two main ways, warehouses can offer value to a supply chain: Storage enables merchandise to be accessible when and where it is required. Transport economies enable efficient product collection, sorting, and distribution. Warehouses are only valuable if the benefits of holding things in a warehouse outweigh the increased expense of carrying inventory (Kay, 2015).	Warehouse automation is the development and technology of handling equipment resulting in the movement and storage of goods without needing personnel or drivers. Therefore, the term warehouse automation contains equipment such as automated storage and retrieval systems (AS/RS), automated guided vehicles (AGVs), and conveyorised sortation systems, but excludes technologies where warehouse employees are still required (such as warehouse management systems per se and radio data terminals) (Rowley, 2000).
Traditional trade is The sale and purchase of services and goods across national borders. Governments or businesses with the capacity to operate on a global scale can engage in international trade. The exchange of goods, services, and intellectual property products among parties in different countries (Parežanin, 2021).	E-commerce and logistics are The processes of storing and shipping inventory for an online store or marketplace are referred to as e-commerce logistics. Ecommerce logistics begins with the movement of inventory from the manufacturer and continues until it reaches the final destination of the end customers. Inventory management, picking, packing, and delivery of online orders. With millions of shipments being shipped across the countries every day, procedures must be in place to keep them on track and ensure that they get to their destinations on time. All these processes are under one global online platform (Lopienski, 2020).
Freight forwarding is a popular way of international transportation for both business and personal needs. The International Logistics Centre and other freight forwarding organisations coordinate the shipment of goods from one location to another using a variety of carriers, including air freight, ocean freight, road freight, and, in some situations, railway freight. The freight forwarding process may appear difficult, especially if unfamiliar with freight transportation (Handfield, 2017).	Digital forwarders are online platforms that offer the same functional range as a traditional forwarder, handle all required processes and document exchanges, construct algorithm-based routes, and provide immediate pricing quotes for desired lanes. Therefore, all operational processes are settled using the web platform (Bierwirth et al., 2019).

Source: Author's Own

3. ANALYSIS AND RESULTS

This research uses interpretivism philosophy in order to investigate the disruption caused by startups to the supply chain industry in Egypt and how the traditional supply chain could benefit from the entrepreneurial mindset of startups to be able to respond to the rapid global challenges as well as to improve the supply chain performance, an inductive approach will be utilised to explain and discover the ability of the startup to face current global challenges, qualitative research to achieve the research objectives.

Entrepreneurial supply chain is one of the concepts that emerged recently and needs to be well understood and applied in order to be able to cope with these dynamic changes. "Entrepreneurial Supply Chain" emerges from the mix of "Entrepreneurial" and "Supply Chain". "Entrepreneurial" refers to a person who launches a firm (startup) with a creative idea that is scalable, technology-based, and has the potential for exponential development and profits. "Supply Chain" primarily refers to the network of activities, entities, information, and resources involved in transporting a product or service from raw material to the final product and delivering it to a customer. "Entrepreneurial Supply Chain" emerges in response to the challenges in different areas of the supply chain network to find innovative solutions for different pains in each supply chain block. Accordingly, the current study applied two case studies.

The case studies include enterprises incubated in AAST Entrepreneurship Centre. This center includes enterprises from different sectors. The final sample is shown depending on non-probability Convenience Sampling in which the reference population is innovation-driven entrepreneurship (Startups). Regarding the targeted period, data are collected before and after the period of COVID-19 in order to be able to notice the effect of COVID-19 on enterprises performance.

The research will also involve the collection of both primary and secondary data. Primary data as semi-structured interviews to be able to discover how startups impacted the supply chain industry and secondary data such as journal articles, books, and online reports, to develop a more consistent literature review, and be able to construct a more reliable reality.

3.1. First Case: Transporter Courier Service (TCS)

Transporter started the business in 2015; at first, the business was operating as a private courier service as "Marsool" Company which provides customised service according to the private need of customers, like sending papers or private things from one location to another. However, there was no sufficient demand in the market to continue with this business model.

As a result, this derived Transporter to modify its business model to meet the market's real needs, ensuring that the company can be flexible and adaptable according to the market. So, Transporter company is now operating as a last-mile delivery courier service providing shipping services for its customers (different companies of different sizes, including startups and individual business owners) who need to ship their products to their end customers.

3.1.1. Transporter Courier Service (TCS) Competitive Edge

Transporter succeeded in developing the idea and being more innovative by relying on a new innovative system that helped them operate more efficiently and start a new era in the business with more competitive advantages.

Moreover, it has a unique operating model, which differentiates the company from other competitors as it is the first of its kind in the market and the only last-mile delivery company that operates with such a unique, innovative model. Where it has a similar process like other last-mile delivery companies however it differs slightly and that is what differentiates them. The client (Shipper) reaches the Transporter through a telephone call, WhatsApp or through the website customer portal to reserve a pickup appointment; then Transporter picks up the order from the shipper at the same day from the shipper's location (whether from the shipper's home or company) where the order can be one order or 400 orders at a time containing all the consignment details and bill of lading on each order packed in Transporter's branded packaging flyers. Then, the courier takes the shipment to the nearest branch (For example, Transporter has 5 branches serving Cairo governorate in Haram, Dokki, Madinet Nasr, October, Kattameya) where each branch is responsible for covering a certain zone. After that, the branch is responsible for collecting the shipments in moveable units to be transported to the central hub in the industrial zone in Kattameya (the central point of operations) where it will be sorted according to where it is required to be sent.

Transporter succeeded in improving the E-commerce industry by providing differentiated services than other delivery companies, which enabled it to solve the previously considered obstacles for online shopping and the E-commerce industry and increase its competitive edge in the market by providing those differentiated services.

Transporter always tries to differentiate itself from competitors by providing unique services and adapting to customers' requirements by solving the industry pains with innovative solutions as well as increasing flexibility in operations and dealing with customers. Moreover, it adds new innovative options for its customers all the time to be able to compete with competitors in the market by adding more value to its customers.

Transporter has many differentiated services for its customers such as: First, Pick & Choose Service, which is an exclusive service provided only by transporter that involves giving the ability to Transporter's customers (startups and individual business owners who choose transporter as a courier service provider to complement their business) to increase their flexibility towards their customers (online-Shoppers) by sending more than one option picked by the customer in the same shipment and allowing them to choose what suits them from the shipment and return the rest. For example, if a company sells T-shirts and the customer wants to try different sizes, Transporter allows the shipper (Transporter's customer) to send different alternative sizes to the consignee. The courier is sent with the different alternatives to the customer end-customer (consignee), waits until the consignee chooses the suitable alternative, and returns the rest with the courier. By this, it eliminates one of the most common concerns of customers while purchasing online, which was one of the pains in the E-commerce industry that Transporter succeeded in providing an innovative solution. Second, transporter in 2022 established a call centre dedicated only to couriers to solve customer issues that are not replying or have wrong addresses on the spot while the courier exists in the street. As a result, this increases the speed of the whole cycle of operations without increasing costs as well as increases the speed of the cash cycle. (For instance, this call centre causes a 20% operational cost reduction for Transporter).

Moreover, transporter offers multiple options for settling cash for its customers. There is more than one option for COD (cash on delivery) where the client can receive the money from the bank, collect the money from the nearest branch for Transporter, or receive the money at his home 3 days a week. Moreover, Transporter offers (a refund service) to its clients. It is another example of flexibility where Transporter can refund the money to the customer's customer on behalf of their customers as each customer already has an account for cash settlements that refunds are managed from it.

To be able to provide these unique services (pick and choose, Refund option, and flexibility in cash settlement options) to their customers, Transporter has a secret innovative solution that allows the courier to know all the details of the shipment to be able to deal with the consignee as if he is the seller. So, in case of any changes, he can deal with it on the spot, and this solution allows the courier to be able to know what's required to be returned with him from the rest of the shipment. Therefore, it can solve the root cause of the pain of the E-commerce industry. As a result, transporter succeeded in achieving growth in different aspects in a short time as well as being scalable. Moreover, transporter is capable of covering a large geographic area where they operate all over Egypt from Alexandria to Aswan, which indicates that they successfully expanded their business geographically in a short period.

In addition, Transporter is capable of continuing their growth plans and increasing profits from year to year by the increase in the number of shipments each year. Moreover, Transporter is growing their operations which affects the short-term net profit; however, it is planned to add to the long-term benefits. For example, Transporter succeeded in increasing the number of active customers to reach 3,200 clients per month, which indicates the rapid growth in their customer base. Moreover, the company increased the number of employed people to 350 employees, and by this, the company is providing more job opportunities for youth, which helps reduce unemployment levels and contributes to economic development. Also, Transporter succeeded in increasing the number of transactions, which indicates that it seeks to grow and have a scalable mindset that aids them in increasing the scalability of the business by expanding operations and adding more solutions. In addition, Transporter tries to operate the business based on the light-asset model as much as possible to reduce their costs. They operate through 15 branches, all rented and a central hub, also rented. However, recently they got an offer from (Banque du Caire) to lease the cars they use in their operations, which means that they are paying rent for it for a certain period of time (5 years) which is equivalent to an instalment and after that period (after 5 years) it becomes theirs as an asset.

This shows that the business benefit from the entrepreneurial mindset to seize the emerging opportunities in the market as by seizing this opportunity Transporter will be able to expand their operations as well as to have more assets in the long run without costing the company extra costs.

Also, Transporter has high adaptability according to the customer's requirements and market changes. For example, Transporter dedicated another central hub, especially for Alexandria shipments as it has many shipments that need to be shipped to different locations in Alexandria and other governorates, which requires more work than any other governorate. This shows that Transporter reacts to the market requirements and customer needs and adapts accordingly.

Moreover, Transporter like any other company, is affected by the current global crises. However, the Covid-19 pandemic affected Transporter positively, affecting the whole E-commerce industry since people became more used to online shopping due to ban restrictions. Transporter obtained a legal permit to work during the time of the ban, so it could continue working and take advantage of the situation.

On the contrary, the current global supply chain shortage, importing problems, and restrictions affected the business negatively as this caused a general shortage in goods, which decreased the demand in the market and consequently decreased the demand for Transporter's services and the number of shipments. However, Transporter has been able to mitigate this risk by diversifying its customer base and adding new customers to its customer base to be able to offset the loss in the number of shipments from each customer by adding new customers to return to the previous operating capacity in terms of many shipments. This demonstrates the ability to mitigate risks and confront global challenges by relying on their entrepreneurial mindset while responding to challenges with innovative solutions and a distinct way of thinking quickly and effectively.

In general, Transporter tries to plan for future risks and to be proactive rather than active in facing challenges and risks through trying to predict the risk and finding an innovative solution that will be able to respond to that risk as well as starting in applying this solution rapidly in order to cope with the rapid changes in the market. However, in case of unpredicted risks, Transporter can respond to it rapidly and effectively by establishing team meetings on the spot to find a rapid, effective solution. For example; By providing (Pick & Choose) unique service to customers, this increases flexibility in an E-commerce business which benefits the business owners who choose Transporter as a service provider that complements their businesses and increases their sales as this option encourages their end-customers to buy more through online-shopping since it eliminates the associated fear with E-commerce of having the wrong item as well as it increases the speed of the purchasing cycle and therefore the cash cycle of the business owners (Transporter's customers) and Transporter company as it helps the end-customers in picking their suitable items in one delivery order instead of making the shipping courier return back and forth to replace wrong items with new ones.

3.2. Second Case: Teradix Startup

Teradix startup Started in 2019, Where it took a year to prepare to start the startup. Then, it started working and entering the market in 2020, where it was just providing help to small-sized companies to connect them with suitable suppliers. However, they launched the system with its current innovative state in 2022, which can serve both small and large-sized companies. Teradix is a cloud-based software for procurement that enables companies to manage their spending efficiently, including purchase requisitions, eRFx, reverse auctions, supplier management, spend analytics, and contract management, while generating greater cost savings and maximising transparency for accelerated audit cycles and improved decisions for the business.

3.2.1 Teradix: Competitive advantage

Teradix succeeded in providing a digital tool that helps eliminate traditional procurement problems and facilitates the procurement process through a technologically innovative solution. This digitalised process will help face corruption by eliminating the need for paperwork (that may contain errors and fraud) and instead relying on software. Moreover, the provided solution will increase the transparency of the process and will decrease the waste of time and effort.

Teradix Solution specialised in the sourcing part of the process, solved it efficiently, and provided a solution that complements large companies' operations.

After the process of registering the request on the company's internal ERP system, the request is automatically transferred to Teradix system, where all the trusted suppliers only are registered. There is no possibility for the existence of fake suppliers on the system as the system guarantees the security for its users by verifying the suppliers' existence through verifying the E-mail and mobile number automatically through the system as well as checking a set of documents (like commercial registration and tax card) to ensure the validity of Suppliers to be part of a successful fair cycle and to ensure for companies that there is no tampering.

In addition, Teradix succeeded in gaining more advantage and offering customers a competitive advantage through verifying suppliers, so instead of being verified by the company Teradix saves time and effort for its clients by enabling them to shorten this step Which provides more security for companies in dealing with suppliers as well as reducing costs.

Teradix has a competitive edge over the traditional procurement process as it succeeded in causing radical changes in the procurement sector through digitalising and providing innovative solutions to the market. Moreover, Teradix eliminates a lot of paperwork and complicated procedures related to the traditional process and replaces them with more digitalised solutions that facilitate the process, make it more reliable and consistent, as well as minimising errors and allowing more flexibility in choosing and dealing with suppliers and in modifying purchase orders.

Teradix is revolutionising how businesses procure and source by offering the most innovative and intelligent procurement solutions that are simple, easy to use, yet packed with unique complementary features and insights. Moreover, Teradix was designed with simplicity in mind to guarantee ease of use, but it has also assured that the customer will earn substantial savings with Teradix sourcing module (eRFx & Reverse Auction), which applies pricing feedback to the customers' suppliers, so that they can bargain more effectively on customer behalf. Also, it provides each department with the appropriate capabilities, from management to requesters and buyers to suppliers. For example, it increases visibility and control as Teradix allows managers to have complete visibility and control by analysing data collected using Teradix customised expenditure reports to uncover savings possibilities and maximise productivity. As it helps the managers to operate and take the right decisions effectively. Also, From the most advantages that Teradix provide for its customers through using the system is that it increases the speed of operations and processes as well as allows cost reductions as Teradix provide Simplified sourcing events, reverse auctions, supplier management, supplier onboarding, analytics, and most crucially, reporting savings and lead time. Moreover, Teradix Supplier Portal makes sourcing events notifications, legal documents, communication, and submitting quotations simple, which allows faster engagement throughout the company departments and managers.

Teradix offers innovative procurement and sourcing solutions to assist companies in digitalising their procurement and sourcing processes and making smarter spending decisions. The innovative solutions that Teradix provides offer the suppliers the opportunity to have immediate detailed feedback from the system for their prices to be able to adjust their prices within minutes from the offerings according to the market and other supplier's offerings, which indicates a new era of fair competition in the market without bias for large companies. Moreover, this technological advance allows buyers to reduce costs through the system and have the best offerings for their requirements. For example, some companies based on true numbers succeeded in reducing costs by 30% through the Teradix system.

Also, Teradix's (reverse auction) innovative service allows companies to reduce costs in large orders through online real-time anonymous bidding with the ability to avoid problems of offline bidding between suppliers, such as favouritism, gratuity, and prior agreements on who will be awarded the bidding. Moreover, the system enforces the lowest minimum decrement by the supplier, which guarantees the buyers the lowest possible offer from the supplier. This experience of reverse auction can reduce costs by 25-30% in large orders. (For example, this service already reduced costs for a certain company from 1,200,000 to 820,000).

As a result, Teradix succeeded in growing reasonably quickly despite being a new idea that needs radical changes in employees' mindsets who might face the idea by refusal due to their fear that the system might replace the need for procurement employees. Moreover, Teradix has succeeded in growing despite the corruption in companies which is one of the main challenges to overcome, and at the same time, it has been able to be a solution to eliminating corruption through targeting to convince the decision-maker in the company who will benefit from Teradix then benefit from the network effect. Teradix depends on its growth strategy on the network effect of making delightful experiences to its customers to benefit from their word of mouth to convince other customers to try the system with increasing interest and awareness about the system. For example, the number of orders increased to nearly 45,000 as well as the number of suppliers on the system is more than 50,000, which indicates growth in the system as this will increase the available database of suppliers on the system.

Moreover, Teradix succeeded in adapting quickly and effectively to the current global crises as the company reacts to those crises as an opportunity for Teradix and manage to adapt be taking advantage of the crisis and convince the managers of their increased need for Teradix system during the crisis as all companies need to reduce overall costs. Teradix can quickly help companies to reduce overall costs (for example, through reducing the number of employees as well as allowing the company to know how much expenses are paid and how much is also saved Teradix offers low prices over a good service that will reduce overall costs, efforts and time).

This embedded technology in the system allows companies, whether suppliers or buyers, to be more agile towards changes in prices as it allows them to be flexible as well as speed in their response to price changes, and it allows them to be updated with real-time information that helps the companies to take agile on the spot yet reliable decisions.

Teradix provides exclusively a quotation system where suppliers can automatically offer their item prices and can help suppliers calculate the total cost for the quotation offer, including VAT (value-added Tax) and different currency options. The provided embedded quotation system gives the suppliers and buyers more flexibility to modify the prices of items and calculate them automatically and easily with just one click, allowing buyers to compare offered prices easily and suppliers to modify their prices easily. Moreover, the system provides updated information on a real-time basis which allows flexibility and, at the same time, ensures accuracy and speed.

4. DISCUSSION

To summarise, each startup disrupts the Supply Chain differently and in a different sector. However, the two Startups were able to increase the supply chain's agility, flexibility, and adaptability and were able, with their different, innovative solutions, to face the global challenges in the market. They were able to disrupt the supply chain and to change the processes used in their related business sectors as well as change the mindset of business owners and supply chain partners who became more flexible toward changing, digitalising, and innovation as this shift in mindset led to more profits to their companies as well as increasing their competitive edge. Moreover, the interviewed startups solved existing pains in the market and improved parts of the supply chain.

From that, it is clearly shown that the current study succeeded in achieving its aim, which is investigating the disruption caused by startups to the supply chain industry in Egypt as well as it shows how startups succeeded in overcoming the current challeunges and how they are able to make the supply chain and its activities more innovative, scalability, adaptable, and flexible. The following table shows a summary of these achieved points.

Table 5. Summary of findings

Startup	Innovation	Scalability and Growth	Adaptability	Flexibility
Transporter	Unique operation model and differentiated services	Expanding operations (continuous growing)	covid-19 pandemic affected Transporter positively (high adaptability)	Proactive rather than active
Teradix	Software solution for procurement problems	Expand and increase target market and operations (continuous expanding)	Reacts to those crises as an opportunity (high adaptability)	Agile on the spot yet reliable decisions

5. CONCLUSION AND RECOMMENDATIONS

This section will conclude the knowledge gained from reviewing the literature and the key findings of the case study and provide recommendations based on the contribution to the topic.

5.1. Conclusion

This case study examined the role of entrepreneurial thinking in promoting supply chain performance by focusing on startups in Egypt. The research aimed to investigate the disruption caused by startups to the supply chain industry in Egypt and how the traditional supply chain can benefit from the entrepreneurial mindset of startups to improve performance. The study used a qualitative approach, specifically case studies, to conduct semi-structured interviews with startups in different sectors. The research found that entrepreneurship causes tremendous disruption to the supply chain industry, where each startup disrupts the supply chain differently and in a different sector, leading to improvements in the agility, flexibility, and adaptability of the supply chain to face global challenges the market.

The study highlighted the importance of the Entrepreneurial Supply Chain concept as it emphasises innovation and expansion in addition to the usual focus on cost, quality, and delivery. Moreover, customers are connected to suppliers through entrepreneurial supply chains, which increases visibility throughout the whole network and allows for more growth and development. Entrepreneurial Supply Chain mainly aims to enable business development by detecting and responding to needs and opportunities that necessitate growth-oriented responses.

The research contributed to closing the gap in the existing literature by identifying the impact of entrepreneurship on disrupting the supply chain industry and providing insights into how traditional supply chains can benefit from the disruptive nature of startups. The research also highlighted the importance of the Entrepreneurial Supply Chain concept and its ability to solve industry challenges as well as to convert the pains into opportunities by making the supply chain and its activities more agile, efficient, adaptable, and flexible.

In addition, the case study found that startups in Egypt, such as TCS and Teradix, have the ability to provide innovative solutions for existing pains in the supply chain, which facilitates the traditional process and enhances performance. Both startups have successfully disrupted the supply chain industry in different sectors by introducing new and innovative solutions that improve efficiency, transparency, and security. TCS introduced a unique last-mile delivery service that improved its competitiveness, while Teradix introduced a cloud-based software for procurement that streamlined the procurement process and eliminated traditional problems.

Furthermore, the findings show the potential for traditional supply chains to benefit from the entrepreneurial mindset of startups. Startups often have a more agile, flexible, and adaptable approach to problem-solving that can be applied to traditional supply chains to improve performance. Besides, startups can provide new perspectives and innovative solutions that traditional supply chains may not have considered.

In conclusion, this case study emphasises the importance of entrepreneurship in the supply chain industry, particularly in the context of startups in Egypt. It highlights the potential for traditional supply chains to benefit from the disruptive nature of startups and the innovative solutions they provide. The research also contributes to the limited literature on Entrepreneurial Supply Chain by providing insights and practical examples of how it can be applied in the real world. This research can be used as a guide for traditional supply chains to learn from the entrepreneurial mindset of startups and apply it to their own operations to achieve better performance.

5.2. Recommendations

Entrepreneurship has greatly affected the supply chain and caused great disruption in the supply chain industry. Also, a lack of awareness on the topic of the Entrepreneurial Supply Chain is considered a limitation. So as a result, recommendations have been made in order to be able to benefit from this disruption. Recommendations are provided to policy makers, entrepreneurs, and potential entrepreneurs.

5.2.1 Policy Makers

- The government and educational institutions, should increase awareness and knowledge of the topic of the Entrepreneurial Supply Chain and its importance, as the topic is still new and needs more understanding.
- More Incubation Programs that are dedicated to entrepreneurship and supply chain at the same time (Entrepreneurial Supply Chain), such as the one provided by the AAST Entrepreneurship center should be provided by the government in order to be able to motivate more people and supports them to initiate more innovative ideas that help to cure more pains of the supply chain.
- The government should continue encouraging those entrepreneurial Startups as their Entrepreneurial Supply Chains are the new era towards growth and survival by providing more facilities on the financial and legal aspects that aid and give them more flexibility to work as well as reducing legal restrictions and complexities as it is considered barriers for Startups.
- The government should also provide more incentives and support for startups in the supply chain industry, such as tax breaks, grants, and access to funding, to encourage innovation and growth in the field.
- Banks should also increase banking facilitation and privileges for Startup owners that help them finance their innovative ideas.

5.2.2 Entrepreneurs

- Enterprises must be proceeded on different sectors to be able to discover more insights and aspects and demonstrate changes that happened to the supply chain in different sectors as this study is limited to only two sectors, and there are still more sectors across the supply chain that needs to be studied.

- Traditional Supply chains should start to increase Supply Chain Entrepreneurial Ebeddedness (SCEE), which involves embedding entrepreneurial thinking and entrepreneurial orientation throughout the supply chain by monitoring and taking advantage of the entrepreneurial mindset of startups that disrupt the supply chain and causing radical changes to be able to respond to these changes and take advantage.

5.2.3 Potential Entrepreneurs

- Always working on innovating new ideas and features that make them ready to face any sudden challenge.
- Train all its employees on how to understand their supply chain quiet well in order to be able to solve any unexpected problems faces by this chain.

CASE SUPPORT MATERIAL GUIDELINES

Questions and Answers

1. **How can traditional supply chains benefit from the entrepreneurial mindset of startups?**

Traditional supply chains can benefit from the entrepreneurial mindset of startups by collaborating with them to find innovative solutions for existing pains in the supply chain. Startups bring a fresh perspective and new ideas that can disrupt the industry, increase efficiency, and reduce costs. By collaborating with startups, traditional supply chains can gain access to new technologies, digitalisation, and sustainable practices that can help them to adapt to the changing market conditions and stay competitive. Additionally, startups can help traditional supply chains to become more agile, flexible and adaptable to face the global challenges in the market.

2. **What are the benefits of digitising procurement processes?**

Digitising procurement processes can bring a number of benefits to companies. One of the main benefits is that it can reduce errors and increase transparency throughout the process. This can be achieved by eliminating paperwork and instead relying on software to manage the process. Additionally, digitising procurement processes can improve supplier management by enabling companies to more easily identify and select suppliers, as well as monitor supplier performance. Furthermore, it can also increase the level of security as the system automatically verifies the E-mail and mobile number of suppliers to ensure that they are legitimate and trustworthy. By digitising procurement processes, companies can gain a competitive advantage by being more efficient and reducing costs.

3. **How can startups disrupt the supply chain industry?**

Startups can disrupt the supply chain industry by bringing new ideas and innovative solutions to the market. They can do this by developing new technologies, digitalising processes, and promoting sustainable practices. Startups can also challenge traditional business models and create new opportunities for growth and development. They can also bring a fresh perspective to the industry and help identify new innovation areas. Additionally, startups can help to create new jobs and support economic growth. In general, startups can disrupt the supply chain industry by causing radical changes in the industry and providing more efficient and cost-effective solutions to the market.

4. **What are the benefits of sustainable practices in the supply chain industry?**

Sustainable practices in the supply chain industry can bring a number of benefits to companies. One of the main benefits is that it can reduce environmental impact and promote sustainable practices throughout the supply chain network. Additionally, by promoting sustainable practices, companies can improve their reputation and attract more customers who are conscious of environmental and social issues. Moreover, sustainable practices can also lead to cost savings in the long run as it can decrease resource usage and environmental impact. Furthermore, sustainable practices can also help companies to comply with the regulations and laws related to the environment and sustainability.

5. **How can government and educational institutions increase awareness and knowledge of the Entrepreneurial Supply Chain?**

Government and educational institutions can increase awareness and knowledge of the Entrepreneurial Supply Chain by providing training and education programs for industry professionals and students. This can include workshops, seminars, and online courses that focus on the concept of Entrepreneurial Supply Chain and its importance in the industry. Additionally, government and educational institutions can also support research and development in the field, by funding studies and providing resources for researchers. Furthermore, they can also support the development of entrepreneurship and supply chain incubation programs, which can help to nurture new ideas and startups in the field. By providing these resources and support, government and educational institutions can help to increase awareness and knowledge of the Entrepreneurial Supply Chain and its importance in the industry.

6. What are the benefits of collaboration between traditional supply chains and startups?

Collaboration between traditional supply chains and startups can bring a number of benefits to companies. One of the main benefits is that it can increase efficiency and reduce costs by providing access to new technologies, digitalisation, and sustainable practices that can help to improve supply chain performance. Additionally, collaboration can also help to increase agility, flexibility, and adaptability in the face of global challenges in the market. Furthermore, startups can bring a fresh perspective and new ideas to the industry, which can help to identify new areas for innovation and growth. By collaborating with startups, traditional supply chains can gain a competitive advantage and stay relevant in the changing market conditions.

7. What are the key performance indicators that companies should monitor in order to improve supply chain performance?

Companies should monitor a variety of key performance indicators in order to improve supply chain performance. Some of the most important indicators include:

- Lead time: The amount of time it takes to fulfill a customer order
- On-time delivery: The percentage of orders that are delivered on time
- Inventory turnover: The rate at which inventory is sold and replenished
- Cost of goods sold: The total cost of producing and delivering products to customers
- Customer satisfaction: The degree to which customers are satisfied with the company's products and services
- Supplier performance: The performance of suppliers in terms of quality, delivery, and cost. By monitoring these indicators, companies can identify areas for improvement and take action to improve supply chain performance. Additionally, monitoring these indicators can also help to improve communication and collaboration throughout the supply chain network.

8. In what ways can traditional supply chains increase their Supply Chain Entrepreneurial Embeddedness (SCEE) to respond to disruptive changes in the industry?

Traditional supply chains can increase their Supply Chain Entrepreneurial Embeddedness (SCEE) by taking a number of actions. One of the main ways is to actively monitor and take advantage of the entrepreneurial mindset of startups that disrupt the supply chain. This can be achieved by engaging with startups and collaborating to gain access to new technologies, digitalisation, and sustainable practices that can help improve supply chain performance. Additionally, traditional supply chains can also increase their SCEE by investing in research and development to identify new areas for innovation and growth. Furthermore, companies can also increase their SCEE by encouraging employees to think entrepreneurially and providing them with the necessary resources and support to develop new ideas and solutions.

9. How do incubation programs for entrepreneurship and supply chain support the growth and development of the Entrepreneurial Supply Chain?

Incubation programs for entrepreneurship and supply chain support the growth and development of the Entrepreneurial Supply Chain by providing startups with the necessary resources and support to develop and scale their innovative solutions. These programs offer access to business mentorship, networking opportunities, and funding to help startups overcome the common challenges of starting a business. Incubation programs also provide startups with the knowledge and resources needed to understand and navigate the supply chain industry, which is essential for creating solutions that can disrupt the traditional supply chain and improve performance. Furthermore, incubation programs also bring together startups, traditional supply chains, and other stakeholders to promote collaboration and knowledge sharing, which can lead to developing more sustainable and efficient supply chain practices.

Lessons Learned

The case study of the role of entrepreneurial thinking in promoting supply chain performance in Egypt provided several key lessons, which include the following:

1. **Entrepreneurial thinking is essential for supply chain innovation and disruption.** The case study highlighted how startups were able to disrupt the supply chain industry in Egypt by bringing new ideas and innovative solutions to the market. This disruption led to improvements in the supply chain's agility, flexibility, and adaptability to face global challenges.
2. **Collaboration between traditional supply chains and startups can bring significant benefits.** The case study showed how traditional supply chains could benefit from the entrepreneurial mindset

of startups by collaborating with them to find innovative solutions for existing pains in the supply chain.

3. **New technologies can bring significant improvements to supply chain performance.** The case study highlighted how startups were able to use new technologies, such as cloud-based software, to improve efficiency, transparency, and security in the supply chain.
4. **Streamlining procurement processes can bring significant benefits.** The case study highlighted how startups were able to digitise paperwork and automate certain tasks to reduce errors, increase transparency, and improve supplier management.
5. **Startups can disrupt the supply chain industry in different ways.** The case study showed that the two startups studied disrupted the supply chain industry differently, but both positively impacted supply chain performance.
6. **Entrepreneurial Supply Chain is a relatively new concept requiring more research and understanding.** The case study highlighted the gap in the existing literature on the topic and the need for more research to fully understand the concept and its impact on the supply chain industry.
7. **Incubation programs are crucial for fostering entrepreneurship in the supply chain industry.** The case study highlighted the importance of incubation programs in providing resources and support for startups to develop their ideas and bring them to market.
8. **Government and private sector play a crucial role in supporting and encouraging entrepreneurship in the supply chain industry.** The case study highlighted the role of government and private sector in providing funding, resources, and incentives to support startups and foster entrepreneurship in the supply chain industry.
9. **Transparency and data analysis are essential for supply chain performance**. The case study highlighted the importance of data analysis and monitoring key performance indicators to identify areas for improvement and make data-driven decisions.
10. **Sustainable practices are crucial for supply chain performance.** The case study highlighted the importance of sustainability in reducing environmental impact and promoting sustainable practices throughout the supply chain network.

ACKNOWLEDGMENT

The authors would like to express sincere gratitude to Dr Hesham Al Araky for his support and networking with startups to learn the real ground insights; without his support and experience, this paper would not exist. We also highly appreciated the hard work of data collection carried out by Mohanad Hossam, Yasmine Ahmed, Passant Hany and Nada Abd El Naby.

REFERENCES

Abdalla, S. S., & Nakagawa, K. (2022, March). Entrepreneurial Leadership, Supply Chain Innovation, and Adaptability: A Cross-national Investigation. *Operations Research Forum*, *3*(1), 1–21. doi:10.100743069-022-00135-x

Aday, S., & Aday, M. S. (2020). Impact of COVID-19 on the food supply chain. *Food Quality and Safety*, *4*(4), 167–180. doi:10.1093/fqsafe/fyaa024

Akbar, I., Muzaffar, M., & Cheema, K. (2012). Entrepreneurial supply chain management competence: performance of manufacturing small and medium enterprises. *Available at SSRN 2386969.*

Akbari, M., Didehkhani, H., Shojaei, S., & Mehrabian, A. (2021). Designing an Entrepreneurial Supply Chain Model during Disasters in Iran. *Quarterly Scientific Journal of Rescue and Relief*, *13*(1), 9–15.

Al-Dhaafri, H. S., & Al-Swidi, A. (2016). The impact of total quality management and entrepreneurial orientation on organisational performance. *International Journal of Quality & Reliability Management*, *33*(5). Advance online publication. doi:10.1108/IJQRM-03-2014-0034

Al-Hakimi, M. A., & Borade, D. B. (2020). The impact of entrepreneurial orientation on the supply chain resilience. *Cogent Business & Management*, *7*(1), 1847990. doi:10.1080/23311975.2020.1847990

Amanor-Boadu, V., Marletta, P., & Biere, A. W. (2009). Entrepreneurial supply chains and strategic collaboration: The case of Bagòss Cheese in Bagolino, Italy. *International Food and Agribusiness Management Review*, *12*, 49-68.

Armor, D. A., & Taylor, S. E. (2003). The effects of mindset on behavior: Self-regulation in deliberative and implemental frames of mind. *Personality and Social Psychology Bulletin*, *29*(1), 86–95. doi:10.1177/0146167202238374 PMID:15272962

Aulet, W., & Murray, F. (2013). A tale of two entrepreneurs: Understanding differences in the types of entrepreneurship in the economy. *Available at SSRN 2259740.*

Baker, W. E., & Sinkula, J. M. (2009). The complementary effects of market orientation and entrepreneurial orientation on profitability in small businesses. *Journal of Small Business Management*, *47*(4), 443–464. doi:10.1111/j.1540-627X.2009.00278.x

Barot, H. (2015). Entrepreneurship–A Key to Success. *International Journal of Business and Management*, *3*(1), 163–165.

Bressanelli, G., Perona, M., & Saccani, N. (2019). Challenges in supply chain redesign for the Circular Economy: A literature review and a multiple case study. *International Journal of Production Research*, *57*(23), 7395–7422. doi:10.1080/00207543.2018.1542176

Chan, H. K., & Chan, F. T. (2010). Comparative study of adaptability and flexibility in distributed manufacturing supply chains. *Decision Support Systems*, *48*(2), 331–341. doi:10.1016/j.dss.2009.09.001

Christopher, M., & Jüttner, U. (2000). Developing strategic partnerships in the supply chain: A practitioner perspective. *European Journal of Purchasing & Supply Management*, *6*(2), 117–127. doi:10.1016/S0969-7012(99)00038-6

Covin, J. G., & Slevin, D. P. (1989). Strategic management of small firms in hostile and benign environments. *Strategic Management Journal*, *10*(1), 75–87. doi:10.1002mj.4250100107

Croom, S., & Brandon-Jones, A. (2007). Impact of e-procurement: Experiences from implementation in the UK public sector. *Journal of Purchasing and Supply Management, 13*(4), 294–303. doi:10.1016/j.pursup.2007.09.015

Davis, M. H., Hall, J. A., & Mayer, P. S. (2016). Developing a new measure of entrepreneurial mindset: Reliability, validity, and implications for practitioners. *Consulting Psychology Journal, 68*(1), 21–48. doi:10.1037/cpb0000045

Diandra, D., & Azmy, A. (2020). Understanding definition of entrepreneurship. International Journal of Management. *Accounting and Economics, 7*(5), 235–241.

Forsberg, J., & Towers, N. (2007). Creating agile supply networks in the fashion industry. *Journal of the Textile Institute, 98*(4), 377–386. doi:10.1080/00405000701502925

Frank, H., Kessler, A., & Fink, M. (2010). Entrepreneurial orientation and business performance—A replication study. *Schmalenbach Business Review, 62*(2), 175–198. doi:10.1007/BF03396804

Fujita, K., Gollwitzer, P. M., & Oettingen, G. (2007). Mindsets and pre-conscious open-mindedness to incidental information. *Journal of Experimental Social Psychology, 43*(1), 48–61. doi:10.1016/j.jesp.2005.12.004

Gedeon, S. (2010). *What is Entrepreneurship?* Retrieved 29 May 2022, from https://www.academia.edu/35644718/What_is_Entrepreneurship?from=cover_page

Gligor, D., Gligor, N., Holcomb, M., & Bozkurt, S. (2019). Distinguishing between the concepts of supply chain agility and resilience: A multidisciplinary literature review. *International Journal of Logistics Management, 30*(2), 467–487. doi:10.1108/IJLM-10-2017-0259

Gollwitzer, P. M. (2012). Mindset theory of action phases. Handbook of theories of social psychology, 1, 526-545.

Gonzalez-Padron, T., Hult, G. T. M., & Calantone, R. (2008). Exploiting innovative opportunities in global purchasing: An assessment of ethical climate and relationship performance. *Industrial Marketing Management, 37*(1), 69–82. doi:10.1016/j.indmarman.2007.06.013

Guo, Y., Wang, L., & Chen, Y. (2020). Green entrepreneurial orientation and green innovation: The mediating effect of supply chain learning. *SAGE Open, 10*(1), 2158244019898798. doi:10.1177/2158244019898798

Habbershon, T. G., Nordqvist, M., & Zellweger, T. (2010). Transgenerational entrepreneurship. *Transgenerational entrepreneurship: Exploring growth and performance in family firms across generations*, 1-38.

Habib, M. A., Bao, Y., Nabi, N., Dulal, M., Asha, A. A., & Islam, M. (2021). Impact of strategic orientations on the implementation of green supply chain management practices and sustainable firm performance. *Sustainability, 13*(1), 340. doi:10.3390u13010340

Handfield, R., Petersen, K., Cousins, P., & Lawson, B. (2009). An organisational entrepreneurship model of supply management integration and performance outcomes. *International Journal of Operations & Production Management, 29*(2), 100–126. doi:10.1108/01443570910932011

Hornsby, J. S., Kuratko, D. F., & Zahra, S. A. (2002). Middle managers' perception of the internal environment for corporate entrepreneurship: Assessing a measurement scale. *Journal of Business Venturing*, *17*(3), 253–273. doi:10.1016/S0883-9026(00)00059-8

Hsu, C. C., Tan, K. C., Laosirihongthong, T., & Leong, G. K. (2011). Entrepreneurial SCM competence and performance of manufacturing SMEs. *International Journal of Production Research*, *49*(22), 6629–6649. doi:10.1080/00207543.2010.537384

Ivanov, D., Sokolov, B., & Kaeschel, J. (2010). A multi-structural framework for adaptive supply chain planning and operations control with structure dynamics considerations. *European Journal of Operational Research*, *200*(2), 409–420. doi:10.1016/j.ejor.2009.01.002

Janvier-James, A. M. (2012). A new introduction to supply chains and supply chain management: Definitions and theories perspective. *International Business Research*, *5*(1), 194–207.

Jeong, Y. M., Ali, M., Zacca, R., & Park, K. (2019). The effect of entrepreneurship orientation on firm performance: A multiple mediation model. *Journal of East-West Business*, *25*(2), 166–193. doi:10.1080/10669868.2018.1536013

Jiang, Z. E. M., Liu, Y., Liu, J., & Li, Y. (2017). Study of manufacturing resource perception and process control of a radio-frequency-identification-enabled decentralised flexible manufacturing system. *Advances in Mechanical Engineering*, *9*(1), 1687814016687449. doi:10.1177/1687814016687449

Ketchen, D. J. Jr, & Hult, G. T. M. (2007). Bridging organisation theory and supply chain management: The case of best value supply chains. *Journal of Operations Management*, *25*(2), 573–580. doi:10.1016/j.jom.2006.05.010

Kraus, S., Harms, R., & Fink, M. (2010). Entrepreneurial marketing: moving beyond marketing in new ventures. *International Journal of Entrepreneurship and Innovation Management, 11*(1).

Kreiser, P. M., & Davis, J. (2010). Entrepreneurial orientation and firm performance: The unique impact of innovativeness, proactiveness, and risk-taking. *Journal of Small Business and Entrepreneurship*, *23*(1), 39–51. doi:10.1080/08276331.2010.10593472

Kropp, F., Lindsay, N. J., & Shoham, A. (2006). Entrepreneurial, market, and learning orientations and international entrepreneurial business venture performance in South African firms. *International Marketing Review*, *23*(5), 504–523. doi:10.1108/02651330610703427

Kuratko, D. F., & Welsch, H. P. (1994). *Entrepreneurial strategy: Text and cases*. Dryden Press.

Kurgun, H., Bagiran, D., Ozeren, E., & Maral, B. (2011). Entrepreneurial marketing-The interface between marketing and entrepreneurship: A qualitative research on boutique hotels. *European Journal of Soil Science*, *26*(3), 340–357.

Le, T. T., Vo, X. V., & Venkatesh, V. G. (2022). Role of green innovation and supply chain management in driving sustainable corporate performance. *Journal of Cleaner Production*, *374*, 133875. doi:10.1016/j.jclepro.2022.133875

Lee, C. S., Cheang, P. Y. S., & Moslehpour, M. (2022). Predictive analytics in business analytics: Decision tree. *Advances in Decision Sciences*, *26*(1), 1–29. doi:10.47654/v26y2022i1p1-29

Lee, H. L. (2004). The triple-A supply chain. *Harvard Business Review, 82*(10), 102–113. PMID:15559579

Lin, H., & Lin, Q. (2018). Research on the impact of supply chain integration of startups: Service supply chain perspective. *Open Journal of Social Sciences, 6*(4), 255–274. doi:10.4236/jss.2018.64022

Liu, Y., Lee, J. M., & Lee, C. (2020). The challenges and opportunities of a global health crisis: The management and business implications of COVID-19 from an Asian perspective. *Asian Business & Management, 19*(3), 277–297. doi:10.105741291-020-00119-x

Lumpkin, G. T., & Dess, G. G. (2001). Linking two dimensions of entrepreneurial orientation to firm performance: The moderating role of environment and industry life cycle. *Journal of Business Venturing, 16*(5), 429–451. doi:10.1016/S0883-9026(00)00048-3

Marcus, I. (2010). 'Agile supply chain: Strategy for competitive advantage'. *Journal Of Global Strategic Management, 7*(6), 5–17.

Marshall, D., McCarthy, L., McGrath, P., & Claudy, M. (2015). Going above and beyond: How sustainability culture and entrepreneurial orientation drive social sustainability supply chain practice adoption. *Supply Chain Management, 20*(4), 434–454. doi:10.1108/SCM-08-2014-0267

Matthyssens, P., & Vandenbempt, K. (2008). Moving from basic offerings to value-added solutions: Strategies, barriers and alignment. *Industrial Marketing Management, 37*(3), 316–328. doi:10.1016/j.indmarman.2007.07.008

McCullen, P., Saw, R., Christopher, M., & Towill, D. (2006, January). The F1 supply chain: adapting the car to the circuit-the supply chain to the market. In Supply chain forum: an international journal (Vol. 7, No. 1, pp. 14-23). Taylor & Francis. doi:10.1080/16258312.2006.11517154

Mentzer, J. T., Stank, T. P., & Myers, M. B. (2007). Why Global Supply Chain Management? Handbook of global supply chain management, 1-16.

Naldi, L., Nordqvist, M., Sjöberg, K., & Wiklund, J. (2007). Entrepreneurial orientation, risk taking, and performance in family firms. *Family Business Review, 20*(1), 33–47. doi:10.1111/j.1741-6248.2007.00082.x

Namagembe, S., Ryan, S., & Sridham, R. (2017). Enviropreneurial orientation in SME supply chains: Construct measurement development. *World Journal of Entrepreneurship, Management and Sustainable Development, 13*(2), 128–150. doi:10.1108/WJEMSD-08-2016-0036

Okangi, F. P. (2019). The impacts of entrepreneurial orientation on the profitability growth of construction firms in Tanzania. *Journal of Global Entrepreneurship Research, 9*(1), 1–23. doi:10.118640497-018-0143-1

Oliva, R., & Watson, N. (2011). Cross-functional alignment in supply chain planning: A case study of sales and operations planning. *Journal of Operations Management, 29*(5), 434-448.

Paritala, P. K., Manchikatla, S., & Yarlagadda, P. K. (2017). Digital manufacturing-applications past, current, and future trends. *Procedia Engineering, 174*, 982–991. doi:10.1016/j.proeng.2017.01.250

Paul, S. K., Chowdhury, P., Moktadir, M. A., & Lau, K. H. (2021). Supply chain recovery challenges in the wake of COVID-19 pandemic. *Journal of Business Research, 136*, 316–329. doi:10.1016/j.jbusres.2021.07.056 PMID:34538979

Pibernik, R., & Sucky, E. (2007). An approach to inter-domain master planning in supply chains. *International Journal of Production Economics, 108*(1-2), 200–212. doi:10.1016/j.ijpe.2006.12.010

Ratten, V. (2020). Coronavirus (covid-19) and entrepreneurship: Changing life and work landscape. *Journal of Small Business and Entrepreneurship, 32*(5), 503–516. doi:10.1080/08276331.2020.1790167

Richey, R. G., Tokman, M., & Wheeler, A. R. (2006). A supply chain manager selection methodology: Empirical test and suggested application. *Journal of Business Logistics, 27*(2), 163–190. doi:10.1002/j.2158-1592.2006.tb00221.x

Rocha, H. O. (2004). Entrepreneurship and development: The role of clusters. *Small Business Economics, 23*(5), 363–400. doi:10.100711187-004-3991-8

Rowley, J. (Ed.). (2000). *The principles of warehouse design*. Institute of Logistics and Transport.

Sarkis, J. (2020). Supply chain sustainability: Learning from the COVID-19 pandemic. *International Journal of Operations & Production Management, 41*(1), 63–73. doi:10.1108/IJOPM-08-2020-0568

Saunders, M., Lewis, P., & Thornhill, A. (2009). *Research methods for business students*. Pearson education.

Scala, B., & Lindsay, C. F. (2021). Supply chain resilience during pandemic disruption: Evidence from healthcare. *Supply Chain Management, 26*(6), 672–688. doi:10.1108/SCM-09-2020-0434

Schumpeter, J. (1961). The theory of economic development: an inquiry into profits, capital, credit, interest, and the business cycle. Oxford University Press. (Original publication 1934)

Seelos, C., & Mair, J. (2004). *Social entrepreneurship-The contribution of individual entrepreneurs to sustainable development*. Academic Press.

Stank, T. P., Daugherty, P. J., & Ellinger, A. E. (1999). Marketing/logistics integration and firm performance. *International Journal of Logistics Management, 10*(1), 11–24. doi:10.1108/09574099910805905

Tahmasebifard, H., Zangoueinezhad, A., & Jafari, P. (2017). The role of entrepreneurial orientation in achieving agility capability. *Journal of Applied Economics & Business Research, 7*(2), 137–156.

Tang, C., & Tomlin, B. (2008). The power of flexibility for mitigating supply chain risks. *International Journal of Production Economics, 116*(1), 12–27. doi:10.1016/j.ijpe.2008.07.008

Van Hoek, R. I. (2006). Moving forward with agility–a little faster. *International Journal of Physical Distribution & Logistics Management, 36*(6). Advance online publication. doi:10.1108/ijpdlm.2006.00536faa.002

Wagner, S. M. (2021). Startups in the supply chain ecosystem: An organising framework and research opportunities. *International Journal of Physical Distribution & Logistics Management, 51*(10), 1130–1157. doi:10.1108/IJPDLM-02-2021-0055

Wales, W. J., Gupta, V. K., & Mousa, F. T. (2011). 201 1, Empirical Research on Entrepreneurial Orientation: An Assessment and Suggestions for Future Research. *International Small Business Journal*, 13. Advance online publication.

Whitten, G. D., Green, K. W., & Zelbst, P. J. (2012). Triple-A supply chain performance. *International Journal of Operations & Production Management*.

Wong, C., Skipworth, H., Godsell, J., & Achimugu, N. (2012). Towards a theory of supply chain alignment enablers: A systematic literature review. *Supply Chain Management*, *17*(4), 419–437. doi:10.1108/13598541211246567

Wong, W. P., & Wong, K. Y. (2007). Supply chain performance measurement system using DEA modeling. *Industrial Management & Data Systems*, *107*(3), 361–381. doi:10.1108/02635570710734271

Wu, C., & Barnes, D. (2012). A dynamic feedback model for partner selection in agile supply chains. *International Journal of Operations & Production Management*, *32*(1), 79–103. doi:10.1108/01443571211195745

Wu, L., Park, D., Chinta, R., & Cunningham, M. (2010). Global entrepreneurship and supply chain management: A Chinese exemplar. *Journal of Chinese Entrepreneurship*.

Chapter 10
The Role of Online Platforms in Enhancing Logistics Activity Performance:
Case Study – Salla Platform: KSA

Sandra Samy Haddad
Arab Academy for Science, Technology, and Maritime Transport, Egypt

Nourhan Foaad Nasib
Arab Academy for Science, Technology, and Maritime Transport, Egypt

EXECUTIVE SUMMARY

Technology has progressed from being a supporter of the fundamental element of today's economy. The "digital economy" includes digital sectors, such as media, e-commerce, as well as traditional industries that have been touched by digitalization to varying degrees. This case study focuses on the Saudi e-commerce retail industry and how much it has grown exponentially through increased internet penetration, use of smartphones, and language diversity on e-commerce platforms. Moreover, the adoption of digital wallets is now more prevalent, supported by a general shift towards digital payments. The development of transport and logistics systems is based on digital platforms, such as Salla platform, which has a significant impact on the efficiency and competitiveness of supply chains and the logistics activities in KSA. Salla connects its sellers and customers. The platform provides companies with many advantages and tools.

BACKGROUND

Coordination, transaction information, customer services, inventory, and standardization of the system are all part of supply chain integration (Kang et al., 2018). Therefore, the perspective of the entire supply chain integration requires the use of emerging technology to improve the performance of logistics activities, follow of information, and enable, in the process, the monitoring of physical goods. Since

DOI: 10.4018/978-1-6684-4686-7.ch010

2010, many supply chains have been automated to control demand, complexity, and integration (Bahrin et al., 2016).

The importance of implementing digitalization and automation in the supply chain can be summarized as enhancing data availability, interactions, collaboration, and market information. This data enables the firm to improve the usefulness, production, and credibility of its products for the consumer (Buyukozkan & Gocer, 2018). Furthermore, quick and flexible responses to customer demand, moreover, decrease delivery lead time, (Spro'e et al., 2017). Automation and centralization of processes help companies make their workers more effective, have better visibility, and support firms to reduce and manage cost-effectively. Process automation usually results in up to 20% cost savings for the related cost base (Raab and Cryan, 2019). The future of digitalization in the supply chain will be critical due to the potential impact of a 75% reduction in inventory and a 30% reduction in operating costs (Ferrantino & Koten, 2019).

E-commerce refers to digital commerce, which is the ability of electronic media and the internet to sell products and services over the internet, thus e-retailing. E-retailing is one of the main logistics activities which expanded due to the speed and ease of use for customers (Kurtz, 2016). Also, selling online can help startups and SMEs to expand their market and increase their sales and revenues. E-commerce activities, such as selling online, can be directed to consumers or other businesses. Business to Consumer (B2C) involves the online sales of goods, services, and provision of information directly to consumers, while Business to Business (B2B) refers to the online selling of products, services, or information between businesses. (Jain et al., 2021).

After COVID-19, consumer behavior has altered globally, accelerating e-domination commerce in the retail industry. E-commerce businesses have included elements that are particularly appealing to customers to draw in more customers, like multi-category product ranges, ratings and reviews, discounted deals, inexpensive delivery, free exchanges and returns, competitive price, and 24/7 availability. The value of the e-commerce market increased by 40% between 2015 and 2020, reaching USD 9.8 billion, and Saudi Arabia was among the top 26 e-commerce markets worldwide. Saudi Arabia stands out among the gulf cooperation council due to its big GDP, vast size, enormous population, impressive purchasing power, high concentration of oil and gas, and extensive mineral and metal resources. In addition, the country now has the second-highest number of social media, smartphone, and internet platforms after the United Arab Emirates, and 70% of its people purchase online. KSA has invested USD 21.3 billion in services and goods across 45,000 stores and e-commerce platforms. China accounts for 46% of all cross-border e-commerce in the Kingdom of Saudi Arabia (gov.sa, 2022).

Vision 2030 of the Kingdom of Saudi Arabia (KSA) is to improve efficiency and become one of the world's leading economies. Part of Saudi Arabia's growth is the assurance to increase the retail segment and confirm that modern business and e-commerce will account for 80% of the retail segment by 2020. E-commerce allows customers to shop whenever and wherever they want. Given Saudi Arabia's appetite for Internet dissemination and e-commerce, commercial activities in KSA will be strengthened by Internet support. For example, the homecentre.com website is the first of many phases designed to provide devoted consumers with online-channel familiarity as well as a more appropriate shopping experience (Khwaja, 2017).

On the other hand, the Vision has identified that traditional retailing controls approximately 50% of the market in Saudi Arabia, compared to 20% in the Gulf Cooperation Council (GCC), with the retail shop suffering from inadequate dissemination of modern business and e-commerce. The administration intends to increase the contribution of modern trade and e-commerce to 80% in the retail segment by 2030. This is intended to be accomplished by appealing to both local and global retail stakeholders, aggregating funding for minor retail firms in order to inspire their growth and expansion and reducing restrictions on proprietorship and external investment (Khwaja, 2017).

These plans were interrupted due to the COVID-19 pandemic, which impacted all sectors worldwide from economic and environmental fluctuations to changes in income, education, employment, and more. The retail industry is one of the industries where the impact of the pandemic was very evident as it operates at the downstream supply chain and is in direct contact with the end consumers. Nevertheless, KSA as described before already had plans in place for boosting e-commerce, especially in the retail segment which was a great enabler to return back on track. The problem that resides is that the retail industry in KSA is still fragmented and not well connected to the rest of the supply chain partners and logistics service providers electronically. Moreover, given the lockdown situation, retailers who were going online as a substitute needed to cover larger geographical locations, thus, needed more than ever to connect to other supply chain partners and logistics service providers.

Accordingly, this case discusses the importance and development of pioneer e-logistics platforms and how they helped the fragmented retail industry to overcome challenges during COVID-19. E-logistics platforms, such as Salla, contributed to the enhancement of retail and logistics activities, which has significantly impacted the efficiency and competitiveness of supply chains in KSA. Thus, the case demonstrates the concept of developing fully integrated logistics platforms that support SMEs with many advantages and tools to positively affect their management of logistics activities through full technological connectivity and ease of communication among members of the supply chain.

A case study technique was used for a better understating of the situation and to analyze the industry's position and capabilities to face the consequences of the pandemic. Salla platform is used as a best practice and pioneer in the Middle East as its role was not only concerned with addressing the challenges of setting up the business and convincing the customers of online retailing, but its services included setting up dedicated e-stores for each retailer, customer service, goods tracking and logistics activities offered to retailers such as shipping, distribution, and warehousing to facilitate the reach of the good nationwide. This qualitative research is based on global and country reports, literature, interviews with the CEO and founder of Salla platform, and company reports.

THE IMPACT OF E-COMMERCE ON THE RETAIL INDUSTRY IN KSA

The digitalization of the economy, through using new technology, which has long been characterized by exponential growth (e.g., mobile, internet, tablets), has created a vicious circle with various economic advantages. The digital economy has always been an interesting area of discussion for society as well as for nations, as it particularly contributes to the economic and technical development of a country. In general, the digital economy is understood as an economy based entirely on information and innovative technology. It involves every stage of education, from education, culture, and training to the manufacturing of computer parts, including hardware and software programs, such as smartphone programs, mobile applications, and other internet-based programs. It is widely believed that the digital economy of a country cannot be created without adequate higher-level legislation from the respective governments; the primary aim of KSA's national transformation plan or national vision is to invest in the digital economy through the financial balance program or the financial sector development program. This financial balance program monitors and evaluates the financial performance of the nation by maximizing non-oil revenue,

Figure 1. Increased number of users of e-commerce in billion
Source: Statista (2021)

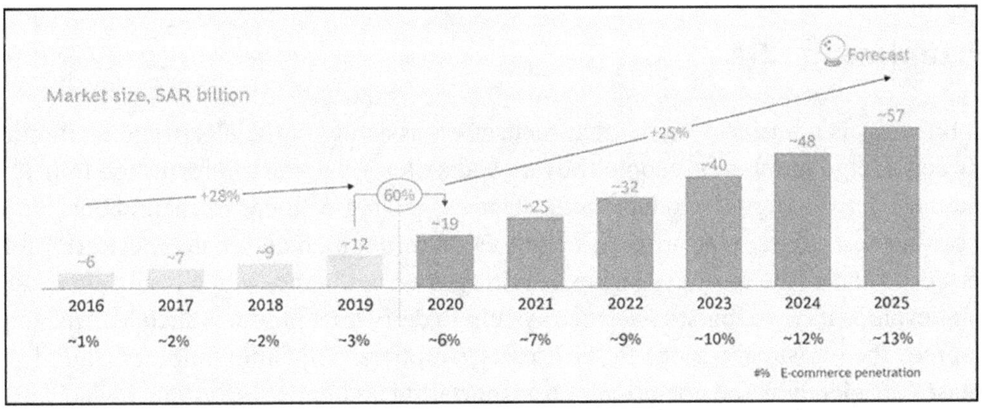

increasing the spending efficiency of the government, managing the associated risks, and maintaining financial reserves to achieve financial sustainability (Wolff, 2020).

E-commerce has the potential to be a big contributor to the Saudi economy. Some of its benefits include the fact that enterprises will be available to all citizens, not only on a regional level but also on a worldwide scale. Operational cost savings: The expenses of creating, processing, distributing, storing, and retrieving paper-based information will be greatly reduced, especially in the long run. E-Commerce has revolutionized the way people buy things by allowing mass customization for economies of scale. Citizens' needs can be met by tailoring products and services. Shopping on the internet allows residents to purchase or do other transactions 24 hours a day, 7 days a week, all year from nearly any location in any Arab country, which will significantly improve accessibility for the laggard countries. E-commerce has improved the shipping process. This can include everything from instant delivery of digital or electronic items to online tracking of package delivery progress. E-commerce will abolish monopolistic markets, creating a more competitive environment (Arab Vision for Digital Economy, 2020).

During and even before the pandemic situation, conventional retailers in Saudi Arabia were not doing well (Ministry Media, 2020; Saudi Arabia Retail Report, 2017). Even in earlier times, conventional retail sales performance had declined significantly from 6.1% in 2013 to 2.2% in 2016 (GCC Retail Industry, 2017). Previous studies have shown that the reason behind the decline in conventional retail sales is due to an exponential growth in the number of e-retailer customers in KSA from 10.5 million in 2016 to 19.3 million in 2022. Increasing performance trends of e-retailers posed a significant threat to brick-and-mortar retail outlets (Statista, 2021).

In KSA E-commerce market has been exponential growth during the covid -19. According to Figure 1 the number of e-commerce is expected to hit SAR 50 billion by 2025. A 7% and a 5% additional growth is anticipated, respectively, due to the effects of the pandemic between 2020-2022 and 2023-2025. The trend however gained momentum during the corona pandemic as the movement was curtailed and so do social isolation. The trend was fast picked by fast foods, regular restaurants, and other retailers who were utilizing different mobile applications to divert customers and adopt the new trends offered by e-business trends. The model was quickly adopted by some of the retailers including Carrefour and Hyper panda which included free home delivery with certain limitations, to attract the customer base. Saudi Arabia's e-commerce is still in a nascent phase. In 2020, it accounted for just 6% of total retail sales, compared to leading e-commerce markets, whose global penetration reached 18% in 2020 (Satista, 2022).

Digital Platforms in KSA

A platform business is a business model that focuses on assisting in the electronic facilitation of interactions between a large number of people (buyers and sellers). Digital platforms are transforming how we consume and deliver digital products and services, posing a threat to incumbents. In contrast to traditional businesses, digital platforms co-create value through an automated network of agents. The logistics service is one of the most expensive activities in e-commerce, which is why, in most situations, the platform develops its own logistics service system to deliver its products such as Amazon, while the seller outsources the logistical service to third-party suppliers. This integration of digital platforms in Leeds increases efficiency in the operation of transportation and logistics systems, which are the fundamental connection and the core of supply chain information and analysis (National Digital Transformation Indicators and Achievements Report, 2019). The number of electronic stores in the KSA has increased by 12.45%, reaching 28,676 stores, in addition to the emergence of platforms that facilitate the creation of electronic stores, such as Salla, Shopify, Expand cart, and Zid Platforms.

Saudis have been embracing digital platforms to study, shop, and work since the emergence of COVID-19. That is why KSA has high hopes of becoming a global leader in the field of digital government by utilizing a "smart digital government concept," which entails using data and emerging technology to build user-centric platforms that deliver services to individuals, the public sector, and commercial organizations, enhancing efficiencies and facilitating access to everyone. KSA aims to enable digital platforms that deliver social prosperity and economic growth through the effective adoption of digital technologies and modern innovative business models, as well as controls and regulations that balance investor and user rights to foster a safe and competitive environment for the development of such platforms (National Digital Transformation Indicators and Achievements Report, 2019).

Factors Enabling Online Platforms to Succeed in KSA

These factors involve Saudi Arabia's telecommunications, internet, legislation, and financial services that support the Salla platform. Saudi consumers have shifted from using PCs to smartphones as they preferred devices for online shopping. KSA boasts one of the highest smartphone penetration rates (97%) in the world, which enabled around 60% of Saudi customers to discover new sellers through social networks in 2020. (Mastercard., 2020).

A widespread boom occurred after the primary three months of the COVID-19 spread. E-commerce around the world witnessed increasing speed due to the lockdown measures. For many shoppers, online retail was a reasonable arrangement to buy basic things while following stay-at-home orders. In June 2020, retail e-commerce site activity around the world recorded more than 21.9 billion monthly visits compared to 16.2 billion in June 2019, according to statistics. Saudi Arabia is the foremost alluring showcase within the Middle East for an e-commerce retailer to work in. The youthful population is energetic and uses their devices for versatile shopping. The past challenges of hesitance towards online payments have presently broken up due to the Covid-19 situation, pushing numerous merchants to utilize e-commerce platforms (GOV. SA Unified National Platform, 2022).

The Agility of Change of Laws According to the E-Commerce Industry

The government has made an effort to enhance the regulatory environment. The government implemented the E-commerce Law in October 2019, which was designed to regulate digital payments and improve transparency, and the Ministry of Commerce and Investment adopted the E-commerce Law Implementing Regulations on January 31, 2020, which added increased oversight to areas like personal data protection, consumer rights, and disclosure obligations.

The government wants to boost the proportion of online payments to 70% by 2030, up from the 2020 objective of 28%, as part of the Financial Sector Development Program, which is also part of Vision 2030. Logistics and infrastructure are expected to grow during the projection period due to the considerations outlined above. According to (Yahoo Finance, 2021), all these elements have bolstered the platform, despite the Saudi consumer's preference for online shopping. To begin with, convenience has risen to the top of the consumer priority list, with 90% of Saudi Arabians actively seeking methods to save time and simplify their lives (Meta for Business, 2020).

Reliable Network of Roads and Services

Despite the Kingdom's extensive land, air, and sea transportation networks, HRH the Crown Prince's strategy intends to position the Kingdom as the world's fifth-largest air transit passenger route, increase international destinations to 250 destinations, and launch a new national carrier. Regarding air cargo capacity, we want to increase it to more than 4.5 million tons. His Royal Highness, the Crown Prince, has set a target of exceeding 40 million containers each year in maritime shipping. In addition, the strategy will increase the total future length of railways to an estimated 8,080 kilometers, including the flagship "Land Bridge" project, which will span over 1,300 kilometers and connect the Kingdom's ports from the Arabian Gulf to the Red Sea, with a capacity of over 3 million passengers and 50 million tons per year. All of this progress will lead to a significant improvement in the logistic network, which will be managed intelligently (Ministery of Transport and Logistics Services, 2022).

SALLA PLATFORM

Salla Platform was founded in 2016, by Nawaf Hareeri and Salman Butt. Salla is a platform for e-commerce with a new retail concept, especially in the Middle East as it allows retailers to set up their online stores in their own names and provide them with a range of free basic packages or paid packages (Salla plus or Salla pro) linked with social media. It acts like a hub for retailers, like an online mall where retailers can have their own stores and get extra marketing and logistics services. The platform started through the website linked to Instagram at the beginning because Salla entrepreneurs noticed that most Saudi merchants are using Instagram to sell their products through it. Also, Salla believed in the importance of Instagram in achieving sales by reaching the whole Saudi market, and it is a well-known easy-to-use application. Furthermore, Instagram allowed Salla to increase its market share through different advertising and promotions that attract and link different Instagram users, as in the beginning they focused on small businesses because Salla can assist them in expanding their business into new markets and increasing sales and revenues, which has opened the way for the platform to work with larger businesses (Salla.sa, 2022).

Salla users linked their URLs with Instagram. The services provided by the platform were initially limited to the product catalog, price, and quantity. Over time, the services provided by Salla have been developed to include integrated payment solutions, order tracking, generating reports, and listing products. Moreover, Salla has offered quality inspection and monitoring services, along with its warehousing solutions and other logistics services. Nowadays, Salla has more than thirteen thousand electronic stores providing different products and services with a revenue of more than SAR 5 billion and 20 million orders (Salla.sa, 2022).

The Importance of the Salla Platform

Salla platform is considered a pioneer and a best practice in the Middle East given the model it presents, which is different from most other online retail platforms. It is a local online platform that enables sellers to create their own e-stores in the form they want. In addition, it provides users with a range of professional designs at the lowest cost, with free hosting and periodic, no - commission sales updates. The ease with which sellers manage their inventory and products is due to the consolidation between the Salla platform and the ERP programs that regulate the functioning of the inventory, whether the products are digital, on-demand, or actual. One of the most important features of the Salla platform is that it supports all means of payment, starting with bank transfer, payment on receipt, credit card payment, as well as payment through PayPal and Apple Pay. The platform helps sellers increase their stores' sales by providing a range of marketing tools that enable them to run marketing campaigns and target the right segment of customers. Not only does the platform provide sellers with building their stores, following their sales, and managing their products but it also provides them with detailed reports and tools that help store owners with automatic invoices, integration, Instagram, customer database, the ability to block customers, pin favorite products, having offers and discounts, and measuring the performance of the store, so sellers will be able to make the best decisions that are useful to their work. The platform also offers warehousing services through 3rd party logistics providers (3PL). Thus, Salla presents a wide range of retail, marketing, reporting, and other logistics services.

In addition, Salla allows unhappy consumers to submit complains and considers these complaints as areas for improvement. When customers contact Salla to complain about a bad experience, they are given top attention and a 24/7 live chat with a trained representative who knows how to deal with irate customers (S. Butt, personal communication, February 21, 2022).

Comparison Between Salla and Amazon

Some of the world's major e-commerce players, such as Amazon, eBay, and Alibaba Group's All Express, are already present in Saudi Arabia's marketplace. Moreover, the highly viewed e-commerce websites in Saudi Arabia are Souq.com, Haraj.com.sa, and Amazon. Souq.com is a common website for the Middle East that is more like Amazon.com. The existence of these two websites on the list advocates high assurance in e-commerce dealings. Amazon completed its acquisition of e-commerce Souq.com in Saudi Arabia. Amazon has developed a strong logistics system, as it has developed its own warehousing operating systems and deployed analytical solutions for tracking, storing, and analyzing vast amounts of historical data from earlier transactions. Furthermore, it was able to understand consumer preferences from previous sales using AI and machine learning. Data analytics made it feasible to predict future sales. The "just-in-time" technology used by Amazon increased its storage capacity while also streamlining

Table 1. Comparison between Amazon and Salla

Salla Platform	Amazon.com
· Salla is an online platform allows merchants to build their own online store. · Salla gives merchants a free domain (www.sellername.com). · Salla offers three packages to merchants, and they can choose one of the packages according to their needs. However, one of these packages is free. · Salla offers an integrated supply chain. · Salla overcoming supply chain challenges (such as shipping, warehousing, and distribution costs) by linking the merchants to logistics service providers. · Availability of various and secure electronic payment methods and services (such as PayPal and Apple pay). · The ability to provide detailed reports on the performance of your online store. · Salla use smart technology such as artificial intelligence, data science, and expert system.	· Amazon is an online store, and brands can build their own online store within the Amazon store. · No domain for merchants. · The cost to ship your orders depends on whether merchants use Fulfillment by Amazon (FBA), or self-ship on their own. · Fulfillment by amazon starts at 5 SAR per unit, which varies by the size of the unit. · Independent third-party sellers sold more than a billion items in 2019. · Have their own warehousing operating system. · Offer forecasts of upcoming sales using artificial intelligence and machine learning.

the management of inventories (Istizada, 2019). The following Table presents a comparison between the global online retailer Amazon.com and Salla.

Thus, what mainly differentiates Salla from Amazon and other retail platforms is that it is mainly about providing space for local retailers to thrive as they offer them free domains, their own online stores, customized marketing services, different payment methods, performance measurement reports, and tailored logistical services through 3PLs such as shipping, distribution, and warehousing such allowed many local retailers to reboot operations during COVID-19, get access to new customers, serve bigger geographical areas, thus, overcome the pandemic challenges to a great extent.

During the pandemic and lockdown, the successful models presented by Salla and some other online platforms led to increased competition in the e-commerce space among existing players, and new entrants attracted by the striving market. Providing logistical services and matchmaking with 3PLs is Salla's strength and competitive advantage in the marketplace, thus it contracted nearly forty logistics companies, including international companies and local companies, to support this advantage such as:

1. E-fulfillment companies:
    - Fulfillment of all online store orders from the store or pick-up points; once an order is placed on the website, the platform provides fulfillment solutions, including warehousing, picking, packaging, customer services, and shipping of products. After that, products are sent for processing based on the delivery location at the processing. Organizations can use a fulfillment service to manage customer orders, send shipments on time, and get dated information on products for restocking.
2. Shipping companies only:
    - When any request comes to the merchant, it automatically turns to the shipping company and ships it to the customer's door.
3. Logistics company such as SAMSA Express (SAMSA Express, 2022):
    - Absolute security: personal ID and address validation, plus a dedicated call center in which all calls are recorded.
    - Transparency and traceability: online tracking and SMS updates in real-time.

- Mailroom management: mail reception, dispatch, and distribution services enhance productivity while reducing error and expense.
- Fast and cost-effective: service throughout the country, 6 days a week.
- A proven track record: in the country's financial sector.
- International and domestic freight – road, sea, and air.
- Customs brokerage and insurance.
- Oversized or special cargo.
- Extensive global network for international freight.
- Handling of oversized, delicate, and/or dangerous cargo.
- Door-to-door, hold-for-pick-up, or drop-off service.
- "Next-flight" urgent delivery.
- Tracking in real-time and online.
- Sub-assembly and kitting to speed up/simplify the supply chain.
- Storage solutions including warehouse and inventory management.
- In-plant logistics and support.
- Line-side feeding.
- Integrated services for an optimized supply chain.
- Fully automated ordering/shipping system customized to your needs.
- Packing – consolidation, pillarization, wrapping, and returnable assets.
- Pre-market customization (kitting and bundling).
- Fast turnaround and competitive pricing.
- Repair and return.

COMPARISON BETWEEN THE CONVENTIONAL RETAIL MARKET SITUATION AND THE SITUATION AFTER THE ENTRANCE OF UNCONVENTIONAL E-PLATFORMS SUCH AS "SALLA" IN KSA

Traditional retailers in Saudi Arabia have underperformed during and even before the pandemic situation (Ministry Media, 2020; Saudi Arabia Retail Report, 2017). Even in earlier dates, conventional retail sales performance had declined significantly from 6.1% in 2013 to 2.2% in 2016 (GCC Retail Industry, 2017). Salla entrepreneurs noticed this situation and wanted to use this gap in the fragmented domestic retail market. The operations of the conventional Saudi market are shown in Figure 2, where merchants used to face numerous challenges such as the inability to cover all Saudi regions due to, for example, the rising cost of transportation. In addition, each retailer had to contact different logistics providers to deliver the products consuming a lot of time and effort during communications, negotiations, and papers paperwork. Also, logistics service providers charged individual retailers highly, especially if they are first-time customers and/or have small cargo volumes, so the retailers were obliged to increase their shipment numbers to reduce the logistics activities price provided by 3PLs. Moreover, the logistics providers set various conditions for retailers to obtain lower prices. For example, they must be initially contacted by the company with an annual contract. Salla's founders saw the opportunity to improve this system and offer innovative solutions to the Saudi retail market by implementing the e-retail and logistics system to help Saudi merchants solve the logistics providers' high rates and improve customer service. That is why Salla had always arranged with its channel partners for opportunities to apply organizational techniques

Figure 2. The conventional retail market situation in KSA
Source: The authors

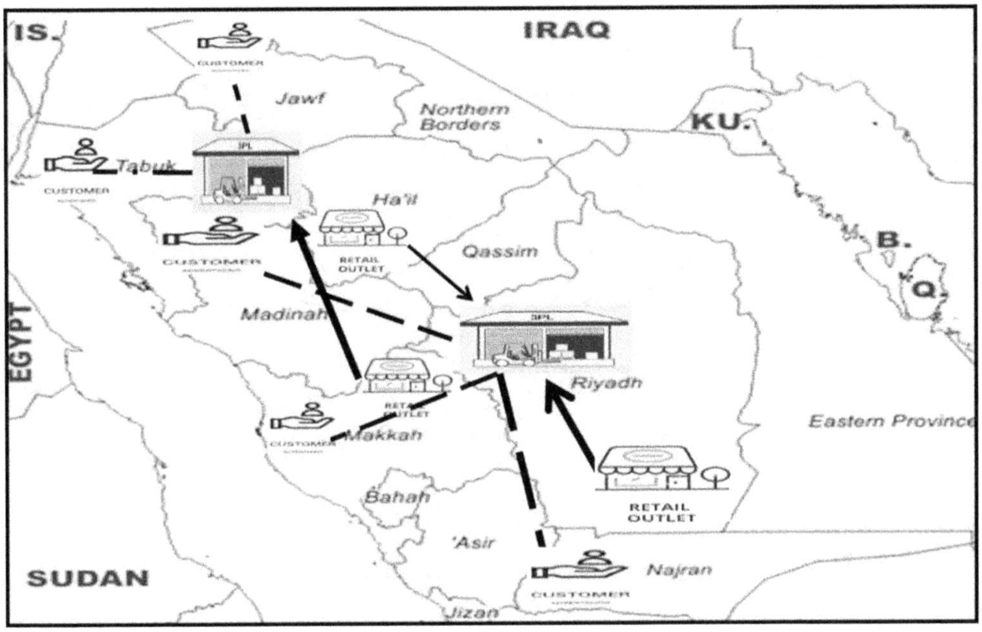

and technologies that could accelerate transaction and information transfer speed and cement channel loyalties (S. Butt, personal communication, February 21, 2022).

The platform started with online contracting of logistics service providers' startups and Small and Medium-size Enterprises (SMEs) as Salla's entrepreneurs knew they would be an easy target to contract given the fact that they need the platform to expand their sales and business outside the local area and that Salla will later pave the way for those startups to compete on a global scale. Nowadays, Salla deals with a wide range of logistics companies. In addition, Salla offers marketing services for its logistics partners through the platform as they provide competitive prices for Salla's retailers. The platform aims to issue bills of leading for its customers in the so-called Salla contract and made many agreements with shipping companies to get reduced prices. Salla made a deal with SMSA to achieve a specific number of shipments to get discounted prices and was able to achieve the target of shipments in the first week. Even more, within 30 days, it was able to achieve two times the target, as more than a million shipments were delivered not only issued. Thus, SMSA agreed on a low unified price for all Salla customers. Based on this experience with SMSA, Sala managed to deal with different logistics service providers. Thus, as shown in Figure 3, Salla presents a successful fully integrated e-supply chain model for Saudi retailers through its platform that serves consumers in all cities of Saudi Arabia (S. Butt, personal communication, February 21, 2022).

The main difference between the model proposed in this case study Figure 3 and the conventional retail situation shown in Figure 2 is that the retail market was scattered, and the retailers were not able to meet the demand of customers, especially during COVID-19 because of numerous factors including the lockdown, the increase in transportation prices, inability to contract convenient logistics service providers to store and deliver the products which was not required before the pandemic. Salla platform saved the seller from the trouble of contracting with various companies. Once the seller opens the online store, the

Figure 3. Retail market with Salla
Source: The authors

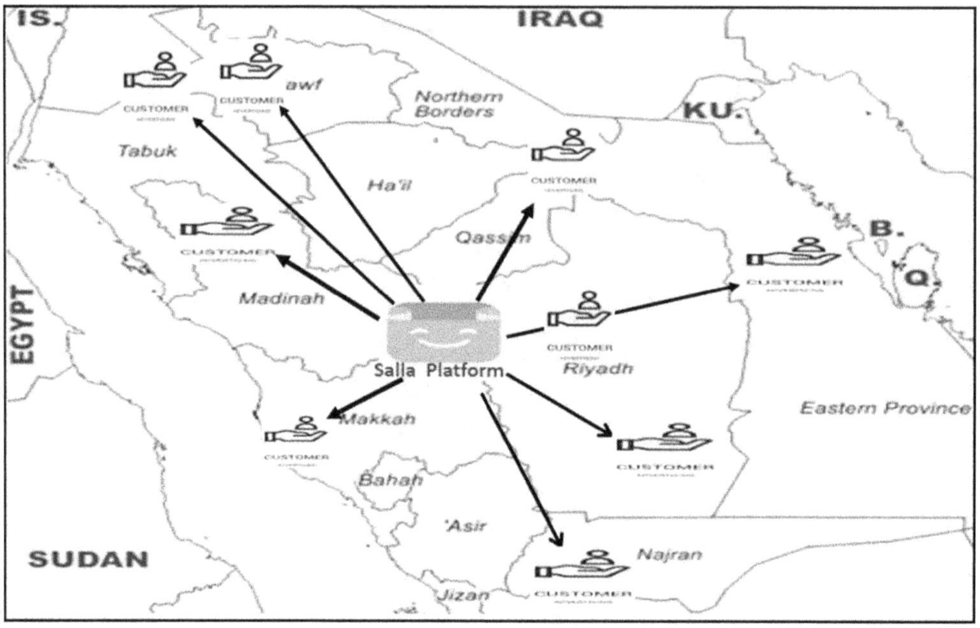

platform provides a direct linkage service with various logistics service providers (shipping, warehousing, distribution etc.) by contracting different 3PLs companies, such as Saudi Post, Jack, Pick, Aramex, Fetchr, Fastlo, DHL and others, which facilitated the movement of products in KSA (Salla.sa, 2022).

Salla platform provides quick delivery by linking the seller to a logistics service provider, which provides rapid delivery to the customer offered at home or pick-up locations within two hours of placing the order, plus cargo insurance up to 5000 SAR (BARQ, 2021).

OTHER SERVICES AND BENEFITS OF SALLA

The Salla platform has a positive impact on logistics activities and their cost. The platform offers users inventory management and marketing tools, as well as detailed reports on store performance and automatic invoices for orders, enabling e-commerce retailers to set up, maintain, and increase sales through their stores without fees or commissions. Furthermore, due to a variety of payment and logistic partnerships, e-commerce store owners who are using Salla do not have to worry about payment or delivery challenges once their store goes live – it is all taken care of by Salla. It also provides companies with many other benefits, such as (Salla.sa, 2022):

Data Analytics

The platform provides the merchant detailed reports to measure the performance of the store, which helps companies to get all the information to evaluate the performance of the store and try to fix the problems resulting from the evaluation, including the following:

1. The number of store visitors per month.
2. Orders that are done monthly.
3. Sales during the month.
4. Customers' details (Gender, Age, Adders)

Moreover, Salla provides merchants with a direct link to Google analytics and other applications, which gives the merchants the free tools they need to analyze data for their business in one place, and the tools they need to better understand their customers. Also, it gives retailers a space to put their recommendations, whether they have recommendations to add new services through the Salla platform or add new logistics companies. The survey is provided to attain customers' opinions about the services provided by the company.

Warehousing and Inventory Management

The warehouse is a significant component of logistics as it performs a valuable function that supports the movement of materials, storing goods, processing products, grouping vehicle loads, creating stock-keeping unit collections, and assembling shipments (Miralam, 2017).

Salla platform contributes to improving inventory management in Saudi companies as companies can use the drop-shipping system available on the platform which is a retail method in which the online store does not keep any of its products displayed in the store, instead, it enters a partnership with a supplier to store its stock. Once the customer requests the purchase of the product, it transfers this request and shipping details to the supplier so that he ships the order directly to the customer. The organization receives an order with payments for a product listed on the website, and this order, along with shipping details, can be passed on to the supplier, usually, the wholesaler or manufacturer with whom the founder has built a relationship, and pays for the product at a lower price. On the other hand, for retailers not using the drop-shipping system, the platform also provides a feature of the minimum order quantity to alert the merchant, meaning that when the safety limit is reached, the platform alerts the merchant to re-order the product, to ensure that the product is available at the external customer's request at any time needed.

Salla Platform Integrated With M5azn Platform

One of the platforms that use the drop-shipping system is "M5AZN", which Salla platform provides a direct linkage service to by purchasing policies with "M5AZN" (salla.sa, 2021). M5AZN is a Saudi platform that stands by online stores with full logistics support. It supports Salla platform sellers by offering them storage, packaging, shipping services, andlectronic payment gateways (M5AZN, 2022).

Activating Logistics Service Providers in the Retailers' E-Stores on Salla Platform

The retailer can activate the logistics services on Salla platform in order to enjoy efficiency, on-time deliveries, reduced lead time, inventory levels, documentation, and delays. The merchant/retailer first establishes the online store, then accesses the shipping application and selects the companies that are available in his/her city. After that, he/she chooses the applicable shipping and logistics companies to activate the 3PL's account and link to the store. Then Salla's system automatically transfers the retailer's

Figure 4. How Salla platform functions
Source: The authors

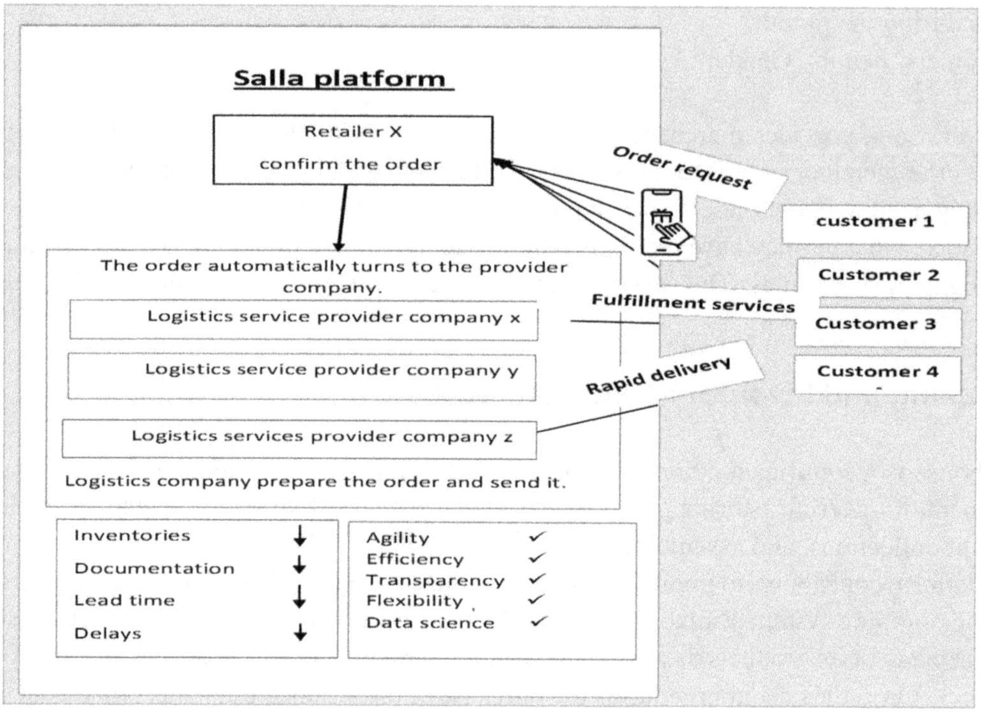

data to the logistics company, and the retailer's account is automatically created with the 3PL. Once the logistics company is activated and integrated within the retailer's store on the platform, the information about the logistics company and its services (price list, different delivery periods, and all services) appears in the retailer's store. As shown in Figure 4 when any order is placed with the retailer, it automatically turns to the logistics company. After that, the logistics company receives the product from the retailer and performs the required services till the product reaches the customer. The retailer pays for the logistics services using Salla's special discounts. Therefore, Salla emerges as the technology to facilitate more agile and accurate decision-making, moreover, decreasing delivery lead time, as shown in Figure 4.

SWOT Analysis for Salla Platform

The following is Salla's SWOT analysis formulated in this case study based on the reports and reliable information gathered during the interviews conducted. As mentioned, Salla has key strengths that are not possessed by its competitors such as complete e-store management with an unlimited number of products, customers, and requests. Moreover, high-quality customer service by implementing a live chat service for 24/7 accessibility for customers and a domain for sellers (www.sellername.com). It acts as a hub for retailers and logistics service providers. Merchants/retailers can reach their target audience easily. They can use Salla's analytical tools to analyze customer preferences to satisfy them, align with the changes in customer needs, and forecast and track orders. Also, Salla offers flexibility in dealing with clients, reducing the total cost of logistics activities and setup costs. It reduces the fixed cost associated with the opening of a business. Salla has a competitive advantage in the ease of documentation required to open

Figure 5. Individuals using the internet (% of population): Saudi Arabia
Source: World Bank

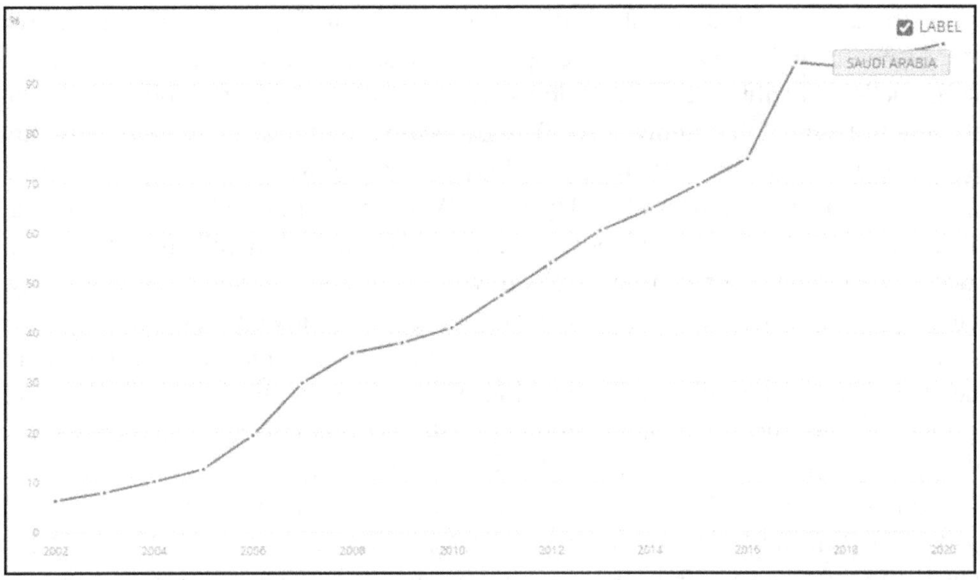

the business. Also, it helps the vendors to target their audience using its data analysis tools, which can be beneficial in the marketing process and logistics transparency. Moreover, it makes the operation easy to set and measure the key performance indicators and offers customized online marketing programs. However, Salla has some weaknesses, such as a lack of international products and a low market share compared to other e-commerce platforms operating in KSA. Also, the platform does not offer multiple languages. On the other hand, Salla foresees major opportunities in the Saudi market, such as the 80 billion SAR size of the e-commerce market, with a growth of 14% from last year (Zid.sa, 2022). As shown in Figure 5, according to the World Bank, 98% of KSA's population uses the internet. Many of the younger generations are more dynamic when purchasing via electronic communications or the Internet.

Other significant opportunities are the growth of online shopping in Saudi Arabia, as well as the country's budget, which energizes investment, demonstrating the presence of money circulation. There is also a serious vision and plan by the Saudi government for the development of the economy and the electronic environment. Another opportunity is the diversity of foreign and local logistics businesses in KSA which encourages more reliable delivery procedures. Furthermore, Saudi customers' strong purchasing power provides an opportunity for the Salla platform. Despite the opportunities, the Saudi market presents threats as KSA is already famous for its technological and economic stability, however, it is challenging for businesses to convince customers of the quality of their products in the absence of a physical product. Furthermore, many customers do not trust online shopping because of privacy issues as it involves transferring personal information, specifically financial details. In addition, competition from local and international companies may be encouraged to follow Salla's successful model and copy it to its current strength points (S. Butt, personal communication, February 21, 2022).

The Impact of the Salla Platform on KSA Retail Market

The Salla platform is considered one of the digital innovators in KSA. Salla differentiates its services from other competitors and strengthens its competitive advantage. It was the first to take its e-business even further in the KSA facilitating different logistics activities, such as warehousing, picking, packing, and delivery as a full part of the supply chain. Thus, it positively impacts customer satisfaction and improves logistics agility and resilience. Moreover, this platform helps in improving the competition in the supply chain environment in Saudi Arabia. The Saudi Arabian retail, freight, and logistics industry can develop further through E-commerce activities (S. Butt, personal communication, February 21, 2022).

Salla allows the customer to purchase whatever, whenever, however and at the price they want from its numerous merchants/ retailers Salla. Salla gives sellers many advantages, such as expanding business and expanding sales outside the local area. Salla enhances customer services by providing a wide range of merchants' support processes and functions focused on enabling a close relationship-building experience with the consumer, including customer profile management, account management, information gathering, and implementation of a live chat service from the platform site to be accessible 24/7. An easy way to issue electronic bill payments (S. Butt, personal communication, February 21, 2022).

The results of the current study have shown that the Salla platform has a positive impact on logistics activities and their cost. The SME industry is expanding and has had a positive impact on Saudi Arabia's economy. Salla's online platform offers more tools to connect and collaborate digitally with stakeholders in the supply chain for lower freight costs, and a better customer care experience, thus, improving the supply chain operations in KSA. It helps youth to become entrepreneurs and supports the entrepreneurship and startup ecosystem in Saudi Arabia, which fosters the economy in different sectors in the field of E-commerce, generates revenue, and may contribute to KSA's GDP. Fully integrated online platforms such as Salla may mitigate the risks that could affect the business in turbulent times taking the COVID-19 pandemic as an example.

Growth Trend

Growth in sales of the Salla platform initially increased by 6 times since its start in 2016; in the last 2 years, its sales more than doubled annually, while growth in the number of merchants participating in the platform is 1.5 merchants in comparison to last year. In general, the number of shipments in 2021 was between 200,000 and 300,000 per month. In 2022, the number of shipments is approximately 500,000 deliveries per month. According to Figure 6, exports of goods and services in Saudi Arabia reach 289.82 billion U.S. dollars in 2021. Salla's founder and CEO claims that Salla may have participated in increasing the Saudi export roughly by a percentage of 5% - 7% as it contributed to linking local companies and retailers to other partners in the supply chain, including international logistics service providers such as Aramex and DHL which paved the way for export opportunities (S. Butt, personal communication, February 21, 2022).

CONCLUSION

In conclusion, the case study of the Salla platform in the Kingdom of Saudi Arabia (KSA) illustrates the potential benefits of e-logistics platforms in enhancing logistics activities and performance. The study

Figure 6. Exports of goods and services $: Kingdom of Saudi Arabia
Source: World Bank

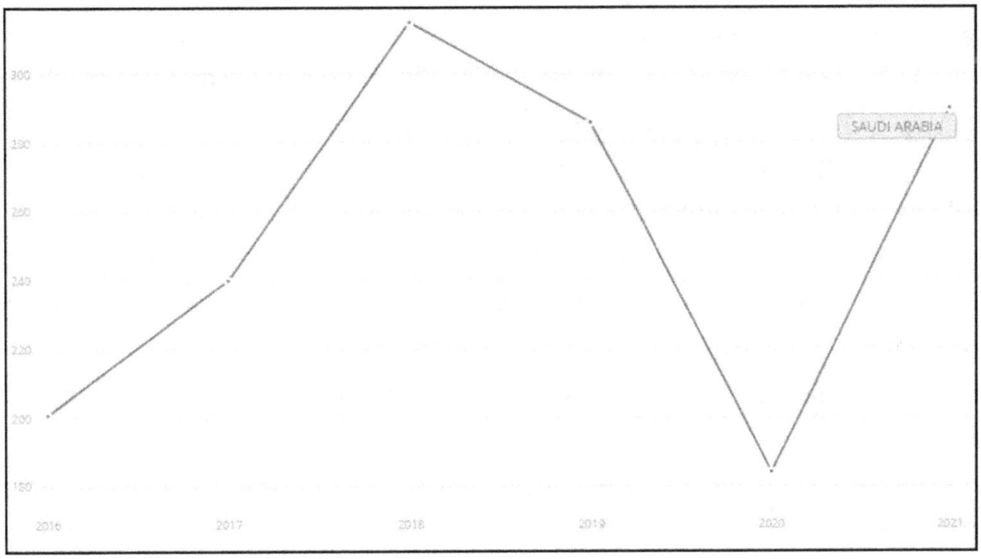

highlighted the challenges faced by the retail industry in KSA, particularly in the wake of the COVID-19 pandemic. However, e-logistics platforms, such as Salla, have contributed to the enhancement of transport and logistics activities, which has had a significant impact on the efficiency and competitiveness of supply chains in the KSA. The Salla platform, in particular, has been able to differentiate its services from competitors by offering a fully integrated e-supply chain model that includes logistics activities such as warehousing, picking, packing, and delivery. This has led to improved customer satisfaction and logistics agility and resilience, and has helped to improve competition in the supply chain environment in KSA.

Furthermore, the Salla platform has played a role in expanding the SME industry and positively impacting the economy of Saudi Arabia. It also supports youth entrepreneurship and the startup ecosystem in Saudi Arabia. The platform offers tools for digital connectivity and collaboration among members of the supply chain, which enables SMEs to more effectively manage logistics activities and reduce costs. The study also highlighted the growth trend of the Salla platform, which has experienced significant growth in sales and merchant participation, and is expected to continue to grow in the future.

Lastly, the case of Salla platform in KSA illustrates the potential benefits of e-logistics platforms in enhancing logistics activities and performance, particularly for SMEs. The platform offers a fully integrated e-supply chain model, which enables SMEs to more effectively manage logistics activities and reduce costs, while also providing support for youth entrepreneurship and the startup ecosystem in Saudi Arabia. The study also highlights the growth trend of the platform, which is expected to continue to grow in the future. The case of Salla can serve as a best practice for other e-logistics platforms to follow and can provide insights for other countries looking to improve their logistics activities and performance.

REFERENCES

BARQ. (2021). *Fast and flexible delivery.* https://www.barqfleet.com

Buyukozkan, G., & Gocer, F. (2018). Digital Supply Chain: Literature review and a proposed framework for future research. *Computers in Industry*, *97*, 157–177. doi:10.1016/j.compind.2018.02.010

Chen, Y., & Xie, J. (2008). Online consumer review: Word-of-mouth as a new element of marketing communication mix. *Management Science*, *54*(3), 477–491. doi:10.1287/mnsc.1070.0810

Crook, J. (2016). *Walmart squares up against amazon with 2-day delivery across the us techcrunch.* Retrieved May 2022 from https://techcrunch.com/2016/06/30/walmart-squares-up-against-amazon-with-2-day-delivery-across-the-u-s

Duneja, R., Sethi, R., & Vinas, M. (2021). *Digital KSA: Assessment and way forward for the digital economy*. https://www.adlittle.com/en/digital-ksa-assessment-and-way-forward-digital-economy

Elgazzar, S. H. (2021). Investigating Digital Supply Chain Transformation Drivers: An Empirical Study. *Journal of Alexandria University for Administrative Sciences*, *58*(5), 139–170.

Faridi, M. (2020). *Digital transformation in supply chain, challenges and opportunities in SMEs: A case study of Al-Rumman Pharma*. Academic Press.

Ferrantino, M.J., & Koten, E.E. (2019). Understanding Supply Chain 4.0 and its potential impact on global value chains. *Global Value Chain Development Report, 103.*

GCC Retail Industry. (2017). *Alpen Capital.* Author.

gov.sa. (2022). *Digital transformation in the kingdom of Saudi Arabia*. https://www.my.gov.sa/wps/portal/snp/aboutksa/digitaltransformation

Grand, W. K. S. (2020). *Assessing Saudi vision 2030: A 2020 Review*. Https://Www.Atlanticcouncil.Org/Wp-Content/Uploads/2020/06/Assessing-Saudi-Vision-2030-A-2020-Review.Pdf

Istizada. (2019). https://istizada.com/ecommerce-in-saudi-arabia-the-complete-guide/

Jain, V., Arya, S., & Bindoo, M. (n.d.). An overview of electronic commerce. *Journal of Contemporary Issues in Business and Government*, *27*(3).

Khwaja. (2017). *Technology, Media & Telecommunications*. Dubai International Financial Centre.

Kutz, M. (2016). *Introduction to E-Commerce: Combining Business and Information Technology*. The eBook Company.

League of Arab States. (2020). *Arab digital economy vision towards a sustainable inclusive and secure digital future report.* Arab Economic Unity Council.

M5azn. (2023). Why ma5azn. https://m5azn.com/en

Merlino, M., & Sproģe, I. (2017). The augmented supply chain. *Procedia Engineering*, *178*, 308–318. doi:10.1016/j.proeng.2017.01.053

Ministry of Logistics and Transport. (2022). *Logistics in Saudi Arabia.* https://mot.gov.sa/ar/AboutUs/Pages/Logisticsplatform.aspx

Miralam, M. (2017). Impact of Implementing Warehouse Management system on Auto Spare Part Industry Market in. *Review of Integrative Business and Economics Research, 6*(3).

National Digital Transformation Unit. (2019). *National Digital Transformation indicators and Achievements.* https://ndu.gov.sa/en/our-reports

National Digital Transformation Unit. (2021). *Digital Economy policy in the kingdom of Saudi Arabia report.* Ministry of Communication and Transformation Technology.

Neffati, M. (2019). Socioeconomic Impacts of Digitization in Saudi Arabia. *International Journal of Economics and Finance, 9*(3).

Othman, A.A., Sundram, V.K., Sayuti, N.M., & Bahrin, A.S. (2016). The relationship between supply chain integration, just-in-time and logistics performance: A supplier's perspective on the automotive industry in Malaysia. *International Journal of Supply Chain Management, 5*(1), 44-51.

Ross, D. (2003). *Introduction to E-Supply Chain Management.* St. Lucie Press.

Satista Reports, (2021). https://www.statista.com/statistics/698675/saudi-arabia-number-of-organizedretailers

Shou, Y., Li, Y., Park, Y., & Kang, M. (2018). Supply chain integration and operational performance: The contingency effects of production systems. *Journal of Purchasing and Supply Management, 24*(4), 352–360. doi:10.1016/j.pursup.2017.11.004

Speedtest. (2022). *Saudi Arabia's Mobile and Broadband Internet Speeds – Speed test Global.* https://www.speedtest.net/global-index/saudi-arabia

Whiteley, D. (2000). *E-Commerce strategy, Technologies, and Application.* McGraw-Hill Publishing Company.

World Bank. (2022). *Individuals using the Internet (% of population) - Saudi Arabia | Data.* worldbank.org

Zid.sa Platform. (2022). https://blog.zid.sa/products-update-q1-2022/

Section 4

Conflicts and Challenges in Logistics and Supply Chain Management

Chapter 11
The Role of Logistics Operations in Humanitarian Aids:
Lessons Learned From the Syria Crisis

Islam Abdelbary
https://orcid.org/0000-0003-1727-9071
Arab Academy for Science, Technology, and Maritime Transport, Egypt

Rasha Hassan Elshawa
Faculty of Economics and Political Science, Cairo University, Egypt

EXECUTIVE SUMMARY

Logistics in humanitarian aid is critical for effectively utilising humanitarian operations and initiatives. This chapter tries to explain the important role that humanitarian logistics plays in relief efforts. It uses the Syria crisis as an example to evaluate the performance of humanitarian logistics in Syria, especially in the healthcare sector. Over 470,000 people have died in the Syrian Civil War, and half of the country's population have been forced to leave their homes. The study determined the humanitarian logistics gaps and bottlenecks in Syria, such as physical access restrictions, a lack of logistical information, operational challenges, the need for integrated logistical coordination, and the increasing need for specialised logistical capacity-building programs. After explaining humanitarian logistics implementation in the healthcare sector in detail, the research draws on the lessons learned and drives recommendations for the future of the Syrian operation itself and identifies best practices for other operations in any humanitarian intervention.

1. BACKGROUND

The concept 'logistics' initially began as a military term, which refers to the process of getting and delivering equipment and supplies to troops (Tomasini et al., 2009). Because of the increasing complexity

DOI: 10.4018/978-1-6684-4686-7.ch011

of supplying businesses with materials and shipping out products in the 1950s, logistics has grown as a business concept. Currently, it is defined as the efficient flow and storage of goods from the point of origin to the end of consumption. Logistics has become a vital part of supply chain management utilised to plan, implement, and control the flow and storage of goods and services to meet customers' requirements(Sahay et al., 2016).

Humanitarian logistics (HL) is a type of logistics that focuses on the crisis management system's preparations and response stages. HL can be defined as the process of planning, implementing, and controlling the efficient, cost-effective flow and storage of goods and materials, as well as associated information, from the point of origin to the point of consumption to alleviate the suffering of vulnerable people (Regis-Hernández et al., 2022). The role covers a variety of tasks, including planning, procurement, transportation, warehousing, tracking and tracing, and customs clearance.

Logistics operations in humanitarian aid are critical for effectively utilising humanitarian operations and initiatives. The disaster risk management cycle includes three main stages: Pre-disaster, disaster response, & post-disaster. The pre-disaster phase is concerned with assessing all the potential risks and mitigating and preventing the risks. It is also called the preparedness phase. Once the disaster strikes, all humanitarian efforts are focused on evacuation, saving people, and providing immediate assistance. In this phase, the damage is assessed. Post-disaster, ongoing assistance is obtained, including restoration of infrastructural services, economic and social recovery, and ongoing development activities.

During the pre and post-disaster periods, these logistical systems are typically required to buy, store, and transport food, water, medication, and other supplies, as well as human resources, vital machinery and equipment. Because the diversity of logistical operations involved in disaster relief is wide, humanitarian logistics is the most expensive component of disaster relief efforts, accounting for roughly 80% of total costs(Nikbakhsh & Farahani, 2011).

Therefore, this chapter attempts to clarify the critical role of humanitarian logistics in relief efforts, with an application to the Syria crisis, where the humanitarian response to it has been one of the largest in living memory. The scale of this crisis continues to require a large-scale, sustained and comprehensive response from the humanitarian community to provide the affected population with critical cross-sectoral assistance.

Based on this background and through content analysis of the available literature, the overall objectives of this study are:

- To highlight the humanitarian logistics strategies. The strategies proposed in this study can develop the ability to respond more quickly to the crisis so that its effect decreases and assistance operations are facilitated.
- To assess the performance and the logistics activities undertaken in Syria, especially in the healthcare sector, to support the humanitarian community in reaching people in need of assistance. The operation is assessed in terms of the degree to which it was relevant, effective and efficient in identifying the gaps and addressing the needs of the humanitarian community.
- To draw lessons and recommendations from the Syria crisis related to logistics business for further improved performance in the future in the country and other areas under military conflicts through the identification of best practices across operations.

2. THE CONCEPT OF HUMANITARIAN LOGISTICS

2.1 Introduction

Logistics of the humanitarian supply chain refers to the effective and efficient planning, implementation, and control of product, material, and information flows from donors to affected people in order to meet their survival needs. According to Van Wassenhove (2006), The logistics planning strategy consists of five key components:

1. **Human Resource Deployment:** Recruitment and training of individuals who will coordinate and intervene in the event of a disaster.
2. **Knowledge Management:** Collect, code, and use data from previous events to improve prevention and support strategies.
3. Operations management in various scenarios, including the location of collection centres and shelters, support resource distribution routes, and evacuation routes.
4. **Financial Resources:** Monetary resources allocated to aid operations.
5. **Collaboration:** Identify the various actors (government, private institutions, NGOs, and the community) in the event of a disaster and coordinate the humanitarian logistics effort among them.

While logistics has historically been associated with business supply chains, it is also a critical component of disaster relief operations. Humanitarian logistics is a subset of logistics that specialises in managing the transportation and storage of supplies to affected areas and individuals during natural disasters or complicated events. However, this definition focuses exclusively on the actual movement of commodities to their final destinations, whereas humanitarian logistics is significantly more complex and entails planning and optimising resource allocation, maintaining inventory, and communicating information. Thus, a good broader definition of humanitarian logistics is the process of planning, implementing, and controlling the efficient, cost-effective flow and storage of goods and materials, as well as associated information, from the point of origin to the point of consumption to alleviate vulnerable people's suffering (Fritz Institute, 2022).

Humanitarian space is supported by fundamental principles to ensure the safety of the vulnerable people and those who provide the aid. These principles include Humanity, Impartiality, and neutrality. Humanity implies that human suffering should be relieved wherever found. Impartiality indicates that assistance should be provided without discrimination and given priority to the most urgent needs. Neutrality implies that relief should be provided without bias or affiliation to a party in the conflict.

The most dramatic problems are frequently the direct result of an emergency: natural disasters destroying transportation infrastructure, conflict zone front lines severing regular supply routes, or systematic resource diversion to or away from warring parties.

Additionally, during times of crisis, there can be intense competition for vehicles and gasoline, as existing cars may be in bad condition, and the importation of new ones is slow and logistically challenging. Vehicles utilised by aid agency logistics staff are essential to impoverished militias that can seize them. Local drivers may also be scarce or unwilling to participate if the populace has fled a crisis, and in some places of the world, only a minority of people can drive.

The high level of uncertainty is one of the significant challenges the humanitarian supply chain face. Thus, logisticians may face difficulties due to insecurity, even in peaceful countries hit by disaster. In-

Figure 1. Humanitarian supply chain strategies
Source: Cano-Olivos et al. (2022)

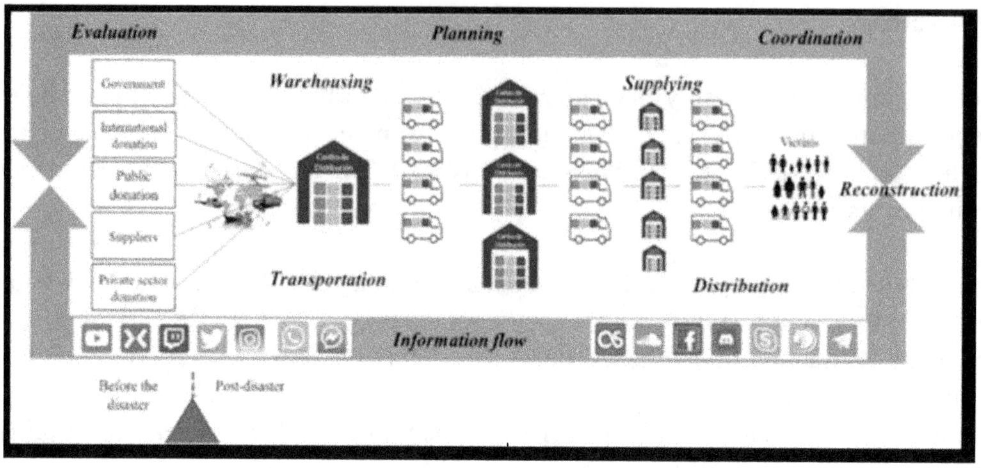

security may include ambushes, raids, and other forms of banditry on roads, poorly supervised police, army, or militia, or 'informal 'informal taxation' taxation' of road users at unofficial roadblocks. Incidents can be minimised by designing routes carefully to avoid ambush points and conflict zones, and varying journey timings. As predictably planned, high-value cargo journeys are ripe for theft.

Additionally, funding can be a difficulty. While news broadcasts elicit greater public sympathy and mobilise significantly more funding in rapid-onset disasters, protracted crises sometimes run out of resources as media attention and public interest shift elsewhere.

Preparing for disasters/ conflicts is difficult, but there are some areas where you can get better results when implementing strategies. According to Cano-Olivos, Sánchez-Partida, Caballero-Morales, and Martínez-Flores (2022), Ideal strategies for improving the performance of a comprehensive humanitarian supply chain, i.e. reducing the impact of disasters or conflicts, are required. (1) planning, (2) information flow, (3) evaluation, (4) coordination, (5) supplying, (6) warehousing, (7) transportation, (8) distribution, and (9) reconstruction are the nine strategies identified in this study. These strategies should be directly linked and reviewed for updates before and after the disaster.

2.2 Humanitarian Supply Chain Strategies

Logistical performance in humanitarian aid is more challenging than commercial activities. Humanitarian logistics performance can be measured by appeal coverage, donation-to-delivery time, financial efficiency, and assessment accuracy. These indicators create a "scorecard" to help the logistics department gauge performance during and after a relief operation.

Therefore, under the constraints of limited funds, efficient and effective supply chain management allows humanitarian organisations to use resources best to address high-priority needs in the shortest time possible. Humanitarian logistics are highly fluid, frequently improvised, and far from unified. In these circumstances, it is critical to identify the key strategies for improving the humanitarian supply chain's performance.

2.2.1 Planning

Planning is an important strategy at any stage of humanitarian logistics; for example, the government must prepare and continually revise the National Emergency Plan and keep it up to date before a disaster, which is necessary for its proper post-disaster operation. Prior to the tragedy, planning necessitates a significant investment of time and effort, but it aids in improving knowledge of potential areas of operation, identifying strengths and weaknesses, as well as solutions and alternatives. The geographical, social, political, and physical context of the areas where managers will carry out logistical activities should be considered when planning. Governments and society should dispel the myth that disaster logistics is improvised because the disasters to which society is exposed and the needs they generate are predictable. The National Emergency Plan should be linked to infrastructure vulnerability and resource analysis, as well as the specific plans of disaster-affected organisations.

Infrastructure risk evaluation should assess the strength and weaknesses of the country's or region's strategic real estate works and assets under consideration, as well as potential solutions in the event of infrastructure collapse. To do so, government and humanitarian organisations must:

- Systematically map and review key aspects of the national transportation infrastructure, such as strategic route capabilities and challenges, potential slowdowns, communications resource availability, risks, and blockages due to the impact of an event. Analyse annual climate records to determine the weather's impact on the transportation system's capacity at different times of the year.
- Monitor major modifications or constructions that could result in bottlenecks or alternate temporary routes on a regular basis.
- The availability of strategic resources for logistics support is constantly changing, so periodic reviews must be current. The private, public, and non-governmental sectors, domestic and international, are all included in this resource review. As a result, it will have:
- A list of sources and locations for various types of supplies, as well as delivery times for critical resources such as medical and rescue equipment, food, clothing, and fuel that victims may require in an emergency.
- Inventory of transportation modes for the mobilisation of people and supplies, including fleet size, type, capacity, location, rates, and availability, among other things.
- A list of locations for the logistics operation, depots, and fuel supply centres, including public and private facilities, ample storage complexes, factories, and other adaptable facilities.
- Determine the locations and capabilities of ports and airports in order to handle emergency supplies in various scenarios.
- A list of possible escape routes in the event of an emergency.

2.2.2 Information Flow

Maintaining information flow with all identified potential actors in the humanitarian supply chain is critical for developing effective response and recovery plans based on lessons learned from previous disasters. Regarding UNOCHA (2013), the information flow incorporates technology, actors in the humanitarian supply chain, and the affected community; however, there are three basic principles to improve the quality of information:

1. Information is a basic need.
2. Everyone can generate valuable information (disaster victims, society, and supply chain actors).
3. Information creates more value when it is widely and freely shared.

Even if the internet is unavailable, the community can contribute helpful information. It is possible to send messages between mobile devices without using the internet or a cellular network, thanks to free applications developed for mobile devices. As a result, people serve as sensors, collecting and sharing data to aid in the recovery process (Laituri & Kodrich, 2008). So, if a person has interpretation and integration skills that vary depending on their experiences, they are considered a mobile smart sensor. Mobile phones with integrated GPS, digital cameras, and tracking devices can help users improve their skills (Manfré et al., 2012).

Enhance information systems to provide real-time, up-to-date, and integrated data so that realistic recovery plans and needs can be developed and implemented quickly in each territory. Large amounts of data can be verified and systematised in real-time, thanks to the standardisation of collaborative technology platforms. As a result, citizens locate family members and neighbours, as well as alert rescuers to disaster areas, by coordinating the changing needs. Furthermore, having a logistics information system available in a disaster situation aids in the efficient management of aid.

2.2.3 Evaluation

The evaluation will determine a rough estimate of the residents' logistical and supply needs, as well as the local capacities, restrictions, and facilitation in the disaster zone. This evaluation should thoroughly determine the type and extent of damage, as well as the most critical areas for intervention. Because requests for supplies will be made based on evaluators' ability to initiate the most urgent actions even if the rescue is not complete, the speed and quality of this assessment are critical. To perform the functions correctly in an emergency, it is critical to understand the logistical requirements. The determination of available and missing resources is simplified when planning is effective.

On the other hand, supply needs are frequently dynamic and changing, so the assessment should identify current needs and anticipate future needs. The evaluations will reveal more specific aspects of the required care in the short term. Generally, the possible basic survival needs are Health, Water, Food, Shelter and Sanitation.

Assessing capacities entails understanding the resources available in operations as well as the local factors that may help or hinder supply management. Religious, political, or health reasons sometimes restrict the entry of any product or material into the country, in addition to the regulation for mobilisation in the affected areas. On the other hand, some governments go above and beyond to make it easier for organisations working to help victims and to allow for more flexible procedures for humanitarian aid entry. Restrictions and/or facilities in displacing work equipment and supplies must be mentioned in the evaluation.

2.2.4 Coordination

Humanitarian supplies must be beneficial to populations in crisis, and logistics systems must be transparently coordinated. The various actors who assist the affected people come from various backgrounds, have different mandates and work in different ways. Despite everyone's desire to help, delays in victim care, duplication of effort, and waste of resources are caused by a lack of coordination, poor information flow, and minor teamwork. To reduce obstacles and increase resources, assistance tasks necessitate coordination. Before disasters strike, coordination should begin with a cross-sectoral, inter-agency, and interdisciplinary vision and be strengthened immediately afterwards. Minor emergencies are handled by national agencies and occasionally by international organisations, while major events are handled by a variety of national and international actors, including:

- Local population
- Neighbouring communities or regions
- National or local government
- Foreign governments
- Multilateral agencies
- National and international non-governmental organisations
- The private and commercial sector
- Specialised institutions
- Military forces

Agreements must be concrete and feasible, rather than eliciting expectations of noncompliance; the effort must be geared toward cooperation and mutual support, allowing for quick and diverse assistance. When the disaster's effects outstrip the country's ability to respond adequately, the federal government will request humanitarian aid from the international community, usually channelled through the United Nations and diplomatic missions abroad. Similarly, some international organisations national subsidiaries will apply to their respective headquarters or other counterparties in the region.

2.2.5 Supplying

Once the impacted area's requisitions are understood, it's time to identify sources and modes of acquisition, as well as the conditions of preparation and shipment and shipping methods. Requisitions must be precise and specific in order for supplies to be delivered as promptly and accurately as feasible. Order forms can help avoid requisition errors by specifying the articles' details, priority, volume, and frequency. Emergency supplies come from various places; whether organisations buy them directly, the national and international society donates them, or collaborators give them. All of these modalities are combined in a disaster. However, selecting the most appropriate option from among them is not always possible. To reduce response times, managers must make decisions based on technical criteria. In humanitarian logistics, the preparation of shipments is critical. The shipped supplies would be separated and classified in an ideal world to make humanitarian aid delivery easier in the affected area. Do not send products that are not in good enough shape or quality. Because inquiries are inappropriate in an emergency, the shipment of supplies must follow a procedure to ensure everything is correct and transparent.

2.2.6 Warehousing

Collection centres (courtyards, offices, garages, and other locations) are frequently set up to receive donations during emergencies. However, the lack of space makes organising a storage system in these locations difficult. Collection centres, on the other hand, can sort and classify donations, sending only those deemed helpful to warehouses. On the other hand, warehouses must keep supplies safe until they are distributed or used. Still, having storage space and an organised system that allows knowing the type, quantity, and location of existing provisions is essential. A warehouse's organisation must have the necessary standards to ensure that supplies are properly cared for. However, in an emergency, it is often necessary to work with what is available (schools, communal centres, gyms, etc.) that were not designed for storage. Nonetheless, warehouses should consider effective and efficient operations even in these circumstances.

2.2.7 Transportation

Different routes and modes of transportation have different characteristics and requirements that reflect advantages and disadvantages depending on the operation's situation, ranging from costs to capabilities. However, other factors such as identified needs and specific and accessible options play a role in determining the mode of transportation. Managers will not always have the financial resources to pay for ideal transportation, so perfect transportation will not always be available. Furthermore, even if a specific mode of transportation is available, the conditions of access to the area will prevent its use. As a result, the challenge is not only to identify needs but also to consider real options and alternatives. There should be an alternative plan for each planned mode of transportation in case it cannot be used due to unforeseen circumstances.

2.2.8 Distribution

Distribution cannot be a blanket, indiscriminate action; instead, it must be proportional and controlled. While each organisation has its policies and motivations when it comes to disaster relief, some criteria must be applied as fundamental principles to ensure more equitable and effective distribution. On the other hand, to maintain continuously updated inventories, it is necessary to control and monitor revenues, dispatches, and outputs of products from warehouses, as well as proof of distribution. Physical verification at distribution sites should be supplemented by document revision, not only for accounting purposes but also for observing and determining the adequacy of the procedures used, identifying needs, correcting problems, etc.

2.2.9 Reconstruction

It is focused on restoring normalcy to life, so it is critical to reactivate community services and sanitation. Rehabilitation, demolition, enablement, repair, reconstruction, construction, and other activities should be prioritised. Reconstruction is frequently conceived and designed to restore normal development conditions to the pre-disaster state. Often leads to the reconstruction of existing risk conditions prior to the disaster, as well as disaster preparedness and possibly contributing to the country's debt levels rising due to reconstruction loans. Similarly, people begin to recover on their own, rebuilding and to reproduce even more dangerous conditions than before the disaster. As a result, by providing early technical support for recovery efforts, risk management and reduction considerations can be incorporated into initiatives, avoiding risk reconstruction and addressing underlying causes.

3. HUMANITARIAN LOGISTICS IN SYRIA CRISIS

3.1 The Crisis's Overview

The Syrian crisis started in 2011 when anti-government rallies spread across the country, and violent conflicts erupted, which President Assad attempted to silence with ruthless force (Abdelbary, 2021). As a result, protestors organised themselves into organisations and eventually armed themselves against the regime, and the whole country turned into a civil war in the first quarter of 2012 (Abdelbary & Benhin, 2019).

Since the war had also flamed on endlessly, several non-state armed groups, including radical Islamist groups, especially the so-called Islamic State (ISIS), emerged. Thus far, the international relations system has failed to serve the interests of the Syrian people, who require an end to hostilities and a genuine political settlement to re-establish their society. Alternatively, regional and international actors' intervention in the conflict has successfully financed and fuelled its escalation. Military violence has wreaked havoc on the humanitarian situation, resulting in one of the worst humanitarian crises since World War II, killing over 470,000 people and displacing half of Syria's total internal or external population. It has also dragged regional and international powers into a proxy war, resulting in spill-over impacts within and outside the region.

Syrians fleeing the conflict have now become the world's fastest-growing refugee population. Syrian refugees are overtaking more than five million Palestine refugees living in Jordan, Lebanon, Syria, and Palestine since the 1948 conflict as the world's most prominent contemporary refugee population. Hundreds of thousands of Syrian refugees have been distributed across 130 countries, while 6.7 million Syrians, including an estimated 2.5 million children, have been internally displaced (UNOCHA, 2021).

This horrific humanitarian cost of the armed conflict is only one facet of broad social and political deterioration, which includes a devastating war on development and economic well-being from which Syria's economy would take decades to recover. The conflict's continued escalation has resulted in armed parties damaging the country's economic and productive capabilities and diverting resources from productive to destructive operations (SCPR, 2013). According to the UNESCWA (2021), physical capital destruction at $117.7 billion and the economic damage in terms of lost Gross Domestic Product at $324.5 billion - putting the cost of the conflict at about $442.5 billion, which represents about 54% of real GDP in pre-conflict.

Syria's geophysical position, combined with its distinct demographic qualities, significantly impacts the country's ongoing turmoil. Syria's position has made it a deciding element in the prospect of two significant gas pipelines: the Iran-Iraq-Syria pipeline and the Qatar-Saudi Arabia-Jordan-Syria-Turkey pipeline, which supply gas from Iran and Qatar to Europe (Staněk, 2017). The UN Security Council has failed to promote effective steps to stop the civil war and resolve the current humanitarian crisis.

Based on all these grievous circumstances and more, the Syrian humanitarian crisis originated to be considered the worst humanitarian crisis in modern history. This ongoing conflict also includes frequent violations of international humanitarian law. For instance, regarding the European Commission (2017), civilians, who are primary victims of the war, are subjected to direct violence, forced displacement, terrorist attacks, recruitment of children into military units, and in many cases serving as "live shields". Tens of thousands of civilians fled due to ISIS's brutal rule and feared U.S., Russian, and Syrian government airstrikes. Indiscriminate attacks against civilians have led many to flee the dangers of being caught in the crossfire or deliberately targeted by armed forces.

Figure 2. The Syrian crisis' geopolitics map
Source: Barabandi (2021)

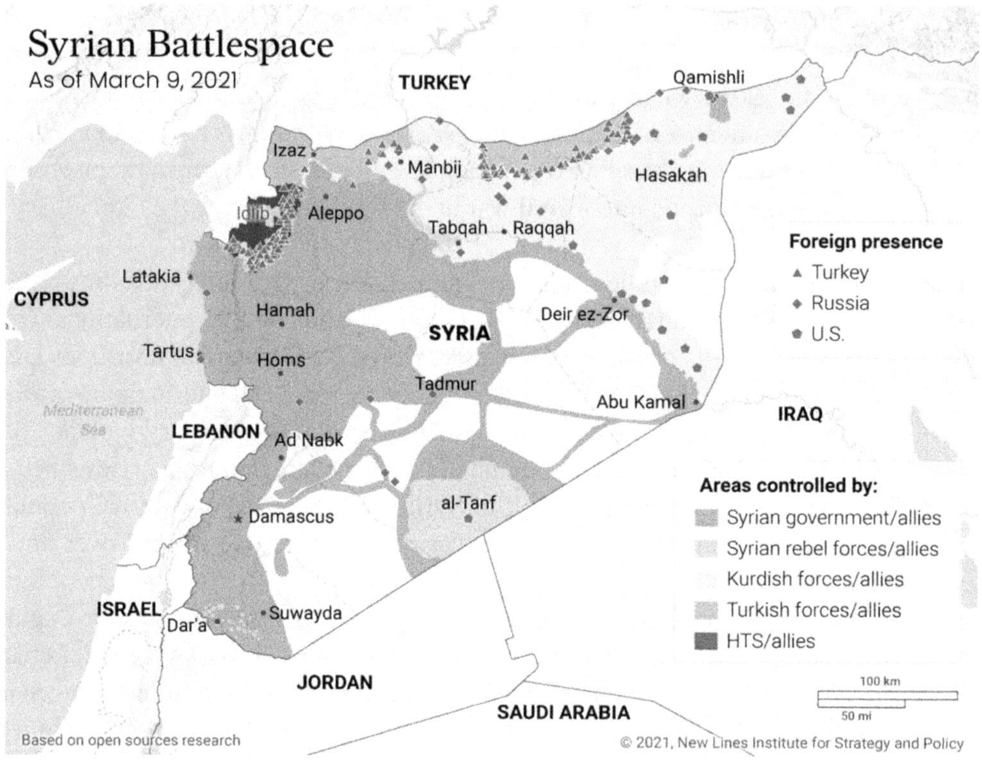

Figure 3. Syrian people in need from 2012-2022
Source: UNOCHA (2021)

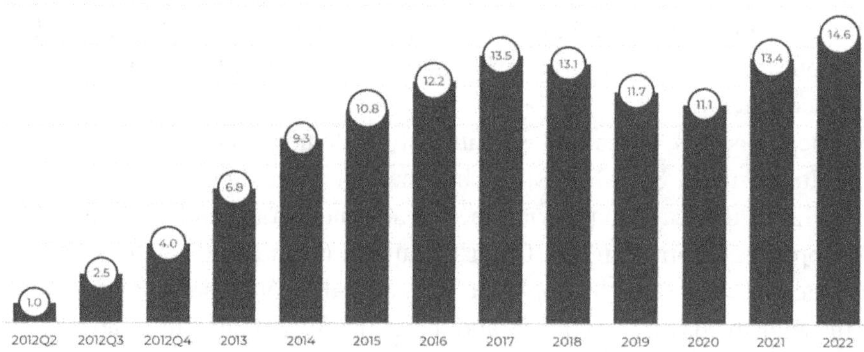

At present, humanitarian actors are struggling to respond to multiple mega-crises. Over the past eleven years, the escalation of the conflict has had severe humanitarian consequences. As rebel forces seized control of towns in several parts of the country and as front lines shifted, sometimes on a daily or hourly basis, accessing Syrian civilians in need of assistance became more difficult. Also, not only do front lines keep moving but so do large numbers of Syrians seeking to escape the violence. Displacement within and from Syria has been massive, dynamic, and rapid (Ferris & Kirisci, 2016b).

3.2 Humanitarian Logistics Gaps and Bottlenecks in Syria

Access and security concerns continue to be the humanitarian community's primary obstacles to reaching vulnerable areas within Syria with life-saving aid supplies. Based on several reports for international originations working in Syria such as Averre and Davies (2015); UNOCHA (2021); WFP (2022), the main gaps identified regarding humanitarian logistics in Syria were:

1) Limited access to certain areas: Due to ongoing conflict and security concerns, humanitarian organizations and workers face significant challenges in accessing certain areas of Syria, particularly in the north and east of the country. This limits the ability of aid groups to deliver assistance and support to people in need.
2) Insufficient infrastructure and logistics capacity: Syria's infrastructure and logistics capacity have been severely damaged as a result of the conflict, making it difficult for aid organizations to transport goods and supplies to those in need. This includes road networks, airports, and ports, all of which are essential for the delivery of humanitarian aid.
3) Difficulty in coordinating and cooperating: With a large number of humanitarian organizations and actors operating in Syria, coordination and cooperation among them can be difficult, leading to inefficiencies and duplicated efforts. This can also make it harder for aid to reach those who need it most.
4) Limited funding and resources: The ongoing conflict in Syria has led to a significant increase in the number of people in need of assistance, while at the same time, funding for aid has decreased. This has led to a significant shortfall in resources and funding for humanitarian organizations, which can make it difficult for them to carry out their work effectively.
5) Difficulty in reaching vulnerable and marginalized populations: Syria's conflict has led to the displacement of millions of people, many of whom are vulnerable and marginalized, including women, children, and people with disabilities. Reaching these populations can be difficult due to security concerns, lack of infrastructure and logistics capacity, and lack of funding.
6) Lack of clear and reliable data and information: With the ongoing conflict, it can be difficult to obtain clear and reliable data and information on the needs of the population and the response of humanitarian organizations. This can make it difficult to make informed decisions and plan effective responses.
7) Challenges in managing and distributing aid: Humanitarian organizations face a number of challenges in managing and distributing aid in Syria, including issues with transportation and storage. This can lead to delays in the delivery of assistance and can make it difficult to reach those who need it most.
8) Limited ability to predict and respond to sudden changes: The ongoing conflict in Syria, along with other factors such as natural disasters or outbreaks of disease, can lead to sudden changes in the situation. Humanitarian organizations may have limited ability to predict and respond to these changes, which can make it difficult to provide effective assistance.

4. HUMANITARIAN HEALTHCARE IN SYRIA

4.1 Introduction

Numerous additional problems are unique to healthcare delivery in crises. In this environment, disease outbreaks are expected and will spread rapidly. When a refugee camp is established, immediate immunisation programmes are frequently recommended. However, a logistical challenge is maintaining storage and warehousing facilities for vaccines and other heat-sensitive pharmaceuticals, including a cold chain (a relay of refrigerated facilities during the voyage). If the cold chain is breached before the medication reaches the patient, it may become inactive or potentially unsafe to use (Çelik et al., 2012).

It cannot be overstated how critical strong logistical support is to crisis response. This is a critical area of work at the heart of humanitarian response, involving complex problems and the potential to provide significant and life-saving help to those affected by catastrophes.

Amid significant challenges encountered by humanitarian groups attempting to act independently in Syria, conflict players who routinely exploit aid as a weapon of war broke the core principles of humanitarian activity. As is the case in most regions hit, organisations wishing to offer humanitarian aid in the country, especially in opposition-held areas, must first obtain permission from the local authorities of the Syrian government.

Access to conflict victims – particularly those trapped in besieged areas – represented de facto the main challenge of this crisis, a challenge that cannot be overcome without humanitarian logistics tailored to these types of constraints. The employment of siege methods reached about 1.5 million Syrians in 2016 trapped in besieged areas (Boulet-Desbareau, 2016). The number of people surrounded in Syria is out of proportion to other sieges, such as those in Sarajevo during the Bosnian conflict. While the war was ongoing, the intensity of these sieges increased dramatically, with more restrictions on the movement of commodities and persons imposed at checkpoints. One of the primary reasons for these additional limitations is to prevent the unnoticed transfer of medical supplies into besieged areas.

4.2 Challenges of Medical Care During the Conflicts

1. Targeting and attacking the medical care facilities and workers

When the initial anti-government demonstrations began in March 2011 from Deera in southern Syria, strikes by the Syrian military forces and private militias were immediately directed toward medical personnel attempting to rescue demonstrators. Many doctors and first-responders accused of treating injured protesters were detained and tortured. Attacks on medical assistance resulted in a major migration of doctors and surgeons from Syria (Boulet-Desbareau, 2016).

The number of hospitals destroyed in Syria has remained unprecedented since WWII (MSF, 2016). Between March 2011 and February 2016, PHR (2019) documented the deaths of over 720 healthcare professionals in Syria.

The number of logisticians arrested or killed while acquiring, storing, or transporting medical supplies for clandestine healthcare structures is more difficult to calculate. Nonetheless, from January to April 2015, incident reports documented by several hospital networks in besieged areas revealed that twice as many logisticians died for every member of medical personnel murdered. Persons illegally transporting medical supplies are frequently shot or killed by mine explosions when crossing siege lines or arrested by armed forces (PHR, 2019).

These numerous forms of violence were apparently perpetrated according to a calculated and organised movement of repression, in plain defiance of the Geneva Conventions on protecting health professionals and patients. Moreover, the causes of this violence mainly were focused on three aspects:

a. To punish Syrians who oppose Bashar Al Assad's government by denying citizens access to primary healthcare.
b. Weakening opposing armed groups and slowing their advance interfere with their ability to care for war-wounded.
c. To eliminate the prospect of medical acknowledgement of the number of injured and dead documented in healthcare systems, allowing large-scale crimes to be committed with complete impunity.

2. The limits of international humanitarian organisations

The Syrian government's restrictions on providing medical care to people opposing its control mostly affect international humanitarian organisations operating out of Damascus. Despite Security Council resolutions unanimously passed in 2014 on humanitarian access to besieged areas, the regime continues to deny humanitarian agencies access to certain areas, citing humanitarian aid, notably medical care, serves the interests of ''terrorist' fighters.

As a result, distributions of humanitarian materials sent from Damascus have frequently been arranged during the well-known 'Reconciliation Committees' that Syrian security forces organised with local representatives of a besieged area. Although international humanitarian organisations based in Damascus were the primary suppliers of these relief commodities, they were not invited to these committee sessions. With the absence of any international agency involvement during assistance distribution, humanitarian commodities brought to the Syrian government-controlled areas were assigned to recipients in a discriminatory manner based on supposed political membership (MSF, 2016). Faced with this persistent blockage of any sort of medical help to those in true need of healthcare, virtually all international groups located in Damascus have given up. They understandably prefer to direct their assistance to other programmes involving water supply, sanitation, education, and/or agriculture.

Therefore, of the mounting frustrations caused by the repeated obstructing of international aid, several governments have begun to pursue unconventional kinds of involvement. Airdrop operations were suggested in 2016 despite risks usually associated with this type of practice when there is no ground control (military-humanitarian confusion, tensions in drop zones, uncontrolled distribution of items dropped, etc.) (Bertini, 2016). Additionally, medical help delivered to Syria by humanitarian via cross-border activities, primarily from Turkey, was likewise severely curtailed in many ways. Few relief organisations have been able to propose healthcare services in severe crises, particularly when performing battlefield surgery. Therefore, most INGOs have been obliged to construct proxy interventions in Syria by employing solely Syrian workers in existing healthcare structures or subcontracting medical treatment to local NGOs or other groups identified within the Syrian diaspora. Due to the unusual challenges posed by the Syrian crisis, many of these international organisations have been used systematically as a finance bridge between institutional donors and local NGOs. Unfortunately, many of these agencies' budgets have grown dramatically as a result, and they lack the logistical capacity to keep up with the financial expansion. As a result, certain INGOs have been subjected to large-scale fraud (Boulet-Desbareau, 2016).

3. Medical networks in besieged areas

The scope and severity of the violence against medical treatment in Syria explain why, from the start of the protests, medical associations decided to collaborate to establish mobile medical teams and underground supply networks in order to operate in hidden health structures. Clandestine networks of doctors operating mostly in metropolitan towns such as Damascus, Hama, and Homs relied on remote support offered by some international medical organisations. Hundreds of surgery and first aid kits were delivered daily to demonstration sites, allowing medical networks to organise covert emergency care. War surgery training sessions were also held in adjacent countries to improve the abilities of medical teams that were inexperienced in dealing with battle injuries (PHR, 2019).

Since 2012, military siege methods grew, along with increasing restrictions on the movement of people and goods, primarily on Damascus' outskirts. More and more underground transportation networks were established in an attempt to circumvent military checkpoints and assure the continued supply of supplies to medical teams besieged in these locations. To meet these siege situations, the scope and severity of which had never been seen before in a fight, underground medical networks expanded as medical assistance and logistics systems adapted to these new and harsh circumstances. The Syrian government opted to impose strict control on humanitarian medical structures in general, and on medical treatment in particular, by voting in an anti-terrorism law to outlaw, any medical assistance supplied to members of the Syrian opposition. During that time, Damascus authorities issued orders preventing public and private medical structures from serving displaced families from areas retaken by the Syrian army (MSF, 2016).

4.3 Humanitarian Logistics Implementation

4.3.1 Analysis of Needs and Logistics Feasibility

Because of the increasing number of support requests, organisations already working in medical support programmes in Syria have adopted operating rules and admission requirements. These principles and criteria were updated regularly in response to medical needs, the reality of the Syrian context, and the dynamics of remote support programmes. In this framework, identifying and assessing healthcare structures and their needs was critical to ensuring conformity with principles and maintaining support supplied to a medical structure. In addition to these early assessments, logistics feasibility analyses (transportability, road access negotiations, checkpoints) were carried out in each besieged pocket were supporting health structures were located. Logistics methods and tools were developed to guarantee that equipment shipped to health structures matches the demands specified by doctors (kind of required item, expected quantity/quality) and, above all, that it has arrived at the required place and time of delivery at destination.

4.3.2 Ordering Systems

One of the most difficult challenges was establishing an "end-to-end" supply chain in collaboration with medical teams and hospital administrators who had never worked in an acute humanitarian crisis prior to the Syrian conflict. In addition to precarious installations, supported medical facilities frequently ran out of drugs and emergency equipment during large influxes of injured. Logically, from the start of assistance activities, the order system was based on standard lists of emergency kits that were straightforward to supply and use. Only once it became clear that siege methods would endure considerably longer, depriving entire regions of access to needed pharmaceuticals for an extended period, were these order lists, which were initially fairly basic, expanded. In addition to kits, a larger assortment of medical materials was given via a pull dynamic that enabled medical teams to order specific items based on their needs. In addition to providing emergency care to the injured, the ordering system's pull dynamic aimed to give doctors the ability to treat chronic and acute diseases, as well as provide delivery services and therapy support to thousands of people traumatised by Syria's war atrocities.

The ordering process was also greatly simplified to allow supporting medical teams to place orders, typically late at night over internet networks, without having to deal with a complex administrative system. It was also necessary to codify order processes and monitoring tools to reduce the chance of medical structures being identified as legitimate targets. Codifying order list items and supported healthcare structures has accelerated the need to harmonise data management for the numerous support projects.

Based on preliminary needs expressed by recipient structures to the support organisation, a more formal external request document was produced and included in the order validation/rejection procedure. Some support businesses have developed an integrated ERP-type software package to increase the performance of logistics data processing, which can sometimes be hefty. Although developing this type of software in an environment such as Syria was difficult, it can help with ordering management linked to stock status and continuing shipments. Currently, most preliminary requests are specified by 'Request Packages,' which include medical, logistical, and human resource needs in a single table. Humanitarian agencies gradually formed support level agreements (SLA) ranging from six to twelve months, with some hospitals receiving regular support over the years. These SLAs enable them to rely on more flexible material and financial support, as well as to obtain resources needed for the structure of their healthcare services throughout time. Some businesses consolidated the preliminary proposal into a more comprehensive package request that included medical products, non-medical items, and HR incentives.

4.3.3 Purchasing Procedures

Since 2012, support activities for health structures began to be handled through cross-border logistics operations during the armed opposition's territorial overflow of Damascus authorities. The great majority of humanitarian organisations were then obliged to operate from outside Syria, relying on an international procurement process for emergency equipment that was eventually delivered to Syria. Due to the gradual closure of Syrian borders with Lebanon and Jordan beginning in 2013 and Turkey two years later, aid organisations had to adjust their procurement strategy for humanitarian materials. To deal with this constraint, several assistance organisations have decided to reduce overseas purchases and increase capacity for local purchases.

Although the implementation was complicated, the shift in procurement techniques permitted, on the one hand, to reduce hazards connected with medical supplies transportation over shorter distances and, on the other hand, to boost reactivity. After mid-2013, it became impossible to supply some besieged pockets without making local pharmaceuticals and medical equipment purchases. At the same time, some foreign organisations ceased support activities in these areas because their purchasing practices could no longer meet the requirements of their financial backers. Compliance with typical purchasing procedures (tenders, preliminary quote requests, supplier selection, etc.) was impossible in Syria's war-torn environment. To continue serving besieged areas inaccessible via cross-border routes, organisations involved in healthcare structures working in these areas had to devise new sourcing techniques. Some of them decided to include Syrian pharmaceutical professionals in their support teams to ensure the availability of local medication markets (quality, quantity, and price) as well as their dependability in a volatile environment.

To be effective, the parallel pharmaceutic market monitoring system must also contain control mechanisms such as reconciliation work performed by purchasers and procurement authorities. Without a reliable invoicing system, which often did not even exist, it was required to ensure that commodities purchased were efficiently delivered to beneficiary health facilities in the proper quantity, quality, and time. Despite bank limits and counter-terrorism pressure measurements, the other key restraint was aggregating financial transactions meant to pay suppliers through informal value transfer channels (Hawala). In light of the increasing dangers of goods interception by governmental troops during their shipment up to besieged areas, an increasing number of suppliers proposed additional purchase prices that include access security, often via corrupted networks linked to the regime. As a result, the decision to buy drugs inside Syria raised a slew of ethical concerns that had to be addressed before approving this last-resort alternative.

4.3.4 Warehouse Management

The gradual closure of primary entry points at Syrian borders significantly impacted purchasing methods and the warehousing of humanitarian materials headed for active hospitals in besieged areas. Initially, medical donations were removed from humanitarian organisation warehouses in adjacent countries by logistical departments of the medical networks. Furthermore, cross-border humanitarian activities have become more complex and dangerous to organise since 2013. Borders were gradually shutting due to saturation of neighbouring countries – mostly Lebanon and Jordan – as well as escalating tensions with migrants, and cross-border movements orchestrated by medical networks pose considerable risks for transporters.

Despite these replenishment limits and the risk of bombardment or looting, central inventories earmarked to support activities were gradually relocated within Syria, primarily from Turkey, to consolidate the increasing volume of supplies. However, deploying stock within Syria – including advanced depots near or within besieged areas – allowed for greater flexibility in medical supplies transit. Support efforts gained greatly in reactivity due to these clandestine humanitarian depots, which were usually kept distinct from military storage. These advanced depots also aided in establishing security stocks, which might be deployed in the event of stress within the besieged region or when purchase prices on reselling markets become excessively high. Using these inventories also allowed support agencies to balance price variations in parallel markets in the event of an unexpected spike. The usage of food reserves during high inflation forces suppliers to re-establish more affordable purchase prices. Since mid-2015, a new limitation has arisen regarding covert warehouse security – primarily for food inventories in besieged areas before dispatch to distribution sites. Some starving people looted warehouses or threatened food distribution points during several high severity peaks.

4.3.5 Cross-Border Shipments

Logistical divisions of medical networks typically organise medical supplies from humanitarian organisations for safety reasons. In order to avoid the dangers of smuggled drugs, access highways to besieged areas were permanently redefined based on military checkpoints, as well as opportunities to cross both borders and front lines. While transporting medical supplies into besieged areas, many logisticians were detained or killed. Aside from the perils associated with persecution by the regime and its supported troops, another significant risk of supplies in besieged areas was the possibility of theft or requisition by opposition armed groups during shipment to beneficiary hospitals. Whereas medical supplies were not usually targeted by robbery or military requisitions, sensitive products (fuel for hospital generators, money for staff salaries, etc.) were. Since the beginning of the crisis, escalating inflation and a sharp depreciation of the Syrian pound have made this mode of transportation more vulnerable.

Given the numerous risks of interruption, diversion, and requisition during shipment, humanitarian commodity shipping in besieged areas has two primary challenges:

- The ability to trace items throughout their transportation until they arrive at their destination and recognise receipt
- The ability to provide bargaining leverage in order to force material reparation in the instance of interception during transportation or robbery by some medical employees.

Clearly, these advantages were almost non-existent in terms of restoration of equipment detained by government forces, private militias, or security agencies. They were, however, far more effective in cases of requisition by opposing armed groups or robbery. There were numerous ways to put pressure on the government to return the equipment. The most expedient and legal option is to suspend support efforts until the intercepted/stolen equipment is returned, despite the caused dangers of treatment disruption.

Because logistics restrictions typically take precedence over medical requirements when it comes to accessing besieged areas, support was predicated on strategic considerations for specific health buildings that serve as mandatory points of entry to other areas.

It was based on numerous alert networks placed on various parts of specified routes that are not necessarily connected to follow up on equipment transit and detect eventual diversions. Various local NGO representatives, activist networks, combatants, local authorities, and other focal points are committed on a daily basis to informing humanitarian organisations of the proper passage of their consignment and, if necessary, of their interception. Prior work on information network maintenance was therefore required before delivering equipment within Syria or any other besieged territory. Some humanitarian groups have set up "Big Data" systems – that is, the tracing of information circulating on the internet – to evaluate the reliability of the information networks that had been developed. Warning messages are frequently posted on Facebook, Twitter, and other social media platforms when cargo heading for a besieged area is intercepted, or equipment is diverted after arrival.

5. CONCLUSION

Syria's war, violence, and the international community's incapacity to stop or mitigate its devastation have shattered humanitarian norms and established new operational models for organisations that seduce victims with aid.

Over 150 years ago, Henri Dunant established the groundwork for humanitarian action by establishing three fundamental principles:

- Conflict victims no longer belong to one camp, they are neutral, and we must be neutral to aid them.
- Aid organisations must be permanently prepared for the expected event.
- In war, humanitarian law is only required when violence and war prevail.

In the Syrian context, these principles were patently impractical because the majority of war-injured people were not treated by humanitarian groups, but by doctors, nurses, and other non-neutral health workers. On the other hand, because the vast majority of health structures were located in besieged areas, these structures were not protected by Geneva conventions. Medical assistance supplied to thousands of victims on a daily basis was not recognised as a humanitarian effort but rather as untrustworthy activity fueled by a partisan mindset.

This perception derives from a rejection of the reality of international humanitarian organisations operating in war zones with an average of 80% local workers, despite their claims of neutrality and impartiality. This contrast in humanitarian terms was also striking when it comes to criticising major and recurring violations of international humanitarian law in Syria. Consequently, while support efforts for health facilities in besieged areas did not strictly adhere to humanitarian principles, they did succeed in ensuring minimal healthcare access for thousands of people and averting the burden rise associated with this cruel war. Support for populations labelled by the United Nations as "hardly reachable" was only made possible by the incredible resolve and self-sacrifice of some logisticians who daily attempt to breach siege methods in order to transport medical supplies to besieged areas at the risk of their lives.

To provide an effective emergency response to that complicated humanitarian conflict, humanitarian organisations adhered to several critical rules:

1. Avoid copying and pasting into the humanitarian response: emergency teams must avoid replicating intervention strategies used in previous crisis contexts. If innovation is not the goal, as opposed to efficiency, it is critical to consider the unique characteristics of crisis contexts in order to adjust the humanitarian situation appropriately.
2. To achieve an acceptable balance of humanitarian risk and impact, unavoidable operational risk-taking must be linked to significant humanitarian impact, even if this impact is effective and apparent (and hence quantifiable) only after humanitarian response deployment.
3. To provide maximum operational transparency, risks faced by emergency team members will involve their organisation and funders – whether institutional or private – who finance this type of dangerous activity. That risk-taking must be recognised at all organisational levels, as evidenced by regular reports on effect achieved, risks incurred in achieving it, and mitigation actions to avoid or mitigate these risks.

LESSONS LEARNED

The primary objective of this chapter was to draw on the lessons learned and derive recommendations for the future of the Syrian operation itself and identify best practices for other operations in any humanitarian intervention. Based on the lessons learned from the Syrian crisis, there are several key implications for global humanitarian logistics:

1. **Access and security are critical:** The ongoing conflict in Syria has highlighted the importance of access and security in humanitarian logistics operations. Aid organizations must have robust security protocols in place and work closely with local partners to ensure the safe and secure delivery of aid.
2. **Coordination and cooperation are essential:** With a large number of aid groups operating in Syria, coordination and cooperation have been essential to ensure that aid is reaching those who need it most and to avoid duplicated efforts.
3. **Logistics capacity and infrastructure are critical:** The conflict in Syria has severely damaged the country's infrastructure and logistics capacity, making it difficult for aid organizations to transport goods and supplies to those in need. Investing in logistics capacity and infrastructure is essential to ensure that aid can be delivered effectively.
4. **Reliable and accurate data and information are important:** With the ongoing conflict, it can be difficult to obtain clear and reliable information on the needs of the population and the response of humanitarian organizations. Investing in data and information management systems is essential to ensure that decisions can be made based on accurate and up-to-date information.
5. **Flexibility and adaptability are necessary:** The Syrian crisis has highlighted the need for flexibility and adaptability in logistics operations. Aid organizations must have contingency plans in place and be able to adapt their logistics operations to changing circumstances.
6. **Funding and resources are crucial:** The ongoing conflict in Syria has led to a significant increase in the number of people in need of assistance, while at the same time, funding for aid has decreased. This has led to a significant shortfall in resources and funding for humanitarian organizations, which can make it difficult for them to carry out their work effectively.
7. **Reaching vulnerable and marginalized populations is a major challenge:** Syria's conflict has led to the displacement of millions of people, many of whom are vulnerable and marginalized, including women, children, and people with disabilities. Reaching these populations can be difficult due to security concerns, lack of infrastructure and logistics capacity, and lack of funding.
8. **Logistics operations should be integrated with overall humanitarian response:** Logistics operations should be integrated with overall humanitarian response, so that humanitarian aid can reach those in need in an efficient and effective manner.

Based on the lessons learned from the Syrian crisis, there are additional key insights for logistics activities in general:

1. The importance of planning and forecasting: Effective logistics operations require careful planning and forecasting to anticipate and respond to the needs of the situation.
2. The need for efficient and reliable transportation: Adequate and reliable transportation is crucial for the effective delivery of goods and supplies.
3. The value of effective inventory management: Proper inventory management is essential to ensure that goods and supplies are available when and where they are needed.
4. The benefit of technology and automation: The use of technology and automation can improve the efficiency and accuracy of logistics operations.
5. The importance of cost-effectiveness: Logistics operations must be cost-effective to ensure they are sustainable in the long term.

6. The need for effective communication and coordination: Clear communication and coordination among all stakeholders is essential for successful logistics operations.
7. The importance of flexibility and adaptability: Logistics operations must be able to adapt to changing circumstances and unexpected events.
8. The need for compliance with regulations and standards: Logistics operations must comply with relevant regulations and standards to ensure the safety and security of goods and people.
9. The importance of sustainability in logistics: Logistics operations should be designed and implemented with a focus on sustainability and minimizing the environmental impact.

Questions and Answers

Q1: How do relief supply chains differ from commercial ones? And which contextual issues challenge how the supply chain is managed?

Within commercial logistics, the typical issue is to try to maximise profits. The objective is to maximise profits, whereas, in humanitarian logistics, we talk about minimising losses. The demand in commercial logistics is stable and predictable, whereas, in humanitarian logistics, it's highly variable in terms of timing, locations, and products. If we'd look at the distribution networks, we have an accurate determination of the number and location of distribution centres within commercial logistics, whereas, in humanitarian logistics, we have unknown locations, poor infrastructure, and unexpected events. Commercial logistics inventory management is more accessible because of well-defined inventory levels based on the lead time, demand average, and target service levels. In humanitarian logistics, this is challenging because of high variability in lead time, demand, and locations. In commercial logistics, information systems are reliable, thanks to advanced technology. In humanity logistics, it's often unreliable, incomplete, or nonexistent.

Q2: If you were to deliver relief items immediately after a disaster, which would be your first consideration? How would these change if you were to deliver them during the recovery phase rather than the response phase? And during the preparedness phase?

For the immediate response phase, the considerations are always preserving the life and safety of individuals and communities. The focus would be water, food, sanitation, clothing, and shelter for distribution items. Safety items would be based on the scenario - do we have access to light, WASH supplies, are medical supplies needed for injured people, PPE, etc. Consider both the communities impacted and the teams responding. Other considerations would include that which upholds the dignity of the person - do they have sanitary products, infant care needs, appropriate clothing (i.e. that which takes into account both the physical and cultural/religious environment), medications etc.

In mid-to-long-term recovery, needs are assessed on a case-by-case basis. If available, caseworkers should be on the ground listening to the community and individual needs and seeking to meet those accordingly. In a well-coordinated recovery, you don't assume people's needs as this reduces trust and creates tension. Similarly, in the preparedness phase, risks are identified with community consultation, and aid workers should seek to fill the gaps whilst promoting self-efficacy.

Q3: Draw a humanitarian supply chain (HSC): Based on your knowledge, list the different supply chain processes (procurement, warehousing, etc.) that take place inside an international humanitarian organisation and then draw its supply chain including:

- The focal organisation (the NGO)

- The supplier's supplier for 3 relief items
- The implementing partner (local chapter of the NGO)
- The beneficiary

Remember to include the information flow coming from the beneficiary and going upstream through the focal organisation, the supplier's supplier and imagine which type of data would that flow represent (number of beneficiaries, number of items, locations, etc.)

Plan, Assessment to identify beneficiaries with disaster organisations, Source suppliers quotations, Bidding, Warehousing & transportation i.e. WFP, Red Cross and Government. Operation, purchasing and distribution Government, Red Cross, WFP & UN. They all work together by reporting to one cluster, which is the focal organisation.

Q4: What is meant by food security, and how does it relate to the humanitarian and development discourse?

Food security means that a person has access to food that is nutritious and sufficient in quantity. It is both a humanitarian and development concern. Many countries around the world are facing food insecurity due to population growth, increased demand for food, food price, the disappearance of agricultural plant species, an increase in the area of scarcity water and the limitation of the availability of land and food losses and food waste.

Q5: How do ensure the safety and security of people and goods in humanitarian operations?

The first thing that we need to do is information. Humanitarian logistics about goods, information, and finances. The same is in the safety and security. A more complex situation is even in the conflict zones, when we have multiple layers, we have different actors, we have different problems, we have things which are from the past, like landmines, and we need to understand that wherever we are going and before we go there. Each humanitarian aid organisation should have policies, reports, and reviews about security and safety, and that should be the first place to understand where we are going and the intervention.

The second is planning. We need to understand what to do, and also we have to be prepared. It means training, first aid training, communication, ability to respond to different situations. And that's necessary. And that should be before are going to the field because when we are there, it can be simply too late.

But whatever we do, planning is the first thing, but when we are there in the field, there are three strategies which are taken.

- The first is about acceptance to show that the humanitarian organisation is not a threat; they should be accepted and not be attacked.
- The second is protection, so passive measures to be sure that nothing happens. And that could be anything from selecting the right site, building the shelters, applying, creating, and wearing the protection and equipment during the conflict zones.
- The third one is deterrence. This is especially visible in conflicts when we have the involvement of military actors.

Q7: According to the case, what are the challenges facing humanitarian aid for healthcare in Syria?

Targeting and attacking the medical care facilities and workers: The number of hospitals destroyed in Syria has remained unprecedented since WWII. Between March 2011 and February 2016, PHR (2019) documented the deaths of over 720 healthcare professionals in Syria. The number of logisticians arrested or killed while acquiring, storing, or transporting medical supplies for clandestine healthcare structures is more difficult to calculate.

The Limits of International Humanitarian Organisations: The Syrian government's restrictions on providing medical care to people opposing its control mostly affect international humanitarian organisations operating out of Damascus. As a result, distributions of humanitarian materials sent from Damascus have frequently been arranged during the well-known 'Reconciliation Committees' that Syrian security forces organised with local representatives of a besieged area. Faced with this persistent blockage of any medical help to those in true need of healthcare, virtually all international groups located in Damascus have given up. They understandably prefer to direct their assistance to other water supply, sanitation, education, and/or agriculture programmes.

Medical networks in besieged areas: The scope and severity of the violence against medical treatment in Syria explain why, from the start of the protests, medical associations decided to collaborate to establish mobile medical teams and underground supply networks in order to operate in hidden health structures. Clandestine networks of doctors operating mostly in metropolitan towns such as Damascus, Hama, and Homs relied on remote support offered by some international medical organisations. Hundreds of surgery and first aid kits were delivered daily to demonstration sites, allowing medical networks to organise covert emergency care.

Q8: What is the difference between humanitarian aid and development assistance?

Humanitarain aid is short term oriented, designed to alleviate the suffering of vulnerable people immediately aftermath of emergencies. The aid is delivered in the disaster zones.

The development aid refers to the ongoing long term assistance that focuses on economic, social and political development. Such type of aid is mainly concerned with developing countries.

Development aid and humanitarian aid can be independent. Development aid can exist in developing countries that do not necessarily have humanitarian crisis. But also they can be interdependent, where development and humanitarian aid both exists during and after crisis.

Q9: How to improve communication between humanitarian aid agencies and affected people?

There are three main global trends that has lead to the improvement of communication between humanitarian aid actors. These trends includes: the proliferation of humanitarian quality and accountability initiatives; the increased availability and use of information and communication technology ICTs in developing countries; and changes in the role of media actors in humanitarian response.

Quality and accountability initiatives in the humanitarian sector proliferation started since mid 1990s where communicating with affected people changed from just being a human right and duty morale to be an essential element to effective and accountable humanitarian aid. Accountability initiatives included: providing accessible and timely information to affected populations and enabling affected populations to play an active role in the decision-making processes that affect them.

Media actors , have played an increasing role in humanitarian response not just as providers of news, but also of humanitarian information of practical value to crisis-affected populations.

ICTs have been significantly more accessible and widely adopted over the past ten years, giving people around the world previously unheard-of chances to access information, connect with one another, and have their voices heard. A paradigm shift in the way the aid sector employs communication tools to better understand and serve crisis-affected populations is being prompted by the speed with which people in the developing world are embracing mobile phone and internet technology and discovering creative uses for them.

Source: https://www.alnap.org/system/files/content/resource/files/main/np74-infoasaid-paper.pdf

Q10: What are the principles of humanitarian assistance?

The principles of humanitarian assistance are a set of guidelines that guide the actions of humanitarian organizations and aid workers in their efforts to provide assistance to those in need. These principles include:

1. Humanity: Humanitarian assistance must be provided in a manner that preserves human dignity and respects the rights and needs of those affected by crisis.
2. Neutrality: Humanitarian assistance must be provided without discrimination and without taking sides in conflicts or political disputes.
3. Impartiality: Humanitarian assistance must be provided to those in need based on need alone, without regard to race, religion, nationality, or other factors.
4. Independence: Humanitarian assistance must be provided independently of political, economic, or military interests.
5. Unity of effort: Humanitarian assistance must be coordinated among all actors, including humanitarian organizations, government, and the private sector, to ensure that aid reaches those in need in an efficient and effective manner.
6. Minimum standards: Humanitarian organizations must adhere to minimum standards for the delivery of aid, including those related to the protection of beneficiaries, the provision of food, water, and shelter, and the prevention of sexual exploitation and abuse.
7. Do no harm: Humanitarian organizations must take steps to ensure that their actions do not cause harm or increase the vulnerability of those they are trying to help.
8. Transparency and accountability: Humanitarian organizations must be transparent and accountable in their actions and must report regularly on their activities and the use of resources.

Source: https://www.paho.org/disasters/dmdocuments/pedhumen.pdf

REFERENCES

Abdelbary, I. (2021). *Reviving Arab Reform: Development Challenges and Opportunities*. Emerald Group Publishing. doi:10.1108/9781839823183

Abdelbary, I., & Benhin, J. (2019). The Economic Reform and Political Transitions: Potentials and Challenges of Arab Development. In P. W. Zgheib (Ed.), *Impacts of political instability on economics in the MENA region* (pp. 145–184). IGI Global. doi:10.4018/978-1-5225-8247-2.ch006

Averre, D., & Davies, L. (2015). Russia, humanitarian intervention and the Responsibility to Protect: The case of Syria. *International Affairs*, *91*(4), 813–834. doi:10.1111/1468-2346.12343

Barabandi, B. (2021). *Shifting Stakeholder Positions & Conflict Resolution in Syria*. Retrieved from https://newlinesinstitute.org/syria/shifting-stakeholder-positions-conflict-resolution-in-syria/

Bertini, C. (2016). *U.N. Struggles To Reach Besieged Areas Of Syria With Aid Air Drop Plan/Interviewer: M. Kelemen*. NPR.

Boulet-Desbareau, P. (2016). *Underground humanitarian logistics in Syria: the invisible driving force of medical care in besieged areas*. Retrieved from http://emergency-log.weebly.com/uploads/2/5/2/4/25246358/ehl_in_syria-jul16.pdf

Cano-Olivos, P., Sánchez-Partida, D., Caballero-Morales, S.-O., & Martínez-Flores, J.-L. (2022). Strategies that Improve the Performance of the Humanitarian Supply Chain. In *Humanitarian Logistics from the Disaster Risk Reduction Perspective* (pp. 119-140). Springer.

Çelik, M., Ergun, Ö., Johnson, B., Keskinocak, P., Lorca, Á., Pekgün, P., & Swann, J. (2012). *Humanitarian logistics New directions in informatics, optimisation, logistics, and production*. INFORMS.

European Commission. (2017). *ECHO Factsheet – Syria crisis*. Retrieved from Brusel: https://reliefweb.int/sites/reliefweb.int/files/resources/syria_en_22.pdf

Ferris, E., & Kirisci, K. (2016a). *The consequences of chaos: Syria's humanitarian crisis and the failure to protect*. Brookings Institution Press.

Ferris, E., & Kirisci, K. (2016b). The context, causes, and consequences of Syrian displacement. *The Consequences of Chaos: Syria's Humanitarian Crisis and the Failure to Protect*, *1*, 32.

Fritz Institute. (2022). *About Humanitarian Supply Chain Management (SCM)*. Retrieved from https://fritzinstitute.org/humanitarian-scm/

Kovacs, G., & Spens, K. M. (2012). *Relief supply chain management for disasters: humanitarian aid and emergency logistics*. Information Science Reference. doi:10.4018/978-1-60960-824-8

Laituri, M., & Kodrich, K. (2008). On line disaster response community: People as sensors of high magnitude disasters using internet GIS. *Sensors (Basel)*, *8*(5), 3037–3055. doi:10.33908053037 PMID:27879864

Manfré, L. A., Hirata, E., Silva, J. B., Shinohara, E. J., Giannotti, M. A., Larocca, A. P. C., & Quintanilha, J. A. (2012). An analysis of geospatial technologies for risk and natural disaster management. *ISPRS International Journal of Geo-Information*, *1*(2), 166–185. doi:10.3390/ijgi1020166

Meier, P. (2015). *Digital humanitarians: how big data is changing the face of humanitarian response*. Crc Press. doi:10.1201/b18023

MSF. (2016). *Documenting war-wounded and war-dead in MSF-supported medical facilities in Syria*. Retrieved from https://doctorswithoutborders.org/sites/default/files/2018-08/syria_2015_war-dead_and_war-wounded_report_en.pdf?_ga=2.111148227.771097555.1650825169-1469270171.1650825169

Nikbakhsh, E., & Farahani, R. Z. (2011). Humanitarian logistics planning in disaster relief operations. *Logistics operations and management: Concepts and models, 291*.

PHR. (2019). *The Syrian Conflict: Eight Years of Devastation and Destruction of the Health System*. Retrieved from https://phr.org/wp-content/uploads/2019/03/PHR-Syria-2019-Fact-Sheet.pdf

Regis-Hernández, F., Mora-Vargas, J., Sánchez-Partida, D., & Ruiz, A. (2022). *Humanitarian Logistics from the Disaster Risk Reduction Perspective*. Springer. doi:10.1007/978-3-030-90877-5

Sahay, B., Gupta, S., & Menon, V. C. (2016). *Managing humanitarian logistics*. Springer. doi:10.1007/978-81-322-2416-7

SCPR. (2013). *Syria- War on Development: socioeconomic monitoring report of Syria, second quarterly report (April – June 2013)*. Retrieved from https://reliefweb.int/sites/reliefweb.int/files/resources/md_syr-rprt_q2fnl_251013.pdf

Staněk, M. (2017). The humanitarian crisis and civil war in Syria: Its impact and influence on the migration crisis in Europe. *Kontakt*, *19*(4), e270–e275. doi:10.1016/j.kontakt.2017.09.013

Tomasini, R., Van Wassenhove, L., & Van Wassenhove, L. (2009). *Humanitarian logistics*. Springer. doi:10.1057/9780230233485

UNESCWA. (2021). *Syria at War: Eight Years On*. Retrieved from Beirut: https://publications.unescwa.org/projects/saw/sdgs/pdf/en/Syria-at-War-8-years-on-Report-Final.pdf

UNOCHA. (2013). *Humanitarianism in the Network Age; Including World Humanitarian Data and Trends 2012*. Retrieved from https://reliefweb.int/sites/reliefweb.int/files/resources/Humanitarianism%20in%20the%20Network%20Age.pdf

UNOCHA. (2021). *Humanitarian Needs Overview: Syrian Arab Republic*. Retrieved from New York: www.unocha.org/syria

Van Wassenhove, L. N. (2006). Humanitarian aid logistics: Supply chain management in high gear. *The Journal of the Operational Research Society*, *57*(5), 475–489. doi:10.1057/palgrave.jors.2602125

WFP. (2022). *Concept of Operations*. WFP.

Wielan, C. (2021). *Syria and the Neutrality Trap: Dilemmas of Delivering Humanitarian Aid through Violent Regimes*. Bloomsbury Publishing Plc.

Zeimpekis, V., Ichoua, S., & Minis, I. (2014). *Humanitarian and relief logistics: Research issues, case studies and future trends* (Vol. 54). Springer.

Zobel, C. W., Altay, N., & Haselkorn, M. P. (2015). *Advances in managing humanitarian operations*. Springer.

Zwitter, Lamont, Heintze, & Herman. (2014). Humanitarian Action: Global, Regional and Domestic Legal Responses. Cambridge University Press.

Chapter 12
Investigating the Conflicts in a Multi-Actor Logistics Incident

Seda Özcan
Izmir University of Economics, Turkey

Onur Aksaray
Izmir University of Economics, Turkey

Bengü Sevil Oflaç
Izmir University of Economics, Turkey

EXECUTIVE SUMMARY

The objectives of the case study are to highlight the possible challenges/disruptions arising from having a joint operation with multiple companies, to demonstrate operational problems encountered in the business process, and to illustrate the approach of the companies to the problems in this process and subsequent reconciliation process. Furthermore, this study aims to uncover conflict and power relations, which dominate the whole process between companies, based on some theoretical perspectives of power and conflict in distribution channels. By using a real case involving multiple players of the supply chain, this study contributes to transportation disruption and conflict management domains.

INTRODUCTION

Since organizations are formed as interdependent units and view the same issues through different lenses, conflict seems inevitable in the business environment. When conflict is not well-managed, it leads to negative consequences for all parties involved. Therefore, understanding conflict and its resolution can help parties to foster their relationships, especially in the service industry (Leung, 2009). Resolution of problems requires a range of coordination mechanisms, which are perceived as a prerequisite for integrating operations of supply chain entities to achieve common goals (Kanda & Deshmukh, 2008). In business transactions, conflicts may occur due to conflicting goals and objectives (goal conflict), disagreements over the domain of decisions and actions (domain conflict), and differences in perceptions of reality

DOI: 10.4018/978-1-6684-4686-7.ch012

in joint decision making (perceptual conflict) (Wood et al., 2012). Conflicts pose a risk for the supply chain members and thereby, increase the level of vulnerability. These conflicts can disrupt supply chain operations and affect customer metrics such as on-time delivery and quality (Blackhurst et al., 2008). Supply chain disruptions may occur in various operations in supply, in transportation, at facilities, in freight, in communications, and in demand at diverse levels (Rice & Caniato, 2003).

Logistics and international transport provide one of the most important services in the modern globalized world. The management of the transportation process is intrinsically complex, as it comprises different types of flows among a large number of self-interested agents having distinctive roles and service quality levels (Reis & Macedo, 2019). In line with this, the complexity created by different factors in planning and organizing increases with a progressively higher number of linkages between partners in the transportation process (Creazza et al., 2010). Therefore, such interconnectivity and interdependence between partners trigger a high level of interaction, and affect the functioning of the networks (de Nooy et al., 2006). Moreover, this complexity may result in more frequent disruptions by increasing operational loads in terms of transaction and coordination costs (Iftikhar et al., 2022). This results in a range of challenges and problems in the management and execution of logistics services.

In the current supply chain literature, conflicts often arise in the context of single and dyadic relationships (Krafft et al., 2015) and single level perspectives including the organizational level or the individual level are more dominant (Reimann et al., 2017). However, disruptions and response processes are inherently a multi-level phenomenon (Lumineau et al., 2015), the advancement of conflict research requires moving beyond a single firm's perspective and integrating a multilevel lens incorporating perceptions of all partners. Apart from the dyadic relationship context (e.g., Feng et al., 2017; Liu et al., 2019; Fan et al., 2020; Loske, 2020; Cai et al., 2022), there is considerable conflict research in logistics service industry literature focusing on triadic (e.g., Jakubicek & Woudsma, 2011; Bolumole et al., 2016; Song et al., 2018; Deng et al., 2022; Hu et al., 2022) and quadratic or other myriad relationships (e.g., Liu et al., 2017; Lukinskiy & Pletneva, 2018; Wang & Vogt, 2019; Brettmo & Williamsson, 2020; Lindroth et al., 2020; Rogerson et al., 2022). In all of these types of B2B relationships, partnership success can be established through certain relational attributes, such as coordination, trust, commitment, and information sharing (Odonto et al., 2016; Abidi et al., 2019; Swierczek, 2020). Additionally, as a network theory supports, the network includes the inner workings of companies and vertical cooperative relations between firms, where "interaction", "relationship" and "network" are the main units of analysis (Sousa, 2010).

With the effect of globalization, the logistics sector witnessed a series of structural changes and international logistics operations became more complex. Considering the challenges in carrying out international transport effectively, global players started to outsource subsequent activities to their partners, subcontractors, or even other freight forwarders to integrate their efforts (Skiba & Karas, 2022). Therefore, we believe that more research is needed, particularly involving such complex transportation networks and focusing on disruptions in multi-actor transport, rather than single or dyadic contexts. In this regard, we discuss a multi- actor logistics incident that occurred in a Middle East logistics operation. More specifically, we address a transportation disruption, a temporary interrupted transit flow within a multi-actor setting, involving actors at different levels: shipper, importer, vessel-container operator, integrated logistics service providers, lashing service provider and transportation company. All actors in this case operate or/and have headquarters in the Middle East region. As stated in the related literature, transportation disruption, although quickly handled in this case, incapacitates the entire supply chain by causing late deliveries, operations shutdown, lost sales, and loss of reputation (Paul et al., 2019).

The objective of the case study is to discover possible challenges and resulting disruptions arising from a joint operation with multiple companies; to demonstrate operational problems encountered in the business process; and to identify the companies' approach to the problems within this process, and subsequent reconciliation process. Furthermore, this study aims to explain conflict and power relations, which dominate the whole process by basing on some theoretical perspectives of conflict in distribution channels. In this sense, this study expands the existing knowledge on the problems occurring during the configuration of international logistics networks within a multi-relational context, reveals the complex and dynamic interactions by highlighting the real-time decision-making of logistics parties, and deepens the understanding of self- interest-oriented management of the network agents in the disruption process.

Our research questions are as follows:

1. What are the challenges and resulting disruptions in this international operation?
2. What are the sources of conflict in this multi-agent international operation?
3. Which conflict resolution strategies can be adopted for the parties involved?

Case study methodology was employed in this research by adopting multiple data collection techniques including archival company reports, business agreements, financials, published consultant reports, and narratives of critical incidents under confidentiality.

Case Description and Involved Parties[1]

Company A was one of Turkey's leading construction companies. Several years ago, an economic crisis in the home market forced the company to initiate export operations with crane and machinery items on an occasional basis. Lack of experience in export resulted in difficulties in new market entry. In order to overcome the possible problems derived from inexperience and international operation incapability, they started to work on EX-Works[2].

Company B, a Qatar-based crane dealer company, was involved in lending and procuring heavy construction equipment from all around the world. They were the first movers when UAE cities initiated the reconstruction revolution in 2001 and experienced accelerating business growth with the large construction projects. With its strong capital structure, this company was considered among the leaders in the heavy construction equipment industry.

Company C, an international logistics company with a history of over 15 years in Qatar and, had established an extensive distribution network with a considerable number of agencies, which enabled it to provide high levels of service quality and coverage in global operations. With project transportation and partial services, they achieved high market shares in air, sea, and land transportation. This company provides full insurance for the freight in order to prevent possible problems in its responsibility zone.

Company D, an integrated logistic service provider serving a wide range of customers, intensified its operations on both third-party logistics services and port management areas. In addition to the local services, Company D provides international transportation, storage, and distribution services within an extensive network, managed by its four offices in Spain, Austria, Hong Kong, and Belgium. In addition to these services, Company D is also an expert in project transportation with over gauge. This company provided full insurance for their freight transportation in order to prevent possible problems in its responsibility zone.

Company E, a global vessel-container operator headquartered in Singapore, provided container service, and additionally shipping services generally on a niche basis to a limited number of countries. This company, a medium-sized company in terms of the number of loads carried, was established in 1974 and merged with another liner company to gain more coverage in the market. With 59 offices all around the world, their vessels operated in over 70 countries. With feeder vessels, the company was serving Europe, the Middle East, and the United States. Their special transport equipment (e.g., open-top containers) and project transportation services had positioned them as one of the pioneering companies in the global container/vessel operation business.

Company F, an internal transportation company established in 2003 carrying the specified containers to the loading site and full containers to the port. This company's vessels provided service to over 74 countries. This company was certified employing drivers, yet, due to competition and cost considerations, these had limited foreign language abilities. This company works with brokers in addition to the direct business with importers and exporters and leases the trucks from private carriers to meet the excess demand and 90% of these leases involve drivers. All company transport activities are insured against damage and accidents.

Company G, a certificated Turkish lashing service provider, mainly serves in customized project transportation, mostly in sea transportation. In order to get the lashing licenses, this company complied with the industry regulations in certification and qualified labor requirements.

The story started with an order from a crane dealer company (Company B) in UAE. When Company A, a construction company in Turkey, received the order for a large crane, negotiations among the parties immediately started. Soon after the initial negotiations, the parties reached an agreement. According to the agreement, Company B undertook the transportation operations. Due to the very large parts in a disassembled crane, the transportation was out of gauge requiring 6-7 parties in shipment and special equipment such as flat rack-open-top containers. Considering the high cost and special requirements of the transportation, Company B aimed to select the most reliable transport company for this project while ensuring the best price possible. Company B began to receive quotations from logistics companies and at the end of the bidding process, the contract was awarded to Company C which had a reputation as a reliable supplier. These two companies did a vast amount of business together, constituting 20% of Company C's annual turnover. During the agreements, the below points were taken into consideration:

As a rule of thumb, in seaway container transportation, transport prices between two countries are determined at the export ports. Therefore, the country in which the transport price is formed becomes an export country without considering the country in which transportation cost is billed.

Based on the given requirement, Company C was in need of a partner in Turkey to carry out an export operation and to deal with pricing issues. They received offers from several logistics companies including Company D. Company C and D were the members of a well-known logistics network, which enabled them to become partners. Membership of various global logistics networks facilitated global collaboration and business matching, as it ensured compliance with the rules and norms. Additionally, logistics network membership can act as a conflict prevention and resolution platform through the conflict mediation services offered to its members. In this network of over 300 independent international forwarders from 75 countries, membership provided payment assurances in conflicts occurring among its members. The security amount was up to USD 20,000, according to the length of membership, and insurance coverage was implemented instantly upon the approval of the membership.

In terms of overall pricing and base pricing line, the representative of Company C received offers from many logistics companies, including Company D and presented these figures to Company B. Meanwhile, Company B received many transportation offers, as it was in simultaneous negotiations with many Dubai-based logistics companies. Company B prefers to work with Company C, its long-term partner, the price quoted by Company C was selected as the target price.

At the end of several rounds in negotiation, Company D was the awarded supplier due to its strong financial power and business experience in logistics operations in the Middle East. Moreover, Company D had included the provision of lashing services in the offer. Soon after, Company D started the negotiation process with five ship owners serving the route between Turkey and the target region. At the end of the process, Company E was selected as the main ship-owner, and Company F and G, as subcontractors (for more explanation of the process, see Figure 1).

Figure 1. Logistics network diagram of the international logistics operation

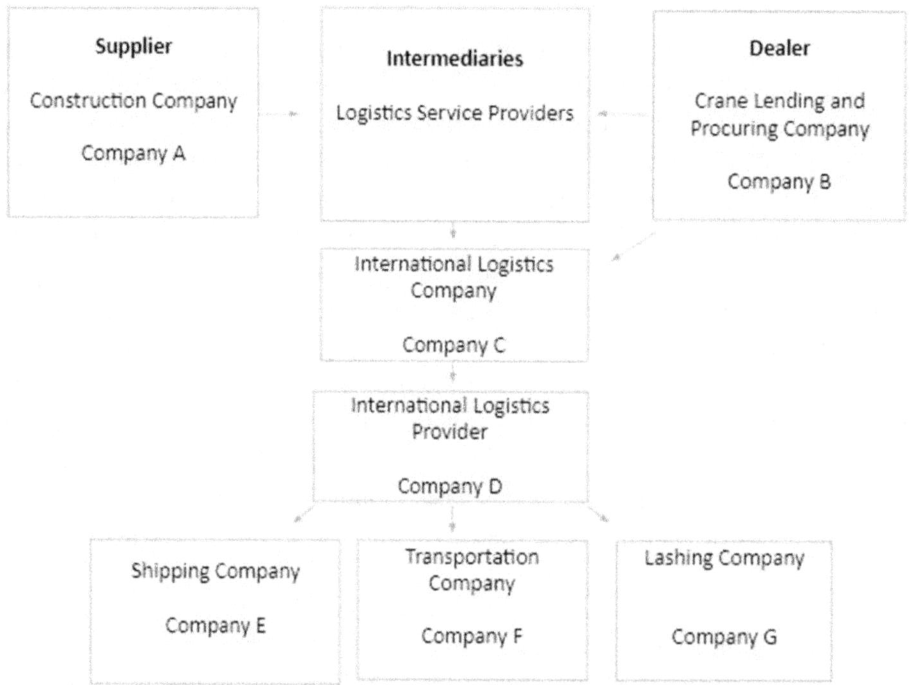

OPERATIONAL PROCESS

Company E identified the transit time between Turkey and Dubai as approximately 18 days. The details of the first batch loading were delivered by Company A as 8 x 40'ft (flat rack container)- 12x40'ot (open top containers) and 6x 40'hc (high cube container), with dimensions of the load, and then calculations were made. These container types (ot' and ft' equipment) are considered as special equipment and at the bid stage, no free time in the export port was considered[3]. Subsequently, the offers were prepared with this content in the proposals submitted from D to C and from C to B. The port storage cost was calculated grounding on the formula below:

Port storage cost: (the day the container enters the port - declared ship departure date) x (storage cost per day)

In Company D's offer, storage cost was determined as 150 $ for ft' and 50 $ for ot'. Company C carried out a special study with Company D in order to minimize the storage cost. Company E determined the cutoff date of the loading ship. The following players were scheduled to be ready in the loading area on the loading day: owner of Company B, dedicated loading team, officials and senior manager of Company A, experts from Company G and Company F truck drivers.

PROBLEM STATEMENT

On the loading day, containers went to the operation area 5-6 hours later than expected due to a supply shortage in Company E. Immediately, officials of Company B charged Company C for this delay issue. In the meantime, officials from Company F and G were unable to communicate with the authorities of Company B due to language barriers. To overcome this issue, they sought the help of Company D officials via phone.

Company F requested extra money from Company B for the delivery of the container. In case of no payment, they declared business would be delayed. This triggered a multi-level incident resulting in a complaint flow in the operational process. All the complaints were transferred respectively from Company B to Company C, from Company C to Company D, and eventually from Company D to its subcontractor Company F and G.

After the loading was completed, it was understood that Company A had misreported the dimensions of the loads when transferring the loading details and it was found that the total height was above the limits allowed on the highway. As a result, Company F refused to carry containers to the port. Consequently, containers entered the port the day after they were loaded, and Company B and C were expecting just 1-day of storage cost. However, since the ship had arrived at the port 2 days late, Company G specified a new cutoff date. With this update, the new storage cost was calculated for 3 days. Company B and C strongly objected to the cost, and passed the responsibility to Company D. Although the expected time of arrival (ETA) was 18 days, delays and lost times on the road had exceeded 20 days. Due to this timing problem, Company B delayed the sales in Qatar, and they wanted to pass on the cost of this delay to Company C. Following this, Company C reported these costs to Company D.

Later, loading measures were revised from 7 x 40'ft - 14x40' ot and 6 x 40'hc to 6 x 40'ft – 12 x40'ot and 6x40'hc. On the grounds of Lloyd's Law[4], which limits the liability of the ship owners, Company E demanded compensation from Company D for delayed return of containers, and did not take any responsibility, other than apologizing. Taking into consideration that Company D and Company E had undertaken many transportation agreements in recent years, Company D wanted to maintain a good relationship with E due to the competitive conditions in the market. The fact remains that Company C and D were affiliated to the network as logistics service providers, while all other companies were sub-contractors.

CURRENT CHALLENGES FACED BY COMPANIES

Supply risk or supply disruptions are emerging as a major challenge for supply chain management primarily in terms of profit-based concerns (Li et al., 2016). In general, all parties seek penalties for delays and operational malpractices. The recovery and compensation negotiations can be problematic in business transactions, due to their criticality and the high penalties that can result (Zhu & Cao, 2021).

Transportation disruptions can severely damage the supply chain, particularly as goods may not arrive on time, jeopardizing promises to customers and level of service (Albertzeth et al., 2020). With even a slight operational disruption, the domino effect can affect all parties. In this case, the main problems that caused international transportation disruption are seen to be related to information sharing, operational planning, and inter-firm relationships.

1. Information Sharing Related Concerns

In this case, each level of transport operation planning seems to face specific information-sharing problems, which result in inefficient coordination of actions throughout the process (Lotfi et al., 2013). At the operational level, information flow is essential by providing answers to the questions of what, with whom, how and when to share (Popp & Yen, 2006).

As Khan et al. (2019) and Yang and Chang (2019) state, communication problems between business partners result in serious costs. During the loading process, Company F and G experienced difficulties in finding interlocutors due to problems in the operation. As they could not contact Company B due to language problems, communication was established via Company D by telephone. Herein, it is also clearly observed that lack of trained and qualified personnel in companies had an adverse effect on the flow of information and interoperability.

Inaccurate information is considered as one of the risk factors that lead to distortion in information sharing (Sharma & Routroy, 2016). Company A misreported the dimensions of the loads when transferring the detailed description of the loading process and created a domino effect for the other parties involved. For Company D, the storage cost proposed in their initial offer was increased with the change in the load size, contradicting the agreement between Company C and Company D for zero or minimum storage costs. Furthermore, when it was found that total height was above the highway limits, Company F refused to carry containers to the port. It was also a problem for company E since the loads occupied more space than planned.

As Wang et al. (2016) pointed out, timely information sharing in case of a disruption contributes to overall flexibility and service quality, allowing them to develop appropriate business continuity solutions. As it is stated in the case, the container arrived 6 hours late at the operation area on the loading day. Aside from taking no precautions beforehand, no additional or up-to-date information regarding delay was provided.

2. Operational Planning Concerns

Minimization of cost items is the primary objective of operational planning and routing in service networks (Mutlu et al., 2017). However, problems encountered in operational planning, especially where there is a need for real-time decision making, become more complex, dynamic, and stochastic (Crainic et al., 2009; Mutlu et al., 2017). In this case, miscalculations in storage costs and delayed sales resulted in enormous costs for companies involved, caused by inefficiencies in operational planning.

In this case, containers did not reach the port until the day after they were loaded due to the disruption. According to the calculations of Company B and C, 1-day storage cost had been foreseen. However, since the ship had arrived at the port 2 days late, the cutoff date was updated as 2 days later, and the storage cost was wrongly calculated at customs for 3 days rather than 4. Company B was planning to minimize the storage cost by exerting pressure on firm C, and this serious miscalculation severely strained their relationship. In this regard, while responsibilities and delays before customs concern Companies C and D, liability was transferred to Company A after customs.

When service providers do not perform as required and do not meet agreed quality standards, risk surcharge is determined by the reclamation costs (Gudehus & Kotzab, 2012). As indicated by Kohtamäki and Farmer (2017), this type of cost also represents a key measure of company performance. As a result of the late arrival of the ship on the loading day and lost time on the road due to the disputes originating from the size of the load, the sale of the crane had been delayed. Since Company C failed to meet the delivery terms of the procurement agreement, this naturally led to the emergence of reclamation costs claimed by Company B.

3. Inter-Firm Relationship Concerns

Relationship issues are acknowledged as one of the challenges while dealing with supply chains and networks (Arlbjorn et al., 2010). In this context, behavioral alignments seem to have a serious impact on the structure, performance, and thus success of the supply chain (Kehoe et al., 2007). Similarly, Fawcett and McCarter (2008) indicate that inter-organizational negotiation, considered as one of the most discussed behavioral issues in SCM literature, creates supply chain problems among partners. According to their study, parties who adopt distributive bargaining strategies strive for domination through persuasive arguments or threats during negotiations, which create ‘conflict spirals’ including emotional conflict, refusal to compromise, impasse, and ultimately, the loss of mutual benefit.

In this international operation, aggressive business behaviors such as threatening turned out to be a major problem for companies.

SOURCES OF THE CHALLENGES

The dynamic complexities in logistics networks brought various challenges and problems for logistics actors. Considering transportation disruptions/problems experienced by international logistics companies in this case study, main challenges were found to be related with information sharing, operational planning, and behavioral issues.

Within the context of principal and the agent relationships, the agent behaves in opposition to the interests of the principal, creating goal incongruence between supply chain partners (Rokkan & Buvik, 2003). In this case, goal incongruence was generally expressed in financial terms among all parties. For instance, while Company B and C attempted to avoid as far as possible the storage costs arising from 3-day late arrival, Company E suffered losses due to late completion of the transactions and therefore requested compensation. In the same vein, with the concern that the dimensions of the load may cause Company F some transport-related operational problems, the company asked an additional fee from Company B. Similarly while Company D pursued the goal of minimizing cost in sales and supply operations through identifying appropriate partners, Company B wanted to pass on the sales loss to this company, as Company E was selected based on D's preference, and caused a decrease in customer service. According to Liche (2021), the best solution to the goal conflict between agent and principle is to bridge the gap in objectives that can emerge over time, and make conflict an invalid option.

On the other hand, perceptual conflicts appear when the parties read the marketplace differently due to their particular perception of reality (Moore et al., 2004) and indicate different bases of actions in response to specific situations. A perceptual difference of dependence was likely to be a source of channel conflict in this case (Jia & Yang, 2019). Company D believed that their dependence on Company E was limited because they could find similar services from other ship-owners, but preferred maintaining a good relationship with company E because of the competitive conditions in the market. However, Company E considered that Company D was highly dependent on them, therefore, assumed no responsibility other than apologizing. Due to the perceptual difference on this dependence issue, Company E acted differently from Company D's expectation. Additionally, Company E exercised legitimate power deriving from Lloyd's Terms (Gauci, 1995). The favorable concessions granted through these terms strengthened Company E's position, giving it a privileged status over other parties.

Apart from this, channel members' expectations may differ due to their access to different information and their different information processing capacities (Etgar, 1979). Developing greater sensitivity to the business culture of other channel members is of key importance for cultivating proper business relationships, yet, in our case, it is seen that failure to recognize cultural and sub-cultural differences exacerbated the perceived channel conflict. For example, business etiquette is crucial when doing business in the Middle East; punctuality and attentive demeanor are considered as a sign of respect. From this perspective, delays exceeding 5-6 hours caused by the ship-owner were regarded as a great disrespect. In a similar way, along with good manners and courtesy, which are highly prized attributes, business conversations are predicated on relationship-building and developing trust, instead of threatening and aggressive behaviors in the case of operational complexities.

Conflict also arises when a channel member perceives that the other party is not taking full responsibility in its appropriate domain (Taek et al., 2010). As an example, Company F, a subcontractor company, works under cost pressure, and uses low technology and low-profile employees, was responsible for conveying the timing of loading to Company E. Due to communication problems that occurred during the loading process, Company D had to be involved in the process to save time and money by providing document flows to connect the parties. This issue was a domain conflict, which arose from the parties' failure to carry out their responsibilities.

SOLUTIONS AND RECOMMENDATIONS

In this case, institutional information intensive mechanisms, third party mechanisms, incentives, relational and contractual governance mechanisms (Lumineau & Malhotra, 2011; Palmatier et al., 2020; Ryciuk, 2020; Shahzad et al., 2020) are found to be applicable as conflict resolution methods (Table 1).

Members create *information intensive mechanisms* by sharing information and devoting resources to communicating for conflict resolution (e.g., Luo, 2005; Jia et al., 2020). As stated by Eshghi (2018), communication often emerges as one of the most preferred solutions to perceptual conflict. By employing constructive conflict processes with cooperative social interaction and open discussions, parties can resolve misunderstandings and ambiguities (Li et al., 2011). These information-intensive mechanisms enable better assessments for the parties. Thus, it does not just help business partners to work effectively, but also leads them to better evaluate each other's abilities and attitudes. Communication technologies can help to facilitate inter-organizational business practices by improving communication and enabling firms to work in a more integrated and collaborative fashion (Loosemore & Lim, 2015). Within this context, through information technologies such as use of blockchain and ERP, sharing information can be facilitated among the conflicting parties (e.g., among Company F, G and B).

Providing *contractual governance* by defining the roles and duties of the parties are some of the efficient ways to deal with conflict. It can be adopted to resolve inter-firm conflict when the relationship is characterized by strong joint dependency (Eckerd & Sweeney, 2018). Herein, a formal and detailed written contract can delineate the responsibilities of each party in possible conflicts and specify the appropriate actions in conflict resolution (e.g., Luo, 2005; Jia et al., 2020). Through the attention to contractual details, likely contingencies can also be planned to a certain point and the parties involved benefit from solutions and knowledge coming through contract governance (Dwivedi et al., 2018). In this case, Company F requested extra money from Company B for the delivery of the container and they declared to delay the business in case of no payment. In order to resolve the problem, which triggered a multi-level incident resulting in a complaint flow in the operational process, a detailed contract dividing the responsibilities of above-mentioned parties (especially F, D, B and C) is needed. Besides, the problem of misreported dimensions between Company A and Company B can be resolved through contingency plannings by taking into consideration all loading details, total height, and highway limits.

Within the context of *contractual governance*, Standard Operational Procedures (SOPs) define the activities required to complete tasks in accordance with industry regulations, state laws, and even companies' own standards to run the business (Khairuddin et al., 2018). By establishing customs duty management strategy as a part of SOP with regard to Edward Deming's cycle of plan- do-check- act to prevent the possible additional storage costs in customs (e.g., incident among Company B, C, G, D). This may ensure that each customs declaration properly reflects the facts (Millar, 2015).

Moreover, building *relational governance* based on informal mechanisms such as trust, reciprocity or social embedding is another way of conflict resolution. Regarding this case, it is known that long term business relations take place among the parties (e.g., Company B and Company C). Based on these relational ties between partners, relational norms can be promoted and facilitated as resolutions.

If the conflict becomes more severe and exceeds the payment security provided by the network, as another *third-party mechanism*, arbitration can be employed through applying to the related institutions such as the International Chamber of Commerce. Sequencing in which both mediation and arbitration take place may be preferred. Additionally, business norms may be shaped by joint membership in logistics networks, whose regulations enforce compliance. Other than forming business norms among its members, joint memberships can facilitate the mediation process for the conflicts among its members. In this regard, due to having membership in the same network, Company C and Company D can apply to the network for resolution.

Lastly, aligning some economic *incentives* offer a way out before the conflict gets much worse. Referring to the case, after misreporting the dimensions of the loads, Company F refused to carry containers to the port. At this point, giving an incentive by Company D can ensure the continuation of the operation.

Table 1. Suggested resolution methods for the involved parties

Companies	Possible Solutions and Recommendations	
-Company F, Company D, Company G, Company B	cooperative social interaction and open discussion processes, assisting timely communication, and using improved communication technologies, etc. (e.g., Rhodes & Dawson, 2013; Barua & Mani, 2014; Loosemore & Lim, 2015, Eshghi, 2018)	Information intensive mechanisms
-Company F and Company D, Company C, and Company B -Company A and Company B -Company B, Company C, Company G, and Company D	formal and detailed written contracts delineating the responsibilities and contingency plannings (e.g., Luo, 2005; Eckerd & Sweeney, 2018; Dwivedi et al., 2018; Jia et al., 2020)	Contractual governance mechanisms
-Company E, Company B, Company C, and Company D	development of personal relationships to provide the basis for the strong initial trust, reaching shared understanding, proposing co-creative win-win solutions etc. (e.g., Yu et al., 2006; Zhu et al., 2017)	Relational governance mechanisms
Company C and Company D	third parties for conflict resolutions in terms of negotiation, mediation, arbitration, or upper industrial regulatory institutions (e.g., Greenberg et al., 2008; Guo et al., 2021)	Third-party mechanisms
Company F and Company D	compensation mechanisms, aligning, and specifying the responsibilities and incentives (e.g., Eriksson, 2010, Wallensteen, 2018)	Using incentives

CONCLUSION AND IMPLICATIONS

In this case, we address transportation disruption caused by temporary interruptions in transit of goods (Chaghooshi & Hajimaghsoudi, 2014). Paul et al. (2019) note that a potential transportation disruption is a source of risk and that it could quickly spread through the entire supply chain by causing late deliveries, operations shutdown, lost sales, and loss of reputation.

As stated in the literature, complexities increase dependency and interconnectedness, and require logistics players to work towards a unified system in a coordinated and cooperative manner to deal with disruptions (Arshinder et al., 2011; Iftikhar et al., 2022). In this regard, the process of working together through pursuing mutual gains leveraged the operational excellence of the parties in their operations (Mangla et al., 2020). However, looking at the case in general, it can be seen that, at some point, self-serving behavior of the parties overshadows mutual effort and reciprocity while executing the transportation operations. According to the view of Zou and Wang (2022), potential malafide actions of the parties, including individualistic and self-centered behavior is possible as the context shifts from dyads to multi actors, and the network becomes more complex requiring dependency on multiple partners. In this sense, partners' observed self-serving and opportunistic behaviors are highly in line with the premises of agency theory, which is widely used in the multi-actor service literature (Sengupta et al., 2018; Zou & Wang, 2022).

Several case studies focus on international transportation and logistics sectors and disruption under the impact of environmental uncertainties (e.g., Adams et al., 2012; Becker & Caldwell, 2015; Nižetić, 2020; Sugiono et al., 2022). However, this study, using a real case involving multiple supply chain players, offers a much more comprehensive approach addressing not only disruptions/problems, but also sources of conflicts and generated conflict resolution strategies in international transportation operations. In this sense, this study contributes to transportation disruption and conflict management domains and supports conceptual knowledge by providing in-depth, as well as up-to-date information in the disciplines of logistics and supply chain management. Besides, this study supports the findings of prior studies (e.g., Kim et al., 2015; Ganin et al., 2017, Golan et al., 2020) which emphasize that, particularly during a pandemic, proper transportation network management is crucial in maintaining a resilient supply chain.

Considering business side practical implications, this study contributes to the literature by focusing on international multi-agent logistics problems. In this regard, the practical findings of the study are in line with prior studies (Yang & Chang, 2019) and it emphasizes the importance of transit time, logistics costs, and service reliability and efficient communication, which emerge as the key challenges faced by companies in Middle East countries. In addition, the case offers insights to practitioners regarding the strategies used by players in multi-actor transport networks to cope with the interconnected negative effects of a transport disruption. Lastly, the findings of the research enlighten practitioners in terms of real-time decision-making situations, and enable them to move away from the "wait and see" approach (Yuan et al., 2022) by preparing them for dynamic unpredictable business environments which pose global challenges and require greater coordination among the players.

Moreover, this problem in business logistics provides an opportunity to highlight the role of the international exchange of information between practitioners and academic scholars and will greatly contribute to the applied science of logistics in the business environment, especially for the Middle East. In terms of academic study, it offers an excellent opportunity for preparing students in business administration, supply chain and logistics management and global business at the undergraduate and master level for real-life decisions.

LIMITATION AND FUTURE RESEARCH DIRECTIONS

This case study is subject to several limitations. First, a greater number of critical incidents would provide more ground for generalization of the findings. Second, the world experienced COVID-19, which has caused disruptions in global production lines and global supply chains in various networks. The effects of such disruptions can be also examined, and the findings can be compared to the past impacts. Finally, the incidents in this study were collected at a single point in time, and therefore longitudinal research could be employed to indicate changes in perceptions of logistics operations factors over time.

REFERENCES

Abidi, H., Dullaert, W., De Leeuw, S., Lysko, D., & Klumpp, M. (2019). Strategic partner evaluation criteria for logistics service provider networks. *International Journal of Logistics Management*, *30*(2), 438–466. doi:10.1108/IJLM-07-2017-0178

Adams, T. M., Bekkem, K. R., & Toledo-Durán, E. J. (2012). Freight resilience measures. *Journal of Transportation Engineering*, *138*(11), 1403–1409. doi:10.1061/(ASCE)TE.1943-5436.0000415

Albertzeth, G., Pujawan, I. N., Hilletofth, P., & Tjahjono, B. (2020). Mitigating transportation disruptions in a supply chain: A cost-effective strategy. *International Journal of Logistics Research and Applications, 23*(2), 139–158. doi:10.1080/13675567.2019.1648640

Arlbjørn, J. S., De Haas, H., Mikkelsen, O. S., & Zachariassen, F. (2010). *Supply chain management.* Academica.

Arshinder, K., Kanda, A., & Deshmukh, S. G. (2011). A review on supply chain coordination: coordination mechanisms, managing uncertainty and research directions. In *Supply chain coordination under uncertainty*. Springer. doi:10.1007/978-3-642-19257-9_3

Barua, A., & Mani, D. (2014). Augmenting conflict resolution with informational response: A holistic view of governance choice in business process outsourcing. *Journal of Management Information Systems, 31*(3), 72–105. doi:10.1080/07421222.2014.995530

Becker, A., & Caldwell, M. R. (2015). Stakeholder perceptions of seaport resilience strategies: A case study of Gulfport (Mississippi) and Providence (Rhode Island). *Coastal Management, 43*(1), 1–34. doi:10.1080/08920753.2014.983422

Blackhurst, J., Wu, T. T., & Craighead, C. W. (2008). A systematic approach for supply chain conflict detection with a hierarchical Petri Net extension. *Omega, 36*(5), 680–696. doi:10.1016/j.omega.2006.02.001

Blecker, T. (Ed.). (2014). Innovative methods in logistics and supply chain management: Current issues and emerging practices (Vol. 19). epubli.

Bolumole, Y. A., Grawe, S. J., & Daugherty, P. J. (2016). Customer service responsiveness in logistics outsourcing contracts: The influence of job autonomy and role clarity among on-site representatives. *Transportation Journal, 55*(2), 124–148. doi:10.5325/transportationj.55.2.0124

Brettmo, A., & Williamsson, J. (2020). The Role of 'Influencers' as Drivers of a More Sustainable Urban Freight Sector. *Sustainability, 12*(7), 2850. doi:10.3390u12072850

Cai, J., Cheng, J., Shi, H., & Feng, T. (2022). The impact of organisational conflict on green supplier integration: The moderating role of governance mechanism. *International Journal of Logistics Research and Applications, 25*(2), 143–160. doi:10.1080/13675567.2020.1818198

Chaghooshi, A. J., & Hajimaghsoudi, M. (2014). Reducing the risk of transportation disruption in the supply chain: Integration of FUZZY-AHP and TOPSIS. *Global Journal of Management Studies and Researches, 1*(1), 1–9.

Crainic, T. G., Gendreau, M., & Potvin, J. Y. (2009). Intelligent freight-transportation systems: Assessment and the contribution of operations research. *Transportation Research Part C, Emerging Technologies, 17*(6), 541–557. doi:10.1016/j.trc.2008.07.002

Creazza, A., Dallari, F., & Melacini, M. (2010). Evaluating logistics network configurations for a global supply chain. *Supply Chain Management, 15*(2), 154–164. doi:10.1108/13598541011028750

de Nooy, W., Mrvar, A., & Batagelj, V. (2006). *Exploratory social network analysis with Pajek.* Cambridge University Press.

Deng, G., Chen, J., & Liu, Q. (2022). Influence mechanism and evolutionary game of environmental regulation on green port construction. *Sustainability*, *14*(5), 2930. doi:10.3390u14052930

Dwivedi, Y. K., Shareef, M. A., Mukerji, B., Rana, N. P., & Kapoor, K. K. (2018). Involvement in emergency supply chain for disaster management: A cognitive dissonance perspective. *International Journal of Production Research*, *56*(21), 6758–6773. doi:10.1080/00207543.2017.1378958

Eckerd, S., & Sweeney, K. (2018). The role of dependence and information sharing on governance decisions regarding conflict. *International Journal of Logistics Management*, *29*(1), 409–434. doi:10.1108/IJLM-12-2016-0301

Eriksson, P. E. (2010). Partnering: What is it, when should it be used, and how should it be implemented? *Construction Management and Economics*, *28*(9), 905–917. doi:10.1080/01446190903536422

Eshghi, K. (2018). *Distribution Channel Conflict: Implications for Channel Governance, and Performance* [Doctoral dissertation].

Etgar, M. (1979). Sources and types of intra-channel conflict. *Journal of Retailing*, *55*(1), 61–78.

Fan, Y., Behdani, B., & Bloemhof-Ruwaard, J. M. (2020). Refer logistics and cold chain transport: A systematic review and multi-actor system analysis of an un-explored domain. *European Journal of Transport and Infrastructure Research*, *20*(2), 1–35.

Fawcett, S. E., & McCarter, M. W. (2008). Behavioral issues in supply chain collaboration: Communicating the literature via interactive learning. *International Journal of Integrated Supply Management*, *4*(2), 159–180. doi:10.1504/IJISM.2008.016616

Feng, F., Pang, Y., Lodewijks, G., & Li, W. (2017). Collaborative framework of an intelligent agent system for efficient logistics transport planning. *Computers & Industrial Engineering*, *112*, 551–567. doi:10.1016/j.cie.2016.12.044

Ganin, A. A., Kitsak, M., Marchese, D., Keisler, J. M., Seager, T., & Linkov, I. (2017). Resilience and efficiency in transportation networks. *Science Advances*, *3*(12), e1701079. doi:10.1126ciadv.1701079 PMID:29291243

Gauci, G. (1995). Limitation of liability in maritime law: An anachronism? *Marine Policy*, *19*(1), 65–74. doi:10.1016/0308-597X(95)92573-P

Golan, M. S., Jernegan, L. H., & Linkov, I. (2020). Trends and applications of resilience analytics in supply chain modeling: Systematic literature review in the context of the COVID-19 pandemic. *Environment Systems & Decisions*, *40*(2), 222–243. doi:10.100710669-020-09777-w PMID:32837820

Greenberg, P. S., Greenberg, R. H., & Antonucci, Y. L. (2008). The role of trust in the governance of business process outsourcing relationships: A transaction cost economics approach. *Business Process Management Journal*, *14*(5), 593–608. doi:10.1108/14637150810903011

Gudehus, T., & Kotzab, H. (2012). *Comprehensive logistics*. Springer Science & Business Media. doi:10.1007/978-3-642-24367-7

Guo, W., Straub, D., Zhang, P., & Cai, Z. (2021). How Trust Leads To Commitment On Microsourcing Platforms: Unraveling The Effects Of Governance And Third-Party Mechanisms On Triadic Microsourcing Relationships. *Management Information Systems Quarterly*, *45*(3), 1309–1348. doi:10.25300/MISQ/2021/14349

Hu, X., Fu, K., Chen, Z., & Du, Z. (2022). Decision-Making of Transnational Supply Chain Considering Tariff and Third-Party Logistics Service. *Mathematics*, *10*(5), 770. doi:10.3390/math10050770

Iftikhar, A., Purvis, L., Giannoccaro, I., & Wang, Y. (2022). The impact of supply chain complexities on supply chain resilience: The mediating effect of big data analytics. *Production Planning and Control*, 1–21. doi:10.1080/09537287.2022.2032450

Jakubicek, P., & Woudsma, C. (2011). Proximity, land, labor and planning? Logistics industry perspectives on facility location. *Transportation Letters*, *3*(3), 161–173. doi:10.3328/TL.2011.03.03.161-173

Jia, F., & Yang, Z. (2019). Perceptual difference of dependence and trust in marketing channel: Reconsideration of dependence measurement. *Asian Business & Management*, 1–27.

Jia, Y., Wang, T., Xiao, K., & Guo, C. (2020). How to reduce opportunism through contractual governance in the cross-cultural supply chain context: Evidence from Chinese exporters. *Industrial Marketing Management*, *91*, 323–337. doi:10.1016/j.indmarman.2020.09.014

Kanda, A., & Deshmukh, S. G. (2008). Supply chain coordination: Perspectives, empirical studies and research directions. *International Journal of Production Economics*, *115*(2), 316–335. doi:10.1016/j.ijpe.2008.05.011

Kehoe, D. F., Dani, S., Sharifi, H., Burns, N. D., & Backhouse, C. J. (2007). Demand network alignment: Aligning the physical, informational and relationship issues in supply chains. *International Journal of Production Research*, *45*(5), 1141–1160. doi:10.1080/00207540600635219

Khairuddin, M. M., Rahman, N. A. A., Mohamad, M. F., Majid, Z. A., & Ahmad, M. F. (2018). Regulator perspective on Halal air cargo warehouse compliance. *International Journal of Supply Chain Management*, *7*(3), 202–207.

Khan, S. A. R., Jian, C., Zhang, Y., Golpîra, H., Kumar, A., & Sharif, A. (2019). Environmental, social and economic growth indicators spur logistics performance: From the perspective of South Asian Association for Regional Cooperation countries. *Journal of Cleaner Production*, *214*, 1011–1023. doi:10.1016/j.jclepro.2018.12.322

Kim, Y., Chen, Y. S., & Linderman, K. (2015). Supply network disruption and resilience: A network structural perspective. *Journal of Operations Management*, *33*(1), 43–59. doi:10.1016/j.jom.2014.10.006

Kohtamäki, M., & Farmer, D. (2017). *Real-time Strategy and Business Intelligence*. Springer International Publishing. doi:10.1007/978-3-319-54846-3

Krafft, M., Goetz, O., Mantrala, M., Sotgiu, F., & Tillmanns, S. (2015). The evolution of marketing channel research domains and methodologies: An integrative review and future directions. *Journal of Retailing*, *91*(4), 569–585. doi:10.1016/j.jretai.2015.05.001

Leung, Y. F. (2009). *Conflict management and emotional intelligence* [Doctoral Thesis]. Southern Cross University, Lismore, Australia.

Li, Y., Liu, Y., & Liu, H. (2011). Co-opetition, distributor's entrepreneurial orientation and manufacturer's knowledge acquisition: Evidence from China. *Journal of Operations Management, 29*(1-2), 128–142. doi:10.1016/j.jom.2010.07.006

Li, Y., Zhen, X., Qi, X., & Cai, G. G. (2016). Penalty and financial assistance in a supply chain with supply disruption. *Omega, 61*, 167–181. doi:10.1016/j.omega.2015.12.011

Liche, M. B. (2021). *Technology Development Practice in Ethiopian Science and Technology Universities*. Academic Press.

Lindroth, E., Huong, H., & Bergqvist, R. (2020). Port-related conflict at port of Gothenburg–consequences from a fashion retailer's perspective. *Journal of Shipping and Trade, 5*(1), 1–17. doi:10.118641072-020-00059-x

Liu, D., Kuang, H., & Huang, M. (2017, May). Graph model for conflict resolution in the information sharing conflict of the fourth party logistics. In *2017 29th Chinese Control and Decision Conference (CCDC)* (pp. 6545-6550). IEEE. 10.1109/CCDC.2017.7978351

Liu, F., Wang, J., Liu, J., & Kong, Y. (2019). Coordination of port service chain with an integrated contract. *Soft Computing*, 1–14.

Loosemore, M., & Lim, B. (2015). Inter-organizational unfairness in the construction industry. *Construction Management and Economics, 33*(4), 310–326. doi:10.1080/01446193.2015.1057193

Loske, D. (2020). The impact of COVID-19 on transport volume and freight capacity dynamics: An empirical analysis in German food retail logistics. *Transportation Research Interdisciplinary Perspectives, 6*, 100165. doi:10.1016/j.trip.2020.100165 PMID:34173456

Lotfi, Z., Mukhtar, M., Sahran, S., & Taei Zadeh, A. (2013, June). Information sharing in supply chain management. *The 4th International Conference on Electrical Engineering and Informatics.*

Lukinskiy, V., & Pletneva, N. (2018). Impact of solutions for goods transportation on business efficiency and traffic safety. *Transportation Research Procedia, 36*, 459–464. doi:10.1016/j.trpro.2018.12.125

Lumineau, F., Eckerd, S., & Handley, S. (2015). Inter-organizational conflicts: Research overview, challenges, and opportunities. *Journal of Strategic Contracting and Negotiation, 1*(1), 42–64. doi:10.1177/2055563614568493

Lumineau, F., & Malhotra, D. (2011). Shadow of the contract: How contract structure shapes interfirm dispute resolution. *Strategic Management Journal, 32*(5), 532–555. doi:10.1002mj.890

Luo, Y. (2005). Transactional characteristics, institutional environment and joint venture contracts. *Journal of International Business Studies, 36*(2), 209–230. doi:10.1057/palgrave.jibs.8400125

Mangla, S. K., Kusi-Sarpong, S., Luthra, S., Bai, C., Jakhar, S. K., & Khan, S. A. (2020). Operational excellence for improving sustainable supply chain performance. *Resources, Conservation and Recycling, 162*, 105025. doi:10.1016/j.resconrec.2020.105025 PMID:32834482

Millar, M. (2015). *Global supply chain ecosystems: strategies for competitive advantage in a complex, connected world.* Kogan Page Publishers.

Moore, C. M., Birtwistle, G., & Burt, S. (2004). Channel power, conflict and conflict resolution in international fashion retailing. *European Journal of Marketing, 38*(7), 749–769. doi:10.1108/03090560410539230

Mutlu, A., Kayikci, Y., & Çatay, B. (2017). Planning Multimodal Freight Transport Operations: a Literature Review. *Proceedings of the 22nd International Symposium on Logistics*, 535–542.

Nižetić, S. (2020). Impact of coronavirus (COVID-19) pandemic on air transport mobility, energy, and environment: A case study. *International Journal of Energy Research, 44*(13), 10953–10961. doi:10.1002/er.5706

Odongo, W., Dora, M., Molnár, A., Ongeng, D., & Gellynck, X. (2016). Performance perceptions among food supply chain members: A triadic assessment of the influence of supply chain relationship quality on supply chain performance. *British Food Journal, 118*(7), 1783–1799. doi:10.1108/BFJ-10-2015-0357

Palmatier, R. W., Sivadas, E., Stern, L. W., & El-Ansary, A. I. (2020). Marketing Channel Strategy (9th ed.). Academic Press.

Paul, S. K., Asian, S., Goh, M., & Torabi, S. A. (2019). Managing sudden transportation disruptions in supply chains under delivery delay and quantity loss. *Annals of Operations Research, 273*(1-2), 783–814. doi:10.100710479-017-2684-z

Popp, R. L., & Yen, J. (Eds.). (2006). *Emergent information technologies and enabling policies for counterterrorism* (Vol. 6). Wiley-IEEE Press. doi:10.1002/047178656X

Ramanathan, U., Williams, N. L., Zhang, M., Sa-nguanjin, P., Garza-Reyes, J. A., & Borges, L. A. (2020). A new perspective of E-trust in the era of social media: Insights from customer satisfaction data. *IEEE Transactions on Engineering Management.*

Reimann, F., Kosmol, T., & Kaufmann, L. (2017). Responses to supplier-induced disruptions: A fuzzy-set analysis. *The Journal of Supply Chain Management, 53*(4), 37–66. doi:10.1111/jscm.12141

Reis, V., & Macedo, P. (2019). Mapping and evaluating the complexity of information flows in freight transport chains. *Transportation Planning and Technology, 42*(8), 757–776. doi:10.1080/03081060.2019.1675312

Rhodes, L., & Dawson, R. (2013). Lessons learned from lessons learned. *Knowledge and Process Management, 20*(3), 154–160. doi:10.1002/kpm.1415

Rice, J. B., & Caniato, F. (2003). Building a secure and resilient supply network. *Supply Chain Management Review, 7*(5), 22–30.

Rogerson, S., Svanberg, M., & Santén, V. (2022). Supply chain disruptions: Flexibility measures when encountering capacity problems in a port conflict. *International Journal of Logistics Management, 33*(2), 567–589. doi:10.1108/IJLM-03-2020-0123

Rokkan, A. I., & Buvik, A. (2003). Inter-firm cooperation and the problem of free riding behavior: An empirical study of voluntary retail chains. *Journal of Purchasing and Supply Management*, *9*(5-6), 247–256. doi:10.1016/j.pursup.2003.09.004

Ryciuk, U. (2020). Supply Chain Governance Mechanisms: A Review and Typology. *Eurasian Business Perspectives*, 145-159.

Sengupta, S., Niranjan, T. T., & Krishnamoorthy, M. (2018). Trends and directions in service triads research. *International Journal of Physical Distribution & Logistics Management*, *48*(3), 333–360. doi:10.1108/IJPDLM-02-2017-0095

Shahzad, K., Ali, T., Kohtamäki, M., & Takala, J. (2020). Enabling roles of relationship governance mechanisms in the choice of inter-firm conflict resolution strategies. *Journal of Business and Industrial Marketing*, *35*(6), 957–969. doi:10.1108/JBIM-06-2019-0309

Sharma, S., & Routroy, S. (2016). Modeling information risk in the supply chain using Bayesian networks. *Journal of Enterprise Information Management*, *29*(2), 238–254. doi:10.1108/JEIM-03-2014-0031

Skiba, S., & Karaś, A. (2022). The Changing Role of a Freight Forwarder in Modern Supply Chains. *European Research Studies*, *25*(1), 341–351. doi:10.35808/ersj/2856

Song, Z., He, S., & Xu, G. (2018). Decision and coordination of fresh produce three-layer E-commerce supply chain: A new framework. *IEEE Access: Practical Innovations, Open Solutions*, *7*, 30465–30486. doi:10.1109/ACCESS.2018.2881106

Sousa, F. J. (2010). Markets-as-networks theory: A review. *Organizational culture, business-to-business relationships, and interfirm networks*.

Sugiono, A., Rahayu, A., & Wibowo, L. A. (2022). Environmental Uncertainty Factor, Incoterm and Implication For A Strategic Alliance In Freight Forwarder Companies Case Study In Indonesia. *Asian Journal of Logistics Management*, *1*(1), 1–15. doi:10.14710/ajlm.2022.14230

Swierczek, A. (2020). Relational orientation of triadic supply chains with structural holes: An empirical comparison of rents derived from bridging the structural holes. *Supply Chain Management*, *25*(5), 565–583. doi:10.1108/SCM-10-2019-0382

Taek Yi, H., Lee, J., & Dubinsky, A. J. (2010). An empirical investigation of relational conflicts in co-marketing alliances. *Journal of Business-To-Business Marketing*, *17*(3), 249–278. doi:10.1080/10517120903465350

Wallensteen, P. (2018). Understanding conflict resolution. *Sage (Atlanta, Ga.)*.

Wang, L., Pfohl, H. C., Berbner, U., & Keck, A. K. (2016). Supply chain collaboration or conflict? Information sharing and supply chain performance in the automotive industry. In *Commercial Transport*. Springer. doi:10.1007/978-3-319-21266-1_20

Wang, P., & Vogt, J. (2019). Untangling process complexity in logistics delivery services with unpredictable service sequences: A mixed-method study of chemical tanker port calls. *Maritime Policy & Management*, *46*(3), 344–366. doi:10.1080/03088839.2018.1543908

Wood, L. C., Reefke, H., & Breidbach, C. F. (2012). *A typology of service supply chain strategies-pathways between agility and efficiency*. Academic Press.

Yang, C. C., & Chang, Y. K. (2019). Crucial factors influencing international logistics operations for African landlocked countries–A case study of Burkina Faso. *Maritime Policy & Management*, *46*(8), 939–956. doi:10.1080/03088839.2019.1606464

Yu, C. M. J., Liao, T. J., & Lin, Z. D. (2006). Formal governance mechanisms, relational governance mechanisms, and transaction-specific investments in supplier–manufacturer relationships. *Industrial Marketing Management*, *35*(2), 128–139. doi:10.1016/j.indmarman.2005.01.004

Yuan, R., Luo, J., Liu, M. J., & Yu, J. (2022). Understanding organizational resilience in a platform-based sharing business: The role of absorptive capacity. *Journal of Business Research*, *141*, 85–99. doi:10.1016/j.jbusres.2021.11.012

Zhu, Q., Feng, Y., & Choi, S. B. (2017). The role of customer relational governance in environmental and economic performance improvement through green supply chain management. *Journal of Cleaner Production*, *155*, 46–53. doi:10.1016/j.jclepro.2016.02.124

Zhu, X., & Cao, Y. (2021). The optimal recovery-fund based strategy for uncertain supply chain disruptions: A risk-averse two-stage stochastic programming approach. *Transportation Research Part E, Logistics and Transportation Review*, *152*, 102387. doi:10.1016/j.tre.2021.102387

Zou, Q., & Wang, Y. (2022). Understanding opportunism in buyer–supplier–supplier triadic relationships: The role of power asymmetry. *Management Decision*, *60*(11), 2952–2971. doi:10.1108/MD-05-2021-0654

KEY TERMS AND DEFINITIONS

Cut Off Date: Is the last date that the container can be returned to the port terminal in order to make the schedule that is requested.

EX Works (EXW): Indicates an international trade contract in which the seller has the goods ready for pickup from an agreed-on location and (often the seller's factory) buyer is responsible for all operations including pickup, export responsibilities, and all transportation.

Expected Time of Arrival (ETA): Is the time when a ship, vehicle, aircraft, cargo, emergency service, or person is expected to arrive at a certain place.

Flat Rack Container (FT): Is usually for the transportation or storage of cargo with unique dimensions. Flat racks only have sides on the short side of the container, the bulkheads, so the cargo can stick out the side of the container during transportation.

High Cube Container (HC): Is similar to the 40ft standard containers in length and breadth but have a height difference of exactly 1 foot. That gives the high cubes an additional ~344 cubic feet of storage capacity. The extra height also means that the containers are heavier than the standard.

Lloyd's Law: Means law of liability insurance that indemnifies liability to third persons, thus providing cover against a consequent depletion of the insured's assets.

Open Top Container (OT): Is a type of container unit that is unique in structure. It is characterized by an open-top that is covered by a tarpaulin. It is specifically built to store large unwieldy cargo that cannot be transported by conventional containers.

Reclamation Cost: Is the process of getting back any customs fees that were paid to import a product when it is returned to the country of origin.

ENDNOTES

1 Due to the confidentiality, company names are named as A, B, C, D, E, F, and G.

2 EX-works indicates an international trade contract in which the seller has the goods ready for pickup from an agreed-on location and (often the seller's factory) buyer is responsible for all operations including pickup, export responsibilities, and all transportation.

3 For open top and flat rack container operations at ports, free time application was not being applied in storage and demurrage.

4 Lloyd's Law means law of liability insurance that indemnifies liability to third persons, thus providing cover against a consequent depletion of the insured's assets.

Section 5

Sustainable Logistics and Supply Chain Management

Chapter 13
The Role of Technology in Enabling Sustainable Road Freight Transport Operation:
Challenges and Opportunities

Sohaila Hassan Elgazar
Arab Academy for Science, Technology, and Maritime Transport, Egypt

Nicoleta Tipi
Open University, UK

Eric Tchouamou Njoya
The University of Huddersfield, UK

EXECUTIVE SUMMARY

The aim of this case study is to summarize the most recent contributions by reviewing recent papers conducted on the adoption of innovative practices in the freight transport sector in addition to how their implementation in this sector will contribute to enhancing the road freight transport sector by concluding an overview of the obstacles and challenges standing against their incorporation in developing countries such as those in the Middle East. The role of the freight transport sector is increasing dramatically in most countries because most cargo is transported from point of origin to point of destination via roads.

INTRODUCTION

The aim of this case study is to summarise the most recent contributions by reviewing recent academic papers debating the adoption of innovative practices in the freight transport sector, in addition to how their implementation in this sector will contribute in enhancing the road freight transport sector by concluding an overview of the obstacles and challenges standing against their incorporation in developing countries, such as the Middle East. The role of the freight transport sector is increasing dramatically in

DOI: 10.4018/978-1-6684-4686-7.ch013

most countries as there is more and more demand for door-to-door delivery, and more goods are transported from point of origin to point of destination via roads (Sorrell et al., 2018). On the other hand, there is a negative impact generated due to these activities that have a direct effect on the environment and put social pressures, such as traffic jams, gas emissions and an increase in traffic accidents.

Winebrake et al. (2015) and Sorrell et al. (2018) state that road freight transport activities account for more than one third of different countries' economies. However, it is responsible for more than 60% of their gas emissions and environmental problems. The dependency on inland transport for moving freight is mainly on roads, and it is higher than the dependency on transporting passengers. Even though, the movement of excessive numbers of empty running trucks leads to the generation of cost. Furthermore, substituting road transport with any other inland mode for moving cargoes is limited because it provides door-to-door services with reasonable prices and large quantities. Still, most countries need to maintain and further develop their road infrastructures and transportation networks. Moreover, there is a rapid increase in the development of technological applications and innovative solutions for this sector. It is also recognised that road freight transport companies are still further adopting them effectively as they require a large investment and well-maintained infrastructures and highways (Liang et al., 2016; Naletina et al., 2019). Accordingly, governments and policymakers are expected to cooperate with the private sector in order to invest more in incorporating technological applications and innovative solutions to enhance and improve the performance of this sector to reduce its negative impacts towards sustainability.

Therefore, it has been suggested that the adoption of technology and innovative solutions would assist in reducing these negative impacts because their application has shown positive signs in this sector. Still, their applicability has been limited due to several factors: high investments, high drivers' turnover and inefficient infrastructures' maintenance in some countries (Kluschke et al., 2019; Naletina et al., 2019) as well as required knowledge to use this technology. Li et al. (2015), Abate et al. (2018), and Noguerol et al. (2018) recommend that some of the innovative solutions should assist in mitigating the environmental and social issues. For example, 75% of the gas emissions are caused by road freight transport; hence, it is considered that by substituting fuel with another environmentally-friendly one, like biofuel or electricity, its negative effect will be reduced. Moreover, the use of information and communication technologies (ICT) is another solution that could reduce these negative impacts. Route optimization and eco-driving systems are other operational solutions that could have a significant effect to reduce the negative impact on the environment.

Naletina et al. (2019), Sullivan et al. (2018), and Tejada et al. (2017) suggest that substituting petroleum oil with the use of natural gas or electric vehicles would encourage lessening the percentages of gas emissions and noise pollution, produced as a result of the truck engines moving by diesel. Another point of view is that adopting innovative practices assists in increasing reliability and security levels, which leads to rebounding effects on the road freight transport sector. The adoption of ICT on a wider range, such as electronic devices, tracing systems and telecommunication processes, should positively impact the performance of road freight transport companies (Muerza et al., 2017).

However, the implementation of innovative solutions and technology applications is still limited in the road freight transport sector, especially in developing countries, as road infrastructures still need higher maintenance and development to be able to adopt new technologies (Nazir et al., 2016; Tobgue et al., 2018). There are also external risks, such as the acts of terrorism in some regions, that require higher investments and enforcement of legislation and policies, which some countries still lack (Ranieri et al., 2018: Carlan et al., 2019).

To that point, it seems that the importance of road transport is increasing massively, especially in transporting freight as it is considered as a safe mode of transporting large quantities of goods with reasonable prices over long distances and adopting technologies and innovative solutions would assist in lessening negative impacts and enhancing the performance of the whole sector toward sustainability (Li et al., 2015; Abate et al., 2018). However, the incorporation of the technological applications and innovative practices is still limited in the road freight transport sector due to the several factors discussed above (Tobgue et al., 2018). Therefore, this case study improves students' understanding of the role of adopting technologies in the road transport sector by discussing the opportunities of their implementation and challenges standing against their execution in this market. An empirical study will be conducted in the Egyptian road freight transport sector as a representative to the Middle East countries to investigate the current situation of adopting technologies in this sector and identifying the challenges that would stand against adopting them.

METHODOLOGY

In this case study, the most recent papers conducted on the impact of adopting ICTs and technological practices on the development of road freight transport, infrastructures' developments and reducing the sustainable road transport problems and issues will be summarised. Then, semi-structured interviews have been conducted with different stakeholders (freight transport companies' managers and truck drivers) in the Egyptian road freight transport sector to sum-up the challenges and problems facing the road freight transport sector in Egypt and to highlight the main obstacles that stand against adopting technologies appropriately in this sector.

In conducting the literature review, different steps have been followed, such as:

- Acknowledged research areas and keywords, such as sustainable road transport problems, ICTs and innovative practices in road transport, infrastructures development and road freight transport challenges.
- Determining the databases and the selected years of search.
- Reviewing and choosing the most relevant papers on the research topic. These keywords have been identified to capture the most recent road freight transport problems and their impacts on different sustainable aspects, the challenges and obstacles standing against the enhancement of this sector, the benefits of adopting ICTs and innovative solutions in the road freight transport sector performance and the role of developing infrastructures in relationships with ICTs adoption. The research took place from 2010 to 2020, where 60 papers have been collected and narrowed down to 40 papers. The databases selected for search were Summon, Sustainable journals, Scopus, Elsevier and Transportation management. Accordingly, the following table has been created and grouped studies based on their areas, where authors' names and years are presented.

Based on the review of the previous studies conducted in this area, the semi- structured interview questions have been formulated as follow:

Three questions have been asked for each participant:

Q1: What are the main problems facing the Egyptian road freight transport sector?

Table 1. Identification of research areas, authors, and year of publications

No.	Author name, (Year)	Area
1	Sanchez-Rodrigues et al. (2010)	Road Transport Sustainable Issues
2	Novadata (2011)	Infrastructures Development in Road Transport
3	Keeling and Mooney (2011)	The Adoption of Sustainable Practices on Road Transport
4	Arentze, Feng, Timmermans, and Robroeks (2012)	Infrastructures Development in Road Transport
5	Litschke and Knitschky (2012)	Road Freight Transport Environmental Problems
6	Armstrong (2013)	Main Issues and Challenges in Road Transport
7	Islam et al. (2013)	Infrastructures Development in Road Transport
8	Santen (2013)	Road Freight Transport Logistics Operations
9	Liimatainen, Hovi, Arvidsson, and Nykänen (2013)	Technological Practices and Innovative Solutions in Road Transport
10	Evangelista, McKinnon, and Sweeney (2013)	Road Transport Sustainable Issues
11	Winebrake et al. (2015)	Technological Practices and Innovative Solutions and Infrastructures Developments
12	Li et al. (2015)	The Impact of Adopting ICTs on Road Freight Transport
13	Nuzzolo et al. (2015)	Technological Practices and Innovative Solutions in Road Transport
14	Liang et al. (2016)	Technological Practices and Innovative Solutions in Road Transport
15	Nazir et al. (2016)	Technological Practices and Innovative Solutions and Infrastructures Developments
16	Mommens, Van Lier, and Macharis (2016)	Issues and Problems Facing the Road Transport Sector
17	Martin et al. (2016)	Road Transport and Economic Development
18	Bedinger et al. (2016)	The Adoption of Sustainable Practices on Road Transport
19	Liang et al. (2016)	The Impact of Technological and Innovative Solutions on Road Transport
20	Holden et al. (2016)	Technological Practices and Innovative Solutions in Road Transport
21	Muerza et al. (2017)	Road Freight Transport Sustainability
22	Tejada et al. (2017)	Technological Practices and Innovative Solutions in Road Transport
23	Muerza et al. (2017)	The Impact of Adopting ICTs on Road Freight Transport
24	Arias et al. (2017)	Road Freight Transport Performance Measures System
25	Li and Yu (2017)	The Impact of Adopting ICTs on Road Freight Transport
26	Parihar (2017)	The Impact of Adopting ICTs on Road Freight Transport
27	Sorrell et al. (2018)	Road Freight Transport Sustainability
28	Abate et al. (2018)	The Impact of Adopting ICTs on Road Freight Transport
29	Noguerol et al. (2018)	Technological Practices and Innovative Solutions in Road Transport
30	Sullivan et al. (2018)	The Impact of Adopting ICTs on Road Freight Transport
31	Tobgue et al. (2018)	The Impact of Adopting ICTs on Road Freight Transport
32	Ranieri et al. (2018)	Logistics Innovations on Transport Cost Reductions
32	Karla Gonzalez Carvajal and Saroj Ayush (2018)	Road Transport Sustainable Issues
33	Tob-ogu, Kumar, and Cullen (2018)	Technological Practices and Innovative Solutions in Road Transport
34	Kluschke et al. (2019)	Technological Practices and Innovative Solutions in Road Transport
35	Naletina et al. (2019)	The Impact of Adopting ICTs on Road Freight Transport
36	Naletina et al. (2019)	Technological Practices and Innovative Solutions in Road Transport
37	Carlan et al. (2019)	The Impact of Adopting ICTs on Road Freight Transport
38	Settey et al. (2019)	Technological Practices and Innovative Solutions in Road Transport
39	Roso et al. (2019)	Road Freight Transport Issues and Problems
40	Kyoung et al. (2020)	ICT and Transport Infrastructure Development

Q2: How could the adoption of technologies enhance or assist in enhancing this sector?

Q3: What are the main challenges that stand against adopting technologies in the Egyptian road freight transport sector?

The semi-structured interview has been conducted with different stakeholders in the Egyptian road freight transport sector as a representative of the Middle East countries to conclude an overview of the various problems facing the Egyptian road freight transport sector and also to highlight the role of the adoption of technologies in enhancing or assisting in enhancing this sector and to highlight the main challenges that stand against adopting technologies in the Egyptian road freight transport sector. Egypt has been selected as a representative of the Middle East countries, as the road freight transport sector is one of the important resources for the country's economy, and still the adoption of technologies is lacking in this sector.

ROAD FREIGHT TRANSPORT PROBLEMS

By reviewing the previous conducted studies, the following discussion has been concluded.

First, the major road freight transport problems and issues presented are related to different sustainable aspects. Some major problems have been concluded, such as congestion problems, infrastructure developments, drivers' qualifications and lack of adopting ICTs and innovative practices (Roso et al., 2019; Sorrell et al., 2018; Gonzalez Carvajal &Ayush, 2018). Moreover, it has been witnessed that the lack of enforcing rules and regulations and the lack of adopting a performance measures system for measuring the road freight transport companies are some of the main challenges and obstacles facing this sector (Muerza et al., 2017; Evangelista et al., 2013; Armstrong, 2013).

Therefore, governments and private sectors should cooperate to pin out key performance measures and develop infrastructures to facilitate the adoption of innovative practices and ICTs. Additionally, further research studies are needed in order to investigate the impacts of developing performance measuring systems in relationship to mitigating road freight transport problems and enhancing performance to reach sustainability (Litschke & Knitschky, 2012; Sanchez-Rodrigues et al., 2010; Mommens et al., 2016).

Second, the role of the ICTs and infrastructure developments is investigated as empirical studies have been conducted to show the positive relationship between developing and maintaining the infrastructures and the adoption of ICTs (Kyoung et al., 2020; Nazir et al., 2016). To that point, it has been observed that infrastructures need to be developed in order to allow for the implementation of the ICTs, which will benefit the road freight transport sector deeply through tracing, tracking and identifying any technical problems faced by the drivers during their trips (Winebrake et al., 2015; Islam et al., 2013; Novadata, 2011).

Third, for technologies and ICTs, it is worth mentioning that technologies play a vital role in achieving sustainability in the road freight transport sector and enable managers, cargo owners and drivers to find cargoes, trace them and reduce gas emissions (Liimatainen et al., 2013; Li et al., 2015; Liang et al., 2016). However, their adoption is lacking in this sector due to some economic problems, such as high cost and low investments and logistics problems, such as lack of infrastructures developments, lack of drivers' trainings and the limited use of performance measures systems (Nuzzolo et al., 2015; Holden et al., 2016; Liang et al., 2016; Li & Yu, 2017). Parihar (2017), Tejada et al. (2017), Muerza et al. (2017), Arias et al. (2017), Ranieri et al. (2018), and Abate et al. (2018) suggest that the adoption of different technological apps ought to facilitate the processes of transporting freight from one point to another, increase the drivers' safety on roads and reduce the road freight transport problems towards sustainability. Hence, it is highly recommended that governments support companies to purchase and adopt ICTs and innovative practices and build scenarios to investigate the situation of relevant companies and the sector before and after the adoption of technologies (Noguerol et al., 2018; Tob-ogu et al., 2018; Sullivan et al., 2018; Kluschke et al., 2019; Naletina et al., 2019; Naletina et al., 2019; Carlan et al., 2019; Settey et al., 2019).

As mentioned before, the demand for transporting freight by road has increased in societies nowadays as road freight transport is a necessary economic activity. This is due to the fact that countries' economies would not perform well without it (ERTRAC, 2019). For instance, the road transport dependency percentage in European countries has been extended to more than 50%, and, in Middle East, 95% of the freight is transported by road. This means that the reliance on transporting cargoes through roads is increasing (Road Freight Transport Statistics, 2019). However, a number of problems should be recognized and a set of performance measures identified to be capable of managing and reducing these problems. Nevertheless, the road freight sector within the EU has developed dynamically at quite a fast rate. Consequently, it is helpful for policy makers, stakeholders, and alternative interested parties to possess up-to-date data on the structure of the business and on major trends (Armstrong, 2013; Road Freight Transport Vademecum Report, 2010).

However, there are various challenges and obstacles facing this sector and impacting it negatively since the movement of a huge amount of freight by road leads to different negative effects that impact our health, such as emissions, noise and accidents and affect the economy through congestion (Mommens, Van Lier & Macharis, 2016). Therefore, public and private sectors should cooperate to understand the existing road freight transport systems and their impact in order to work on mitigating the negative impacts produced from them to be able to enhance performance and achieve sustainability (Karla Gonzalez Carvajal and Saroj Ayush, 2018). Another key point aspect highlighted is the lack of infrastructure investments that would benefit the whole sector as they will ease the accessibility level and assist in reducing travel time (Islam et al., 2013).

Additionally, some reasons for the disturbances within road freight operations occur due to the problems related to the control of the logistics operations. Moreover, transport as a whole is a main aspect in the economic development of a country, and particularly road transport. However, road freight operations are known for their very low-profit margins because of the fuel cost and related taxes (Martin et al., 2016; Santen, 2013). Therefore, it is important to avoid any unnecessary travel. In addition, the studies emphasize the importance of road freight transport in the development of a country's economy, and they state that it is considered as a key component in supporting and securing sustainability and the health of a national economy as well. They add that while road freight transport is considered a key aspect in securing social and economic welfare, it also imposes negative environmental impacts. In order to reduce climate change, it is imperative to minimize greenhouse gas (GHG) emissions in all sectors of the economy, especially in road freight transport (Liimatainen et al., 2013; Novadata, 2011; Sanchez-Rodrigues et al., 2010; McKinnon et al., 2009).

Moreover, it has been further noticed that there are some popular technological systems that should be adopted in road freight transport, such as navigation systems that most trucks are equipped with. These navigation systems are provided with tracking and tracing systems in order to allow the road freight transport companies to monitor the truck and the driver while transporting goods as well as provide the trucks with important information throughout their trips, such as the trip's time to reach the desired destination, the congestion area to be avoided, alternative routes to use and the rate of fuel consumption

(Settey et al., 2019). However, despite their importance, there is still a lack of efficient use. For example, the infrastructures are not maintained and constructed in order to cope with the technologies adopted. In addition, there are limitations and constraints in some areas regarding the use of innovative trucks equipped with navigation systems (Arentze et al., 2012).

To conclude, this case study highlights the fact that researchers, practitioners, and governments have recognised the role of sustainable development in enhancing various sectors, especially the transport sector, as it reduces environmental and social burdens, all the while promoting countries' economies. However, there is still a lack of adopting efficient sustainable practices by the road freight transport sector as a result of the absence of a unified set of rules and regulations to manage the road freight transport sector (Bedinger et al., 2016). Above all, there is an insufficient adoption of technological and innovative solutions to assist in enhancing the performance of the road freight transport sector. Since most of these solutions are of high cost, not all road freight transport companies are capable of adopting them (Tob-ogu et al., 2018). To that point, the issues and challenges facing the road freight transport and the adoption of ICTs have been discussed.

ROAD FREIGHT TRANSPORT AND ICTs

The importance of freight transport is expanding and growing rapidly in most countries around the world as it directly impacts the countries' economies and most of the freight transported from point to point by road transport. However, this type of transport increases the burden on the environmental and social aspects because of its negative impacts, such as congestion, air and noise pollutions, accidents and the excessive number of empty running trucks (Evangelista et al., 2013). These problems in turn increase cost. Moreover, there is a huge development in technological apps, such as ICT, even though they cannot be incorporated and adopted efficiently because this requires high investments and well-structured and maintained infrastructures (Liang et al., 2016).

It has been noted that the application of e-commerce is rare in this sector, despite its benefits and its role in improving the sector's overall performance. Road freight transport companies should trace and control emissions produced from freight transported by road in order to enhance their performance in the future. To this end, a predefined performance measures' system is needed to measure their performance from an environmental perspective (Nuzzolo et al., 2015). However, innovative solutions are more expensive than traditional ones because the former have been launched recently. In addition, three actors (researchers, governments, and road freight transport companies' managers) would have to cooperate in order to apply sustainable and innovative practices. On the other hand, the presence of various actors and stakeholders often leads to a conflict of interest when applying innovative solutions (Holden et al., 2016).

Arias et al. (2017), Roso et al. (2019), and Settey et al. (2019) focus particularly on the regulatory measures suggested by researchers in order to overcome the road freight transport's negative environmental impacts, such as congestion problems and air pollution. Thus, technological readiness is needed to enhance any system of measurement. Furthermore, the European Commission aims to substitute the use of fuel by moving trucks with any other environmentally-friendly source in order to reduce gas emissions, especially that road freight transport is increasing dramatically, and there is a huge dependency on transporting freight through road. The road freight transport sector has a share in a country's economic growth. The dependency on transporting freight by road is increasing in most countries nowadays. It has been recognized that road transport contributes to 85% of the total CO_2 emissions domestically (Litschke & Knitschky, 2012).

Accordingly, it has been recommended that launching innovative practices decreases the CO_2 emitted from road transport sectors, such as vehicle fuel efficiency, the carbon intensity of the fuel used and the road freight transport network optimization and consolidation. The development of information and communication technologies (ICT) has been increasing in recent years; accordingly, road freight transport companies have depended more on adopting ICT in order to enhance the performance of their processes (Li & Yu, 2017; Parihar, 2017).

Governments should further cooperate with the road freight transport companies to reconstruct and maintain the infrastructures and bridges in order to cope with the innovative solutions adopted to be able to achieve sustainability. Moreover, the government should set guidelines and policies to manage the road freight transport sector adequately (Keeling & Mooney, 2011; Besselink et al., 2016; Tubis & Wojciechowska, 2017). The adoption of technologies in transport, development of road freight transport technologies, and the rise of awareness concerning the importance of applying information and telecommunication systems and sustainable transportation development would all lead to improving the overall performance of road freight transport companies, by improving flexibility, productivity, quality, susceptibility, resilience and the reliability of road freight transport chains, activities and processes (Naganathan & Chong, 2017).

To that end, it has been observed that the adoption of technology is a key element in improving and enhancing the road freight transport sector as it aids the road freight transport companies to be more competitive and reduce the negative externalities produced from this sector. This sector has negative economic, social and environmental effects (Marchet et al., 2009; Perego et al., 2009; Parihar, 2017). The adoption of technology also assists the road freight transport companies to be more reliable, flexible and capable of tracking and monitoring all their processes efficiently. Therefore, the benefits achieved from adopting ICTs are presented.

THE IMPLEMENTATION OF TECHNOLOGIES IN DIFFERENT AREAS OF ROAD FREIGHT TRANSPORT TO ACHIEVE SUSTAINABILITY

It has been witnessed that adopting technologies increases the companies' competitive advantage as most companies are competing in a dynamic environment. For that reason, companies should always look forward to adopting new innovative technologies in order to achieve competitiveness (Liang et al., 2016). Another point of view states that recent technologies and e-commerce have been growing dramatically throughout the past few decades. The dependency on transporting freight through road has also been increasing (Bonilla, 2016).

Subsequently, it can be argued that adopting information and communication technologies and innovative strategies would benefit the road freight transport sector. Until recently, innovative systems have been fully implemented, where infrastructures still need development and improvement (Arias et al., 2017; Kyoung et al., 2020). Since the road freight transport market is dynamic, measuring, tracking and managing performance should be implemented in any road freight transport company for the sake of sustainability. Successful management and setting goals, mission and vision are very effective in meeting corporate goals (Roso et al., 2019).

Table 2. Some of the technological contributions in road freight transport sector

Some of the Technological Contributions in the Road Freight Transport Sector	Authors	Year
Innovative practices and e-commerce	Bonilla	2016
ICT and innovative strategies for road infrastructures	Arias et al. Kyoung et al.	2017 2020
Cargo owner apps (tracking, tracing, picking cargoes)	Marchet et al. Perego et al.	2009 2009
Driver's apps (picking drivers)	Parihar	2017

Accordingly, it is highly recommended that road freight transport companies are in need of creating and implementing a performance measures' system in order to achieve competitiveness (Settey et al., 2019). Therefore, Marchet et al. (2009) and Perego et al. (2009) suggest that freight apps ought to improve road freight transport companies and assist in reducing fuel consumption and carbon dioxide emissions per ton/kilometre. In addition, in logistics, apps can be used by both cargo owners and drivers. On one hand, cargo owners can announce sources of goods and pick the drivers needed, whereas drivers can identify the available trucks and search for the goods.

The apps used by cargo owners are mainly designed to assist them in ordering, tracking, account checking and inquiry. These apps can also be used for managing road freight transport by logistics companies that own their trucks or out-source trucks. These apps can include management functions, such as vehicle archiving and vehicle dispatching and tracking. The drivers' apps focus on announcing the source of trucks, finding the goods and reviewing the transportation process (Parihar, 2017). To that point, it has been observed that the adoption of ICTs ought to add value to the road freight transport sector whether through mitigating the issues and challenges facing this sector or through enhancing the road freight transport companies' performance. In Table 2, some of the technological contributions toward sustainability in road freight transport sector will be presented.

There are various problems facing the road freight transport in the Middle East countries and especially in Egypt, which limits the adoption of technologies. Hassan (2019) suggests that road infrastructures in most African countries, especially Egypt, have dominated the transportation of both freight and passengers. However, road infrastructures require high maintenance to be sustainable. Some African countries, such as Egypt, Nigeria, and Ethiopia, are limited in achieving road transport infrastructures' sustainability as various challenges are facing them, such as insufficient funds, lack of rules and regulations enforcement and the scarcity of professional human resources (Egypt Freight Transport Shipping and Port; Shipping Report, 2018).

In addition, as most African economies depend on oil products for industrial and domestic production, the demands of fuelling trucks for transportation are increasing heavily, and these transport operations usually include significant human, social, environmental, and economic costs. Cases in point include a series of fuel tanker truck accidents linked to injuries and deaths (Porter, 2014).

Moreover, there is a lack in the adoption of Information and Communication Technologies (ICT), Intelligent Transport Systems (ITSS) and innovative solutions in Egypt due to their high cost, poor infrastructures, and the scarcity of qualified drivers (El-Husseiny et al., 2017).

There are different challenges and problems facing the road freight transport sector in Egypt, including the increasing cost of petroleum products because the consumption is extremely infrequent, and sometimes there is a shortage in the availability of fuels (Porter, 2014).

Also, road transport crashes have been considered as a massive and hazardous issue, since over 26% of road accidents occur in Egypt every year (World Health Organisation, 2015; Elshamly et al., 2017). Therefore, road transport accidents should be reduced marginally through the adoption of innovative information and communication systems (Federal Road Safety Corps, 2015). This adopted policy has been identiðed as a key point to enhance the performance of road freight transport (WHO, 2015).

Indeed, the road transport sector in Egypt is facing various problems, such as congestion problems, limited infrastructure maintenance, high accident rates and truck drivers' fatigue. In addition, there is a lack of rules' enforcement in this sector, and there are no unified management systems for the road freight transport companies. These problems lead to a lack in the adoption of technological systems, such as ITSS, ICT and eco-driving systems, that all should enhance this sector through increasing safety and mobility and reducing the negative externalities imposed by the road transport sector (Faajir et al., 2016; Havenga et al., 2016; El-Husseiny et al., 2017).

To this point, the current situation of the road freight transport sector in the Middle East countries and especially in Egypt have been addressed. Therefore, the following section will present the semi-structured interview's main findings.

THE EMPIRICAL STUDY FINDINGS AND DISCUSSION

The interview results revealed that the main problems facing the Egyptian road freight transport sector are lack of adopting technologies, congestion, infrastructure maintenance and drivers' scarcity because these problems directly affect the road freight transport sector negatively from different environmental, social and economic aspects. The interviewees suggested that the truck drivers in Egypt are in need of more training programs and sessions to deal with different types of cargoes transported via road and to increase their awareness about being sustainable and avoiding drugs.

According to the interviewees, the adoption of technological aids can reduce the above-mentioned problems of the road freight transport sector because technologies would assist managers to measure their companies' performances and identify problems faced by their drivers. Through identifying the problems, managers will be able to set decisions to mitigate these problems towards sustainability.

The discussion revealed that the main challenges that stand against adopting technologies in the Egyptian road freight transport sector are the absence of rules and regulations for managing the road transport sector in Egypt, the culture of the Egyptian market; competition is more about the cost of the trip, rather than the quality of the trip and the scarcity of professional drivers and un-planned circumstances and crises, such as the existence of COVID-19, which have affected the whole industry negatively and stood against its enhancement and development. To this point, challenges and problems standing against adopting technologies in the Egyptian road freight transport sector have been discussed. The following section will draw up a conclusion for the whole case study, where the case study limitations will be highlighted, in addition to an agenda for further research.

CONCLUSION

The case study focuses on identifying the road freight transport problems, the road freight transport and ICT, the role of adopting technologies and innovative practices to enhance the road freight transport sector, and implications in the context of the Middle East sector. By illustrating the main problems facing this sector, the role of the technologies has been highlighted and presented and how it could assist in reducing the impact of these problems. Also, an overview of the technological practices used for this sector were discussed. Then, a practical implication has been presented through conducting semi-structured interviews in the Egyptian road freight transport sector to highlight the various problems facing this sector from a sustainable perspective to conclude the role of adopting technologies in this sector to enhance it and the challenges and obstacles that stand against adopting technologies in the Egyptian market.

Case Study Limitations

This case study focuses on the role of technologies and innovative practices in the Egyptian road freight transport sector only. Semi-structured interviews have been used as a tool for collecting data, in which other data collection methods ought to change the results concluded. Participants selected were road freight transport managers and drivers. The selection for other participants may lead to other results.

Further Research Agenda

According to the conclusion drawn up and the case study limitation, the following agendas are recommended for further research:

- An implication in another context rather than the Middle East would be conducted to show the differences between results.
- A comparative analysis between the different technologies adopted in this sector in different countries could be highlighted to identify their impacts on mitigating this sector problems from a sustainable perspective.
- Different data collection tools could be selected rather than semi-structured interviews, such as surveys to test the relationship between adopting technologies and enhancing the road freight transport sector.

KEY LEARNING POINTS FROM THIS REVIEW

Four main learning points have been concluded from this case study:

1. Reviewing the main findings and contributions from recent papers conducted in this area, in addition to identifying further work needed to enhance this sector.
2. Investigating the role of technology in enabling sustainable road freight transport operation.
3. Identifying the challenges and obstacles facing the road freight transport sector to adopt ICTs and technologies, as well as identifying the main problems facing this sector with different sustainable aspects.

4. Highlighting the benefits of ICTs adoption in this sector, whether in relation to the infrastructures development, drivers' enhancement, or road freight transport problems mitigation.

REFERENCES

Abate, M., Vierth, I., Karlsson, R., de Jong, G., & Baak, J. (2019). A disaggregate stochastic freight transport model for Sweden. *Transportation, 46*(3), 671-696. http://dx.doi.org.libaccess.hud.ac.uk/10.1007/s11116-018-985 6-9

Agamez-Arias, A., & Moyano-Fuentes, J. (2017). Intermodal Transport in Freight Distribution: A Literature Review. *Transport Reviews, 37*(6), 782–807. doi:10.1080/01441647.2017.1297868

Arentze, T., Feng, T., Timmermans, H., & Robroeks, J. (2012). Context-dependent influence of road attributes and pricing policies on route choice behavior of truck drivers: Results of a conjoint choice experiment. *Transportation, 39*(6), 1173–1188. doi:10.100711116-012-9391-z

Armstrong, A. (2013). *Transport Purchasing and Environmental Impacts.* http://www.diva-portal.org/smash/get/diva2:1309436/FULLTEXT0 1.pdf

Carlan, V., Sys, C., & Vanelslander, T. (2019). Innovation in road freight transport: Quantifying the environmental performance of operational cost-reducing practices. *Sustainability, 11*(8), 2212. doi:10.3390u11082212

Frizzo-Barker, J., Chow-White, P. A., Adams, P. R., Mentanko, J., Ha, D., & Green, S. (2020). Blockchain as a disruptive technology for business: A systematic review. *International Journal of Information Management, 51*, 102029. doi:10.1016/j.ijinfomgt.2019.10.014

Goldmann, K. (2019). Time-declining risk-adjusted social discount rates for transport infrastructure planning. *Transportation, 46*(1), 17-34. http://dx.doi.org.libaccess.hud.ac.uk/10.1007/s11116-017-978 0-4

Kluschke, P., Gnann, T., Plötz, P., & Wietschel, M. (2019). Market diffusion of alternative fuels and powertrains in heavy-duty vehicles: A literature review. *Energy Reports, 5*, 1010–1024. doi:10.1016/j.egyr.2019.07.017

Li, J., Lu, Q., & Fu, P. (2015). Carbon footprint management of road freight transport under the carbon emission trading mechanism. *Mathematical Problems in Engineering, 2015*, 1–13. doi:10.1155/2015/814527

Li, L., & Li, L. (2019). Structure and influencing factors of CO2 emissions from transport sector in three major metropolitan regions of china: Estimation and decomposition. *Transportation, 46*(4), 1245–1269. doi:10.100711116-017-9827-6

Li, Y., & Yu, Y. (2017). The use of freight apps in road freight transport for COORW1S-34RfeSDcfkexd09rT421RW1S34RfeSDcfkexd09rT4 reduction. *European Transport Research Review, 9*(3), 1-13. http://dx.doi.org.libaccess.hud.ac.uk/10.1007/s12544-017-025 1-y

Liang, K., van de Hoef, S., Terelius, H., Turri, V., Besselink, B., Mårtensson, J., & Johansson, K. H. (2016). Networked control challenges in collaborative road freight transport. *European Journal of Control, 30*, 2–14. doi:10.1016/j.ejcon.2016.04.008

Lietuvnikė, M. M., Vasilis Vasiliauskas, A., Vasilienė-Vasiliauskienė, V., & Sabaitytė, J. (2018). Peculiarities of illegal immigrant's intrusions into road freight transport units in the france - UK corridor. *Entrepreneurship and Sustainability Issues*, *5*(3), 634–647. doi:10.9770/jesi.2018.5.3(16)

Mes, M. R. K., Schutten, J. M. J., & Zijm, W. H. M. (2018). Freight consolidation in intermodal networks with reloads. *Flexible Services and Manufacturing Journal, 30*(3), 452-485. doi:http://dx.doi.org.libaccess.hud.ac.uk/10.1007/s10696-016-9259-1

Muerza, V., Larrodé, E., & Moreno-Jiménez, J. M. (2017). Identification and selection of ICTs for freight transport in product service supply chain diversification. *Industrial Management & Data Systems*, *117*(7), 1469–1484. doi:10.1108/IMDS-09-2016-0375

Na, K. Y., Kim, D. H., Park, B. G., Yoon, S. W., & Yoon, C.-H. (2020). ICT and transport infrastructure development: An empirical analysis of complementarity. *Applied Economics*, *52*(2), 195–211. doi:10.1080/00036846.2019.1640860

Naletina, D., Petljak, K., & Rožić, T. (2020). Outsourcing as a challenge for achieving competitive advantage in road freight industry – The case of Croatia. *Promet – Traffic & Transportation, 32*(1), 127-139. doi:. doi:10.7307/ptt.v32i1.3198

Nazir, E., Nadeem, F., & Véronneau, S. (2016). Road safety challenges in Pakistan: An overview. *Journal of Transportation Security, 9*(3-4), 161-174. http://dx.doi.org.libaccess.hud.ac.uk/10.1007/s12198-016-0172-3

Osorio-Tejada, J. L., Llera-Sastresa, E., & Scarpellini, S. (2017). Liquefied natural gas: Could it be a reliable option for road freight transport in the EU? *Renewable & Sustainable Energy Reviews*, *71*, 785–795. doi:10.1016/j.rser.2016.12.104

Parihar, M. (2017). Using Intelligent Transport System (ITS) to Solve Problems of Road Freight Transportation Industry in India. *Supply Chain Pulse*, *8*(1), 6–12.

Ranieri, L., Digiesi, S., Silvestri, B., & Roccotelli, M. (2018). A review of last mile logistics innovations in an externalities cost reduction vision. *Sustainability*, *10*(3), 782. doi:10.3390u10030782

Roso, A., & Labas, D. (2019). Use of Performance Measurement Methods in Croatian Firms. *Economic and Social Development: Book of Proceedings*, 114-122.

Sarmento, H., Clemente, F. M., Araújo, D., Davids, K., McRobert, A., & Figueiredo, A. (2017). 2018;). What performance analysts need to know about research trends in association football (2012–2016): A systematic review. *Sports Medicine (Auckland)*, *48*(4), 799–836. doi:10.100740279-017-0836-6 PMID:29243038

Sorrell, S., & Stapleton, L. (2018). Rebound effects in UK road freight transport. *Transportation Research Part D, Transport and Environment*, *63*, 156–174. doi:10.1016/j.trd.2018.05.006

Sullivan, J. L., Lewis, G. M., & Keoleian, G. A. (2018). Effect of mass on multimodal fuel consumption in moving people and freight in the U.S. *Transportation Research Part D, Transport and Environment*, *63*, 786–808. doi:10.1016/j.trd.2018.06.019

Tob-Ogu, A., Kumar, N., Cullen, J., & Ballantyne, E. (2018). Sustainability intervention mechanisms for managing road freight transport externalities: A systematic literature review. *Sustainability*, *10*(6), 1923. doi:10.3390u10061923

Valentin Carlan, C. S., & T. V. (2019). *Innovation in Road Freight Transport : Quantifying the Environmental Performance of Operational*. Academic Press.

Vázquez-Noguerol. González-Boubeta, Domínguez-Caamaño, & Prado-Prado. (2018). Best practices in road transport: An exploratory study. *Journal of Industrial Engineering and Management, 11*(2), 250-261. http://dx.doi.org.libaccess.hud.ac.uk/10.3926/jiem.2525

Winebrake, J. J., Green, E. H., Comer, B., Li, C., Froman, S., & Shelby, M. (2015). Fuel price elasticities in the U.S. combination trucking sector. *Transportation Research Part D, Transport and Environment*, *38*, 166–177. doi:10.1016/j.trd.2015.04.006

Chapter 14
Obtaining Green Warehouse From the Movement of Trucks Through Piezoelectric Tiles:
Case Study (Kinda Foods Warehouse)

Bassma Sameer Abdelaleem
College of International Transport and Logistics, Egypt

Amal Lotfy Sakr
Arab Academy for Science, Technology, and Maritime Transport, Egypt

EXECUTIVE SUMMARY

The use of clean and renewable sources of energy is a global trend in preserving the environment. In addition, in the long run, the cost of renewable energy is lower than the energy generated by fuels. By extension, if clean energy is used in industry, it will have a very strong impact on all supply chains, both service and productivity. This case study highlighted the technical potential and economic feasibility of the activation the transformation of kinetic energy of trucks to electrical power using piezo-electric tiles, its effect in Kinda Food's warehouse, its impact on the supply chain, and the economic feasibility of its long-term application. This case explained how to convert regular warehouses into green warehouses, explained the usage of alternative energy in warehouses, explained the difference in cost of using renewable energy and fuel energy in warehouses, and obtained the benefits.

ORGANIZATION BACKGROUND

Kinda Foods Factory is a local factory in Alexandria located in the Apis Industrial Zone. Mr. Mohamed Kabbary is the owner of this factory. Kinda Foods Factory started in 2017 as a local factory. This factory produces different types of juices distributed and sold in the Egyptian countryside. The juice industry is one of the important industries that face many competitors due to its spread and the spread demand for ready-made juices, whether in the sectors of schools, hospitals, and various establishments (Yiqun Huang

DOI: 10.4018/978-1-6684-4686-7.ch014

et, al.,2009). (This factory is not one of the huge factories with a huge administrative, and organizational structure, it consists of the chairman of the board of directors and the production department and quality, packing and warehouse management, as many small business owners start by structuring the business by trial and error, or haphazardly, therefore, the organizational structure of the factory is simple because the factory is based on local trade and a small regional scale. The culture of this institution is based on the idea of reducing the cost of juice because it targets villages and Upper Egypt to sell it in large quantities, but at a price lower than the market price, as it is common knowledge that regions and rural areas can market products of medium quality, not very high due to the different cultures of customers, for example, customers do not care The material of the packed carton or in the form of bottles that are packaged as a design, but they care about the taste, whether it is good or not, and equivalent to its cost or not. Therefore, Kinda Foods focused on the regional market and Upper Egypt due to its low costs compared to capital markets such as Cairo and Alexandria were targeted due to the lack of competition in Upper Egypt. And its ferocity in the capital. The company's situation is like most of the industrial sector, which is the high electricity costs, as any industry consumes a lot of electricity. The government also holds the commercial segment at a price per watt higher than the natural consumption, as it reaches that the price of a kilowatt reaches one pound and 60 piasters. The company faces the problem of electricity in the warehouse explicitly because it consumes electricity in a large volume due to the use of refrigerators to maintain the appropriate temperature for juices so that they do not spoil (EEHC, 2019). So, the main problem in the factory is the warehouse because the warehouse, as monthly electricity cost of the warehouse is very high and reaches 17,000 pounds per month, which reduces the factory's profits and also it raises the inventory price, therefore, the price of juice relatively compared to what the company wants to achieve the lowest price available in the market (personal communication, May 3, 2019).

SETTING THE STAGE

In this case study, the piezoelectric technique was used, which is a technique that relies on converting kinetic energy into electrical energy through a specific type of crystal that converts kinetic energy into electrical energy. Those crystals were discovered in France in 1880 by two brothers, Pierre, and Paul (Hari Anand et al., 2019), and crystals work by converting Vibrations resulting from feet or moving anything on them to electricity, as shown in Figure 1. Piezoelectric tiles are made using special materials, such as crystals and ceramics, in which electric charge builds up when mechanical stress is applied" such as a foot pressing down (Zack Mester et al., 2012). The piezoelectric effect is very useful in many applications involving the production and detection of sound, generation of high voltages, electronic frequency generation, microbalances, and ultra-fine focusing of optical assemblies (Yanfang Meng et al., 2022). It is also the basis of several scientific instrumental techniques with atomic resolution, such as scanning probe microscopes (STM, AFM, etc.) (Zinc-Based Nanostructures for Environmental and Agricultural Applications, 2021). The piezoelectric effect also has its use in more mundane applications as well, such as acting as the ignition source for cigarette lighters (TK Basu, 2010). Due to the intrinsic characteristics of piezoelectric materials, numerous applications benefit from their use: High Voltage and Power Sources; an example of applications in this area is the electric cigarette lighter, where pressing a button causes a spring-loaded hammer to hit a piezoelectric crystal, thereby producing a sufficiently high voltage that electric current flows across a small spark gap, heating and igniting the gas. Most types of gas burners and ranges have a built-in piezo-based injection system. Sensors, the principle of operation of a piezoelectric sensor is that a physical dimension, transformed into a force, acts on two opposing faces of the sensing element. The detection of pressure variations in sound is the most common sensor application, seen in piezoelectric microphones and piezoelectric pickups for electrically amplified guitars. Piezoelectric sensors are used with high-frequency sound in ultrasonic transducers for medical imaging and industrial nondestructive testing (B. Chandra Sekhar et al., 2021). Piezoelectric Motors, because very high voltages correspond to only tiny changes in the width of the crystal, this crystal width can be manipulated with better-than-micrometer precision, making piezo crystals an important tool for positioning objects with extreme accuracy, making them perfect for use in motors, such as the various motor series offered by Nano motion. Regarding piezoelectric motors, the piezoelectric element receives an electrical pulse, and then applies directional force to an opposing ceramic plate, causing it to move in the desired direction. Motion is generated when the piezoelectric element moves against a static platform (such as ceramic strips). The characteristics of piezoelectric materials provided the perfect technology upon which Nano motion developed our various lines of unique piezoelectric motors. Using patented piezoelectric technology, Nano motion has designed various series of motors ranging in size from a single element (providing 0.4Kg of force) to an eight-element motor (providing 3.2Kg of force) (Neelima Sharad Vatkar & Yogesh Sharad Vatkar,2016). Nano motion motors can drive both linear and rotary stages, have a wide dynamic range of speed, from several microns per second to 250mm/sec, and easily mount to traditional low friction stages or other devices. The operating characteristics of Nano motion's motors provide inherent braking and the ability to eliminate servo dither when in a static position (www.valin.com).

Figure 1. Piezoelectric tile layout
Source: Shreeshayana et al. (2017)

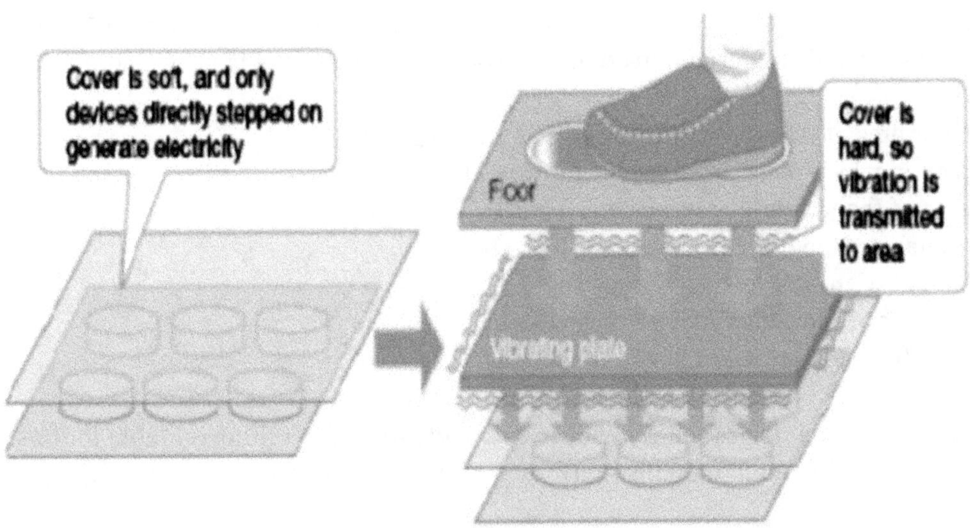

CASE DESCRIPTION

Recently, all companies are currently aspiring to make their supply chain green to coincide with the vision of sustainable development for the year 2030 as an overview of the supply chains, it turns out that one of the most important facilities that consume fuel energy and non-renewable energy are factories, followed by warehouses, especially warehouses in which it is stored The consumables that need special refrigerators to provide the appropriate temperatures for the products so that they do not spoil as a result of the high temperatures in the warehouses, so, in this case, study the warehouse was chosen as one of the most important facility along the supply chain that may consume energy and cause harmful emissions to the environment (Warehouse Carbon Footprint Calculation 101, 2015). Therefore, all institutions that have warehouses seek to convert them into green warehouses, which are warehouses that operate using renewable energy, whether solar or wind energy and other renewable energies, including electromagnetic energy generated from piezoelectric tiles to reduce carbon emissions from regular electricity (APC, 2015). Warehouses were chosen in general, and Kinda Foods warehouse, because it is not a very large warehouse that piezoelectric tiles can be applied to and without high costs due to its small size to answer several questions, which are:

1. What is the meaning of green warehouses?
2. To what extent can normal warehouses be converted into green warehouses?
3. Does the use of alternative energy affect costs?
4. How can the energy generated by piezoelectric tiles be calculated?
5. How can we make the most of the energy generated by the piezoelectric slab?
6. Is it possible to rely on piezoelectric tiles completely or not?
7. Can several types of tiles be combined or not?
8. Is the period of recovery of technology costs feasible or not compared to the period of consumption of tiles?

It was necessary to collect specific details about the warehouse, such as the area, weight of trucks that enter the warehouse, the number of times trucks, the weight of loaded juice cartons and the rent cost of the warehouse, and this information collected from the owner of the factory, and it found as follows:

1. The floor area of the store is 17 * 22 = 374 square meters.
2. The path in which the trucks move is 6 * 3 = 18 square meters.
3. The area of the warehouse entrance is 4 * 3 = 12 square meters.
4. The tonnage of the truck is 2 tons.
5. The weight of the truck is 4500 tons.
6. The number of charging times per day is three times.
7. The monthly electricity cost is 17,000 pounds

To study the consumption of the warehouse and study the types of tiles suitable for this warehouse, it is necessary to calculate the monthly consumption of electricity and know the appropriate need for the warehouse:

The warehouse rent costs 17,000 pounds per month, the price of a kilowatt = 1.60 pounds
So, the monthly warehouse consumption of kilowatts = 17000/1.60 = 10,625 kilowatts
Daily consumption of watts = 10,625/30 = 354 kilowatts approximately = 354,000 watts

Table 1. Prices of the Egyptian Electricity Company for the year 2019/2020 (www.eehc.gov.eg)

New Electricity Prices for Households DAILY NEWS EGYPT

Consumption Bracket	New Tariff	Old Tariff	% Hike
0-50 Kw	EGP 0.38	EGP 0.30	27%
51-100 Kw	EGP 0.48	EGP 0.40	20%
101-200 Kw	EGP 0.65	EGP 0.50	30%
201-350 Kw	EGP 0.96	EGP 0.82	17%
351-650 Kw	EGP 1.18	EGP 1	18%
651-1000 Kw	EGP 1.18	-	-
Above 1000 Kw	EGP 1.60	EGP 1.45	90 %

And these calculations are based on the prices of the Egyptian Electricity Company for the year 2019/2020 shown in Table 1.

After clarifying the above calculations, the appropriate type of piezoelectric tiles was chosen, as there are many types of tiles, as shown in Table 2.

1. Selected type of piezoelectric

The piezoelectric slab selected was a Sustainable Energy Floor (SEF) (Figure 2).

a. Usage of (SEF)
   § It is used in sidewalks and high-altitude areas such as airports.
   § Sports arenas, shopping malls, railway stations, offices, and apartments.
   § Electric streetlights and signature systems and units can be fully customized.
   § Used in many projects, such as the Nissan Innovation Station in 2015.
b. Characteristics of (SEF) tiles
   § Width: 750 mm width.
   § Depth: 750 mm depth.
   § Height: 115 mm high.
   § Weight: 15-45 kg.

Through Table 2, it becomes clear to us that one tile has an area of 75 cm * 75 cm, and one tile produces electrical energy from 20 to 50 watts, and from Figure No. "5" the power generated by the number of 50 tiles is though the number of people who have stepped on those tiles times the power generated per tile. The table shows that 50 tiles can generate 12,498 kilowatts if 249 steps are taken.

Table 2. Types and cost of Piezoelectric tiles (Moussa & Rania, 2019)

No.	Company-Technology	Product Dimension	Generated Energy	Price\Egyptian Pounds	Estimated Lifespan per Year
1	Waynergy Floor	40*40 cm tile	10 W per step	4000	20
2	Sustainable Energy Floor (SEF)	75*74 cm tile 50*50 cm tile	Up to 30 Watt of continuous output. Typical power output for continuous stepping by a person lies between 1 and 10 W nominal output per module (average 7 W)	15000	15
3	Pavegen tiles	V3 tile, 50 cm each edge	5 Watts continuous power from footsteps	35000	20
4	(EAPs) electroactive polymers	Sheets	1 Watt	Unknown	20
5	Sound Power	50*50 cm tile	0.1 Watt per 2 steps	Unknown	20
6	PZT ceramic (Lead Zirconate Titanate)	Manufacturing in a small size	8.4mW	Unknown	20
7	Parquet PVDF layers	Layers	2.1mWs per pulse with a load of about 70 kg	Unknown	20
8	Drum Harvesters Piezo puzzar piezoelectric ceramics	Vary	Around 2.463mW	Estimated 500 per tile	20
9	Power Leap PZT	Tile 24*24	0.5mW per step	The project has stopped	20
10	Hybrid Energy Floor combines human power with solar energy	75*75 cm tile 1*2-meter tile	Up to 60kWh per year, per tile Up to 250kWh per year, per tile	Estimated 15000	20
11	PZT nanofiber nanogenerator & PZT textile nanogenerator	Sheets the volume of the material used in 0.2cm3	6mW/cm3 0.03 μW power destiny up to 2.4 μW/cm3	Available commercially at law cost and in a variety of designs	20
12	PVDF nanofiber	....	4μW/cm3, 7.2 pW	Unknown	20
13	ZnO nanowire VINGs	....	5pW 11mW/cm3 2.7mW/cm3	Very economically	20
14	BaTiO3	....	~7mW/cm3	Available commercially at law cost and in a variety of design	....

The price of this SEF tile, in addition to the installation cost, is 15,000 pounds per tile, and the shelf life is 15 years for the slab, as shown in Figure 2.

1. How to calculate the cost of piezoelectric tiles in the warehouse

   a. calculate the number of tiles that the warehouse needs

Figure 2. (SEF) tiles (www.rdso.indianrailways.gov)

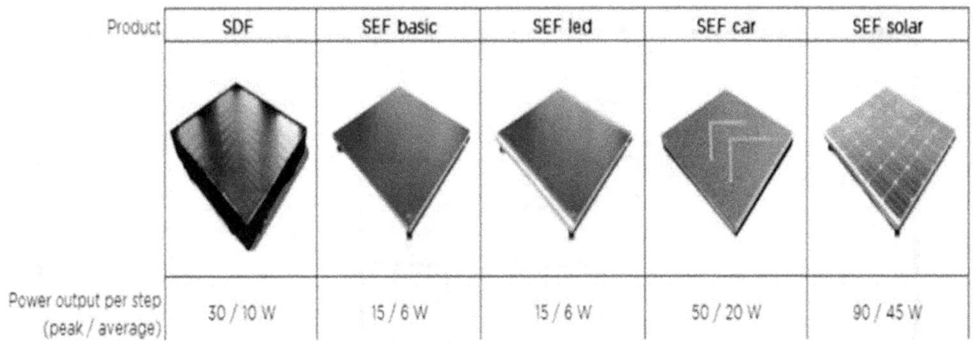

In Figure 3 a simple shape of the warehouse and the locations of the piezo-electric tiles that are placed in the place where the truck is traveling to and from the warehouse are shown, in addition to placing the piezo-electric tiles in the locations of truck wheels inside the warehouse.

In Figure 3, the piezo-electric tiles will be shown in the itinerary of the truck wheels, whether in the entrance of the store or in the path of the store inside it, but how do we know the required number of piezo-electric tiles, it will become clear as follows:

The piezoelectric slab has an area of 75 * 75 cm, and we will need only one tile width along the entrance and corridor only because the width of the tile is 75 cm.

First, the entrance is 3 meters long and the slab is 75 cm, i.e., 4 tiles are the length of the entrance, so 75 * 4 = 300 cm = 3 meters. The corridor then has 16 piezoelectric tiles, so the number of tiles required in the warehouse is = 16 + 8 = 24 piezoelectric tiles.

The cost of the tiles used in its installation is 24 tiles * 15,000 pounds = 360,000 pounds.

b. Calculate the energy produced by trucks in human steps instead of tons

The human steps are calculated on that slab and the pressure of the steps on that slab is electrical energy measured in watts, and the average human weight is calculated as 80 kilograms, and to facilitate the calculation of the energy resulting from the pressure of the truck on the piezoelectric tiles, we will accurately calculate the weight of the load and the truck and converting them to human steps, as they were used in previous research and studies.

Table 3. Energy generated by 50 tiles in watt per hour (www.rdso.indianrailways.gov)

Proposed No of Tiles	Pedestrians per Hour	Electricity Generated = Tiles* Pedestrian per Hour	Kilo Watt Hour
50	2638	131900-watt hour	131.9 KWH
50	2186	109308-watt hour	109.308 KWH
50	249	12498-watt hour	12.498 KWH

Figure 3. Simple design of Kinda Foods Warehouse

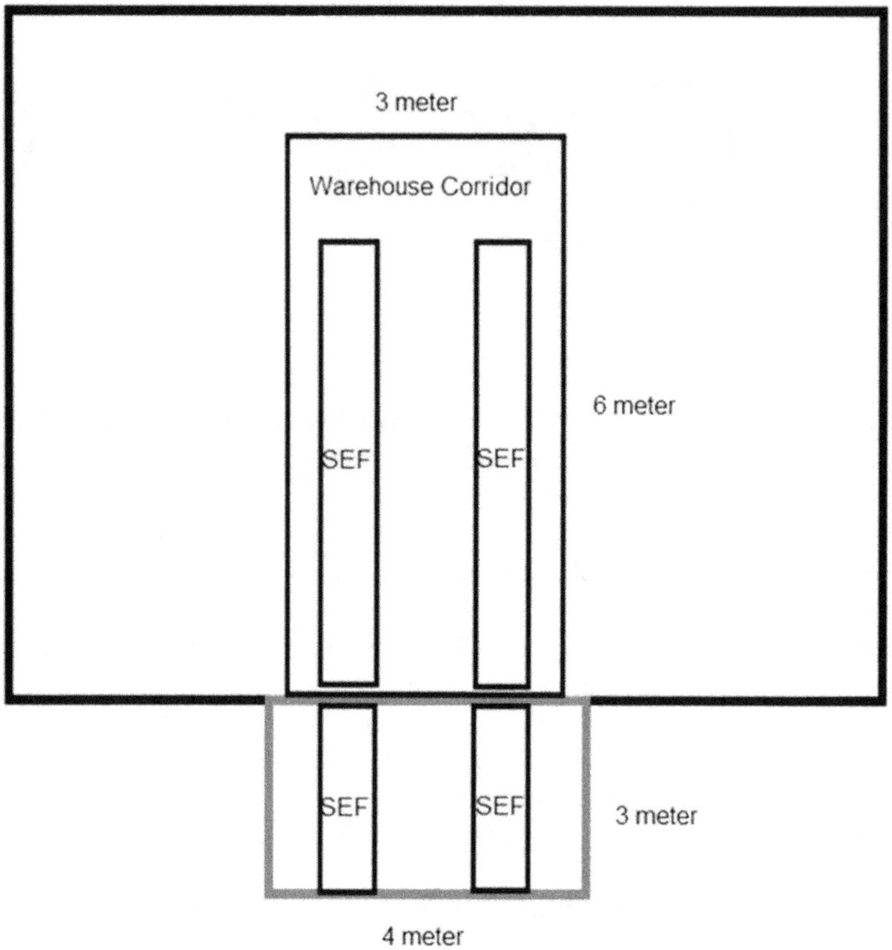

§ The number of trucks traveling in the warehouse and passing on the path that was clarified is 3 trucks daily, and those trucks are traveling three times on that path, once with a load of 2 tons and once empty each time.

§ The weight of the empty truck = 4500 kg, the load weight = 3000 kg, so there will be six lanes, three with a weight of 7500 kg (truck + goods) and three with a weight of 4500 kg (an empty truck).

§ Now we will calculate the energy resulting from the movement of the truck twice, once by the weight of the truck only and once by the weight of the truck with the load, three times daily.

I. Calculating the energy resulting from entering the truck three times a day with the load:

§ The truck weighs (4500 kg) and it is transporting a load inside the warehouse that weighs (3000 kg), meaning that the weight of the truck with the load is (7500 kg).

§ The payload of 7500 kg is distributed on 4 axles, which are (truck wheels), meaning that each truck wheel carries several kilograms distributed between the weight of the truck and the load itself, so we will calculate for each wheel (truck weight above one wheel + weight of the load on one wheel) and therefore each wheel passes on each slab, it passes a weight = 7500/4 = 1875 kg.

Table 4. Energy produced from the truck three times a day with the load

Weight of Truck	Load of Truck	Weight of Truck + Load of Truck	Distribution of the Load on the Wheel Axles	Weigh Each Axis in Human Steps	Energy Produced by One Wheel	Energy Generated by 24 Tiles Pressed by Two Wheels on Each Side (46 Steps on the Slab)	Final Energy of the Truck Running Is Loaded Three Times a Day
4500 KG	3000 KG	7500 KG	1875 KG	23 STEPS	=23*50 1150 WATTS	1150*24*2= 55200 WATTSS	=55200*3165600 165.6= K WATTS

§ The truck has two wheels on each side (meaning that each tile while the truck passes over it, a front wheel weighing 1875 kg and a rear wheel weighing 1875 kg) passes on it in the right wheels and the left wheels.

§ To calculate the energy, we will convert kilograms into human steps by dividing the truck's weight by 80 kg, the average weight of people, and therefore 1875 kg / 80 kg (the average human weight) = 23 people approximately, or 23 steps on one slab.

§ So, one wheel = 23 steps, and there are two wheels on the right side and two wheels on the left side, meaning that each slab will be pressed by two wheels while entering on each side of the truck track, i.e., 23 * 2 = 46 steps on one slab.

§ One tile produces from 20 to 50 watts, but we will calculate the maximum energy produced because the load that is pressing on the slab generates the maximum energy from the tile, so we will calculate the energy to generate 50 watts of energy, meaning that the two wheels travel on one tile generate 46 * 50 = 2300 watts per tile. And we have 24 tiles, and the slab produces 2300 watts, so the 24 produces energy = 2300 * 24 = 55,200 watts.

§ So, the energy generated at one time for the truck to enter the warehouse is 55,200 watts, the truck enters three times, so the energy generated by the truck entering the store three times = 55,200 * 3 = 165,600 watts = 165.6 kilowatts.

Table 4 explains the previous calculation.

II. Calculation of the empty truck going out three times a day from the warehouse

§ The truck is empty and weighs 4500 kg after the load is unloaded. Of course, since the truck enters the warehouse three times, it exits three times and travels on the same tiles, but with less weight and fewer steps.

§ Just as we calculated the power to be taken from the truck with a full load, we will also calculate it empty; we will calculate the weight distribution on the four axes, so the weight of each axle of the truck is 4500/4 = 1125 kg per wheel.

§ Converting each wheel weight to human steps, so we calculate it as follows (1125/80 = approximately 14 steps) for each wheel.

§ There are two wheels on the right side and two wheels on the left side meaning that each tile is pressed twice by two wheels while entering on each side in the truck track, i.e., 28 steps per slab.

§ Calculating that the tile produces 50 watts, so the output of one tile = 28 * 50 = 1400 watts.

Table 5. Energy generated from the empty truck going out three times a day from the warehouse

Truck Weight Empty	Distribution of the Load on the Wheel Axles	Weigh Each Axis in Human Steps	Energy Produced by One Wheel	Energy Generated by 24 Tiles Pressed by Two Wheels on Each Side (28 Steps on the Slab)	Final Energy of the Truck Running Is Loaded Three Times a Day
4500 KG	1125 KG	14 STEPS	14*50 700= WATTS	700*24*2 33600= WATTS	33600*3 100800= 100.8= K WATTS

Table 6. Explain the energy saved from piezoelectric tiles

Percentage of Energy Saved per Day	The Difference Between the Energy Produced and Consumed	Energy Consumed by the Warehouse Daily	Energy Generates From Piezoelectric Tiles	Number of Daily Steps
266.4/354*100 %75.25= Almost 75%	354-226.4 127.6= K WATTS	354 K WATTS	266.4 K WATTS (74*50*24*3)	74 Step for one tile

§ There are 24 tiles at the entrance and corridor of the store, so the total output power = 1400 * 24 = 33,600 watts

§ The truck comes out empty three times from the store, so the generated energy = 33,600 * 3 = 100,800 watts = 100.8 kilowatts.

Table 5 explains the previous calculation.

Table 7. Explain monthly energy saved from piezo electric tiles

Percentage of Energy Saved per Month	The Difference Between the Energy Produced and Consumed	Energy Consumed by the Store per Month	Energy Produced From Piezo Electric Tiles	Monthly Steps
7,992/10,620*100 =75.25% Almost 75%	10,620-7,992 =2,628 K WATTS	10,620 K WATTS	7,992 K WATTS (2220*50*24*3)	=222074*30 steps per one tile

Table 8. explain yearly energy saved from piezoelectric tiles

Percentage of Energy Saved per Year	The Difference Between the Energy Produced and Consumed	Energy Consumed by the Store per Year	Energy Produced From Piezo Electric Tiles	Yearly Steps
95,904/127440*100 =75.25% almost 75%	127440-95904 =31536 K watts	10,620*12 =127440 K watts	95,904 K watt (26640*50*24*3)	74*30*12 26640= step per one tile

From Table 4 and Table 5, energy generated because of the piezo-electric tiles because of the entry and exit of the truck during charging and unloading, as the energy resulting from entering the truck three times = 165.6 kilowatts.

And the energy produced by leaving the truck empty three times = 100.8 kilowatts.

So, the total energy generated by the truck traveling daily to and for = 165.6 + 100.8 = 266.4 kilowatts.

2. Calculation of the energy saved from piezoelectric tiles compared to the use of the store

After reviewing how to calculate the number of tiles and the resulting energy, it is possible through Table 6 to compare the daily output and consumed energy available from piezoelectric tiles.

Table 7 explains monthly energy saved from piezoelectric tiles, and Table 8 explains yearly energy that could be saved from piezoelectric tiles.

From the previous tables, it appears clearly that the percentage of savings in electricity is 75%, in theory with accurate calculations, but in reality, the actual useful generated energy is less than the theoretical calculated energy due to many factors such as tiles maintenance program, tiles components aging, power loss due to voltage conversion from the tile output voltage to store operating voltage (as 220 V.ac), change of stepping conditions. So, on the average, the actual useful generated energy is 80% of the theoretical calculated energy, which makes the actual savings percentage as shown in Table 9.

Table 9. Explain the actual saving percentage per year

Annual Energy Generated From Tiles	Actual Power Consumed by Store	Energy Consumed From the Warehouse Annually	Difference Between the Energy Consumed From the Warehouse and the Energy Generated by the Tiles	Actual Savings Percentage per Year
95,904 K WATTS	95,904*80% 76,723.2= K WATTS	127440 K WATTS	127440 76,723.2- 50717= K WATT	76,723.2/127440 *100 =60.2% Almost 60%

It is evident that the warehouse's normal energy consumption (fuel energy) decreases by about 60% and reaches 50,717 kW annually, down from 127440 kW.

The factory manager used to pay a monthly bill for the warehouse of 17,000 pounds, or 204,000 pounds per year, but after using the tiles, we will find that an annual financial value of 50717*1.60=81147.2 pounds will be paid, i.e. savings 122852.8 pounds annually, which is the 60% savings in value Financially, meaning that in a month it consumes (50,717 kilowatts / 12 months = 4226.4 kilowatts) and the manager will pay the warehouse electricity cost 6752.24 pounds per month, which means that the kilowatt cost has decreased from 1.6 pounds to 63 piasters per month (6752.24/10620=0.63)

III. Study the value of recovering the cost of installing piezoelectric tiles

Replacement costs must be considered, i.e., the cost of laying new tiles instead of the tiles that were consumed and that are 15 years old, meaning that those tiles must be replaced after 15 years with new ones, and it is a cost that the store must consider while calculating the cost savings so that the energy produced continues in a manner Good and bigger.

§ The costs of installing the tiles are 360,000 pounds, and their life span is 15 years.
§ To calculate the replacement cost after 15 years, we do the following, which is calculating the cost of tiles per month for 15 years (assuming no change in tile cost after 15 years).
§ 360000 / 15 years = 24000 pounds per year, that is, 2000 pounds per month.
§ This means that the store must consider that there are 2000 pounds that are held per month for 15 years for the replacement process later when the new tiles are installed, and it will be added to the monthly electricity bill.
§ The warehouse will pay 6752.24 pounds per month, in addition to the fact that 2000 pounds must be retained as replacement expenses, so the actual cost that the warehouse will pay per month = 8,752.24 pounds per month.
§ The actual value of savings after adding tile replacement expenses becomes 17000-8,752.24 = 8247.76 pounds per month, so savings per month = (8247.76 / 17,000) *100=48.5%, 17000 pounds is the monthly electricity bill before tile installation.
§ Table 10 shows the recovery time of the tiles installation value that the store paid in addition to the value of the savings over a period of 15 years after the redemption of the value of the tiles.

Table 10. Recovery time of the tile's installation value

<table>
<tr><th colspan="2">Saving From the 1st Year</th><th colspan="3">Saving From 2nd Year</th><th colspan="2">Saving From 3rd Year</th><th colspan="4">Savings From the 4th Year</th></tr>
<tr><td colspan="2">17000
-8752.24
=8247.76
per month
* 12 months
=98973.12
L.E per year</td><td colspan="3">98973.12
L.E per year</td><td colspan="2">98973.12
L.E per year</td><td colspan="4">First half of the year
8247.76=49486.56 L.E*6 months
+7TH month
8247.76 L.E</td></tr>
<tr><td colspan="2"></td><td colspan="3"></td><td colspan="2"></td><td colspan="4">Only the eighth month, 5346.32 pounds is calculated from it, to complete the recovery period of the amount of 360000 pounds, leaving 2901.44 pounds unused savings that are calculated in the total savings + the month from the ninth to the twelfth month, any amount (8247.76 * 4) + 2901.44
So, the saver from the fourth year after recovery = 35892.48 pounds</td></tr>
<tr><td colspan="11">So, the payback period is 3 years and eight months, and from the ninth month the savings are calculated over the years of operation</td></tr>
<tr><td>5TH year</td><td>6th year</td><td>7th year</td><td>8th year</td><td>9th year</td><td>10th year</td><td>11th year</td><td>12th year</td><td>13th year</td><td>14th year</td><td>15th year</td></tr>
<tr><td colspan="11">Savings from the fourth year = 35892.48 + (98973.12 per year * 11 (the number of years remaining in the validity of the tiles)
So, savings within 15 years of using piezo-electric tiles after calculating the recovery
=1,124,596.8 L. E</td></tr>
</table>

The warehouse before the piezoelectric tiles for 15 years, its costs in the electricity bill are = 17,000 pounds * 12 months * 15 years = 3,060,000 pounds

But after installing the tiles, its costs during 15 years = 8752.24 pounds * 12 months * 15 years = 1,575,403.2 pounds

That is, the warehouse has saved = 3,060,000 – 1,575,403.2 = 1,484,596.8 pounds

And after deducting replacement costs, the total savings = 1,484,596.8 – 360,000 = 1,124,596.8 pounds

By numbers and calculations, we are assured that the financial savings amount to 51.4% (1,575,403.2/3,060,000 * 100).

From the previous calculations, it is not only clear the costs that piezoelectric tiles can save, but also, it is clear how to convert warehouses that are powered by electrical energy resulting from hydrocarbons into green warehouses that are powered by renewable energy, such as the energy produced from piezoelectric tiles, which were used in many institutions outside Egypt, whether in schools, roads, etc. (Solban & Moussa, 2019). Thus, green warehouses can be defined as making updates that reduce the amount of energy used, tap into sustainable energy sources and materials, and reduce the amounts of non-recyclable waste created during warehouse operations. Progress towards a greener warehouse can be measured tangibly by seeking building certifications that will evaluate performance across metrics that are often tied to Environmental, Social, and Governance (ESG) criteria (Ranpak, 2022).

CURRENT CHALLENGES FACING THE ORGANIZATION

Although the piezoelectric tiles technology has proven its efficiency and the extent to which it provides alternative energy for non-renewable energy, there are many challenges that faced the implementation of the technology in the warehouse at the beginning, and among those challenges are the following points:

1. Fear of experimenting with modern technologies in the industrial culture in Egypt, because it is not known to most people.
2. Experimenting with a certain number of piezoelectric tiles, as the warehouse is not one of the large warehouses, and therefore the number of tiles was limited in the truck tracks.
3. Changing the infrastructure and connecting the tiles to the electricity network that runs the warehouse.
4. Training drivers on the slab track, specifically in the middle, to obtain the highest amount of electricity generated.
5. The different types of piezoelectric tiles and their different prices were among the challenges that faced the warehouse because the warehouse is small in size, so it was necessary to choose a type of slab that generates large electrical energy and in a limited area.

SOLUTIONS AND RECOMMENDATIONS

The problems encountered in implementing the piezoelectric technology are not as big or as difficult as it was impossible to solve, and each problem was solved as follows:

1. The CEO was persuaded to adopt the idea of piezoelectric tiles, which will bring him financial benefit first, before transforming the warehouse into a green warehouse and ensuring the transformation.

2. The number of tiles was calculated in proportion to the size and trajectory of the trucks in the warehouse, and all places were used to achieve maximum benefit.
3. Changing the infrastructure was not very difficult because only the trucks track and not the entire warehouse was taken.
4. Training drivers to walk in a certain way on the tiles was not difficult, as the space of the tiles is sufficient for the truck tires to pass smoothly.
5. Choosing the appropriate piezoelectric tile of the SEF type, which has a suitable area and a large power generation.

CONCLUSION

After studying the case of the Kinda Food Store for Food Industries and making a study of the costs of installing piezoelectric tiles that produce electrical energy as soon as the trucks pass them and light up the store, and by comparing the costs of monthly consumption of regular electricity (fuel energy electricity) over a 15-year period (the validity period of the tiles) The following conclusion: -

1. Placing 24 piezo-electric tiles in the Kinda Food store, which converts the truck's movement energy into electrical energy that can provide the store with electricity amounting to 76,723.2 kilowatts annually, meaning that it provides 60% of the store's needs annually.
2. The cost of laying the tiles is 360,000 pounds, the value of which will be recovered within 3 years and eight months, after calculating the replacement cost, which is the installation of new tiles after 15 years.
3. The financial value of the actual electricity bill decreases from 17,000 pounds to 6752.24 pounds, and the amount of 2000 pounds increases to the electricity bill to collect the replacement value later, meaning that the store's monthly cost decreases from 17,000 to 8752.24 pounds.

That is, the electricity bill decreases by 51.4%, which makes the value of a kilowatt approximately drop from 1.60 pounds to 65 piasters.

4. The store, within 15 years, will have a net saving of 1,124,596.8 pounds that can be used to develop the store, develop the industry, expand the company's industry itself, or improve the product.
5. Through the case study, it can be said that the warehouse can be transformed into a green warehouse by 60%, meaning that it works with renewable energy, which is the energy of movement that turns into electrical energy, which is a very feasible percentage as a small start.
6. One of the important conclusions is that the lower the costs of the store in terms of the electricity bill, of course, the cost of maintaining inventory for the stored products will decrease, and therefore it will benefit the price of the product or the value of the profits achieved for the company, because storage is one of the most material costs on products and the lower cost in Warehousing means either an increase in profits or a decrease in the price of the product being stored according to the vision of the factory management.
7. It is also clear from the case study that providing electricity from piezo-electric tiles is a practical and easy solution to implement in theory and in practice as well but is also available in the Arab

Republic of Egypt, which means that it is possible to dispense with non-renewable energy sources and replace those tiles that generate Energy from motion instead.

8. The economical return resulting from the installation of piezoelectric tiles is large, and not only the economical return but also the return on the environment. Operating the store with kinetic energy that turns into electrical energy is entering the store within the framework of the environmentally friendly green circle, which means reducing pollution and emissions resulting from the use of non-renewable energy.

Through the case study of the Kinda Foods warehouse and the extent of the change and benefit that occurred because of the introduction of piezoelectric technology, but there are some points that were ignored, but if attention is paid to them, the performance of the warehouse will be improved from the use of energy and these points are:

1. Placing piezoelectric tiles at the human entrances to the warehouse or to the factory itself, as from the case study it becomes clear the extent of the economic feasibility on the store, and the application can be expanded for the company and the factory itself because of its energy and cost savings of up to 60%.
2. It is possible to reduce the monthly electricity cost more by reducing the lighting a little and using saving lamps and reducing their number if they are not directly needed during the entry and exit of stored goods.
3. Use of tiles with built-in solar cells (hybrid), which are designated for pedestrian paths as well, and workers' paths can be made, so these tiles form energy by collecting solar and kinetic energy together and produce twice the energy produced from ordinary piezo-electric tiles and use them to collect greater energies in the areas were labor movement.

REFERENCES

Abd-elsalam, K. A. (2021). *Zinc-Based Nanostructures for Environmental and Agricultural Applications*. https://www.bookdepository.com

Anand, H., & Singh, B. (2021). Piezoelectric energy generation in India: An empirical investigation. *Energy Harvesting and Systems.*, *1*(3-4), 1–8. doi:10.1515/ehs-2020-0002

Anand, H., & Singh, B. (2021). Piezoelectric energy generation in India: An empirical investigation. *Energy Harvesting and Systems.*, *1*(3-4), 1–8. doi:10.1515/ehs-2020-0002

Anand, H., & Singh, B. K. (2019). Piezoelectric energy generation in India: An empirical investigation. *Energy Harvesting and Systems*, *6*(3-4), 69–76. doi:10.1515/ehs-2020-0002

EEHC. (2019). www.eehc.gov.eg

Huang, Y., & Barbara, A. (2009). Infrared Spectroscopy for Food Quality Analysis and Control. Academic Press.

Industrial Distribution. (2015). *Warehouse Carbon Footprint Calculation 101*. https://www.inddist.com/

IRWG. (2015). www.rdso.indianrailways.gov

Meng, Y., Chen, G., & Huang, M. (2022). Piezoelectric Materials: Properties, Advancements, and Design Strategies for High-Temperature Applications. *Nanomaterials, 12*(7), 1171. doi:10.3390/nano12071171

Ranpank. (2022). 3 Trends Elevating the Importance of Green Warehousing. *Sustainability.*

Sekhar, B. C., Dhanalakshmi, B., Rao, B. S., Ramesh, S., Prasad, K. V., Rao, P. S., & Rao, B. P. (2021). Piezoelectricity and Its Applications. In Multifunctional Ferroelectric Materials. IntechOpen. doi:10.5772/intechopen.96154

Solban, M. M., & Moussa, R. R. (2019). *IOP Conf. Ser.: Earth Environ. Sci.* https://iopscience.iop.org/article/10.1088/1755-1315/397/1/012020/meta

Vatkar, N. S., & Vatkar, Y. S. (2016). Piezoelectric motors & its applications. *IRJET, 3*(6), 65-72. https://www.irjet.net/archives/V3/i6/IRJET-V3I6186.pdf

Chapter 15
The Tendency Toward Producing Ecologically Friendly Products at Toshiba in the Middle East

Ahmed Hussein Ali
https://orcid.org/0000-0002-2626-3293
College of International Transport and Logistics Arab Academy for Science, Technology and Maritime Transport, Alexandria, Egypt

Habiba Sherif El-Rouby
College of International Transport and Logistics Arab Academy for Science, Technology and Maritime Transport, Alexandria, Egypt

Sarah Yousry El-Gamal
College of International Transport and Logistics Arab Academy for Science, Technology and Maritime Transport, Alexandria, Egypt

Ahmed Saad Zaghloul
Elaraby Group, Egypt

EXECUTIVE SUMMARY

The case deals with decreasing environmental harm and pollution in all industries. The corporations have followed worldwide environmental standards to replace toxic materials with environmentally acceptable alternatives, such as lead-free glass used in producing L.E.D. lamps and Freon R410 used in the production process of air conditioners and refrigerators. ELARABY Group is one of the few enterprises in the Middle East specialized in electronics. It designed and applied a system to face the challenges, consequences, and results of replacing harmful materials with environmentally friendly ones. The case followed a qualitative approach through conducting interviews with experts in order to collect data.

DOI: 10.4018/978-1-6684-4686-7.ch015

INTRODUCTION

The fast growth in industrialisation in the last century has produced a difficult challenge related to environmental degradation in the world; in addition, the increase in the human population has caused a huge depression on resources. In 1987, the World Commission on Environment and Development (WCED) launched sustainability initiatives to reduce the damage on the environment, society, and community. The role of sustainability started to be shown since Malthus (1872) was concerned about how Britain's apparently unstoppable rise in population could be sustained by a limited amount of land. As a result, the consumption of energy increases with a limited quantity of coal. Moreover, people start to face a lot of challenges, especially the damage related to social, economic, and environmental resources, which are connected. Furthermore, these challenges could be solved by a newly integrated system of thinking to take action that creates a future where human society and nature can live with common advantages and where the suffering caused by natural resource abuse is finished.

Environmental problems related to waste and emissions come from supply chain activities; moreover, reduction and deterioration of natural resources and the high environmental pressure have forced organisations to recognise, realise and manage their supply chain to make it environmentally friendly.

Toshiba Elaraby is one of the electronic companies in Egypt that started to follow the same approach, starting from raw materials selection until they reach the end user, as the headquarter in Japan has followed the same approach to adopt the sustainability practices. Toshiba Elaraby took the initiative to follow the same approach. Therefore, this study aims to find the consequences of using environmentally friendly raw materials "Lead-Free Glass" and Freon.

ORGANISATION BACKGROUND

Since its establishment in 1964, ELARABY Group has grown from a joint stock family enterprise to one of the largest industrial and commercial corporations in Egypt, the Middle East, and Africa. ELARABY Group operates through 16 commercial, industrial, medical, and service companies, in four different governorates with 26 industrial facilities, and 2 hospitals. In 2020, ELARABY Group's workforce exceeded 40,000 employees. Elaraby's brand portfolio consists of 14 global brands with 25 product categories and more than 4,000 variations. With regards to the domestic and international markets, Toshiba Elaraby's figures continue to grow by exporting to over 60 countries across the globe. In the domestic market, one of ELARABY Group's strongest assets is the vast distribution network, which consists of more than 3,000 sales partners and 20 branded stores, backed by more than 600 after-sale service centres. In a society consisting of more than 100 million Egyptians who trusted ELARABY Group over the years, ELARABY Group gives back to the community through implementing and adopting various developmental projects in education, healthcare, environmental well-being, and social solidarity.

Since 1964, ELARABY Group has been associated with major international companies and has commercial relations with these companies in the marketing and manufacturing of electronic and electrical devices. 1974 is considered the starting point in its historical relationship with the Japanese ELARABY Group, the company that is credited with providing technical and technological support to ELARABY Group when it entered the battlefield of manufacturing for the first time.

In 2002, ELARABY Group was associated with another Japanese giant, which is the Japanese SHARP Company, and then rolled out global partnerships to make ELARABY Group a partner for major companies in the world, such as (Japanese HITACHI - Italian LA GERMANIA - N.E.C. Japanese - SEIKO and ALBA Japanese Company - Italian HOOVER - Japanese giant SONY - Italian Candy).

ELARABY Group is involved in both manufacturing and marketing engineering products, which has a great role in enhancing the Egyptian economy. ELARABY Group is providing a high-quality product that includes high technology, to achieve customer satisfaction and fulfil their needs. ELARABY Group started to take a serious step starting from 2015 to ensure sustainability and continuity of all industries to save resources and reduce pressure on the environment.

"Natural resources are limited; we have to do our best to keep them safe and secured for the coming generations by consuming less."

Eng. Mahmoud Elaraby

The C.E.O. of Elaraby Group

Setting the Stage

By the end of 1990, businesses began to take into consideration the environmental issues in each department in the company's and firm's structure (Welford 2016, P1), despite the appearance of the International Organization for Standardization (ISO) in 1994, which encouraged organisations to set environmental management systems. These systems encompass rules for environmental policies, practices, objectives, and targets. However, it was stated that (ISO) became a weak tool with the huge challenges and pressures that demand protecting the environment and the social and economic aspects. Studer, Welford, et al. (2006) illustrated that companies should use the environmental management systems with the additional main points of sustainability to figure out a new way to manage the business. Moreover, Evans and Sawyer (2010) clarified that firms still have the main goal to achieve the profit plan, but the change in economic, social, and environmental perspectives led them to consider profitability as a late prior target. Furthermore,White and Lee (2009) also confirmed that companies took into account the term sustainability and became more interested in environmental issues. Organisations increasingly tend to integrate sustainability into their business strategies to explore opportunities for creating competitive advantage and achieving sustainable business (Bielak, Bonini et al. 2007).

Many researchers have recognised the role of sustainability in the electronic industry, as indicated in Table 1. The sustainability aspects related to electronics supply chains have been indicated. Fritz, Schöggl et al. (2017) presented sustainability aspects related to the electronic departments; these aspects consider the key of applying sustainability practices in organisations. They indicated that these aspects are the first points to evaluate the sustainability of the supply chain.

The electronic industry has faced many challenges related to sustainability practices. Wasylka and Wojnowski (2021) and Hjort et al. (2019) explained the materials related to the electronic sectors and demonstrated that manufacturers should reduce the amount of usable hazardous materials in the production operation. Moreover, Simon (2022) and Hawken et al. (2010) concentrated on the waste side, and they recommended using environmentally friendly materials to reduce the total of Greenhouse gases and reduce the carbon footprint. In addition, Yingying(2011); Konstantinos (2013); Hawken et al. (2010); Guomin et al. (2019) and Giacomo et al. (2021) highlighted that energy is one of the most important factors in the electronic industry. Manufacturers need to consider and reduce the amount of energy con-

Table 1. Sustainability practices in the electronic industry. Source:Fritz, Ruel et al. (2021)

Sustainability categories	Sustainability aspects	References
Materials	Avoidance of hazardous substances in products and production. Sustainable production and use of renewable materials (e.g., from sustainable forestry)	Commission of the European € Communities (2009); European Chemicals Agency (2012); European Parliament and Council of the European Union (2002a); Wasylka and Wojnowski (2021); Hjort et al. 2019
Product and services responsibility	Product quality and safety (including customer health)	Commission of the European Communities (2009); Wurzel rt al. 2019; Frederiksen et al. (2021); Antrim (2019)
Wastes	Prevention, reuse, collection, separation, recovery, and safe disposal.	Simon (2022); Hawken et al. (2010)
Emissions	Reduction and prevention of Greenhouse Gas emissions (GHG)/ Carbon footprint	Kalkanci 2020; Hockerts et al. (2012)
Energy	Production of energy-efficient products and services, initiatives to reduce indirect energy consumption, and Energy-efficient production.	Yingying(2011); Konstantinos (2013); Hawken et al. (2010); Guomin et al. 2019; Giacomo et al. 2021.
Water	Water consumption/reuse of water/water Footprint	European Chemicals Agency (2012); Remco et al. (2020); Water Footprint Network (2011).
Biodiversity	Reduction of impacts of activities/products/ services	Baumgartner 2019; Barbu 2019; Korhonen 2020

sumed and energy-efficient production. European Chemicals Agency (2012); Remco et al. (2020), and Water Footprint Network (2011) mentioned that water is one of the factors that need to be considered while producing products. They stated that water conservation and reducing water footprint are important factors that need to be considered, and they recommend that water desalination plants be constructed. Furthermore, Baumgartner (2019); Barbu (2019) and Korhonen (2020) illustrated that reduction of impacts of activities/products/services is an essential factor in achieving better sustainability practices.

According to the changes in environmental requirements and how they could affect their supply chain operations, companies developed environmental management strategies and long-term plans to deal with this development (Nkrumah, Asamoah et al. 2020). Green supply chain management (GSCM) is considered to be an environmental innovation that uses the integrated environmental thinking into supply chain management. "GSCM aims to eliminate wastes, including hazardous chemicals, emissions and energy and solid wastes along the supply chain, such as product design, material resourcing and selection, manufacturing process, delivery of the final product and end-of-life management of the product" (Chin, Tat et al. 2015, P 1). With the new era of GSCM, companies have to address their responsibilities for new issues, such as human rights, the safety of the workers and society as a whole, for enhancing the quality of life; therefore, they started to take serious steps toward applying a new concept to serve not only the environmental part but also the social and economic parts. The idea of integrating these three factors is to develop a concept of Sustainable Supply Chain Management (SSCM).

In response to evolving and tightening environmental laws and restrictions around the world, the electronics industry must provide products that meet applicable regulations. Current environmental initiatives confronting electronics manufacturers include requirements under a variety of regulations and proposed regulations from jurisdictions worldwide that will regulate or restrict the use of lead and other substances, or impose additional requirements when these substances are used in products. The RoHS

Directive, which went into effect on July 1, 2006, states that the use of lead and certain other substances in products placed on the market in the European Union must be regulated. Other international markets, including China and Korea, are also planning hazardous substance regulations shortly (Toshiba, 2022).

Moreover, United Nations launched sustainability goals in 2015 to be achieved by 2030. Sustainability includes features in three dimensions: environment, society, and economy. Carter and Rogers (2008) mentioned that using those three dimensions "strategically and contemporarily" leads to higher economic performance. Environmental sustainability is one of the most important elements of sustainability, which includes environmental responsibilities and environmentally friendly technologies (Winter and Knemeyer 2013). A lot of researchers have introduced environmentally friendly practices, starting with Carter and Rogers (2008), who introduced environmentally friendly practices, such as using friendly materials in packaging and fuel-efficient transportation; moreover, they identified them as efficient and environmentally friendly material sources, low carbon emissions and energy-efficient machines. Furthermore, Brandenburg, Govindan et al. (2014) described using renewable energy sources, water and energy consumption, waste management, and pollution. Ahi and Searcy (2013) mentioned that managers should take into consideration many points while applying sustainability in a supply chain that includes efficient end-of-life product management, product reuse, product recovery, reverse logistics, and closed-loop supply chains.

Egypt is a developing country with huge activity on domestic and international levels. The Egyptian government has set 2030 sustainability goals to apply sustainability practices in different sectors and levels1[1].

Sustainable Development Strategies are considered to be a basic step in the march of country-wide development in Egypt, which links all organisations, companies, firms, and associations to achieve specific goals that serve the cooperate social responsibility (CSR) and sustainable development. Furthermore, they characterised the path of advantages and use of competitiveness. These strategies aim to guarantee a convenient and dignified life for the Egyptians by achieving their dreams. The Egyptian constitution's amendment targets the economy's growth through sustainable development and social fairness, and grantees balance between development and growth by taking into account the environmental dimension[2].

By applying sustainability goals in 2015 and 2030 with knowledge and creativity, Egypt will have a highly competitive, stable and balanced economy. It will also have social justice with stable ecosystems, taking advantage of human capabilities and resources to save quality life for Egyptians. All these aspects give the government hopes to put Egypt in highly-ranked positions among countries in these fields: "economic development indicators, fighting corruption, human development, markets' competitiveness, the quality of life and environmental protection". However, the Egyptian government and other organisations will face a lot of challenges in applying sustainability goals: creativity and innovation systems that are rare in our society; scarcity of natural resources, such as energy, land, and water; the negative effect on the environmental usage and weakness of human resource development "including population, health and education". Sustainability goals seek to adopt those challenges and find the best solutions to beat them in a way that keeps and does not affect the rights of the next generations.

The challenges that exist in the Egyptian environment are considered the map that is used to build the sustainable strategies' goals. Therefore, the next section will explain the main challenges briefly. One of the main goals was to extract the main challenges and their relationships with the private sector or the public sector. The classification of challenges has been divided into three main groups: the first one was related to resources (including human, natural, and financial resources), which means the availability of the resources to achieve sustainable goals; after that comes the infrastructure, which means each of the main fundamentals to reach the expected results, and finally the legislative environment, which is concerned with the natural relationships between parties and the constitutional law. The strategy also recognised some of the challenges facing foreign policy and national security, including internal situations, such as insecurity (terrorism, the problem of traffic, and security of citizens); food security; water security (low per capita, the lack of water necessary to increase the agricultural area); low economic growth and social justice (Nations 2016).

Egypt has developed 8 sustainability goals based on the United Nations sustainability goals 2030 which are(Ali, Melkonyan et al. 2021, Ali, Gruchmann et al. 2022):

1- Achieve a better quality of life for the Egyptian citizens.
2- Fairness and justice.
3- Social inclusion.
4- Competitive and diversified economy
5- knowledge
6- Innovation and scientific research.
7- Integrated and sustainable ecosystems
8- governance of the state and community institutions

Companies tended to follow environmental standards that would reduce pressure on environmental resources and use ecologically friendly products due to the increased environmental pollution, increased percentages of greenhouse gases, and the increased demand for the use of environmental resources. Furthermore, businesses agreed to implement these environmental criteria to perform exporting and importing processes, as some importing countries have prohibited importing products that contain harmful materials or do not follow ISO standards. EL ARABY Group, as one of the largest industrial and commercial corporations in Egypt, was encouraged to follow the new sustainability aspects. Toshiba has many international activities and practices to apply sustainability practices and reduce the amount of CO_2 emitted (see Figure 1). The figure indicates the amount of CO_2 emissions in the headquarter in Japan and also the other sites of Toshiba around the world. The company also has a vision related to environmental practices to be applied by 2050 (see Figure 2). Toshiba took the initiative of replacing the use of glass that contains a high percentage of lead with another, which is lead-free,e, and also replaced the use of Freon R22 with R 410, which is more environmentally friendly.

Data Collection

To gain the research data required for describing the challenges, consequences, and results gained from the shift to more environmentally friendly material in production, this case followed the qualitative approach. Interviews are one of the main tools of qualitative research. Interviews are interactive by talking to people, making it one of the most effective methods of gathering and collecting data; moreover, face-to-face interviews will provide the research with clear answers and allow the chance to go into more details. Miller and Crabtree (1999) stated that interviews are the most common communication method used among people. Semi-structured interviews have been conducted with experts in the ELARABY Group. Three online interviews were conducted with the head of the lighting technology sector at ELARABY Group Corporation, and the other two interviews were conducted with two experts from the Quality management department. Each interview lasted for nearly 45 minutes. The interviewee was asked about

Figure 1. CO2 emission at manufacturing sites. Source: https://www.toshibatec.com/company/csr/environment/process/energy.html

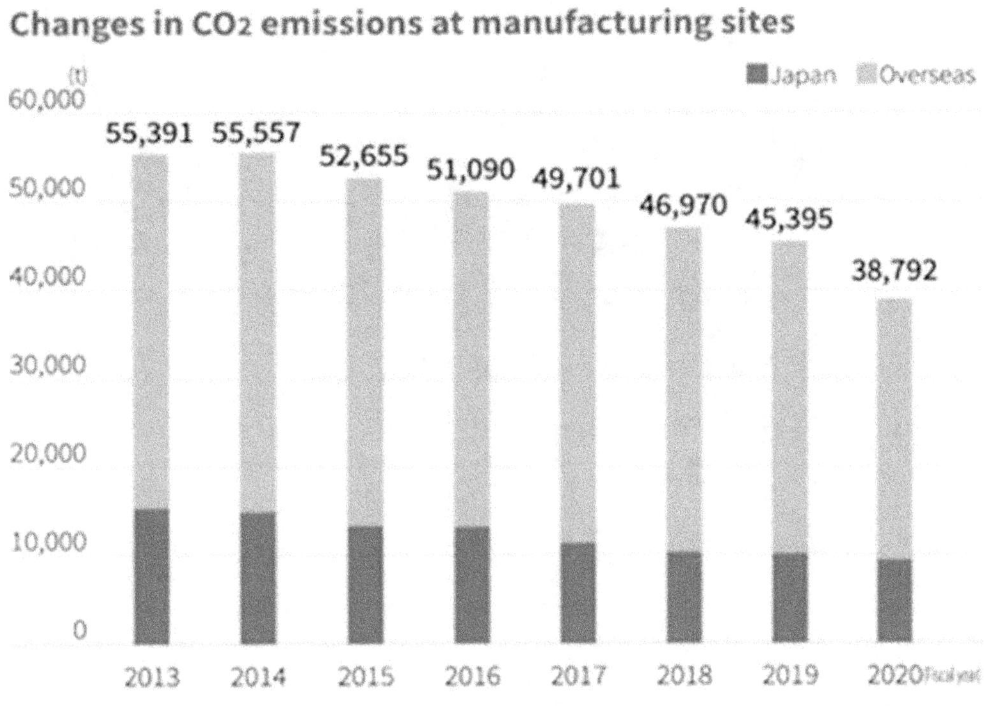

the main reasons that encouraged the company in the first place to use different materials, the materials used instead and their utilisation in products, challenges faced, results gained, and plans.

CASE DESCRIPTION

EL ARABY Group strives to implement continuous improvement plans within its companies and factories, including the use of environmentally friendly materials, as well as the continuous improvement of its employees and the development of their skills to deal with technological advancement and keep pace with local and international requirements.

Lead-Free Glass

Using Lead (Pb) in production has become restricted as various regulations admitted that, accordingly the term Lead (Pb)-Free" or "Pb-Free" has developed to be used in the electronics industry as the most suitable term to be compatible with these regulations. EL ARABY Group presents Lead (Pb)-Free to deal with the standards of the electronics industry "as no more than 0.1 percent Lead (Pb) by weight in Homogeneous Materials".

Electrical and Electronic Equipment (RoHS) Directive aims to decrease the risks to the environment and humans through using environmentally friendly materials, EL ARABY Group tries to follow the main rule of RoHS as the device must comprise no more than the maximum threshold level.

Figure 2. Environmental future vision. Source: https://www.toshibatec.com/company/csr/environment/vision/

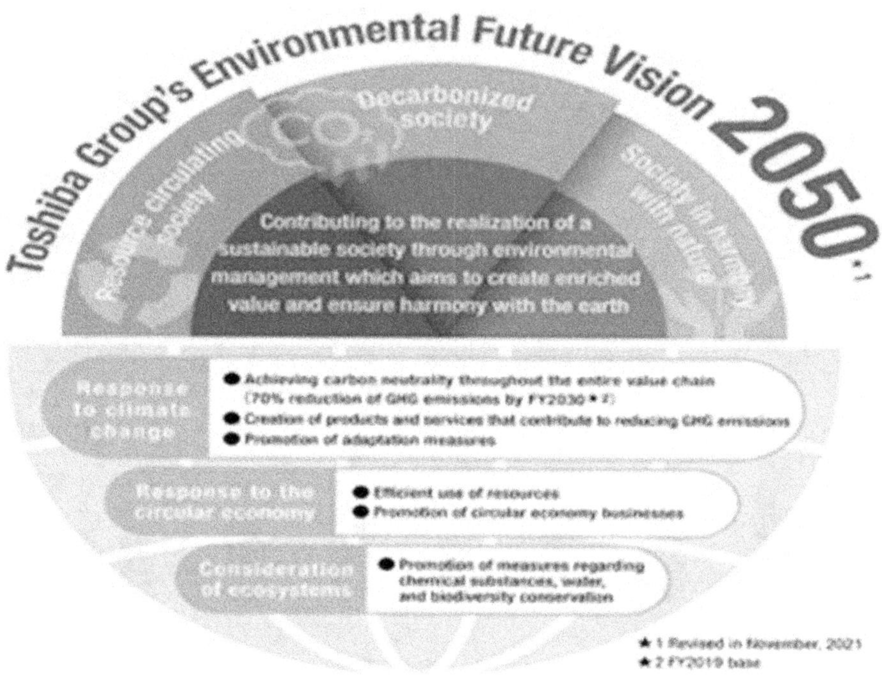

One of the most significant developments that ELARABY Group sought to implement in its factories was lead-free glass, rather than glass containing an amount of lead. Normal glass is one of the main raw materials that ELARABY Group uses to produce its products, as they melt the glass and reform it to use it in the production line. However, it has a huge negative impact on the environment; using lead increases CO2 emissions, emitting Nitrogen oxides (NOx) due to the high melting temperatures, and melting the glass leads to releasing particles into the atmosphere. Therefore, ELARABY Group was encouraged to use environmentally friendly glass (Lead-Free Glass).

Starting with the glass that contains lead, it is considered one of the most important products used in the manufacturing process of ELARABY Group products. Its easy shaping helped reduce defects in the product and increase products' productivity. However, if we look at the negative side of the glass that contains lead, it is considered one of the products that have harm and a negative impact on the environment, as lead and mercury are heavy metals (toxic), which are prohibited by Egyptian Law No. (94/4) that states the usage percentage of lead that should not be exceeded in the manufacturing process.

The United Nations Organization issued a set of goals, which is called the Sustainable Development Goals 2030, which encourage companies and business organisations to abandon the usage of harmful materials that harm the environment and use environmentally friendly ones. Thus, ELARABY Group began to make double efforts to implement environmentally friendly systems through the use of Lead-free glass in its production process to conform with international and local specifications, aiming to manufacture a product of high quality and comply with environmental standards, as the company is considered one of the leading exporters in Egypt.

Table 2. Challenges facing companies implementing green practices

Author(s)	Challenges	
(shedid, Hewedi, Mosaad, & Ali, 2022)	Lack of sustainable resources. Lack of sustainable audits and certifications.	A scarcity of long-term resources for implementing sustainable purchasing practices, like a lack of finding alternative green materials for the manufacturing process. Sustainable audits and certifications are few.
(Akbar & Ahsan, 2021) (Hasan & Zhang, 2016)	Cost and financial concerns.	Firms face significant challenges in keeping production costs to a minimum, and implementing sustainability initiatives requires significant initial investment and upfront costs.
(Luo, Chau, Fan, & Chen, 2021) (Mbasera & Plessis, 2017)	Lack of environmental awareness.	It can be challenging for businesses to embrace green practices if consumers, employees, and suppliers are not environmentally conscious.
(Hasan & Zhang, 2016) (Konys, 2019)	Limited availability of green suppliers and information.	The companies face a significant challenge in locating an alternative supplier who will provide them with green materials of high quality at reasonable prices.

Freon

Since the company is one of the most important companies in manufacturing electronic and industrial products, Freon is used in the production process of these products. Freon has many uses within the production processes in ELARABY Group, although it is important to note that Freon has a negative impact one way or another as it is very harmful to the environment and human health. Hence, the company had to take some measures and follow modern standards in changing this raw material to be environmentally friendly, as Toshiba has started following the requirements of organisations that call for the manufacture of environmentally friendly products, as well as the application of these standards within their products.

CURRENT CHALLENGES FACING THE ORGANISATION

Lead- Free Glass and Freon were the two most negative elements impacting the environment, so the company decided to go through these challenges and take a step forward to solve this problem. ELARABY Group faced many challenges due to the new steps that have been taken to adopt the new environmentally friendly materials, as many challenges exist in the industry, see Table 2. Firstly, supplier selection was one of the main obstacles, as the company sought to find the most suitable suppliers to provide it with the raw materials it needed. Secondly, the manufacturing process was challenging for the company, as the product needs special treatment while using it. The following section will illustrate in detail the main two obstacles.

Lead-Free Glass

In the process of converting from ordinary glass to lead-free glass, some obstacles and challenges appeared that hindered the purchase of the new product; the company began to take initiatives to overcome these challenges:

1. Supplier Selection

One of the most important obstacles ELARABY Group faces is the process of selecting a supplier who can provide lead-free glass with high quality and suitable price, attempting to avoid influencing the final price and product quality. This is due to the limited number of suppliers providing lead-free glass, unlike other suppliers who provide ordinary glass. As a result, the company began to search for suppliers through the Logistics Department, who are capable of supplying the environmentally friendly product, and it will have to reconsider the evaluation of the suppliers to ensure that the suppliers follow the same quality system as Toshiba, and to ensure if the new suppliers will carry out the product's examination procedures that the company demands and adheres to.

The company discovered a group of suppliers from countries that signed the (Mini Mata) agreement, which is a global agreement ratified by the United Nations and signed by 114 countries. The agreement forbids the use of any hazardous or non-environmentally friendly materials in a company's manufacturing processes. Japan was one of these countries that signed this agreement, and through it, Toshiba reached suppliers in Japan. However, there were some challenges and obstacles that faced the company in the beginning: the high cost of raw materials for this new product, first and foremost, and the scarcity of suppliers responsible for selling environmentally friendly materials, secondly.

The Japanese side implemented this policy of using environmentally friendly materials in their industries, and as a result, ELARABY Group Egypt, in collaboration with the parent company in Japan, held numerous meetings and interviews in Osaka, Tokyo, and Egypt, to use their expertise in the conversion process and the use of friendly applications. The Japanese side also presented methods for selecting suppliers by establishing various criteria for their selection (price, inspection, environmentally friendly materials and quality).

Initially, finding suitable suppliers was critical, but after a lengthy search, ELARABY Group discovered two suppliers in Japan and another in Seoul, South Korea. Dealing with them was complicated at first due to the high costs of raw materials and the logistics activities associated with them, such as transporting, storing, and packing, but a final agreement was reached between the two parties through negotiations.

2. Manufacturing Processes

The use of lead-free glass has become one of the basic requirements in the production of the company's products; however, to produce, the company must use some applications and replace some of the equipment used to produce this type of environmentally friendly product. Initially, the company faced many difficulties in production, which affected the quality of the final product, as well as its supply chain, and thus the final customer's satisfaction, as the damage from the use of these materials was estimated to be 15%. As a result, the company has undertaken some initiatives that would benefit the techniques used in production by utilising environmentally friendly materials. The company has hired a group of chemical engineering consultants to solve the crisis that the company encountered when using the new raw materials. This group of consultants has come up with new production procedures needed to manufacture the company's products, using the new environmentally friendly material; high heat to form the product, and distinctive fermentation and formation processes from the standard product.

Hence, the consultants delivered a series of lectures to train the workers on how to work with this type of raw material, shape it by incorporating it into manufacturing processes, and use the newly purchased machines and equipment.

Freon

Previously, the company was using Freon R22, which has a huge negative impact on the environment, but with the modern trend to protect the environment, the company began using Freon 410, but it turned out that this type of Freon also harms the environment but to a lesser degree than the first Freon R22. Despite its high price, the company makes a concentrated effort to use this type of Freon.

SOLUTIONS AND RECOMMENDATIONS

After using lead-free glass, ELARABY Group has become one of the leading companies in manufacturing by using this material and expanding using it into manufacturing other products. Moreover, the company achieved the best result, 1.5% waste, compared to the international loss, which is 9% percent, which is considered superior to Japanese factories and others. The company was also honoured by its main company in Japan for the achievement of approaching this level of production and for its capabilities of a successful transition from using environmentally harmful resources to other environmentally friendly materials. In addition to the previous achievements, other benefits were gained. The weight of the glass decreased by a large percentage, affecting the company's profitability, which increased by 18%, providing a high-quality product to the end customer despite the difficulties in dealing with this type of glass at first, lowering logistics costs and increasing productivity (if a kilo of ordinary glass yields seventy bulbs, a kilo of lead-free glass yields five hundred bulbs).

Through the research and development department, the company aims to reduce waste operations to be less than 1.5% by making the best use of resources, training workers, and producing a defect-free product with a competitive advantage.

The company decreased its negative impact on the environment to a lesser degree by using Freon 410 instead of Freon R22; however, still more efforts are required in the coming period in order to search for a better alternative with lower effects.

The company achieved a very critical part in their industrial operations. The authors have recommended points that should be taken into consideration for further research:

1- Increasing the awareness of sustainability and supply chain across the Egyptian organisations through presenting specialised training courses for the employees and workers.
2- Companies must take serious steps to adopt sustainability practices in their organisations, as (Bask, Halme et al. (2020)) stated that sustainability is a potential source of competitive advantage for companies.
3- The government should provide a financial incentive for producers who start using environmentally friendly materials.
4- For academics and researchers, the field of sustainability and supply chain needs more investigation in different sectors in Egypt.

CONCLUSION

Sustainable manufacturing strategies strive to maximize a company's production efficiency while reducing the environmental effects of manufacturing processes. Products are now evaluated based on the sustainable business practices adopted by companies rather than their pricing. Traditionally, efforts to lessen the negative environmental effects of manufacturing activities have been seen as a barrier to efficiency and profitability. However, research has shown that adopting sustainable manufacturing techniques is advantageous for businesses. (Nordin, Ashari, & Rajemi, 2014).

ELARABY Group is one of Egypt's leading electronic industry companies. Applying sustainability practices is the most priority of the ELARABY group. Using lead free-glass and using Freon, which has less CO2 emission on the environment, where the company's first step to take a green initiative. The initiation also sounded tempting at the beginning was not an easy task for a large organization as ELARABY group. New supplier selection criteria besides changes in manufacturing processes were some of the main obstacles. These obstacles are currently faced by many organizations.

Based on interviews, it could be concluded that manufacturing companies must always be ready with multiple supplier selection strategies/criteria to cope with the continuously changing environment. In addition, when applying new practices at the company, the top management must follow different strategies in order to reach the best offers. Moreover, companies need to. need to add value continuously to their products by considering the future organizations and customers trends and needs, and requirements.

Furthermore, they indicated that companies need to consider some factors while taking a new initiative such as cost, quality & safety, social responsibility, convenience/simplicity, risk and agility. They added that the successful of adopting green products in the manufacturing would be a successful for all supply chain partners starting from suppliers to the customers. Moreover, adopting green product successfully will also be reflected on the society and increase the quality of life.

On the other side, Organizations must continuously work on increasing employers' qualifications in order to be ready for any changes. Adopting adequate crisis management strategies are also equally important for companies' survival nowadays.

Applying the initiatives has led to increasing the company's performance, which agreed with the studies of Younis, Sundarakani et al. (2019) and Safa, Green et al. (2022). In addition, applying these practices would increase the cooperation with customers, suppliers and distribution partners regarding related environmental issues(Saeed, Rasheed et al. 2021). Moreover, using environmentally friendly materials will also improve the efficiency of manufacturing processes and enhance the customer satisfaction of ELARABY group. Kim, Lee et al. (2016) stated that using environmentally friendly materials will enhance the company's operation, which is also supported by Samad, Nilashi et al. (2021) and Lin (2022).

This study has been able to highlight four main strategies of sustainable manufacturing processes which are: 1. Sustainable material and design, 2. Responsive product strategy, 3. Lean practices, and 4. Supply chain restructuring. Using the data obtained by employing a semi-structured interview from the chosen case company, it could be concluded that:

1. Sustainable design and materials strategy refers to the usage of materials that don't harm the environment or potential customers. Sustainable design is cost-effective, accessible, and recyclable.
2. Responsive product strategy refers to Concentrating the company's efforts on providing goods with competitive components in terms of originality, adaptability, and continuous offerings.

3. Lean practices refer to reducing waste, boosting quality, and boosting productivity while continuously optimizing the entire business process from sourcing to delivery by equipping the workforce with improved sets of skills and experience.
4. Supply chain restructuring refer to globalization, the expansion of suppliers with manufacturing and service skills, and the availability of outsourcing.

Following the implementation of these four key tactics, any business will be able to:

- Advance in terms of certifications and compliance with environmental regulations as by integrating best practices, the company minimizes the need to later modify its operations to comply with newly proposed legislation.
- Reduce operations costs, one of the main barriers that prevent manufacturers from adopting sustainable practices is cost. They think that altering their production processes will increase their costs without offering them much in return. However, sustainable manufacturing practices advocate for a corporation to utilize fewer resources and generate less waste.
- Positively Affect the Environment as by using sustainable manufacturing techniques, you can preserve the planet's finite natural resources and aid the ecosystem in the long run.
- Enhance company's reputation.

REFERENCES

Ahi, P., & Searcy, C. (2013). A comparative literature analysis of definitions for green and sustainable supply chain management. *Journal of Cleaner Production*, *52*, 329–341. doi:10.1016/j.jclepro.2013.02.018

Ali, A. H., Gruchmann, T., & Melkonyan, A. (2022). Assessing the impact of sustainable logistics service quality on relationship quality: Survey-based evidence in Egypt. *Cleaner Logistics and Supply Chain*, *4*, 100036. doi:10.1016/j.clscn.2022.100036

Ali, A. H., Melkonyan, A., Noche, B., & Gruchmann, T. (2021). Developing a sustainable logistics service quality scale for logistics service providers in Egypt. *Logistics*, *5*(2), 21. doi:10.3390/logistics5020021

Antrim, L. N. (2019). The United Nations conference on environment and development. In The Diplomatic Record 1992-1993. Routledge.

Barbu, C. M., Logofătu, M., & Olari, C. (2019). ISO 26000: A Vital Vector in Interconnecting the Human Resource Management Standards. In ISO 26000-A Standardized View on Corporate Social Responsibility. Springer.

Bask, A., Halme, M., Kallio, M., & Kuula, M. (2020). Business students' value priorities and attitudes towards sustainable development. *Journal of Cleaner Production*, *264*, 121711. doi:10.1016/j.jclepro.2020.121711

Bielak, D., Bonini, S. M., & Oppenheim, J. M. (2007). CEOs on strategy and social issues. *The McKinsey Quarterly*, *4*, 1–8.

Brandenburg, M., Govindan, K., Sarkis, J., & Seuring, S. (2014). Quantitative models for sustainable supply chain management: Developments and directions. *European Journal of Operational Research, 233*(2), 299–312. doi:10.1016/j.ejor.2013.09.032

Carter, C. R., & Rogers, D. S. (2008). A framework of sustainable supply chain management: Moving toward new theory. *International Journal of Physical Distribution & Logistics Management, 38*(5), 360–387. doi:10.1108/09600030810882816

Chin, T. A., Tat, H. H., & Sulaiman, Z. (2015). Green supply chain management, environmental collaboration and sustainability performance. *Procedia CIRP, 26*, 695–699. doi:10.1016/j.procir.2014.07.035

Communities, C. E. (2009). *Communication from the Commission to the European Parliament, the Council, the European Economic and Social Committee and the Committee of the Regions: A Strategy for ICT R&D and Innovation in Europe: Raising the Game*. Office for Official Publications of the European Communities.

Di Foggia, G. (2021). Energy-efficient products and competitiveness in the manufacturing sector. *Journal of Open Innovation, 7*(1), 33. doi:10.3390/joitmc7010033

Evans, N., & Sawyer, J. (2010). CSR and stakeholders of small businesses in regional South Australia. *Social Responsibility Journal, 6*(3), 433–451. doi:10.1108/17471111011064799

Frederiksen, C. S., Pedersen, D. B., Nielsen, M. E. J., & Idowu, S. O. (2021). Corporate Social Indices: Refining the Global Reporting Initiative. In Global Challenges to CSR and Sustainable Development. Springer.

Fritz, M., Ruel, S., Kallmuenzer, A., & Harms, R. (2021). Sustainability management in supply chains: The role of familiness. *Technological Forecasting and Social Change, 173*(C), 121078. doi:10.1016/j.techfore.2021.121078

Fritz, M. M., Schöggl, J.-P., & Baumgartner, R. J. (2017). Selected sustainability aspects for supply chain data exchange: Towards a supply chain-wide sustainability assessment. *Journal of Cleaner Production, 141*, 587–607. doi:10.1016/j.jclepro.2016.09.080

Hix, S., & Høyland, B. (2022). *The political system of the European Union*. Bloomsbury Publishing.

Hjort, Skobelev, Almgren, Guseva, & Koh. (2019). Best available techniques and sustainable development goals. *International Multidisciplinary Scientific GeoConference: SGEM, 19*(4.2), 185-192.

Kim, J., Lee, W. J., & Park, H. W. (2016). The state of the art in the electron beam manufacturing processes. *International Journal of Precision Engineering and Manufacturing, 17*(11), 1575–1585. doi:10.100712541-016-0184-8

Korhonen, J. (2020). *The circular economy as a complex adaptive system. In Handbook of the circular economy*. Edward Elgar Publishing.

Li, G., Li, W., Jin, Z., & Wang, Z. (2019). Influence of environmental concern and knowledge on households' willingness to purchase energy-efficient appliances: A case study in Shanxi, China. *Sustainability, 11*(4), 1073. doi:10.3390u11041073

Lin, H.-F. (2022). IT resources and quality attributes: The impact on electronic green supply chain management implementation and performance. *Technology in Society*, *68*, 101833. doi:10.1016/j.techsoc.2021.101833

Malthus, T. R. (1872). *An Essay on the Principle of Population*. Academic Press.

Nations, U. (2016). *Sustainable development goals knowledge platform*. Academic Press.

Nkrumah, S. K., Asamoah, D., Annan, J., & Agyei-Owusu, B. (2020). Examining green capabilities as drivers of green supply chain management adoption. *Management Research Review*.

Płotka-Wasylka, J., & Wojnowski, W. (2021). Complementary green analytical procedure index (ComplexGAPI) and software. *Green Chemistry*, *23*(21), 8657–8665. doi:10.1039/D1GC02318G

Saeed, A., Rasheed, F., Waseem, M., & Tabash, M. I. (2021). Green human resource management and environmental performance: The role of green supply chain management practices. *Benchmarking*.

Safa, M., Green, K. W., Zelbst, P. J., & Sower, V. E. (2022). Enhancing Supply Chain through Implementation of Key IIoT Technologies. *Journal of Computer Information Systems*, 1–11. doi:10.1080/08874417.2022.2067792

Salonitis, K., & Ball, P. (2013). Energy efficient manufacturing from machine tools to manufacturing systems. *Procedia CIRP*, *7*, 634–639. doi:10.1016/j.procir.2013.06.045

Samad, S., Nilashi, M., Almulihi, A., Alrizq, M., Alghamdi, A., Mohd, S., Ahmadi, H., & Azhar, S. N. F. S. (2021). Green Supply Chain Management practices and impact on firm performance: The moderating effect of collaborative capability. *Technology in Society*, *67*, 101766. doi:10.1016/j.techsoc.2021.101766

Seow, Y., & Rahimifard, S. (2011). A framework for modelling energy consumption within manufacturing systems. *CIRP Journal of Manufacturing Science and Technology*, *4*(3), 258–264. doi:10.1016/j.cirpj.2011.03.007

Studer, S., Welford, R., & Hills, P. (2006). Engaging Hong Kong businesses in environmental change: Drivers and barriers. *Business Strategy and the Environment*, *15*(6), 416–431. doi:10.1002/bse.516

Weiss, R. S. (1994). *Learning from strangers: The art and method of qualitative interview studies*. Free Press, Inc.

Welford, R. (2016). *Corporate environmental management 3: Towards sustainable development*. Routledge.

White, L., & Lee, G. J. (2009). Operational research and sustainable development: Tackling the social dimension. *European Journal of Operational Research*, *193*(3), 683–692. doi:10.1016/j.ejor.2007.06.057

Winter, M., & Knemeyer, A. M. (2013). Exploring the integration of sustainability and supply chain management. *International Journal of Physical Distribution & Logistics Management*, *43*(1), 18–38. doi:10.1108/09600031311293237

Wurzel, R. K., Liefferink, D., & Di Lullo, M. (2019). The European Council, the Council and the Member States: Changing environmental leadership dynamics in the European Union. *Environmental Politics*, *28*(2), 248–270. doi:10.1080/09644016.2019.1549783

Younis, Sundarakani, & O'Mahony. (2019). *Green supply chain management and corporate performance: Developing a roadmap for future research using a mixed method approach*. Academic Press.

ENDNOTE

1 https://www.mped.gov.eg/EgyptVision?lang=en

Compilation of References

Abate, M., Vierth, I., Karlsson, R., de Jong, G., & Baak, J. (2019). A disaggregate stochastic freight transport model for Sweden. *Transportation, 46*(3), 671-696. http://dx.doi.org.libaccess.hud.ac.uk/10.1007/s11116-018-9856-9

Abd Elsalam, S. R. (2021). *Measuring transparency in the Egyptian pharmaceutical system.* Academic Press.

Abdalla, S. S., & Nakagawa, K. (2022, March). Entrepreneurial Leadership, Supply Chain Innovation, and Adaptability: A Cross-national Investigation. *Operations Research Forum, 3*(1), 1–21. doi:10.100743069-022-00135-x

Abdelbary, I. (2021). *Reviving Arab Reform: Development Challenges and Opportunities.* Emerald Group Publishing. doi:10.1108/9781839823183

Abdelbary, I., & Benhin, J. (2019). The Economic Reform and Political Transitions: Potentials and Challenges of Arab Development. In P. W. Zgheib (Ed.), *Impacts of political instability on economics in the MENA region* (pp. 145–184). IGI Global. doi:10.4018/978-1-5225-8247-2.ch006

Abd-elsalam, K. A. (2021). *Zinc-Based Nanostructures for Environmental and Agricultural Applications.* https://www.bookdepository.com

Abegunde, O. (2020). *Understanding the sector impact of COVID-19 Oil and Gas.* www.deloitte.com.ng

Abidi, H., Dullaert, W., De Leeuw, S., Lysko, D., & Klumpp, M. (2019). Strategic partner evaluation criteria for logistics service provider networks. *International Journal of Logistics Management, 30*(2), 438–466. doi:10.1108/IJLM-07-2017-0178

Aboualmal, A. (2018). *Artificial Intelligence for IoT & Smart Cities.* Academic Press.

Adams, T. M., Bekkem, K. R., & Toledo-Durán, E. J. (2012). Freight resilience measures. *Journal of Transportation Engineering, 138*(11), 1403–1409. doi:10.1061/(ASCE)TE.1943-5436.0000415

Aday, S., & Aday, M. S. (2020). Impact of COVID-19 on the food supply chain. *Food Quality and Safety, 4*(4), 167–180. doi:10.1093/fqsafe/fyaa024

Agamez-Arias, A., & Moyano-Fuentes, J. (2017). Intermodal Transport in Freight Distribution: A Literature Review. *Transport Reviews, 37*(6), 782–807. doi:10.1080/01441647.2017.1297868

Agility. (2018). *Agility is First Forwarder to Work with Maersk IBM on Blockchain Solution.* Agility. https://www.agility.com/en/agility-first-forwarder-work-maersk-ibm-blockchain-solution/

Agility. (2022a). *About Us.* Agility Logistics. https://www.agility.com/en/about-agility-3pl-company/

Agility. (2022b). *Supply Chain Services and Innovation.* Agility. https://www.agility.com/en/

Ahi, P., & Searcy, C. (2013). A comparative literature analysis of definitions for green and sustainable supply chain management. *Journal of Cleaner Production*, *52*, 329–341. doi:10.1016/j.jclepro.2013.02.018

Akbar, I., Muzaffar, M., & Cheema, K. (2012). Entrepreneurial supply chain management competence: performance of manufacturing small and medium enterprises. *Available at SSRN 2386969.*

Akbari, M. (2018). Logistics outsourcing: A structured literature review. *Benchmarking*, *25*(5), 1548–1580. doi:10.1108/BIJ-04-2017-0066

Akbari, M., Didehkhani, H., Shojaei, S., & Mehrabian, A. (2021). Designing an Entrepreneurial Supply Chain Model during Disasters in Iran. *Quarterly Scientific Journal of Rescue and Relief*, *13*(1), 9–15.

Akinboro, S., Adeyiga, J., Omotosho, A., & Akinwunmi, A. (2017). Mobile road traffic management system using weighted sensors. *International Journal of Interactive Mobile Technologies*, *11*(5), 147–160. doi:10.3991/ijim.v11i5.6745

Al-Abaid, S. A. F. (2020). A Smart Traffic Control System Using Image Processing: A Review. *Journal of Southwest Jiaotong University*, *55*(1), 31. doi:10.35741/issn.0258-2724.55.1.31

Alavi, A. H., Jiao, P., Buttlar, W. G., & Lajnef, N. (2018). Internet of Things-enabled smart cities: State-of-the-art and future trends. *Measurement: Journal of the International Measurement Confederation*, *129*(July), 589–606. doi:10.1016/j.measurement.2018.07.067

Al-Badri, I. (2021). *alahramgate*. https://gate.ahram.org.eg/News/2807065.aspx

Albertzeth, G., Pujawan, I. N., Hilletofth, P., & Tjahjono, B. (2020). Mitigating transportation disruptions in a supply chain: A cost-effective strategy. *International Journal of Logistics Research and Applications*, *23*(2), 139–158. doi:10.1080/13675567.2019.1648640

Al-Dhaafri, H. S., & Al-Swidi, A. (2016). The impact of total quality management and entrepreneurial orientation on organisational performance. *International Journal of Quality & Reliability Management*, *33*(5). Advance online publication. doi:10.1108/IJQRM-03-2014-0034

Algamili, A. S., Khir, M. H. M., Dennis, J. O., Ahmed, A. Y., Alabsi, S. S., Ba Hashwan, S. S., & Junaid, M. M. (2021). A Review of Actuation and Sensing Mechanisms in MEMS-Based Sensor Devices. *Nanoscale Research Letters*, *16*(1), 16. Advance online publication. doi:10.118611671-021-03481-7 PMID:33496852

Al-Hakimi, M. A., & Borade, D. B. (2020). The impact of entrepreneurial orientation on the supply chain resilience. *Cogent Business & Management*, *7*(1), 1847990. doi:10.1080/23311975.2020.1847990

Al-Hammouri, A. T., Liberatore, V., Al-Omari, H., Al-Qudah, Z., Branicky, M. S., & Agrawal, D. (2007). A co-simulation platform for actuator networks. International Conference on Embedded Networked Sensor Systems. https://doi.org/10.1145/1322263.1322306

Ali, A. H., Gruchmann, T., & Melkonyan, A. (2022). Assessing the impact of sustainable logistics service quality on relationship quality: Survey-based evidence in Egypt. *Cleaner Logistics and Supply Chain*, *4*, 100036. doi:10.1016/j.clscn.2022.100036

Ali, A. H., Melkonyan, A., Noche, B., & Gruchmann, T. (2021). Developing a sustainable logistics service quality scale for logistics service providers in Egypt. *Logistics*, *5*(2), 21. doi:10.3390/logistics5020021

Almurisi, S. H., Al Khalidi, D., Al-Japairai, K. A., Mahmood, S., Chilakamarry, C. R., Kadiyala, C. B. N., & Mohananaidu, K. (2020). *Impact of COVID 19 Pandemic Crisis on the Health System and Pharmaceutical Industry*. Academic Press.

Aly, H. (2019). *Low power IoT based automated manhole cover monitoring system as a smart city application.* http://search.ebscohost.com/login.aspx?direct=true&db=ddu&AN=035B68D36D29E1CB&site=ehost-live

Alyavina, E., Nikitas, A., & Tchouamou Njoya, E. (2020). Mobility as a service and sustainable travel behavior: A thematic analysis study. s.l. *Transportation Research Part F: Traffic Psychology and Behaviour, 73*, 362–381. doi:10.1016/j.trf.2020.07.004

Amanor-Boadu, V., Marletta, P., & Biere, A. W. (2009). Entrepreneurial supply chains and strategic collaboration: The case of Bagòss Cheese in Bagolino, Italy. *International Food and Agribusiness Management Review, 12*, 49-68.

AmCham Egypt. (2020). *COVID-19 Impacts on Egypt's Transportation Sector.* AmCham Egypt. https://www.amcham.org.eg/information-resources/covid-19-response/covid-19-impacts-on-egypts-transportation-sector

AmCham. (2020a). *COVID-19 Impacts on Egypt's Petroleum Sector.* AmCham Egypt. https://www.amcham.org.eg/information-resources/covid-19-response/impacts-of-covid-19-pandemic-on-egypts-petroleum-secto r

AmCham. (2020b). *Impacts of COVID-19 Pandemic on Egypt's Petroleum Sector.* Author.

Anand, H., & Singh, B. (2021). Piezoelectric energy generation in India: An empirical investigation. *Energy Harvesting and Systems., 1*(3-4), 1–8. doi:10.1515/ehs-2020-0002

Anca, V. (2019). Logistics and Supply Chain Management: An Overview. *Studies in Business and Economics, 14*(2), 209–215. doi:10.2478be-2019-0035

Anderson, J. M., Kalra, N., Stanley, K. D., Sorensen, P., Samaras, C., & Oluwatola, O. A. (2014). Brief History and Current State of Autonomous Vehicles. *Autonomous Vehicle Technology: A Guide for Policymakers*, 55-74. https://www.jstor.org/stable/10.7249/j.ctt5hhwgz

Angerholzer, M., III, Mahaffee, D., Vale, M., Kitfield, J., & Renner, H. (2017). *The Autonomous Vehicle Revolution: Fostering Innovation with Smart Regulation.* http://www.thepresidency.org/sites/default/files/pdf/The Autonomous Vehicle Revolution—Fostering Innovation with Smart Regulation.compressed.pdf%0Ahttps://trid.trb.org/view/1491418

Angert, S. (2019). *Blockchain technology implementation in the US customs environment.* Naval Postgraduate School. Retrieved from apps.dtic.mil/sti/pdfs/AD1086921.pdf

Antrim, L. N. (2019). The United Nations conference on environment and development. In The Diplomatic Record 1992-1993. Routledge.

Arabia, S. (2020). *The Impact of COVID-19 on Natural Gas Markets.* Academic Press.

Araújo, N., Pacheco, V., & Costa, L. (2021). Smart Additive Manufacturing: The Path to the Digital Value Chain. *Technologies, 9*(4), 88. doi:10.3390/technologies9040088

Arentze, T., Feng, T., Timmermans, H., & Robroeks, J. (2012). Context-dependent influence of road attributes and pricing policies on route choice behavior of truck drivers: Results of a conjoint choice experiment. *Transportation, 39*(6), 1173–1188. doi:10.100711116-012-9391-z

Arlbjørn, J. S., De Haas, H., Mikkelsen, O. S., & Zachariassen, F. (2010). *Supply chain management.* Academica.

Armor, D. A., & Taylor, S. E. (2003). The effects of mindset on behavior: Self-regulation in deliberative and implemental frames of mind. *Personality and Social Psychology Bulletin*, *29*(1), 86–95. doi:10.1177/0146167202238374 PMID:15272962

Armstrong, A. (2013). *Transport Purchasing and Environmental Impacts*. http://www.diva-portal.org/smash/get/diva2:1309436/FULLTEXT01.pdf

Arshinder, K., Kanda, A., & Deshmukh, S. G. (2011). A review on supply chain coordination: coordination mechanisms, managing uncertainty and research directions. In *Supply chain coordination under uncertainty*. Springer. doi:10.1007/978-3-642-19257-9_3

Asariotis, W. J. R., Assaf, M., Ayala, G., Ayoub, A., Benamara, H., Chantrel, D., Hoffmann, J., Larouche-Maltais, A., Premti, A., Rodríguez, L., Sun, S., Youssef, F., Abbas, H., Bradford, G., Cariou, P., Crowe, T., Davidson, N., Manuel, J., Orejas, D., … Verhoeven, P. (2020). *Review of Maritime Transport 2020*. Academic Press.

Ashraf, M., Caruso, P., & Pensado, P. G. G. (2020). *Reinventing the oil and gas industry: compounded disruption*. World Economic Forum. https://www.weforum.org/agenda/2020/09/reinventing-the-oil-and-gas-industry-compounded-disruption/

ASI Sealants and Adhesives Industry. (2021). *H.B. Fuller to Build New Facility in Egypt*. Retrieved from: www.adhesivesmag.com/articles/98765-hb-fuller-to-build-new-facility-in-egypt

Assaad, R. (2020). *Prospects for Egypt's Population and Labor Force: 2000 to 2050*. Economic Research Forum.

Auer, A., Feese, S., & Lockwood, S. (2016). History of Intelligent Transportation Systems. Intelligent Vehicle Systems Joint Program Office, 1–56.

Aulet, W., & Murray, F. (2013). A tale of two entrepreneurs: Understanding differences in the types of entrepreneurship in the economy. *Available at SSRN 2259740*.

Averre, D., & Davies, L. (2015). Russia, humanitarian intervention and the Responsibility to Protect: The case of Syria. *International Affairs*, *91*(4), 813–834. doi:10.1111/1468-2346.12343

Awad, E. (2021). *Measuring logistics performance in ports: a case of Alexandria in Egypt*. World Maritime University Dissertations. 1678. Retrieved from https://commons.wmu.se/all_dissertations/1678

Ayati, N., Saiyarsarai, P., & Nikfar, S. (2020). Short and long term impacts of COVID-19 on the pharmaceutical sector. *Daru: Journal of Faculty of Pharmacy, Tehran University of Medical Sciences*, *28*(2), 799–805. doi:10.100740199-020-00358-5 PMID:32617864

Bachar, Y. (2004). Developing Controllers for Biped Humanoid Locomotion. *Science*, 1–137. http://citeseerx.ist.psu.edu/viewdoc/download?doi=10.1.1.66.2645&rep=rep1&type=pdf

Bahlol, M. M., & Lagutkina, T. P. (2016). Pharmaceutical marketing communication tools and company activities orientation. In Актуальные вопросы медицины в современных условиях (pp. 179-182). Academic Press.

Bahlol, M., & Dewey, R. S. (2021). Pandemic preparedness of community pharmacies for COVID-19. *Research in Social & Administrative Pharmacy*, *17*(1), 1888–1896. doi:10.1016/j.sapharm.2020.05.009 PMID:32417070

Baker, W. E., & Sinkula, J. M. (2009). The complementary effects of market orientation and entrepreneurial orientation on profitability in small businesses. *Journal of Small Business Management*, *47*(4), 443–464. doi:10.1111/j.1540-627X.2009.00278.x

Balcerzak, A. P., Nica, E., Rogalska, E., Poliak, M., Kliestik, T., & Sabie, O. M. (2022). Blockchain Technology and Smart Contracts in Decentralised Governance Systems. *Administrative Sciences, 12*(3), 96. doi:10.3390/admsci12030096

Balci, G. (2021). Digitalization in container shipping: Do perception and satisfaction regarding digital products in a non-technology industry affect overall customer loyalty? *Technological Forecasting and Social Change, 172*, 121016. doi:10.1016/j.techfore.2021.121016

Barabandi, B. (2021). *Shifting Stakeholder Positions & Conflict Resolution in Syria*. Retrieved from https://newlinesinstitute.org/syria/shifting-stakeholder-positions-conflict-resolution-in-syria/

Barbu, C. M., Logofătu, M., & Olari, C. (2019). ISO 26000: A Vital Vector in Interconnecting the Human Resource Management Standards. In ISO 26000-A Standardized View on Corporate Social Responsibility. Springer.

Barot, H. (2015). Entrepreneurship–A Key to Success. *International Journal of Business and Management, 3*(1), 163–165.

BARQ. (2021). *Fast and flexible delivery*. https://www.barqfleet.com

Barshikar, R. (2020). Covid 19–Impact and new normal for pharmaceutical industry (Part–I). *Journal of Genetic Medicine, 16*(3), 112–119.

Barua, A., & Mani, D. (2014). Augmenting conflict resolution with informational response: A holistic view of governance choice in business process outsourcing. *Journal of Management Information Systems, 31*(3), 72–105. doi:10.1080/07421222.2014.995530

Bask, A., Halme, M., Kallio, M., & Kuula, M. (2020). Business students' value priorities and attitudes towards sustainable development. *Journal of Cleaner Production, 264*, 121711. doi:10.1016/j.jclepro.2020.121711

Bauer, M., Sanchez, L., & Song, J. (2021). Iot-enabled smart cities: Evolution and outlook. *Sensors (Basel), 21*(13), 1–29. doi:10.339021134511 PMID:34209436

Bavassano, G., Ferrari, C., & Tei, A. (2020). Blockchain: How the shipping industry is dealing with the ultimate technological leap. *Research in Transportation Business & Management, 34*. doi:10.1016/j.rtbm.2020.100428

Bawack, R. E., & Kala Kamdjoug, J. R. (2022). (Preprint). Managing client–consultant relationships to derive benefits from ERP projects. *Information Technology & People*. Advance online publication. doi:10.1108/ITP-07-2021-0573

Becker, A., & Caldwell, M. R. (2015). Stakeholder perceptions of seaport resilience strategies: A case study of Gulfport (Mississippi) and Providence (Rhode Island). *Coastal Management, 43*(1), 1–34. doi:10.1080/08920753.2014.983422

Belu, M. G. (2020). Blockchain Technology and Customs Procedures. *Romanian Economic Journal, 23*(78), 13–26.

Benevolo, C., Dameri, R., & D'auria, B. (2016). Smart mobility in a smart city. In Empowering organizations. doi:10.1007/978-3-319-23784-8_2

Bertini, C. (2016). *U.N. Struggles To Reach Besieged Areas Of Syria With Aid Air Drop Plan/Interviewer: M. Kelemen*. NPR.

Bezerra, B. (2019). Road Safety and Sustainable Development. *CHAP*, 1-13.

Bielak, D., Bonini, S. M., & Oppenheim, J. M. (2007). CEOs on strategy and social issues. *The McKinsey Quarterly, 4*, 1–8.

Blackhurst, J., Wu, T. T., & Craighead, C. W. (2008). A systematic approach for supply chain conflict detection with a hierarchical Petri Net extension. *Omega, 36*(5), 680–696. doi:10.1016/j.omega.2006.02.001

Blecker, T. (Ed.). (2014). Innovative methods in logistics and supply chain management: Current issues and emerging practices (Vol. 19). epubli.

Blunt, R., Thomson, P., & Bory, O. (2020). *International: The Impact of COVID-19 on the Oil & Gas Industry.* Baker McKenzie InsightPlus. https://insightplus.bakermckenzie.com/bm/energy-mining-infrastructure_1/international-the-impact-of-covid-19-on-the-oil-gas-industry_2

BMI Research. (2019). *Egypt Pharmaceuticals and Healthcare Report.* https://nationsemergentes.org/wp-content/uploads/2019/02/egypt-pharmaceutical

Bolumole, Y. A., Grawe, S. J., & Daugherty, P. J. (2016). Customer service responsiveness in logistics outsourcing contracts: The influence of job autonomy and role clarity among on-site representatives. *Transportation Journal, 55*(2), 124–148. doi:10.5325/transportationj.55.2.0124

Boulet-Desbareau, P. (2016). *Underground humanitarian logistics in Syria: the invisible driving force of medical care in besieged areas.* Retrieved from http://emergency-log.weebly.com/uploads/2/5/2/4/25246358/ehl_in_syria-jul16.pdf

Brandenburg, M., Govindan, K., Sarkis, J., & Seuring, S. (2014). Quantitative models for sustainable supply chain management: Developments and directions. *European Journal of Operational Research, 233*(2), 299–312. doi:10.1016/j.ejor.2013.09.032

Breisinger, C., Raouf, M., Wiebelt, M., Kamaly, A., & Karara, M. (2020). *Impact of COVID-19 on the Egyptian economy: Economic sectors, jobs, and households* (Vol. 6). Intl Food Policy Res Inst.

Bressanelli, G., Perona, M., & Saccani, N. (2019). Challenges in supply chain redesign for the Circular Economy: A literature review and a multiple case study. *International Journal of Production Research, 57*(23), 7395–7422. doi:10.1080/00207543.2018.1542176

Brettmo, A., & Williamsson, J. (2020). The Role of 'Influencers' as Drivers of a More Sustainable Urban Freight Sector. *Sustainability, 12*(7), 2850. doi:10.3390u12072850

BSI. (2018). *BSI & TT Club Cargo Theft Report H1 2018.* Available at: https://www.ttclub.com/fileadmin/uploads/tt-club/Documents/BSI_TT_ClubCargoTheftReportH1_2018_FinalRev.pdf

BSI. (2020). *BSI and TT Club Cargo Theft Report 2020.* Available at: bsigroup.com/supplychain.

Bull. (2017). *Traffic congestion: the problem and how to deal with it.* ECLAC.

Burges, D. (2012). *Cargo Theft, Loss Prevention, and Supply Chain Security.* Available at: https://books.google.com.eg/books?hl=ar&lr=&id=Fk2AK3pAkQkC&oi=fnd&pg=PP1&dq=cargo+theft+crime+pdf+&ots=9XITY3QrO_&sig=24TV_SYzP53cU-0snsGDnJZQjUM&redir_esc=y#v=onepage&q&f=false

Burges, D. (2013). Truckload Theft. *Cargo Theft, Loss Prevention, and Supply Chain Security*, 17–33. . doi:10.1016/B978-0-12-416007-1.00002-9

Burks, A., & Davidson, E. (1999). Introduction to "The ENIAC.". *Proceedings of the IEEE, 87*(6), 1028–1030. doi:10.1109/jproc.1999.763315

Buyukozkan, G., & Gocer, F. (2018). Digital Supply Chain: Literature review and a proposed framework for future research. *Computers in Industry*, *97*, 157–177. doi:10.1016/j.compind.2018.02.010

Cai, J., Cheng, J., Shi, H., & Feng, T. (2022). The impact of organisational conflict on green supplier integration: The moderating role of governance mechanism. *International Journal of Logistics Research and Applications*, *25*(2), 143–160. doi:10.1080/13675567.2020.1818198

Calia, E., & D'Aprile, D. (2020). Industry 4.0. *Analytics for the Sharing Economy: Mathematics, Engineering and Business Perspectives*, 309–333. doi:10.1007/978-3-030-35032-1_18

Caliskan, A., & Ozturkoglu, Y. (2016). Maritime logistics. In Handbook of Research on Military, Aeronautical, and Maritime Logistics and Operations (pp. 361–384). IGI Global. doi:10.4018/978-1-4666-9779-9.ch019

Cano-Olivos, P., Sánchez-Partida, D., Caballero-Morales, S.-O., & Martínez-Flores, J.-L. (2022). Strategies that Improve the Performance of the Humanitarian Supply Chain. In *Humanitarian Logistics from the Disaster Risk Reduction Perspective* (pp. 119-140). Springer.

Capmas. (2020). *Central Agency for Public Mobilization and Statistics*. https://www.capmas.gov.eg/

CAPMAS. (2021). *The annual bulletin results of car and train accidents*. Central Agency for Public Mobilization and Statistics.

Carlan, V., Sys, C., & Vanelslander, T. (2019). Innovation in road freight transport: Quantifying the environmental performance of operational cost-reducing practices. *Sustainability*, *11*(8), 2212. doi:10.3390u11082212

Carter, C. R., & Rogers, D. S. (2008). A framework of sustainable supply chain management: Moving toward new theory. *International Journal of Physical Distribution & Logistics Management*, *38*(5), 360–387. doi:10.1108/09600030810882816

CBP. (2022). *ACE Automated Broker Interface (ABI)*. CBP and Trade Automated Interface Requirements (CATAIR). Retrieved from www.cbp.gov/trade/ace/catair

CEIC. (2020). *Egypt Container Port Throughput, 2008 – 2022*. CEIC Data. https://www.ceicdata.com/en/indicator/egypt/container-port-throughput

Çelik, M., Ergun, Ö., Johnson, B., Keskinocak, P., Lorca, Á., Pekgün, P., & Swann, J. (2012). *Humanitarian logistics New directions in informatics, optimisation, logistics, and production*. INFORMS.

Chaghooshi, A. J., & Hajimaghsoudi, M. (2014). Reducing the risk of transportation disruption in the supply chain: Integration of FUZZY-AHP and TOPSIS. *Global Journal of Management Studies and Researches*, *1*(1), 1–9.

Chan, H. K., & Chan, F. T. (2010). Comparative study of adaptability and flexibility in distributed manufacturing supply chains. *Decision Support Systems*, *48*(2), 331–341. doi:10.1016/j.dss.2009.09.001

Charles, H. K. (2005). Miniaturized electronics. *Johns Hopkins APL Technical Digest*, *26*(4), 402–413.

Chataut, R., & Akl, R. (2020). Massive MIMO systems for 5G and beyond networks—Overview, recent trends, challenges, and future research direction. *Sensors (Switzerland)*, *20*(10), 1–35. doi:10.339020102753 PMID:32408531

Cheese, P. (2016). Managing risk and building resilient organizations in a riskier world. *Journal of Organizational Effectiveness: People and Performance*.

Chen, H.-P., & Ni, Y.-Q. (2018). Introduction to Structural Health Monitoring. *Structural Health Monitoring of Large Civil Engineering Structures,* 1–14. doi:10.1002/9781119166641.ch1

Chen, Y., Liu, Y., & Wang, D. (2020). Impact of COVID-19 on the global steel industry. *Journal of Cleaner Production*, 121738.

Chen, Y., & Xie, J. (2008). Online consumer review: Word-of-mouth as a new element of marketing communication mix. *Management Science*, *54*(3), 477–491. doi:10.1287/mnsc.1070.0810

Cherian, T. M., & SJ, C. J. A. (2021). Digital Transformation in Supply Chain Management: A conceptual framework for construction industry. *Indian Journal of Economics and Business*, *20*(3), 1167–1187.

Chin, T. A., Tat, H. H., & Sulaiman, Z. (2015). Green supply chain management, environmental collaboration and sustainability performance. *Procedia CIRP*, *26*, 695–699. doi:10.1016/j.procir.2014.07.035

Choo, E. K., & Rajkumar, S. V. (2020, June). Medication shortages during the COVID-19 crisis: What we must do. *Mayo Clinic Proceedings*, *95*(6), 1112–1115. doi:10.1016/j.mayocp.2020.04.001 PMID:32312491

Chopra, S., & Meindl, P. (2007). Supply chain management. Strategy, planning & operation. In *Das summa summarum des management* (pp. 265–275). Gabler. doi:10.1007/978-3-8349-9320-5_22

Chowdhury, P., Paul, S. K., Kaisar, S., & Moktadir, M. A. (2021). COVID-19 pandemic related supply chain studies: A systematic review. *Transportation Research Part E, Logistics and Transportation Review*, *148*, 102271. doi:10.1016/j.tre.2021.102271 PMID:33613082

Christopher, D., & Fredrick, K. (2019). *Investigative analysis of CRM system implementation and the challenges attached to its integration into the existing ERP system From an organization perspective: A case study of a Freight Forwarding Company in Sweden*. Academic Press.

Christopher, M., & Jüttner, U. (2000). Developing strategic partnerships in the supply chain: A practitioner perspective. *European Journal of Purchasing & Supply Management*, *6*(2), 117–127. doi:10.1016/S0969-7012(99)00038-6

Clover, M. (2021). *The Future Of Freight Forwarding In A Post-Covid World Survey*. Bolloré Logistics.

Communities, C. E. (2009). *Communication from the Commission to the European Parliament, the Council, the European Economic and Social Committee and the Committee of the Regions: A Strategy for ICT R&D and Innovation in Europe: Raising the Game*. Office for Official Publications of the European Communities.

Covin, J. G., & Slevin, D. P. (1989). Strategic management of small firms in hostile and benign environments. *Strategic Management Journal*, *10*(1), 75–87. doi:10.1002mj.4250100107

Crainic, T. G., Gendreau, M., & Potvin, J. Y. (2009). Intelligent freight-transportation systems: Assessment and the contribution of operations research. *Transportation Research Part C, Emerging Technologies*, *17*(6), 541–557. doi:10.1016/j.trc.2008.07.002

Creazza, A., Dallari, F., & Melacini, M. (2010). Evaluating logistics network configurations for a global supply chain. *Supply Chain Management*, *15*(2), 154–164. doi:10.1108/13598541011028750

Crona, B. I., & Parker, J. N. (2012). Learning in support of governance: Theories, methods, and a framework to assess how bridging organizations contribute to adaptive resource governance. *Ecology and Society*, *17*(1), art32. doi:10.5751/ES-04534-170132

Crook, J. (2016). *Walmart squares up against amazon with 2-day delivery across the us techcrunch*. Retrieved May 2022 from https://techcrunch.com/2016/06/30/walmart-squares-up-against-amazon-with-2-day-delivery-across-the-u-s

Croom, S., & Brandon-Jones, A. (2007). Impact of e-procurement: Experiences from implementation in the UK public sector. *Journal of Purchasing and Supply Management*, *13*(4), 294–303. doi:10.1016/j.pursup.2007.09.015

Davis, M. H., Hall, J. A., & Mayer, P. S. (2016). Developing a new measure of entrepreneurial mindset: Reliability, validity, and implications for practitioners. *Consulting Psychology Journal*, *68*(1), 21–48. doi:10.1037/cpb0000045

Dawood, H., & Wang, Y. (2013). An efficient emergency message broadcasting scheme in vehicular ad hoc networks. *International Journal of Distributed Sensor Networks*, *9*(11), 232916. doi:10.1155/2013/232916

de Nooy, W., Mrvar, A., & Batagelj, V. (2006). *Exploratory social network analysis with Pajek*. Cambridge University Press.

Deng, G., Chen, J., & Liu, Q. (2022). Influence mechanism and evolutionary game of environmental regulation on green port construction. *Sustainability*, *14*(5), 2930. doi:10.3390u14052930

Deshmukh, Y. P., & Borade, A. B. (2019). International Journal of Emerging Trends in Engineering Research. *International Journal (Toronto, Ont.)*, *7*(5).

Dezdar, S., & Ainin, S. (2011). The influence of organisational factors on successful ERP implementation. *Management Decision*, *49*(6), 911–926. doi:10.1108/00251741111143603

Di Foggia, G. (2021). Energy-efficient products and competitiveness in the manufacturing sector. *Journal of Open Innovation*, *7*(1), 33. doi:10.3390/joitmc7010033

Dia, H., & Panwai, S. (2014). December. Intelligent Mobility for Smart Cities: Driver Behavior Models for Assessment of Sustainable Transport. *IEEE Fourth International Conference on Big Data and Cloud Computing*, 625-632.

Diandra, D., & Azmy, A. (2020). Understanding definition of entrepreneurship. International Journal of Management. *Accounting and Economics*, *7*(5), 235–241.

Dillmann, R. (2016). Digital Transformation in Supply Chain Management. *BearingPoint*, *1*(2). https://www.onenetwork.com/supply-chain-management-solutions/digital-transformation/

Dimapindan, P. R. (2014). *An Integrated Framework to Evaluate Customer Service Delivery: A Study of Electronic Systems at FDA's Los Angeles Import Operations Branch*. University of Southern California.

Dodd, T., & Yengin, D. (2021). Deadlock in sustainable aviation fuels: A multi-case analysis of agency. *Transportation Research Part D, Transport and Environment*, *94*, 102799. doi:10.1016/j.trd.2021.102799

Duneja, R., Sethi, R., & Vinas, M. (2021). *Digital KSA: Assessment and way forward for the digital economy*. https://www.adlittle.com/en/digital-ksa-assessment-and-way-forward-digital-economy

Duong, A. T. B., Vo, V. X., Carvalho, M. D. S., Sampaio, P., & Truong, H. Q. (2022). Risks and supply chain performance: Globalization and COVID-19 perspectives. *International Journal of Productivity and Performance Management*. Advance online publication. doi:10.1108/IJPPM-03-2021-0179

Dwivedi, Y. K., Shareef, M. A., Mukerji, B., Rana, N. P., & Kapoor, K. K. (2018). Involvement in emergency supply chain for disaster management: A cognitive dissonance perspective. *International Journal of Production Research*, *56*(21), 6758–6773. doi:10.1080/00207543.2017.1378958

Eckerd, S., & Sweeney, K. (2018). The role of dependence and information sharing on governance decisions regarding conflict. *International Journal of Logistics Management*, *29*(1), 409–434. doi:10.1108/IJLM-12-2016-0301

Economics, C. (2020). *Economic consequences of the COVID-19 Pandemic.* https://copenhageneconomics.com/publication/economic-consequences-of-the-covid-19-pandemic

EEHC. (2019). www.eehc.gov.eg

EGPC. (2021). http://www.egpc.com.eg/About_EGPC.aspx

Egyptian Customs Authority. (2022). *Advance Cargo Information.* Retrieved from www.customs.gov.eg/Services/Customs_Clearance/ACI

EIFFA. (2020). https://www.eiffa.com/april-2020/

Ekwall, D., & Lantz, B. (2015). Cargo theft at non-secure parking locations. *International Journal of Retail & Distribution Management, 43*(3), 204–220. doi:10.1108/IJRDM-06-2013-0131

El Baz, J., & Ruel, S. (2021). Can supply chain risk management practices mitigate the disruption impacts on supply chains' resilience and robustness? Evidence from an empirical survey in a COVID-19 outbreak era. *International Journal of Production Economics, 233.* doi:10.1016/j.ijpe.2020.107972

Elbahy, R. (2021). *The Egyptian battle against the coronaviruses: policies and tools.* Institute of International Politics and Economics.

El-Baz, M. (2011). Fuzzy performance measurement of a supply chain in manufacturing companies. *Expert Systems with Applications, 38*(6), 6681–6688. doi:10.1016/j.eswa.2010.11.067

Elgazzar, S. H. (2021). Investigating Digital Supply Chain Transformation Drivers: An Empirical Study. *Journal of Alexandria University for Administrative Sciences, 58*(5), 139–170.

El-Kadi, A.-W. (2013). Suggested Solutions for Traffic Congestion in Greater Cairo. *Journal of Sustainable Development, 6*, 106-107.

Elsafty, A., & Osman, M. (2021). The Impact of COVID-19 on the Efficiency of Packing Lines in Pharmaceutical Manufacturing Sites in Egypt. *International Journal of Business and Management, 16*(7), 57–72. doi:10.5539/ijbm.v16n7p57

Elzarka, S. (2019). *A study on logistics risk assessment: The case of container shipping in Egypt.* Research Gate. https://www.researchgate.net/publication/354423556_A_STUDY_ON_LOGISTICS_RISK_ASSESSMENT_THE_CASE_OF_CONTAINER_SHIPPING_IN_EGYPT

Eriksson, P. E. (2010). Partnering: What is it, when should it be used, and how should it be implemented? *Construction Management and Economics, 28*(9), 905–917. doi:10.1080/01446190903536422

ESCAP. (2017). Cross-border paperless trade and single window in East and North-. *East Asia.*

Eshghi, K. (2018). *Distribution Channel Conflict: Implications for Channel Governance, and Performance* [Doctoral dissertation].

Essam, M. (2020). *A boom in the road network. and experts: Egypt built 250 new bridges and accidents decreased.* https://akhbarelyom.com/news/newdetails/3172829/1/%D8%B7%D9%81%D8%B1%D8%A9-%D9%81%D9%8A-%D8%B4%D8%A8%D9%83%D8%A9-%D8%A7%D9%84%D8%B7%D8%B1%D9%82-%D9%88%D8%AE%D8%A8%D8%B1%D8%A7%D8%A1-%D9%85%D8%B5%D8%B1-%D8%B4%D9%8A%D8%AF%D8%AA-250-%D8%AC

Etgar, M. (1979). Sources and types of intra-channel conflict. *Journal of Retailing, 55*(1), 61–78.

European Commission for Industry Technologies. (2020). Advanced technologies for industry. In *Product watch: IoT components in connected and autonomous vehicles.* Author. doi:10.2826/70918

European Commission. (2017). *ECHO Factsheet – Syria crisis.* Retrieved from Brusel: https://reliefweb.int/sites/reliefweb.int/files/resources/syria_en_22.pdf

European Commission. (2021). *Import Control System Trader Guide.* Retrieved from www.revenue.ie/en/customs-traders-and-agents/documents/electronic/ics-trade-guide.pdf

European Pharmaceutical Review. (2020). COVID-19 update: Coronavirus and the pharmaceutical supply chain. *European Pharmaceutical Review.* https://www.europeanpharmaceuticalreview.com/article/116145/covid-19- update-coronavirus-and-the-pharmaceutical-supply-chain/

European Union. (2019). *The Food and Beverage Market Entry Handbook: Egypt. A Practical Guide to the Market in Egypt for European Agri-food Products and Products with Geographical Indications.* doi:10.2818/256126

Evans, N., & Sawyer, J. (2010). CSR and stakeholders of small businesses in regional South Australia. *Social Responsibility Journal, 6*(3), 433–451. doi:10.1108/17471111011064799

Ewald, L., Hjortstam, A., & Wilén, J. (2021). *Blockchain Technology in Transportation Management - A case study with Rhenus Logistics AB (Undergraduate).* Linnaeus University, School of Business and Economics, Department of Management Accounting and Logistics.

Ezz Steel. (2022). *About Ezz Steel.* Retrieved from: www.ezzsteel.com/about-ezz-steel

Fan, Y., Behdani, B., & Bloemhof-Ruwaard, J. M. (2020). Refer logistics and cold chain transport: A systematic review and multi-actor system analysis of an un-explored domain. *European Journal of Transport and Infrastructure Research, 20*(2), 1–35.

Faridi, M. (2020). *Digital transformation in supply chain, challenges and opportunities in SMEs: A case study of Al-Rumman Pharma.* Academic Press.

Fawcett, S. E., & McCarter, M. W. (2008). Behavioral issues in supply chain collaboration: Communicating the literature via interactive learning. *International Journal of Integrated Supply Management, 4*(2), 159–180. doi:10.1504/IJISM.2008.016616

Feng, F., Pang, Y., Lodewijks, G., & Li, W. (2017). Collaborative framework of an intelligent agent system for efficient logistics transport planning. *Computers & Industrial Engineering, 112*, 551–567. doi:10.1016/j.cie.2016.12.044

Ferrantino, M., & Koten, E. E. (2019). Understanding Supply Chain 4.0 and its potential impact on global value chains. *Global Value Chain Development Report: Technological Innovation, Supply Chain Trade, and Workers in a Globalised World.* Available at: https://www.wto.org/english/res_e/booksp_e/gvc_dev_report_2019_e.pdf

Ferrantino, M.J., & Koten, E.E. (2019). Understanding Supply Chain 4.0 and its potential impact on global value chains. *Global Value Chain Development Report, 103.*

Ferris, E., & Kirisci, K. (2016a). *The consequences of chaos: Syria's humanitarian crisis and the failure to protect.* Brookings Institution Press.

Ferris, E., & Kirisci, K. (2016b). The context, causes, and consequences of Syrian displacement. *The Consequences of Chaos: Syria's Humanitarian Crisis and the Failure to Protect*, *1*, 32.

FIATA. (2021). *International Federation of Freight Forwarders Associations (FIATA) Digitalization and logistics resilience: lessons learned from COVID-19 and challenges ahead*. FIATA.

Ford Motor Company. (2019). *Ford - Volkswagen expand their global collaboration to advance autonomous driving, electrification and better serve customers*. Ford Media Center. https://media.ford.com/content/fordmedia/fna/us/en/news/2019/07/12/ford-vw.html

Forsberg, J., & Towers, N. (2007). Creating agile supply networks in the fashion industry. *Journal of the Textile Institute*, *98*(4), 377–386. doi:10.1080/00405000701502925

Frankenfield, J. (2021). *Cryptocurrency*. Retrieved from: www.investopedia.com/terms/c/cryptocurrency.asp

Frank, H., Kessler, A., & Fink, M. (2010). Entrepreneurial orientation and business performance—A replication study. *Schmalenbach Business Review*, *62*(2), 175–198. doi:10.1007/BF03396804

Frederico, G. F. (2021). From Supply Chain 4.0 to Supply Chain 5.0: Findings from a Systematic Literature Review and Research Directions. *Logistics*, *5*(3), 49. doi:10.3390/logistics5030049

Frederiksen, C. S., Pedersen, D. B., Nielsen, M. E. J., & Idowu, S. O. (2021). Corporate Social Indices: Refining the Global Reporting Initiative. In Global Challenges to CSR and Sustainable Development. Springer.

Fritz Institute. (2022). *About Humanitarian Supply Chain Management (SCM)*. Retrieved from https://fritzinstitute.org/humanitarian-scm/

Fritz, M. M., Schöggl, J.-P., & Baumgartner, R. J. (2017). Selected sustainability aspects for supply chain data exchange: Towards a supply chain-wide sustainability assessment. *Journal of Cleaner Production*, *141*, 587–607. doi:10.1016/j.jclepro.2016.09.080

Fritz, M., Ruel, S., Kallmuenzer, A., & Harms, R. (2021). Sustainability management in supply chains: The role of familiness. *Technological Forecasting and Social Change*, *173*(C), 121078. doi:10.1016/j.techfore.2021.121078

Frizzo-Barker, J., Chow-White, P. A., Adams, P. R., Mentanko, J., Ha, D., & Green, S. (2020). Blockchain as a disruptive technology for business: A systematic review. *International Journal of Information Management*, *51*, 102029. doi:10.1016/j.ijinfomgt.2019.10.014

Fujita, K., Gollwitzer, P. M., & Oettingen, G. (2007). Mindsets and pre-conscious open-mindedness to incidental information. *Journal of Experimental Social Psychology*, *43*(1), 48–61. doi:10.1016/j.jesp.2005.12.004

FullerH. B. (2022). *About us*. Retrieved from: www.hbfuller.com/en/north-america/about-us/

Gams, M., & Kolenik, T. (2021). Relations between electronics, artificial intelligence and information society through information society rules. *Electronics (Switzerland)*, *10*(4), 1–16. doi:10.3390/electronics10040514

Ganapati, P. (2009, December 23). Dec. 23, 1947: Transistor Opens Door to Digital Future. WIRED. https://www.wired.com/2009/12/1223shockley-bardeen-brattain-transistor/

Ganin, A. A., Kitsak, M., Marchese, D., Keisler, J. M., Seager, T., & Linkov, I. (2017). Resilience and efficiency in transportation networks. *Science Advances*, *3*(12), e1701079. doi:10.1126ciadv.1701079 PMID:29291243

Garcia-Lozano, E., Barba, C., Igartua, M., & Campo, C. (2013). *A distributed, bandwidth-efficient accident prevention system for interurban VANETs*. IEEE. doi:10.1109/SaCoNeT.2013.6654564

Gauci, G. (1995). Limitation of liability in maritime law: An anachronism? *Marine Policy*, *19*(1), 65–74. doi:10.1016/0308-597X(95)92573-P

GCC Retail Industry. (2017). *Alpen Capital*. Author.

Gedeon, S. (2010). *What is Entrepreneurship?* Retrieved 29 May 2022, from https://www.academia.edu/35644718/What_is_Entrepreneurship?from=cover_page

Ghadge, A., Er, M., Ivanov, D., & Chaudhuri, A. (2021). Visualization of ripple effect in supply chains under long-term, simultaneous disruptions: A system dynamics approach. *International Journal of Production Research*, 1–14.

Ghoneim. (2021). *Egypt Digitalization*. Academic Press.

Girteca. (2021). *Carrying high-value goods on the road: Challenges and requirements*. Girteka Logistics. Available at: https://www.girteka.eu/carrying-high-value-goods-on-the-road-challenges-and-requirements/

Gligor, D., Gligor, N., Holcomb, M., & Bozkurt, S. (2019). Distinguishing between the concepts of supply chain agility and resilience: A multidisciplinary literature review. *International Journal of Logistics Management*, *30*(2), 467–487. doi:10.1108/IJLM-10-2017-0259

Global Chains Company. (2019). Available at: https://global-chains.com/

Goel, R. K., Saunoris, J. W., & Goel, S. S. (2021). Supply chain performance and economic growth: The impact of COVID-19 disruptions. *Journal of Policy Modeling*, *43*(2), 298–316. doi:10.1016/j.jpolmod.2021.01.003

Göl, H., & Çatay, B. (2007). Logistics Outsourcing and 3Pl Selection :A Case Study in an Automotive Supply Chain. *Engineering*.

Golan, M. S., Jernegan, L. H., & Linkov, I. (2020). Trends and applications of resilience analytics in supply chain modeling: Systematic literature review in the context of the COVID-19 pandemic. *Environment Systems & Decisions*, *40*(2), 222–243. doi:10.100710669-020-09777-w PMID:32837820

Goldmann, K. (2019). Time-declining risk-adjusted social discount rates for transport infrastructure planning. *Transportation, 46*(1), 17-34. http://dx.doi.org.libaccess.hud.ac.uk/10.1007/s11116-017-9780-4

Gollwitzer, P. M. (2012). Mindset theory of action phases. Handbook of theories of social psychology, 1, 526-545.

Gonzalez-Padron, T., Hult, G. T. M., & Calantone, R. (2008). Exploiting innovative opportunities in global purchasing: An assessment of ethical climate and relationship performance. *Industrial Marketing Management*, *37*(1), 69–82. doi:10.1016/j.indmarman.2007.06.013

GoodFirms. (2022). *Agility Reviews & Profile*. GoodFirms. https://www.goodfirms.co/company/agility

gov.sa. (2022). *Digital transformation in the kingdom of Saudi Arabia*. https://www.my.gov.sa/wps/portal/snp/aboutksa/digitaltransformation

gov.uk. (2022). https://www.gov.uk/government/publications/road-congestion-and-travel-times-statistics-guidance/travel-time-statistics-background-quality-report

Grainger, A. (2007). Government Actors in international supply chain operations: Assessing requirements for skills and capabilities. In *Logistics research network conference proceedings* (pp. 293-298). Doi:10.1.1.621.1935

Grand, W. K. S. (2020). *Assessing Saudi vision 2030: A 2020 Review*. Https://Www.Atlanticcouncil.Org/Wp-Content/Uploads/2020/06/Assessing-Saudi-Vision-2030-A-2020-Review.Pdf

Greenberg, P. S., Greenberg, R. H., & Antonucci, Y. L. (2008). The role of trust in the governance of business process outsourcing relationships: A transaction cost economics approach. *Business Process Management Journal*, *14*(5), 593–608. doi:10.1108/14637150810903011

Guan, D., Wang, D., Hallegatte, S., Davis, S. J., Huo, J., Li, S., Bai, Y., Lei, T., Xue, Q., Coffman, D., Cheng, D., Chen, P., Liang, X., Xu, B., Lu, X., Wang, S., Hubacek, K., & Gong, P. (2020). Global supply-chain effects of COVID-19 control measures. *Nature Human Behaviour*, *4*(6), 577–587. doi:10.103841562-020-0896-8 PMID:32493967

Gudehus, T., & Kotzab, H. (2012). *Comprehensive logistics*. Springer Science & Business Media. doi:10.1007/978-3-642-24367-7

Guinness World. (2021). *Largest floating roof tank*. Guinness World Records. https://www.guinnessworldrecords.com/world-records/631865-largest-floating-roof-tank?fbclid=IwAR3In9XVH1YefZNsSWhHNQOiTU4og-4ZwP6Cmp9wCevLtHp-dye-mSywEkw

Guo, W., Straub, D., Zhang, P., & Cai, Z. (2021). How Trust Leads To Commitment On Microsourcing Platforms: Unraveling The Effects Of Governance And Third-Party Mechanisms On Triadic Microsourcing Relationships. *Management Information Systems Quarterly*, *45*(3), 1309–1348. doi:10.25300/MISQ/2021/14349

Guo, Y., Wang, L., & Chen, Y. (2020). Green entrepreneurial orientation and green innovation: The mediating effect of supply chain learning. *SAGE Open*, *10*(1), 2158244019898798. doi:10.1177/2158244019898798

Gupta, A. K. (2019). Creating the smart cities of the future: A three-tier development model for digital transformation of citizen services. *1PwC/World Economic Forum*, 1–16. https://www.pwc.com/gx/en/sustainability/assets/creating-the-smart-cities-of-the-future.pdf

Habbershon, T. G., Nordqvist, M., & Zellweger, T. (2010). Transgenerational entrepreneurship. *Transgenerational entrepreneurship: Exploring growth and performance in family firms across generations*, 1-38.

Habib, M. A., Bao, Y., Nabi, N., Dulal, M., Asha, A. A., & Islam, M. (2021). Impact of strategic orientations on the implementation of green supply chain management practices and sustainable firm performance. *Sustainability*, *13*(1), 340. doi:10.3390u13010340

Haddad, S. (2020). Developing an e-business system to improve the downstream Pharmaceutical supply chain (a study on the Egyptian market. *Proceedings of the 8th International Conference on Advanced Materials and Systems (ICAMS)*. 10.24264/icams-2020.III.7

Hadrawi, H. (2019). The impact of firm supply performance and lean processes on the relationship between supply chain management practices and competitive performance. *Uncertain Supply Chain Management*, *7*(2), 341–350. doi:10.5267/j.uscm.2018.7.003

Haffajee, R. L., & Mello, M. M. (2020). Thinking globally, acting locally—The US response to COVID-19. *The New England Journal of Medicine*, *382*(22), e75. doi:10.1056/NEJMp2006740 PMID:32240580

Handfield, R., Petersen, K., Cousins, P., & Lawson, B. (2009). An organisational entrepreneurship model of supply management integration and performance outcomes. *International Journal of Operations & Production Management, 29*(2), 100–126. doi:10.1108/01443570910932011

Harrison, L. (2022, April 7). Standards And Threat Testing For Secure Autonomous Vehicles. Semiconductor Engineering. https://semiengineering.com/standards-and-threat-testing-for-secure-autonomous-vehicles/

Hasegawa, T. (2015). Chapter 5-Intelligent Transport System. *Traffic and Safety Science - Interdiciplinary Wisdom of IATSS*, 212. http://www.iatss.or.jp/en/publication/commemorative-publication/

Hendrickx, A. (2020). *Infosys Annual Report 2020-21*. Available at: https://www.infosys.com/investors/reports-filings/annual-report/annual/documents/infosys-ar-21.pdf

Hix, S., & Høyland, B. (2022). *The political system of the European Union*. Bloomsbury Publishing.

Hjort, Skobelev, Almgren, Guseva, & Koh. (2019). Best available techniques and sustainable development goals. *International Multidisciplinary Scientific GeoConference: SGEM, 19*(4.2), 185-192.

Holland, O. (2003). The first biologically inspired robots. *Robotica, 21*(4), 351–363. doi:10.1017/S0263574703004971

Hornsby, J. S., Kuratko, D. F., & Zahra, S. A. (2002). Middle managers' perception of the internal environment for corporate entrepreneurship: Assessing a measurement scale. *Journal of Business Venturing, 17*(3), 253–273. doi:10.1016/S0883-9026(00)00059-8

Hosny, K. (2021). *How did Egypt succeed in reducing the number of accidents by 29% in 2020?- 4500 km of roads were built.* Alarabiya. Retrieved from https://www.alarabiya.net/aswaq/economy/2021/11/05/%D9%83%D9%8A%D9%81-%D9%86%D8%AC%D8%AD%D8%AA-%D9%85%D8%B5%D8%B1-%D9%81%D9%8A-%D8%AE%D9%81%D8%B6-%D8%B9%D8%AF%D8%AF-%D8%A7%D9%84%D8%AD%D9%88%D8%A7%D8%AF%D8%AB-29-%D9%81%D9%8A-2020%D8%9F

Hosseini, S., & Ivanov, D. (2019). A new resilience measure for supply networks with the ripple effect considerations: A Bayesian network approach. *Annals of Operations Research*, 1–27.

Hsu, C. C., Tan, K. C., Laosirihongthong, T., & Leong, G. K. (2011). Entrepreneurial SCM competence and performance of manufacturing SMEs. *International Journal of Production Research, 49*(22), 6629–6649. doi:10.1080/00207543.2010.537384

Huang, Y., & Barbara, A. (2009). Infrared Spectroscopy for Food Quality Analysis and Control. Academic Press.

Huff, H. R. (2003). *John Bardeen and transistor physics.* doi:10.1063/1.1354371

Hu, X., Fu, K., Chen, Z., & Du, Z. (2022). Decision-Making of Transnational Supply Chain Considering Tariff and Third-Party Logistics Service. *Mathematics, 10*(5), 770. doi:10.3390/math10050770

Hyams, J. (1999). *Autonomous Multi-Agent Docking using Color Segmentation.* Academic Press.

IEA. (2021). *Oil 2021.* International Energy Agency. www.iea.org

Iftikhar, A., Purvis, L., Giannoccaro, I., & Wang, Y. (2022). The impact of supply chain complexities on supply chain resilience: The mediating effect of big data analytics. *Production Planning and Control*, 1–21. doi:10.1080/09537287.2022.2032450

IMF. (2021). *Egypt: Overcoming the COVID Shock and Maintaining Growth.* https://www.imf.org/en/News/Articles/2021/07/14/na070621-egypt-overcoming-the-covid-shock-and-maintaining-growth

Industrial Distribution. (2015). *Warehouse Carbon Footprint Calculation 101.* https://www.inddist.com/

International Trade Administration. (2021). *Import Requirements & Documentation.* Retrieved from www.trade.gov/country-commercial-guides/egypt-import-requirements-documentation

International Trade Center. (2018). *Customs procedures guide to import and export in Egypt.* Retrieved from euromed.tradehelpdesk.org/euromed/ar/market-access-info/customs-procedures-guides/download?reporter=818

Introduction to Computers/Networks - Wikiversity. (n.d.). https://en.wikiversity.org/wiki/Introduction_to_Computers/Networks

Irish Tax and Customs. (2021). *Import Control System (ICS).* Retrieved from www.revenue.ie/en/customs/businesses/electronic-systems/import-control-system.aspx

IRWG. (2015). www.rdso.indianrailways.gov

Istizada. (2019). https://istizada.com/ecommerce-in-saudi-arabia-the-complete-guide/

ITA. (2020). *Energy Resource Guide - Egypt - Oil and Gas.* https://www.trade.gov/energy-resource-guide-egypt-oil-and-gas

Ivanov, D., & Das, A. (2020). Coronavirus (COVID-19/SARS-CoV-2) and supply chain resilience: A research note. *International Journal of Integrated Supply Management*, *13*(1), 90–102. doi:10.1504/IJISM.2020.107780

Ivanov, D., Sokolov, B., & Kaeschel, J. (2010). A multi-structural framework for adaptive supply chain planning and operations control with structure dynamics considerations. *European Journal of Operational Research*, *200*(2), 409–420. doi:10.1016/j.ejor.2009.01.002

Jain, V. N. (2019). Robotics for Supply Chain and Manufacturing Industries and Future It Holds! *International Journal of Engine Research*, *V8*(03), 66–79. doi:10.17577/ijertv8is030062

Jain, V., Arya, S., & Bindoo, M. (n.d.). An overview of electronic commerce. *Journal of Contemporary Issues in Business and Government*, *27*(3).

Jakubicek, P., & Woudsma, C. (2011). Proximity, land, labor and planning? Logistics industry perspectives on facility location. *Transportation Letters*, *3*(3), 161–173. doi:10.3328/TL.2011.03.03.161-173

Janvier-James, A. M. (2012). A new introduction to supply chains and supply chain management: Definitions and theories perspective. *International Business Research*, *5*(1), 194–207.

Japan International Cooperation Agency. (2008). *The study on multimodal transport and logistics system of the eastern Mediterranean region and master plan in the Arab Republic of Egypt.* Retrieved from openjicareport.jica.go.jp/pdf/11893450_01.pdf

Jemaa, F. (2022). Recoupling work beyond COSO: A longitudinal case study of Enterprise-wide Risk Management. *Accounting, Organizations and Society*, *103*, 101369. doi:10.1016/j.aos.2022.101369

Jeong, Y. M., Ali, M., Zacca, R., & Park, K. (2019). The effect of entrepreneurship orientation on firm performance: A multiple mediation model. *Journal of East-West Business*, *25*(2), 166–193. doi:10.1080/10669868.2018.1536013

Jia, F., & Yang, Z. (2019). Perceptual difference of dependence and trust in marketing channel: Reconsideration of dependence measurement. *Asian Business & Management*, 1–27.

Jiang, Z. E. M., Liu, Y., Liu, J., & Li, Y. (2017). Study of manufacturing resource perception and process control of a radio-frequency-identification-enabled decentralised flexible manufacturing system. *Advances in Mechanical Engineering*, *9*(1), 1687814016687449. doi:10.1177/1687814016687449

Jia, Y., Wang, T., Xiao, K., & Guo, C. (2020). How to reduce opportunism through contractual governance in the cross-cultural supply chain context: Evidence from Chinese exporters. *Industrial Marketing Management*, *91*, 323–337. doi:10.1016/j.indmarman.2020.09.014

Justus, M., Ceccato, V., & Kahn, T. (2018). *Crime Against Trading: The Case of Cargo Theft in São Paulo*. doi:10.1007/978-3-319-73065-3

Kamel, S. (2021). *The Potential Impact of Digital Transformation on Egypt*. https://erf.org.eg/publications/the-potential-impact-of-digital-transformation-on-egypt/

Kanda, A., & Deshmukh, S. G. (2008). Supply chain coordination: Perspectives, empirical studies and research directions. *International Journal of Production Economics*, *115*(2), 316–335. doi:10.1016/j.ijpe.2008.05.011

Karthik Kumar Vaigandla, Sandyarani Bolla & Radhakrishna Karne. A Survey on Future Generation Wireless Communications-6G: Requirements, Technologies, Challenges and Applications. (2021). *International Journal of Advanced Trends in Computer Science and Engineering*, *10*(5), 3067–3076. https://doi.org/ doi:10.30534/ijatcse/2021/211052021

Kassai, E. T., Azmat, M., & Kummer, S. (2020). Scope of Using Autonomous Trucks and Lorries for Parcel Deliveries in Urban Settings. *Logistics*, *4*(3), 17. doi:10.3390/logistics4030017

Keen, R. (2020). *Covid-19 crisis emphasises the key role of freight forwarders, says logistics association*. BIFA. https://bifa.org/news/articles/2020/mar/covid-19-crisis-emphasises-the-key-role-of-freight-forwarders-says-logistics-association

Kehoe, D. F., Dani, S., Sharifi, H., Burns, N. D., & Backhouse, C. J. (2007). Demand network alignment: Aligning the physical, informational and relationship issues in supply chains. *International Journal of Production Research*, *45*(5), 1141–1160. doi:10.1080/00207540600635219

Kerpedzhiev, G., König, U., Röglinger, M., & Rosemann, M. (2017). Business Process Management in the Digital Age. *BPTrends, 4801*, 1–6. www.bptrends.com

Kersten, W., & Blecker, T., & M., R. C. (2017). Digitalization in supply chain management and logistics. *Proceedings of the Hamburg International Conference of Logistics (HICL)*. doi:10.15480/882.1442

Ketchen, D. J. Jr, & Hult, G. T. M. (2007). Bridging organisation theory and supply chain management: The case of best value supply chains. *Journal of Operations Management*, *25*(2), 573–580. doi:10.1016/j.jom.2006.05.010

Kewalram, B. (2020a). *Data-Driven Decision Making and How to Get There*. Agility Logistics. https://www.agility.com/en/blog/data-driven-decision-making-and-how-to-get-there/

Kewalram, B. (2020b). *Part 1: A Conversation with the Chief Digital Officer*. Agility. https://www.agility.com/en/a-conversation-with-biju-kewalram-chief-digital-officer-of-agility-gil-part-one/

Khairuddin, M. M., Rahman, N. A. A., Mohamad, M. F., Majid, Z. A., & Ahmad, M. F. (2018). Regulator perspective on Halal air cargo warehouse compliance. *International Journal of Supply Chain Management*, *7*(3), 202–207.

Khalifa, N., Abd Elghany, M., & Abd Elghany, M. (2021). Exploratory research on digitalisation transformation practices within supply chain management context in developing countries specifically Egypt in the MENA region. *Cogent Business and Management*, *8*(1), 1965459. doi:10.1080/23311975.2021.1965459

Khan, S. A. R., Jian, C., Zhang, Y., Golpîra, H., Kumar, A., & Sharif, A. (2019). Environmental, social and economic growth indicators spur logistics performance: From the perspective of South Asian Association for Regional Cooperation countries. *Journal of Cleaner Production*, *214*, 1011–1023. doi:10.1016/j.jclepro.2018.12.322

Kherbash, O., & Mocan, M. L. (2015). A Review of Logistics and Transport Sector as a Factor of Globalization. *Procedia Economics and Finance*, *27*, 42–47. doi:10.1016/S2212-5671(15)00969-7

Khwaja. (2017). *Technology, Media & Telecommunications*. Dubai International Financial Centre.

Kim, S. (2019). *Micro-LEGO for MEMS*. Academic Press.

Kim, J., Lee, W. J., & Park, H. W. (2016). The state of the art in the electron beam manufacturing processes. *International Journal of Precision Engineering and Manufacturing*, *17*(11), 1575–1585. doi:10.100712541-016-0184-8

Kim, Y., Chen, Y. S., & Linderman, K. (2015). Supply network disruption and resilience: A network structural perspective. *Journal of Operations Management*, *33*(1), 43–59. doi:10.1016/j.jom.2014.10.006

Kluschke, P., Gnann, T., Plötz, P., & Wietschel, M. (2019). Market diffusion of alternative fuels and powertrains in heavy-duty vehicles: A literature review. *Energy Reports*, *5*, 1010–1024. doi:10.1016/j.egyr.2019.07.017

Kohtamäki, M., & Farmer, D. (2017). *Real-time Strategy and Business Intelligence*. Springer International Publishing. doi:10.1007/978-3-319-54846-3

Korhonen, J. (2020). *The circular economy as a complex adaptive system. In Handbook of the circular economy*. Edward Elgar Publishing.

Korpela, K., Hallikas, J., & Dahlberg, T. (2017). Digital Supply Chain Transformation toward Blockchain Integration. *Proceedings of the 50th Hawaii International Conference on System Sciences*, 4182-4191. Available at: http://hdl.handle.net/10125/41666

Kovacs, G., & Spens, K. M. (2012). *Relief supply chain management for disasters: humanitarian aid and emergency logistics*. Information Science Reference. doi:10.4018/978-1-60960-824-8

Krafft, M., Goetz, O., Mantrala, M., Sotgiu, F., & Tillmanns, S. (2015). The evolution of marketing channel research domains and methodologies: An integrative review and future directions. *Journal of Retailing*, *91*(4), 569–585. doi:10.1016/j.jretai.2015.05.001

Kraus, S., Harms, R., & Fink, M. (2010). Entrepreneurial marketing: moving beyond marketing in new ventures. *International Journal of Entrepreneurship and Innovation Management, 11*(1).

Kreiser, P. M., & Davis, J. (2010). Entrepreneurial orientation and firm performance: The unique impact of innovativeness, proactiveness, and risk-taking. *Journal of Small Business and Entrepreneurship*, *23*(1), 39–51. doi:10.1080/08276331.2010.10593472

Kropp, F., Lindsay, N. J., & Shoham, A. (2006). Entrepreneurial, market, and learning orientations and international entrepreneurial business venture performance in South African firms. *International Marketing Review*, *23*(5), 504–523. doi:10.1108/02651330610703427

Kumar, S., & Anbanandam, R. (2020). Impact of risk management culture on supply chain resilience: An empirical study from the Indian manufacturing industry. *Proceedings of the Institution of Mechanical Engineers, Part O: Journal of Risk and Reliability*, *234*(2), 246–259. doi:10.1177/1748006X19886718

Kuratko, D. F., & Welsch, H. P. (1994). *Entrepreneurial strategy: Text and cases*. Dryden Press.

Kurgun, H., Bagiran, D., Ozeren, E., & Maral, B. (2011). Entrepreneurial marketing-The interface between marketing and entrepreneurship: A qualitative research on boutique hotels. *European Journal of Soil Science*, *26*(3), 340–357.

Kutz, M. (2016). *Introduction to E-Commerce: Combining Business and Information Technology*. The eBook Company.

Laituri, M., & Kodrich, K. (2008). On line disaster response community: People as sensors of high magnitude disasters using internet GIS. *Sensors (Basel)*, *8*(5), 3037–3055. doi:10.33908053037 PMID:27879864

League of Arab States. (2020). *Arab digital economy vision towards a sustainable inclusive and secure digital future report*. Arab Economic Unity Council.

Lee, C. S., Cheang, P. Y. S., & Moslehpour, M. (2022). Predictive analytics in business analytics: Decision tree. *Advances in Decision Sciences*, *26*(1), 1–29. doi:10.47654/v26y2022i1p1-29

Lee, H. L. (2004). The triple-A supply chain. *Harvard Business Review*, *82*(10), 102–113. PMID:15559579

Le, T. T., Vo, X. V., & Venkatesh, V. G. (2022). Role of green innovation and supply chain management in driving sustainable corporate performance. *Journal of Cleaner Production*, *374*, 133875. doi:10.1016/j.jclepro.2022.133875

Leung, Y. F. (2009). *Conflict management and emotional intelligence* [Doctoral Thesis]. Southern Cross University, Lismore, Australia.

Li, Y., & Yu, Y. (2017). The use of freight apps in road freight transport for CO0R-W1S34RfeSDcfkexd09rT421RW1S34RfeSDcfkexd09rT4 reduction. *European Transport Research Review, 9*(3), 1-13. http://dx.doi.org.libaccess.hud.ac.uk/10.1007/s12544-017-0251-y

Liang, K., van de Hoef, S., Terelius, H., Turri, V., Besselink, B., Mårtensson, J., & Johansson, K. H. (2016). Networked control challenges in collaborative road freight transport. *European Journal of Control*, *30*, 2–14. doi:10.1016/j.ejcon.2016.04.008

Liche, M. B. (2021). *Technology Development Practice in Ethiopian Science and Technology Universities*. Academic Press.

Lietuvnikė, M. M., Vasilis Vasiliauskas, A., Vasilienė-Vasiliauskienė, V., & Sabaitytė, J. (2018). Peculiarities of illegal immigrant's intrusions into road freight transport units in the france - UK corridor. *Entrepreneurship and Sustainability Issues*, *5*(3), 634–647. doi:10.9770/jesi.2018.5.3(16)

Li, G., Li, W., Jin, Z., & Wang, Z. (2019). Influence of environmental concern and knowledge on households' willingness to purchase energy-efficient appliances: A case study in Shanxi, China. *Sustainability*, *11*(4), 1073. doi:10.3390u11041073

Li, J., Lu, Q., & Fu, P. (2015). Carbon footprint management of road freight transport under the carbon emission trading mechanism. *Mathematical Problems in Engineering*, *2015*, 1–13. doi:10.1155/2015/814527

Li, L., & Li, L. (2019). Structure and influencing factors of CO2 emissions from transport sector in three major metropolitan regions of china: Estimation and decomposition. *Transportation*, *46*(4), 1245–1269. doi:10.100711116-017-9827-6

Li, L., & Zhou, H. (2020). A survey of blockchain with applications in maritime and shipping industry. *Information Systems and e-Business Management, 19*(3), 789–807. doi:10.100710257-020-00480-6

Lindroth, E., Huong, H., & Bergqvist, R. (2020). Port-related conflict at port of Gothenburg–consequences from a fashion retailer's perspective. *Journal of Shipping and Trade, 5*(1), 1–17. doi:10.118641072-020-00059-x

Lin, H.-F. (2022). IT resources and quality attributes: The impact on electronic green supply chain management implementation and performance. *Technology in Society, 68*, 101833. doi:10.1016/j.techsoc.2021.101833

Lin, H., & Lin, Q. (2018). Research on the impact of supply chain integration of startups: Service supply chain perspective. *Open Journal of Social Sciences, 6*(4), 255–274. doi:10.4236/jss.2018.64022

Liu, D., Kuang, H., & Huang, M. (2017, May). Graph model for conflict resolution in the information sharing conflict of the fourth party logistics. In *2017 29th Chinese Control and Decision Conference (CCDC)* (pp. 6545-6550). IEEE. 10.1109/CCDC.2017.7978351

Liu, F., Wang, J., Liu, J., & Kong, Y. (2019). Coordination of port service chain with an integrated contract. *Soft Computing*, 1–14.

Liu, Y., Lee, J. M., & Lee, C. (2020). The challenges and opportunities of a global health crisis: The management and business implications of COVID-19 from an Asian perspective. *Asian Business & Management, 19*(3), 277–297. doi:10.105741291-020-00119-x

Liu, Y., & Wang, D. (2020). The impact of COVID-19 on global supply chains and the role of technology. *Journal of Business Research, 117*, 275–289.

Li, X., Li, D., & Liu, Y. (2019). Advanced analytics and IoT technologies for real-time monitoring and inventory management in supply chain. *Journal of Business Research, 96*, 365–372.

Li, Y., Liu, Y., & Liu, H. (2011). Co-opetition, distributor's entrepreneurial orientation and manufacturer's knowledge acquisition: Evidence from China. *Journal of Operations Management, 29*(1-2), 128–142. doi:10.1016/j.jom.2010.07.006

Li, Y., Zhen, X., Qi, X., & Cai, G. G. (2016). Penalty and financial assistance in a supply chain with supply disruption. *Omega, 61*, 167–181. doi:10.1016/j.omega.2015.12.011

Logfret. (2021). *How is technology changing the future of freight forwarders?* Logfret. https://logfret.com/how-is-technology-changing-the-future-of-freight-forwarders/

Logistics, B. (2022). *3 Tips For Protecting Freight From Cargo Theft with Technology*. Available at: https://mybluegrace.com/bluegrace-logistics/protecting-freight-from-cargo-theft-with-technology/

Loosemore, M., & Lim, B. (2015). Inter-organizational unfairness in the construction industry. *Construction Management and Economics, 33*(4), 310–326. doi:10.1080/01446193.2015.1057193

Lorenc, A., & Kuźnar, M. (2018). An intelligent system to predict risk and costs of cargo thefts in road transport)-System for proactive management and analysis of resources View project An Intelligent System to Predict Risk and Costs of Cargo Thefts in Road Transport. *International Journal of Engineering and Technology Innovation, 8*(4), 284–293.

Loske, D. (2020). The impact of COVID-19 on transport volume and freight capacity dynamics: An empirical analysis in German food retail logistics. *Transportation Research Interdisciplinary Perspectives, 6*, 100165. doi:10.1016/j.trip.2020.100165 PMID:34173456

Lotfi, Z., Mukhtar, M., Sahran, S., & Taei Zadeh, A. (2013, June). Information sharing in supply chain management. *The 4th International Conference on Electrical Engineering and Informatics.*

Luke, R. (2020). The impact of COVID-2019 on transport in South Africa. *Journal of Transport and Supply Chain Management, 14*(1), 1–5. doi:10.4102/jtscm.v14i0.545

Lukinskiy, V., & Pletneva, N. (2018). Impact of solutions for goods transportation on business efficiency and traffic safety. *Transportation Research Procedia, 36*, 459–464. doi:10.1016/j.trpro.2018.12.125

Lumineau, F., Eckerd, S., & Handley, S. (2015). Inter-organizational conflicts: Research overview, challenges, and opportunities. *Journal of Strategic Contracting and Negotiation, 1*(1), 42–64. doi:10.1177/2055563614568493

Lumineau, F., & Malhotra, D. (2011). Shadow of the contract: How contract structure shapes interfirm dispute resolution. *Strategic Management Journal, 32*(5), 532–555. doi:10.1002mj.890

Lumpkin, G. T., & Dess, G. G. (2001). Linking two dimensions of entrepreneurial orientation to firm performance: The moderating role of environment and industry life cycle. *Journal of Business Venturing, 16*(5), 429–451. doi:10.1016/S0883-9026(00)00048-3

Luo, Y. (2005). Transactional characteristics, institutional environment and joint venture contracts. *Journal of International Business Studies, 36*(2), 209–230. doi:10.1057/palgrave.jibs.8400125

M5azn. (2023). Why ma5azn. https://m5azn.com/en

Mahase, E. (2020). Covid-19: *Demand for dexamethasone surges as RECOVERY trial publishes* preprint. *BMJ, 369*, 2512. doi:10.1136/bmj.m2512 PMID:32576548

Mahmood, F., Khan, A. Z., & Bokhari, R. H. (2020). ERP issues and challenges: A research synthesis. *Kybernetes, 49*(3), 629–659. doi:10.1108/K-12-2018-0699

Maier, R., Passiante, G., & Zhang, S. (2011). 'Creating value in networks. *International Journal of Innovation and Technology Management, 8*(3), 357–371. doi:10.1142/S0219877011002416

Malthus, T. R. (1872). *An Essay on the Principle of Population*. Academic Press.

Manfré, L. A., Hirata, E., Silva, J. B., Shinohara, E. J., Giannotti, M. A., Larocca, A. P. C., & Quintanilha, J. A. (2012). An analysis of geospatial technologies for risk and natural disaster management. *ISPRS International Journal of Geo-Information, 1*(2), 166–185. doi:10.3390/ijgi1020166

Mangla, S. K., Kusi-Sarpong, S., Luthra, S., Bai, C., Jakhar, S. K., & Khan, S. A. (2020). Operational excellence for improving sustainable supply chain performance. *Resources, Conservation and Recycling, 162*, 105025. doi:10.1016/j.resconrec.2020.105025 PMID:32834482

Manuj, I., & Mentzer, J. T. (2008). Global supply chain risk management strategies. *International Journal of Physical Distribution & Logistics Management, 38*(3), 192–223. doi:10.1108/09600030810866986

Marcus, I. (2010). 'Agile supply chain: Strategy for competitive advantage'. *Journal Of Global Strategic Management, 7*(6), 5–17.

Marshall, D., McCarthy, L., McGrath, P., & Claudy, M. (2015). Going above and beyond: How sustainability culture and entrepreneurial orientation drive social sustainability supply chain practice adoption. *Supply Chain Management, 20*(4), 434–454. doi:10.1108/SCM-08-2014-0267

Másilková, M. (2017). Health and social consequences of road traffic accidents. *Kontakt*, 43-47.

Mathew & Bombay. (2014). Intelligent Transportation Systems. In Transportation System Engineering. Indian Institute of Technology Bombay.

Matthews, K. (2020, June 4). The 4 cities competing to fully implement autonomous vehicles. IoT Times. https://iot.eetimes.com/the-4-cities-competing-to-fully-implement-autonomous-vehicles/

Matthyssens, P., & Vandenbempt, K. (2008). Moving from basic offerings to value-added solutions: Strategies, barriers and alignment. *Industrial Marketing Management*, *37*(3), 316–328. doi:10.1016/j.indmarman.2007.07.008

Mazareanu, E. (2021b, April 6). *Logistics - Leading ocean freight forwarders worldwide 2020*. Statista. https://www.statista.com/statistics/254936/leading-ocean-freight-forwarders-worldwide-based-on-market-share/

Mazareanu. (2021a). *COVID-19 impact on the global freight forwarding market*. Statista. https://www.statista.com/statistics/1115277/year-on-year-change-freight-forwarding-market-worldwide/

McCullen, P., Saw, R., Christopher, M., & Towill, D. (2006, January). The F1 supply chain: adapting the car to the circuit-the supply chain to the market. In Supply chain forum: an international journal (Vol. 7, No. 1, pp. 14-23). Taylor & Francis. doi:10.1080/16258312.2006.11517154

McKinsey. (2019). *Industrial robotics - Insights into the sector's growth dynamics*. McKinsey & Company. https://www.mckinsey.com/industries/advanced-electronics/our-insights/growth-dynamics-in-industrial-robotics

Medhat, M. A., & El Kassas, M. (2020). COVID-19 in Egypt: Uncovered figures or a different situation? *Journal of Global Health*, *10*(1), 010368. doi:10.7189/jogh.10.010368 PMID:32566159

Meier, P. (2015). *Digital humanitarians: how big data is changing the face of humanitarian response*. Crc Press. doi:10.1201/b18023

Mele, J. (2021). *What is ACI?* Retrieved from cargoxhelp.zendesk.com/hc/en-us/articles/360018855758-What-is-ACI-

Meltzer, J. P. (2018). *The impact of artificial intelligence on international trade*. Brookings Institution.

Meng, Y., Chen, G., & Huang, M. (2022). Piezoelectric Materials: Properties, Advancements, and Design Strategies for High-Temperature Applications. *Nanomaterials*, *12*(7), 1171. doi:10.3390/nano12071171

Menon, A. (2021). *10 Major Ports in China*. https://www.marineinsight.com/know-more/10-major-ports-in-china/

Mentzer, J. T., Stank, T. P., & Myers, M. B. (2007). Why Global Supply Chain Management? Handbook of global supply chain management, 1-16.

Merlino, M., & Sproģe, I. (2017). The augmented supply chain. *Procedia Engineering*, *178*, 308–318. doi:10.1016/j.proeng.2017.01.053

Merzouk, S., Cherkaoui, A., Marzak, A., & Nawal, S. (2020). IoT methodologies: Comparative study. *Procedia Computer Science*, *175*, 585–590. doi:10.1016/j.procs.2020.07.084

Mes, M. R. K., Schutten, J. M. J., & Zijm, W. H. M. (2018). Freight consolidation in intermodal networks with reloads. *Flexible Services and Manufacturing Journal, 30*(3), 452-485. doi:http://dx.doi.org.libaccess.hud.ac.uk/10.1007/s10696-016-925 9-1

Millar, M. (2015). *Global supply chain ecosystems: strategies for competitive advantage in a complex, connected world.* Kogan Page Publishers.

Ministry of Commerce People's Republic of China. (2021). *Customs Clearance Procedures.* Retrieved from: http:// english.mofcom.gov.cn/

Ministry of Communication and Information Technology. (2022). Available at: https://mcit.gov.eg/en/ICT_Strategy

Ministry of Finance. (2013). *Introduction of the Advance Filing Rules on Maritime Container Cargo Information Guidance*. Customs and Tariff Bureau Ministry of Finance. Retrieved from www.wcoomd.org/-/media/wco/public/global/pdf/topics/wto-atf/dev/japan-_-advance.pdf?la=en

Ministry of Logistics and Transport. (2022). *Logistics in Saudi Arabia.* https://mot.gov.sa/ar/AboutUs/Pages/Logistic-splatform.aspx

Miralam, M. (2017). Impact of Implementing Warehouse Management system on Auto Spare Part Industry Market in. *Review of Integrative Business and Economics Research, 6*(3).

Moneim, D. (2021). *Egypt aims to be logistics hub for global trade flow: ETA head.* https://english.ahram.org.eg/NewsContent/3/12/413251/Business/Economy/Egypt-aims-to-be-logistics-hub-for-global-trade-fl .aspx

Moore, C. M., Birtwistle, G., & Burt, S. (2004). Channel power, conflict and conflict resolution in international fashion retailing. *European Journal of Marketing, 38*(7), 749–769. doi:10.1108/03090560410539230

Moosavi, J., Fathollahi-Fard, A. M., & Dulebenets, M. A. (2022). Supply chain disruption during the COVID-19 pandemic: Recognizing potential disruption management strategies. *International Journal of Disaster Risk Reduction, 75*, 102983. doi:10.1016/j.ijdrr.2022.102983 PMID:35475018

Mordor Intelligence. (2022). *Egypt Freight and Logistics Market Size, Share, Trends (2022 - 27).* https://www.mordorintelligence.com/industry-reports/egypt-freight-logistics-market-study

MSF. (2016). *Documenting war-wounded and war-dead in MSF-supported medical facilities in Syria.* Retrieved from https://doctorswithoutborders.org/sites/default/files/2018-08/syria_2015_war-dead_and_war-wounded_report_en.pdf?_ga=2.11 1148227.771097555.1650825169-1469270171.1650825169

Muerza, V., Larrodé, E., & Moreno-Jiménez, J. M. (2017). Identification and selection of ICTs for freight transport in product service supply chain diversification. *Industrial Management & Data Systems, 117*(7), 1469–1484. doi:10.1108/IMDS-09-2016-0375

Murphy, J., Paul, R., & Knemeyer, A. M. (2009). Contemporary Logistics. Pearson.

Mutlu, A., Kayikci, Y., & Çatay, B. (2017). Planning Multimodal Freight Transport Operations: a Literature Review. *Proceedings of the 22nd International Symposium on Logistics*, 535–542.

NAFEZA. (2021). *Your Comprehensive (ACI) Guide.* Retrieved from www.nafeza.gov.eg/en

Na, K. Y., Kim, D. H., Park, B. G., Yoon, S. W., & Yoon, C.-H. (2020). ICT and transport infrastructure development: An empirical analysis of complementarity. *Applied Economics*, *52*(2), 195–211. doi:10.1080/00036846.2019.1640860

Naldi, L., Nordqvist, M., Sjöberg, K., & Wiklund, J. (2007). Entrepreneurial orientation, risk taking, and performance in family firms. *Family Business Review*, *20*(1), 33–47. doi:10.1111/j.1741-6248.2007.00082.x

Naletina, D., Petljak, K., & Rožić, T. (2020). Outsourcing as a challenge for achieving competitive advantage in road freight industry – The case of Croatia. *Promet – Traffic & Transportation, 32*(1), 127-139. doi:. doi:10.7307/ptt.v32i1.3198

Namagembe, S., Ryan, S., & Sridham, R. (2017). Enviropreneurial orientation in SME supply chains: Construct measurement development. *World Journal of Entrepreneurship, Management and Sustainable Development, 13*(2), 128–150. doi:10.1108/WJEMSD-08-2016-0036

National Digital Transformation Unit. (2019). *National Digital Transformation indicators and Achievements.* https://ndu.gov.sa/en/our-reports

National Digital Transformation Unit. (2021). *Digital Economy policy in the kingdom of Saudi Arabia report.* Ministry of Communication and Transformation Technology.

Nations, U. (2016). *Sustainable development goals knowledge platform.* Academic Press.

Nazir, E., Nadeem, F., & Véronneau, S. (2016). Road safety challenges in Pakistan: An overview. *Journal of Transportation Security, 9*(3-4), 161-174. http://dx.doi.org.libaccess.hud.ac.uk/10.1007/s12198-016-0172-3

Neely, A. D., Adams, C., & Kennerley, M. (2002). *The performance prism: The scorecard for measuring and managing business success.* Prentice Hall Financial Times.

Neffati, M. (2019). Socioeconomic Impacts of Digitization in Saudi Arabia. *International Journal of Economics and Finance*, *9*(3).

Neuweiler, L., & Vanessa Riedel, P. (2017). *Autonomous Driving in the Logistics Industry* [Thesis]. Jönköping University.

Nicola, M. E., Alsafi, Z., Sohrabi, C., Kerwan, A., Al-Jabir, A., Iosifidis, C., Agha, M., & Agha, R. (2020). The socio-economic implications of the coronavirus pandemic (COVID-19): *A Review. International Journal of Surgery*, *78*, 185–193. doi:10.1016/j.ijsu.2020.04.018 PMID:32305533

Nikbakhsh, E., & Farahani, R. Z. (2011). Humanitarian logistics planning in disaster relief operations. *Logistics operations and management: Concepts and models, 291.*

Nižetić, S. (2020). Impact of coronavirus (COVID-19) pandemic on air transport mobility, energy, and environment: A case study. *International Journal of Energy Research*, *44*(13), 10953–10961. doi:10.1002/er.5706

Nkrumah, S. K., Asamoah, D., Annan, J., & Agyei-Owusu, B. (2020). Examining green capabilities as drivers of green supply chain management adoption. *Management Research Review*.

NMI. (2021). E-Governance and Digital Transformation - Egypt. NMI.

Odongo, W., Dora, M., Molnár, A., Ongeng, D., & Gellynck, X. (2016). Performance perceptions among food supply chain members: A triadic assessment of the influence of supply chain relationship quality on supply chain performance. *British Food Journal*, *118*(7), 1783–1799. doi:10.1108/BFJ-10-2015-0357

OECD. (2020a). *COVID-19 crisis response in MENA countries*. OECD. https://read.oecd-ilibrary.org/view/?ref=129_129919-4li7bq8asv&title=COVID-19-Crisis-Response-in-MENA-Countries&_ga=2.27386362.736981282.1637125248-1008574582.1623229278

OECD. (2020b). *The impact of Coronavirus (COVID-19) and the global oil price shock on the fiscal position of oil-exporting developing countries*. OECD. https://read.oecd-ilibrary.org/view/?ref=136_136801-aw9nps8afk&title=The-impact-of-Coronavirus-COVID-19-and-the-global-oil-price-shock-on-the-fiscal-position-of-oil-exporting-developing-countries&_ga=2.2246262.736981282.1637125248-1008574582.1623229278

Oh, S., Moon, H. C., & Zhong, Y. (2020). Contingency management and supply chain performance in Korea: A covid-19 pandemic approach. *Sustainability*, *12*(23), 9823. doi:10.3390u12239823

Okangi, F. P. (2019). The impacts of entrepreneurial orientation on the profitability growth of construction firms in Tanzania. *Journal of Global Entrepreneurship Research*, *9*(1), 1–23. doi:10.118640497-018-0143-1

Olaverri & Monreal. (2016). Intelligent technologies for mobility in smart cities. *Hiradastechnika*, *71*, 29–34.

Olesen, T. R. (2015). Value Creation in the Maritime Chain of Transportation: The Role of Carriers, Ports and Third Parties in Liner and Bulk Shipping (2nd ed.). CBS Maritime.

Oliva, R., & Watson, N. (2011). Cross-functional alignment in supply chain planning: A case study of sales and operations planning. *Journal of Operations Management, 29*(5), 434-448.

Omran, H. (2020). *Egypt's maritime, air freight sectors hit by COVID-19: AmCham*. Daily News Egypt. https://dailynewsegypt.com/2020/04/29/egypts-maritime-air-freight-sectors-hit-by-covid-19-amcham/

OPEC. (2020). *OPEC: The 10th (Extraordinary) OPEC and non-OPEC Ministerial Meeting concludes*. https://www.opec.org/opec_web/en/press_room/5891.htm

Osama, A., Elgarhy, A., & Elseddawy, A. (2022). *A Proposed Framework for Enhancing the transportation systems based on the physical internet and data science techniques. In Proceedings of the Future Technologies Conference (FTC) 2022*. Springer. Retrieved from https://link.springer.com/chapter/10.1007/978-3-031-18461-1_38

Osorio-Tejada, J. L., Llera-Sastresa, E., & Scarpellini, S. (2017). Liquefied natural gas: Could it be a reliable option for road freight transport in the EU? *Renewable & Sustainable Energy Reviews*, *71*, 785–795. doi:10.1016/j.rser.2016.12.104

Othman, A.A., Sundram, V.K., Sayuti, N.M., & Bahrin, A.S. (2016). The relationship between supply chain integration, just-in-time and logistics performance: A supplier's perspective on the automotive industry in Malaysia. *International Journal of Supply Chain Management*, *5*(1), 44-51.

Paksoy, T., Koçhan, C., & Ali, S. S. (2021). *Logistics 4.0: Digital transformation of supply chain management*. CRC Press.

Palmatier, R. W., Sivadas, E., Stern, L. W., & El-Ansary, A. I. (2020). Marketing Channel Strategy (9th ed.). Academic Press.

Palmer, J. S. (2010). *The Cargo Theft Threat*. Inbound Logistics. Available at: https://www.inboundlogistics.com/cms/article/the-cargo-theft-threat/

Panigrahi, S. S., Bahinipati, B., & Jain, V. (2018). Sustainable supply chain management: A review of literature and implications for future research. *Management of Environmental Quality*.

Parihar, M. (2017). Using Intelligent Transport System (ITS) to Solve Problems of Road Freight Transportation Industry in India. *Supply Chain Pulse*, *8*(1), 6–12.

Paritala, P. K., Manchikatla, S., & Yarlagadda, P. K. (2017). Digital manufacturing-applications past, current, and future trends. *Procedia Engineering*, *174*, 982–991. doi:10.1016/j.proeng.2017.01.250

Paul, S. K., Asian, S., Goh, M., & Torabi, S. A. (2019). Managing sudden transportation disruptions in supply chains under delivery delay and quantity loss. *Annals of Operations Research*, *273*(1-2), 783–814. doi:10.100710479-017-2684-z

Paul, S. K., Chowdhury, P., Moktadir, M. A., & Lau, K. H. (2021). Supply chain recovery challenges in the wake of COVID-19 pandemic. *Journal of Business Research*, *136*, 316–329. doi:10.1016/j.jbusres.2021.07.056 PMID:34538979

Pfeiffer, S. (2017). The Vision of "Industrie 4.0" in the Making—A Case of Future Told, Tamed, and Traded. *NanoEthics*, *11*(1), 107–121. doi:10.100711569-016-0280-3 PMID:28435474

Pharco. (2021). *Pharco Reports*. Pharco Corporation in Egypt.

PHR. (2019). *The Syrian Conflict: Eight Years of Devastation and Destruction of the Health System.* Retrieved from https://phr.org/wp-content/uploads/2019/03/PHR-Syria-2019-Fact-Sheet.pdf

Phuong Vu, T., Grant, D. B., & Menachof, D. A. (2020). Exploring logistics service quality in Hai Phong, Vietnam. *The Asian Journal of Shipping and Logistics*, *36*(2), 54–64. doi:10.1016/j.ajsl.2019.12.001

Pibernik, R., & Sucky, E. (2007). An approach to inter-domain master planning in supply chains. *International Journal of Production Economics*, *108*(1-2), 200–212. doi:10.1016/j.ijpe.2006.12.010

Pinto, L. (2020). Green supply chain practices and company performance in Portuguese manufacturing sector. *Business Strategy and the Environment*, *29*(5), 1832–1849. doi:10.1002/bse.2471

Płotka-Wasylka, J., & Wojnowski, W. (2021). Complementary green analytical procedure index (ComplexGAPI) and software. *Green Chemistry*, *23*(21), 8657–8665. doi:10.1039/D1GC02318G

Poongodi, T., Rathee, A., Indrakumari, R., & Suresh, P. (2019). Iot sensing capabilities: Sensor deployment and node discovery, wearable sensors, wireless body area network (WBAN), data acquisition. *Intelligent Systems Reference Library*, *174*(July), 127–151. doi:10.1007/978-3-030-33596-0_5

Popp, R. L., & Yen, J. (Eds.). (2006). *Emergent information technologies and enabling policies for counterterrorism* (Vol. 6). Wiley-IEEE Press. doi:10.1002/047178656X

Priswanto, A., Maryanto, S., & Santoso, R, D. (2019). Wireless sensor module for 3-axis vibration and tilt monitoring on the structural building. *Journal of Physics: Conference Series*, *1153*, 012040. doi:10.1088/1742-6596/1153/1/012040

Qiuxia, H., & Yujie, H. (2022). The Application of Internet of Things Data Analysis in the Development of International Trade. *Computational Intelligence and Neuroscience*, *2022*, 1–8. Advance online publication. doi:10.1155/2022/5507951 PMID:35769269

Queiroz, M. M., Ivanov, D., Dolgui, A., & Fosso Wamba, S. (2020). Impacts of epidemic outbreaks on supply chains: mapping a research agenda amid the COVID-19 pandemic through a structured literature review. In Annals of Operations Research. Springer US. doi:10.100710479-020-03685-7

Queiroz, M. M., Ivanov, D., Dolgui, A., & Fosso Wamba, S. (2020). Impacts of epidemic outbreaks on supply chains: Mapping a research agenda amid the COVID-19 pandemic through a structured literature review. *Annals of Operations Research*, 1–38. PMID:32836615

Queiroz, M. M., Pereira, S. C. F., Telles, R., & Machado, M. C. (2019). *Industry 4.0 and digital supply chain capabilities A framework for understanding digitalisation challenges and opportunities. Benchmarking: An International Journal.* doi:10.1108/BIJ-12-2018-0435

Raats, K., Fors, V., & Pink, S. (2020). Trusting autonomous vehicles: An interdisciplinary approach. *Transportation Research Interdisciplinary Perspectives*, *7*, 100201. doi:10.1016/j.trip.2020.100201

Radwan, A. (2015). *Intelligent transportation system as a tool in solving Cairo's transportation problems.* Academic Press.

Rai Technology University. (2012). *Import-Export Management.* Retrieved from www.raitechuniversity.in

Ramanathan, U., Williams, N. L., Zhang, M., Sa-nguanjin, P., Garza-Reyes, J. A., & Borges, L. A. (2020). A new perspective of E-trust in the era of social media: Insights from customer satisfaction data. *IEEE Transactions on Engineering Management.*

Ranieri, L., Digiesi, S., Silvestri, B., & Roccotelli, M. (2018). A review of last mile logistics innovations in an externalities cost reduction vision. *Sustainability*, *10*(3), 782. doi:10.3390u10030782

Ranpank. (2022). 3 Trends Elevating the Importance of Green Warehousing. *Sustainability.*

Raslan, W. E. (2021). Fractional mathematical modeling for epidemic prediction of COVID-19 in Egypt. *Ain Shams Engineering Journal*, *12*(3), 3057–3062. doi:10.1016/j.asej.2020.10.027

Ratten, V. (2020). Coronavirus (covid-19) and entrepreneurship: Changing life and work landscape. *Journal of Small Business and Entrepreneurship*, *32*(5), 503–516. doi:10.1080/08276331.2020.1790167

Regis-Hernández, F., Mora-Vargas, J., Sánchez-Partida, D., & Ruiz, A. (2022). *Humanitarian Logistics from the Disaster Risk Reduction Perspective.* Springer. doi:10.1007/978-3-030-90877-5

Reidy, S. (2020). *Cargo Theft: An unavoidable problem within your supply chain.* Available at: https://arviem.com/cargo-theft-problem-supply-chain/

Reimann, F., Kosmol, T., & Kaufmann, L. (2017). Responses to supplier-induced disruptions: A fuzzy-set analysis. *The Journal of Supply Chain Management*, *53*(4), 37–66. doi:10.1111/jscm.12141

Reis, V., & Macedo, P. (2019). Mapping and evaluating the complexity of information flows in freight transport chains. *Transportation Planning and Technology*, *42*(8), 757–776. doi:10.1080/03081060.2019.1675312

Reuters. (2022). *Egypt's 2021 petroleum exports revenue up 84.3% to $12.9 bln -minister.* Reuters. https://www.reuters.com/article/egypt-petroleum-exports-idUSS8N2SK06R

Rhodes, L., & Dawson, R. (2013). Lessons learned from lessons learned. *Knowledge and Process Management*, *20*(3), 154–160. doi:10.1002/kpm.1415

Rice, J. B., & Caniato, F. (2003). Building a secure and resilient supply network. *Supply Chain Management Review*, *7*(5), 22–30.

Richey, R. G., Tokman, M., & Wheeler, A. R. (2006). A supply chain manager selection methodology: Empirical test and suggested application. *Journal of Business Logistics*, *27*(2), 163–190. doi:10.1002/j.2158-1592.2006.tb00221.x

Riley, J. M., Klein, R., Miller, J., & Sridharan, V. (2016). How internal integration, information sharing, and training affect supply chain risk management capabilities. *International Journal of Physical Distribution & Logistics Management, 46*(10), 953–980. doi:10.1108/IJPDLM-10-2015-0246

Rocha, H. O. (2004). Entrepreneurship and development: The role of clusters. *Small Business Economics, 23*(5), 363–400. doi:10.100711187-004-3991-8

Rockwell Anyoha. (2020, April 23). The History of Artificial Intelligence. Science in the News. https://sitn.hms.harvard.edu/flash/2017/history-artificial-intelligence/

Rogerson, S., Svanberg, M., & Santén, V. (2022). Supply chain disruptions: Flexibility measures when encountering capacity problems in a port conflict. *International Journal of Logistics Management, 33*(2), 567–589. doi:10.1108/IJLM-03-2020-0123

Rojko, A. (2017). Industry 4. 0 Concept. *Background and Overview., 11*(5), 77–90.

Rokkan, A. I., & Buvik, A. (2003). Inter-firm cooperation and the problem of free riding behavior: An empirical study of voluntary retail chains. *Journal of Purchasing and Supply Management, 9*(5-6), 247–256. doi:10.1016/j.pursup.2003.09.004

Roso, A., & Labas, D. (2019). Use of Performance Measurement Methods in Croatian Firms. *Economic and Social Development: Book of Proceedings*, 114-122.

Ross, D. (2003). *Introduction to E-Supply Chain Management.* St. Lucie Press.

Rowley, J. (Ed.). (2000). *The principles of warehouse design.* Institute of Logistics and Transport.

Rozhkov, M., Ivanov, D., Blackhurst, J., & Nair, A. (2022). Adapting supply chain operations in anticipation of and during the COVID-19 pandemic. *Omega, 110*, 102635. doi:10.1016/j.omega.2022.102635 PMID:35291412

Ryciuk, U. (2020). Supply Chain Governance Mechanisms: A Review and Typology. *Eurasian Business Perspectives,* 145-159.

Sadouskaya, K. (2017). *Adoption of Blockchain Technology in Supply Chain and Logistics.* Retrieved from www.semanticscholar.org/paper/Adoption-of-Blockchain-Technologyin-Supply-Chain-Sadouskaya/2ed7baf04dc202f1e

Saeed, A., Rasheed, F., Waseem, M., & Tabash, M. I. (2021). Green human resource management and environmental performance: The role of green supply chain management practices. *Benchmarking.*

Safa, M., Green, K. W., Zelbst, P. J., & Sower, V. E. (2022). Enhancing Supply Chain through Implementation of Key IIoT Technologies. *Journal of Computer Information Systems*, 1–11. doi:10.1080/08874417.2022.2067792

Sahay, B., Gupta, S., & Menon, V. C. (2016). *Managing humanitarian logistics.* Springer. doi:10.1007/978-81-322-2416-7

Salonitis, K., & Ball, P. (2013). Energy efficient manufacturing from machine tools to manufacturing systems. *Procedia CIRP, 7*, 634–639. doi:10.1016/j.procir.2013.06.045

Salvatore, D. (2020). Growth and trade in the United States and the world economy: Overview. *Journal of Policy Modeling, 42*(4), 750–759. doi:10.1016/j.jpolmod.2020.03.001 PMID:32362694

Samad, S., Nilashi, M., Almulihi, A., Alrizq, M., Alghamdi, A., Mohd, S., Ahmadi, H., & Azhar, S. N. F. S. (2021). Green Supply Chain Management practices and impact on firm performance: The moderating effect of collaborative capability. *Technology in Society, 67*, 101766. doi:10.1016/j.techsoc.2021.101766

Samih, H. (2019). Smart cities and internet of things. *Journal of Information Technology Case and Application Research, 21*(1), 3–12. doi:10.1080/15228053.2019.1587572

Samir, N. (2022). *Egypt acts as hub for global trade routes: South Korean Ambassador.* Daily News Egypt. https://dailynewsegypt.com/2022/05/31/egypt-acts-as-hub-for-global-trade-routes-south-korean-ambassador/

Sarkis, J. (2020). Supply chain sustainability: Learning from the COVID-19 pandemic. *International Journal of Operations & Production Management, 41*(1), 63–73. doi:10.1108/IJOPM-08-2020-0568

Sarmento, H., Clemente, F. M., Araújo, D., Davids, K., McRobert, A., & Figueiredo, A. (2017). 2018;). What performance analysts need to know about research trends in association football (2012–2016): A systematic review. *Sports Medicine (Auckland), 48*(4), 799–836. doi:10.100740279-017-0836-6 PMID:29243038

Satista Reports, (2021). https://www.statista.com/statistics/698675/saudi-arabia-number-of-organizedretailers

Saunders, M., Lewis, P., & Thornhill, A. (2009). *Research methods for business students.* Pearson education.

Scala, B., & Lindsay, C. F. (2021). Supply chain resilience during pandemic disruption: Evidence from healthcare. *Supply Chain Management, 26*(6), 672–688. doi:10.1108/SCM-09-2020-0434

Schumpeter, J. (1961). The theory of economic development: an inquiry into profits, capital, credit, interest, and the business cycle. Oxford University Press. (Original publication 1934)

SCPR. (2013). *Syria- War on Development: socioeconomic monitoring report of Syria, second quarterly report (April – June 2013).* Retrieved from https://reliefweb.int/sites/reliefweb.int/files/resources/md_syr-rprt_q2fnl_251013.pdf

Seelos, C., & Mair, J. (2004). *Social entrepreneurship-The contribution of individual entrepreneurs to sustainable development.* Academic Press.

Sekhar, B. C., Dhanalakshmi, B., Rao, B. S., Ramesh, S., Prasad, K. V., Rao, P. S., & Rao, B. P. (2021). Piezoelectricity and Its Applications. In Multifunctional Ferroelectric Materials. IntechOpen. doi:10.5772/intechopen.96154

Selby, L. M., Hewlett, A. L., Cawcutt, K. A., Wood, M. G., Balfour, T. L., Rupp, M. E., & Starlin, R. C. (2021). Effect of severe acute respiratory coronavirus virus 2 (SARS-CoV-2) mRNA vaccinations in healthcare workers with high-risk coronavirus disease 2019 (COVID-19) exposure. *Infection Control and Hospital Epidemiology, 42*(10), 1281–1282. doi:10.1017/ice.2021.193 PMID:33934742

Sengupta, S., Niranjan, T. T., & Krishnamoorthy, M. (2018). Trends and directions in service triads research. *International Journal of Physical Distribution & Logistics Management, 48*(3), 333–360. doi:10.1108/IJPDLM-02-2017-0095

Seow, Y., & Rahimifard, S. (2011). A framework for modelling energy consumption within manufacturing systems. *CIRP Journal of Manufacturing Science and Technology, 4*(3), 258–264. doi:10.1016/j.cirpj.2011.03.007

Shahin, M. (2021). *Trade Facilitation Profile.* Retrieved from www.idsc.gov.eg/

Shah, S., Logiotatopouloh, I., & Menon, S. (2019). Industry 4.0 and Autonomous Transportation: The Impacts on Supply Chain Management. *International Journal of Trasportation Systems, 4*, 45–50. http://www.iaras.org/iaras/journals/ijts

Shahzad, K., Ali, T., Kohtamäki, M., & Takala, J. (2020). Enabling roles of relationship governance mechanisms in the choice of inter-firm conflict resolution strategies. *Journal of Business and Industrial Marketing, 35*(6), 957–969. doi:10.1108/JBIM-06-2019-0309

Sharma, S., & Routroy, S. (2016). Modeling information risk in the supply chain using Bayesian networks. *Journal of Enterprise Information Management*, *29*(2), 238–254. doi:10.1108/JEIM-03-2014-0031

Shigehiro, M., Miyakawa, T., & Masuda, T. (2012). Road traffic control is based on a genetic algorithm for reducing traffic congestion. *Electronics and Communications in Japan*, *95*(4), 11–19. doi:10.1002/ecj.10421

SHIPA. (2022). *About Us*. https://www.shipafreight.com/about-us/

Shou, Y., Li, Y., Park, Y., & Kang, M. (2018). Supply chain integration and operational performance: The contingency effects of production systems. *Journal of Purchasing and Supply Management*, *24*(4), 352–360. doi:10.1016/j.pursup.2017.11.004

Skiba, S., & Karaś, A. (2022). The Changing Role of a Freight Forwarder in Modern Supply Chains. *European Research Studies*, *25*(1), 341–351. doi:10.35808/ersj/2856

Solban, M. M., & Moussa, R. R. (2019). *IOP Conf. Ser.: Earth Environ. Sci.* https://iopscience.iop.org/article/10.1088/1755-1315/397/1/012020/meta

Song, R., Huang, L., Cui, W., Óskarsdóttir, M., & Vanthienen, J. (2020). Fraud detection of bulk cargo theft in port using bayesian network models. *Applied Sciences (Switzerland)*, *10*(3), 1056. doi:10.3390/app10031056

Song, Z., He, S., & Xu, G. (2018). Decision and coordination of fresh produce three-layer E-commerce supply chain: A new framework. *IEEE Access: Practical Innovations, Open Solutions*, *7*, 30465–30486. doi:10.1109/ACCESS.2018.2881106

Sorrell, S., & Stapleton, L. (2018). Rebound effects in UK road freight transport. *Transportation Research Part D, Transport and Environment*, *63*, 156–174. doi:10.1016/j.trd.2018.05.006

Sousa, F. J. (2010). Markets-as-networks theory: A review. *Organizational culture, business-to-business relationships, and interfirm networks*.

Spectral Engines. 2018. Industry 4.0 and how smart sensors make the difference. https://www.spectralengines.com/articles/industry-4-0-and-how-smart-sensors-make-the-difference

Speedtest. (2022). *Saudi Arabia's Mobile and Broadband Internet Speeds – Speed test Global.* https://www.speedtest.net/global-index/saudi-arabia

StanczykA. (2022). https://link.springer.com/article/10.1057/s41301-022-00335-2

Staněk, M. (2017). The humanitarian crisis and civil war in Syria: Its impact and influence on the migration crisis in Europe. *Kontakt*, *19*(4), e270–e275. doi:10.1016/j.kontakt.2017.09.013

Stank, T. P., Daugherty, P. J., & Ellinger, A. E. (1999). Marketing/logistics integration and firm performance. *International Journal of Logistics Management*, *10*(1), 11–24. doi:10.1108/09574099910805905

Statista. (2022). *Blank and skipped sailings worldwide.* Statista. https://www.statista.com/statistics/1223853/blank-and-skipped-sailings-worldwide/

Stevens, P. (2020). *Oil plunges 24% for worst day since 1991 after OPEC deal failure sparks price war.* https://www.cnbc.com/2020/03/08/oil-plummets-30percent-as-opec-deal-failure-sparks-price-war-fears.html

Stewart, P., Broom, R., & Ahmed, N. (2020). *How Can the Oil and Gas Industry Prepare to Deal With the Impact of COVID-19?* https://www.eia.gov/beta/international/analysis_includes/countries_long/United_Arab_Emirates/uae.pdf

Stojanović, D. M., & Velickovic, M. (2019). *Freight forwarding industry-The contemporary role and development trends in Serbia.* https://www.researchgate.net/publication/340446983

Straight, B. (2020). *Cargo theft on the rise.* FreightWaves. Available at: https://www.freightwaves.com/news/cargo-theft-on-the-rise

Strong, S., Delzell, P., Trygstad, W., Fitzpatrick, G., Haley-Hyer, P., Bates, A., & Awwad, M. (2020, January). The impact of covid-19 on the pharmaceutical supply chain. In *2nd African International Conference on Industrial Engineering and Operations Management* (pp. 565-572). IEOM.

Studer, S., Welford, R., & Hills, P. (2006). Engaging Hong Kong businesses in environmental change: Drivers and barriers. *Business Strategy and the Environment, 15*(6), 416–431. doi:10.1002/bse.516

Sturmanis, A., Hudenko, J. & Jurušs, M. (2020). *The Application of Blockchain Technologies for Rail Transit Customs Procedures.* . doi:10.1007/978-3-030-44610-9_26

Subhashini, S., & Preetha, S. (2018). An empirical analysis of service quality factors pertaining to ocean freight forwarding services. *Maritime Business Review, 3*(3), 276–289. doi:10.1108/MABR-01-2018-0004

Sugiono, A., Rahayu, A., & Wibowo, L. A. (2022). Environmental Uncertainty Factor, Incoterm and Implication For A Strategic Alliance In Freight Forwarder Companies Case Study In Indonesia. *Asian Journal of Logistics Management, 1*(1), 1–15. doi:10.14710/ajlm.2022.14230

Sullivan, J. L., Lewis, G. M., & Keoleian, G. A. (2018). Effect of mass on multimodal fuel consumption in moving people and freight in the U.S. *Transportation Research Part D, Transport and Environment, 63*, 786–808. doi:10.1016/j.trd.2018.06.019

Sun, N. (2021). Intelligent Transportation System Planning in the Age of Artificial Intelligence. *E3S Web of Conferences, 253*, 4–8. doi:10.1051/e3sconf/202125301036

Swierczek, A. (2020). Relational orientation of triadic supply chains with structural holes: An empirical comparison of rents derived from bridging the structural holes. *Supply Chain Management, 25*(5), 565–583. doi:10.1108/SCM-10-2019-0382

Swiss Embassy in Egypt. (2016). *Egypt: New Import Procedures/Measures. Cairo: State Secretariat for Economic Affairs SECO.* Retrieved from www.sage.com/sites/default/files/mig/sites/default/files/EGYPT-Import_April.pdf

Syed, A. S., Sierra-Sosa, D., Kumar, A., & Elmaghraby, A. (2021). Iot in smart cities: A survey of technologies, practices and challenges. *Smart Cities, 4*(2), 429–475. doi:10.3390martcities4020024

Taek Yi, H., Lee, J., & Dubinsky, A. J. (2010). An empirical investigation of relational conflicts in co-marketing alliances. *Journal of Business-To-Business Marketing, 17*(3), 249–278. doi:10.1080/10517120903465350

Tahmasebifard, H., Zangoueinezhad, A., & Jafari, P. (2017). The role of entrepreneurial orientation in achieving agility capability. *Journal of Applied Economics & Business Research, 7*(2), 137–156.

Tang, C. S. (2006). Perspectives in supply chain risk management. *International Journal of Production Economics, 103*(2), 451–488. doi:10.1016/j.ijpe.2005.12.006

Tang, C., & Tomlin, B. (2008). The power of flexibility for mitigating supply chain risks. *International Journal of Production Economics, 116*(1), 12–27. doi:10.1016/j.ijpe.2008.07.008

Taulli, T. (2019). *Artificial Intelligence Basics*. Artificial Intelligence Basics. doi:10.1007/978-1-4842-5028-0

Tay, H. L., & Loh, H. S. (2021). Digital transformations and supply chain management: A Lean Six Sigma perspective. *Journal of Asia Business Studies*. doi:10.1108/JABS-10-2020-0415

Tay, S. I., Lee, T. C., Hamid, N. A. A., & Ahmad, A. N. A. (2018). An Overview of Industry 4.0: Definition, Components, and Government Initiatives. *Journal of Advanced Research in Dynamical and Control Systems, Safety and Environmental Protection, 117*, 408–425.

Thakurdesai, H. M., & Aghav, J. V. (2020). Autonomous Cars: Technical Challenges and a Solution to Blind Spot. Advances in Intelligent Systems and Computing, 533–547. https://doi.org/ doi:10.1007/978-981-15-1275-9_44

Thapa, B. (2014). *Adoption of new technology in supply chain management: A survey of Nepalese organizations*. Academic Press.

The Economic Times. (2020a). COVID-19 impact: Drugs essential, ancillaries not so, means supplies take a hit. *The Economic Times*. https://economictimes.indiatimes.com/industry/healthcare/biotech/pharmaceuticals/drugsessential-ancillaries-not-so-means-supplies-take-a-hit/articleshow/75038462.cms?from=mdr

The Egyptian Centre for Economic Studies. (2019). *Egypt Pharmaceuticals and Healthcare Report*. https://nations-emergentes.org/wp-content/uploads/2019/02/egypt-pharmaceutical-survey.pdf

The Story of the Chinese Abacus. (n.d.). http://en.chinaculture.org/classics/2010-04/20/content_383263.htm

The World Bank for Egypt's Economic Update. (2020). *Impact of Covid-19 on Egypt's Economy*. https://www.worldbank.org/en/country/egypt/publication/economic-update-october-2020

Thompson, D. D., & Anderson, R. (2021). The COVID-19 response: Considerations for future humanitarian supply chain and logistics management research. *Journal of Humanitarian Logistics and Supply Chain Management, 11*(2), 157–175. doi:10.1108/JHLSCM-01-2021-0006

Tob-Ogu, A., Kumar, N., Cullen, J., & Ballantyne, E. (2018). Sustainability intervention mechanisms for managing road freight transport externalities: A systematic literature review. *Sustainability, 10*(6), 1923. doi:10.3390u10061923

Tomasini, R., Van Wassenhove, L., & Van Wassenhove, L. (2009). *Humanitarian logistics*. Springer. doi:10.1057/9780230233485

Tsiulin, S., Reinau, K., Hilmola, O., Goryaev, N., & Karam, A. (2020). Blockchain-based applications in shipping and port management: A literature review towards defining key conceptual frameworks. *Review of International Business and Strategy, 30*(2), 201–224. doi:10.1108/RIBS-04-2019-0051

UN Comtrade. (2021). *Egypt | Imports and Exports | World | ALL COMMODITIES | Value (US$) and Value Growth, YoY (%) | 2009 - 2020*. https://trendeconomy.com/data/h2/Egypt/TOTAL

UNCTAD. (2017). *Review of Maritime Transport*. https://unctad.org/system/files/official-document/rmt2017_en.pdf

UNCTAD. (2020). *COVID-19 and maritime transport: Impact and responses*. UNCTAD.

UNESCWA. (2021). *Syria at War: Eight Years On*. Retrieved from Beirut: https://publications.unescwa.org/projects/saw/sdgs/pdf/en/Syria-at-War-8-years-on-Report-Final.pdf

UNOCHA. (2013). *Humanitarianism in the Network Age; Including World Humanitarian Data and Trends 2012*. Retrieved from https://reliefweb.int/sites/reliefweb.int/files/resources/Humanitarianism%20in%20the%20Network%20Age.pdf

UNOCHA. (2021). *Humanitarian Needs Overview: Syrian Arab Republic*. Retrieved from New York: www.unocha.org/syria

USDA. (2021). *Egypt Postpones Launch of the Advanced Cargo Information System to Oct 1*. Global Agriculture Information Trade. Retrieved from www.fas.usda.gov/

USITC. (2020). *The Impact of the COVID-19 Pandemic on Freight Transportation Services and U.S. Merchandise Imports*. https://www.usitc.gov/research_and_analysis/tradeshifts/2020/special_topic.html

Valentin Carlan, C. S., & T. V. (2019). *Innovation in Road Freight Transport : Quantifying the Environmental Performance of Operational*. Academic Press.

Van der Meer, J. J., Hassan, S., Lofink, O., Jones, R., & Hagedorn, R. (2018). *AI and robotics automation in consumer-driven supply chains*. https://www.theconsumergoodsforum.com/wp-content/uploads/2018/04/201805-CGF-AI-Robotics-Report-with-PA-Consulting.pdf

van der Merwe, B. (2021). *How Covid created shipping's container shortage*. Investment Monitor. https://www.investmentmonitor.ai/analysis/covid-global-shipping-container-shortage

Van Hoek, R. I. (2006). Moving forward with agility–a little faster. *International Journal of Physical Distribution & Logistics Management*, *36*(6). Advance online publication. doi:10.1108/ijpdlm.2006.00536faa.002

Van Wassenhove, L. N. (2006). Humanitarian aid logistics: Supply chain management in high gear. *The Journal of the Operational Research Society*, *57*(5), 475–489. doi:10.1057/palgrave.jors.2602125

Varley, K., & Koh, A. (2022). *Supply-Chain: China Port Congestion Worsens as 477 Bulk Ships Waiting to Berth*. https://www.bloomberg.com/news/articles/2022-04-11/477-bulk-ships-wait-off-east-china-s-ports-amid-virus-lockdowns

Vasileska, D., Khan, H. R., & Ahmed, S. S. (2008). Modeling Coulomb Effects in Nanoscale Devices. *Journal of Computational and Theoretical Nanoscience*, *5*(9), 1793–1827. doi:10.1166/jctn.2008.901

Vatkar, N. S., & Vatkar, Y. S. (2016). Piezoelectric motors & its applications. *IRJET, 3*(6), 65-72. https://www.irjet.net/archives/V3/i6/IRJET-V3I6186.pdf

Vázquez-Noguerol. González-Boubeta, Domínguez-Caamaño, & Prado-Prado. (2018). Best practices in road transport: An exploratory study. *Journal of Industrial Engineering and Management, 11*(2), 250-261. http://dx.doi.org.libaccess.hud.ac.uk/10.3926/jiem.2525

Volkswagen. (2019). *Mobility for generations to come*. Volkswagen. https://www.volkswagenag.com/presence/investorrelation/publications/annual-reports/2020/volkswagen/Y_2019_e.pdf

Vorotyntseva, T., Nemirova, G., & Vinichenko, A. (2020). Problems of application of digital technologies in international trade. In New Silk Road: Business Cooperation and Prospective of Economic Development (NSRBCPED 2019) (pp. 452-456). Atlantis Press. doi:10.2991/aebmr.k.200324.085

Wagner, S. M. (2021). Startups in the supply chain ecosystem: An organising framework and research opportunities. *International Journal of Physical Distribution & Logistics Management, 51*(10), 1130–1157. doi:10.1108/IJPDLM-02-2021-0055

Wales, W. J., Gupta, V. K., & Mousa, F. T. (2011). 201 1, Empirical Research on Entrepreneurial Orientation: An Assessment and Suggestions for Future Research. *International Small Business Journal*, 13. Advance online publication.

Wallensteen, P. (2018). Understanding conflict resolution. *Sage (Atlanta, Ga.)*.

Wallis & Lupton. (2019). *The Problem with Congestion*. World Highways. https://www.transport.govt.nz/assets/Uploads/Paper/DefiningCongestion.pdf

Wang, L., Pfohl, H. C., Berbner, U., & Keck, A. K. (2016). Supply chain collaboration or conflict? Information sharing and supply chain performance in the automotive industry. In *Commercial Transport*. Springer. doi:10.1007/978-3-319-21266-1_20

Wang, P., & Vogt, J. (2019). Untangling process complexity in logistics delivery services with unpredictable service sequences: A mixed-method study of chemical tanker port calls. *Maritime Policy & Management, 46*(3), 344–366. doi:10.1080/03088839.2018.1543908

Wang, S., Chaovalitwongse, W., & Babuška, R. (2012). Machine learning algorithms in bipedal robot control. *IEEE Transactions on Systems, Man and Cybernetics. Part C, Applications and Reviews, 42*(5), 728–743. doi:10.1109/TSMCC.2012.2186565

Wang, Y. (2022). Optimal Design of International Trade Logistics Based on Internet of Things Technology. *Computational Intelligence and Neuroscience, 2022*. Advance online publication. doi:10.1155/2022/8781095 PMID:35479599

WEF. (2021). *The Global Risks Report 2021: 16th Edition*. https://www3.weforum.org/docs/WEF_The_Global_Risks_Report_2021.pdf

Weiss, R. S. (1994). *Learning from strangers: The art and method of qualitative interview studies*. Free Press, Inc.

Welford, R. (2016). *Corporate environmental management 3: Towards sustainable development*. Routledge.

WFP. (2022). *Concept of Operations*. WFP.

White, L., & Lee, G. J. (2009). Operational research and sustainable development: Tackling the social dimension. *European Journal of Operational Research, 193*(3), 683–692. doi:10.1016/j.ejor.2007.06.057

Whiteley, D. (2000). *E-Commerce strategy, Technologies, and Application*. McGraw-Hill Publishing Company.

Whitten, G. D., Green, K. W., & Zelbst, P. J. (2012). Triple-A supply chain performance. *International Journal of Operations & Production Management*.

WHO. (2020). *Archived: WHO Timeline - COVID-19*. https://www.who.int/news/item/27-04-2020-who-timeline---covid-19

WHO. (2022). *Road traffic injuries*. Retrieved from https://www.who.int/news-room/fact-sheets/detail/road-traffic-injuries

Wielan, C. (2021). *Syria and the Neutrality Trap: Dilemmas of Delivering Humanitarian Aid through Violent Regimes*. Bloomsbury Publishing Plc.

Winebrake, J. J., Green, E. H., Comer, B., Li, C., Froman, S., & Shelby, M. (2015). Fuel price elasticities in the U.S. combination trucking sector. *Transportation Research Part D, Transport and Environment*, *38*, 166–177. doi:10.1016/j.trd.2015.04.006

Winter, M., & Knemeyer, A. M. (2013). Exploring the integration of sustainability and supply chain management. *International Journal of Physical Distribution & Logistics Management*, *43*(1), 18–38. doi:10.1108/09600031311293237

Wong, C., Skipworth, H., Godsell, J., & Achimugu, N. (2012). Towards a theory of supply chain alignment enablers: A systematic literature review. *Supply Chain Management*, *17*(4), 419–437. doi:10.1108/13598541211246567

Wong, W. P., & Wong, K. Y. (2007). Supply chain performance measurement system using DEA modeling. *Industrial Management & Data Systems*, *107*(3), 361–381. doi:10.1108/02635570710734271

Wood, L. C., Reefke, H., & Breidbach, C. F. (2012). *A typology of service supply chain strategies-pathways between agility and efficiency*. Academic Press.

World Bank. (2022). *Individuals using the Internet (% of population) - Saudi Arabia | Data*. worldbank.org

World Customs Organization. (2018). *Advance Cargo Information (ACI) Implementation Guidelines*. Retrieved from www.wcoomd.org/

World Health Organization. (2020). *Impact of Coronavirus disease (COVID-19) on pharmaceutical sector*. https://www.who.int/emergencies/diseases/novel-coronavirus-2019

World Trade Organization. (2018). The future of world trade: How digital technologies are transforming global commerce. *World Trade Review*, *17*(4), 707–709. doi:10.1017147474561800028

Wu, L., Park, D., Chinta, R., & Cunningham, M. (2010). Global entrepreneurship and supply chain management: A Chinese exemplar. *Journal of Chinese Entrepreneurship*.

Wu, C., & Barnes, D. (2012). A dynamic feedback model for partner selection in agile supply chains. *International Journal of Operations & Production Management*, *32*(1), 79–103. doi:10.1108/01443571211195745

Wurzel, R. K., Liefferink, D., & Di Lullo, M. (2019). The European Council, the Council and the Member States: Changing environmental leadership dynamics in the European Union. *Environmental Politics*, *28*(2), 248–270. doi:10.1080/09644016.2019.1549783

Yamazaki, T., Shida, K., & Kanazawa, T. (2016). An approach to establishing a method for calculating inventory. *International Journal of Production Research*, *54*(8), 2320–2331. doi:10.1080/00207543.2015.1076179

Yang, C. (2019). Maritime shipping digitalization: Blockchain-based technology applications, future improvements, and intention to use. *Transportation Research Part E, Logistics and Transportation Review*, *131*, 108–117. doi:10.1016/j.tre.2019.09.020

Yang, C. C., & Chang, Y. K. (2019). Crucial factors influencing international logistics operations for African landlocked countries–A case study of Burkina Faso. *Maritime Policy & Management*, *46*(8), 939–956. doi:10.1080/03088839.2019.1606464

youmatter. (2021). https://youmatter.world/en/definition/definitions-sustainability-definition-examples-principles

Younis, Sundarakani, & O'Mahony. (2019). *Green supply chain management and corporate performance: Developing a roadmap for future research using a mixed method approach*. Academic Press.

Yuan, R., Luo, J., Liu, M. J., & Yu, J. (2022). Understanding organizational resilience in a platform-based sharing business: The role of absorptive capacity. *Journal of Business Research*, *141*, 85–99. doi:10.1016/j.jbusres.2021.11.012

Yu, C. M. J., Liao, T. J., & Lin, Z. D. (2006). Formal governance mechanisms, relational governance mechanisms, and transaction-specific investments in supplier–manufacturer relationships. *Industrial Marketing Management*, *35*(2), 128–139. doi:10.1016/j.indmarman.2005.01.004

Zaid, M. A. (2020). *Kuwait's Agility signs contract to operate Egypt's Gosoor Project*. Arab News. https://www.arabnews.com/node/1780871/business-economy

Zambonelli, F. (2016). Towards a discipline of IoT-Oriented software engineering. *CEUR Workshop Proceedings*, *1664*, 1–7.

Zamil Steel. (2022). *About the company*. Retrieved from www.zamilsteel.com/peb/en/the-company

Zeimpekis, V., Ichoua, S., & Minis, I. (2014). *Humanitarian and relief logistics: Research issues, case studies and future trends* (Vol. 54). Springer.

Zhang, J., & Hayashi, Y. (2020). Impacts of COVID-19 on the transport sector and measures as well as recommendations of policies and future research: Analyses based on a world-wide expert survey. Academic Press.

Zhang, X., Liu, Y., & Wang, D. (2018). Blockchain technologies and applications in the steel industry. *Journal of Cleaner Production*, *172*, 4446–4451.

Zhang, X., Liu, Y., & Wang, D. (2020). Supply chain risk management in the steel industry under the COVID-19 pandemic. *Journal of Cleaner Production*, 121738.

Zhu, Q., Feng, Y., & Choi, S. B. (2017). The role of customer relational governance in environmental and economic performance improvement through green supply chain management. *Journal of Cleaner Production*, *155*, 46–53. doi:10.1016/j.jclepro.2016.02.124

Zhu, X., & Cao, Y. (2021). The optimal recovery-fund based strategy for uncertain supply chain disruptions: A risk-averse two-stage stochastic programming approach. *Transportation Research Part E, Logistics and Transportation Review*, *152*, 102387. doi:10.1016/j.tre.2021.102387

Zid.sa Platform. (2022). https://blog.zid.sa/products-update-q1-2022/

Zobel, C. W., Altay, N., & Haselkorn, M. P. (2015). *Advances in managing humanitarian operations*. Springer.

Zou, Q., & Wang, Y. (2022). Understanding opportunism in buyer–supplier–supplier triadic relationships: The role of power asymmetry. *Management Decision*, *60*(11), 2952–2971. doi:10.1108/MD-05-2021-0654

Zwitter, Lamont, Heintze, & Herman. (2014). Humanitarian Action: Global, Regional and Domestic Legal Responses. Cambridge University Press.

About the Contributors

Islam Abdelbary is an Egyptian economist, an economic researcher at the University of Plymouth, and also a lecturer of economics at the Arab Academy for Science and Technology since 2007. He holds a PhD from the University of Plymouth in the UK, and his BSc and MSc degrees in Economics from Alexandria University. Abdelbary's current research focuses on Institutional Economics, Sustainability and economic development. He has published several research papers in ranked journals on topics in development reform policy in developing countries and particularly in the MENA region, besides presented numerous working papers at international conferences. His research has been awarded several international prizes, such as the Ibn Khaldun Prize 2018. Abdelbary also works as an independent researcher in several multi-disciplinary research projects for national and international organisations.

Sandra Haddad is an Assistant Professor in Marketing and Supply Chain Management at the Arab Academy for Science, Technology and Maritime Transport - College of International Transport and Logistics. She is acting as the vice dean for postgraduate studies and research. Dr. Haddad holds a Bachelor's degree in Business Administration (major in marketing) and a postgraduate diploma from the School of Management - Arab Academy for Science, Technology and Maritime Transport. She obtained her MSc in Shipping Management from the World Maritime University in Malmoe, Sweden, and her PhD in Supply Chain Management from Liverpool John Moores University in the UK. Dr. Haddad was awarded the Fellowship of the British Higher Education Academy (AFHEA) in 2013, and she is a certified Higher Fiata diploma and International Road Union (IRU) instructor. Moreover, Dr. Haddad works as a professional consultant for several businesses, in addition to managing several EU and US Aid projects.

Ghada Elkady is an Assistant Professor in supply chain and logistics modelling in the College of International Transport & Logistics, Arab Academy for Science, Technology and Maritime Transport. Her research interests include both serious games and their applications in education and training, as well as simulation modelling for Retail Industry, insight and prediction. Ghada has published some researches in the field of simulation modelling, blockchain in agri-food and big data analytics in retail sector. she recently member of System Dynamics Society (US) and the UK Chapter of the System Dynamics Society. she currently reviewer in some journals and international conferences such as Journal of Transport & supply chain management and Cogent journal.

* * *

Bassma Abdelaleem is a master's student at the Arab Institute for Trade & Commodity Exchange (AITC), College of International Transport and Logistics, Arab Academy for Science and Technology and Maritime Transport (AASTMT), Alexandria. She holds a bachelor's degree in International Transport and Logistics, major Supply Chain Management. She is working as a Graduate Teaching Assistant in the College of International Transport and Logistics, Department of Supply Chain Management, AASTMT, Alexandria, Egypt. She has taught many courses related to supply chain and logistics management.

Ahmed Ahmed is currently the Export Head of (SEDICO), one of the largest pharmaceutical companies in Egypt. He was the Export Manager of Pharco Pharmaceuticals Group till 2021. Ahmed holds an MBA from the Arab Academy for Science Technology and Maritime Transport (AASTMT) "International Business Major". He is a part-time instructor at the AASTMT – College of International Transport and Logistics and is a DBA researcher at the AASTMT since 2020 (Marketing Major).

Onur Aksaray received his undergraduate education at Dokuz Eylül University, Department of General Business Administration. During his undergraduate education, he spent 3 months each in Mercedes Benz & Bayer AG, Istanbul (Turkey) as a marketing trainee. After graduation, he was accepted to begin as a Customer Representative / Business Development Specialist in one of the biggest Shipping Liner in Turkey who is named Arkas Line, part of Arkas Holding. He lives currently in Dusseldorf Germany , with leading the same tasks in the name of Borusan Logistics.

Ahmed Al is a Lecturer at Arab Academy for Science, Technology and Maritime Transport - College of International Transport and Logistics (CITL), He has graduated from CITL year 2010. In 2014, he has awarded Master degree in Supply chain and logistics. In 2021, he has awarded PhD at Duisburg-Essen university in Transport system and Logistics.

Hesham Aly is an Assistant Professor of the Electronics and Communication Engineering Department at the Arab Academy for Science and Technology and Maritime Transport (AASTMT). In 2019, he obtained his PhD from Staffordshire University- UK. His research focuses on implementing AI concepts on software and hardware for Smart City applications based on IoT systems.

Remonda Ashraf holds a bachelor's degree in International Transport and Logistics - Supply Chain major, from the Arab Academy for Science, Technology and Maritime Transport. Currently working as a Teaching Assistant at College of International Transport and Logistics, Smart village campus.

Hany Ayad is Assistant Professor of Entrepreneurship, Logistics, and Supply Chain Management And Associated Dean for Students Affaires at the Arab Academy for Science Technology and Maritime Transport. He has obtained his Ph.D in Green Supply chain Management from Strathclyde University UK.

Ashish Bagwari is Head of Electronics and Communication Engineering Department, Women's Institute of Technology (WIT) (Institute of State Government) Dehradun, Constituent College of Uttarakhand Technical University (State Government Technical University), Dehradun, India. He has more than 8.0 years' experience in industry, academic, and research. Dr. Bagwari is received various awards as the Best WIT Faculty award in 2013, 2015, Best Project Guide Award in 2015, Corps of Electrical and Mechanical Engineers Prize from the Institution of Engineers, India (IEI) in December 2015. Dr.

Bagwari has published more than 65 research papers in various international journals (including ISI/SCI indexed) and IEEE international conferences. He is a member of IEEE-USA, MIR Laboratories India, IETE, ACM, and IAENG. He has also been an editor, an advisor, and a reviewer for several well-known international journals published by IEEE, Elsevier, Springer, etc. Dr. Bagwari organized several conferences and has been invited as a key speaker in various workshops/conferences. Dr. Bagwari has filed one patent. He has written two books and a few book chapters in CRC Press/other reputed publications.

Amr Ekram is a Teaching Assistant at the Arab Academy for Science Technology and Maritime Transport, College of International Transport and Logistics, Department of Energy and Petroleum Logistics Management. He teaches oil and gas operations management and energy management systems. He holds a master's degree in supply chain management.

Rawan El Haddad is an executive project manager and content creator at Puzzle Business Development. She is certified by the Ministry of Communications and Information Technology for completing the Digital marketing professional nanodegree program by Udacity. She was an ocean operation executive at Agility Egypt for shipping and freight. Also, she was a teaching assistant at the College of International Transport and Logistics at the Alamein branch of the Arab Academy for Science, Technology, and Maritime Transport (AASTMT). She holds a bachelor's degree in International Transport and Logistics, major Supply chain management at AASTMT. Lastly, she is about to obtain her MSC degree in Business administration from the College of Management and Technology at AASTMT.

Rowan Abd El-bary is a teaching assistant at the Arab Academy for Science and Technology and Maritime Transport, College of International Transport and Logistics, Logistics and Supply Chain Management Department. Bachelor's degree in Logistics and supply chain management (2018) at Arab Academy for Science and Technology and Maritime Transport. Spent one semester in an exchange program at Shanghai Maritime University, Shanghai, China (2015). Studying for a master of science in the College of Management and Technology at the Arab Academy for Science and Technology and Maritime Transport from 2019 to 2023. Studied for one semester in an Erasmus+ program at the University of Maribor, Maribor, Slovenia (2018).

Zeina El-Desouky is a Teaching Assistant at the Arab Academy for Science Technology and Maritime Transport - College of International Transport and Logistics. She teaches International Marketing, Strategic Management, Principles of Marketing, Managerial accounting and cost accounting. She holds a Bachelor degree in International Transport and Logistics major Logistics of International Trade.

Sarah El-Gamal, Assistant professor in e-Business and the Head of Logistics and Supply Chain Management Department - College of International Transport and Logistics. I started my professional career in 2004 as a graduate teaching assistant in the Productivity and Quality Institute (PQI) after graduating from the Faculty of Engineering - Electronics and Communication Department and joined the Master Program of Total Quality Management where I graduated in 2006. In 2009, I joined the University of Northumbria, UK to continue further investigations in Learning Management Systems as a PhD candidate, where I was granted my PhD in 2014. Since then, I been specialised in the teaching and design of master and diploma courses specialised in the field of Management Information Systems at the PQI, besides tutoring in various quality management training courses (ISO 9001, 14001, 18001 &

27001) as a certified tutor from International Register for Certified Auditors (IRCA). I held the position of the Head of Quality Assurance from 2018 to 2020, where I was in charge of national and international accreditation files such as ISO 900, NAQAAE, and AACSB.

Habiba El-Rouby is a Graduate Teaching Assistant at Arab Academy for Science, Technology and Maritime Transport - College of International Transport and Logistics (CITL), she has graduated from CITL in 2019.

Aya Mostafa Rabie ElGarhy is a Lecturer and Head of Supply Chain Department, Smart Village campus at College of International Transport & Logistics, Arab Academy for Science, Technology and Maritime Transport. She holds B.SC. Degree and M.Sc. Degree in International Transport & Logistics Management from Arab Academy for Science, Technology and Maritime Transport. Aya holds PhD degree In International Logistics, Supply Chain and Shipping Management, University of Plymouth, In the United Kingdom. She holds a Professional Certificate "Instruction of the IRU Academy CPC Manager Programme". And Aya participated in some reports and project that are raised from the ministry of transport to be done by the Arab Academy "Collage of International Transport & Logistics". Her current research focuses on International Logistics, Supply Chain and Shipping Management.

Sohaila El-Gazar is an Assistant Professor in the Transport Logistics Management Department at the Arab Academy for Science, Technology and Maritime Transport - College of International Transport and Logistics. PhD from Huddersfield University, UK. Cooperated in different projects such as Tech-Log, EU. She previously taught courses in Air Transport Management, Freight Forwarding Management, Liner Trade, Multi-Modal Transport Management, Inland Transport, and Import and Export Management in the BSc program. Currently she is a manager for the educational section of the FIATA Diploma.

Sara ElGazzar is Dean of College of International Transport and Logistics at Arab Academy for Science, Technology & Maritime Transport.

Hebatallah ElMesmary is Vice Dean for Education Affairs - College of International Transport and Logistics.

Rasha Elshawa is a political science researcher who graduated from Cairo University's college of economics and political science with multiple academic certificates in project management, public administration, and international relations. Mrs. Elshawa has 15 years of experience managing multiple development projects with numerous local and international partners, including Save the Children, the British Council, UNHCR, and the Arab Academy for Science and Technology. She also has experience in child protection, political and social research, and social development. She has published and presented her research findings in multiple international publications and conferences, such as the American Political Science Association. Her current study concentrates on humanitarian studies, international relations, and social development.

Nourhan Foaad is a Graduated Teaching Assistant at the Arab Academy for Science, Technology and Maritime Transport - College of International Transport and Logistics. She teaches strategic management, Quality Management, and Financial Accounting in the BSc programs. Ms. Nourhan foaad holds a Bachelor degree in Logistics and supply chain management (major logistics of international trade). She now studying masters in supply chain management at the Arab Academy for Science, Technology, and Maritime Transport.

Gamal Haikal is an assistant professor of financial economics at the Arab Academy for Science Technology and Maritime Transport. He has worked for a number of universities around the world including University of Business and Technology, Arab University, Poletenica University, Cardiff Metropolitan, and others. In addition to his different academic positions as vice dean for International affairs, Vice-dean for training, and Vice Dean for student affairs. Dr. Haikal served as a consultant for different companies organizations and governments. Including the Egyptian, Saudi, and Emarti governments, European Union along with different companies over the Middle East including Ernst and Young, HP, and others. His research track includes researchers in financial economics and supply chain management. He innovated 6 simulations in the field of business management learning. He utilized it by serving L&D functions in tens of corporations and organizations.

May Mohamed is Assistant Professor at College of International Transport and Logistics, Transport Logistics Management Department @ AASTMT. May Salah received her PhD in applied science from University of Huddersfield- UK. In 2014. She was the Head of Logistics and Supply Chain Management Department in 2017. Now, she is the Vice Dean for Training Affaires and Community Services since 2018 till now. Her research is situated in the field of International transport and Logistics, with a special focus on Transport Logistics management. May participated in number of national projects in relation to the development of Egyptian ports according to the government's plan 2030. She also organizes all the college's workshops in relation to developing the students' skills and become aware of all the new in the practical market. She also has the responsibility to provide CITL students with all the training opportunities offered by the companies related to the field of international transport and logistics.

Saurav Negi is a Faculty of Logistics and Supply Chain with Modern College of Business and Science, one of the prestigious and leading higher academic institution in Muscat, Oman, affiliated with University of Missouri, St. Louis, USA and Franklin University, USA. He has done his Doctorate (PhD) and Masters (MBA) in the domain of Logistics and Supply Chain Management. As an academician, he has participated in various national and international conferences, and has published more than 25 scholarly papers in international journal of repute (some of them are indexed and listed in Web of Science, Scopus and ABDC) and in edited books in the field of Logistics and Supply Chain Management. He teaches Logistics and Supply Chain Management courses such as Introduction to Logistics Management; Advanced Business Logistics; Supply Chain Management; Retail Logistics; Transportation Safety; Hazardous Material Transportation; and Total Quality Management. He has guided more than 40 Bachelors and Post-graduate Management students' through their dissertations' successfully.

Eric Tchouamou Njoya is a Senior Lecturer in Air Transport Economics and Corse Leader of Transport and Logistics Courses at the Department of Logistics, Marketing, Hospitality and Analytics at the Huddersfield Business School. He also serves as Cluster Co-Director at the Behavioural Research Centre of Huddersfield Business School and Deputy Director of Future Mobility Lab. He is an Associate Editor of the Journal of Aerospace Technology and Management and Topic Editor of Sustainability. He has published in highly ranked international journals including among others Transportation Research

Part A, Journal of Travel Research, Journal of Sustainaable Tourism and Tourism Management. He has successfully completed transport related research projects for various institutions, including the European Investment Bank, the European Commission, the European Subsea Cables Association, and The Korea Transport Institute. He has worked on FP7 research initiatives and participated in EU COST projects. He has also been visiting scholar to various universities including the University of Las Palmas Gran Canaria, Dublin City University, University of Thessaly and the Free University of Brussels. His current work involves the economic impacts of transport infrastructure investments and policies.

Bengü Oflaç received her bachelor's degree from Izmir Dokuz Eylül University, Faculty of Economics and Administrative Sciences in 2003.After getting her MA in marketing from Izmir Dokuz Eylül University (2006), she took a scholarship from Izmir University of Economics and became a Phd candidate in Business Administration with Logistics Management major. She took TUBITAK BIDEB scholarship and became a visiting researcher at University of Illinois at Urbana Champaign, USA in 2009. She received her PhD degree from Izmir University of Economics in 2011 and was assigned as a Asst. Prof. Dr. in the Department of Logistics Management in 2012.

Ashrakat Osama is an Egyptian teaching assistant at Arab Academy for science technology and maritime transport – smart village campus. She holds an academic MBA from the graduate school of business and bachelor's degree from the college of international transport and logistics.

Seda Özcan received her undergraduate education with a 100% Academic Success Scholarship at Izmir University of Economics, Department of Logistics Management and the Department of International Trade and Finance with the Double Major Program. During her undergraduate education, she spent 6 months at the Netherlands HanzehogeSchool Applied Sciences University with the Erasmus Exchange Programme. After graduation, she was accepted as a Project Scholar by The Scientific and Technological Research Council of Turkey (TUBITAK) to the "Shipment Consolidation and Planning Problems" project, then continued to Izmir University of Economics Logistics Management Master's Program with an Education and Research Support Scholarship. She is currently a research assistant at İzmir University of Economics and continues her studies in Business Administration Doctorate Program.

Bojan Rosi is an experienced full professor with a demonstrated history of working in the higher education industry. Skilled in Research, Negotiation, English, Management, and Strategic Planning. Strong education professional with a Ph.D. focused in Business/Managerial Economics from University of Maribor, Faculty of Economics and Business.

Farah Samir holds a BSc in International Transport and Logistics - Transport Logistics Management major, from the Arab Academy for Science and Technology. Currently working as a Logistics assistant, specializing in import logistics, at HB Fuller Egypt.

Karim Soliman holds a PhD from the University of Plymouth, UK. He is currently the Vice Dean for Education Affairs at the Graduate School of Business, Smart Village Campus. He conducted several pieces of training in logistics and supply chain management. Moreover, Soliman participated in several studies for the Ministry of Transport and the EU. Moreover, Soliman is a freelancer and business consultant in the supply chain and logistics management fields. Furthermore, Soliman is an International Instructor in the Freight Forwarding Int. Association (FIATA) teaching the FIATA diploma.

Nicoleta Tipi is a Senior Lecturer in the area of operations and supply chain management at the Open University UK. Her area of research includes aspects of developing performance measurement systems, modeling and analytics in the supply chain and developing enquiries for Sustainability and resilience in the area of supply chain and logistics.

Index

F

G

H

I

K

L

M

O

P

R

S

T

U

V

Z

www.ingramcontent.com/pod-product-compliance
Lightning Source LLC
LaVergne TN
LVHW060414300926
849162LV00006B/1422